FILM QUARTERLY

Film Quarterly

FORTY YEARS—
A SELECTION

EDITED BY
BRIAN HENDERSON
AND ANN MARTIN
WITH LEE AMAZONAS

UNIVERSITY OF CALIFORNIA PRESS
Berkeley   Los Angeles   London

University of California Press
Berkeley and Los Angeles, California

University of California Press, Ltd.
London, England

© 1999 by
The Regents of the University of California

Film Quarterly: Forty years—a selection / edited by Brian Henderson
    and Ann Martin, with Lee Amazonas.
        p.   cm.
    Includes bibliographical references and index.
    ISBN 0-520-21602-4 (alk. paper). — ISBN 0-520-21603-2 (pbk. : alk. paper)
    1. Motion pictures. I. Henderson, Brian. II. Martin, Ann.
III. Amazonas, Lee. IV. Film quarterly.
PN1994.F439135   1998
791.43—dc21   98-28889
                                                         CIP

Printed in the United States of America
9 8 7 6 5 4 3 2 1

In Memoriam

In fond memory of our dear friend and irreplaceable colleague
Albert Johnson, Assistant Editor 1958–1961, board member 1961–1998

CONTENTS

ACKNOWLEDGMENTS

This volume developed in the best sense as a group project, and my deepest gratitude for their guidance and participation goes to the *Film Quarterly* editorial board members—Leo Braudy, Ernest Callenbach, Brian Henderson, Albert Johnson, Marsha Kinder, and Linda Williams—without whom this book, both in concept and in form, could not have appeared. Board member and co-editor Brian Henderson brought his long history with *FQ* and a wonderful intellectual rigor and imagination to the introductions he wrote for this volume; I value the time we worked together and the contribution he made. I must also make particular and affectionate mention of *FQ*'s founding editor, whose editorial sense and sensibility is reflected throughout this selection: Ernest Callenbach's generosity to me is constant and his example an inspiration. And I'm sure he joins me in gratitude not only to those authors whose writings appear in these pages, but also to the many authors who have contributed their work to the journal over the years; they have made *FQ* a fine publication indeed.

For their invaluable assistance with film stills, all thanks go to Nancy Goldman and Jason Sanders at the Pacific Film Archive, Mary Corliss and Terry Geesken at the Museum of Modern Art Film Stills Archive, and Robert Haller at Anthology Film Archives. My thanks also to Rebecca Simon and the staff of the Journals Department at the University of California Press for their patience and support, and to Ed Dimendberg, former humanities editor at the press, for his calmly dispensed words of advice and reassurance. And, though definitely not last, to my invaluable assistant and researcher, Lee Amazonas, heartfelt thanks for her hard work in hard times.

A note about editing: it was decided to publish these articles in their original form, which basically meant "warts, inconsistencies, and all." Proofreader/copy editor Virginia Clark—whose work was, as usual, impeccable—was thus forced to see many of her thoughtful changes and suggestions rejected. Errors have, of course, been corrected and inconsistencies resolved when they might have caused confusion; where errors and confusing inconsistencies still occur, the fault is mine.

Frame enlargements and film stills are included by courtesy of the following: Pacific Film Archive, the Museum of Modern Art Film Stills Archive, Anthology Film Archives, Twentieth Century Fox, Turner Entertainment, Paramount Pictures, Warner Bros., Columbia Pictures, Universal Pictures, Les Filmes Galaxies, Greenwich Film Productions, First Run/Icarus, New Day Films, Miramax Films, New Yorker Films, Zipporah Films, Clarity Films, Canyon Cinema, California Newsreel, Third World Newsreel, China Film Imp/Exp LA, the Academy of Motion Picture Arts and Sciences, UC Media, Ken Stein, Mark Lipson, Bruce Baillie, and L. Roger Turner.

Not all photos included in the original publication of the articles could be found and included despite efforts made to locate and acquire them; our thanks to the many contributors who provided assistance (and, in some cases, the original photographs). In a few instances, where illustrations seemed necessary and the originals were unavailable, similar photographs have been included in their place. Every effort was also made to track down contributors and notify them of their inclusion in this anthology; where we were unsuccessful, we apologize.

ANN MARTIN
BERKELEY
JUNE 1998

INTRODUCTION

BRIAN HENDERSON

Film Quarterly (Fall 1958 to the present) had two antecedents: *Hollywood Quarterly* (October 1945–Summer 1951) and *Quarterly of Film, Radio, and Television* (Fall 1951–Summer 1957). *Hollywood Quarterly* was launched in 1945 as a joint venture of the Hollywood Writers Mobilization and the University of California Press. The association began as a wartime collaboration between educators and media workers in response to social needs occasioned by the war. Playwright and screenwriter John Howard Lawson and Franklin Fearing, a university supporter, were co-editors; two additional industry representatives, including writer-director Abraham Polonsky, and three university representatives made up the editorial board. The first issue, which appeared just after the end of the war, posed the question: "What part will the motion picture and the radio play in the consolidation of the victory, in the creation of new patterns in world culture and understanding?" The first issue featured Fearing's article "Warriors Return: Normal or Neurotic?" and "The Case of David Smith," a radio play by Polonsky on a similar subject. High standards were maintained in subsequent issues as representatives from many areas of the industry contributed essays on their respective crafts. These included writers Philip Dunne, Lester Cole, and John Paxton; directors Irving Pichel and Curtis Harrington; composers Franz Waxman and Adolph Deutsch; costume designer Edith Head; and others. In late 1946 the earliest phase of postwar Red hunting targeted Lawson, among others.

According to Alan Gevinson's profile of *Film Quarterly* in Anthony Slide's *International Film, Radio, and Television Journals* (1985), Lawson resigned from his position as co-editor when "the provost of the University of California told him the journal would have to fold or dissociate itself from the university if Lawson continued his position." Polonsky took over as co-editor and continued Lawson's policies, among other ways by writing excellent and socially conscious reviews of *Odd Man Out* and *Monsieur Verdoux*. But the journal, according to Gevinson, "eventually lost its critical bite and turned academic, emphasizing studies, albeit excellent ones in many cases, of foreign and past filmmakers, Shakespearean adaptations, and television programming." *Hollywood Quarterly* was cited in a House Un-American Activities Committee hearing as a Communist organ; in 1951 its name was changed to *Quarterly of Film, Radio, and Television.* The new journal stated that it no longer spoke for the Hollywood community. It published, said Gevinson, "high quality but politically safe pieces on a variety of subjects," including an article on the history of the horror film by Curtis Harrington, Norman McLaren's "Notes on Animated Sound," and T.W. Adorno's "How to Look at Television." August Frugé, director emeritus of the University of California Press, notes in his book *A Skeptic Among Scholars* (1993) that the *Quarterly of Film, Radio, and Television* gradually ran down "—or so I seem to remember—as the emphasis became more sociological and less cinematic." A series of assistant editors who worked under the editorial board "did not always fit in well." The last of these, says Frugé, often threatened to resign to get her way. At last he accepted her offer. Frugé expected trouble with the editorial board, but the board's chairman, Kenneth MacGowan, professor emeritus of theater arts at UCLA, understood and wondered if another qualified person could be found. "In the end, and after a quiet talk, he sighed and said that perhaps the time had come to bring the enterprise to a halt." Frugé speculates that MacGowan, who once again had become involved in theater—his first love— had lost some of his former interest in film.

"That should have been the end of the affair," says Frugé, "but I hesitated." The *Quarterly of Film, Radio, and Television* had what was then called a university subvention (that is, a subsidy), as did other journals, and he did not want it to revert to the state. Frugé looked at *Sight and Sound* and *Cahiers du cinéma.* "There was no American review comparable to these two, intellectual but not academic and devoted to film as art and not as communication. By accident we found ourselves with the means to publish one—if we chose and if we knew how."

Frugé had been talking to Andries Deinum, his one friend in the film business. Deinum had been teaching film at the University of Southern California, but in 1955 he was called before the House Un-American Activities Committee; he testified that for a time he had been a member of the Communist Party in Hollywood, but he refused to name names. As a result, he was dismissed from his position at USC. Deinum's knowledge and "his great ability to talk and, talking, to enlighten" impressed Frugé; hence he asked whether, if a new journal were started, he would serve as editor. Deinum declined, on the basis that the university would never hire him. Frugé disagreed: in the expanded university, President Sproul was "no longer second-guessing our decisions." Frugé speculates that Deinum's incomparable ability with the spoken word may have decided him against an editor's role. (In any case, Deinum took a teaching position soon after, which he held for the rest of his career, at Portland State University.) Deinum suggested that Frugé instead consider someone on Frugé's own staff: Ernest Callenbach, of whose work as a film critic, including contributions to the *Quarterly of Film, Radio, and Television,* Frugé was unaware. Frugé recalls that Callenbach was reluctant to take the job, mindful of the other activities that such a move might forestall. Before making up his mind, Callenbach suggested Pauline Kael, who had made a local reputation writing blurbs for a repertory movie house near campus. Kael came in for a discussion, and "almost immediately it became clear that she and I did not think alike and would never be able to work together. For one thing, she wanted a completely free hand, which we would not give."

Callenbach agreed to a one-year trial and was aided by an advisory board composed of Deinum; Gavin Lambert, a former editor of *Sight and Sound* and then a screenwriter in Hollywood; Albert Johnson; Hugh Gray; Paul Jorgensen; and Colin Young of UCLA. The first issue of *Film Quarterly,* as the new journal was called, appeared in Fall 1958. In the Fall 1991 issue—thirty-three years later—Callenbach penned his "Founding Editor's Farewell," in which he announced both his retirement from the editorship and his participation on the editorial board to continue his association with the journal. Callenbach had overseen the production of 133 issues of *Film Quarterly.*

The present editor is Ann Martin, who has worked at *American Film* and *The New Yorker,* edited a series of monographs for the American Film Institute, and worked in film and video production. Martin has been the editor of *Film Quarterly* since the Winter 1991–92 issue; the Fall 1998 issue marked the completion of seven years—twenty-eight issues—under her leadership. It is possible to argue that the successful transfer of the editorship of *Film Quarterly* from Callenbach to Martin is the most important moment in the history of the journal since its founding forty years ago. One need only look around a bit to see how rare such a peaceful transition is. In most cases, either a venerable journal is scrapped when a longtime editor retires, or the appointment of a successor coincides precisely with its decline. There are many exceptions, of course, but with dictatorships—however benevolent and effective—and with journals—however brightly and long they burn—the problem that is never quite worked out is that of transition.

THE PHYSICAL JOURNAL

What follows will explore only a few aspects of *Film Quarterly's* first forty years. "Where to begin?" is not only the title of an essay by Roland Barthes, but also a conundrum faced on any sort of writing occasion. We might take a cue from Dziga Vertov's *The Man with a Movie Camera*: the camera itself is the first thing we see in the film and virtually the last. As the star of the show, the camera takes a mechanical bow to the audience near the end of the film. So we will begin with the physical journal itself, reminding us that it has an existence—a life?—of its own that is affected by, but independent of, publisher, editor, board, contributors, and readers.

The journal that was born fully grown in 1958 measured a svelte $6^3/_4$ by $8^3/_8$ inches. Unlike the rest of us, it stayed that way for twenty-three years, including, of course, the twentieth-anniversary issue of Fall 1978. Beginning with the Fall 1981 issue, the format expanded to $6^3/_4$ by $9^3/_4$ inches; that is, the width remained the same, but $1^3/_8$ inches were added at the top. In the Fall 1989 issue the format expanded to the dimensions of a ream of letter-quality computer paper. The first format lasted twenty-three years, the second eight years, and the third completed its ninth year with the Summer 1998 issue. Phenomenologically speaking, the first format suggested a radical pamphlet that one could stuff in one's pocket and read at any time, secretly if necessary. Familiar as it was then, it is now almost impossible to visualize the tiny envelopes that issues from that period arrived in. Unpacking the contents must have recalled to some the long-gone thrill of opening a mailed Captain Midnight decoder, with instructions. Once the shock of change wore off, the new appearance was accepted as the "natural" form of *Film Quarterly* of the then present. (It is disconcerting to recall that this format corresponded almost exactly to the two Reagan terms: 1981–1989.) By contrast, the expansion to $8^1/_2$ by 11 inches took place with no more than a "Not again!" Let me note— before some other pundit does—that the format changes of the last seventeen years have seemed no more than two double-clicks on a computer keyboard, the first achieving a somewhat taller screen and the second a fuller one.

An indication of the shock of the first format change in nearly a quarter century may be found in the Editor's Notebook in the Fall 1981 issue. Under the title "Our New Format," the column explained:

> Three issues back, we adopted a new cover design for *Film Quarterly*. With this issue we are enlarging our pages and switching to a larger, more readable type size. The editorial policies of the magazine remain the same: as a journal published by a university press, we print the most intransigently intelligent film criticism that we can find.
>
> The appearance of *Film Quarterly* did not change except in minor details for more than twenty years. But the marketplace in which we compete—the newsstands and bookstores of the nation—has changed a great deal. In time the austere Roman elegance of our old cover design tended to disappear in a welter of increasingly flashy commercial magazines. Our new cover, with a larger area of color and the title in bolder lettering, makes *Film*

Quarterly more visible; it has already helped us begin to attract more of the new subscribers we depend upon for our survival. . . . These changes should make the contents more visually appealing to new readers and old, as we continue our familiar mix of articles, interviews, reviews, and book reviews—all with the lively seriousness that befits a scholarly journal.

The editor here assures the reader that the change in the journal's size will not affect editorial policy and the categories of material that will appear in its pages—interviews, articles, film reviews, and book reviews. Some might ask why an additional $1^{3}/_{8}$ inches at the top of a journal should change its contents. But the size, shape, and typeface of a magazine or journal determine how one holds it, how one turns the pages, and how one's eye traverses the page (whether text is arranged in columns or across the page); in short, how the physical journal disposes and interacts with the body of the reader. As Norman O. Brown said, all categories are bodily categories.

As noted, the format of the journal changed again in the Fall 1989 issue. What were the editor's reflections on this change? We do not know, because by then the institution of the Editor's Notebook no longer existed. (Its last appearance was in the Summer 1986 issue.) Its disappearance was due to another redesign of the contents page, in the excised right column of which the Editor's Notebook had appeared for twenty-eight years. One might argue, on the other hand, that the excitement of the cinema that emerged in the late fifties, sixties, and seventies had shifted to business-as-usual in the mid-eighties. The mining of viewers for cinematic gold perhaps required more patience, more systematic search; it was no longer everywhere to be found. As a result, the avidity for chats and discussions of all kinds diminished, including perhaps the Editor's Notebook. Hegel once said that the Owl of Minerva takes flight only after sunset; that is, we attain wisdom about events only after they are completed. The eighties and nineties may not be a conspicuously innovative period in cinema, but the articles, reviews, interviews, and book reviews of this era have seemed to probe more deeply and attain more understanding than before.

A GALAXY OF WRITERS

The principal glory of *Film Quarterly* has been its contributors. Some journals have proceeded with more or less the same group of writers, with only occasional replenishment by others over the years. In each of its main time periods, *Film Quarterly* has had a far greater diversity among both regular and occasional contributors.

From 1958 to 1965, a number of writers who were well known—either then or later, or both—wrote for *Film Quarterly*. These included Arlene Croce,

Parker Tyler, Vernon Young, Eugene Archer, and Gavin Lambert, among others. What these superb writers contributed to the journal were almost exclusively film reviews. (Noël Burch wrote articles as well as reviews during this period.) There was also, beginning in 1961, a regular feature called "Films of the Quarter," in which a group of professional film critics—Dwight Macdonald, Stanley Kauffmann, Pauline Kael, Jonas Mekas, and Gavin Lambert—discussed what they regarded as the best films of the preceding three months. It was when Andrew Sarris (Mekas's fellow writer on the *Village Voice*) joined the group that sparks began to fly. In the Spring 1963 issue Pauline Kael attacked Sarris and auteurism in an article called "Circles and Squares." In the Summer 1963 issue Sarris responded in his article "The Auteur Theory and the Perils of Pauline." For a short while "Films of the Quarter" continued alongside these heated exchanges. In the Fall 1963 issue, Dwight Macdonald resigned:

> I've been wondering, for various reasons, whether to keep on contributing to "Films of the Quarter," but now that Andrew Sarris has been added to the stable, I feel the decision has been made for me. I am not willing to appear under the same rubric as a "critic" who thinks *The Birds* "finds Hitchcock at the summit of his artistic powers." His simplistic coarsening of Truffaut's *auteur* theory has produced a dogma so alien to the forms of reasoning and sensibility I respect as to eliminate any basis of discussion.

Not long after, "Films of the Quarter" quietly disappeared. Pauline Kael, who had contributed articles, film reviews, and other material to the journal between 1961 and 1965, reprinted a great deal of that material in her first book, *I Lost It at the Movies* (1965).

The later sixties and early seventies introduced a number of new writers to *Film Quarterly,* each of whom was to contribute to the journal over a long period. These include Stephen Farber, who first wrote for *Film Quarterly* in 1965; James Roy MacBean (1968); Leo Braudy (1968); Joan Mellen (1971); Michael Dempsey (1971); Brian Henderson (1971); and Marsha Kinder and Beverle Houston (1973). This group brought to the journal a new seriousness about film criticism and scholarship and took a longer-range view of commentary on film than did the "Films of the Quarter" group, whose polemics and turf wars, moreover, did not interest the newcomers. Not least, it was members of this group who introduced to *Film Quarterly* an abiding interest in film theory and theoretically inflected criticism. This interest quickly became and has remained one of the distinctive features and commitments of the journal. Those who wrote for the journal between other assignments included Estelle Changas,

Claire Clouzot, Richard Corliss, David Denby, Peter Harcourt, Richard T. Jameson, Richard Kozarski, Max Kozloff, Joseph McBride, Harriet Polt, Paul Schrader, and Paul Warshow.

Film Quarterly writers who have emerged since those early days include longtime contributors Jonathan Rosenbaum, Karen Jaehne, Tania Modleski, William F. Van Wert, Peter Brunette, and James Naremore, as well as the journal's Rome editor, Gideon Bachmann, and its New York editor, William Johnson. The journal's outstanding book reviewers, including Tom Gunning, Dana Polan, and others too numerous to name here, should also be acknowledged.

A few words about this book are in order. It is not, sadly, a representative selection of *Film Quarterly* and its writers over forty years and 160 issues. It contains one interview (out of well over a hundred), no film reviews (out of many hundreds), and no book reviews (out of perhaps thousands). Its organization and selections were determined at two extraordinary meetings of the editorial board, in which a much-too-large proposed book was whittled down and merged with a composite of other choices and categories. This most stimulating process went through many stages and hours before resulting in a conclusion acceptable to all. The editors of this volume wish to thank the editorial board—Leo Braudy, Ernest Callenbach, Albert Johnson, Marsha Kinder, and Linda Williams—for its labors and unceasing perspicacity. Thanks also to the expert advice of experienced page counters at our planning meeting for telling us, to paraphrase Cocteau, how far we could go too far. They kept all of us firmly under the rule of the reality principle. No one emerges from such a regimen without fantasies, however; each of us had at least several pieces, and—these failing—one last one that we still wished were included.

Over forty years, the pages of *Film Quarterly* have reflected not only many interests, but also many kinds of interests. These are reflected in the section headings of this book: Theory, Genre, Documentary, Technologies, Historical Revisions, and, under the heading of Group Texts, the avant-garde on the one hand, and feminism and the narrative film tradition on the other. In the necessarily compressed dimensions of this book we have tended toward articles that in one way or another combine two or more of these categories. To compare *Film Quarterly* to other journals, there are certainly others that specialize in feminism or in the avant-garde, and hence perhaps treat them more extensively than we do. In documentary coverage, and especially in documentary theory—although other journals have articles and features in this field—the position of *Film Quarterly* is especially strong. Superb as they are, the articles and interview in this book only sample the abiding commitments of the journal over forty years. But what is unique about *Film Quarterly* is not any one of these specialty areas, but all of them. No other film journal has embraced and kept up with all of these fields as *Film Quarterly* has.

Two topics not yet dealt with are theory and *Film Quarterly*'s annual book review issue. The massive annual review coverage of the year's film books is unique; no other film journal in the United States or elsewhere offers anything like this systematic coverage. (The genesis and development of the book issue are discussed in the introduction to Part One, "Early Days.")

As for theory, it is a more complex question—of course! What else would it be? *Film Quarterly* has published theoretical work by André Bazin, Umberto Eco, and Jean-Louis Baudry, among other Europeans, and a very considerable body of indigenous work as well. Theory has included narrative theory and, as mentioned, feminist, documentary, and avant-garde theory. *Film Quarterly* remains open to—indeed is hoping for—both articles on general theory and theoretical work addressing particular fields. Recently, under the rubric "anti-theory," some have proposed the end of theory. At *Film Quarterly,* we are waiting for the theoretical and other kinds of work that will frame the course of film and television studies in the new century. And one last minor note: although the essays in each section are listed chronologically in the table of contents, the introductions to four of the sections—Theory, Genre, Technologies, and Historical Revisions—depart from temporal order to develop thematic points among the pieces included.

PART ONE

EARLY DAYS

From *Film Quarterly*'s first issue in Fall 1958 through the Spring 1961 issue, Albert Johnson was the journal's assistant editor, the only one it has ever had. Thereafter he became a member of the editorial board, on which he is active to this day. This is by far the longest service on the board that anyone has had: thirty-seven years. Johnson's long career as a teacher and his participation in film festivals and colloquia around the globe have enriched the journal many times over, particularly as Johnson is the only member to have seen many of the films that contributors have reviewed or discussed in articles submitted to the journal's editorial board. His encyclopedic knowledge of the entire work of a staggering number of filmmakers has aided the board in its deliberations and, through the editor, helped contributors avoid errors and expand the scope and applicability of their arguments.

Johnson's article "Beige, Brown, or Black" (Fall 1959) concerns the treatment of blacks in Hollywood film in the 1950s but begins with a brief summary of the late 1940s, "a brief period of sociological experiment in American film." Several works dealt specifically with "problems involving Negro characters." These included *Home of the Brave, Pinky, Lost Boundaries*, and *No Way Out*. Of the 1950s generally, he notes that American drama has suffered from a lack of Negro playwrights and screenwriters able to present their characters "in authentic and dramatically informative situations." In "The Negro in American Films: Some Recent Works," a seventeen-page article that appeared in Fall 1965, Johnson drew attention to, among other issues, later Sidney Poitier films and what might be called the Diahann Carroll–Diana Sands era, literally a pivotal time for African American characters—and players—in film.

Thirty-two years after "Beige, Brown, or Black," in the Winter 1990–91 and Spring 1991 issues, Johnson published a two-part article entitled "Moods Indigo: A Long View." Filling a gap in film scholarship, this article became an instant classic, remarkable for its intellectual acuity, breadth and firmness of grasp, and subtlety and grace of writing style. Johnson's opinions are also sometimes controversial—for instance, his reservations about some aspects of Spike Lee's work—but this controversy too provides impetus for critical thought. Comprising thirty pages of *Film Quarterly*'s then relatively new 8$^1/_2$-by-11 format, "Moods Indigo" already constitutes a short book. Indeed, Johnson's colleagues—on *Film Quarterly* and elsewhere—urged him to gather the articles mentioned, along with his two-part article on Vincente Minnelli and his writings on the musical (including reviews of *West Side Story* and *The Young Girls of Rochefort*), into the confines of a book.

Founding editor Ernest Callenbach's twenty-two-page article "Recent Film Writing: A Survey" (Spring 1971) appeared in the journal's fourteenth year. Of course, *Film Quarterly* had published a number of book reviews over the years. Some issues had five book reviews; most had two or three; quite a few had none at all. Callenbach wrote many of the reviews; in the Spring 1967 issue, for instance, he reviewed *A World on Film* by Stanley Kauffmann and *Josef von Sternberg* by Herman G. Weinberg. But there were other reviewers also, such as Hugh Kenner (author of books on Ezra Pound, Buckminster Fuller, and Chuck Jones, among others), who reviewed *One Reel a Week*, accounts by filmmakers of cinema's early days; Rudi Blesch's biography of Keaton; and other books.

But "Recent Film Writing" was something new. Its immediate impetus was a quantum leap in the number of film books published. Callenbach's article was divided between attempting to understand this phenomenon and trying to catch up with it.

> There have been a tremendous number of film books published in the past year or so, although the output relative to that of the established fields like English or sociology is still modest. Once, we could have the easy feeling that we could read everything that came out. We now face a situation like that in older fields, where specialization is forced on us whether we like it or not: nobody has the time to read all the books that are appearing. I regret this, personally speaking, because it means a kind of fragmentation and dispersion of intellectual activity, but it seems to be inevitable whenever any subject is attacked by large numbers of people.

It may be stretching a point, but one might link Callenbach's lament to the early writings of Marx, in which the division of labor is seen as a kind of Original Sin, which occasions the fragmentation not only of fields of knowledge, but also of the self.

Callenbach's article in its complete form (it has been edited for this anthology) lists sixty-six books and discusses six additional books, in greater depth than the other books, in the long "Criticism" section (reproduced here). With this number of books, the author felt it necessary to devise a system of categories, which was no more perhaps than a pragmatic breakdown according to the topics they treated. The nine sections of the article covered anthologies, interviews, how-to-do-it books, scripts, director studies, histories, reference books, miscellaneous, and criticism. The first eight sections—one to three pages each—comprise ten pages of the article; the "Criticism" section comprises thirteen pages.

These categories and the article itself are important as the precursor, indeed the actual beginning, of what eventually became a *Film Quarterly* regular feature, if not an institution: the annual book review issue, which is now the summer issue of each year. Tracing briefly the development of these surveys or round-ups, as they came to be called, might be illuminating. For one thing, Callenbach's article marked the first and last time that a survey of the year's film books was done by a single person; many hands have accomplished all later book issues. Regular journal features rarely spring up all at once, and the annual book issue is no exception. It took several years before the survey was established as an annual summer event. Moreover, the book issue has never quite congealed into a fixed entity: its format and categories have changed over time. Since 1984, for instance, the summer book issue has more often than not spilled over into the fall issue also.

There was no book issue in 1973, but there has been one in every year since. Nearly all issues since 1975 have referred to the book issue—on the cover and inside—as a "round-up": "Another Round-up at the *FQ* Corral" or "Another Giant Film Book Round-up." This became more or less standardized in 1985 as "Annual *Film Quarterly* Book Round-up." This metaphor refers not to the actual West, of course, but to the Western genre. Taken literally, the term suggests a correspondence between a gathering of film books and a gathering of cattle into a herd. One can imagine individualistic authors who might not enjoy that metaphor. ("Don't Fence *Me* In" might be their anthem.) For perhaps a larger number of writers, the prospect of a review, even a lackluster one, is a promotional opportunity not lightly cast aside. Accepting an uncertain fate—or pessimistic about the whole matter—"I'm a-headin' for the last round-up" might be their lament of choice.

One might speculate also about the lingering doubt editors and board members might have over how readers react to the perpetually spilling-over book review coverage. In this event, the Western terminology and tongue-in-cheek Paul Bunyan hyperbole—"Gargantuan! Colossal! Stupendous!"—may be attempts to overcome the long stretches of extended book reviews, short notes, and annotations. Matthew Arnold said that religion had "lighted up" morality, meaning—it has been supposed—that the burdens of morality may be carried more easily with the aid of the light, sound, music, and other consolations of religious experience. So perhaps with the phraseology of hoopla that dominates the covers and insides of book issues. Very few complaints have been received about the book issues, however, and much praise. Book reviews provide abundant materials for conversations about film—as much as interviews, articles, and film reviews—which is presumably a principal reason people read film journals.

Equally important for the future of *Film Quarterly* are Callenbach's remarks in the long "Criticism" section of the piece. Sometimes explicitly, sometimes between the lines, he considers where film criticism—and, implicitly, *Film Quarterly*—has been and where it is going/should go. His theme is stated in the section's first paragraph:

> It seems to me that we now have critical resources that greatly surpass those of a decade ago; our general-audience magazines, in particular, are now immensely better served, and the critical books which have flowed from the journalistic work seem to me to constitute a remarkable outpouring of critical energy, knowledge, and intelligence. Many new and good critics continue to develop within the specialized film journals. As a congenital pessimist, I choke to say it, but we *have* never had it so good.

That general magazines are now "immensely better served" surely refers to several well-known critics, but it refers especially perhaps to Pauline Kael. From 1961 to 1965 Kael contributed a considerable amount of material to *Film Quarterly,* including her best, most amusing blasts at the flat-footed pretensions of Hollywood filmmaking; her contributions to "Films of the Quarter," a regular *FQ* feature for some years; and her notorious article "Circles and Squares." After writing for *Vogue* and the *New Republic,* Kael became a permanent regular film critic at *The New Yorker.*

What Callenbach seems to be thinking through in the "Criticism" section is the question of the future, specifically the weekly critical format of the general magazines versus the ideas, including theoretical ones, of a younger generation (or half generation). This is not an "either/or" in relation to ultimate values, but a question of where the future lies, especially for a journal the size of *Film Quarterly,* its mission at least partly defined by its university-sponsored status. His conclusion is perhaps implicit in his remarks on method at the outset: "Nevertheless, speaking more as an editor than a critic, I would like . . . to make some sense of what has been happening in film criticism recently on the level of ideas."

He cites the ideational limits of weekly reviewing—"You can imply theoretical matters, but in the general press you had better be sure they don't get too heavy." Also, each review has to be freestanding; one can't expect the reader to keep a connected argument in mind from one week to the next. A review done by a skilled writer is a special-purpose item that cannot easily be put to other purposes. Finally, especially with foreign films now having a hard time entering the U.S. market, there are not necessarily films worthy to review every week. Regarding Kael's then recent collection *Going Steady,* he says that of seventy-six films discussed, only ten seem to matter to her as films.

On the other side, Callenbach notes:

> The theorist must attempt to "rise above" individual cases, to arrive at large generalizations. . . . Theorizing can be a pleasure quite in itself, of course, just as playful activity. . . . Criticism *needs* ideas, however, and I would like to spell out some of the reasons, perhaps a bit painfully. Criticism cannot in fact rely upon "taste" alone; every good critic's way of thinking rests upon a pattern of assumptions, aesthetic and social; and it employs a constellation of terms appropriate to those assumptions. The act of "criticism," in essence, as opposed to the mere opinion-mongering of most of the daily press, is the application of such terms to the realities of a given film: describing it, analyzing it, evaluating it, and in the process also refining the terms and assumptions.

Nobody would enjoy this process if carried out in an obvious and mechanical way: "there are benefits to be gained by carrying it out with more intellectual elegance and determination than are customary among our film critics." He also notes:

> Assumptions and terms reasonably suitable for dealing with conventional narrative fictions have been around for a long time. Basically "realist" in tenor, these ideas have never applied very well to non-narrative and expressionist forms, especially experimental ones; the neglect of experimental film by critics has been due at least as much to practical embarrassment at this as to the inaccessibility or low quality of the films.

Callenbach concludes this section of his article with a brief mention of a filmmaker-theorist such as Eisenstein and, with qualifications, Godard. "But aside from such rare exceptions, we will get our ideas about what is going on from critics, or we will not get them at all. It would be a good thing if our critics could, over the next couple of years, come up with some new and coherent ones."

ALBERT JOHNSON

BEIGE, BROWN, OR BLACK

Tropical dilemma: Joan Fontaine and
Harry Belafonte in *Island in the Sun.*

Vol. 13, no. 1 (Fall 1959): 38–43.

The late nineteen-forties, a brief period of sociological experimentation in American film-making, contained several works dealing specifically with problems involving Negro characters. Such films as *Home of the Brave, Pinky, Lost Boundaries,* and *No Way Out* were particularly memorable because they attempted to portray the Negro in a predominantly white environment; as a figure of dramatic importance, the Negro has long been overlooked or carefully avoided on the screen, chiefly because of the refusal of Southern theater exhibitors to book such films. The U.S. Motion Picture Code's rule regarding the depiction of Negro characters, notoriously outdated, has only managed to keep in effect a rigidly stereotyped view of a race whose economic and intellectual status has risen to such a degree since 1919 that one tends to look upon most Negro screen actors as creatures speaking the language of closet-drama.

American drama has suffered from a lack of Negro playwrights (not to mention Negro screen writers) who are able to present their characters in authentic and dramatically informative situations, for certainly few racial groups in this country flourish so actively on a level of melodrama, except perhaps the Puerto Ricans in New York, and yet, the two most successful stage works about contemporary Negro life are based upon the same rather bland premise: the sudden acquisition of a large sum of money by a middle-class family (*Anna Lucasta* and *A Raisin in the Sun*). These plays succeed because they honestly develop character in an all-Negro milieu on a nonstereotyped basis—they reveal the Negro to audiences with the same sympathy and insight with which Sean O'Casey exhibited the Irish in *Juno and the Paycock*. So far, so good, but what has happened in the American cinema since the forties regarding the plight of the Negro?

First of all, the Supreme Court decisions regarding integration of Southern schools, in 1954, once more brought the entire question of Negro-white relationships to the attention of the world. The incidents ensuing from this historic decree have yet to be conveyed in either stage or screen terms, and apparently, no one is courageous enough to do anything about it, but, at any rate, the Arkansas affair stirred interest in the Negro race once more as a focus for drama. Secondly, it was apparently decided by various Hollywood producers that a *gradual* succession of films about Negro-white relationships would have a beneficial effect upon box-office returns and audiences as well. The first of these films, *Edge of the City* (1956), is the most satisfactory because it is the least pretentious. The performance by Sidney Poitier (the Negro actor whose career has most benefited by the renaissance of the color theme) was completely authentic, but true to the film code, any hint of successful integration must be concluded by death, usually in some particularly gory fashion, and so Poitier gets it in the back with a docker's bale-hook. The most constructive contribution of *Edge of the City* to film history is one sequence in which Poitier talks philosophically to his white friend, using language that rings so truthfully and refreshingly in the ears that one suddenly realizes the tremendous damage that has been nurtured through the years because of Hollywood's perpetuation of the dialect-myth. The film was praised for its honesty, but its conclusion was disturbing; audiences wanted to know *why* the Negro had to be killed in order for the hero to achieve self-respect.

Strangely enough, this promising beginning of a revival of American cinematic interest in interracial relationships took a drastic turn with Darryl F. Zanuck's lavish production of *Island in the Sun* (1957). The focus changed from concern for an ordinary friendship between men of different racial backgrounds to the theme of miscegenation, considered to be, in Hollywoodian terms, a much bolder and more courageous source of titillation.

This film, made solely for sensationalistic reasons, was supposed to depict racial problems on the fictional West Indian island of Santa Marta, but it became simply a visually fascinating document without a real sense of purpose. Against a background of tropical beauty, a series of romantic attachments and longings are falsely attached to a group of famous personalities, each of whom is given as little to do as possible.

Harry Belafonte, a Negro singer who has risen to the astonishing and unprecedented stature of a matinee idol, was presented as David Boyeur, a labor leader for the island's native population, and his obvious attractions for a socially distinguished white beauty, Mavis (Joan Fontaine), created a furor among the Southern theater exhibitors, who either banned the film or deleted the Belafonte-Fontaine sequences. Actually, there were no love scenes between the two, only glances of admiration and dialogue of almost Firbankian simplicity. In fact, Boyeur's decision not to make love to Mavis is evasive and full

American film mythology: Integration leads to death. Kathleen Maguire, Sidney Poitier, and John Cassavetes in scenes from *Edge of the City.*

of chop-logic, and every indication is given that poor Mavis will literally pine away thereafter among the mango trees. On the other hand, a Negro girl, Margot (Dorothy Dandridge), is allowed to embrace and eventually marry a white English civil servant (John Justin) and, although their life on Santa Marta is segregated, they finally sail happily off to England together at the end of the film. And so, the crux of the matter of miscegenation is again at the mercy of the film production code. Although "color" is the most important problem on the island, it seems that a white man may marry a Negro girl and not only *live,* and live happily, but that a Negro man and a white woman dare not think of touching. There is an odd moment in *Island in the Sun* when (after watching Mavis yearn for Boyeur in sequence after sequence) the Negro reaches up and lifts her slowly from a barouche, holding her waist. The shock-effect of this gesture upon the audience was the most subtle piece of eroticism in the film, and only the lack of honesty in the work as a whole made this hint of a prelude-to-embrace seem realistic.

Island in the Sun also stirred other concepts about color, for the problem of concealed racial ancestry is introduced, bringing out all sorts of moody behavior on the part of a young girl, Jocelyn (Joan Collins), and her brother, Maxwell (James Mason). Jocelyn attempts to break off her engagement to an English nobleman, but he ignores her racial anxieties and is willing to chance the improbabilities of an eventual albino in the family. Maxwell, however, is driven into gloom, drink, and eventual murder, one feels, because the Negro skeleton in the family closet has thoroughly rattled him. The entire film is certainly important as a study of the tropical myth in racial terms, and even Dandridge's character, though she comes out of the whole business fairly happily, is not entirely free from the stereotype of the Negro as sensualistic, for, at one point, she performs a rather unusual Los Angeles–primitive dance among the Santa Marta natives, an act that is quite out of character, if one knows anything at all about the problem of class consciousness among the Negroes themselves in the West Indies.

Miss Dandridge has been continually cast as the typically sexy, unprincipled lady of color, in all-Negro films like *Carmen Jones* (1956) and *Porgy and Bess* (1959), as well as in a singularly appalling film called *The Decks Ran Red* (1958), in which she is the only woman aboard a freighter in distress and, naturally, is pursued by a lusty mutineer, with much contrived suspense and old-hat melodrama. It is ironic, under the circumstances, to recall that this actress's dramatic debut in films coincided with that of Belafonte in *Bright Road* (1955), a minor work about a gentle schoolteacher and a shy principal in a Southern school.

The commercial success of *Island in the Sun* led to the decisive movement in Hollywood to make films dealing specifically with the theme of miscegenation. The color question appeared in the most unusual situations, particularly *Kings Go Forth* (1958), an epic cliché of wartime in France, where two soldiers (Frank Sinatra and Tony Curtis) find it nicer to be in Nice than at the front. Sam (Sinatra) falls in love with Monique Blair (Natalie Wood), whose parents are American, although she has been reared in France. Monique lives with her widowed mother, and reveals to Sam that her father was a Negro. Exactly *why* this is introduced is never really clear unless it was intended to bring some sort of adult shock to a basically *What Price Glory* situation, for even Mademoiselle from Armentières is fashionably under the color line in contemporary war

American film mythology: American GIs are more susceptible to miscegenation. *Far left*: Natalie Wood and Frank Sinatra, *right*: Tony Curtis, in *Kings Go Forth*.

films. There is also a triangle complication, for while Sam is away, Monique becomes infatuated with Britt (Curtis) after hearing him play a jazz solo on a trumpet. This implies that even Monique's French upbringing cannot assuage the jazz-tremors of her American Negro heritage. Of course, nothing is solved in the film. Although Sam and Britt go through a baptism of fire and limb-loss, their characters are molded out of a screen clay pit as tough-talking, hard-drinking, callous hedonists, and the fact that both love *and* racial awareness are merged in their personalities is supposed to be basis for poignancy; besides, marriage with Monique is only weakly suggested at the conclusion of the film. Perhaps the most unfortunate part of *Kings Go Forth* was its adherence to the lamentable Hollywood practice of casting a white actress in the part of a mulatto heroine, thereby weakening even further an already unsuccessful attempt to jump on the bandwagon of popular film concepts regarding hardhearted American officers falling madly in love with foreign girls of another race. *Kings Go Forth* convinced one that racial films were once more in vogue, and the so-called taboo theme was simply a "gimmick."

Although it attempts boldness, *Night of the Quarter Moon* (1959) only belabors the question of intermarriage. Ginny (Julie London) marries a wealthy San Franciscan, Chuck Nelson (John Drew Barrymore), while on a vacation in Mexico. When she reveals that their marriage might cause them trouble because of her racial background (she is one-quarter Portuguese-Angolan, which is, one supposes, cause for some sort of genetic alarm), Chuck tells her that such statistics only bore him. However, the film erupts into a succession of violent and racially antagonistic episodes on the part of Chuck's society-minded mother (Agnes Moorehead), the San Francisco police force, and the neighbors. The fact that Chuck is a Korean war veteran, susceptible to mental blackouts and fatigue, creates an odd impression about American film myths of this nature. It would seem that war veterans are more susceptible to miscegenation, and that certain environments, like the Caribbean or Mexico, actually put one into that frame of mind which considers racial backgrounds to be of major insignificance, eventually leading to intermarriage. All of this chaos leads to one of the most incredible courtroom sequences in film history, during which Ginny's Negro lawyer (James Edwards) strips the blouse from her back in front of the judge so that her skin color can be revealed as white. *Night of the Quarter Moon* did contain one notable feature, however. It showed an adjusted, sophisticated, and extremely articulate interracial couple, Cy and Maria Robbin (Nat Cole and Anna Kashfi), and Maria's summation of a white man's general attitude toward a quadroon is a very forthright and adult statement that takes one by surprise.

It is, indeed, the social position of an individual who is able to pass for white that seems to bear most interest for film-makers, and it was only a matter of time (28 years) before a remake of *Imitation of Life* (1959) would appear. Fannie Hurst's novel, a tear-jerker, could possibly have been a fine film, considering the different film techniques and audience attitudes of 1931 and 1959. However, the earlier version of the film is the more honest of the two, if only for the fact that the mulatto girl, the true figure of pathos, was played by Fredi Washington, a Negro actress. But the basic premise that any Negro girl with a white skin is doomed to despair on a social level is maintained in a most unreal and almost farcical manner. The clichés are kept intact and aimed at the tear ducts, and once more, one cannot help feeling that a Negro screen writer might have been able to bring subtlety into the characterizations. *Imitation of Life* is a hymn to mother love, a popular fable of ironic contrasts between the light and the dark realms of racial discrimination. A famous actress, Lora Meredith (Lana Turner), and her daughter, Susie (Sandra Dee), are devoted to the Negro maid, Annie Johnson (Juanita Moore), and her mulatto child, Sarah Jane (Susan Kohner). But it is the behavior of Sarah Jane as a beautiful young woman that is handled falsely. Living in a nonsegregated environment in a Northern metropolis, surrounded by the glamour of Lora's world of the theater, it is inconceivable that Sarah Jane would be made to feel inferior by people around her, especially since she is not, by any stretch of the imagination, obviously a Negro. It is equally incomprehensible that Sarah Jane's taste in clothes would not be affected by the chic apparel of both Lora and Susie, both of whom symbolize a world to which she very much wants to

"Ironic contrasts between the light and the dark realms" of mother love. *Above*: Sandra Dee and Lana Turner, *below*: Susan Kohner and Juanita Moore, in *Imitation of Life*.

belong. The final stroke of absurdity lies in the sequence in which Sarah Jane is savagely beaten by her white boyfriend (Troy Donahue) when he learns that she is a Negro, implying that anyone who attempts to step out of an established class structure, racially or otherwise, must be subjected to physical violence. This attitude (equally out of place in a film like *Room at the Top*) comes as a shock and reflects a dangerous kind of moralizing. As if inner anguish is not enough for an individual who is unable to successfully "pass" for white, or move from one social stratum to another, one must behold such a character actually beaten up and thrown into the gutter.

In *Imitation of Life*, Annie's funeral is epic sentiment in the charlotte russe tradition, complete with a spiritual by Mahalia Jackson—an episode that is

The hero in isolation:
Harry Belafonte in
*The World, the Flesh
and the Devil.*

completely fictional and as incredible to Negro spectators as it is to white; and Sarah Jane's psychological maladjustment never leads one to imagine that she would so blatantly embrace her Negro heritage by hysterically throwing herself upon her mother's coffin; also one is never told what the girl eventually does or becomes. What is not understood by the makers of *Imitation of Life* is that a Negro's sympathies are with Sarah Jane, *not* Annie, and that contemporary audiences are able to discern the finely hypocritical dictums of the fake solution, the outdated stereotypes of the code, and, in a sense, the anti-integrationist's point of view.

The Negro character in the nineteen-fifties is very much the hero or heroine in isolation, and the cinema never quite illustrates this quality of "invisibility" and frustration as often as it should. Perhaps the most effective presentation of this particular aspect of racial adjustment is *The World, the Flesh and the Devil* (1959), in which Ralph Burton (Harry Belafonte) finds that he is the only person alive in New York City after some great destructive force has swept away all human existence. The horror of loneliness in New York, a potential Angkor Wat surrounded by steel foliage, is brilliantly evoked, at once underlining one's contemporary fears of sudden radioactive destruction, and emphasizing the symbolic figure of the Negro hero alone in society.

The appearance of two white people throws the film back into the world of color consciousness. Sarah Crandall (Inger Stevens) meets Ralph, and for a time they exist together, but he insists upon maintaining separate living quarters. The racial issue remains symbolically in his mind, though, in reality, it is gone with the civilization around them. When Benson Thacker (Mel Ferrer) arrives, however, a triangle is created, a wall of simple-minded clichés obscures the true situation, and, after a gun battle and fight, the men declare peace, join hands with Sarah, and walk into the oblivion of Wall Street together.

This parable exemplifies today's approach to the theme of interracialism: vague, inconclusive, and undiscussed. Like a fascinating toy, American filmmakers survey the problem from a distance, without insight, and guided by a series of outmoded, unrealistic concepts regarding minorities. The major irony is this: that in a country where life is actually lived quite freely with races so intermingled, it is still difficult to capture this sense of freedom, of humanity, this robust diversity of backgrounds of American life upon the screen. As far as motion pictures are concerned, the Negro character remains mysterious because he is the most diversified by background, by color, and by regional dialect, and, considering the number of films involving Negroes, the race as a whole is inadequately represented on the screen. Represented solely by limited night-club entertainers and recording artists, and only a few outstanding young actors (Poitier, Belafonte, and Henry Scott, who has appeared in only one small role so far), it is no wonder that audiences cannot get a sense of truth between the black, brown, or beige images that vary so greatly from celluloid to reality, from mythology and stereotype to history and drama.

ERNEST CALLENBACH

RECENT FILM WRITING

A Survey

When I was little, I wanted to be a mathematician. I have always been fasci-nated by those who do pure research, by the great mathematicians who, by making an advance in one direction, unlock years of fruitful research pos-sibilities for succeeding generations. This taste for research is quite personal and absolutely irrational.

—JEAN-LUC GODARD TO JEAN COLLET,
SEPT. 1963

Vol. 24, no. 3 (Spring 1971): 11–32.

Ernest Callenbach © Ken Stein

It's a satisfaction to film people, in a general way, that so many film books are now being published. After the long lean years, it's comfortable to think that our faith in the art is at last being justified. For if anything signifies Seriousness, it is books. Yet a publisher and editor like myself must be constitutionally skeptical, in hopes of conserving both sanity and trees. The motives people have for wanting to publish are, to say the least, mixed—though we have only recently begun to receive in the film field any sizable number of manuscripts that are clearly sprung from the publish-or-perish fount, that source of so much academic intellectual corruption (not to mention the waste of paper). And especially in a field where the pace of publication has increased so fast, we need to stop and try to take stock of the purposes and worth of what has been done. There have been a tremendous number of film books published in the past year or so, although the output relative to that of the established fields like English or sociology is still modest. Once, we could have the easy feeling that we could read everything that came out. We now face a situation like that in older fields, where specialization is forced on us whether we like it or not: nobody has the time to read all the books that are appearing. I regret this, personally speaking, because it means a kind of fragmentation and dispersion of intellectual activity, but it seems to be inevitable whenever any subject is attacked by large numbers of people; in science, matters have gone so far that the dozen or so workers really concerned with a given problem communicate with each other by telephone, xerox, or at worst mimeograph, between Berkeley, Cambridge, Dubna, or wherever, and only see other scientists at occasional meetings; publication itself is a side product of the process—not unimportant, of course, but it merely memorializes what has happened, and adds to the problems of the abstracters and information-retrievers. (When Watson and Crick had cracked the DNA structure, they took pains to bring their report down to a crisp 600 words, and could hardly be accused of littering up the intellectual universe.)

Film is still, however, within the domain of the humanities for most writers who address themselves to it. An occasional sociologist ventures some notions, usually with a generality that film historians consider flimsy; an occasional psychologist uses film as a research recording tool. There are probably some curious scientific problems involved in film perception, but so far no psychologists have found them interesting. People writing about film have usually been interested in it either because it's an art that intrigues them (like most critics) or because it's a mass medium they hope can be turned to political advantage (a tradition going back to John Grierson, who was a political scientist and socialist agitator). We are now, however, coming to a point where both of these emphases seem limited and insufficient, and people seem to be getting ready to try integrating them, to deal with film as an art that is inherently political even in the most apolitical hands. . . .

It seems to me that we now have critical resources that greatly surpass those of a decade ago; our general-audience magazines, in particular, are now immensely better served, and the critical books which have flowed from this journalistic work seem to me to constitute a remarkable outpouring of critical energy, knowledge, and intelligence. Many new and good critics continue to develop within the specialized film journals. As a congenital pessimist, I choke to say it, but we *have* never had it so good.

Nevertheless, speaking more as an editor than a critic, I would like to try here to make some sense of what has been happening in film criticism recently on the level of ideas. I do not propose another round of critical arm-wrestling, of which I am probably more tired than any reader could be. Nor do I have a defensive attitude about film criticism's contribution to our culture. It is reported that when an actor attacked John Simon, in a television debate, Simon tried to justify his role as a critic by lamely recounting how he had worked in dramatic productions and so on; even Pauline Kael, when attacked along the line of how can you know anything about it if you've never done it, once retreated to telling of her work with the San Francisco underground. Such arguments are farcical because they ignore the fact that criticism is an art in its own right. Writers who can get hundreds of thousands of intelligent persons to read their stuff are clearly practitioners with some kind of real skill; but it's not the same skill that film-makers have, much less actors. Like film-making, criticism is a kind of culture-secretion, and they share a few elementary prerequisites like taste and intelligence; but the working requirements of the two are utterly different. We might as well demand of an actor that he be able to write a readable, stimulating, informative critique as ask a critic to act (or direct, for that matter). The business of the film-maker is to make films; the business of the critic is to react to them—as sensitively and intelligently and wisely and interestingly as he can. I don't find a balance of presumption on either side. There is a plainly visible Darwinian selection process among critics, just as among actors; if you can act or write so that it impresses and interests people, and have reasonable luck, you'll be able to work and become known. It would be excellent if more critics tried their hand at scriptwriting or directing, and more directors tried their hand at writing criticism, but it isn't obligatory; they are working opposite sides of the same movie street, and should have the mutual regard of good gunfighters or good con men or good trial lawyers.

Our critics span a range of philosophical assumptions and tastes which is broad enough (though so far entirely bourgeois) to cope with almost all films produced in recent years, one way or another; you have always been able to find a critic who could deal with films in a way that seemed reasonable to you, whether your tastes ran to Hawks, Kramer, or Bergman.

In what way, then, can this body of critical work be considered deficient?

One way to begin is by noting that practically nobody writes *books* of film criticism. If this seems a strange statement after a year when more film books have probably been published than in all previous publishing history, consider that among the books that could be considered as serious, major criticism only a tiny handful were original, "real" books—Wood on Bergman and Higham on Welles, above all. For the rest—Kael, Farber, Sarris, Pechter (and Youngblood to a lesser extent)—all was packaging together of previously written material. I indicated earlier one practical reason for this—you can make a living by writing for magazines, and you can't just by writing books. Robin Wood, I believe, mainly teaches to live; so does another excellent British writer, Raymond Durgnat. But in this country our film teachers don't seem to include talented critical writers, with the exception of Sarris, who has begun to teach at Columbia.

Now journalism is not necessarily a bad thing for writers. Bazin was, after all, a journalist, and a harried one at that. Some of Shaw's best writing was done under journalistic pressure. A weekly deadline can be an inspiration, and so can the fact that in weekly criticism you get no chance for second thoughts or leisurely revision. Nonetheless, writing in the review format has drastic limitations. You can imply theoretical matters, but in the general press you had better be sure they don't get too heavy. You can revert to themes broached in another piece, but you had better make every review essentially free-standing— you can't depend on the reader keeping a connected argument in mind from one to the next. You can mention old films, but you had better organize your reviews around current ones, and if you generate any historical perspectives, you had better keep them light. Moreover, the finer a writer you are, the harder it becomes to turn your reviews into genuine chapters of a book (even supposing editors encouraged you to try); for a review done by a skilled writer is a special-purpose item that cannot easily be put to other purposes. From a practical working standpoint, thus, reviews aren't really useful grist for an integrated book—they may, indeed, be outright obstacles.

An equally severe problem with working as a weekly critic is that it forces you to waste your time: especially with today's situation where foreign films are having a hard time entering the U.S. market and domestic production is falling off, there simply isn't a film worth writing about every week. (Or indeed sometimes every month.) And this disability is simply memorialized in the ensuing books. In *Going Steady,* for instance, out of some 76 films Kael discusses, about 10 seem to matter to her as films. She has important and intriguing things to say about many of the unimportant films; but when the balance tips this far one feels it as a waste of talent—not only is criticism here an independent art, but a superior one; it's like devoting an orchid-grower's finesse to the production of snap beans. There is no question that the ordinary output of an art-industry like film deserves some attention, above all because the first works of promising talents generally fall into the less-than-triumphant category, and also because film criticism is inevitably cultural criticism and must convey to the reader some sense of the general cultural output surrounding works of unusual interest. But what we most relish in good criticism is the sense of a fine mind responding to a fine work: in fact, it is the excitement of this give-and-take process, which Kael is extraordinarily good at conveying, that makes criticism an art: who really reads critics to obtain ratings for movies? Sometimes, indeed, the critique that fascinates us most is busily setting forth an opinion on a film utterly different from our own. (Just as, in science, we may admire a co-worker's experimental technique but believe that his results must be interpreted differently.)

As a group, our American big-time critics are very good at responding to movies; in one way or another, they make you feel that it would be simply marvelous to hang around listening to them in person. (Complaints have even been heard about the cult of personality in film criticism, where the critic becomes the star just as the director has.) They are sensitive and witty people, often with a stunning gift of phrase. I think it not far off to say, however, that general ideas do not much interest them. Why this is, I do not pretend to know; perhaps there is something about the very act of writing criticism which means that one tends to so intently focus upon the work in immediate question that sensitivity in that context triumphs over all more general kinds of mental activity. Theorizing, that particular speculative curiosity which motors science, takes after all a very special mental set. Its presumption may even be inherently at odds with art, which is by nature unsystematic, ad hoc, furtive, messy, vital. (Or so at least I would imagine Pauline Kael might argue.) The theorist must attempt to "rise above" individual cases, to arrive at large generalizations—a process which inevitably dissociates his sensibility from actual films, at least to some extent. It is significant that Bazin, the most theoretical critic of our times, also relied constantly on scientific allusions and metaphors in his work.

Theorizing can be a pleasure quite in itself, of course, just as playful activity. But as a kind of intellectual work it appeals to disappointingly few people. Besides, it's scary; as Kael remarks, "In the arts, one can never be altogether sure that the next artist who comes along won't disprove one's formulations." However, this is a risk any person who indulges in what we might very loosely call "scientific" thinking has to take. Indeed it is practically foregone that one will look a bit silly, for every generation of scientists reworks and refines previous thought—sometimes even throwing it out bodily. There is no reason to hope that criticism (even Bazin's!) can be exempt from this process; nor can concentrating on the refinement of taste exempt one—for tastes too change, indeed even more rapidly and irrationally.

Criticism *needs* ideas, however, and I would like to spell out some of the reasons, perhaps a bit painfully. Criticism cannot in fact rely upon "taste" alone; every good critic's way of thinking rests, if we bother to analyze it carefully, upon a pattern of assumptions, aesthetic and social; and it employs a constellation of terms appropriate to those assumptions. The act of "criticism," in essence, as opposed to the mere opinion-mongering of most of the daily press, is the application of such terms to the realities of a given film: describing it, analyzing it, evaluating it, and in the process also refining the terms and assumptions. Nobody would enjoy it much if the process were carried out in an obvious and mechanical way; on the other hand, there are benefits to be gained by carrying it out with more intellectual elegance and determination than are customary among our film critics. For the terminologies current today really don't seem to be suitable for coping with crucial current developments;

they leave the sensitivity and intelligence of the critics stranded whenever a difficult new film appears—a *Persona, Weekend,* or *Rise to Power of Louis XIV.*

Assumptions and terms reasonably suitable for dealing with conventional narrative fictions have been around for a long time. Basically "realist" in tenor, these ideas have never applied very well to non-narrative and expressionist forms, especially experimental ones; the neglect of experimental film by critics has been due at least as much to practical embarrassment at this as to the inaccessibility or low quality of the films. They have also, as Brian Henderson suggests . . . not been very useful for analyzing internal ("part-whole") relationships in works of art—precisely the kind of formal analysis we need to fall back on in a period like the present when relations to reality have become largely moot.

Realist assumptions tend to deal in terms of essences, but film has no single essence such as Bazin sought—it is a multiform medium, and all signs point to our entering a period of increasing fragmentation. We may never reach another consensus, such as underlay traditional Hollywood craftsmanship, as to what film is or ought to be. Assumptions may henceforth have to be couched in terms of polarities, or "ideal types." The notions that will seem natural to the future are almost literally invisible to us, because they will make assumptions we cannot entertain. It seems certain, however, that any new nomenclature must include terms for dealing with the relations between the art's materials and its forms, and the relations between the work and its viewer. Surrounding and to some extent subsidiary to such terms will be various others concerned with technique or style: questions on the level our criticism now chiefly deals with. But where are the critics who are developing new terms? (I must reserve judgment about the "structuralist" school of analysis until it shows itself more clearly in English; so far, work under this banner has seemed either conventionally literary-thematic analysis or "iconography" on a stupefyingly naive level.)

The critic needs new ideas because otherwise it is impossible to articulate what the new film-maker feels and does; otherwise the most delicate critical faculties can register only zeroes. Most artists, of course, have ideas they are plenty willing to express, and indeed often talk in a strongly programmatic style. (The Flaherty Seminars were an attempt to institutionalize this phenomenon.) It's seldom, however, that artists have an interest in or grasp of large trends in their art, and the root act of artistic creation is in any event not ideational. A rare film-maker, like Eisenstein, happens to be good at theorizing about his own kind of work; Godard, in his elliptical and maddening way, seems to be the only one around at present. But aside from such rare exceptions, we will get our ideas about what is going on from critics, or we will not get them at all. It would be a good thing if our critics could, over the next couple of years, come up with some new and coherent ones.

Every critic worth reading has some heresy to propound, and William Pechter's in *Twenty-four Times a Second* (New York: Harper & Row, 1971. $8.95) is that of revelation: he believes that the truth is ready to hand, if only somebody will come forward to seize it, like Lancelot picking up the magic sword. Thus he tends to be a little scornful of other views, brashly overconfident that he is of the Elect. In fact, when he is good he is very good, but sometimes he is not. His explication of *Breathless* is acute, energetic—his abilities outstretched to cope with a challenging work. His defense of de Broca's *Five Day Lover,* and of de Broca's essentially noncomic talent, is the kind of clarification of style and genre we badly need and rarely get. But his attempted clearing of the air about *Marienbad* gets nowhere because he is unwilling to entertain the possibility that the film is as psychological as it is, and as un"moral"—he writes of its containing "scarcely a line of dialogue that one can imagine being spoken." Yet clearly, if the film makes any sense to anybody at all, this can't be true. And it seems in fact that most of us, though perhaps not Pechter, do indeed "imagine" dialogue like *Marienbad*'s in plenty of our adolescent and not-so-adolescent fantasies. It's bad dialogue, perhaps; but that doesn't keep us from imagining it—quite the contrary, for it is a minor subspecies of pornography, whose necessary repetitiousness and obsessiveness it shares. The *Marienbad* case sets one limit for Pechter's method; to his relentless moral tests, the film yields no clear pink or blue reaction. It makes no *statement;* yet it exists, it *presents* something. But that something is not of the order which Pechter can analyze; he complains, thus, that "the deeper we probe into the characters' consciousness, the less we know and understand them." But what if the film is not "probing," or at least not probing "characters"—what if it is the complex embodiment of fantasy, something like visual dreaming? Pechter even ventures to speak confidently of "failure" when he surely must have considered that he could be misunderstanding the film's intention. At the end of his essay, conscious of the problem, he poses it in fancifully stark terms: whether art serves beauty or knowledge. He declares roundly that the end "must, of internal necessity, be that of knowledge"—but only after qualifying this to apply only "where the subject of art is the human being, at least, the human being as protagonist of an action." Thus finally he must beg the question—for whatever *Marienbad* is, it does not seem to be that sort of art. It is, rather, some weird transitional variant between the film drama we are familiar with and some as-yet-undefined species toward which film is moving. As Kipling had it in his story, something that is neither a turtle nor a hedgehog may still come into existence and survive, and somebody will come along to name it arma-dillo. But poor *Marienbad* has no category in Pechter's nomenclature.

Nor is Pechter, to my way of thinking, really any more reliable than most critics on more conventional fare. In dealing with *The Wild Bunch*, he neglects the important *machismo* side of Peckinpah's personality (the film in fact owes major debts to a Mexican novel). Pechter thinks Nicholson the only interest-ing thing in *Easy Rider,* whereas his actorish performance seemed to me the major tonal flaw in the film—entertaining, but as out of place as an interjected juggling performance might have been.

Pechter's essay against Eisenstein is a bold attempt at a major overhauling job, but it still seems to me rather perverse. This is not because of its judg-mental side—I am not greatly agitated by the question of whether or not *Potemkin* is a Great Classic, though I think it is rather more humanly inter-esting in an allegorical way than Pechter does—but because his essay merely sets up an undergraduate dichotomy and plumps for one side of it: Bazin and Renoir over Eisenstein and montage. But in the art history that must some day be written about film, no film-maker is an island; and Eisenstein, whose thought is immensely more complicated and subtle than Pechter admits, will have to be evaluated not only in the circumstances of the deadly society he in-habited but also in the context of a larger world artistic tendency with coun-terparts in other arts. Pechter skirts edges of this large problem here and there—he quotes Eisenstein on Joyce, thinking to ridicule only Eisenstein—but doesn't try to do anything with it.

Of Bergman, Pechter has little good to say—and even less of the recent films, where morality has given way to psychology and what Bergman also thinks of as a kind of music. He is good on *Psycho;* though (as I did too at the time) he misapprehends the ironies of the phony psychological ending. He makes a valiant defense of *The Birds* on the grounds that it is about "Nature outraged, nature revenged"—a kind of premature ecology story, with Jobian overtones—which I find clever but hopeless, fundamentally a city person's mis-placed fantasy ("nature's most beautiful and gentle creatures . . .").

Was will der Mensch? one of my philosophy professors used to begin by asking. And in Pechter's case the dominant underlying concern seems to be with the question, "Is this film or film-maker truly great?" The question can be interesting, and attempted answers to it can be interesting; but as an orga-nizing principle of analysis it seems to me somehow deficient—its role really ought to be that of a working hypothesis, as it was for Bazin, but not the *end* of enquiry. Assuming and believing that *Bicycle Thief* is great, or that *Diary of a Country Priest* is great, Bazin always goes on to propound ideas of another order: ideas having to do with how the films work upon us, what their aes-thetic assumptions and strategies are, ideas in short having to do with style, in the largest sense. Pechter has some ideas about style, but they largely boil down to negative propositions. Eisenstein is a bad artist (and a bad man, as well as a bad writer) because he elevated art above truth, thus betraying both man and art. *Marienbad* is a bad film because it is not about character and plot in a manner that provides "meaning" or truth. Bergman is a bad director because his is an art of surfaces.

Well then, what *is* this truth? Don't stay for the answer, because there really isn't one. Each artist has his own truth: Buñuel's that "this is the worst of all possible worlds" (I'd like to verify the original on that some day—did he say "the worst" or "not the best"?); Welles's, Renoir's, Fellini's. It seems to be, in fact, essential to a great artist that his truth cannot be described. But it is the role of the critic to discern and announce its existence, and to excoriate all those false artists who don't tell the truth.

Whatever its virtues, this is a narrower conception of the critic's task than most critics accept. Consequently, Pechter heaps much scorn for their laxness upon film magazines, film books, other film critics, and "film enthusiasts," and thus generates unfulfillable expectations in the reader that his own book will somehow be a quantum jump ahead of other film writing. Pechter is a most intelligent and sensitive critic; disconcertingly, what keeps him from the very front ranks is precisely a certain hubris, a prideful fastidiousness which can become suspect even though it never becomes crippling as it does in the work of John Simon. Pechter quotes Lionel Trilling, on Agee, as saying that "nothing can be more tiresome than protracted sensibility"; but his 300 pages of careful, judicious, humane prose end merely with a section called "Theory," leading to the conclusions that critical consideration of art must be whole, cannot concentrate on mere technique, and is inherently dependent upon reactions to "the aesthetic ramifications of art's meaning."

It is any critic's right to imply that his candlepower exceeds others' by a significant margin, or that the darkness is denser in film than in other parts. But it is more accurate, as well as more modest, when critics recognize that their work is part of an inherently confused welter by which tastes and ideas rub upon created works and little by little give off the light, such as it is, by which we and posterity understand them. Bazin, who seems to me the most important film thinker of our times, was too busy analyzing films, trying out his ideas on them, constantly testing and revising and rethinking, to be much concerned with the sort of ultimate, permanent critical purity Pechter envisages as the goal. I would be the last to deny that film criticism could use a lot more sensibility of the kind Pechter possesses; but in itself that is not enough. We also need new ideas; and the fundamental ideas lurking in *Twenty-four Times a Second*, as in virtually all other current film writing, are still Bazinian. It is as if Bazin had thoroughly ploughed the field of film aesthetics right up to the edge of the precipice. We can retrace his work, refine it, even eke out a corner here or there that he missed. But nobody has yet figured how to fly off into the space at the edge.

Ironically, the only critic around with a patent on a theory is Andrew Sarris, whose success as popularizer of the "*auteur* theory" was, as he genially points out in the introduction to *Confessions of a Cultist*, entirely inadvertent (New York: Simon & Schuster, 1970. $8.95). Worse still, this theory isn't a theory at all, but a practical critical policy: a good one within obvious limits, but of no analytical significance in itself whatsoever. When we look back over Sarris's columns of critical writing, as assembled in this volume, it's surely just as much a shambles as the film criticism he observed about him in 1955. He's a master of the light phrase ("Neorealism was never more than the Stalinallee of social realism") and he is charming about his extra-theoretical divagations—at least when you share them, as I do about Vitti. Sarris makes a halfhearted attempt to turn the auteur theory into "a theory of film history" in the introduction to *The American Cinema*; but a little later he remarks that it's "not so much a theory as an attitude." Actually, he doesn't have a real theoretical bone in his body; he is a systematizer, but that's quite a different matter, just as entomologists who revise the species classifications for bees are useful scholars, but not doing the same kind of work as researchers who try to figure out how bees fly. Sarris's early formulations of auteurism, as about *The Cardinal*, are significantly evasive: "Preminger's meaning" is said to be strongly expressed visually, but is nowhere described—as indeed, judging even by what else Sarris says of the film, it could hardly be by anybody. Admittedly, in this volume we get only a truncated Sarris. But a truncated pyramid is still visibly a pyramid. When one takes away Sarris's holy categories, however, there is nothing theoretical left; what is left is an urbane, witty writer with an elephantine memory and an accurate eye who often has sensible things to say about individual films and who can occasionally, as in his account of seeing *Madame X* on a transatlantic jet, become quietly and movingly personal. The generalities he will sometimes venture are usually perverse: "The strength of underground cinema is basically documentary. The strength of classical cinema (including Bergman) is basically dramatic. The moderns—Godard, Resnais, Antonioni, Fellini—are suspended between these two polarities." Moreover, by 1968 he could write in the *New York Times* a piece whose defense of auteurism is so mellow that it must seem mild to Pauline Kael (who can, of course, out-*auteur* anybody when she feels like it). At this point it seems clear that Sarris's contribution to American film thought has been massive in transmitting enthusiasms but minimal in analytical ideas.

Perhaps disappointingly, neither *Dwight Macdonald on Film* (New York: Berkeley Books, 1970. $1.50) nor Stanley Kauffmann's new collection, *Figures of Light* (New York: Harper & Row, 1971. $7.95), offer any explicit, coherent view of the new relations developing between art and audience, though they are our two most socially concerned critics. Macdonald was famous for his own attempt at classification, his formula of masscult and midcult and *kitsch*. But as far as analytical ideas go, he cheerfully confesses that "being a congenital critic, I know what I like and why. But I can't explain the why except in terms of the specific work under consideration, on which I'm copious enough. The general theory, the larger view, the gestalt—these have always eluded me." He then trots out a number of rules of critical thumb, but only to prove his honesty by showing how they don't work. It is only in a piece about comedy that he is less diffident, and works out some general principles (he calls them "rules"); but these could apply to novels or plays just as well as to films. His long and careful commentaries on Soviet film, written in the thirties and forties, are to my mind excellent cultural criticism of a kind we also could use, but they don't contain anything original about film style.

Kauffmann, though he is concerned with the new audiences and the delicate balances between commercial hype and genuine novelty in "youth" films, isn't willing to venture any general ideas about what is going on, either; at the end of his new book he takes refuge in the vague notion that "standards in art and life are becoming more and more congruent." In a day when survival is a catchword, it may be true that criticism should select and appraise "the works that are most valuable—most necessary—to the individual's *existence*." But how do we know which works those are? To determine this, we need ideas about the society we must survive in, the role of art in it, how we "use" art, and what makes art "useful."

The virtues of Manny Farber (*Negative Space*. New York: Praeger, 1970. $7.95) have usually been taken to be those of the wise tough guy who looked at movies for their secret pleasures—those precious moments in the action flicks when a clever actor and a "subversive" director got together either to spoof the material or give it an instant of electric life. He liked plain, grubby stories, and he was allergic to pretensions at all levels, including those of auteurists; he could write of Hawks's *Only Angels Have Wings* as a "corny semi-catastrophe" and conclude that "No artist is less suited to a discussion of profound themes."

But there's more to Farber than that. Farber hates what has been happening to movies since about 1950, but that doesn't really matter; he could just as well have loved it—except that adoration has a tendency to blur vision. What counts is that he notices what has been happening, and indeed has been more willing than any other critic to try and elaborate on it in fairly general terms. If he might be called an aesthetic reactionary, at least he's a conscious and articulate one. Like Bazin, of whom one perhaps hears faint indirect echoes in

Farber from time to time, he believes in realism. The excitement of action films comes from the fact that they confront us with the gutty, tough, cynical inhabitants of the American lower depths caught on the fly in miscellaneous unhallowed adventures, racing through stories of greed and desperation under the guidance of skilled and modest craftsmen. Appreciation of such films is a kind of shock-of-recognition operation—the film whirls you through its itinerary and here and there you notice things that matter, because they are *real*. Farber would never presume to hope for what Bazin saw in neorealism—whole, finished works of dense and convincing realism—but he would have wanted it if he thought it could happen here.

Yet Farber never confronts the philosophical or aesthetic or indeed practical problems such a position presents. He is not some kind of Christian like Bazin, so he has no doctrine of immanence or anything like it. Though he is aware that film involves much pretense, he is unwilling to consider that "realism" is itself a set of conventions; his defense of the old style is ultimately an impossibly simplistic "imitation" theory. Thus he can argue: "What is unique in *The Wild Bunch* is its fanatic dedication to the way children, soldiers, Mexicans looked in the small border towns during the closing years of the frontier"—as if he (or we) had to have been there to enjoy or appraise the movie. He never confronts the phenomena of camp, whereby a bit of acting which strikes him as utterly real can seem totally phony to somebody else—especially somebody coming along a couple of decades after. (It has been found that fashions in clothes can't be revived until 30 years have passed; does a similar cycle length perhaps prevail for film acting?)

But, from the standpoint of his devotion to the old Hollywood style, Farber sees pretty clearly what has been happening: how the former "objective" style, the anonymous, geographically reliable world of the Hollywood writer, cameraman, and editor, has given way to far more dubious forms dominated by directors, in which some vague directorial viewpoint or personality or style is supposed to be the center of interest, rather than the plot.

Nor is Farber's perceptiveness only a recent development. As far back as 1952 he was complaining about *A Streetcar Named Desire* that "The drama is played completely in the foreground. There is nothing new about shallow perspectives, figures gazing into mirrors with the camera smack up against the surface, or low intimate views that expand facial features and pry into skinpores, weaves of cloth, and sweaty undershirts. But there is something new in having the whole movie thrown at you in shallow dimension. Under this arrangement, with the actor and spectator practically nose to nose, any extreme movement in space would lead to utter visual chaos, so the characters, camera, and story are kept at a standstill, with the action affecting only minor details, e.g., Stanley's backscratching or his wife's lusty projection with eye and lips . . . the fact is these films actually fail to exploit the resources of the medium in any real sense." He exaggerates, of course; moreover, a few years later Kazan was to be the first director actually to *use* the vast expanses of CinemaScope with any visual activity—in *East of Eden*, a film Farber did not comment on. And we must admit that Farber's analysis is often careless and suspect. Thus he remarks that Toland's camera in *Kane* "loved crane-shots and floor-shots, but contracted the three-dimensional aspect by making distant figures as clear to the spectator as those in the foreground." Would space have been expanded if they were fuzzy? On the contrary, keeping the backgrounds blurry (and the lead players in stronger light than anybody else) was a basic device of standard Hollywood craftsmanship to *avoid* perception of fuller spatial relations, resulting in compositions where the figures stood out but not really against anything—only as differentiated from a background blur, usually of constructed, shallow sets.

Nonetheless, Farber's basic descriptive contention cannot, I think, be escaped: "The entire physical structure of movies has been slowed down and simplified and brought closer to the front plane of the screen so that eccentric effects can be deeply felt." (81) "Movies suddenly [in the early 60's] changed from fast-flowing linear films, photographed stories, and, surprisingly, became slower face-to-face constructions in which the spectator becomes a protagonist in the drama." (190)

Since the Hollywood film is dead, and Farber knows we can never go back to that aesthetic home again, what is left? In a melancholic survey of the 1968 New York Film Festival, he plumps for Bresson's *Mouchette*—because of the girl's toughness, the down-and-out life surroundings taken straight; his terms of praise are that the film is "unrelievedly raw, homely, and depressed," and here for some reason he does not mention Bresson's camera style, or note how odd it is that Bresson's excruciatingly refined and stripped-down handling should be the last refuge of the streamlined naturalism he loved in the action flicks. There's not much left in the cinema to love, for Farber. Some of Warhol's odd characters appeal to him; he approves of Michael Snow's "singular stoicism"; he likes *Ma Nuit chez Maud* because of Trintignant's performance and the richness of its provincial detailing, and *Faces* grabs him because of Lynn Carlin. But no more do we enjoy "the comforting sense of a continuous interweave of action in deep space." We're caught up instead in conversations about movies—"a depressing, chewed-over sound, and . . . a heavy segment of any day is consumed by an obsessive, nervous talking about film."

For readers who only know Farber by his famous piece on "underground" (action) pictures, this new volume will establish that he is indeed one of our first-rank critics, with a very personal vision, an often irritating yet suggestive style, and faster ideational reaction-time than anybody around. But the acuteness of his vision is like looking down the wrong end of a telescope; everything looks very sharp, but small and going away.

In the one corner, thus, we have Farber, stoutly bemoaning the destruction of the movies—the replacement of the plotted and acted picture by exudations of the director's twisted psyche. In the other, we have Gene Youngblood, bemoaning the phoniness and redundancy of the plotted and acted picture and announcing the cinematic millennium because film-makers are at last portraying "their own minds."

I think Youngblood's *Expanded Cinema* (New York: Dutton, 1970. $4.95) is an important book, so I want to get out of the way some minor criticisms of it. Youngblood writes in that blathering style common among media freaks—half Bucky Fuller mooning and half McLuhan "probes"—with a peculiarly alarming Teutonic tendency toward agglomeration. "The dynamic interaction of formal proportions in kinaesthetic cinema evokes cognition in the articulate conscious, which I call kinetic empathy." (Who won World War II, anyway?) He can be staggeringly naive or unperceptive. ("A romantic heterosexual relationship of warm authenticity develops between Viva and Louis Waldron in the notorious *Blue Movie*.") He is prone to wild exaggeration and imprecise logic, but he is also the only film writer on video technology to display mastery of the subject. He is very unhistorical, which may merely be fashionable disdain of the past, but is more probably a youthful lack of familiarity with both the conventional and experimental cinema of the past—however lamentably unexpanded they may have been. Nonetheless, its drawbacks do not prevent the book from being a forceful and clear exposition of a theoretical position, like it or lump it.

Youngblood's view can be sketched thus: all previous cinema has been deficient because it has been falsely and tautologically "about external things, to the neglect of the proper subject of cinema, namely the mind of the film-maker. In the synaesthetic cinema or expanded cinema, however, this dominance of the external is thrown off; all things become subjects of film perception and expression, nothing is taboo, "unfilmic," or impossible to deal with, and people use film as freely or wildly as poets use words. It turns out that the really distinguishing mark of synaesthetic cinema is superimposition, which guarantees that you are not seeing *via* a "transparent" medium, but *via* one which somebody has created—the function of superimposition is perhaps similar to that of the frame or canvas surface in illusionist painting. Sound is dissociated from image—for, as Bazin remarked, the coming of synch sound extinguished "the heresy of expressionism," and Youngblood is reviving it.

All this has some smell of novelty; does it perhaps have the substance as well? What is the philosophical and ideological basis of such a doctrine?

One way of getting at this question is to look back at earlier major shifts in film "theory." We can now see that Bazin crystallized, in his defense of deep-focus and neorealism, the essence of the cinema of Christian Democracy—postwar European liberalism. (As Bazin himself pointed out, it is no argument against this that Italian script teams, for political insurance, customarily included one Communist, one Christian Democrat, one rightist, and one socialist.) Similarly, we can see in Eisenstein the essence of Bolshevik cinema—*montage* was "democratic centralism" in the hands of the film director, while deep-focus and widescreen allowed democratic participation in the image-reading process by the liberal middle-class spectator.

If we can see a similar over-simplified paradigm in Youngblood, it would probably be that of the coming technological slave culture, in which the masses of people are allowed to play with certain fascinating visual toys within a tightly controlled corporate society. At a discussion during the opening festivities of the University's Pacific Film Archive in Berkeley, Youngblood spoke of people playing with visual equivalents of Moog synthesizers—processing bits of film into their own personal video trips, presumably rather as our ancestors used to gather round the piano and sing "Daisy, Daisy." What really catches his imagination is man-machine symbiosis: computers retrieving and storing and diagramming in a playful partnership with people—a sort of benign Big Brother fantasy in both the sibling and sociological senses.

There are two main problems with this kind of notion. One is aesthetic, and was put into blinding focus at the Berkeley symposium when somebody asked John Whitney how long it took him to make *Matrix*, no doubt expecting an answer like six hours. But it took three months of shooting (fully assisted by sophisticated computer hardware) and three more months of editing, filtering, and printing. Now *Matrix* is not a frightfully complex production project in its own area, and it is a highly precise, mathematical kind of work which probably entails less than the usual stresses and indecisions of artistic creation. In short, we are *not* about to enter some kind of aesthetic paradise in which every man can become his own electronic-wizard artist. Indeed the lesson of Youngblood's own tastes is that the best of the "synaesthetic" artists he discusses (Belson, Brakhage, Hindle) don't even use electronic technology, only rather ingenious but conventional home-made rigs, in which the impact of the human hand, brain, and eye can be directly and intimately achieved. I don't wish to assert that there is a simple inverse relation between technological involvement and artfulness—if there were, modelling clay would be our greatest art form. But artfulness does not spring from technology, it *uses* technology. When you ask machines to create something, as in the computer-generated films Youngblood describes, it comes out dreadfully flat and dull. Even the most sophisticated machines so far built have no sense of play.

What they do have is a high price tag, and this connects with the second problem, which is a social one. Modern technology is extraordinarily expensive, and it is owned, in a patent and often in a literal sense, by giant corporations which lease it out. Youngblood talks like some kind of radical, and writes for the underground *LA Free Press,* but he seems surprisingly comfortable with big business, and sometimes seems to think it philanthropically inclined to coddle our perceptions. Yet we must notice that the only way artists have gotten at complex video technology is through the ETV stations in San Francisco and Boston and by the "artist in residence" situation at Bell Telephone and a few other corporations. It is not only chroma-key video equipment which is tightly controlled, either; the coming wave of EVR and other cassette distribution systems is similarly tightly held, with patents flying like shrapnel. The sole aspect of video technology which is freely available to artists and users the world over—largely thanks to Japanese initiative, it seems—is half-inch video tape, a cheap, convenient but shabbily low-definition medium. Anybody using the other systems will not be his own master; he may not be as bad off as artists at the mercy of old-fashioned producers or distributors, but he will be in jeopardy whenever he becomes unorthodox.

Youngblood writes of the new technology creating a technoanarchy in which all men's creativity is freed. This kind of optimism is not just constitutional, of course, but springs from a particular philosophical position—one which, in my opinion, fits neatly into the program of the technofascism which is what is *really* developing in our society. Youngblood's position is a confused and oversimplified one. "We've been taught by modern science that the so-called objective world is a relationship between the observer and the observed, so that ultimately we are able to know nothing but that relationship." (127) A few pages later he breezily remarks, "There's no semantic problem in a photographic image. We can now see through each other's eyes . . ." (130) To compound these basic confusions, he also contends that the "media," by which he and other McLuhanites tend to mean not whole, real-people social institutions but only their technical manifestions, are becoming and will be our only reality: our very minds will be merely extensions of the worldwide media net.

This kind of view has been put so often lately that it is necessary to say why it is not reasonable, or perhaps even sane. First of all, we are creatures with a very detailed biological constitution that has powerful mental components; moreover, the psychological development of a human being takes place on a level of experience quite different from that of the media. Without necessarily being Freudian about it, our minds are much more extensions of our experiences in babyhood and childhood than they are of anything that happens to us later. We must expect the replacement of a good deal of normal parental interaction by interaction with television sets to have significant effects on our children and on their own later child-rearing practices as adults—effects in the direction of depersonalization, passivity, and so on. Even so, the residues and constancies of our biological condition and earliest life persist; they account for the myths that concerned Jung, and in a different sense Bazin. They are, indeed, most of what enables us to continue as viable mammals, rather than appendages of machines.

Second, the development of society, of which the media are only one part, is a material process. "Information" freaks like to argue that objects don't matter anymore—only information is important, and since information is immaterial, we have transcended materialism. This seems to me a gross and pathetic delusion. In fact, the more highly technological our society becomes, the more dependent it is on physical objects, and the more numerous, tightly controlled, and demanding of natural resources those objects become; in short, the more sheer power is at stake, and the more the power relationships of the society come to bear. Since power in our society is chiefly ownership power we can't possibly understand the media and what they are doing to us without understanding who owns them and what their purposes are. In the real world media do not "expand" of their own accord.

Like most idealist positions, Youngblood's is founded on physics metaphors rather than biology ones: despite the seeming modernity of much computer talk, it is still basically nineteenth-century thinking—childishly and enthusiastically fascinated with the machine, eager to assimilate human actions to parallels with machines.

I would like to note two puzzles which arise from the films Youngblood discusses, but which do not seem to worry him. We can see two general trends or types of film in Youngblood's examples—the classic, mathematical, abstract work of the Whitneys, people who work with computer simulation, etc., and another trend in which the imagery is drawn from the real world, though perhaps much transformed—Belson, Baillie, Hindle, Brakhage, Bartlett and DeWitt, etc. The films of the former group are often intriguing, beautiful, or startling; but it is only films in the latter group which are moving. Why is this?

My own guess is that it has to do with the way our perceptual processes work. We do not really perceive abstractions; if Gestalt-oriented psychologists such as Rudolf Arnheim are to be believed, abstractions are indeed inherent parts of the methodology of the perceiving process itself. "Pure" shapes such as those of the Whitney films thus pose a kind of short-circuit situation; in this they are perhaps akin to certain antique mosaics or some op art. They cannot be sufficiently mixed and muddled to be stimulating to our entire perceptual resources, like part of the real world; it is too obvious that they are simply what they are, whereas our evolution has equipped us precisely to cope with those appealing or disturbing things whose nature may not be obvious. Youngblood is scornful of the repetitions and tautologies of the fiction drama film; but repetitions are pretty clearly the stuff of our mental processes, and I would hazard indeed that it is in certain obscure repetitions (perhaps of earlier experiences we happen to share with the film-maker) that we would find the source of what touches us—even in quite abstract films like *Re-Entry*.

The other puzzle concerns the visual characteristics of images that have been passed through a video system—like those of *OffOn, Moon 69, The Leap,* and so on. It seems to me that their characteristic visual style is significant in some way, but I don't know of what. Of course they have scanning lines: a constant visible interference with clear vision. Their colors are photoluminescent, rather than the dye colors of ordinary photography; with such colors it is impossible to achieve quite what we think of as "natural" tones, as of skin, leaves, earth, or water. Moreover, that crucial superimposition is an immensely easier and more flexible technique in video than in conventional film work, and some kinds of color keying and dropping-out can be done in video that cannot be done in film at all, or only through the most tedious kind of hand work. All these qualities of the video image certainly make for a "dramatic" image, that is, an image whose own nature is a strong focus of attention, just as they go against a "realistic" image, that is, an image that seems to be transparent in the way Bazin loved.

It may be that imagery of this sort is properly nameable as *hallucinatory*: vision in which the heuristic or biological function of sight is subsumed to an introspective, purely "visionary" function: one in which we no longer see in order to learn or to act, but in order to enjoy seeing *itself*. (We might, clearly, argue certain parallels between this kind of imagery and modern painting.) Youngblood is curiously reticent about the relation between drugs and "expanded cinema," but it is commonplace among heads that certain films are "trippy" while others are not. Films, indeed, offer the opportunity for a kind of tripping that painting, for instance, cannot offer, no matter how "visionary" the painter tries to be. (Most hip painting, ironically, turns out merely fanciful in a grotesque way, without any of the magical perceptual stimulation of the film trips.)

If we are entering an era of hallucinatory film in some such sense, this may also explain away one difficulty about video transformation work. With a network control room at your disposal you can do what Youngblood visualized as happening at a visual synthesizer: you can transform images according to dozens of technical commands, superimposing, echoing, changing their color, contrast, orientation in space, and so on. Putting into the machine only a few minutes of color film original, you could come out with hours of wildly varied and superimposed material, like a huge symphony based on the theme

"Row, Row, Row Your Boat." But if the conventional narrative film is formalized and redundant, what would we say of such an operation?

No: the artist must still deal with his images; no machine can do it for him. And art is long and madness-making. In the end, Youngblood's heresy is the familiar American one, that technology can save us, that by building a better object we can redeem our souls. In his Los Angeles terminology, this approach leads to "the new man." So it may, alas. But it won't lead to good films.

If, as both Farber and Youngblood imply, we are indeed entering an era of unrealistic or even hallucinatory cinema, in both the feature and underground or independent films, can we foresee anything of the questions that aesthetic theory must try to answer? Rudolf Arnheim, in his pioneer work four decades ago, dwelt on the nonrealistic elements of the film image—those aspects of it which abstracted from (or distracted from) its faithfulness to things photographed. Yet Arnheim was able to do this kind of analysis comfortably precisely because an abiding faith in reality still existed: film might abstract from reality, all right, but everybody knew it was still there, waiting to be kicked, like the tree Johnson used to refute Bishop Berkeley. With Youngblood and other media freaks, this basic certainty has been seriously eroded, though not perhaps as seriously as they like to imagine. But do we therefore face an era solely of what Henderson calls part-whole theories: theories of formal organization, in which what is represented or used as material for art is of little interest compared to the ways in which the artist manipulates it? I think not, basically because there is now a much greater sophistication among us about the relations between artistic styles and social phenomena. Purely formalist theories, thus, are likely to seem empty and decadent to most people who care about such things. Hard though it may be, we are going to have to develop theories which deal both with forms and with their relation to audiences and the societies to which the audiences belong.

Such theories cannot be developed in isolation from the rest of our cultural life, nor in isolation from our personal lives and personal relations with films and other film-goers; we have to try anew to make sense of the current movie-going experience (or the electronic forms that displace it) just as "going to the movies" made social and intellectual sense to Kael or Farber in their youth. No search for meaning or value in art can be conducted on the basis solely of pure sensitivity and intelligence, as Pechter imagines; any search for meaning is inevitably engaged in some kind of social debate or indeed (to use a hackneyed term that is still viable) struggle. A critic's intelligence cannot be "committed," in the sense that Kael has made pejorative, but it cannot help being *engaged* with some explicit sense of the potentialities of film art and of our culture generally. There is no need to conceive these potentialities dogmatically or narrowly; but critics must try to conceive of them in some way, and apply their conceptions aggressively to developments in film-making, if criticism is not to be simply entertaining opinion-mongering.

It would seem, then, that the particular task confronting our little film magazines at present is to seek out and develop critical writing with some theoretical ambitiousness and bite. Obviously no one can will ideas into being; they must come from our social experience, as Eisenstein's were stimulated by the Russian Revolution and Bazin's by the Liberation. But among the many new and good writers who are coming out of the great wave of interest in film, I hope that we editors can manage to find and encourage and publish those who are engaged in developing the genuinely new ideas we need.

PART TWO

THEORY

The five articles in this section are theoretical in different senses, which is congruent with the changed nature of theory in the eighties, the decade in which they all appeared. Each essay must pose the question of theory anew; no method or context can guarantee its occurrence. On the other hand, there is virtually no occasion or writing mode in which theory might not occur. In the eighties, and so far in the nineties as well, there is still theory, or anti-theory, that proceeds from a prior, fixed position and therefore issues mechanically. But theory that emerges in a context that does not determine it or on an occasion that has not been called to summon it for some end, may still surprise writer and reader alike.

As its title indicates, Virginia Wright Wexman's article is concerned with the practices of film analysts and text interpreters, whose work she posits as shaped by "concrete historical processes." She classifies them according to Antonio Gramsci's distinction between (1) traditional intellectuals who serve the dominant group by rationalizing its social hegemony and (2) a more "organic" function "by which a rising group theorizes its own entrance into the upper reaches of the social power structure." Those who argue *Vertigo*'s status as pure cinema serve the power structure by "rationalizing particular cinematic institutions at work in the film." *Vertigo*'s feminist critics belong to a larger group of women intellectuals "who have elaborated a discourse on women at a moment when women have been entering high-level positions both within and outside of the academy."

Wexman cites Donald Spoto's Hitchcock biography to establish that in making *Vertigo*, the director was concerned primarily with the stars and the locations. (She observes astutely that Hitchcock's obsession with his actresses enabled him to function more effectively in "the environment of commercialized eroticism that defined the Hollywood style.") Wexman superbly elucidates the social implications of the Madeleine-Judy contrast and of the role of tourism and travelogue in fiction film, and in *Vertigo* in particular. She also notes that critics have failed to grasp the "displacement of racial and class issues into the sphere of sexuality" in *Vertigo* and other films. She cites an essay by Michael Rogin that uses psychoanalysis with analysis of fifties cold-war America to trace a polarized conception of "otherness." In the popular imagination, Wexman argues, such conceptions were often focused on women. "Images of women were often deployed to displace and domesticate fears of a more ungovernable xenophobic cast, fears of the Russians and of 'subversives.'. . . Hitchcock has masked the ideological workings of racism and xenophobia beneath a discourse of sexuality that is itself idealized as romantic love."

The title of Esther C.M. Yau's article on *Yellow Earth* is precise: "Western Analysis *and* a Non-Western Text," not *of*. *Of* presumes a through reading that reveals the main significations of a text. What this article provides instead is a many-stranded exploration on both its "analysis" and "text" sides. That Yau is highly adept at Western-style analysis and knowledgeable of Chinese history and culture makes this double exploration possible.

The article is dialectical in more ways than one can enumerate without writing a text as long as hers. This dialectic, the back-and-forth between expertises, provides continual illumination and increased admiration for the film, but nothing like resolution. Yau observes that the Chinese audience is used to "tear-jerking" melodramas but that *Yellow Earth*

> has missed most of the opportune moments for dialogue and tension, and is thus unnecessarily opaque and flat. . . . The scenes where Cuiqiao is forced to marry an older stranger, and the one where her tiny boat disappears from the turbulent Yellow River, would both be exploited as moments for pathos. But here they are treated metonymically: . . . the rough dark hand extending from off-screen to unveil the red headcloth of the bride is all one sees of her feudalist "victimizer" [and] the empty shots of the river simply obscure the question of her death. In both situations, some emotional impact is conveyed. . . . But the cinematic construction is incomplete, creating an uncertainty in meaning and a distancing effect in [the] audience.

These are some of the reasons that this apparently simple, visually stunning film is so elusive of interpretation. Thus, the text that Yau begins to explore on the first page of her article, she is still exploring on its last page. Even the Chinese censors were puzzled; they frowned but did not ban.

Yau also seeks to make the text responsive to its historical and political contexts, asking in what way the text is different from and incommensurable with master narratives (socialist dogma, mainstream filmmaking, classical editing, etc.). The main part of Yau's article pursues these and other questions regarding "the interweaving and work of four structurally balanced strands . . . on three levels: a diegetic level, . . . a critical level, . . . and a discursive level." The strands are narrative, but are also "semic" ones, that is, sites of meaning. Yau's analysis illuminates the film, but her question remains: "How does this non-Western text elude the logocentric character of Western textual analysis as well as the sweeping historicism of cultural criticism?"

The point of departure of Manthia Diawara's 1988 article is twenty-five years of African cinema, beginning with *Borom Sarret* (1963), Ousmane Sembene's first film, and proceeding to Cheick Oumar Sissoko's *Nyamanton* (*The Garbage Boys*, 1986) and other films. This work has "necessarily created an aesthetic tradition which African filmmakers use as a point of reference which they either follow or contest." Why has this tradition largely escaped serious attention?

> The lack of African critics who know African traditions is at fault, as well as . . . the ethnocentrism of European and American film critics. . . . They think that [African] cinema is in the process of finding its individuality, that the film-makers have not mastered yet the film medium, that the camera style is still primitive in African films.

Diawara's goal is "to make possible the definition of a dynamic aesthetic proper to Africa." He will do this by developing the relations between African oral tradition and African cinema. An essential part of these relations has to do with the figure of the griot (the bard), who is both a storyteller and the custodian of traditional values. Fundamental for the griot is skill in narration, including detailed, nuanced realization of the story itself. Not only is the filmmaker a kind of griot, but many African films also specifically refer to the griot tradition itself. "When African films are examined," Diawara notes, "one sees that all the directors resort in different ways to oral story-telling forms."

What follows is an illuminating discussion of different manifestations of the griot in a number of important films. Indeed, in the most brilliant turn of this influential article, Diawara demonstrates how each film's realization of the griot positions it socially and ideologically. For instance, *Borom Sarret* shows a fat griot with a gold tooth taking a cart driver's morning wages to tell him a story. The griot's narrative, authoritative in oral tradition, here exploits his listener and omits contemporary realities that oppress him. But Ababakar Samb's *Jom* (1981) surrenders its narrative authority to the griot and thus positions the spectator to identify uncritically with tradition, with which everything positive is associated, just as everything negative is placed on the side of modernism.

The articles by Marsha Kinder and Brian Henderson concern the applicability of Gérard Genette's categories of narrative analysis (as set out in "Discours du récit" [1972]) to film—a realm of inquiry about which Genette himself says nothing. Henderson considers Genette's five main topics—order, duration, frequency, mood, and voice—in relation to film. Narrative order chiefly involves what Genette calls analepses, which go backward in time, and prolepses, far less frequent, which go forward in time. If a work has no temporal variations, its order is called straight chronology. It seems that the majority of films of every era are told in straight chronology, whereas, according to Genette, such order is the exception in novels. The article discusses many examples of analepsis in classical cinema, American and European, and in the avant-garde. Because there is no "normal" reading speed, duration in literature has to do with the *relative* speeds of different passages, determined by comparing the number of pages devoted to different time periods, and dates these sections by the story time they cover. Films, on the contrary, have fixed viewing times; one may compare a length of film measured in minutes and seconds or in feet, to a portion of story, or vice versa, and one may assemble these findings in an exact table.

Narrative frequency—what Genette calls the iterative—has to do with relations of repetition between a narrative and a story. The most common of these—to narrate once what happened many times—is the iterative, strictly speaking, in which a single utterance takes upon itself several occurrences of the same event. Henderson discusses several instances of iteration in classical cinema before launching into an extended analysis of the Huw-narrated opening passage of *How Green Was My Valley*, which makes repeated use of the word "would," the principal verb form for the iterative in English. The almost imperceptible shift from the iterative to the singulative mode in Huw's narration raises the question of how such a slippage is possible in cinema. Are the images neutrally either iterative or singulative, depending upon a voice-over to define their temporal status? Another issue concerns what Genette calls the pseudo-iterative: scenes presented, particularly by their wording in the imperfect, as iterative, whereas their richness and precision of detail ensure that no reader can seriously believe they occur and reoccur in that manner, several times, without variation. This happens occasionally in Proust; in cinema it is pervasive because "richness and precision of detail" seem to be inherent in cinematography and sound recording. Genette's chapters on mood and voice painstakingly distinguish them. His shorthand for the difference is that mood has to do with who sees and voice has to do with who speaks. Voice in literature can be complex indeed, but someone—a major or minor character or an identified narrator (or a succession of these)—is understood to be speaking the words of the novel or poem. In cinema, it is unclear who "speaks" the images, music, sound effects, dialogue, and graphic material that comprise a film.

Marsha Kinder begins with a discussion of Genette on the literary and Henderson on the filmic iterative. Genette speaks of Proust's "intoxication with the iterative" and Henderson of an ultra-literal position according to which cinema, because of its precision and detail, is inherently singulative. Kinder then says:

> I am arguing precisely the opposite position: namely, that the iterative is inherent in cinema, either through the pseudo-iterative . . . or through the iterative implication (where the acknowledgement of the iterative repetition is only implicit and positioned within a scene presented as singulative). . . . Genette confines the iterative to temporal relations and to utterances about past events. Yet by acknowledging that iterative repetition depends on the mental construction of a class . . . of similar instances, he opens a space within the iterative for the issue of typicality. Since temporality . . . is not foregrounded in film the way it is in literature, I am arguing that it is this issue of typicality that is usually foregrounded by the iterative in cinema.

Kinder analyzes the opening of *Duel in the Sun* as an instance of Hollywood's intoxication with the singulative, where the iterative implications of scenes are used to naturalize the singulative and render the slippage between the two invisible. In neorealism, by contrast, the iterative background is not subordinate, "but at least coequal, normative, and determinant in ideological terms. . . . Individuals and their actions are chosen precisely because they are representative and typical in an iterative sense." In *Umberto D*, the maid's ordinary morning routine foregrounds the iterative. What Kinder calls "the spectatorial retraining function of the neorealist pseudo-iterative" is "perhaps most notable" in *Il Posto* (*The Job*). The film concerns the entry of a young man from Lombardy into the dehumanizing world of the Milanese bureaucracy. The character's typicality is underlined by the scores of other young people who are seen at his workplace, on the streets of Milan, in his suburban tenement, etc. Indeed, at a certain point, there is a sudden slippage into the iterative, as we see a series of brief scenes showing how each of five clerks from the office typically spends his evenings. In these sequences from both films, "the neorealist intoxication with the iterative immerses the spectator, not in the emotional intensity of personal memory as in Proust, but in the ideological relations between individual and collective experience." Chantal Akerman's *Toute une nuit* (*The Whole Night*) "goes much further in deconstructing traditional narrative." We see the beginnings of a series of meetings between various actual or potential lovers, but none is continued to produce anything like narrative development, let alone closure. Kinder argues that there is an important iterative aspect to this film also: "the brief scenes are presented in such a way as to suggest that these or similar events occur every night—an aspect that was already implicit in the title *Toute une nuit*."

BRIAN HENDERSON

TENSE, MOOD, AND VOICE IN FILM

(Notes After Genette)

Vol. 36, no. 4 (Summer 1983): 4–17.

*Narrative Discourse** is a translation of "Discours du récit," which is the major part of *Figure III* (1972) by Gérard Genette. Genette's topics are traditional ones of literary theory and criticism: order, duration, frequency, mood, and voice in classical fiction and the subversion of these in modern texts. Genette offers no new method of literary analysis but a clarification, systematization, and extension of older ones, amounting to a transformation of them. The book is immensely stimulating and has already been quite influential.

Aside from a reference or two, Genette does not treat film, and his work cannot be directly applied to film. Each of his categories must be rethought on the ground of film analysis, a project whose value is argued below.

What does *Narrative Discourse* do? It studies Proust's *A la recherche du temps perdu* and it studies narrative discourse; it is at once the criticism of one text and a theory of narrative. To do both without subordinating one to the other is a paradox; but it permits "a refreshing rotation and mutual entertainment between theoretical dryness and critical meticulousness." Genette compares the project to an insomniac turning over and over in search of a better position.

His study of narrative discourse is limited to the narrative text itself. He does not compare the *Recherche* to actual events, as one might a history, nor to the circumstances of its production, as might a biography of Proust. Rather he addresses the relationship between a narrative discourse and the events that it recounts and the relationship between the discourse and the act that produces it. But it is the narrative discourse alone that informs us both of the events that it recounts and of the activity that supposedly gave birth to it.

Narrative Discourse, An Essay in Method, translated by Jane E. Lewin (Ithaca: Cornell, 1980). *Figures of Literary Discourse*, translated by Alan Sheridan (New York: Columbia University Press, 1982) comprises translations of Genette essays from *Figure I* (1966), *Figure II* (1969), and an additional essay from *Figure III*. See also Seymour Chatman, *Story and Discourse: Narrative Structure in Fiction and Film* (Ithaca: Cornell, 1978), especially pp. 63-79.

Genette distinguishes three aspects of narrative reality within the narrative text: *story* refers to the narrative content, that is, to the chronological order of events implied by the narrative; *narrative* refers to the narrative discourse or text; *narrating* refers to the producing narrative action.

Having made these distinctions, Genette turns to method. Since any narrative is a linguistic production, telling of one or several events, he argues that it is legitimate to treat it as the development given to a verbal form, in the grammatical sense of the term: the expansion of a verb. "*I walk, Pierre has come* are for me the minimal forms of narrative, and inversely the *Odyssey* or the *Recherche* is only, in a certain way, the amplification (in the rhetorical sense) of statements such as *Ulysses comes home to Ithaca* or *Marcel becomes a writer.*" This perhaps authorizes us to formulate the problems of analyzing narrative discourse according to categories borrowed from the grammar of verbs. Genette reduces these to three basic classes of determination: tense, mood, and voice. Tense, which includes order, duration, and frequency, has to do with temporal relations between narrative and story. Mood has to do with the modalities, i.e., the forms and degrees of narrative representation. Voice has to do with the mode of action of the verb in its relations with the subject of the statement, not an actual writer or speaker, but the subject of the enunciating itself; more broadly, it has to do with what Genette calls the narrative situation and its two protagonists: the narrator and his audience, real or implied. These terms are borrowed from the grammar of verbs for narrative analysis; Genette claims no rigorous homology between the two instances.

To study the tense of a narrative is first of all to compare the order in which events are arranged in the narrative discourse with the order of succession these events have in the story. Types of order include straight chronology and anachronies, a general name for deviations from straight chronological order. Anachronous narratives begin, in one way or another, *in medias res* then go backwards (analepses) or, much less frequently, forwards (prolepses). Analepses are external when their entire extent happens before the beginning of the first narrative, commonly used to give background to the present action. They are internal when they fill in gaps occurring later than the start of the novel. There are also lateral ellipses, in which the narrative sidesteps an element within a chronological passage. Genette calls this paralipsis, ellipsis to the side; like a temporal ellipsis it may be filled in later.

It is not difficult to apply Genette's basic concepts of order to cinema. It seems that the majority of films of every era have been told in straight chronological order whereas, according to Genette, such order is the exception among novels. Prolepses are relatively rare in the novel but they are even rarer in cinema. Flashforwards are sometimes used by Resnais and Roeg, on the whole integrally to their projects; in some sixties and early seventies films they were used rather unsystematically as instances of "mind" or "cinema" or both, e.g., *Easy Rider*.

Anachronies in cinema come down mainly to analepses. Such figures are extremely rare in the first twenty years of film history, although one does find there dreams, visions, and even "reviews" of material shown earlier in some sequels, episodes of serials, etc. In *Broken Blossoms* (1919), Griffith introduces Battling Burrows then flashes back to his recent victory in the ring to explain his bad temper at having to keep in training; he introduces Lucy then flashes back to her encounters with a weary wife and with some prostitutes to show the options that hem her in. In the manner of classical fiction, *The Cabinet of Dr. Caligari* (1919) casts its main story as a long analepsis inside a framing story set in the present; but like *Last Year at Marienbad* (1961), this "past" may be delusional and therefore the "remembering" itself a strictly present action. Victor Sjöström's *The Phantom Chariot* (1920) exhibits a remarkable mastery of cinematic tenses, at one point presenting a flashback within a flashback.

The greatest period for analepsis in classical cinema was undoubtedly 1941–1957, that maturity of the sound film marked by *Citizen Kane* (1941) and *How Green Was My Valley* (1941). The latter begins with an older Huw leaving the valley and remembering it as it was; the rest of the film presents that remembering and never returns to the framing story, recurring at the end to memory images from the early part of the analepsis itself, in a kind of looping of the past. More usual is the analeptic structure of *All About Eve* (1950), which returns to the framing story at the end and carries it forward for an additional scene or two. *Citizen Kane, Double Indemnity* (1944), and *Sunset Boulevard* (1950) follow this pattern, as indeed do most analeptic films of the classical period.

Analepses in the cinema have nearly always involved the use of language, sometimes explicit dialogue setting up a return to the past, more often the direct intervention of language in the form of titles or voice-over. Without such linguistic cues, and quite often with them, analepses in classical cinema are usually marked redundantly by plot, indirect dialogue, music (dreamlike or "mental"), and optical devices such as blurs, rippling, fades, or dissolves. Classical cinema reacts to a tense shift as though to a cataclysm; the viewer must be warned at every level of cinematic expression, in sounds, in images, and in written language, lest he/she be disoriented.

Why is this? Cinema has no built-in tense system as language does. One cannot write a sentence without indicating tense but one can apparently make a shot, and therefore perhaps a film, without indicating tense. In written discourse the tense structure must be renewed with every sentence and, concomitantly, a single sentence may subvert that structure; Genette pauses over the tense structure of several individual sentences by Proust and their implications for the narrative as a whole. In the cinema, one is tempted to say, if the camera keeps running or if there is a cut to another angle within the scene, continuous temporality is the result; the cut to another sequence is read as straight chronological order, unless otherwise marked. One must do something, indeed a great deal, if a comprehensible shift of tenses is to be achieved in cinema. So, at any rate, classical cinema has persuaded us by making straight chronological order seem natural and inevitable. Cinema, unlike language, is, in Barthes's terms, a "complex system in which different substances are engaged," in which "the senses are subjected to the concerted action of a collection of images, sounds, and written words." Language need only change a word-ending to indicate tense shifts; cinema must pass from one complex conjunction of communication channels to another and provide a plausible transition between them, all without an explicit tense system.

This is one reason why films like *Wild Strawberries* (1957) and *8¹/₂* (1963) made such an impact when they appeared and have had such influence. They went back and forth between past and present without explicit linguistic cuing and with a subtlety as to other signals that made the old ways seem heavy-handed. These films seemed to abolish the rhetoric of tense shifts in cinema; in fact they substituted new rhetorics for old. *8¹/₂* in particular convinced viewers that it had achieved the seamless interaction between past and present that it had aimed for. Any spoken version of "I remember" would have defeated the film's psychological subtlety and cinematic fluidity. But other, well-hidden signals prepare the audience for tense shifts and guide it back smoothly. These include the context of setting and plot and Fellini's isolation of Guido by reframing or character movement just before a return to the past. There are also at times different optical treatment of past and present, wind sounds, fading of present voices, etc. Rota's music is used to bridge time shifts expertly as is Mastroianni's detachment and bemusement, his inwardness amidst public scenes, slight modulations of which carry him (and us) from something in the present to something in the past. He is passive yet alert to his own visions, as though receiving them from outside and shaping them at the same time. Indeed Fellini brings in a pair of mind-readers to keep his hero from introducing the past on his own ("Asa Nisi Masa").

Certain films undermine our ability to distinguish analepses from straight chronological order and thereby subvert narrative order itself. These include works by Buñuel, Duras, and Rainer, not to mention the semi-narrative films of the avant-garde. Made well before *Marienbad*—and more lucidly—Maya Deren's *Meshes of the Afternoon* (1943) tempts us to discover a single narrative order; our effort is necessary to the film's operation but is of course doomed to fail.

Perhaps the most formidable subversion of order specifically, of order as order, is *Not Reconciled* (1965) by Jean-Marie Straub, an adaptation of

Mastroianni as
Guido in *8½*

Heinrich Böll's long *Billiards at Half-Past Nine* (1962) into a 53-minute film. The story deals with three generations of a Cologne family and the resistance of some of its members to militarism in World War I, in the thirties, and in the postwar period in which it is set; it all takes place on Heinrich Fähmel's eightieth birthday, a *Ulysses*-like day on which various characters remember the past. Straub actually straightens out the novel's jumbling of the events of the day and eliminates most of its flashbacks. Nevertheless the film is vastly harder to follow than the novel because Straub has omitted most of the signals that cue viewers as to time shifts.* He uses straight cuts to go to the past and to return; there are no optical devices and no music cues. Voice-over is used for the past

*The film begins with a three-second shot of a man playing billiards, saying to a bellboy, "Tell me what, boy?", which is followed by eight shots with voice-over concerning boys involved in political conflicts at a high school. Then there is a shot of the billiard player ordering a cognac and five shots of the bellboy going to get it, including two flashbacks concerning his life at the hotel. A shot back in the billiard room, in which the bellboy asks if there is more to the story, is followed by twelve more shots, with voice-over, of one of the schoolboys being beaten, being smuggled out of the country, etc. At this point, less than seven minutes into the film, first- and even second-time viewers have no idea where they are and have no way to regain their footing for the rest of the film. For a fuller treatment, see Richard Roud, *Jean-Marie Straub* (New York: Viking, 1972), which remains the best introduction to its subject.

material itself, but not to bridge present-past shifts. Plot context and period detail are probably what viewers most rely upon to construct the narrative order of a work. Here too Straub withholds orientation: he makes his thirties shots and his fifties shots virtually indistinguishable in dress, environment, gestures, mode of speech, etc., which is also a thematic statement. (Some of the World War I–era shots have period flavor.) Also, there is never enough context provided to know with certainty which shots belong to which period, let alone how the various events depicted relate to one another. It is only upon multiple screenings or upon reading about the film, or both, that we realize that some of the characters are the same characters at different ages; there are two Roberts, two Schrellas, two Johannas, and two Heinrichs. Most remarkable of all is the temporal coherence of *Not Reconciled* when one has studied it carefully. Its order is straight chronology with three major analepses (Robert's two-part story of the thirties and Heinrich's story of 1910–1918) and two minor ones (Hugo the bellboy's life at the hotel). Straub is right in calling it a simple film but it takes a great deal of work to understand that.

All of our examples, from Griffith to Straub, have stayed within Genette's basic categories of straight chronology and analepsis. It is notable that he himself does not stay within these simple concepts. Thus he finds in Proust "repeating prolepses" (playing a role of advance notice), "prolepsis on analepsis," "analepsis on prolepsis," "analepsis on paralipsis," etc. Our discussions indicate that cinema has not (yet) developed the complexity of tense structures found in literary works. They also indicate that in cinema analysis the interesting questions have to do not with narrative order itself, but with *how* films indicate this order, both straight chronology and deviations from it.

For Genette, duration is a more difficult question than that of order or frequency because the time needed to read a text depends upon factors external to it. There is no "normal" reading speed so one cannot pose a hypothetical equality between narrative time and story time, against which to measure variations. One can, however, compare parts of the narrative discourse to each other to determine their *relative* speeds. This method applies only to the large narrative articulations of a work and not to detailed studies of rhythm, which, Genette notes, would lack rigor. Thus he divides Proust's text according to its principal temporal and spatial breaks, determines the number of pages devoted to each, and dates these sections by the story time they cover. He then expresses these findings in an overall ratio: the Combray episode devotes 140 pages to ten years, the Gilberte episode devotes 200 pages to two years, etc. On the basis of this table Genette assigns a range of variations to the Proustian text: from 150 pages for three hours to three lines for twelve years. He also notes a durational evolution in the overall text: a gradual slowing of the narrative through longer and longer scenes and a corresponding increase in the number and length of ellipses between such scenes. Genette calls such variations of speed, which all narratives have, anisochronies or effects of rhythm.

Films, of course, have fixed viewing times. One may compare a length of film, measured in minutes and seconds or in feet, to a portion of story, or vice versa, and one may assemble these findings in an exact table. One may examine the large narrative articulations of a whole film or the microrhythms of very short passages. Genette's account of duration does not enlarge these methodological options; he is dealing with a less exact case. But by making the question of duration newly interesting, he provides new motivation to make such analyses.

Duration in cinema is a very delicate matter, as anyone knows who has shown Straub or Michael Snow to an unreceptive audience. Even viewers sophisticated in other respects become angry if their sense of proper filmic duration is challenged.

If Straub's transgressions in *Not Reconciled* have to do with order, those of his *Chronicle of Anna Magdalena Bach* (1968) have to do with duration. The 93-minute film consists almost entirely of images and sounds of musicians in period costume playing Bach's works. An account of the circumstances of the composing and playing of these works, of Bach's financial difficulties, of the births and deaths of their children—and of little else—is spoken over the images and music by Anna Magdalena. She usually speaks over the ending of one work and the beginning of another or in very brief intervals between them. She also speaks very rapidly, as though speaking of family matters and external circumstances hurriedly between musical performances. Straub calls it a Marxist film because it presents the actual production of music (directly recorded), to which Bach's waking hours were massively devoted, as well as his marginal economic status and his struggle for the right to select his musicians. Despite superb performances of well-chosen Bach works, *Chronicle* still has the power to empty theaters and classrooms.

In the commercial realm, Frank Capra reports in his autobiography that the first version of *Lost Horizon* (1937) was too long and had too much background to the main story. As a result, the preview audience was restless throughout the screening. A durational miscalculation at the beginning threw off the reception of the entire film. Capra's response was to "Burn the first two reels," his chapter title for the incident, an indication of how strongly the durational code is enforced.

Film's multi-channelled textuality raises durational problems, and opportunities, not found in literature. Image, dialogue, voice-over, music, sound effects, and written materials may contribute, complementarily or redundantly, to a single duration; or they may create multiple, simultaneous, or contradic-

The Chronicle of
Anna Magdalena Bach

tory temporalities. Modern films have exploited such possibilities in a variety of ways. In *Le Petit Soldat* (1960), like *The Lady from Shanghai* (1948) before it, a final shot of the hero is held while the voice-over summarizes a much larger time period:

> It was after killing Palivoda that I learned of Veronica's death. Only one thing was left to me: learn not to be bitter. But I was happy, because I had a lot of time in front of me.

Similarly, *Badlands* (1973) opens with a long take of Holly in bed playing with her dog, over which we hear her voice-over:

> My mother died of pneumonia when I was just a kid. My father had kept their wedding cake in the freezer for ten whole years. After the funeral he gave it to the yard man. He tried to act cheerful but he could never be consoled by the little stranger he found in his house. Then one day, hoping to begin a new life away from the scene of all his memories, he moved us from Texas to Fort Dupree, South Dakota.

The classical cinema is not without its durational contradictions either, although one must look more carefully to find them. *How Green Was My Valley* (1941) covers many years of its novel source in less than one year, including births, deaths, two sets of emigrations, the transformation of the valley from garden to slagheap, etc. In the same year Huw begins school, graduates, and goes to work in the mines. The decision to use Roddy McDowall as Huw

Le Petit Soldat

throughout the film imposes this durational contradiction: Huw does not age while events around him suggest years going by. The other players do seem to get older—there is even an excuse for his mother's hair turning white suddenly. The duration of the plot and that implied by the performance level are contradictory, something that could not happen in literature.

Genette continues his discussion of duration and prepares for his discussion of frequency by proposing a general system of narrative speeds. In theory there is a continuous gradation from the infinite speed of ellipsis, defined as story time without discourse time, to the absolute slowness of descriptive pause, defined as discourse time without story time. In fact the narrative tradition has reduced that liberty to four basic relationships that Genette calls the canonical forms of novelistic tempo. Besides ellipsis and descriptive pause, there are the scene, most often in dialogue, realizing an equality of time between narrative and story, and the summary, a form with variable tempo—that of the other three is fixed—that covers the entire range between scene and ellipsis. Summary remained, to the end of the nineteenth century, the most usual transition between scenes, the background against which scenes stood out, and thus the connective tissue par excellence of novelistic narrative, whose fundamental rhythm was defined by the alternation of summary and scene. Genette ingeniously shows that, despite appearances, there are almost no summaries in Proust and no descriptive pauses. Proustian descriptions are always grounded in a character's perception and therefore are parts of scenes. Moreover, narrative cutting in Proust is never accomplished by Balzacian summaries but by a quite different kind of synthesis, that of the frequentive or iterative, which is used in conjunction with ellipses.

The cinematic equivalent of Genette's scene is clear enough; indeed the notion and the prestige of the dramatically present moment were borrowed by the novel from theater. Summary we will consider in relation to the iterative, below. Ellipsis in cinema is a vast topic; aside from single-take films on the Lumière model or virtual long takes like Hitchcock's *Rope* (1948), there can be no cinema without ellipsis. In Rossellini, Godard, and other figures of modern cinema, as in the later *Recherche,* ellipses tend to become longer and more abrupt. The scenes between gaps are not necessarily longer, as in Proust, but may be denser in synthesized content (Rossellini) or in *cinéma-vérité* detail (Godard). Rossellini's ellipses trace the movements of an argument unconcerned with conventional diegesis, though what he does show is usually "neo-realist" in its detail and objectivity. Similarly, but differently, Godard likes to balance the ethnographic detail of actual locations, direct sound, and observed gestures with the arbitrary jumps and *dénouements* of fiction, often expressed through ellipses. (In *Masculin-féminin* [1966], Paul's death occurs between the next-to-last and the last sequences.) Generalizing is hazardous, but both Rossellini and Godard tend to use long takes around their ellipses, as though their abruptness and force would be lost amidst montages.

Description poses special problems for film analysis because every shot serves a descriptive function, whatever else it may do. At the same time no shot is entirely descriptive, therefore cannot be a true descriptive pause, because the fixed time of film viewing makes it dramatic also. Even if no action occurs in this shot or in this setting, the time devoted to them builds expectations for action to come; they too are ticks on the dramatic clock. Indeed few things build more expectancy than silent shots of objects in a narrative film.

Speaking very broadly, some films seem to invent actions to fill out projects descriptive of a time or place (Ford's *Judge Priest*); others describe an environment so that we will understand the action to follow (every heist film). The opening scenes of classical narrative films generally describe a setting while introducing us to the protagonists of the action. The trick in classical script construction, as in the theater before it, was to accomplish this while already advancing the action. The opening sequence of *How Green Was My Valley,* told in the frequentive tense, describes a complex setting in detail, introduces us by name and personality to eight or nine characters, indeed to an entire village, and immerses us in a nostalgic vision of a way of life that will begin to deteriorate in the next sequence.

Description provides a bridge to frequentive or iterative narrative, for as Genette says, "The classic function of iterative narrative is thus fairly close to that of description, with which, moreover, it maintains very close relations." Narrative frequency has to do with the relations of repetition between the narrative and the story. Genette proposes a system of relationships between the capacities for repetition on the part of both the narrated events of the story and the narrative statements of the text. This system is reducible to four virtual types. One may narrate once what happened once; one may narrate *n* times what happened *n* times; one may narrate *n* times what happened once; one may narrate one time what happened *n* times. The last is the frequentive or, as Genette prefers to call it, iterative narrative, in which a single utterance takes upon itself several occurrences of the same event: "For a long time I used to go to bed early."

In classical narrative, iterative sections are almost always functionally subordinate to singulative scenes, for which they provide a sort of informative frame or background. In this the classical function of iterative narrative is fairly close to that of description: both are at the service of the narrative as such, which is the singulative narrative. The first novelist to liberate the iterative from its functional dependence was Flaubert, who constructed entire passages in its mode. But no novel has given the iterative a scope, importance, or technical elaboration comparable to Proust's. Genette develops these points in a series of fine analyses, including a classification of kinds of iteration that need not concern us here. Suffice it to say that his elaboration of the iterative is one of the most original things in *Narrative Discourse*.

In classical cinema, as in the classical novel, the iterative nearly always has an information or background function subordinate to singulative scenes. The exterior shots of trains or buses in backstage musicals signify numberless such journeys. If the words "Baltimore," "Philadelphia," "New Haven" appear under a series of train shots, as in *The Bandwagon*, then there is a narrative summary as well as iterative narrative; a specific itinerary is signified as well as numerous rides on trains. The montages of nightclub signs and clinking champagne glasses in romantic comedies are iterative in function. If they stand for a series of such evenings, they are what Genette calls generalizing or external iteration; if for one of them, what he calls synthesizing or internal iteration.

In *Trouble in Paradise* (1932), Lubitsch shows Mme. Colet's typical activities as head of a company by cutting from her on a stairway to four shots of servants and assistants down below, who say, respectively: "Yes, Mme. Colet," "No, Mme. Colet," "No, Mme. Colet," "Yes, Mme. Colet." This rhyme is itself rhymed later when Gaston has taken over direction of the company. Lubitsch shows this change (summary) and the typical obedience that Gaston now receives (iteration) by cutting from him to another series of servants and subordinates: "Yes, M. LaValle," "No, M. LaValle," "No, M. LaValle," "Yes, M. LaValle." Needless to say, the repeated yesses and nos also echo and mock the sexual oscillation that is going on in the plot.

The opening sequence of *How Green Was My Valley* presents a large and sustained figure of iteration; it takes up over half of the film's entire spoken narration by the older Huw, whose face we never see. As he is leaving it for the last time, Huw remembers his valley as it was when he was a boy, describing a typical day through a repeated use of the word "would," the principal verb form for the frequentive in English.

> Someone would strike up a song and the valley would ring with the sound of many voices . . . Then came the scrubbing . . . Most [of the coal] would come off but some would stay for life . . . There was always a baron of beef or a shoulder or leg of lamb before my father. There was never any talk while we were eating . . . My mother was always on the run . . . After dinner, when dishes had been washed, the box was brought to the table, for the spending money to be handed out. No one in our valley had ever seen a bank. We kept our savings on the mantlepiece.

At this point, when Huw gets his penny, hurries to the candy shop, and meets Bron, his future sister-in-law, the voice-over narration suffers an odd sea-change, dropping almost imperceptibly from the iterative to the singulative mode.

> It was on this afternoon that I first met Bron—Bronwen. She had come over from the next valley for her first call on my father and mother.

> I think I fell in love with Bronwen then.

Which afternoon is "this," since the voice-over has been describing the typical activities of many days but of no particular day? Thematically one might call this a fall into time: out of the frequentive mode, which is preserved, as in Proust, from the ravages of time, into the singulative mode, the order of irreversible time and change, in which the family will be dispersed and the valley destroyed. The fall into time is also a fall from grace, corresponding to Huw's first love attachment outside of the family as well as to his brother's marriage, the first actual division of the family.

Most interesting, theoretically, is how and why such a slippage is possible in cinematic iterative; it would not be in literary narrative. Are the images neutrally either iterative or singulative, depending upon a voice-over to define their temporal status? If so, then the continuity of the images may sustain us through a shift in tense, while the changed verbal tense tells us how to read the images. Or is there a shift of reference here? The images have seemed to follow the voice-over narration, as though illustrating it; perhaps, its introductory function accomplished, the voice-over now refers to the images. "This afternoon" seems to refer to the images we see before us. This shift may prepare us for the withdrawal of the voice-over in favor of the images, which will now be furnished with synchronized dialogue; this is what happens in *How Green Was My Valley*. After Huw describes his love for Bronwen and the scene shifts to her introduction to the family, from which young Huw is pointedly excluded, his voice-over ceases—except for seven or eight more interjections of a clearly summarizing sort throughout the rest of the film.

Our discussion of *How Green Was My Valley* raises the problem of what Genette calls the pseudo-iterative:

> scenes presented, particularly by their wording in the imperfect, as iterative, whereas their richness and precision of detail ensure that no reader can seriously believe they occur and reoccur in that manner, several times, without any variation.

This happens occasionally in Proust; in cinema it is pervasive because "richness and precision of detail" seem to be inherent in photography and sound recording, at least in those practices of them engaged in by most films. Thus Donald Crisp and company walk to the pay window in precisely this way only once, as recorded in the take included in the release print of the film. Some might take an ultra-literal position and say that this makes the iterative impossible in cinema; its images and sounds are always singulative. But, as noted, cinema is a "complex system"; it is the "concerted action" of images, sounds, including voice-overs, and written words that create meaning in cinema, including iterative constructions. And, as Metz once argued, the fact to be understood is that films are understood, including the cinematic iterative.

Nevertheless, the singulative tendency of recorded sounds and images can have a backlash effect on iterative constructions. *How Green Was My Valley* goes from the iterative to the singulative by virtue of a tense change in the voice-over. A much more frequent figure is a scene that begins in the iterative, by virtue of a title or a voice-over, then becomes singulative, as though reverting to the singulative in the absence of continued linguistic definition to the contrary. A title in *Lady Windermere's Fan* (1925) tells us that the way a gentleman rings a lady's doorbell reflects the state of their relationship and we see a tentative finger finally engage the button. "But when he knows her well . . ." says a later title, and we see an impatient finger ringing and ringing. Under the pressure of the title, these images are iterative: they narrate once what happened many times; but in the scenes that follow each image, singulative events occur. One might say that the doorbell images are iterative and the rest of each scene singulative; or better, that the doorbell images have a dual status, belonging both to an iterative construction and to a singulative one.

There is also the opposite problem, what Genette calls "a sort of contamination by the iterative" of a singulative scene. In Proust this is produced by a few iterative sentences within a singulative passage. In cinema, as in the other performing arts, there are many ways to suggest habit, frequency of occurrence, and typicality within a singulative context. Indeed, how many plays and films, from *King Lear* to *On the Waterfront*, open on a scene of habitual order just as it is about to be changed irrevocably.

Genette's chapters on mood and voice painstakingly and brilliantly distinguish them. Perhaps for that reason, his treatment of the two topics is very much intertwined. Strictly speaking, the mood of narrative statements can only be the indicative since the function of a narrative is to report facts, real or fictive, not to give an order (the imperative), to express a wish or state a condition (the subjunctive), etc. Admitting that he is extending the linguistic metaphor, Genette argues that within the indicative there are differences between degrees of affirmation as well as different points of view from which an action may be looked at. One can tell *more or less* what one tells and one can tell it according to one point of view or another; this capacity and the modalities of its use are what Genette's category of narrative mood concerns. Thus the chief subcategories of mood are distance and perspective. The narrative can furnish more or fewer details, rendered in a more or less direct way, and can thus seem to keep at a greater or lesser distance from what it tells. That distance need not be fixed throughout a narrative but may vary according to the knowledge of one or more participants in the story, adopting what is usually called their point of view. Thus the narrative seems to take on, with regard to the story, one or another perspective.

Genette's discussion of distance entails an extended contrast between mimesis and diegesis. Mimesis is direct imitation, as are words and actions on a stage. Written narration cannot be mimetic since it presents words and actions described by an intermediary—the author or, more correctly, the narrative discourse itself. An exception is direct speech, presented in the manner of drama, in which the mediation of the narrator seems to disappear. Genette cleverly shows that the interior monologue, which he prefers to call immediate speech, pushes mimesis to its limit by "obliterating the last traces of the narrating instance and giving the floor to the character right away." Some analysts have called cinema or particular films or passages mimetic, others have called them diegetic; sometimes the terms are used more or less interchangeably. Genette's definitions might make possible a new clarity regarding cinematic instances, although, again, cinema is a more difficult case because it is a "complex system." Films usually present the direct imitation of speech and action but do so in a mediated, or diegetic way. Films may combine mimetic and diegetic elements in a large variety of ways and may also oppose them through slight discrepancies or gaps, as in Bresson's *Diary of a Country Priest* (1951).

Narrative perspective is a second mode of regulating information, turning on the use or absence of a restrictive point of view. Genette confronts at the outset a widespread confusion between mood and voice, between the question: Whose point of view orients the narrative perspective? and the question: Who is the narrator? Or, more simply, between "Who sees?" and "Who speaks?" Genette's clarification of this large, muddied realm is, with his original discussion of frequency, his most conspicuous achievement.

Genette prefers the term "focus of narration" or "focalization" to "point of view." Ishmael and Strether occupy the same focal positions in *Moby-Dick* and *The Ambassadors*, respectively. That Ishmael also narrates while an author absent from the story narrates *The Ambassadors* is a question of voice, not of mood. Wayne Booth's implied author and narrator, the narrator who is dramatized or undramatized, reliable or unreliable, are all categories of voice.

Genette distinguishes nonfocalized narratives, generally the classical narrative, from internally and externally focalized narratives. Internal focalizations are fixed if we rarely leave the point of view of one character; variable if we go back and forth between more than one character; or multiple if the same event is evoked several times according to the point of view of different characters, e.g., *The Sound and the Fury,* certain epistolary novels, or *Rashomon.* In external focalization (some of Hammett and Hemingway), the hero performs in front of us without our knowing his thoughts or feelings. A focalization is not necessarily steady; a work may combine many types of focalization, even all of them, although particular passages are usually focalized in one way rather than another. The division between variable focalization and nonfocalization is sometimes difficult to establish, since the nonfocalized narrative can most often be analyzed as a narrative that is multifocalized *ad libitum.*

Older Huw is the narrator of *How Green Was My Valley*—it is literally his voice that we hear; but this does not control the question of mood. We almost never see things from young Huw's visual perspective. *How Green* is nonfocalized in that no sequence, let alone the whole film, is shot from any one character's perspective. It is variably focalized in that it frequently borrows a character's perspective for one or more shots—sometimes for dramatic reasons, sometimes opportunistically because it yields a stunning image or an efficient view of the action. Huw's arrival at school is shot in a non-focalized way; he is small and timid in the hallway but no character is looking at him in this way. When Huw opens the door, Ford cuts to his point of view of the girls in the class looking hostile, then to the boys in the class, farther away, looking even more hostile. (Both shots cannot be from Huw's perspective, strictly speaking.) Ford then cuts to a shot of the teacher from Huw's point of view but when he is summoned to the front of the room, his point of view is dropped in favor of, more or less, the point of view of the class. Later on, a few shots of Huw's fight in the school yard are taken from the perspective of a girl who is sympathetic to Huw but not otherwise an important character. Ford gives us a few shots from Huw's perspective to register the first impact of school, then proceeds in a nonfocalized or variably focalized way to present the events that happen there.

Several of the film's shots are classical Griffith-Ford iconic images, for some of which, anyway, there can be no character perspective, unless it be that of God or America. Such shots include those of the entire family assembled, for which there can be no character perspective because there is none who is not part of the scene. Many of the final memory images in *How Green,* though not of the entire family, are also of this kind.

Genette's account of voice is particularly long and complex; our remarks will be partial and abbreviated. Genette equates voice with "the narrating instance," that is, with the presence of the narrator in the story he tells. The narrator is not the author and not a character. Even where the narrating is identified with a character, the instances are distinct. The elements of the narrating situation include "time of the narrating," "narrative level," and "person."

The tense structure of language requires a narrator to situate himself temporally in relation to the story he tells—but not spatially. Narrators almost never describe the place where they are narrating; moreover, the narration itself, as opposed to the story, has no apparent duration. In the classical novel, in Proust, "narrating involves an instantaneous action."

Voice-over narrators in cinema are generally shown: Joe Gillis floating dead in a pool in *Sunset Boulevard;* Walter Neff addressing the dictaphone in *Double Indemnity;* Addison DeWitt and Karen Richards sitting at the banquet table in *All About Eve.* In *How Green* we see the older Huw pack his things in order to leave the valley but his face is hidden, as though sharing the shame of the besmirched valley and the degraded present. We do *not* see the writer of *A Letter to Three Wives* (1949), who narrates the film; a more remarkable transgression of this sort is *Le Plaisir* (1951) by Max Ophuls. Over a blank screen, the author, presumably Maupassant (voice of Peter Ustinov), speaks to us:

I have always loved the night, the hours of darkness. That's why I am so grateful to be able to speak to you in the dark. They wanted to photograph me; after all, this is a photographic medium, can one say that? But that I didn't allow. An author's pleasure is to be heard, not seen. I thought the best thing might be if I just told you these stories myself, as if I were sitting beside you and, well, who knows, maybe I am. I will try to speak English, but I have not had as much practice as I would like.

Perhaps you can guess my anxiety. These tales are rather old and you are so very modern, as we all call ourselves while we are still alive. Anyway, be patient with me. Here's the first story.

The instances mentioned all realize that instantaneity of narration of which Genette speaks: Huw packing his things, DeWitt and Richards at the banquet table, and Joe in the pool remember it all and speak it all in a flash. *Not Reconciled* does something different in this respect also. Robert Fähmel, the narrator of the two-part analepsis about the thirties, pauses in the middle of his story for a cognac and the film devotes five shots to the fetching of the cognac. This includes two brief flashbacks concerning the duties of Hugo, Robert's listener, in the hotel. In Straub, even the listener has his own material situation and even listening must be produced; narrating and listening usually take place in an idealist utopia, free of physical and economic constraints.

Genette on person rejects the distinction between "first-person" and "third-person" narratives. Every narrating is, by definition, presented in the first person; this is the only way a narrator can be in his narrative. The real question is whether or not the narrator will use the first person to designate one of his characters; but even when he does, the narrating instance and the character remain distinct; they do not merge. For one thing, the narrator almost always knows more than the hero, even when he is himself the hero. "For the narrator focalization through the hero is a restriction of field just as artificial in the first person as in the third." Marcel the narrator knows everything that will happen to Marcel the character from the moment he begins to narrate. "Between the information of the hero and the omniscience of the novelist is the information of the narrator, who disposes of it according to his own lights and holds it back only when he sees a precise reason for doing so." Advance notices in a narrative, and more generally all prolepses, cannot be the hero's doing, they must be the narrator's.

Thus older Huw knows in advance everything that will happen to the Morgans in the film and withholds information in order to reveal it gradually, as do DeWitt and Richards in *Eve* and other narrators in their films. This follows from the nature of the narrating instance, but something is wrong with this statement. Maybe we do not believe that Huw, DeWitt and Richards, etc., really narrate their entire stories. There is first the fact that many important scenes in each film could not be known by their narrators: the wedding party for Bronwen and Ivor, the scenes between Angharad and Mr. Gryffyd, the town gossip scenes, and others in *How Green*; the intimate scenes between Margo and Bill and between Lloyd and Eve, all the scenes of Eve alone, and others in Eve. Genette defines as "alterations" instances of narrators giving more information (or less) than is within their competence, saying that such momentary infractions of the code governing the narrational context may not call the code itself into question. But these instances go well beyond this definition and make us question what the code of the voice-over narrator in classical films is.

There is also the fact that the narrators of *How Green, Eve,* and other films are actually silent for most of the film. In both instances, there is a good deal of narration at the beginning of the film in order to set the scene and to introduce the main characters; once that is done, the film proceeds in usual scenic fashion, the voice-over brought back from time to time to provide narrative summaries and to bridge ellipses in the long period of time covered by each film. (This is a long year in the case of *How Green;* a theatrical season, October to June, in the case of *Eve.*) The conclusion seems unavoidable that voice-over narration in classical cinema has little in common with character narration in fiction; it is a narrative convenience used and dropped by the film to suit its purposes. Character narration in fiction is often consistent for the whole text; if a character's voice is dropped, it is usually in favor of another character's voice. There are switches from subjective voice to objective voice, as in the final section of *The Sound and the Fury,* but there is usually not then a return to subjective voice. The voice-over in film is usually picked up and dropped by the film at will, according to no principle but expediency. Above all, of course, voice-over narration in cinema does not comprise the whole text. It does not pervade the text or inflect every detail of it, color it, shape it, lend it its entire flavor, as character narration in fiction does. In the "complex system" of cinema, it is just one element among many elements, to be juggled along with them, often in shifting combinations.

A closer look at the functions of the narrators in *How Green* and *Eve* will confirm and amplify these points, since their patterns are typical of voice-over narration in classical cinema generally. Both films begin with long voice-over narrations at the beginning of the film: to describe the setting and general situation and to introduce the characters by name, occupation, and relation to the other characters, as the camera shows us their faces and their physical environment. Both films have an unusually large number of important characters and both attempt to situate them, complexly and fully, in a distinctive milieu, a world. To attempt this through usual, objective exposition seems difficult, if not impossible—though that may be because the devices work so well and are used so skillfully in these two films. It seems undeniable, however, that the convention of the voice-over made possible more complex, "novelistic" projects than formerly.

The function of the voice-over narration in *How Green* and *Eve* is not only to introduce a complex situation but to bridge the transition of the narrative from

All About Eve

present to past, a shift that will hold good for most or all of the rest of the film. (All of it in *How Green;* all but the final scene in *Eve,* which is a kind of epilogue and a looping of the narrative, oddly parallel to the looping of visuals at the end of *How Green.*) If we recall the crisis of order posed to classical cinema by an analepsis, we appreciate the importance of this function. One wonders, indeed, if bridging the transition from present to past may not be the primary function of voice-overs in the classical period; that is, whether "voice" is not determined by "order" in classical narrative films, at least in part.

Often, as in *How Green* and *Eve,* a voice-over will continue for a certain duration after the bridge from present to past: to insure continuity, to provide orientation and exposition within the world of the flashback, and to reintroduce characters and plot situation within the flashback. Then, when the analepsis is well launched, the film characteristically drops the voice-over and proceeds for the main part of the film in an objective way. About two-thirds of Huw's total narration in *How Green* is spoken in the opening sequence of the film, until the formal introduction of Bronwen to the family, a duration of about ten minutes. The first 14 of the 25 voice-over speeches in *Eve* occur in the opening sequence of the film, until we see Eve in the theater alley as she approaches Karen Richards. Also, in both films, the voice-over recedes just before the first big, objective scene, in both cases a vivid set-piece serving to make us forget the introductory voice and to launch the world of the flashback on its own: the wedding of Bronwen and Ivor and the party that follows in *How Green;* the introduction of Eve to Margo and company in *Eve.* Thereafter, in both films, the voice-over returns occasionally to provide brief narrative summaries and to bridge transitions within the analepsis. This happens 8 times in *How Green*, 11 times in *Eve*; for example:

> HUW: Twenty-two weeks the men were out, as the strike moved into winter . . .
>
> And so it came to Ianto and Davy, the best paid workers in the colliery, but too highly paid to compete with poorer, more desperate men.
>
> Then Angharad came back from Capetown without her husband . . .
>
> KAREN: It was a cold week-end—outside and in. Bill didn't come at all. Margo didn't know where he was and didn't care—she kept saying. Somehow we staggered through Sunday—and by the time we drove Margo to the station late Monday afternoon, she and Lloyd had thawed out to the extent of being civil to each other . . .
>
> Lloyd never got around, somehow—to asking whether it was all right with me for Eve to play "Cora" . . .
>
> ADDISON: To the Theatre world—New Haven, Connecticut, is a short stretch of sidewalk between the Schubert Theatre and the Taft Hotel, surrounded by what looks very much like a small city. It is here that managers have what are called out-of-town openings—which are openings for New Yorkers who want to go out of town.

Such transition or scene-setting speeches turn their narrators into speaking title cards, pragmatic in the case of *How Green*, ornate and witty in the case of *Eve*. But what a comedown from the high-flown openings of both narrations, which even lead us to believe that the films might be about their speakers! Instead Huw is a bystander in most of the scenes in which he appears and is missing altogether from many others. Addison is a bystander at the party scene and others and is missing altogether from even more scenes. Interestingly, each film gives its forgotten narrator one important scene or sequence later: the school sequence for Huw in *How Green*; Addison's "killer to killer" confrontation with Eve in *Eve*.

The voice-over narrator in classical film is a puppet of the narration. One might say the same of character-narrators in fiction, but they at least are always onstage and are built to withstand observation; they also serve all the functions of the narration. The puppet narrators of cinema are jerked on and off stage in a manner that is quite undignified. They may have integrity as characters but they have no integrity as narrators, no resistance to the demands placed upon them; they are nothing but the functions they serve, a collection of odd jobs. They are reeds buffeted by the winds of the narrative; their voices resonate but they are hollow. An important part of their function is to mimic the novelistic voice, the guarantor of experience, subjectivity, and seriousness, with its "I remember" and "I suffer." In fact these inflated "I"s of classical cinema "open" for the main story; they are second-rate acts that warm up the audience with their sonorities. They are ludicrous stand-ins for the novelistic "I" because, though they wind up elaborately, they have nothing to pitch. For precisely these reasons, of course, voice-over narrators in cinema are interesting; they ruthlessly expose the mechanisms of narration in classical cinema.

This is not to disparage the convention of the voice-over in cinema, which has figured in so many excellent films. It is rather to indicate that if we seek to define voice in cinema, in Genette's sense, we will have to look beyond these voices.

VIRGINIA WRIGHT WEXMAN

THE CRITIC AS CONSUMER

Film Study in the University, Vertigo, *and the Film Canon*

The world of art, a sacred island systematically and ostentatiously opposed to the profane, everyday world of production, a sanctuary for gratuitous, disinterested activity in a universe given over to money and self-interest, offers, like theology in a past epoch, an imaginary anthropology obtained by denial of all the negations really brought about by the economy.

PIERRE BOURDIEU[1]

Vol. 39, no. 3 (Spring 1986): 32–41.

Though critics customarily consider themselves disinterested observers, their activities are shaped by concrete historical processes. The recent development of a group of film intellectuals within the American academy can be examined as an example of this interaction. Given the body of radical theory produced by many members of this newly constituted intellectual group, one might well assume that the function they have served has been a progressive one. However, these progressive goals operate in a far more limited way than is generally understood. Because the work of film intellectuals leads to practical valuations of film texts, one can view current scholarly practices in the light of these valuations. Why are certain cinematic texts chosen for special attention? Which elements in these texts are singled out for critical discussion?

Film studies, with its fluid and shifting canon, lends itself particularly well to this kind of sociologically oriented inquiry. The past ten years have marked a change in *Sight and Sound*'s decennial listings of the ten greatest of all time, suggesting that values held by contemporary film scholars and critics are historically shifting.[2] In 1982, four films appeared on the *Sight and Sound* list that had not appeared on the 1972 list: *Singin' in the Rain* (1952), *The Searchers* (1956), *The Seven Samurai* (1954), and *Vertigo* (1958). The appearance of the three American titles may be partly accounted for by the continuing vitality of the auteur theory. Also, the growing interest in film's status as cultural production entailing a complex industry and elaborating generic models has certainly influenced such preferences—as well as the lower regard for films like *The Passion of Joan of Arc* and *Persona*. Neither of these trends, however, accounts for the fact that three of *Sight and Sound*'s newly canonized films were made in the United States during the cold-war period of the fifties. An analysis of the politics of contemporary film scholarship must take such historical specifics into account.

Of the three American films on the list, *Vertigo* is the text that says most about the relation between film aesthetics and the ideology of criticism. Of the three films, *Vertigo* most owes its preeminence to the opinions of cinema scholars

Vertigo

rather than the enthusiasm of less "committed" film fans. Moreover, unlike *Singin' in the Rain* and *The Searchers*, *Vertigo* has generated a sizable body of conflicting critical writing that can be revealingly classified according to ideological positions. In terms of evaluation, what is noteworthy about this critical writing is the *centrality* it grants to this particular film. The film is canonized even by those who argue against it. As Janet Staiger has pointed out, "Some films will be chosen for extensive discussion and analysis, others will be ignored. . . . As ideal fathers, these select films are given homage or rebelled against."[3]

Critics of *Vertigo* can be broadly divided into two groups. One line of approach, inaugurated by Robin Wood's pioneering 1967 study, speaks to the issue of Hitchcock as an artist, claiming that *Vertigo* masterfully manipulates the codes of "pure cinema," thereby revealing the creative genius of its director. By contrast, for another group of critics *Vertigo*'s value rests on the way it reveals—or enacts—an objectification and fetishization of women which is at the heart of cinema's codes of voyeuristic pleasure. These critical postures correspond closely to the two roles that Gramsci assigns to intellectuals in society. The first role is the one assigned to traditional intellectuals, who are "the dominant group's subalterns, exercising the subaltern's function of social hegemony and political government."[4] Those who argue *Vertigo*'s status as "pure cinema" rationalize the hegemonic functions served by particular cinematic institutions at work in the film. The second role Gramsci assigns to intellectuals is an "organic" one, by which a rising group theorizes its own entrance into the upper reaches of the social power structure. From this perspective *Vertigo*'s feminist critics can be viewed as a subgroup of a larger group of women intellectuals who have elaborated a discourse on women at a moment when women have been entering high-level positions both within and outside of the academy. The progressive project of this group is entangled with methodological constraints that prevent it from addressing broader and more historically specific issues of class, race, and economics.

To better understand the assumptions implicit in the work of the former of these two groups of intellectuals, we can contrast the insights made possible by the task-oriented approach advocated by Wayne Booth, an approach which follows the development of the text with a view to determining what principles governed its shaping. Donald Spoto's recent biography of Hitchcock, which traces the development of *Vertigo* from the director's purchase of the novel *D'entre les morts*, offers a wealth of material apposite to this approach.[5] Hitchcock's difficulties in putting together a screenplay led him to engage several different writers for the project, and he ultimately instructed Samuel Taylor to write a script without reading the original novel. Taylor constructed the film's narrative around the director's conceptions for various individual scenes. In the meantime, however, Hitchcock had committed himself to using James Stewart and Kim Novak, then two of the most popular stars in Hollywood. And he had also sent his production designer Henry Bumstead on several trips to San Francisco to scout locations. These circumstances suggest that the stars and locations were primary considerations in the director's mind, and that the actual script and story were a secondary and contingent concern.

Given Hitchcock's highly developed sensitivities about the commercial appeal of his movies, it is easy to understand why these particular features of the film, its stars and its status as travelogue, should have preoccupied him from the start. In a now-classic study, Edgar Morin has examined the role played by stars—especially female stars—in the film industry, which promoted a cult of romantic love based on the mystification of female beauty, manufacturing what it then called "love goddesses." As a successful practitioner within the Hollywood industry, Hitchcock was adept at exploiting the images of such major Hollywood stars as Cary Grant and Grace Kelly.

In *Vertigo*, Kim Novak's position as a manufactured romantic idol is a crucial component of the film's power. It has often been noted that the story of an ordinary young woman who is transformed into a celestial beauty by a controlling man recreates the director's relationships with his female stars, many of whom were also transformed into erotic ideals under Hitchcock's own tutelage. But such a reading of Novak's Madeleine-Judy role, by emphasizing the control exercised by an individual director-auteur over his star, shifts the focus of discussion away from the meaning inherent in the star's own presence. In fact, Hitchcock's obsession with controlling his leading ladies, which grew as his career in films progressed, can be seen as an adaptation that for a long period of time enabled him to function more effectively in the environment of commercialized eroticism that defined the Hollywood style. This pattern of behavior did not emerge until *after* Hitchcock had embarked on a career in commercial movie-making and did not reach full-blown proportions until the director had established himself in Hollywood. Thus, the individuated analysis of his romantic obsessions posited by Spoto and others requires the addition of the societally determined mediating term represented by the commercialized eroticism of the film industry.

In the case of Kim Novak, control over her image was exercised not just by Hitchcock but more importantly by industry mogul Harry Cohn, president of Columbia Pictures, who arranged to have her constantly watched, forced her to live in her studio dressing room and eat only food prepared by the chef, and called her "the fat Polack."[6] Like Judy, Novak was docile enough to accept this bullying for the most part, while occasionally fighting for a modicum of recognition of her own identity—managing, for instance, to keep her surname despite its ethnic overtones.

Specific aspects of the Novak persona that are invoked in her portrayal of Judy include her well-known preference for the color lavender, brought to mind when Judy tries the appeal she herself might have for Scottie by selecting a lavender dress for their first dinner together. By contrast, Madeleine is associated not with the part of the Novak image that speaks of the ordinary young woman chosen for greatness, but with the star's etherialized, aestheticized beauty. The repeated profile shots of Madeleine not only call to mind Novak's then well-publicised classic profile but also the conventions of relief portraiture found in antique cameos and coins. This association of the star's transcendent beauty with the traditions of high art is further alluded to by the connection between Madeleine and the portrait of Carlotta hanging in the art museum.

The film's skillful manipulation of the Novak persona in the Madeleine-Judy figure opposes the spiritual transcendence of the star as erotic ideal to the quotidian material forces that contribute to her ascendency. Such a portrayal is deeply implicated in the contradictory role assigned to contemporary bour-

Kim Novak
(as Madeleine),
James Stewart

geois women, who act as purveyors of a mystique of beauty at the same time as they are shaped into consumers of the products of a commercial beauty industry. The importance Hitchcock attached to his stars, creating a script individually tailored to these aspects of her image, reflects his understanding of and collaboration with the practical and conflict-ridden nature of the American film industry's investment in such figures.

The star system, however, is not the only cinematic institution addressed in *Vertigo*. Hitchcock's predilection for spectacular settings throughout his career has often been remarked on, and this predilection, like his use of stars, plays a significant part in his commercial appeal. In this, he follows a well-defined tradition, for the first documentary films were travelogues, and the more encompassing institutions of commercial cinema itself are partly involved with the project of taking audiences to attractive faraway locales. Thus, the motto of one early studio became: "The world at your fingertips." The early cinema's concern with glamorous settings is not surprising, given the changes taking place in society as a whole at the end of the nineteenth century. Industrialization and vastly improved transportation systems had by then produced an increasingly mobile middle class with a sizable disposable income to spend on travel, an eager audience for cinematic fantasies of escape to alluring, exotic places. One need only recall films such as *Around the World in Eighty Days* and *Indiana Jones and the Temple of Doom* to appreciate how central such a travelogue function has remained for today's movie audiences.

The cinema's preoccupation with travel is not without ideological implications. In his book *The Tourist: A New Theory of the Leisure Class* (New York: Shocken, 1976), Dean MacCannell argues that "tourist attractions are an unplanned typology of structure that provides direct access to the modern consciousness or 'world view,' that tourist attractions are precisely analogous to the religious symbolism of primitive peoples. . . . This effort of the international middle class to coordinate the differentiations of the world into a single ideology is intimately linked to its capacity to subordinate other peoples to its values, industry and future designs."(2, 13) By disseminating and domesticating the far-off, cinema participates in this rhetoric of tourism.

In *Vertigo* Hitchcock indulges the touristic impulse by showing all the famous sights of the San Francisco Bay area: the Golden Gate Bridge; the Embarcadero; Ernie's, the city's best-known restaurant; the art museum; a forest of giant sequoias; hilly streets; scenic, oceanside highways; and cable cars. As if to emphasize his function as tour guide, Hitchcock even sets the film's climax in a location that exists solely as a tourist attraction (though it was doctored for the purposes of the plot). Here again, as happened in the case of his stars, Hitchcock selected these picture-postcard settings early in the production process and had the movie's script tailored to accommodate them. Like Kim Novak, San Francisco is part of *Vertigo*'s beauty, beauty defined by a consumerist function.

Both the romantic ideal of the love goddess and the escapist ideal of the tourist attraction have a material dimension, for both beauty and travel are multi-billion-dollar industries. Though the traces of these two related cinematic institutions are readily observable in Hitchcock's film, they are ignored in the commentaries of its art-oriented critics. Whether there is or is not an "essential" or "pure" cinema, art-oriented critics have used this concept to avoid confronting the specific commercial strategies on which much of *Vertigo*'s appeal is based. By such time-honored means, borrowed from traditional aesthetics, abstract theoretical formulations enshrine art as a "sanctuary of disinterested activity," while concealing the operations of ideology within it, thereby rationalizing existing social relations.

The feminist critics of *Vertigo* pose a different issue, for as organic intellectuals such critics work within a discernible political agenda designed to further the interests of the group with which they identify. The question here becomes: how does this agenda operate in practice? Who, exactly, profits?

The approach taken by most contemporary feminist film scholarship limits the application of its conclusions to bourgeois women, a limitation which results not only from its selection of cinematic data but also from the methodology most feminist critics commonly use. The methodology at issue here is psychoanalysis. Inspired by Laura Mulvey's essay "Visual Pleasure and Narrative Cinema," which uses *Vertigo* as one of its main examples, feminist critics have used psychoanalytic models to open up cinematic texts to a wealth of reading strategies. Following Mulvey, many feminist critics have accepted psychoanalysis as a key to the essential nature of mainstream cinema. Like traditional film intellectuals, feminists' allegiance to such an idealist position, which some assume explains *all* commercial narrative film, can obscure the workings of more culturally specific codes within the cinematic text. To derive analyses that can articulate the specific operations of patriarchy within a particular culture, psychoanalytic perspectives must be integrated with other critical models.

Christine Gledhill, questioning this use of psychoanalysis, has argued for a form of cultural analysis that looks not simply to idealized psychoanalytic models but to the specific social practices by which such models are activated.[7] The distinct discourses that construct social reality can be obscured by a critical approach that uses an essentializing psychoanalytic methodology to interpolate cinematic material that yields too readily to such an approach. Indeed, it can be argued that Hitchcock's recurrent preoccupation with psychoanalysis in his films has often served as a "MacGuffin" (to use his term), distracting the viewer's attention from other, more hidden aspects of the text, his shrewd co-optation of a popular discourse that could locate the roots of social dis-ease in psychological rather than economic causes.

For an example of Hitchcock's appropriation of such displacements, consider his comments about what attracted him to *Marnie:* "The fetish idea. A man who wants to go to bed with a thief, just like other men have a yen for a Chinese woman or a colored woman."[8] Given the widespread interest in psychoanalytic readings of Hitchcock's films, it is noteworthy that no critic has commented on the director's remarkable equation of fetishism with miscegenation here. And, more importantly, no one has observed the workings of a similar displacement of racial and class issues into the sphere of sexuality functioning in the films themselves. Like Hitchcock, feminists committed to psychoanalysis may interpret all cinematic practices in terms of universalizing concepts of fetishization, lack, and voyeuristic exchange. Whether these psychoanalytic operations actually form the essential base of all cinematic art or not, the feminist critics of Hitchcock sometimes tend to describe his films as though they relied solely on such operations. However, a reading of *Vertigo* which poses history as what Fredric Jameson has called an "absent cause" shows other strategies at work.

In a recent essay Michael Rogin mapped the ideological terrain that forms the background of American films of the cold-war period.[9] Using psychoanalytic theory in conjunction with this historical background, Rogin describes the cold-war period as one in which polarized conceptions of "otherness" were particularly evident. In the popular imagination, such conceptions often focused on women. Images of women were often deployed to displace and domesticate fears of a more ungovernable xenophobic cast, fears of the Russians and of "subversives." Such displacements can be negotiated in the cinematic texts themselves through a strategy of paired oppositions, which develop as the narrative proceeds in such a way as to provide the spectator with increasingly refined definitions of the terms involved. In *Vertigo*, an analysis of these paired oppositions, which center on the Madeleine-Judy figure, suggests the limitations of psychoanalytically based textual approaches. Issues such as gender difference, regression, and the organization of filmic space through the agency of the gaze, the mainstays of many psychoanalytic readings, may be less central to our understanding of the operation of many filmic texts than many feminists now consider them.

In the case of gender difference, it is important to recognize that more culturally specific differences may exist within this universal opposition. In *Vertigo* the first of these culturally specific differences initially emphasizes the class contrast between Madeleine and Midge Wood, with whom we see the film's protagonist Scottie Ferguson at the opening of the film. While the all-American Midge appears untainted by conspicuous marks of class, Madeleine is firmly positioned as upper class. Her family owns a shipyard; she lives in a luxurious apartment building and drives an expensive car. First glimpsed amid the opulent surroundings of an expensive restaurant, she also affects, as do most of Hitchcock's heroines, an upper-class accent. Indeed, Scottie's obsession with her, seen in this context, becomes largely an obsession with money and class.

But Madeleine's upper-class image entails its opposite: the lower-class Judy. Though Scottie spends a considerable amount of money trying to recreate this working-class woman into the upper-class figure he originally idolized, the fruitlessness of his attempt is ultimately exposed when he sees Judy's telltale necklace. Unlike the clothes Scottie buys Judy, this necklace cannot be duplicated. Its status as a symbol of family jewels implies the inherited wealth that marks a truly upperclass person: an aristocrat. In one sense, then, Scottie's shock on seeing this necklace can be construed as the shock of the nouveau-riche aspirant who discovers his inability to buy his way into the upper reaches of old-money society.

Scottie's inchoate identification with aristocratic values grows out of his disdain for work. He rejects the idea of gainful employment for himself at the beginning of the film and later tries to persuade both Midge and Judy to follow his example. Though he succeeds with the malleable Judy, Midge is more resistant. When Scottie rejects Midge's parodic portrait of Carlotta, he is rejecting her Yankee practicality (Midge can't take painting seriously because she has to "make a living") and literalness (she demystifies the portrait by treating its subject as just another woman, equal to herself). Midge alienates herself from Scottie in this scene by refusing to take seriously his un-American fantasies of aristocratic elegance and ease.

These fantasies, which are focused on the figure of Madeleine, are fantasies not of America but of Europe. The old-world idea of aristocracy is evoked in repeated associations between Madeleine and Europe: her husband's British ac-

Kim Novak (as Judy),
James Stewart

cent; the Viennese accent of Pop Liebl, who recounts her history; and the Spanish-style mission she frequents. Yet by further defining her social position, such associations also imply still another opposition, an opposition focused on the figure of Carlotta Valdez. Carlotta, who grew up in a Spanish mission town but "danced in the cabarets," becomes a presence of charged ambiguity. Is she a descendant of old Spanish aristocracy, or is she lower-class Latino? The film never specifies, preferring instead to situate her in a realm of exotic class marginality. *Vertigo*'s series of oppositions, beginning with gender difference, leading to class difference and from there to ethnic difference, must stop short with the image of Carlotta: the racial opposition that is the logical extension of this series remains, for Hitchcock, unrepresentable. Yet it is significant that Scottie's nightmare reveals Elster not with the blonde, patrician Madeleine but instead beside the darkly ambiguous Carlotta. In the nightmare, Carlotta represents what ultimately terrorizes Scottie, and the fears Carlotta arouses in him are more culturally specific than either Hitchcock or his feminist critics are in a position to acknowledge.

Vertigo's buried references to issues of class and race were contained during the fifties as part of a nationalistic ideology that defined American society in terms of its ability to achieve world dominance. In the context of this cultural fantasy, the meaning of the past in *Vertigo*, so often invoked by critics as a sign of psychological regression, takes on a more political coloration. In the figure of Scottie, the past does indeed connote regression; but Scottie's private dilemma displaces more political connotations attached to the invocation of the past. The film's first reference to the past explicitly connects it to the political sphere: Gavin Elster speaks nostalgically of "the old San Francisco," when men had "freedom and power." The cold-war connotations of the phrase "freedom and power" are unmistakable, for America was at the time seeking power on the international scene in the name of freedom, and it justified these aspirations in part by invoking the country's past heroism in "saving the world for freedom" in World War II.

When the past is next invoked in the film, it refers not to politics but to the figure of Carlotta Valdez, whose rich lover long ago abandoned her and took her child. Pop Liebl's explanation of her tragedy recalls Elster's earlier comments: "Men could do these things in those days. They had the freedom and the power." Here the motif of sexual exploitation is central, but Pop Liebl's story also carries overtones of a past era of American imperialism characterized by the freedom and the power to colonize and plunder, whether the object of exploitation was the resources of an underdeveloped country or the body of an underprivileged woman.

As Rogin points out, the word "freedom" has been variously used throughout American history to construct oppositions which could uphold American interests at the expense of a racial, ethnic, or national "other." Such oppositions recast contradictions within American society itself into a discourse of demonology. In the cold-war period, the most salient contradiction existed between the "free" individual and a newly oppressive mass society characterized by sophisticated patterns of surveillance.

In *Vertigo* such issues are raised through the portrayal of law. Scottie, initially presented as a member of the law-enforcement bureaucracy, withdraws from his responsibilities because he feels he has faltered in carrying out his duty as a watchdog of society's interests. He then becomes a "wanderer," free inasmuch as he is detached from the demands of the law and thus disengaged from the functions of surveillance required in the mass society of fifties America. However, Scottie's relationship with the law is not thereby severed but merely mystified, for his surveillance function merely shifts to a more personalized site: Madeleine's body. But the film insures that this site must also be regarded in relation to the law, for later, at the hearing on Madeleine's death, he is severely chastized by the judge for his failure to perform his "duty." This censurious judgment gains the imprimatur of a higher order when Hitchcock reveals two male clerics seated behind Madeleine's "injured" husband. Finally, when a nun appears in the belltower during the film's concluding scene, Scottie's dilemma is finally displaced from a public, male world into a private, female one. What is initially presented as the suffocating obligations felt by a fifties American bureaucratic functionary to a group of ruling males—Scottie's job on the police force—is completely transformed into a motif of religious guilt centered on sexual desire. At the same time, Scottie's statement in this scene that he wishes to be "free of the past" displaces terms initially presented with specific political connotations into the realm of the private and the personal.

America's cold-war aspirations to global supremacy are expressed in *Vertigo* not only by the film's depiction of time but also by its depiction of space. One can speak of two opposed conceptions of space operating in *Vertigo*: the panorama and the vortex. Hitchcock announces this opposition during the credit sequence, in which Saul Bass's abstract designs exploit the cinema's capacity to create two-dimensional patterns that can suggest three-dimensional space by means of an optical illusion. Immediately afterward, in the film's first scene of the rooftop chase, this conception is connected with images of the natural world, images that will be developed throughout the narrative: the panorama of the San Francisco skyline in the background followed by the vortex created by Hitchcock's famous track-out, zoom-in shots depicting Scottie's vertiginous vision of the street below.

The panorama has obvious affinities with the touristic world view described earlier, defining a "picturesque," two-dimensional space that negates the actual forces of production and labor that contributed to its creation. Such a two-dimensional, picture-postcard view appears first in Hitchcock's narrative proper as a backdrop to the apartment belonging to the all-American Midge. Later, however, when Scottie visits Elster's office, the background becomes more ominous, for the scene outside of Elster's window depicts the shipyards, implying another world beyond the ocean and the role played by American industrial supremacy in the domination of this world. At the same time, the dominance-oriented two-shots of Scottie and Elster in this scene shift the terms of spatial perception. In contrast to the shot–reverse shot technique of the earlier scene in Midge's apartment, which isolates characters within their own surrounding space, the power relationships represented in Scottie's first scene with Elster reflect an awareness of how the relative positioning of the human subject within the space may suggest structures of dominance.

As the action progresses, two possible positions are defined: the camera's horizontal tracking movements associated with Madeleine suggest a harmonious integration into the three-dimensional space, while the vertical camera movements associated with Scottie's vertigo suggest the fear of being engulfed by the space. Madeleine is often flanked by portals and archways that begin to define more specifically the depth of the filmic field. The depth of field is more dramatically emphasized in scenes in which the camera tracks toward her and in other scenes where she herself approaches the camera to the strains of Bernard Herrmann's Wagnerian musical score. The alluring invitation implied by this three-dimensional quality, however, accelerates to a frightening pitch of intensity during the vertigo shots. At these points the viewer's harmonious incorporation within the space, which is achieved by the complementary alternation of camera movement toward an object and the movement of the object toward the camera, is compressed into a single, humanly impossible operation. This series of oppositions is initiated by the early scene in Elster's office, which specifically associates the opening out of the cinematic space with American industrial power and expansionist aspirations, thereby adding an explicitly political dimension to the anxieties over spatial dominance that are so pervasive throughout the film.

The process by which such political anxieties about dominance and otherness are displaced in *Vertigo* onto the image of the woman is focused on a specific spatial image: the spiral. This image, repeatedly associated with both Madeleine and Carlotta's hairstyles, strikes Scottie powerfully in the art museum scene. The sequence involves both the camera's tracking movement, which invades the filmic space, and the inviting illusion of depth created by the spiral shape of Madeleine's French twist. Many of the film's suppressed issues are condensed into this spiral image, for through it the promise held out by the blonde Madeleine's seductive presence is represented as an invitation to fuse with a hollow shell. The erotic promise of this image is consummated in the final love scene, where the camera circles around the romantic couple in an active imitation of the contours of the spiral associated with Madeleine. Yet, rather than exposing an enticing void into which male fantasies of power and dominance can be projected, Madeleine's confused dependency may conceal the threatening intractability of the alien Carlotta. Thus the inviting horizontal movement suggested by the women's hair leads to the traumatic vertical oscillations created by the spiral of the stairway during the tower sequences. These sequences depict an ultimate loss of control over the cinematic space, and they end with the fatal fall of an exalted female love object who has represented a projection of male power fantasies.

The implications of the film's spatial oppositions, however, finally culminate not in Madeleine and Carlotta but in Judy. If Madeleine, whose head seen from behind is dominated by the spiral of her hairstyle, invites Scottie to merge with a hollow space, Judy represents not a projective male fantasy but an actual woman. After Scottie's first encounter with her, however, Hitchcock's camera executes a similar track forward into the back of Judy's head. Judy's hair, though, does not coil into an inviting spiral. And this time, rather than losing itself in the woman's body offered as a void, the camera decisively reveals the "other" which has been suppressed by the film's romantic fantasy. For the movement culminates as Judy's head turns toward us, and we are then permitted access to her own mental images, images at odds with Scottie's—and the viewer's—partial and mistaken conceptions about her.

In this image of a woman's head turning, Hitchcock focuses on a representation of otherness that uses gender opposition to emphasize the film's theme of romantic love. But this image of otherness, as we have seen, contains far more complex and localized associations than feminist psychoanalytic theory can account for. As *Vertigo* illustrates, the oppression of women in our culture is intimately related to particular political conditions, and the forms of its representation often exploit such associations. Indeed, the film's abrupt and unresolved ending can be viewed as a signal of its refusal to confront the implications of its strategies. In *Vertigo* Hitchcock has masked the ideological workings of racism and xenophobia beneath a discourse of sexuality that is itself idealized as romantic love.

If the text of Hitchcock's film employs the techniques of cinematic art and the motifs of sexual difference, these techniques and motifs function in part to mask less familiar meanings. Though its rhetorical disguises have seduced film scholars, *Vertigo* is neither a work of pure artistry nor an exercise in essential psychoanalytic truth. Hitchcock, after all, did not create his films in an ivory tower surrounded by cinematic essences; nor did he make them amid the private surroundings of the analytic session. He was a businessman as well as an artist. In 1958 he embarked on a commercial enterprise entitled *Vertigo*, starring Kim Novak and San Francisco. Cinema scholars have now honored this venture as one of their top ten favorites. Such a valuation reflects not only on its object but also on those who sit in judgment. Gramsci's paradigm of the role played by intellectuals in society suggests the ideological stakes involved in interpretations of cultural texts. Film scholars, like others, have class interests at stake: we are not only critics but also consumers.

NOTES

1. Pierre Bourdieu, *Outline of a Theory of Practice*, trans. Richard Nere (New York: Cambridge University Press), p. 197.

2. For the 1982 list, see *Sight and Sound* 51, no. 4 (Autumn 1982): 243. In a 1978 survey of critics conducted by the Belgian Film Archives regarding important American films, *Vertigo* was ranked only eighteenth. See *The Most Important and Misappreciated American Films Since the Beginning of Cinema* (Brussels: Royal Film Archives of Belgium, 1978). This jump in popularity preceded *Vertigo*'s re-release in 1983.

3. Janet Staiger, "The Politics of Film Canons," *Cinema Journal* 24, no. 2 (Spring 1985): 4.

4. Antonio Gramsci, *Selections from the Prison Notebooks*, ed. and trans. Quintin Hoare and Geoffrey Nowell-Smith (New York: International Publishers, 1971), p. 11.

5. Donald Spoto, *The Dark Side of Genius: The Life of Alfred Hitchcock* (New York: Ballantine, 1983). The making of *Vertigo* is discussed on pp. 425–35.

6. See Bob Thomas, *King Cohn: The Life and Times of Harry Cohn* (New York: G. P. Putnam's Sons, 1967), pp. 325–31.

7. Christine Gledhill, "Developments in Feminist Film Criticism," *Re-Vision: Essays in Feminist Film Criticism*, ed. Mary Ann Doane, Patricia Mellencamp, and Linda Williams (Frederick, MD: University Publications of America, 1984), pp. 18–48.

8. François Truffaut, *Hitchcock* (New York: Simon and Schuster, 1984), p. 227.

9. Michael Rogin, "*Kiss Me Deadly:* Communism, Motherhood, and Cold War Movies," *Representations,* no. 6 (Spring 1984): 1–36.

ESTHER C.M. YAU

YELLOW EARTH

Western Analysis and a Non-Western Text

Vol. 41, no. 2 (Winter 1987–88): 22–33.

1984. China. The wounds of the Cultural Revolution have been healing for nearly a decade. After the hysterical tides of red flags, the fanatical chanting of political slogans, and militant Mao supporters in khaki green or white shirts and blue slacks paving every inch of Tienanmen Square, come the flashy Toshiba billboards for refrigerators and washing machines, the catchy phrases of "Four Modernizations," and tranquilized consumers in colorful outfits and leather heels crowding the shops of Wangfujing Street. A context of Change. Yet contradiction prevails. Who are these people flocking to local theaters that posted *First Blood* on their billboards? Are they not the same group that gathered for lessons on anti-spiritual pollution? The Red Book and the pocket calculator are drawn from shirt pockets without haste, just like the old long pipe from the baggy pants of the peasant waiting for the old Master of Heavens to take care of the order of things. In 1984, after the crash of the Gang of Four, when China becomes a phenomenon of the "post"—a nation fragmented by and suffering from the collapse of faith in the modern socialist politics and culture—the search for meaning by the perturbed Chinese character begins to occupy the electric shadows of new Chinese cinema.[1]

At the end of 1984, a few Chinese men who were obsessed with their history and culture—all of them had labored in factories and farms during the Cultural Revolution and just graduated from the Beijing Film Academy—quietly completed *Huang Tudi* in a very small production unit, the Guangxi Studio, in Southern China. A serious feature that had basically eluded political censorship, *Huang Tudi* (which meant *Yellow Earth*) was soon regarded as the most significant stylistic breakthrough in new Chinese cinema. It won several festival prizes, started major debates at home about filmmaking, and interested international film scholars.[2]

Safely set in the 1930s, *Yellow Earth* tells the story of an encounter between a soldier and some peasants. Despite its ambitious attempt to capture both the richly nourishing and the quietly destructive elements of an ancient civilization already torn apart in the late nineteenth century, the film's story and its use of folksongs/folktale as device and structure is deceptively simple and unpretentious. In fact, the film's conception and its musical mode were originally derived from one of the trite literary screenplays which glorified the peasants and the earlier years of socialist revolution: an Eighth Route Army soldier influenced a peasant girl to struggle away from her feudal family.[3] Such a commonplace narrative of misunderstanding-enlightenment-liberation-trial-triumph or its variations would be just another boring cliché to the audience familiar with socialist myths, while the singing and romance could be a welcome diversion. Dissatisfied with the original story but captivated by the folk-tale elements, director Chen Kaige and his young classmates—all in their early thirties—scouted the Shaanxi Province in northwestern China for months on foot. Their anthropological observations of the local people and their subcultures both enriched and shaped the narrative, cultural, and aesthetic elements in the film.[4] Consequently, they brought onto the international screen a very different version of Chinese people—hardworking, hungry, and benevolent peasants who look inactive but whose storage of vitality would be released in their struggles for survival and in their celebration of living. The structure of the original story was kept, but *Yellow Earth* has woven a very troubling picture of Chinese feudal culture in human terms that had never been conjured up so vividly before by urban intellectuals.

The film's narrative: 1937. The socialist revolution has started in western China, but most other areas are still controlled by the Guomindang. Some Eighth Route Army soldiers are sent to the still "unliberated" western highlands of Shaanbei to collect folk tunes for army songs. Film begins. Spring, 1939. An Eighth Route Army soldier, Gu Qing, reaches a village in which a feudal marriage between a young bride and a middle-aged peasant is taking place. Later, the soldier is hosted in the cave home of a middle-aged widower peasant living with his young daughter and son. Gu Qing works in the fields with them and tells them of the social changes brought about by the revolution, which include the army women's chances to become literate and to have freedom of marriage. The peasant's daughter, Cuiqiao, is interested in Gu Qing's stories about life outside the village, and she sings a number of "sour tunes" about herself. The peasant's son, Hanhan, sings a bed-wetting song for Gu Qing, and is taught a revolutionary song in return.[5] The young girl learns that her father has accepted the village matchmaker's arrangement for her betrothal. Soon, the soldier announces his departure. Before he leaves, the peasant sings him a "sour tune," and Cuiqiao privately begs him to take her away to join the army. Gu Qing refuses on grounds of public officers' rules but promises to apply for her and to return to the village once permission is granted. Soon after his departure, Cuiqiao's feudal marriage with a middle-aged peasant takes place. At the army base, Gu Qing watches some peasants drum-dancing to soldiers going off to join the anti-Japanese war. Back in the village, Cuiqiao decides to run away to join the army herself. She disappears crossing the Yellow River while singing the revolutionary song. Another spring comes. There is a drought on the land. As the soldier returns to the village, he sees that a prayer for rain involving all the male peasants is taking place. Fanatic with their prayers, nobody notices Gu Qing's return, except the peasant's young son. In the final shots he rushes to meet the soldier, struggling against the rush of worshippers. End of story.

Yellow Earth poses a number of issues that intrigued both censors and the local audience. The film seems to be ironic: the soldier's failure to bring about any change (whether material or ideological) in the face of invincible feudalism and superstition among the masses transgresses socialist literary standards and rejects the official signifieds. However, such an irony is destabilized or even reversed within the film, in the sequences depicting the vivacious drum-dancing by the liberated peasants and the positive reactions of the young generation (i.e., Cuiqiao and Hanhan) towards revolution. The censors were highly dissatisfied with the film's "indulgence with poverty and backwardness, projecting a negative image of the country." Still, there were no politically offensive sequences to lead to full-scale denunciation and banning.[6] To the audience used to tear-jerking melodramas (in the Chinese case, those of Xie Jin, who is by far the most successful and popular director[7]), *Yellow Earth* has missed most of the opportune moments for dialogue and tension, and is thus unnecessarily opaque and flat. For example, according to typical Chinese melodrama, the scenes where Cuiqiao is forced to marry an older stranger, and the one when her tiny boat disappears from the turbulent Yellow River, would both be exploited as moments for pathos. But here they are treated metonymically: in the first, the rough dark hand extending from off-screen to unveil the red headcloth of the bride is all one sees of her feudalist "victimizer"; in the second instance, the empty shots of the river simply obscure the question of her death. In both situations, some emotional impact is conveyed vocally, in the first by the frightened breathing of the bride, and in the second by the interruption of her singing. But the cinematic construction is incomplete, creating an uncertainty in meaning and a distancing effect in an audience trained on melodrama and classical editing. Nevertheless, when the film was premiered at the 1985 Hong Kong International Film Festival, it was lauded immediately as "an outstanding breakthrough," "expressing deep sentiments poured onto one's national roots" and "a bold exploration of film language." Such an enthusiastic reception modified the derogatory official reaction towards the film (similar to some initial Western reception, but for different political reasons), and in turn prompted the local urbanites to give it some box-office support.[8]

Aesthetically speaking, *Yellow Earth* is a significant instance of a non-Western alternative in recent narrative film-making. The static views of distant ravines and slopes of the Loess Plateau resemble a Chinese scroll-painting of the Chang'an School. Consistent with Chinese art, Zhang Yimou's cinematography works with a limited range of colors, natural lighting, and a non-perspectival use of filmic space that aspires to a Taoist thought: "Silent is the Roaring Sound, Formless is the Image Grand."[9] Centrifugal spatial configurations open up to a consciousness that is not moved by desire but rather by the lack of it—the "telling" moments are often represented in extreme long shots with little depth when sky and horizon are proportioned to an extreme, leaving a lot of "empty spaces" within the frame. The tyranny of (socialist) signifiers and their signifieds is contested in this approach in which classical Chinese painting's representation of nature is deployed to create an appearance of a "zero" political coding. Indeed, the film's political discourse has little to do with official socialism; rather, it begins with a radical departure from the (imported) mainstream style and (opportunist) priorities of narrative film-making in China. One may even suggest that *Yellow Earth* is an "avant-gardist" attempt by young Chinese film-makers taking cover under the abstractionist ambiguities of classical Chinese painting.[10]

To film-makers and scholars, then, *Yellow Earth* raises some intriguing questions: What is the relationship between the aesthetic practice and the political discourse of this film? In what way is the text different from and incommensurable with the master narratives (socialist dogma, mainstream film-making, classical editing style, etc.), in what way is it "already written" (by patriarchy, especially) as an ideological production of that culture and society, and finally, how does this non-Western text elude the logocentric character of Western textual analysis as well as the sweeping historicism of cultural criticism?[11]

This essay will address the above questions by opening up the text of *Yellow Earth* (as many modernist texts have been pried open) with sets of contemporary Western methods of close reading—cine-structuralist, Barthesian poststructuralist, neo-Marxian culturalist, and feminist discursive. This will place *Yellow Earth* among the many parsimoniously plural texts and satisfy the relentless decipherers of signifieds and their curiosity for an oriental text. The following discussion of this text will show that the movement of the narrative and text of *Yellow Earth* involves the interweaving and work of four structurally balanced strands (micro-narratives) on three levels: a diegetic level (for the construction of and inquiry about cultural and historical meaning), a critical level (for the disowning and fragmentation of the socialist discourses), and a discursive level (for the polyvocal articulations of and about Chinese aesthetics and feudalist patriarchy).[12] In this way, I hope to identify certain premises of Chinese cosmological thinking and philosophy as related in and through this text. In this analytic process, the contextual reading of Chinese culture and political history will show, however, the limitations of textual analysis and hence its critique.[13]

I shall begin with a brief description of the organization of the four narrative strands and their function on both diegetic and critical levels. The Lévi-Straussian structural analysis of myths is initially useful: the peasant father imposes feudal rules on Cuiqiao, the daughter (he marries her off to stabilize the kinship system), and the soldier imposes public officers' rules on her as well (he prevents her from joining the army before securing official approval). Thus, even though the host-guest relationship of the peasant and the soldier mobilizes other pairs of antinomies such as agriculture/warfare, subsistence/revolution, backwardness/modernization, the pattern of binaries breaks down when it comes to religion/politics, since both signify, in Chinese thinking, patriarchal power as a guardian figure. In addition, Hanhan, the young male heir in the film, counteracts the establishment (runs in the reverse direction of the praying patriarchs) in the same way Cuiqiao does (rows the boat against the Yellow River currents for her own liberation). Again, the antinomy peasant/soldier is destabilized, as myth is often disassembled in history—that is, the mythic glory of hierarchic dynasties and the revolutionary success of urban militia breaks down when confronted by the historical sensibility of the post–Cultural Revolution period.

There are four terms of description: brother, sister, father, soldier. While there is a relationship of consanguinity and descent, both are complicated by the problematic relation of affinity: Cuiqiao's intimacy with Hanhan and their distance from the peasant father is more excessive while romance is taboo and marriage is ritual in the film. The prohibition of incest among family members (Cuiqiao with her brother or father) is transferred to prohibition of romantic involvement between Cuiqiao and the soldier, enforced at the cost of the girl's life.[14] Hence, the textual alignment of patriarchy with sexual repression. However, the film text is not to be confused with an anthropological account. As both Fredric Jameson and Brian Henderson point out, historicism is at work in the complex mode of sign production and in reading.[15] Hence this text would preferably be read with a historical knowledge of the Communist Party's courtship with the peasants and its reconstruction of man [sic] through the construction of socialist manhood—which reserves desire for the perfection of the ideological and economic revolution, while the liberation of women (its success a much-debated topic) becomes an apparatus for the Party's repression of male sexuality, besides being a means for winning a good reputation. Hence the position of contemporary Chinese women, generally speaking, involves a negotiation between patriarchy and socialist feminism in ways more complicated than what one deduces from the Lévi-Straussian analysis of kinship systems.

Yellow Earth:
Father and daughter

Now I shall proceed to a more detailed (though non-exhaustive) discussion of what is at work in each of the micro-narratives as narrative strands, as well as the contextual readings relevant to the textual strategies.

FIRST NARRATIVE STRAND: THE PEASANT'S STORY

The scenes assembled for the first narrative strand have a strong ethnographic nature: the material relation between the Shaanbei peasants and their land is documented through the repetitive activities of ploughing land on bare slopes, getting water every day from the Yellow River ten miles away, tending sheep, cooking, and quiet residence inside the cave home, while marriages and rain prayers are treated with a moderate amount of exotic interest—of the urban Han people looking at their rural counterparts. The peasants are depicted as people of spare words (Cuiqiao's father even sings little: "What to sing about when [one is] neither happy nor sad?"). They have a practical philosophy (their aphorism: "friends of wine and meat, spouse of rice and flour") and they show a paternal benevolence (Cuiqiao's father only sings for the soldier for fear that the latter may lose a job if not enough folk tunes are collected). Obviously, anthropological details have been pretty well attended to.

Meaning is assigned according to a historical or even ontological dependence of peasants on their motherly Land and River. This signifying structure is first of all spatially articulated: the Loess landscape with its fascinating ancient face is a silent but major figure both in Chinese painting and in this film. Consistent with the "high and distant" perspective in scroll painting is the decentered framing with the spatial contemplation of miniaturized peasants as black dots laboring to cross the vast spans of warm yellow land to get to the river or their cave homes.[16] No collective farming appears in this film, and neither planting nor harvesting modify this relationship. The symbolic representation of an ancient agrarian sensibility is condensed in shots that include the bare details of one man, one cow, and one tree within the frame in which the horizon is always set at the upper level and the land, impressive with deep ravines, appears almost flattened. In an inconspicuous way, the Yellow River's meaning is also contemplated: the peasants are nourished by it and are sometimes destroyed by it. A narrative function is attached: this is a place in dire need of reform, and it is also stubbornly resistant. The state of this land and people accounts for the delay of enlightenment or modernity—there is an unquestioning reliance on metaphysical meaning, be it the Old Master of Heavens or the Dragon King of the Sea, but which is tied so closely to the survival of the village. The narrative refusal of and enthusiasm for revolution are motivated: the ideology of survival is a much stronger instinct than the passion for ideals. But to the peasants, the Party could have been one of the rain gods.

There is a vocal part to this cosmological expression as well, articulated dialectically for a critical purpose. We shall attend to three voices: the first, that of the peasant's respect for the land: "This old yellow earth, it lets you step on it with one foot and then another, turn it over with one plough after another. Can you take that like it does? Shouldn't you respect it?" A classical form of deification borne from a genuine, everyday relationship. Then it is countered by the second, the soldier's voice: "We collect folk songs—to spread out—to let the public know what we suffering people are sacrificing for, why *we farmers* [my emphasis] need a revolution." Gu Qing offers a rational reading of the agrarian beliefs; his statement contains a simple dialectic—the good earth brings only poverty, and the way out is revolution. Yet his statement and his belief are but a modernized form of deification: the revolution and its ultimate signified (the Revolutionary Leader) are offered to replace the mythic beliefs through a (false) identification by the soldier with the peasants ("Our Chairman likes folk songs," says the soldier). Blind loyalty (of peasants to land) finds homology in, and is renarrativized by, a rational discourse (of soldier to his Leader). The ancient structure of power changes hand here; thereafter, the feudalist circulation of women and socialist liberation of women will also remain homological.

As explicit contradiction between the first two voices remains unresolved, a major clash breaks out in the form of a third voice, which appears in the rain prayer sequence. Assembled in their desiccated land, the hungry peasants chant in one voice: "Dragon King of the Sea, Saves Tens of Thousands of People, Breezes and Drizzles, Saves Tens of Thousands of People." Desperation capsuled: the hungry bow fervently to the Heavens, then to their land, and then to their totemic Dragon King of the Sea, in a primitive form of survival instinct. At this moment the soldier appears (his return to the village) from a distance, silent. A 180° shot/reverse shot organizes their (non)encounter: a frontal view of the approaching soldier, followed by a rear view of the peasants whose collective blindness repudiates what the soldier signifies (remember his song "The Communist Party Saves Tens of Thousands of People"). In this summary moment of the people's agony and the film's most searing questioning of the Revolution's potential, the multiple signifieds are produced in and through a mirroring structure: the soldier's failure reflected by the peasants' behavior and the peasants' failure in the soldier's presence.

At the outset, two dialectical relationships are set up explicitly in the text, one against the other: between peasant and nonpeasant, and between peasant and land. The roots of feudalism, through this first narrative strand, are traced to their economic and cultural bases, and are compared in a striking way to Chinese socialism. In this manner, the whole micro-narrative is historicized to suggest reflections on contemporary China's economic and political fiascos. But there is another relationship between the filmic space and the audience's (focal) gaze. The nonperspectival presentation of landscapes in some shots and sequences often leads one's gaze to linear movements within the frame, following the contours of the yellow earth and the occasional appearance and disappearance of human figures in depth on an empty and seemingly flat surface. The land stretches within the frame, both horizontally and vertically, with an overpowering sense of scale and yet without being menacing. In these shots and sequences, the desire of one's gaze is not answered by the classical Western style of suturing; indeed it may even be frustrated.[17] Rather, this desire is dispersed in the decentered movement of the gaze (and shifts in eye level as well) at a centrifugal representation of symbolically limitless space. Such an unfocused spatial consciousness (maintained also by nonclassical editing style) has a dialectical relationship with one's pleasure-seeking consciousness. It frustrates if one looks for phallocentric (or feminist, for that matter) obsessions within an appropriatable space, and it satisfies if one lets the sense of endlessness/emptiness take care of one's desire (i.e., a passage without narrative hold). In these instances, one sees an image without becoming its captive; in other words, one is not just the product of cinematic discourse (of shot/reverse shot, in particular), but still circulates within that discourse almost as "nonsubject" (i.e., not chained tightly to signification).

Within the text of *Yellow Earth*, one may say, two kinds of pleasures are set up: a hermeneutic movement prompts the organization of cinematic discourse to hold interest, while the Taoist aesthetic contemplation releases that narrative hold from time to time. Most of the moments are assigned meaning and absences of narrative image are filled, though some have evaded meaning in the rationalist sense. When the latter occurs, the rigorous theoretical discourses one uses for deciphering are sometimes gently eluded.

SECOND NARRATIVE STRAND: THE DAUGHTER'S STORY

Inasmuch as the sense of social identity defines the person within Chinese society, individuals in Chinese films are often cast as nonautonomous entities within determining familial, social, and national frameworks. Ever since the 1920s, the portrayals of individuals in films have been inextricably linked to institutions and do not reach resolution outside the latter. Hence, unlike the classical Hollywood style, homogeneity is not restored through the reconciliation of female desires with the male ones, and the ways of looking are not structured according to manipulations of visual pleasure (coding the erotic, specifically) in the language of the Western patriarchal order. With an integration of socialism with Confucian values, film texts after 1949 have often coded the political into both narrative development and visual structures, hence appropriating scopophilia for an asexual idealization. In the post–Cultural Revolution context, then, the critique of such a repressive practice naturally falls on the desexualizing (hence dehumanizing) discourses in the earlier years and their impact on the cultural and human psyche.[18]

The plotting of *Yellow Earth*, following the doomed fate of Cuiqiao the daughter, seems to have integrated the above view of social identity with the recent critique of dehumanizing political discourses. Within the second narrative strand, the exchange of women in paternally arranged marriages is chosen as the signifier of feudalist victimization of women, while the usual clichés of cruel fathers or class villains are replaced by kind paternal figures. The iconic use of feudal marriage ceremonies has become common literary and filmic practice since the 1930s, but compared with other texts, this one is more subtle and complex in its enunciation of sympathy for women.[19] In this regard, we may undertake to identify two sets of homological structures in the text that function for the above purpose. It is through the narrative and cinematic construction of these structures that *Yellow Earth* made its statement on patriarchal power as manifested in cultural, social, and political practices.

The first set of homological structures involves the spatial construction of two marriage processions, each characterized by a montage in close-up of the advancing components (trumpet players, donkey, dowry, the red palanquin and its carriers) in more or less frontal views. In each case, the repetitive and excessive appearance of red, which culturally denotes happiness, fortune, and spontaneity, is reversed in its connotative meaning within the dramatic context of the oppressive marriages. More significantly, the absence/presence of Cuiqiao as an intradiegetic spectator and her look become a linchpin to that system of signification. In the first marriage sequence, the bride is led from the palanquin to kneel with the groom before the ancestor's plate and then taken to their bedroom. Meanwhile, Cuiqiao as a spectator is referred to three or four times in separate shots, establishing her looking as a significant reading of the movement of the narrative. Yet she is not detached from that narrative at all. Seeing her framed as standing at the doorway where Confucius's code of behavior for women is written, one is constantly reminded that Cuiqiao's inscription will be similarly completed (through marriage) within the Confucian code.[20] Her look identifies her with the scene of marriage, and also relays to the audience her narrative image as a young rural female. The victimizing structure (feudalist patriarchy) and the potential victim (Cuiqiao) are joined through a shot/reverse-shot method, mobilized by her looking which coded the social and the cultural into the signifying system here.

In the second marriage sequence, the similar analysis in close-up of the advancing procession (by a similar editing style) performs an act of recall, which as a transformed version of the first marriage sequence reminds the audience of Cuiqiao's role as the intradiegetic spectator previously. In this instance, however, Cuiqiao is the bride, locked behind the dull black door of the palanquin covered by a dazzlingly red cloth. The big close-up of the palanquin, however, suggests her presence within the shot (hidden), in depth, and going through the process of "fulfilling" the inscription predicted earlier on for her against her wish for freedom. The palanquin replaces her look but points to her absence/presence. At the same time, Hanhan, her quiet brother, replaces Cuiqiao as an intradiegetic spectator looking (almost at us) from the back of the palanquin, figuring her absence and her silence. Hanhan as the brother represents an ideal form of male sympathy in that context, yet as the son and heir of a feudal system, he is also potentially responsible for the perpetuation of this victimization. In this manner, the text shifts from a possible statement on class (backwardness of peasants before the Liberation) to a statement of culture (the closed system of patriarchy) to locate the woman's tragedy. With an intertextual understanding of most post-1949 Chinese films presenting feudal marriages, this cultural statement becomes a subtle comment on the (pro-revolutionary) textual appropriations of folk rituals for political rhetorics.

The second set of homological structures appears in two pairs of narrative relationships between three characters (between Cuiqiao's father and Cuiqiao, and between Gu Qing the soldier and Cuiqiao) concerning the subject of women's (and Cuiqiao's) fate. Initially, one finds the first relationship a negative one while the second is positive, i.e., the father being feudal but the soldier liberating. This is encapsulated in a dialogue in which the soldier attempts to convince the peasants that women in socialist-administered regions receive education and choose their own husbands, and Cuiqiao's father answers: "How can that be? We farmers have rules." However, when one compares the peasants' exchange of women for the survival of the village and the revolutionaries' liberation of women for the promotion of the cause, then one finds both relationships being similarly fixated on woman as the Other in their production of meaning. Such a homology, nevertheless, is asymmetrical in presentation. On the one hand, the film is direct about the negative implications of the patrilinear family though without falling into a simple feminist logic (Cuiqiao's father sympathizes with women's tragedy in the sour tune he sings for the soldier). On the other, there is no questioning about the socialist recruitment of women (and Cuiqiao's failure to join the army is regarded as regrettable). The critique falls on another issue: Gu Qing's refusal to take Cuiqiao along with him because "We public officers have rules, we have to get the leader's approval." Thus it is nongendered bureaucracy that is at stake here, and not exactly the patriarchal aspects of the feudalist and socialist structures, which can only be identified from an extratextual position.

The suspected drowning of Cuiqiao, then, can be read as the textual negotiation with the symbolic loss of meaning: she is to be punished (by patriarchy, of course) for overturning the peasants' rule (by leaving her marriage), for brushing aside the public officers' rule (by leaving to join the army without permission), and for challenging nature's rule (by crossing the Yellow River when the currents are at their strongest).

When Cuiqiao is alive, the sour tunes she sings fill the film's sound track—musical signifiers narrating the sadness and the beauty of "yin." Her death, though tragic, brings into play the all-male spectacles in the text: drum-dancing and rain-prayer sequences each celebrating the strength and attraction of "yang," so much suppressed when women's issues were part of the mainstream political mores.[21] Here one detects the "split interest" of the text in these instances—the nonpolitical assignment of bearers of meaning (rather than the nonsexist) prescribes a masculine rather than feminine perspective of the narrative images of man and woman. That is to say, since the position of men and women in this patriarchal culture has been rearranged for the last three decades, first according to everyone's class background, then with a paternal favoring (as bias and strategy) of women, the text's critique of socialist discourses become its own articulation of a male perspective. In this way, this text does not escape being "overdetermined" by culture and society, although in some ways by default.

Since the Yan'an Forum for writers in 1942, literary writing in China followed a master narrative that privileged class consciousness over individual creativity.[22] In revolutionary realism, character types (and stereotypes) were considered the most effective methods of interpellating the masses during economic or political movements. Literary and filmic discourses on the social being dictate a structure of dichotomies: proletariat/bourgeois, Party members/non–Party members, allies/enemies, peasants/landlords, etc. It was not until 1978 that "wound literature" gave an ironic bent to the hagiographic mode for Party members and cadres. Still, such writing found shelter in specificity—for example, Xie Jin's *The Legend of Tianyun Mountain* and other adaptations from wound literature were bold in questioning the political persecution of intellectuals during the terrifying decade, unmistakably attributing the causes of people's suffering to the influences of the Gang of Four. Dichotomy, however, was basically maintained even though the introduction of good cadre/bad cadre did cause some reshuffling in the antinomies. Meanwhile, the master narrative remained intact, with authority diminished but the direct questioning of it taboo.[23]

The figure of an Eighth Route Army soldier and Party member in *Yellow Earth*, therefore, was not written without technical caution and political subtleties. A number of alterations to humanize the soldier were made during adaptation which to some extent decentralized his position in the narrative. Nevertheless, the rectitude of a revolutionary perspective and its influence on the peasants were not the least mitigated—that is to say, the third narrative strand sets the three others in motion. Thus, even when the representation of the Party member may be more in line with the popular notion, there is a level of operation that makes socialist interpretation plausible. One may say that with an audience used to being prompted by dialogue and behavior, the figure of Gu Qing does not contest the proper image of a revolutionary military man.

As a signifying structure, the soldier's story functions as (in)difference and as metonymy, which is where the ironic mode works. The figures of that ancient agrarian subculture are no longer the same when Gu Qing, the outsider, enters—they are transformed under the soldier's gaze of bewilderment, which subsequently exerts its critical import. It is the third strand that begins the braiding process among the four and is responsible for the climaxes: the daughter no longer submits to her father's wishes, the son abandons the rain-prayer ceremony. Yet, these changes take place virtually outside Gu Qing's knowledge: he is ignorant of Cuiqiao's dilemma (except about women's fate in a general way) and of the peasants' problem of survival (except in broad terms of their poverty). The Party's political courtship with the peasants is metonymically dealt with here, in the prohibition of romance (as lack of knowledge) between Gu Qing and Cuiqiao, and also powerfully in the last scene of rain prayer which brought into circulation "hunger" as the peasants' signified (versus the power elite's lack of experience of it) for their rural human–land and marriage relationships. Tension between history and ideology was again condensed, the three to four decades' national history of socialism contesting to little avail the five thousand years' national ideology of subsistence. The peasants' hospitable reception of Gu Qing and Cuiqiao's idealistic trust in the Party further reinforce the ironic mode—difference is not a simple dichotomy and often works in the areas least expected. Then, none could go very far: Cuiqiao disappears in the Yellow River, the peasants are dying of drought, while the totemic figure of the Sea Dragon King dominates the scene, lifted by worshippers who want their lives saved. The discourse here is historicist: the cultural and epistemological barriers (of both Party and people) to the capitalist market economy in the 1980s motivates this myth of survival. Yet, it is also historical: the gods, emperors, leaders, all have been sought after by people in disaster, and made disasters by people.

THE FOURTH STRAND: HANHAN'S STORY

A quiet young boy with a blank facial expression, Hanhan moves almost inconspicuously as a curious figure in the scenes. One may even ponder a Brechtian address made possible by this marginal but conscious presence. Almost uninscribed by culture, and, to some extent, by the text itself, Hanhan has the greatest degree of differentiation (i.e., Hanhan = X) and exists to be taken up by the three other narrative strands for signification.[24]

As a peasant's son, Hanhan is heir to land, feudalism, and patriarchy. As a brother to Cuiqiao, he is the displaced site of her repressed feminine love and its failure. As a little pal of Gu Qing's he is the first person to learn the song and spirit of revolution. Yet his story is also underdeveloped. In other words, Hanhan is neither unconnected nor fixated in the textual generation of meaning. Contrary to the marked positions of other song singers (of either sour tunes or revolutionary songs), Hanhan is more ambiguous with his short "bed-wetting song" (which made unrefined jokes with both the Sea Dragon King and the son-in-law) before the soldier recruits his voice for the revolutionary song, which he sings only once. In the scene where he is already made part of the fanatic horde of worshippers, Hanhan turns towards

"The silent, blank face":
Hanhan and the
soldier in *Yellow Earth*

the sight of the soldier as the source of possible change in an act of individual decision.

However, it is not Hanhan the literary figure that escapes inscription. Indeed, pressured by political demands, the textual movement of Hanhan is along the trajectory of "liberation," though there is no intention of completing it. The circulation of Hanhan (as X) along the various narrative strands is, significantly, a production of textual interweaving. When conventional meaning in that society has been fragmented and questioned within the text, Hanhan (as a textual figure) functions as the desire for meaning. One may venture to say Hanhan is the signifier of that meaning—an insight for history and culture with an urge for change, portrayed as a childish moment before inscription, before meaning is fixed at the level of the political and agrarian institutions. Therefore the silent, blank face, because to speak, to have a facial expression, is to signify, to politicize.

A braid? Perhaps, as one woven by culture in society, and not flaunted as a fetish. Since the nineteenth century, major historical events in China (wars, national calamities, revolutions, etc.) have made four topics crucial to national consciousness: feudalism, subsistence, socialism, and modernization, and discourses are prompted in relation to them in numerous literary and cultural texts. In 1984, when contemporary China struggles with the evil spells of the

Cultural Revolution and begins flirting once again with the capitalist market economy, discourses related to the four topics reappear in terms of current issues: will the agrarian mentality of its people prevent China from becoming a modern nation? Will feudal relations persist in spite of the lure of individualist entrepreneurship? Will the country's recent radical economic move (as in the Great Leap Forward) bring another large-scale fiasco? Is the Communist Party leadership still competent for the changing 1980s? Will a second Cultural Revolution occur soon? As technology and business turn corporate and global, the answers to these questions can no longer be found in an isolated situation. The China that partakes in the world's market economy no longer operates in an "ideological context" that is uniquely Chinese (as it had during the Cultural Revolution). Inevitably (and maybe unfortunately), this changing, modernizing "ideological context" in China also informs the "avant-gardist" project of *Yellow Earth* which has focused its criticism only on the patriarchal and feudal ideologies of that culture. Arguably, then, *Yellow Earth*'s modernist power of critique of Chinese culture and history comes from its subtextual, noncritical proposition of capitalist-democracy as an alternative; it is (also arguably) this grain in the text that attracts the global-intellectual as well.

An historicist reading of texts and contexts is a powerful analytic practice. In the case of *Yellow Earth*, such a reading enables one to relate the film's textual strategies to the specific political and cultural context, while at the same time exposing some of the text's symptoms. However, there still remains a need to locate *Yellow Earth*'s difference from other interesting Chinese films made during the same period. Wu Tianming's *Life* (1984), for example, deals with the disparity between intellectual and agrarian life as an important subcultural dichotomy in Chinese identity and boldly pits individual motivation against class issues. Again, such a film is possible in China only in the 1980s. Yet, one may argue that discursive constraints are not fully watertight in their operations. With respect to *Yellow Earth*, there is a presence of a certain "negative dialectics" that seems to run counter to its grain of modernist activities and does not yield to an historicist reading. It is, again, the simple Taoist philosophy which (dis)empowers the text by (non)affirming speaking and looking: "Silent is the Roaring Sound, Formless is the Image Grand." There are many such instances in the film: when the human voice is absent and nobody looks, history and culture are present in these moments of power(lessness) of the text. With this philosophy, perhaps, we may be able to contemplate the power(lessness) of our reading of the text.

NOTES

1. For detailed discussions of the conflict and contradictions involved in recent political and economic formulations of Chinese socialism see Bill Brugger, ed. *Chinese Marxism in Flux: 1978–84, Essays on Epistemotogy, Ideology and Political Economy.* New York: M. E. Sharpe, 1985.

2. In 1985, *Yellow Earth* won five festival prizes—in China, Hawaii, Nantes, Spain, and Locarno. This film's impact on filmmakers and critics in China and Hong Kong was documented in *Talking About Huang Tudi,* Chen Kaiyan, ed. Beijing: China Film Press, 1986. For an English discussion, refer to Tony Rayns's discussion of the dissident "Fifth Generation" of young PRC directors, and also his review of *Yellow Earth* in the BFI *Monthly Film Bulletin,* 10/1986.

3. A number of melodramatic and political clichés in the original essay *Echoes of the Deep Ravine* were dropped in Chen Kaige's adaptation into the screenplay titled *Silent Is the Ancient Plain.* The impressive color tones of the first work print inspired the film's final title, *Yellow Earth.*

4. According to director Chen Kaige, Cuiqiao's father in the film is close to a *vérité* version of a local peasant he met during the walking reconnaissance of Shaanxi Province, and the bachelor singer in the first marriage sequence was also a local recruit. Yet, according to official views, the film's representation of peasants was ethnocentric and derogatory. One may understand this disparity by noting that Chinese socialism has always favored a more progressive image of peasants.

5. "Xintianyou," the folk songs sung in the northern Shaanxi region, provide a rich form for metaphoric expressions and direct telling of the singers' sentiments.

6. The first film completed by a group of Beijing Film Academy '82 graduates, *One and Eight (Yige He Bage,* 1984), was directed by Zhang Junzhao. Cinematographer Zhang Yimou's contribution was already regarded as the major reason for the film's aesthetic excellence. However, the film's entire end-

ing was altered due to censorship and it was still banned from circulation. *Yellow Earth* also had several censorship problems but with its ambiguities it had better luck with the Film Bureau.

7. Examples from Xie Jin's most popular films include *The Red Detachment of Women* (1961), in which a serf girl reacted positively to a soldier's influence and turned herself into a brave red soldier, and *The Legend of Tianyun Mountain* (1978), in which two women were emotionally entangled with a persecuted rightist intellectual. Xie Jin has successfully dealt with topical issues in melodramatic form shot with classical style, which made most of his works tear-jerking successes in China.

8. According to Tony Rayns, the triumph of *Yellow Earth* in film festivals prompted the official accusation of its bad influence on local aspirations to "compete with the ideology of the bourgeoisie at foreign film festivals." On the other hand, it is the film's international reputation that silenced established film-makers and officials.

9. Originally from Lao Tzu's *Daode Jing*, this Taoist concept of representation was developed in two seminal discussions on Chinese aesthetics, "On the Origins and Bases of Chinese and Western Painting Techniques" (written in 1936), and "The Spatial Consciousness Expressed in Chinese Painting and Poetry" (written in 1949) by Zong Baihua and collected in Zong's *A Stroll in Aesthetics*. Shanghai: The People's Press, 1981, pp. 80–113.

10. Some of the principles of Chinese spatial representation have been taken up by the West for interrogation of its own norms, e.g., Beijing Opera by Brechtian theater, and hence what is classical for one cultural system can be appropriated for avant-gardist reasons in another. Here, I would quickly add (with reference to Edward Said's discussion on "Traveling Theory" in *The World, the Text and the Critic*) that while critical consciousness is the issue, classical Chinese painting as the borrowed theory itself is not free of institutional limitations in the local context. On the other hand, the aestheticization of nature in *Yellow Earth* could also be quickly seized by Western audiences for sentimentalized retreats to a preindustrial corner of the world.

11. Culturalist or neo-Marxist criticisms of mass culture focus mostly on sign systems produced within bourgeois capitalism. In general, hardcore propaganda is taken to be characteristic of socialist sign systems, which is a gross simplification of the complicated mediations and processes at work in those economies and cultures. With reference to China, a more complicated view of socialist mass cultures is called for, and Bill Brugger's *Chinese Marxism in Flux* can be read along with Victor F. S. Sit, ed. *Commercial Laws and Business Regulations of the PRC, 1949–1983* (London: Macmillan, 1983) to see that utilitarian individualism, for example, is functional within recent Chinese economic discourses.

12. For substantial discussions of the interweaving of Confucianism, socialism, and patriarchy in contemporary China, see Richard Madsen, *Morality*

and Power in a Chinese Village (Berkeley: University of California Press, 1984) and Judith Stacey, *Patriarchy and Socialist Revolution in China* (Berkeley: University of California Press, 1983).

13.   Refer to Said's discussion of Derrida's and Foucault's approach to texts in "Criticism Between Culture and System," *The World, the Text and the Critic,* pp. 183–225.

14.   The largely asexual representation of revolutionary characters was a major practice in the Revolutionary Model Plays, the only films made during 1970–73. In the post–Cultural Revolution era, the hagiographic mode of representation was debated as suppression of "true human character" in literary and film circles.

15.   Both Brian Henderson's "*The Searchers:* An American Dilemma" (Bill Nichols, ed. *Movies and Methods* Vol. II, pp. 429–49) and Fredric Jameson's *The Political Unconscious* (Ithaca: Cornell University Press, 1981) have informed the historicist reading of this essay. I am also thankful to Nick Browne of UCLA who introduced me to them and gave valuable advice, and to David James of Occidental College for his inspiring comments.

16.   The term "Chinese westerns" was used recently in China to describe films that took to northwestern China for location shooting (e.g., Tian Zhuangzhuang's *On the Hunting Ground,* 1984). Yet, while the American frontier appealed to the immigrants' evolutionist expansion of social and political organization over inanimate nature (according to Frederick J. Turner), the Chinese west evoked a non-aggressive self-reflection; or according to Wang Wei, "The sage, harboring the Tao, responds to eternal objects; the wise man, purifying his emotions, savors the images of things."

17.   While I agree with Heath's critique of Oudart-Dayan's definition of "suturing" in filmic discourse as "narrow," I still refer here, for the sake of convenience, to the privileged example of shot/reverse shot as the suturing approach to spatial articulation.

18.   In this respect, Laura Mulvey's "Visual Pleasure and Narrative Cinema" would not be relevant to many Chinese films, and especially not to those made during the Cultural Revolution, which prohibited erotic codes in its representation of women.

19.   One may suggest, in terms of Teresa DeLauretis's "Desire in Narrative" in *Alice Doesn't* (Bloomington: Indiana University Press, 1984, pp. 139–46), that there are instances in which the girl in *Yellow Earth* moves as "mythical subject" in narrative while men became her topoi; the marriage sequence and the river-crossing sequence are arguable examples.

20.   The four Chinese characters in the shot are "San Cong Si De," meaning "three obediences and four virtues." The "three obediences" for a Chinese woman are obedience to her father at home, to her husband after marriage, and to her son in her widowhood.

21.   "Yin" the female element; "Yang," the male element. These two elements in Chinese cosmology involve symbolic systems and economies present both in the male and the female gender.

110   ESTHER C. M. YAU

22.   "Talks at the Yan'an Forum on Literature and Art," *Mao Zedong on Literature and Art*. Beijing Foreign Language Press, 1977.

23.   Recently, the citing of Mao's "Talks at the Yan'an Forum" as the standard of literary and artistic creation in China is usually indicative of a tightened literary policy. In 1987, with the "anti-bourgeois liberalization" movement, China celebrated the 45th anniversary of the "Talks."

24.   This concept is taken from Gilles Deleuze's "A Quoi Reconnait-on le Structuralisme?" (1973). Hanhan's name in Chinese means simple and lacking the ability to talk well.

MANTHIA DIAWARA

POPULAR CULTURE
AND ORAL TRADITIONS
IN AFRICAN FILM

Vol. 41, no. 3 (Spring 1988): 6–14.

In spite of the increasing number of African films released in the course of the last 20 years (from *Borom Sarret* in 1963 to *Nyamanton* [*The Garbage Boys*] in 1986), there has not been an African film criticism as enlightening and provocative as the criticism generated by the Brazilian Cinema Novo, the theories of Imperfect Cinema, and the recent debates around Third Cinema.[1] This gap must be filled to overcome the repetitious nature of criticism which has addressed itself to African film in the last 25 years and to make possible the definition of a dynamic aesthetic proper to Africa. The lack of African critics who know African traditions is at fault, as well as the critical practice of the West, where the ethnocentrism of European and American film critics has limited them to evaluating African cinema through the prism of Western film language. Thus, they refuse to look at African cinema "straight in the eyes." They think that that cinema is in the process of finding its individuality, that the film-makers have not mastered yet the film medium, that the camera style is still primitive in African films.

European critics are afraid to look at African cinema in the same manner that Africans used to be afraid to watch the first movies from Europe. According to Amadou Hampate Ba, the wise man of Bandiangara, when film was introduced in his village in 1935, the Imam and the head of the village accused it of being loaded with lies, tricks, and anti-Islamic goals. In order to protect the village against this diabolical invention imposed upon them by the colonial administrator, the Imam commanded women and children to stay at home. Only men came to the projection and they closed their eyes for the entire length of the film. At the end, the men told the administrator that women and children could not come because they were afraid of the images in motion on the screen.[2]

Versions of this paper were presented to the colloquium of Film and Oral Literature in Ouagadougou at the 10th Pan-African Film Festival, and to the Center for Black Studies at the University of California, Santa Barbara. I would like to thank the University of California at Santa Barbara for research and travel support in writing the paper.

Today, African cinema must combat this resistance to foreign images. Europeans close their eyes in order not to see the questioning of Western values, the reaffirmation of cultures repressed by the West, and anti-neocolonialist discourses. European critics sent to view these films, in another form of the reactions like those of Amadou Hampate Ba's village chief, bring back inevitably indulgent and nonanalytical comments on African cinema.

To analyze African cinema, one must first understand that 25 years of film production have necessarily created an aesthetic tradition which African filmmakers use as a point of reference which they either follow or contest. An African aesthetic does not come merely from European cinema. To avoid making African cinema into an imperfect appendix to European cinema, one must question Africa itself, and African traditions, to discover the originality of its films. In his article "Sur les formes traditionnelles du roman africain," Mahamadou Kane wrote that "the originality of the African novel must be found more precisely in its relation with the forms of oral literature from 'Black Africa'."[3] In the same article, Kane compared the oral story-teller to the novelist, exploring the themes, the narrative devices, and other features of the novel which also form the basis of the oral tale. He also showed that the novelist, as well as the story-teller, uses realism as a means of expression, resorting to a linear story with one action which enfolds around three units of time (departure, arrival, and return). Like the traditional story-teller, the novelist opts for a didactic enunciation and, consequently, reproduces in the text the apprenticeship of life as well as moral and social codes.

In this article, I will try to bring out the relations between the oral tradition and African cinema in the same manner that Kane does for the novel. I will compare the griot (the bard) to the film-maker, looking particularly at their reproduction of traditional modes of being, so as to show the similarities and the differences between their works.

First of all, it seems logical to underline the fundamental difference between oral literature and cinema. The means put into play in the construction of a film—the camera movement, close-ups, and shot/reverse-shots—are not the same as those used by the story-teller. Indeed, the latter enunciates by incarnating characters one by one, dominating the narrative by his or her presence. The griot depends on spoken language as well as on music to actualize the story. The film-maker, on the contrary, uses the means of mechanical reproduction to give shape to the story. Whereas oral literature speaks of life, cinema reproduces an impression of life.[4]

Putting this difference aside, can one say that the originality of African cinema must be found in the oral tradition? Can one also overlook the notion that African cinema had had nothing to inherit when it started its development?[5] According to this postulate, there would exist only one film language,

Ousmane Sembene's *Xala* (New Yorker Films)

the one to which the West has given birth and which it has perfected. The black film-maker would then only have to place the content of his/her work in a framework that takes its condition of possibility from the rules and precepts already elaborated by Western masters.

However, when African films are examined, one sees that all the directors resort in different ways to oral story-telling forms. As Kane noted in regard to the novelist, the film-maker too is influenced, consciously or unconsciously, by the story-teller's techniques of narrating. "At night, he/she used to be fed with oral tales, historical or cosmogonical legends . . . very often, he/she grew up in a milieu which had a specific mentality as regards the forms of discourse, a sensibility which expressed itself in particular ways."[6]

First it is important to look at the manner in which popular cultures are filmed in African cinema, because such popular practices as song and dance, the performance of the griot, and the representation of African social systems such as polygamy are often used to create the effect of the real in the films. In *Xala* (Ousmane Sembene's 1974 film about independence and the impotence of the new leaders), for example, after the Africans have taken control of the Chamber of Commerce, song and dance are represented to accentuate the transition of power in the story as a return to authenticity. The dance occurring at the beginning of the film, instead of having a fixed exotic meaning as in anthropological films about Africa, is a spectacle open to several interpretations. First one can see in it the desire of the new public employees to be considered traditional, and therefore authentic. But one soon realizes that the dance and music outside are used as masks to hide the incompetence of the new leaders inside, who accept bribes from the very Frenchmen they had kicked out. Finally, the dance connotes in an ironic manner the representation of half-naked Africans who are always dancing in European and American films. At the level of the signified, song and dance in *Xala* position the spectators to criticize the superficial use of tradition by politicians. The opening scene helps the audience build a revolutionary attitude relative to the regressive behavior of the characters in the film.

In *Visages de Femmes* (*Faces of Women*, a 1985 film by Desiré Ecaré, which tells two different stories about two women in Ivory Coast), song and dance are narrative processes which move the story forward. In this film song and dance, at the beginning and end of the river love scene, constitute a mininarrative with a beginning, middle, and end. Through their performance, the women tell the story of how a boy and a girl deceived everybody and met in the river to make love. In *Xala* Sembene negates the Hollywood stereotypes of exotic Africans and gives a contextual interpretation to song and dance, but in *Visages de Femmes* Ecaré emphasizes the manner in which song and dance in Africa are used to inform people of what is taking place behind their backs. This balletic cinema, or a cinema that dances in order to tell its story, has its parallel in at least one West African popular theater, the *Koteba*, which also can imitate all forms of representation through dance.

As the dancers of *Visages de Femmes*, in their colorful attire, move to the beat of the music in harmony with the rhythm of the editing and the camera movements, one cannot help but think that Ecaré has invented a new language for African cinema. But how is this aesthetization of an African popular culture, which pushes the spectator to identify with the dancing women, different from the old tradition of constructing the body of women as the site of desire in Western cinema? Furthermore it seems that the dance scene, through the use of medium close-ups of women's feet, arms, and heads, is addressed to the desire of the male spectator, and thus contradicts the love-making in the river, which seems to proclaim the sexual freedom of African women. In other words, as Ecaré places song and dance in African cinema, away from anthropological and Hollywood films, he surrenders to the sexist codes of African popular culture which undermine his very attempt to keep alive in *Visages de Femmes* the political commitment of African directors.

This brief analysis of the representation of song and dance in *Xala* and *Visages de Femmes* reveals that the appropriation of popular culture by the fiction film in Africa creates a movement away from Western film language, toward a predominance of traditional narrative codes. Sembene leads this movement by first negating European stereotypes of song and dance in Africa, and by putting into question the African elite's attempt to exploit these popular forms for its own gains. Ecaré's desire to let African dance and song speak in a cinematic language coincides with a phallocentric construction of the characters which turns them into objects of desire for the spectator. *Visages de Femmes* teaches us, thus, the necessity for the film-maker to interrogate popular culture in order to divest it of its manifest and/or repressed phallocentrism.

As regards social practices such as polygamy in African film, two examples suffice to illustrate its cinematic representation. In *Sey Seyeti* (*One Man, Several Women*, 1980), Ben Diogaye Beye puts polygamy and modernity into play in order to bring to light the contradictions in a contemporary African society. Beye constructs polygamy as the common denominator of the problems of several men in the film, and ends by focusing on the freedom of a young woman who is forced to marry an older man. There is no central story in *Sey Seyeti*, which tells one anecdote after another, using polygamy as the over-determining factor. This complex film, which runs the risk of confusing the spectator in the West about the relationships among many characters, or of being dismissed as an example of African avant-garde, shocked the inhabitants of Senegal. When it was released, the film provoked an unprecedented reaction in the press from sociologists, ethnologists, and politicians. Beye was accused by some for looking at polygamy, an African custom, with European eyes, and praised by others for boldly exposing a regressive practice which no longer finds its justification in modern Senegal. The fact that *Sey Seyeti* shocked African audiences, while its message remains opaque or confusing to the spectator in the West, indicates that Beye simultaneously fashioned an African film language while attempting to shed light on the repressiveness of a popular practice such as polygamy.

In *Finye* (*The Wind*, by Souleymane Cissé, 1983), polygamy is a principal theme. One of the scenes in this film debunks polygamy by exposing its internal contradictions. Indeed, the youngest of the governor's wives takes the initiative in the quest for a lover by expressing her desire for a young man of her age. The man this young woman chases also happens to be the lover of the governor's daughter. Symbolically, therefore, both women have become the governor's daughters and/or wives because they have the same object of desire. What becomes an issue in this scene is polygamy's inability to answer to the emerging needs of sexual freedom in Africa. But the tradition of polygamy is more seriously questioned in the film by the belittling of its social and economic meaning. Women play the role of respectful spouses, who submit to their husbands in order to cheat on them even better and to get from them what they want. For example, in another scene the oldest and the youngest wives stage a mock fight to distract the husband from his commitment to punish a disloyal daughter. As for the governor/husband marrying three wives, which in the past would have served to emphasize his prestige, this now appears as a movement toward the weakening of moral and social values. The youngest wife squanders his money, drinks whiskey, and smokes in front of him. These signs of depravity in a traditional Islamic society are ascribed to modernity and the persistence of polygamy. An understanding of local culture (anthropological signs) is necessary to appreciate the play of the actors as authoritative and phallocentric husband, or oldest and youngest wives. One has to go beyond the simplistic conception of art as functional in Africa and see, for example, the aesthetics over-determined by polygamy in the comic scene of the mock fight between the wives.

The figure of the griot, symbol of the oral tradition, has also been often represented in African films. Historians of African cinema have already studied the griot's presence in Sembene's films. In a pioneering article on the subject, Mbye Cham argues that Sembene sees himself as "the mouth and ears of his people," and in his role as a film-maker, he "prefers to amalgamate, adapt, develop, and enhance certain features of the *gewel* [griot] and the *Lekbat* [storyteller]."[7] In her book *The Cinema of Sembene Ousmane* (1984), Françoise Pfaff compares Sembene's cinematic techniques with the griot's narrative techniques. She also analyzes the representation of the griot in films such as *Niaye, Borom Sarret, Xala,* and *Ceddo.* I will limit myself to the figure of the griot seen in a scene of *Borom Sarret*: fat, well dressed, and even with a gold tooth. By contrast the "Borom Sarret" (cart driver) is skinny, poorly dressed, and tired from his work. The opposition between these two characters is so striking that it reminds one of an earlier scene where Sembene uses high- and low-angle shots to contrast the cart driver with a crippled beggar who crawls on all fours.

As money is transferred from the cart driver to the griot, one sees tradition as tainted with obvious corruption. The griot turns tradition into a tool of exploitation when he evokes the cart driver's past nobility in order to take away all the money he has earned for the morning labor. The griot's narrative about the cart driver, which would have been authoritative in oral tradition, is debunked here as exploitative and not inclusive of the contemporary realities that oppress the cart driver. Sembene transcends the griot, therefore, and surrounds him and his old narrative with a new vision which traces the mechanism by which people such as the cart driver are exploited. It is important to notice that in the same scene, as the griot goes on taking the cart driver's money, one young boy shines the shoes of another who is stronger and who leaves without paying. Here again Sembene uses high- and low-angle shots, as he does throughout the length of the film to maintain this hierarchy of power not only between people, but also between the two sides of the city.

The richness of this scene is such that it shows the spectator that a return to tradition, to authenticity, does not always bring about solutions to the problems of Africans such as the cart driver. While criticizing the inhuman westernization of the inhabitants of the Europeanized side of the city, the "Plateau," *Borom*

Cart driver and griot:
Borom Sarret
(New Yorker Films)

Sarret questions the unconditional return to tradition. Sembene creates a distance between spectators and the characters in the film which enables the spectators to criticize themselves in their tradition. This cinematic language takes its form and content from the figure of the griot, symbol of the oral tradition which Sembene uses as his point of departure. The difference between this first film by Africa's leading director and Western films resides in Sembene's ability to transform Western cinema's exotic characters like the griot and the cart driver into thematic as well as structural elements for the content and the form of his film language.

In *Djeli* (*The Griot*, 1981), on the contrary, Lancine Fadika-Kramo resists this transcendence of the griot's art form. He posits the griot as the point of departure and the master of narrative. *Djeli* starts with a flashback retracing the griot's mythic origin in order to put into question the hierarchies of the caste system. According to this rhetoric, the griot was originally a hunter who changed trades to become a singer, story-teller, and musician. Interestingly enough, another West African myth of origins, "Gassire's Lute," states that the griot was a brave warrior who, tired of killing, turned into a musician to follow and entertain the warriors.[8] *Djeli* blames the caste system for the contemporary negative image of griots as inferior to other social groups. To show that this definition of griots is opposed to any revolution of ideas, to love and life, Fadika creates a love story between a man from the griot caste and a woman from another social group so as to reveal the regressiveness of caste systems which suppress such a possibility. The aesthetic in *Djeli* defines itself as a movement out of the stagnation of caste hierarchies, towards a transformation of tradition into an equalitarian system. It is in this sense that the film valorizes "Djeli-ya"—the state of being a griot—through beautiful images of the griottes (female artists), slow-motion shots of griottes singing and dancing, and the flashback which shows that griots were originally equal to other groups. The film positions the spectator to get rid of hierarchical notions, to enjoy the art of the griot, and to see a coincidence between the rehabilitation of griots and progress in Africa.

Finally, in *Jom* (1981), Ababakar Samb paints a romantic figure of griots. According to Samb, they are the historians, the educators, and the guardians of people's conscience. In *Jom* the griot is the main character, the omniscient narrator of the different sketches that form the film, and the immortal persona who travels through time and space. He remains unchanged by age and by the weapons used by the enemies of tradition. Neither money nor fear can corrupt him. He is the griot of the poor as well as of the rich. Samb's griot, like Sembene's narrator in *Borom Sarret*, is a committed activist who fights for the right of the oppressed. He provides leadership and moral support to the factory workers who are on strike, ridicules the eccentricities of the *nouveaux riches* in Africa, and praises the courage and dignity of the migrant workers who had to leave their villages because of the drought.

Samb's construction of the griot and his narrative as master and model respectively for African cinema has for a consequence the subordination of the film-maker's narrative to that of the griot and the creation of a nostalgic mood to serve as a refuge for the spectator. The figure of the griot is used to reinvent a beautiful image of the past. Unlike Sembene, who puts the griot's narrative within a larger narrative, Samb surrenders to the narrative authority of the griot. This romanticization of the griot defines Samb's film language, which valorizes tradition as characterized in the film by authenticity, dignity, and truth, and negates modernism as characterized by alienation, colonialism, and exploitation. *Jom* positions the spectator to identify with tradition without any attempt at self-criticism: everything positive is pushed on the side of tradition and everything negative on the side of modernism.

Up to now, I have shown the manner in which elements of popular culture have been incorporated into cinema. I will show now how the structure of oral literature has helped to shape the originality of African cinema. At the beginning of this article, I pointed out that film-makers, like novelists, are influenced, consciously or not, by the narrative forms of the oral story-teller. They have been initiated into oral tradition before going to Western schools. The way the story-tellers narrate becomes their point of reference when they take their first steps at a film school. During the rest of their careers, they are bound to be dealing with oral tradition, to move it sometimes, contrasting it with the modern forms of the novel and of cinema, or even to repress it. One can see the influence of oral tradition in all African films, including *Xala*, *The Money Order*, *Finye*, and *Baara (The Porter)*, even where the narrative forms of the classic novel and cinema dominate.

Sembene's *Ceddo*
(New Yorker Films)

Elsewhere, I showed how Gaston Kabore's *Wend Kuuni (The Gift of God,*
1983) makes orality its subject and questions the hermetic and conservative
structure of tradition in oral literature.[9] One can also mention Sembene's
Ceddo as another film which takes the oral tradition for a principal subject
and transforms its structure into a revolutionary statement. Sembene's *The
Money Order* is a historical landmark because, for the first time in a film by
an African director, the actors speak an African language. But it is in *Ceddo*
that Sembene posits an archeology of discourse in Africa. The richness of the
language in proverbs and sayings, the power of the spoken word and of the
speaker, are all represented in *Ceddo*. In the king's court, the discursive space
defines itself by including some as members of the discourse in a hierarchical
order and by excluding others. The griot, to use the words of Camara Laye, is
master of discourse. He controls its distribution and its impact. He is the one
through whom the speaking members communicate.

Let's examine the manner in which the subject of orality determines the form
of narration in the film. In order to represent the discursive space, the director
creates a *mise-en-scène* in which the griot occupies the center of the circle
formed by the king's court, the Imam, the missionary, and the Ceddoes. The fast
editing style of European films is replaced by long takes in deep-focus shots. It
is as if the camera has taken the griot's position so as to reveal the directions of
speech. There are very few camera movements and close-ups. Shot/reverse-

shots are avoided so as not to give the impression that one is dealing with a dialogue scene similar to the ones in Western films.

However, Sembene, like the griot, also makes his presence felt at several points in the diegesis. He is physically present as a Ceddo, carrying firewood on his head, discussing the issue of exile with other Ceddoes, and during the Imam's baptizing of Ceddoes. The use of close-ups of human faces and of objects, in this film where long shots dominate the narration, reveals a didactic intervention on the part of the director. Thus Sembene, like the oral storyteller, determines the reading of the signs for the viewer.

The travel of initiation or the educational quest, which constitutes the structural cell of oral literature, is also an important motif in African cinema (cf. *Borom Sarret, La Noire de . . . , L'Exile, Lettre Paysanne, Wend Kuuni, Njangane, Touki Bouki*, etc.). The quest defines itself as a movement from the village to the city and ends with the return to the village. One can also interpret it as an alienation and a return to authenticity, as is shown at the end of *Touki Bouki*, for example.

Ceddo also moves its characters so as to bring them to an awakening of consciousness. The princess, first kidnapped by the Ceddoes, realizes the exploitation of her people by the Imam and joins the Ceddoes in their resistance against the tyranny of the Imam. What above all differentiates *Ceddo* from the oral narration is its closure. In the oral tradition, the physical return symbolizes the return to the status quo. The griot is conservative and his story helps to reinforce traditional values. In oral traditions, the story is always closed so as not to leave any ambiguity about interpretations. In *Ceddo*, on the contrary, the return denotes the union of the princess and the Ceddoes. Thus the end of the film, a freeze frame, announces the new day pregnant with several possibilities.

Finally, I will end this study by showing the manner in which one of the best films of the Pan-African Film Festival (FESPACO 1987), Cheick Oumar Sissoko's *Nyamanton* (see *FQ*, Winter 1987–88), continues the African film language I have sought to define above. *Nyamanton* constitutes an educational quest, or an initiation trip for the two main characters, Kalifa and Fanta, who travel daily from their home to the neighborhood where they work. The home symbolizes the interior space where tradition is a refuge, safeguarding parental relations. The children play with their grandparents and the resulting laughs help the family go through their daily difficulties. The city represents the outside, the change of setting and imminent danger. The trips between home and the city enable the children to witness the injustice present in their society and to question its permanence.

Nyamanton, too, like *Ceddo*, goes beyond the mere imitation of orality to question the griot who is the master of discourse. In one scene Kalifa says to his friend, Aliou, that his father is the greatest liar after Jali Baba, Mali's famous griot. Aliou answers that griots do not lie, that what they say is the true story and that Kalifa ignores their value. Aliou then starts imitating Jali Baba and sings his friend's praises. One sees in this scene the definition of the griot as a historian on the one hand and, on the other hand, as an artist whose play with words ranks him with liars. But more important than this reference to the figure of the griot and his narrative is the fact that the director's world view takes the place of that of the griot as the most authoritative in the thematization of the kids' relation to everyday life in Africa. In oral tradition, it is through the griot's point of view that one sees and realizes the universe around one. In film, the camera replaces the griot as the director's eyes and constructs the new images of Africa for the spectator. It is in this sense that one says that the African film-maker has replaced the griot in the rewriting of history.

Nyamanton is constructed mostly with long shots. These shots show clearly the space occupied by the women at the house door and Kalifa's father under the tree. The father has to yell when he communicates with women because of the distance separating them. In order to remain within the limits of realism as regards the representation of such spaces, the camera occupies the center between the women and the father, as was the case with the griot in *Ceddo*. Here, too, close-ups and shot/reverse-shots are avoided as much as possible.

At first sight, this narrative expedient may be dismissed as simply a primitive use of the camera in an attempt to economize on editing. Thus a hasty comparison with Western cinema might bring one to the conclusion that African films lack action. But an analysis based on the forms of oral tradition will highlight the originality of African film language in *Nyamanton*. First, one can see through an ethnographic insight that the long shots serve better to create the effect of verisimilitude in the narrative. The external space in Africa is less characterized by the display of emotion and closeness between man and woman, and more by a designation of man's space and woman's space in society. The narrator imitates this reality by using mostly long shots and by describing the emotion of the characters instead of showing it. The griot's influence on the film-maker brings about the fact that subjective shots do not always have the same significance in African cinema as in Western cinema. Close-ups of a child's face or of a pack of cigarettes in *Nyamanton*, for example, are not objects seen by a character but their description by the director/narrator for the spectator. Even the flashforward in the film is a description of the mother coming to an understanding of the situation in which she finds herself. Instead of effacing himself and realizing the story through different characters' narrations, the director in *Nyamanton* always carries the camera on his shoulder and, like the griot, dominates the narrative with his presence. While Western directors often achieve recognition by letting the story tell itself, African directors, like the griots, master their craft by impressing the spectator with their narrative performance. This may be because, with the griots, one achieves fame not by being the author of new texts but by being able to reproduce the best versions of old texts. *Nyamanton* is a new version of such African films in which tradition clashes with modernity, and the popularity of its director lies in the manner in which he describes the most memorable episodes of the clash.

The choice of *Nyamanton* for the title of the film is also interesting in the context of oral tradition. Etymologically, "Nyamanton" comes from the prefix "Nyama," which in Bambara and Mandinka may be translated as "potentially dangerous forces released through the performance or violation of ritual."[10] "Nyaman" with an "n" at the end means trash. Thus a popular song in West Africa likens Sunjata, King of Mali in the thirteenth century, to a dump-site which hides everything underneath itself, but which cannot be covered by other things. Literally the song refers to Sunjata's vital force which protects his people and which harms his enemies like the plague released from a "Nyama" or from the violation of ritual.[11]

When the title of the film is interpreted in the context of "Nyama" as a West African trope, one sees how Sissoko positions the spectator to take a personal responsibility in reducing the children's future to trash collection, and to fear the retribution of "Nyama." Sunjata, too, had a difficult childhood, and those who were responsible were punished. On the other hand, the likening of the children to Sunjata leads the spectator to identify them with the collective future of Africa. As in *Ceddo*, orality is here again made the subject of the film in order to arraign the repressive forces of tradition and modernism.

Finally, the oral tradition also influenced the French title of the film, *La leçon des ordures (The Lesson of Garbage)*. Sissoko wanted to oppose to "The Lesson of Things," which students in Francophone Africa learn every morning from French textbooks, the lessons learnt about Malian society by Kalifa and Aliou through their work as garbage boys. As "leçon des choses" becomes interchangeable with "leçon des ordures," and both are little more than "Nyaman," the film creates the necessity to question the lessons inherited from the former colonial powers. There is no doubt that the form of African cinema is influenced by its traditional content. Understanding the role played by the oral tradition in African film enables the critic to see how the film-maker has transformed this tradition into a new ideology. But it is also possible to study the way in which the African content has changed the cinematic language of the West. This is what transpires when one examines the strategies by which film has incorporated African traditions. The African director makes conscious and unconscious references to the griot's narrative techniques.

NOTES

1.   Robert Stam and Randal Johnson, *Brazilian Cinema* (East Brunswick: Associated University Press, 1982). Teshome Gabriel, *Third Cinema in the Third World: The Aesthetics of Liberation* (Ann Arbor: UMI Research Press, 1982). Julianne Burton, *Cinema and Social Change in Latin America: Conversations with Film-makers* (Austin: University of Texas Press, 1986). For the recent debates on Third Cinema see Julianne Burton, "Marginal Cinemas and Mainstream Critical Theory." *Screen* vol. 26, no. 3/4 (1985). Teshome Gabriel, "Colonialism and 'Law and Order' Criticism." *Screen*, vol. 27, no. 3/4 (1986). For an overall review, see Roy Armes, *Third World Filmmaking and the West* (Berkeley: University of California Press, 1987).

2.   "Le dit du cinéma africain" in *Films éthnographiques sur l'Afrique Noire,* by Jean Rouch. Paris: UNESCO (1967), pp. 1–9.

3.   In *Revue de Littérature Comparée*, vol. 3, no. 4 (1974), p. 537.

4.   For a recent discussion of codes that are specific to film language see Jacques Aumont et al., *Esthétique du film*. Paris: Editions Fernand Nathan (1983), pp. 138–143.

5.   Jacques Binet, for example, argues that "The African traditions were not prone to an art of images: no fresco, no painting and no drawing." See "Les cultures africaines et les images" in *CinémAction* no. 26 (1982) (special issue: Cinémas noirs d'Afrique), p. 19.

6.   *Revue de Littérature Comparée*, p. 549.

7.   Mbye Cham, "Ousmane Sembene and the Aesthetics of African Oral Traditions," in *Africana Journal* (1982), p. 26.

8.   In *Technicians of the Sacred*, ed. by Jerome Rothenberg. New York: Anchor Books (1969), pp. 184–191.

9.   "Oral Literature and African Film: Narratology in *Wend Kuuni*." *Présence Africaine* no. 142 (1987), pp. 36–49.

10.   Christopher L. Miller, "Orality through Literacy: Mande Verbal Art after the Letter." *The Southern Review*, vol. 23, no. 1 (1987), p. 88.

11.   Massa Makan Diabaté, *Le Lion à l'Arc*. Paris: Hatier (1986), p. 77.

MARSHA KINDER

THE SUBVERSIVE POTENTIAL OF THE PSEUDO-ITERATIVE

Vol. 43, no. 2 (Winter 1989–90): 2–16.

The *iterative* was introduced into contemporary narrative theory by French narratologist Gérard Genette in his ground-breaking work *Narrative Discourse*, where he considers "*narrative frequency*, that is, the relations of frequency (or, more simply, of repetition) between the narrative and the diegesis," which he claims is "one of the main aspects of narrative temporality." He describes the iterative as a type of narrative "where a single narrative utterance takes upon itself several occurrences together of the same event (in other words, . . . several events considered only in terms of their analogy)"—as in the example "every day of the week I went to bed early." Genette acknowledges that the *identity* of these multiple occurrences is debatable (i.e., that each instance of going to bed has its unique variations) and "that the 'repetition' is in fact a mental construction, which eliminates from each occurrence everything belonging to it that is peculiar to itself, in order to preserve only what it shares with all the others of the same class, which is an abstraction." Nevertheless, he defines the iterative as "*narrating one time* (or rather: *at one time*) *what happened* n *times*"; as opposed to narrating one time what happened one time (the *singulative*—as in the example "Yesterday, I went to bed early"); or narrating *n* times what happened *n* times (the *anaphoric*, as in "Monday I went to bed early, Tuesday I went to bed early, Wednesday I went to bed early, etc.," which is merely a multiple form of the singulative); or narrating *n* times what happened one time (the *repeating* narrative, as in "Yesterday I went to bed early, yesterday I went to bed early").[1]

Usually signalled in verbal discourse by the use of the imperfect tense ("I used to go to bed early") and normally limited to a subordinate descriptive function in classical literary narrative, the iterative aspect, according to Genette, can be traced all the way back to Homer, but was first liberated from "functional dependence" by Flaubert in *Madame Bovary* and most fully expanded "in textual scope, in thematic importance and in degree of technical elaboration" by Proust in *A la Recherche du temps perdu*, where it becomes a key component of his radical innovation. What I intend to do in this essay is to explore how the elaboration of the iterative functions in filmic narrative and the filmic means by which it is signalled, particularly in works that attempt to make a radical break from existing narrative conventions.

THE PSEUDO-ITERATIVE IN HOLLYWOOD CLASSICAL CINEMA

Although Genette's elaboration of the iterative is commonly assumed to be one of his most important contributions to narrative theory, there has been surprisingly little application of this concept to cinema. A notable exception is Brian Henderson's essay, "Tense, Mood, and Voice in Film (Notes After Genette)," in which he attempts to describe how the iterative functions in classical Hollywood cinema in contrast to classical literary narrative. After noting that "in classical cinema, as in the classical novel, the iterative nearly always has an information or background function subordinate to singulative scenes," Henderson perceptively observes that what is far more central to cinema than to literature is the "pseudo-iterative"—an unusual mode that Genette finds in Proust and that he defines as "scenes presented, particularly by their wording in the imperfect, as iterative, whereas their richness and precision of detail ensure that no reader can seriously believe they occur and reoccur in that manner, several times, without any variation" (Genette, p. 121). Henderson notes:

> This happens occasionally in Proust; in cinema it is pervasive because "richness and precision of detail" seem to be inherent in photography and sound recording, at least in those practices of them engaged in by most films.[2]

Pursuing his comparison of the ways the iterative functions in cinema as opposed to literature, Henderson describes the opening scene from *How Green Was My Valley* (1941), where Huw's voice-over first establishes the iterative mode through his description of a typical day and through his repeated use of the word "would" (e.g., "Someone would strike up a song and the valley would ring with the sound of many voices . . . ") and then slips almost imperceptibly into the singulative ("It was on this afternoon that I first met Bron . . ."). Henderson observes:

> Most interesting, theoretically, is how and why such a slippage is possible in cinematic iterative; it would not be in literary narrative. Are the images neutrally either iterative or singulative, depending upon a voice-

*How Green
Was My Valley*

over to define their temporal status? If so, then the continuity of the images may sustain us through a shift in tense, while the changed verbal tense tells us how to read the images. (Henderson, pp. 11–12)

Genette interprets analogous slippages in Proust (i.e., when he "inadvertently lets a necessarily singulative *passé simple* into the middle of a scene presented as iterative") as "so many signs that the writer himself sometimes 'lives' such scenes with an intensity that makes him forget the distinction of aspects." Rather than seeing them as a conscious artistic strategy, Genette reads them as "confusions" that "reflect in Proust a sort of *intoxication with the iterative*" (p. 123)—an intoxication that presumably is transmitted to the reader. I would argue that the particular form of pseudo-iterative that operates in classical Hollywood cinema generates in the spectator an *intoxication with the singulative*—an intoxication which uses iterative implications to naturalize the singulative and which renders the slippage between the two aspects invisible.

But this explanation doesn't really address Henderson's question of why subtler slippages are possible in classical cinema in contrast to classical literature. One could argue that (even beyond the issue of fictional reference within the diegesis) the specific nature of the cinematic apparatus constructs an inevitable slippage between the singulative and the iterative, which are established and associated respectively with the stages of production and exhibition. That is, in front of the camera and microphone, the footage seemingly speaks in the singulative, either in the present tense or in the simple past by capturing and embalming the present moment ("this event is happening now as it is being recorded," or "this event happened in front of the camera and microphone").[3] In the theater at the point of exhibition and reception (and even during the post-production stage, where a single utterance may be constructed out of multiple takes), the footage of images and sounds recorded in the past could be read as speaking in the iterative ("the event now being uttered/projected used to occur while this scene was being shot and in all previous projections"). In a discourse that tries to efface all traces of this dual system, such as Hollywood classical cinema, the emphasis is primarily on the singulative and on the illusory construction of a present tense; references to the past tend to be clearly marked out by voice-overs and/or flashbacks, as in the example Henderson cites from *How Green Was My Valley*.

One could also argue that the slippage into the iterative is more easily accomplished in cinema because, unlike the sentence, the film utterance is initially atemporal and its tense is therefore established contextually by discourse. That is, the film utterance is not *required* to have a tense and therefore (unlike the literary utterance) there is not always a clearly established tense for the iterative to suspend or displace. On the other hand, as Edward Branigan has pointed out, spatial relations in the film utterance must be clearly defined (that is, the camera must be *somewhere*).[4] This might suggest that in cinema there is a tendency to spatialize the iterative—i.e., to use spatial relations to generate iterative implications of frequency.

Thus, I would argue that it is not only voice-overs that can redefine the aspect of frequency of any cinematic image or scene, especially those involving spatial relations and representations of typicality, but also other stylistic operations within a narrative. In classical Hollywood cinema, it's the iterative aspect that tends to remain hidden; and that's why, as Henderson observes, when the iterative aspect is acknowledged, it is nearly always subordinated as mere descriptive background to what appear to be singulative events, whose distinguishing details are frequently accentuated by close-ups, editing codes of continuity (such as shot/reverse shot), or foregrounding of linear plot structure. This emphasis is hardly surprising since, as Genette observes, the singulative form of narrative is "so common, and apparently considered so 'normal' that it bears no name" (p. 114); that's why he coins the neologism *singulative*. Thus, it's the singulative nature of cinema that always tends to be foregrounded in classical cinema, even when those singular events take on what I would call an "iterative implication." This implication suggests that this particular narrative is a single telling of a class of events that habitually or typically occur in this set of circumstances, period, or culture—a dimension that is consistent with Aristotelian norms of probability and strongly reinforced by the normative power of popular Hollywood genres. Yet because this iterative aspect is only implicit (and somewhat analogical rather than strictly grammatical) and the precision of rich detail literally foregrounded, "some [as Henderson cautiously observes] might take an ultra-literal position and say that this makes the iterative impossible in cinema; its images and sounds are always singulative" (p. 12).

I am arguing precisely the opposite position: namely, that the iterative is inherent in cinema, either through the pseudo-iterative (as defined by Genette and modified by Henderson, where there is an explicit acknowledgement that the event is presented in the iterative aspect despite the rich perceptual detail in the image), or through the iterative implication (where the acknowledgement of the iterative repetition is only implicit and positioned within a scene presented as singulative). One might reasonably object at this point that my usage of the term iterative may have moved too far away from its strictly grammatical usage in *Narrative Discourse,* yet Genette himself acknowledges that his grammatical terms "are merely borrowed" and that he makes "no pretense of basing them on rigorous homologies" (p. 32).

Genette confines the iterative to temporal relations and to utterances about past events. Yet by acknowledging that iterative repetition depends on the mental construction of a class (or paradigm) of similar instances, he opens a space within the iterative for the issue of typicality. Since temporality, as we have seen, is not foregrounded in film the way it is in literature, I am arguing that it is this issue of typicality that is usually foregrounded by the iterative in cinema. Within Hollywood classical cinema, the combination of rich perceptual detail and strong emphasis on genre not only generates iterative implications, but also uses them to naturalize the singulative event. The combination suggests that this particular narrative utterance is realistic or truthful in the sense of being habitual, typical, or inevitable, while the determination (the diachronic limits of the series) and the specification (of how frequently it occurs) are significantly left indefinite. Often a classical film will begin with scenes depicting normal, typical actions, from which the singulative narrative will soon deviate; though such scenes are technically presented in the singulative, they carry iterative implications (particularly through spatial relations) that are extended to the singulative plot.

Two brief examples should suffice. *Duel in the Sun* (1946) opens with an extravagant prologue, in which a lushly colored landscape and overblown literary voice-over boldly place the story of Pearl Chavez in the mythic past. Although we are told that this legend and the figurative stone that commemorates it have withstood the test of time, it's the dramatic setting (rather than the particular moment) that is truly singular. Pearl's uniqueness is explicitly symbolized by a rare cactus flower that blooms every year, but only here in this unique space where she and her lover died. Though clearly presented as extraordinary, this opening supposedly depicts what happened many times (the blooming of the flower, the survival of the stone, the telling of her story). Yet, this prologue arouses our curiosity not about these repetitions (which are only the background), but about the dramatic climax—the death of "the wild young lovers"—which already occurred in the past, but toward which the singulative narrative will inevitably be moving.

Once inside the story, we are immediately confronted with the same conflation of the habitual action with the extraordinary singulative event. We move directly to a close shot of the young Pearl as she dances seductively for a group of youngsters outside the Presidio, and then inside where her mother is doing a similar dance for scores of men and where her father is losing at cards ("broke again?") and being humiliated by the other players ("he's not so fancy about his wife"). By being introduced to these characters through these actions, we assume that they perform them every night, yet simultaneously we realize that this night will lead to a singulative climax. Both dancers are approached by a man who makes the iterative trace between them explicit (telling Pearl, "like mother, like daughter") and who triggers the slippage into the singulative (by kissing Pearl's mother in front of her husband and by taking her off to make love). While implying the previous series, this single utterance explicitly depicts only the *final* humiliation, which leads Pearl's father to shoot his wife and her lover as Pearl and we look on, intoxicated with the singulative. Yet the prologue enables us to see the iterative implications in this action: to realize that Pearl met a fate similar to her mother's, and to read both of these framing melodramatic climaxes as probable, inevitable, foretold.

A Place in the Sun (1951) opens with a long shot of a hitchhiker with a suitcase trying to thumb a ride from a passing car on a curved highway. It's a familiar image we all recognize, although the time, place, and character are ambiguous. At first we can't see him very well because he has his back to the camera and his body is partially covered by the opening titles which appear over this scene. But, because of his suitcase, we assume he has hitchhiked a long way, and that this filmic utterance is meant to depict an action that has been repeated along many different stretches of highway. Gradually, as the titles conclude, he backs toward the camera in the foreground. As soon as he turns around, this image ceases to function as background and slips into the singulative: for we recognize the extraordinary face of the young Montgomery Clift and the camera moves in for a tight, fully lit close-up of his half smile as something unusual captures his attention. Then there's a cut to the object of his gaze—an outdoor poster of a glamour girl, with the headline "It's an Eastman." At that very moment a horn from a passing car draws his attention back to the road just in time to see Elizabeth Taylor (who turns out to be his rich cousin, an Eastman) driving by in a Cadillac convertible. The contrived convergence of image, name, and vehicle prefigure the inevitable conclusion toward which the singulative linear narrative will be driving. Like the roadside collision of Oedipus and Laius, this coincidence appears to be predestined. It expresses the young man's intoxication with the singulative assumptions of romance: the belief that she's the love of his life, his single chance for happiness, his missed opportunity—a belief that will lead him to consider murder. But now this elusive object of desire drives out of sight and, as if awakened from his revery, he goes over to the dilapidated truck that has stopped to give him a ride. In this opening, the contrast between typicality and singulative romance is figured as a choice between two narrative vehicles (the truck that could have driven out of *Grapes of Wrath* and the glamorous convertible that belongs to bourgeois melodrama) and between the long shot and the large facial close-up. The narrative will constantly maneuver between these two modes, using the iterative traces of drab typicality to intensify the desirability of the singulative romance.

Although (unlike *How Green Was My Valley*) neither of these openings uses the pseudo-iterative, they still use iterative implications to naturalize the linear drive of the narrative and to intensify the intoxication with the singulative. Yet the slippage between the iterative and the singulative remains barely visible.

But if the iterative implications and the slippage between the two aspects were ever foregrounded, then they would potentially call attention to the process of naturalizing ideology through the reading of singulative events of fiction as universal truth, a reading that reinforces the dominant cultural paradigms and genres. This is precisely what happens in a wide range of films where the narrative experimentation is designed to make a sharp break from the prevailing conventions of narrative discourse.

In the rest of this essay, I will explore a few examples of how such foregrounding functions in two quite different filmic contexts: Italian neorealism, where narrative discourse was intentionally distinguished from the dominant practice of Hollywood classical cinema; and the radical feminist avant-garde of the late 1970s and 80s, where one of the primary goals of narrative experimentation was to subvert the sadistic drive of the oedipal plot, that key master narrative of Western patriarchal culture.[5] I will argue that, despite the striking differences in the historical, cultural, and stylistic contexts of these two kinds of subversive film practice, the specific texts under analysis all use the foregrounded slippage between iterative and singulative to undermine the linear drive of the narrative and to retrain the spectator for a more attentive, speculative reading of richly detailed images and sounds. In these analyses, I do not mean to exaggerate the stylistic unity of these two contexts or to suggest that either of them functions as a monolithic entity; rather, I merely want to sketch some broad stylistic tendencies in their usage and signalling of the iterative aspect of narrative.

Within the neorealist aesthetic, rich photographic detail frequently functions to express not the singulative (as in Hollywood classical cinema) but the iterative. Although the iterative is sometimes signalled by voice-overs (as in films like *La Terra Trema*, *Paisà*, and *Amore in città*), it more typically is marked by visual operations, particularly through spatial determinations. The referential interplay between the singulative event and the paradigm it represents is frequently played out spatially in terms of foreground and background. Yet, the iterative background is not merely "descriptive" or subordinate as in Hollywood classical cinema, but at least co-equal, normative, and determinant in ideological terms—relations that can be established by spatial or temporal continuity through depth composition or long takes punctuated by ellipses. Individuals and their actions are chosen precisely because they are representative and typical in an iterative sense; the anonymous characters in the background are not used merely as a backdrop against which to distinguish the singularity of the protagonist (a singularity which then is invisibly transformed into a norm as in classical Hollywood cinema), but rather as a means of explicitly acknowledging the iterative aspect and the slippage between it and the singulative dimensions of this particular occurrence within the series.

For example, the singular protagonists of DeSica's *Bicycle Thief* and *Umberto D* are introduced within a crowd, from which they are visibly selected for foregrounding during an habitual event (a daily hiring of workers, or one of the frequent impromptu demonstrations in postwar Rome). Yet it's the typicality of these characters and their events that are valued and repeatedly emphasized, not their singularity. Similarly, the multiple protagonists of Rossellini's *Open City* and *Paisà* emerge from events involving large numbers of people, events that are already in progress and that are presumed to be illustrative of a common series that frequently occurred during a specific historical period in a specific location. The precision of detail in the image helps identify the paradigm to which the particular characters and events belong; the long take and depth focus, and even the montage structure at the opening of *Umberto D* and *Shoeshine*, continue to acknowledge the connection between the individual and the paradigm, between the singulative and the iterative aspects.

UMBERTO D (1951)

The use of visual codes to express the neorealist intoxication with the pseudo-iterative and to control the slippage between the iterative and the singulative can be demonstrated in a celebrated sequence from *Umberto D*, which is frequently cited as the "purest" example of the neorealist aesthetic. The sequence where the pregnant maid does her morning chores seems to contribute nothing whatever to the advancement of the narrative line; rather, it merely presents her ordinary daily moves. Bazin calls it "a perfect illustration of [the DeSica–Zavattini] approach to narrative, . . . the exact opposite of that 'art of ellipsis' . . . [which] presupposes analysis and choice." He defines it as "the succession of concrete instants of life, no one of which can be said to be more important than another, for their ontological equality destroys drama at its very basis."[6]

By presenting the maid's ordinary morning routines, this totally nonverbal sequence clearly foregrounds the iterative. Yet, perhaps even more important for my argument here, it also trains the spectator in how to read the familiar moves both of the maid and of the camera and editing and to thereby deduce what she is probably thinking. Moreover, these cognitive tasks will be required later in the two singulative events that *are* crucial to the narrative line—the two moments when the old man Umberto contemplates suicide. Thus, in this sense, the sequence *does* contribute to the narrative by renegotiating the relationship between the iterative and the singulative, a relationship which proves essential to our understanding of what happens in the film.

In the representation of this particular morning our attention is first drawn to the old man Umberto who stands in the foreground, phoning the ambulance to take him away to the hospital, arranging a singulative event that will distinguish this day from all others. The maid appears behind him in the background, as part of the ordinary context against which Umberto's singulative event is to be read. When the film cuts to the maid, lying on her back in bed, there is a noticeable slippage to the iterative, which now takes over the foreground. Her ordinary morning routines fill in the time (or temporal gap in the narrative) that it takes the ambulance to come for Umberto. As Bazin suggests, this sequence rejects narrative ellipsis.

Yet Bazin fails to notice that the way her actions are represented visually is not always consistent with what we normally identify as the neorealist aesthetic. For example, this sequence does not rely on the long take, but has at least seventeen intra-sequence cuts. In the very first shot, the maid rubs her eyes, drawing our attention to her gaze. Then there's a cut to the object of her gaze—an upward-angle long shot of a cat walking across the roof seen through a screen-like surface with a striking graphic design. This shot stands out, not because it depicts an unusual event (undoubtedly, like the maid, the cat is pursuing its daily morning routines), but because the almost abstract formalism of the visuals is not characteristic of the neorealist aesthetic. This shot is followed by a cut back to the maid, which then moves in closer to her gaze, anchoring it firmly within the suturing structure (shot/reverse shot/shot) normally associated with classical Hollywood cinema. This suture works toward the kind of emotional identification that is also typical of DeSica and Zavattini. Then the camera follows the

Umberto D

maid into the kitchen where we see her performing a number of household tasks in a series of long and medium shots more typical of neorealism. Three shots later there is a medium shot of her through the window, and then she and the camera move toward each other, a convergence which again calls our attention both to her gaze and to our own. The reverse shot reveals the object of her gaze in an exterior long shot—a white cat walking along the slanted roof, evoking the earlier more abstract image of the cat through the screen, and then there's a cut back to her gaze through the window.

Despite Bazin's claims that no one instant in this sequence is more important than any other, the formal repetition (of the shot/reverse shot suture, of the camera moving in closer to her gaze, and of the cat imagery) privileges these two moments. This repeated pattern leads us not only to identify with the young maid, but also to speculate on her thoughts: perhaps she, too, is identifying with the feline, envying its freedom, particularly in light of her pregnant condition. This hypothesis is strengthened a little later when she looks down at her slightly swollen belly, and the camera moves in tighter, almost to a close-up of her face, which reveals her eyes blinking, as if to ward off the tears that will appear a few moments later. What's really at stake here is not whether we reach a "correct" interpretation of what she is thinking, but rather that we learn how to read the phenomenology of her moves and how to recognize the filmic codes that elicit such speculations.

All three of the visual codes that have been foregrounded in this sequence through repetition—the shot/reverse shot suture, the striking camera movement (or zoom) that closes in on the gaze, and the accelerated tempo of the cutting—are used again later (and intensified through the accompaniment of dramatic non-diegetic music) in the two melodramatic sequences, where Umberto considers suicide: first, when he stands at his window staring at the streetcar tracks below, and finally, when he carries his dog to the railroad tracks and nearly lunges in the path of an on-coming train. In both cases he is prevented from acting out his suicidal impulse by the presence of the dog, another inarticulate creature (like the cat in the maid's morning sequence, or like the anonymous poor backgrounded by the narrative) whose readable gestures serve as the basis of emotional identification for spectators trained by the neorealist aesthetic. If we are *un*able to read these silent moves and gestures (or what Pasolini would later call *im-signs*), then we prove to be less trainable than Umberto's clever little mutt, whose ability to decipher these nonverbal signs saves both himself and his master.

IL POSTO (1961)

The spectatorial retraining function of the neorealist pseudo-iterative is perhaps most notable in Ermanno Olmi's *Il Posto* (*The Job*, aka *The Sound of Trumpets*, 1961). Unlike the earlier classics within the movement, this latter-day neorealist work documents not the economic failure of the poor but rather the "successful" entry of a timid young man from a Lombardy suburb into the dehumanizing world of bureaucracy in Milan—"that city" which (we are told in an opening title) "is primarily a place to work." Not only is Domenico's typicality underlined by this title and by the scores of other young people who surround him at work, in the busy streets of Milan, or in his own suburban tenement, but at one point in this fairly conventional linear narrative there is a dramatic rupture that marks a sudden slippage into the iterative—a rupture that is far more blatant than the maid sequence in *Umberto D.*

Up to that point the narrative has consistently followed the inarticulate Domenico, leading us to focus on his closely observed movements and to read his facial expressions and gestures (almost as if we were watching a silent film). Now it presents a series of brief elliptical scenes (linked by dissolves) which show how five clerks from one office typically spend their evenings: working on a novel, cultivating a dashing appearance, retaining vestigial possessions from a lost aristocratic past, singing arias at a cafe, interacting with a difficult son. Ironically, though these scenes differentiate the clerks by revealing the various ways in which they try to preserve their individual identity, the narrative form in which they are presented suggests an illustrative montage, which stresses the typicality rather than the uniqueness of the behavior depicted. Depending on how one sees its articulation with the scene that introduces it, this sequence could be read either as what Genette calls the *generalizing, external iteration,* where an iterative passage within a singulative scene "opens a window onto the external period," or as the *internal, synthesizing iteration,* where there is an "enumeration of a certain number of classes of occurrences, each of which synthesizes several events . . . not over a wider period of time, but over the period of time of the scene itself" (pp. 118–119).

The series is introduced by a conversation in the office between two co-workers who are speculating about a near-sighted clerk, calling him "a sneaky type." Then there's a cut to that same clerk at home alone in his sparsely furnished room, laboring over a manuscript. When his landlady spies on him through a keyhole, she admits that she's unable to tell what kind of writing he's doing ("God knows what he's writing!") but she does identify the activity as iterative by explicitly telling us that he does it every night. The voyeuristic motivation for the scene, its minimalism and ambiguity, its emphasis on interpretation, its punctuating dissolves—all raise the additional possibility that this scene may represent not what the near-sighted clerk *actually* does on that or any other specific night, but rather merely a reasonable speculation.

By the time we reach the fifth scene, where the middle-aged woman clerk discovers her wallet is empty and painfully concludes that she's been robbed by her son, the narrative seems to have slipped back to the singulative, preparing us for the cut back to the office where the camera pans across the other clerks as they stare at the same poor woman who sits at her desk silently weeping. This narrative continuity tends to anchor this particular elliptical scene temporally, locating it specifically during the previous night, but still leaving ambiguous whether the scenes of the other four clerks also took place during that same night, or whether the scene leading into the montage (the co-workers speculating about the "sneaky" near-sighted clerk) occurred on the same day as the scene that followed it. Yet, since we learned in an earlier scene that this same woman had previously been late to work three times this month (presumably because of similar problems with her son), even this specific incident could be read as merely one typical illustration of what causes her daily misery.

This disruptive sequence of elliptical scenes is evoked again near the end of the film, when there's a direct cut from the gaiety of a New Year's Eve party to the silent panning across the same clerks as they grimly stare at the empty desk of their near-sighted co-worker, and then to a montage of artistic stills of his empty room, linked by dissolves. Not only does this dramatic rupture signify death (both in the narrative and in the linear structure of a man's life), it also creates an opening for the protagonist Domenico, which allows him to advance from messenger boy to clerk. Thus, this rupture helps to transform our reading of the film—from the singulative story of a young white-collar worker finding his place in the world, to an iterative account of the recurring cycle in which workers struggle to maintain their humanity within a dehumanizing bureaucracy, a cycle which is part of Italy's so-called economic miracle. This rupture also exposes the narrative gaps that have been there all along (e.g., the stories of minor characters or losers, like the married man who failed the examination and didn't get the job). It also brings to mind earlier montage sequences in the film, like the montage of urban construction that is part of the literal background for Domenico's and Antonietta's lunch break in the city and also the historical background of industrialization, which proves more instrumental than the narrative in determining their future. And, on a more abstract level, it also reveals the structural similarity between ellipses and montage (which had always been so ambiguous in Bazin's treatment of Rossellini and the neorealist aesthetic).

The blatancy of the iterative dimension in these narrative ruptures also calls attention to the more subtle iterative implications in other, more conventional sequences—i.e., to the various ways in which characters and actions are positioned within paradigms and repetitive cycles. For example, we see how Domenico's interaction with the cold patriarchal boss and his warm, mediating maternal secretary echoes his relationship with his parents. We perceive how the spatial arrangement of the rows of clerks facing their supervisor duplicates the classroom hierarchy between students and teacher. We recognize traces of the dehumanizing fascist aesthetic in the over-sized scale of the corporate lobby, with its rigid rules (only four to an elevator) and uniformed staff (someone even jokingly asks Domenico whether he's a member of the Gestapo). We recall the book-strap that Domenico is forced to pass down to his younger brother in the opening sequence, or his careful observance of other customers in the coffee bar to learn how to tip and what to do with his cup, or his watching through the window to see how the previous group of applicants is responding to the physical exam.

By specularizing this iterative aspect, the film reminds us that we also learn such conventions from watching movies. Even *Il Posto* is self-consciously positioned within the paradigm of neorealism, but with its historical "difference" duly noted. In one scene an old man enters the corporate building, having mistaken it for the welfare office. When he asks for the office that gives out money to the poor, he's told he's in the wrong building. He could just as easily have been told that he's in the wrong movie, for clearly he belongs in a neorealist classic like *Bicycle Thief* or *Umberto D.* Yet it's easy to understand his error

Olmi's *Il Posto:* The spatial arrangement of the rows of desks facing the supervisor duplicates the classroom hierarchy between students and teachers.

because the architecture (of the corporate building and welfare office) and the film aesthetic (of *Il Posto* and neorealist classics) look very similar.

The neorealist classic that is singled out for specific comparison is quite properly *Umberto D*, which helped to mark the end of the movement as well as its entry into the world of middle-class white-collar workers. *Il Posto* recycles many images that are found in *Umberto D*: the cafeteria with its cheap food, the niggardly landlady who harasses the lonely bureaucrat, and the old man with a small dog riding on a streetcar. In one sequence, when the young applicants are being led down the street in an orderly line, an old man with a dog asks what is going on. When Domenico tells him it's for a job, the old man remarks, "That's a laugh!" We can't help but be reminded of the retired bureaucrat Umberto, who knows from bitter experience that disappointment awaits these prospective white-collar workers. Yet while he probably thinks it has to do with material conditions like inadequate pensions, here the problem is seen as the dehumanization of the individual. Such a view can also be found in the silent comedies of Chaplin and Keaton, many of whose conventions are also absorbed in *Il Posto* and whose basic humanism was seen by Bazin as compatible with neorealism. Thus, *Il Posto* is not merely an updated version of *Umberto D*; rather, it offers a different analysis of the problems, one that extends ever further back to the beginnings of both cinema and industrialization. In this way, the film's intertextuality (both with neorealism and American silent comedy) names the paradigm to which the film belongs and becomes another means of marking a slippage into the iterative.

In such a reading of the film, there is no need for narrative closure. Thus, we are not disappointed that we never find out whether Domenico gets the girl or gets ahead to the front row. What we see represented is one man's entry and another's exit from the same subject position, which has been constructed by the economic system of postwar Italy. The linearity of the narrative is shown to be merely an illusion of progress, of getting ahead. This reading is underscored by the emblematic ending, where the "personal" belongings (including the unread life work) of the dead clerk are carelessly tossed aside while another worker turns the handle of a mimeograph machine, producing identical copies from a single master. As we see a large facial close-up of Domenico, blinking with discomfort in his new post, and then see the film title *Il Posto* (which in Italian refers both to the "position" and to the victorious sound of trumpets) superimposed on his face, we hear the repetitive droning of the mimeograph machine. The extreme length of the close-up gives us time to speculate on what the young man may be thinking: perhaps, that this is a sound, not of economic triumph, but of spiritual defeat.

In these sequences from *Umberto D* and *Il Posto*, the neorealist *intoxication with the iterative* immerses the spectator not in the emotional intensity of personal memory as in Proust, but in the ideological relations between individual and collective experience.

THE FEMINIST AVANT-GARDE: THE PSEUDO-ITERATIVE
AS SEMIOTIC TRANSGRESSION IN *TOUTE UNE NUIT*

The radical experimentation in Chantal Akerman's *Toute une nuit* (1982) goes much further in deconstructing traditional narrative and in revealing how the slippage between the iterative and the singulative helps to naturalize dominant ideology. The film challenges not only woman's position in narrative, but also the very structure of narrative and language, for they are the primary signifying systems that have held women in captivity under patriarchy by making their subordination seem natural and inevitable rather than culturally inscribed.

Instead of leading us into emotional identification with the characters on screen, the film enables us to see that, as in all movies, the specific images and sounds have been selected from familiar cultural paradigms and combined to generate narratives. In *Toute une nuit* we find the traditional vocabulary and moves of the melodramatic narrative: the rendezvous, separations, and reunions, the romantic triangles, balcony scenes, and slow dances, the taxis, telephones, and cigarettes, the waiting women and even waiting men—in short, the problems of the couple. Yet there is no driving linear thrust and no climactic "big bang" resolutions. Instead, these familiar components are positioned within a comfortably paced, rhythmic cycle of recurrence that grants us plenty of time for the perceptual pleasure of savoring the painterly visuals (with their strong graphic compositions and lush colors) and the rich textures of sound and image (with their unpredictable rhythms). And also plenty of time for the conceptual pleasure of enjoying the wit and of figuring out how these components are connected.

The title, *Toute une nuit* (a whole night), immediately foregrounds the dual axes of selection and combination—those linchpins of Saussurian and Jakobsonian semiotics. On the one hand, the title designates a temporal unit based on a natural cycle, night and day (a primordial opposition like male and female). Yet, since the film is only 91 minutes long, there must be omissions, so the artistic process of human selection (which is necessarily culturally coded) is also involved. While the *toute* stresses the illusion of unity and completeness, the indefinite article *une* acknowledges the selection of one discrete unit from the paradigm.

Both Roman Jakobson and Roland Barthes recognized that the reversal of these axes of selection and combination is a form of "semiotic transgression" with great subversive potential. According to Barthes,

> It is probably around this transgression that a great number of creative phenomena are situated, as if perhaps there were here a junction between the field of aesthetics and the defections from the semantic system. The chief transgression is obviously the extension of a paradigm on to the syntagmatic plane, since normally only one term of the operation is actualized, the other (or others) remaining potential: this is what would happen, broadly speaking, if one attempted to elaborate a discourse by putting one after the other all the terms of the same declension.[7]

In *Toute une nuit* Akerman commits this "semiotic transgression" by reversing the two axes of selection and combination. Instead of selecting units from different paradigms and combining them together in a linear fashion to create a story, she strings together units from the same paradigm, thereby extending a paradigm on to the syntagmatic plane. This transgression reveals the grammar of melodrama and its naturalized slippage from the singulative to the iterative and frustrates the conventional demand for the linear drive of the story.

The opening montage immediately foregrounds the cinematic process of selection and combination. It selects and combines images—of a street, traffic, a

Toute une nuit

fence, a woman walking, a man going downstairs, someone getting on a street-car, a car driving toward the camera, its headlights beaming, a very young couple huddling together inside—and sounds of traffic, of a pop song on the radio, of footsteps. These typical sights and sounds of a city at night are mobile units of signification that will be recombined in a variety of ways to generate mini-stories in the 90 minutes that follow. We don't yet know whether this is documentary footage of ordinary people or actors performing in a fiction. We don't yet understand the connections between the shots—if the couple in the vehicle is in any way connected to the woman walking or to the man descending the stairs. Yet the formal structure of the editing leads us to consider such connections. This opening also strongly evokes the iterative—or more specifically, what Genette calls "the synthesizing iteration," where the scene is "synthesized by a sort of paradigmatic classification of the events composing it" (pp. 118–119). The brief scenes are presented in such a way as to suggest that these or similar events occur every night—an aspect that was already implicit in the title *Toute une nuit* and that will be intensified in the sequences that follow by having so many different sets of characters of different ages, gender, and class perform similar moves. Thus the film demonstrates the iterative's subtle slippage, not only with the singulative, but also with the anaphoric (narrating *n* times what happens *n* times) and the repeating form of narrative (narrating *n* times what happens once). It extends onto the syntagmatic plane the full paradigm not only of melodrama but also of narrative frequency.

The first dramatic sequence that follows seems to narrow the narrative choices. It moves indoors to observe a single character in a long take with a distanced, static camera. We recognize signifiers of fiction: the actress Aurore

Toute une nuit

Clément, who starred in a previous Akerman film, *Les Rendezvous d'Anna*. We also recognize conventions of melodrama: the red low-cut dress that suggests she's not a virgin. After restlessly pacing, phoning a man and then hanging up, she says dramatically, "I love him." Suddenly she leaves the room and goes out into the night to hail a cab, walking past men loitering in the street and past the cafe which is the diegetic source for the Middle-Eastern music on the sound track. After she and the taxi have driven off, the camera holds on the space, raising the question: what is more important, the characters and their actions, or the spaces in which they are positioned? Such spaces are foregrounded in the film's opening montage, are associated with the role of women in the traditional male-dominated narrative, and are privileged by the Proustian form of iterative (for, as Genette observes, the "Proustian creature" is "as little sensitive to the individuality of moments as he is spontaneously sensitive to the individuality of places," p. 123). Eventually the camera leads us to the woman's destination, the man's apartment where she watches him pacing upstairs, just as she had earlier been pacing.

This sequence leads us to believe *the story has begun,* but it has its deviations from traditional narrative: not only the pause at the space left by the taxi (which suggests a reluctance to pursue the linear drive of the story), but also the reversals in gender. Here it's not the man but the woman who actively pursues erotic desire. Here it's the woman who leads the camera and the story to her destination, controlling the erotic gaze as the voyeur, and the man who is the object of her gaze.

Much later in the film we will return to this same woman, admitting a man (perhaps the same man) into her apartment. And in the final sequence, we will return to this same woman reflecting on this or a similar object of desire, even though she will be in the arms of another man. It doesn't seem to matter whether it *is* the same man, for they all seem to function as substitutable members of the same paradigm, the object of desire, just as she (as a shifter) has been selected from this same paradigm by the man whom we now see embracing her. And we recognize a similar interchangeability for all of the characters in the film—all belonging to the paradigms of pursuer and pursued within this grammar of romance. In the final sequence she will receive a return phone call from her lover and deliver a repetitive monologue on their relationship, which will fragment him as she considers why she loves him ("Maybe it's his mouth . . . or his eyes . . . or his chin . . . or the way he talks . . ."), just as women have traditionally been fragmented in Hollywood classical cinema. This monologue also offers other reasons for her desire that depend on the contexts of the setting ("I'm so tired . . . it's so hot . . . I should have gone on holiday . . . the music is so lovely") and on the strangeness of the narrative ("I can't understand it"). Ironically, these recurrences of this woman's pursuit of desire provide the film with a false promise of narrative continuity and perfect narrative closure for a film without a story, or more precisely, a film with too many stories that are unconventionally short, or a film with all of the linguistic signs of melodrama but combined in an unconventional syntax.

The three brief sequences that follow make us realize that our initial expectations about the first dramatic sequence are wrong. They provide no linear development of that story; the same woman does not reappear. Eventually we realize that all four sequences are examples from the same paradigm: of a man and woman getting (or not getting) together, four variations on the problematic couple in the same situation all strung together on the syntagmatic plane. And this situation is merely one paradigm in the grammar of romance. Moreover, all four sequences function as pseudo-iterative. Like Proust's *A la Recherche du temps perdu*, the narrative which Genette selects as the single focus of his theoretical analysis, *Toute une nuit* liberates the iterative from its purely descriptive function. In showing not what happened a single time, but what used to happen and still happens, typically, regularly, ritually, or every night, it explores and expands the iterative aspect—"in textual scope, in thematic importance, in degree of technical elaboration" (p. 117). Akerman demonstrates how such elaboration can take on a subversive function in cinema where, because of the realistic (or indexical) potential of the photographic image, the iterative aspect calls attention to the process of naturalizing the ideology carried by singulative instances of fiction—as if they were the inevitable Truth, as if we spectators can never escape these paradigms of gender and romance.

Here is what we actually see in these three sequences. In the first, a woman in a red jacket is seated in a cafe, waiting in the foreground, with men shooting pool in the background. A man enters, pauses at the door, and then he and the woman passionately embrace. This scene brings to our attention certain binary oppositions: coming together or not coming together (as in the previous sequence), foreground versus background, stillness versus movement. These binary oppositions apply not only thematically to the issue of romantic relationships but also reflexively to the issue of what constitutes narrative.

In the second sequence, a man and a woman are seated apart at separate tables in a cafe. Each stares at a glass, each turns to the other as the other turns away. The man gets up to leave, then the woman gets up to leave. The man returns and they suddenly embrace. Their actions are separate but parallel, like the sequences in this narrative, but then they unpredictably cohere, like the film's false narrative closure in the final sequence. The dynamics of space and the gestural movements of the characters become pointedly expressive. There is no verbal language to distract us. We recognize the meaning of these gestural movements by comparing and contrasting them with the similar movements we saw in the previous two sequences. The repetitions with variations help to code them and make us read them as language. It's a language we know from our past: from silent cinema, and from our infantile days before speech. It's a gestural language that semioticians like Pasolini and Eco have tried to theorize and that was foregrounded in the sequences we analyzed from *Umberto D* and *Il Posto*. After seeing this sequence in *Toute une nuit*, we will be more conscious of gestural and spatial language in all of the scenes that follow.

In the third sequence, three persons (two young men and a woman) are seated together in the same cafe, smoking. Suddenly one man gets up and leaves, then the second young man follows, then the woman. All three stand outside the cafe in the street. The blond man asks the woman: "Who are you going with?" After pausing a moment and getting no verbal response, both men walk off screen in opposite directions (left and right), and the woman moves directly toward the camera out of the frame. It's the first scene that explicitly foregrounds the romantic triangle and the dynamics of selection that control narrative as well as romance—the choice of which character to follow. It also evokes the first dramatic sequence with Aurore Clément in at least three formal ways: by returning to the use of verbal language (with only the second line of dialogue in the film), by repeating the option of *not getting together,* and by relying on the combination of interior and exterior scenes. In struggling to perceive coherence, we find ourselves making connections between sequences on formal rather than on narrative grounds.

At this point, the film makes another unexpected move. For the first time it returns to characters from an earlier sequence—to the lovers who had sat apart at the cafe. Now we watch them dancing passionately to a romantic song on the juke box. Once again, the narrative rules of the film are altered, causing us to adjust our expectations, but also granting us an immediate sensory pleasure in the schmaltzy music on the sound track and in the lyrical image of the lovers dancing in the smoky cafe. Within the luminous blue-green light, the movements of the woman's vibrant hair and the couple's swaying bodies compete with the slow graceful swirling of the smoke deep in the background. Sound and image also compete for our attention. The emotional excessiveness of the music underlines the recurrence of getting together—not only the romantic reunion of the dancing couple, but also the narrative reunion of subject and spectator.

After this first reappearance of characters, the film can move on to other paradigms—of waiting and meeting, of coming and going, of sleeping and waking. The reappearance of the characters at this point no longer threatens to undermine the radical ruptures of the narrative, but to extend their scope. From here on, there will be many such reappearances, including those of Aurore Clément that offer false narrative continuity and closure. We are led to realize that such reappearances are merely another form of structural repetition—like the reappearance of actions, settings, objects, and sounds. The characters are no longer singular, they no longer hold a privileged place in the narrative; no longer can they draw our attention away from all of the subtle perceptual shifts that comprise the text. The film is free to create a rich intertextuality among its own mini-stories which comprise their own paradigm—one that partially overlaps with melodrama, that most pervasive and malleable of all movie genres.

By repeatedly seeing the same banal actions freed from the context of a single continuous story, we are led to observe (almost from an ethnographic perspective) how the subtle differences in their performance communicate meaning. They become defamiliarized; they become an infinite play of difference within a closed system. For example, one woman leans against a wall as she anxiously waits for her lover, then paces restlessly before she impatiently walks off alone into the night. Later, in a different sequence, another woman, somewhat older, also appears to be waiting as she leans against a wall and smokes a cigarette. Yet she displays no restlessness or impatience, but rather a savoring of the slow pace. Then we hear someone calling "mama" from inside the building. At first the woman doesn't respond. Finally she turns, puts out her cigarette, and goes inside. We realize she hasn't been waiting at all, but temporarily suspending her role as mother, taking a break. (I am told this woman is Chantal Akerman's actual mother.) The single word confirms how we read the subtle differences in the images. It also makes us see how we privilege verbal language, which is controlled by patriarchy, and how we distrust gestural language, so crucial to mother-child intersubjectivity during the pre-oedipal phase.

In another sequence a young girl enters a cafe and approaches a middle-aged man, saying, "Let's dance." He begins to clown, parodying his version of how young people dance these days. But her moves prevail: she wants to slow dance in a close embrace. Despite her age and gender, she leads every aspect of the encounter and also decides when the dance and the sequence are over, as she abandons her partner and the frame. From this point on, we watch the age of the characters more closely and the power dynamics of their movements.

In another sequence a young man goes upstairs with loud footsteps that express a bold defiance and determination mixed with anger. Then he knocks on the door, at first playfully, tapping out a well-known rhythm; then his tone shifts and his knocks become loud, insistent, and aggressive. Suddenly he stops, sits on the stairs and waits, and listens to the footsteps of someone else we never see. The sounds of the footsteps and knockings at the door, which recur throughout the entire film, communicate with such specificity in this sequence that their meanings cannot be missed. They lead us to listen to all other sounds in the film with far greater attention.

By denying us a single unifying story, by frequently pitting word against visual image and nonverbal sound, by discouraging us from identifying with any of the anonymous characters, by denying us a single unified subject position, by calling our attention to the blatant stylization of structure, by reversing the axes of selection and combination, by elaborating the iterative aspect and by foregrounding the slippage between the iterative and the singulative, *Toute une nuit* makes us change the way we read a film.

Though perhaps less radical in their demands on the spectator, the two neorealist films discussed in this essay also require a similar shift in reading, one that de-emphasizes the narrative line and that leads one to interpret gestural language and rich perceptual detail. It's as if the foregrounding of the slippage between the iterative and the singulative helps one to see both the distinctiveness of the present image and its deep immersion in a system of representation. And it's the duality of this perception that helps empower one as an active spectator who is capable of resisting the singular closed reading and of perceiving the iterative traces of collective history and dominant ideology.

NOTES

1. Gérard Genette, *Narrative Discourse: An Essay in Method,* trans. Jane F. Lewin. Ithaca, NY: Cornell University Press, 1980, pp. 113–117.

2. Brian Henderson, "Tense, Mood, and Voice in Film (Notes After Genette)," *Film Quarterly,* XXXVI, No. 4 (Summer 1983), 11–12.

3. Roland Barthes, "The Rhetoric of the Image," in *Image, Music, Text,* trans. by Stephen Heath. New York: Noonday Press, 1977, p. 40.

4. Edward Branigan develops this kind of argument in *Point of View in the Cinema,* where (explicitly echoing Genette) he observes that whereas "in a verbal narrative the temporal determinations of the narrating act are more salient than the spatial determinations. By contrast, this dissymmetry is exactly reversed in pictorial narration . . . The spatial properties of a picture are at least initially more important than other properties and hence may serve as a reference with which to measure the general activity of narration." Edward R. Branigan, *Point of View in the Cinema: A Theory of Narration and Subjectivity in Classical Film.* New York: Mouton Publishers, 1984, p. 45.

5. According to Laura Mulvey, "Sadism demands a story, depends on making something happen, forcing a change in another person, a battle of will and strength, victory/defeat, all occuring in a linear time with a beginning and an end." ("Visual Pleasure and Narrative Cinema," *Screen* [Autumn 1975]). Teresa de Lauretis reverses the formulation, suggesting that all traditional male-dominated narrative demands sadism, figuring women only as obstacles that delay the male quest or as markers of the positions and settings through which the hero and his story move to reach their destination and to accomplish meaning. *(Alice Doesn't: Feminism, Semiotics, Cinema.* Bloomington: Indiana University Press, 1984, pp.103–119.)

6. André Bazin, "*Umberto D*: A Great Work," in *What Is Cinema?,* Vol. II, trans. and ed. by Hugh Gray. Berkeley: University of California Press, 1971, p. 81.

7.   Roland Barthes, *Writing Degree Zero and Elements of Semiology,* trans. Annette Lavers and Colin Smith. Boston: Beacon Press, 1970, p. 86. For an application of this principle to the narrative experimentation of Luis Buñuel, see also Susan Suleiman, "Freedom and Necessity: Narrative Structure in *The Phantom of Liberty,*" *Quarterly Review of Film Studies* (Summer 1978), 277–295.

I wish to thank Edward Branigan, Brian Henderson, and Linda Williams for reading an earlier draft of this essay and for making helpful suggestions.

PART THREE

GENRE

The first two articles in this section have a de facto thematic relationship: Noël Carroll's "Nightmare and the Horror Film" (1981) and J. P. Telotte's "Human Artifice and the Science Fiction Film" (1983). That science fiction and horror film genres intermix and overlap—and not for the first time in *Alien* (1979)—is perhaps more widely accepted now than it was when these articles were written. Thus both articles discuss *Frankenstein, Dr. Jekyll and Mr. Hyde,* and *Invasion of the Body Snatchers,* among other films. What most sharply differentiates the articles are their theoretical orientations, and how these organize the arguments of each.

Carroll notes that the horror and science fiction film are currently in the ascendance because they correspond to a moment of American history in which "feelings of paralysis, helplessness, and vulnerability (hallmarks of the nightmare) prevail." He proposes to extend some points made by Ernest Jones in *On the Nightmare* (1951) to the imagery of the horror/science fiction film. Noting that nightmare has long been associated with horror literature and film, he points to Mary Shelley's *Frankenstein,* Horace Walpole's *The Castle of Otranto,* and R. L. Stevenson's *Dr. Jekyll and Mr. Hyde* as works whose genesis was "fitful sleep" or outright nightmare. Carroll does not adhere to psychoanalysis as a general hermeneutic method, but finds it applicable here because "as a matter of social tradition, psychoanalysis is more or less the *lingua franca* of the horror film and thus the privileged critical tool for discussing the genre." (Thus Carroll arrives at a Freudian method by way of something like Hume's reliance on social convention.)

Jones argues that the object seen in the nightmare is frightful or hideous because the underlying wish is not permitted in its naked form, so that the dream is a compromise between the wish and the fear belonging to its inhibition. Carroll sees this conflict between attraction and repulsion as corrective to approaches that emphasize only one side of this duality; allegorical readings of horror films, for instance, tend not to acknowledge the repellent aspects of the genre. Nevertheless, Carroll "modifies" Jones, whom he calls "a hardline Freudian," by studying the nightmare conflicts embodied in the horror film as "having broader reference than simply sexuality." (It should be noted that since writing this piece, Carroll has abandoned the use of a psychoanalytic framework for dealing with this material and has approached it through the cognitive theory of emotions as set forth in his book *The Philosophy of Horror.*)

Telotte focuses on "the number of recent films that take as their major concern . . . the potential doubling of the human body and thus the literal creation of a human artifice." These include the remakes of *Invasion of the Body Snatchers* and *The Thing, Blade Runner,* and *Alien*. These films reflect uneasiness about human identity, and what makes us human, in an era of cloning and other technologies of human duplication. Telotte begins his survey with the destructive android look-alike of Maria in *Metropolis* and then proceeds to the original *Invasion of the Body Snatchers*, in which individuals are duplicated "cell for cell, atom for atom." *Frankenstein*, subtitled *The Modern Prometheus*, points to the presence in the genre of a Faustian drive for knowledge or power, a dangerous impulse behind the fascination with the power of science. (There is a split between good and bad science in some of these films.) Telotte makes a fascinating point concerning the "lingering Cartesian dualism" between mind and body, thinking and feeling: the fashioning of other bodies, other forms of the self, only reinforces that split and reasserts the hegemony of mind over body.

He sees the monster in *Alien*, invulnerable to normal human defenses, as metaphoric of "some flaw within man." John Carpenter's *The Thing*, which can imitate the form of any human, entails what René Girard discusses as the "close scrutiny" that reveals man's double to be monstrous. When only a black and a white character remain at the end of the film, each eyes the other with the conviction that he is a double fashioned by the alien, which points up the distrust and fear that mark modern society and particularly, of course, its race relations. Telotte's longest discussion, which carries his exploration of the artificial doubling of the human to its farthest point, concerns, not surprisingly, *Blade Runner.*

In "The Sacraments of Genre: Coppola, DePalma, Scorsese," Leo Braudy contrasts André Bazin's definition of neorealism with the orientation of the three Italian-American directors of his title, whose commitment is to genre, which the author calls "the prime seedbed of American films." Concerning an unrealistic but symbolically potent juxtaposition of rooms in Rossellini's *Open City,* Braudy notes that it is "an incantatory moment, a mode of suprarealistic perception that I would like to call a sacramentalizing of the real, not so that it be worshipped but so that its spiritual essence, whether diabolical or holy, inflect what is otherwise a discrete collection of objects in space."

For all the differences among his three directors, Braudy finds in all of them a sense of the importance of ritual narratives, the significance of ritual objects, and a tendency to mine the visual world for its transcendental potential. Objects, people, places, and stories are irradiated by the meaning from within, which the directors seek to unlock. In the work of Francis Ford Coppola, the sense of genre is attached to a feeling for family rituals, including betrayals. As Braudy notes, "Always there is a dream of camaraderie, and invariably that dream turns sour." Orson Welles is Coppola's directorial antecedent, but, unlike Welles, he is unwilling to question his own role as director and *Wunderkind.* Brian DePalma's work is concerned with the interplay between the technological future and the mythic past; like Alfred Hitchcock, his principal inspiration, he is fascinated with significant objects, which in the younger director's work are close to icons. He is also concerned with the power of the mind to move objects, especially in *Carrie* and *The Fury.* His bright young people, like the computer whiz in *Dressed to Kill,* can never reach the greatness of the past, which they turn instead into a machinelike efficiency. Martin Scorsese explores the final and perhaps most pervasive aspect of the intersection of film with Catholicism—the structure of sainthood. Just as *Mean Streets* says you make up for your sins not in church but in the street and at home, so the director places "the performer/saint/devil" at the center of films such as *Taxi Driver, Raging Bull,* and *The King of Comedy.* By casting himself in violent or subservient roles in these films, Scorsese also questions his own authority as director and makes himself complicit in the stories he tells.

Scott MacDonald's "Confessions of a Feminist Porn Watcher" is sacramental in name only—there is no quest for transcendence here. To call his participation in his account complicit does not begin to reveal its courageous, highly personal nature. But what the confessional mode masks is how much the article tells us about porn as an institution and a genre. For this reason alone, a second reading is advantageous. It does not dissolve the article's subjective cast, but reveals a good deal more information and insight through that framework.

The point of departure for the article was a screening of an anti-porn film polemic/documentary and several reviews of it, notably B. Ruby Rich's challenge "for the legions of feminist men" to undertake the analysis of why men like porn. MacDonald, in a remarkably thoughtful way, takes up the challenge. If, as the film said, porn reinforces male domination of women, why then do men pay for fantasy material to this effect; and why is there so much fear and embarrassment about going to porn houses or arcades? MacDonald notes also that "direct sexual experience with a conventionally attractive woman is, or seems, out of the question for many men." Porn provides a compromise by making visual knowledge of such an experience possible. His most trenchant argument has to do with the "unprovoked leers and comments" that women complain of. MacDonald will go to considerable lengths to avoid intruding in this way, but "I have to fight the urge to stare all the time. Some of the popularity of pornography even among men who consider themselves feminists may be a function of its capacity to provide a form of unintrusive leering."

To David James in "Hardcore: Cultural Resistance in the Postmodern," the pornography which Scott MacDonald occasionally seeks out is "industrial" porn, which James also calls "commodity pornography," which he opposes unfavorably to *The Best of Amateur Erotic Video Volume II*, a compilation of four tapes, each fifteen to twenty minutes long, self-photographed and self-produced by middle-class, heterosexual, white couples. Although his article is anything but a confession, James does forthrightly admit that he finds the amateur erotic video compilation, which he greatly prefers on theoretical grounds, "less arousing and so less desirable than its industrial counterpart."

James's article begins with a bleak survey arguing the destruction or co-optation of working-class movements in the United States since the 1930s; the collapse of mobilization around Third World struggles of decolonization since the end of the Vietnam War; and, most recently, the politically effective roll-back of basic Marxist concepts, even that of class. (The article appeared in Winter 1988–89.) The turning to art and culture as a possible refuge for utopian thinking has been a plausible resort at least since the Frankfurt School. The avant-garde film movement in the sixties was an effective refuge of this kind; this was followed by a brief period of alternative video, but later emanations of these movements and of every other potentially oppositional movement has been absorbed into the cultural industry. James identifies two possibilities for opposition: the amateur erotic video movement, which he contrasts favorably with commodity porn in a long, frequently brilliant comparison; and a genuinely local, self-produced alternative punk rock movement that is explicitly and blisteringly political. For those whose exposure is limited to MTV, he notes, this movement is an enormous and pungent surprise.

NOËL CARROLL

NIGHTMARE AND THE HORROR FILM

The Symbolic Biology of Fantastic Beings

Vol. 34, no. 3 (Spring 1981): 16–25.

Whereas the Western and the crime film were the dominant genres of the late sixties and early seventies, horror and science fiction are the reigning popular forms of the late seventies and early eighties. Launched by blockbusters like *The Exorcist* and *Jaws,* the cycle has flourished steadily; it seems as unstoppable as some of the demons it has spawned. The present cycle, like the horror cycle of the thirties and the science fiction cycle of the fifties, comes at a particular kind of moment in American history—one where feelings of paralysis, helplessness, and vulnerability (hallmarks of the nightmare) prevail. If the Western and the crime film worked well as open forums for the debate about our values and our history during the years of the Vietnam war, the horror and science fiction film poignantly express the sense of powerlessness and anxiety that correlates with times of depression, recession, Cold War strife, galloping inflation, and national confusion.

The purpose of this paper is to examine the basic structures and themes of these timely genres by extending some of the points made in Ernest Jones's *On the Nightmare.*[1] Jones used his analysis of the nightmare to unravel the symbolic meaning and structure of such figures of medieval superstition as the incubus, vampire, werewolf, devil, and witch. Similarly, I will consider the manner in which the imagery of the horror/science fiction film is constructed in ways that correspond to the construction of nightmare imagery. My special, though not exclusive, focus will be on the articulation of the imagery of horrific creatures—on what I call their symbolic biologies. A less pretentious subtitle for this essay might have been "How to make a monster."

NIGHTMARE AND THE HORROR FILM

Before beginning this "unholy" task, some qualifications are necessary. Throughout this article I will slip freely between examples drawn from horror films and science fiction films. Like many connoisseurs of science fiction literature, I think that, historically, movie science fiction has evolved as a subclass of the horror film. That is, in the main, science fiction films are monster films, rather than explorations of grand themes like alternate societies or alternate technologies.

Secondly, I am approaching the horror/science fiction film in terms of a psychoanalytic framework, though I do not believe that psychoanalysis is a hermeneutic method that can be applied unproblematically to any kind of film or work of art. Consequently, the adoption of psychoanalysis as an interpretive tool in a given case should be accompanied by a justification for its use in regard to that case. And in this light, I would argue that it is appropriate to use psychoanalysis in relation to the horror film because within our culture the horror genre is explicitly acknowledged as a vehicle for expressing psychoanalytically significant themes such as repressed sexuality, oral sadism, necrophilia, etc. Indeed, in recent films, such as Jean Rollin's *Le Frisson des Vampires* and *La Vampire Nue*, all concealment of the psychosexual subtext of the vampire myth is discarded. We have all learned to treat the creatures of the night—like werewolves—as creatures of the id, whether we are spectators or film-makers. As a matter of social tradition, psychoanalysis is more or less the *lingua franca* of the horror film and thus the privileged critical tool for discussing the genre. In fact horror films often seem to be little more than bowdlerized, pop psychoanalysis, so enmeshed is Freudian psychology with the genre.

Nor is the coincidence of psychoanalytic themes and those of the horror genre only a contemporary phenomenon. Horror has been tied to nightmare and dream since the inception of the modern tradition. Over a century before the birth of psychoanalysis Horace Walpole wrote of *The Castle of Otranto,*

> I waked one morning, in the beginning of last June, from a dream, of which all I could recover was, that I had thought myself in an ancient castle (a very natural dream for a head like mine filled with Gothic story) and that on the uppermost bannister of a great staircase I saw a gigantic hand in armour. In the evening I sat down, and began to write, without knowing in the least what I intended to say or relate. The work grew on my hands and I grew so fond of it that one evening, I wrote from the time I had drunk my tea, about six o'clock, till half an hour after one in the morning, when my hands and fingers were so weary that I could not hold the pen to finish the sentence.

The assertion that a given horror story originated as a dream or nightmare occurs often enough that one begins to suspect that it is something akin to invoking a muse (or an incubus or succubus, as the case may be). Mary Shelley's

Frankenstein, Bram Stoker's *Dracula*, and Henry James's "The Jolly Corner" are all attributed to fitful sleep as is much of Robert Louis Stevenson's output—notably *Dr. Jekyll and Mr. Hyde*.[2] In what sense these tales were caused by nightmares or modeled on dreams is less important than the fact that the nightmare is a culturally established framework for presenting and understanding the horror genre. And this makes the resort to psychoanalysis unavoidable.

A central concept in Jones's treatment of the imagery of nightmare is conflict. The products of the dreamwork are often simultaneously attractive and repellent insofar as they function to enunciate both a wish and its inhibition. Jones writes, "The reason why the object seen in a Nightmare is frightful or hideous is simply that the representation of the underlying wish is not permitted in its naked form so that the dream is a compromise of the wish on the one hand and on the other of the intense fear belonging to the inhibition."[3] The notion of the conflict between attraction and repulsion is particularly useful in considering the horror film, as a corrective to alternate ways of treating the genre. Too often, writing about this genre only emphasizes one side of the imagery. Many journalists will single-mindedly underscore only the repellent aspects of a horror film—rejecting it as disgusting, indecent, and foul. Yet this tack fails to offer any account of why people are interested in seeing such exercises.

On the other hand, defenders of the genre or of a specific example of the genre will often indulge in allegorical readings that render their subjects wholly appealing and that do not acknowledge their repellent aspects. Thus, we are told that *Frankenstein* is really an existential parable about man thrown-into-the-world, an "isolated sufferer."[4] But if *Frankenstein* is part *Nausea*, it is also nauseating. Where in the allegorical formulation can we find an explanation for the purpose of the unsettling effect of the charnel-house imagery? The dangers of this allegorizing/valorizing tendency can be seen in some of the work of Robin Wood, the most vigorous champion of the contemporary horror film. *Sisters*, he writes, "analyzes the ways in which women are oppressed within patriarchal society on two levels which one can define as professional (Grace) and the psychosexual (Danielle/Dominque)."[5]

One wants to say "perhaps but . . ." Specifically, what about the unnerving, gory murders and the brackish, fecal bond that links the Siamese twins? Horror films cannot be construed as completely repelling or completely appealing. Either outlook denies something essential to the form. Jones's use of the concept of conflict in the nightmare to illuminate the symbolic portent of the monsters of superstition, therefore, suggests a direction of research into the study of the horror film which accords with the genre's unique combination of repulsion and delight.

To conclude my qualifying remarks, I must note that as a hardline Freudian, Jones suffers from one important liability; he over-emphasizes the degree to which incestuous desires shape the conflicts in the nightmare (and, by extension, in the formation of fantastic beings) and he claims that nightmares always relate to the sexual act.[6] As John Mack has argued, this perspective is too narrow; "the analysis of nightmares regularly leads us to the earliest, most profound, and inescapable anxieties and conflicts to which human beings are subject: those involving destructive aggression, castration, separation and abandonment, devouring and being devoured, and fear regarding loss of identity and fusion with the mother."[7] Thus, modifying Jones, we will study the nightmare conflicts embodied in the horror film as having broader reference than simply sexuality.

Our starting hypothesis is that horror film imagery, like that of the nightmare, incarnates archaic, conflicting impulses. Furthermore, this assumption orients inquiry, leading us to review horror film imagery with an eye to separating out thematic strands that represent opposing attitudes. To clarify what is involved in this sort of analysis, an example is in order.

When *The Exorcist* first opened, responses to it were extreme. It was denounced as a new cultural low at the same time that extra theaters had to be found in New York, Los Angeles, and other cities to accommodate the overflow crowds. The imagery of the film touched deep chords in our national psyche. The spectacle of possession addressed and reflected profound fears and desires never before explored in film. The basic infectious terror in the film is that personal identity is a frail thing, easily lost. Linda Blair's Regan, with her "tsks" and her "ahs," is a model of middle-class domesticity, a vapid mask quickly engulfed by repressed powers. The character is not just another evil child in the tradition of *The Bad Seed*. It is an expression of the fear that beneath the self we present to others are forces that can erupt to obliterate every vestige of self-control and personal identity.

In *The Exorcist,* the possibility of the loss of self is greeted with both terror and glee. The fear of losing self-control is great, but the manner in which that loss is manifested is attractive. Once possessed, Regan's new powers, exhibited in hysterical displays of cinematic pyrotechnics, act out the imagery of infantile beliefs in the omnipotence of the will. Each grisly scene is a celebration of infantile rage. Regan's anger cracks doors and ceilings and levitates beds. And she can deck a full-grown man with a flick of a wrist. The audience is aghast at her loss of self-control, which begins fittingly enough with her urinating on the living room rug, but at the same time its archaic beliefs in the metaphysical prowess of the emotions are cinematically confirmed. Thought is given direct causal efficacy. Regan's feelings know no bounds; they pour out of her, tearing her own flesh apart with their intensity and hurling people and furniture in every direction. Part of the legacy of *The Exorcist* to its successors—like *Carrie, The Fury,* and *Patrick,* to name but a few titles in this rampant subgenre—is the fascination with telekinesis, which is nothing but a cinematic

"Figures that are simultaneously attractive and replusive": *Dr. Jekyll and Mr. Hyde.*

metaphor of the unlimited power of repressed rage. The audience is both drawn to and repelled by it—we recognize such rage in ourselves and superstitiously fear its emergence, while simultaneously we are pleased when we see a demonstration, albeit fictive, of the power of that rage.[8]

Christopher Lasch has argued that the neurotic personality of our time vacillates between fantasies of self-loathing and infantile delusions of grandeur.[9] The strength of *The Exorcist* is that it captures this oscillation cinematically. Regan, through the machinations of Satan, is the epitome of self-hatred and self-degradation—a filthy thing, festering in its bed, befouling itself, with fetid breath, full of scabs, dirty hair, and a complexion that makes her look like a pile of old newspapers.

The origins of this self-hatred imagery are connected with sexual themes. Regan's sudden concupiscence corresponds with a birthday, presumably her thirteenth. There are all sorts of allusions to masturbation: not only does Regan misuse the crucifix, splattering her thighs with blood in an act symbolic of both loss of virginity and menstruation, but later her hands are bound (one enshrined method for stopping "self-abuse") and her skin goes bad (as we were all warned it would). Turning the head 360 degrees also has sexual connotations; in theology, it is described as a technique Satan uses when sodomizing witches. Regan incarnates images of worthlessness, of being virtually trash, in a context laden with sex and self-laceration. But the moments of self-degradation give way to images that express delusions of grandeur as she rocks the house in storms of rage. She embodies moods of guilt and rebellion, of self-loathing and omnipotence that speak to the Narcissus in each of us.

The fantastic beings of horror films can be seen as symbolic formations that organize conflicting themes into figures that are simultaneously attractive and repulsive. Two major symbolic structures appear most prominent in this regard: fusion, in which the conflicting themes are yoked together in one, spatio-temporally unified figure; and fission, in which the conflicting themes are distributed—over space or time—among more than one figure.

Dracula, one of the classic film monsters, falls into the category of fusion. In order to identify the symbolic import of this figure we can begin with Jones's account of vampires—since Dracula is a vampire—but we must also amplify that account since Dracula is a very special vampire. According to Jones, the vampires of superstition have two fundamental constituent attributes: revenance and blood sucking. The mythic, as opposed to movie, vampire first visits its relatives. For Jones, this stands for the relatives' longing for the loved one to return from the dead. But the figure is charged with terror. What is fearful is blood sucking, which Jones associates with seduction. In short, the desire for an incestuous encounter with the dead relative is transformed, through a form of denial, into an assault-attraction, and love metamorphoses into repulsion and sadism. At the same time, via projection, the living portray themselves as passive victims, imbuing the dead with a dimension of active agency that permits the "victim" pleasure without blame. Lastly, Jones not only connects blood sucking with the exhausting embrace of the incubus but with a regressive mixture of sucking and biting characteristic of the oral stage of psychosexual development. By negation—the transformation of love to hate, by projection—through which the desired dead become active, and the desiring living passive, and by regression—from genital to oral sexuality, the vampire legend gratifies incestuous and necrophiliac desires by amalgamating them in a fearsome iconography.

The vampire of lore and the Dracula figure of stage and screen have several points of tangency, but Dracula also has a number of distinctive attributes. Of necessity, Dracula is Count Dracula. He is an aristocrat; his bearing is noble; and, of course, through hypnosis, he is a paradigmatic authority figure. He is commanding in both senses of the word. Above all, Dracula demands *obedience* of his minions and mistresses. He is extremely old—associated with *ancient* castles—and possessed of incontestable strength. Dracula cannot be overcome by force—he can only be outsmarted or outmaneuvered; humans are typically described as puny in comparison to him. At times, Dracula is invested with omniscience, observing from afar the measures taken against him. He also hoards women and is a harem master. In brief, Dracula is a bad father figure, often balanced off against Van Helsing. who defends virgins against the seemingly younger, more vibrant Count. The phallic symbolism of Dracula is hard to miss—he is aged, buried in a filthy place, impure, powerful, and aggressive.

The contrast with Van Helsing immediately suggests another cluster of Dracula's attributes. He does appear the younger of the two specifically because he represents the rebellious son at the same time that he is the violent father. This identification is achieved by means of the Satanic imagery that contributes to Dracula's persona. Dracula is the Devil—one film in fact refers to him in its title as the "Prince of Darkness." With few exceptions, Dracula is depicted as eternally uncontrite, bent on luring hapless souls. Most importantly, Dracula is a modern devil, which, as Jones points out, means that he is a rival to God. Religiously, Dracula is presented as a force of unmitigated evil. Dramatically, this is translated into a quantum of awesome will or willfulness, often flexed in those mental duels with Van Helsing. Dracula, in part, exists as a rival to the father, as a figure of defiance and rebellion, fulfilling the oedipal wish via a hero of Miltonic proclivities. The Dracula image, then, is a fusion of conflicting attributes of the bad (primal) father and the rebellious son which is simultaneously appealing and forbidding because of the way it conjoins different dimensions of the oedipal fantasy.

The fusion of conflicting tendencies in the figure of the monster in horror films has the dream process of condensation as its approximate psychic prototype. In analyzing the symbolic meaning of these fusion figures our task is to individuate the conflicting themes that constitute the creature. Like Dracula, the Frankenstein monster is a fusion figure, one that is quite literally a composite. Mary Shelley first dreamed of the creature at a time in her life fraught with tragedies connected with childbirth.[10] Victor Frankenstein's creation—his "hideous progeny"—is a gruesome parody of birth; indeed, Shelley's description of the creature's appearance bears passing correspondences to that of a newborn—its waxen skin, misshapen head, and touch of jaundice. James Whale's *Frankenstein* also emphasizes the association of the monster with a child; its walk is unsteady and halting, its head is outsized and its eyes sleepy. And in the film, though not in the novel, the creature's basic cognitive skills are barely developed; it is mystified by fire and has difficulty differentiating between little girls and flowers. The monster in one respect is a child and its creation is a birth that is presented as ghastly. At the same time, the monster is made of waste, of dead things, in "Frankenstein's workshop of filthy creation." The excremental reference is hardly disguised. The association of the creature with waste implies that, in part, the story is underwritten by the infantile confusion over the processes of elimination and reproduction. The monster is reviled as heinous and as unwholesome filth, rejected by its creator—its father—perhaps in a way that reorchestrated Mary Shelley's feelings of rejection by her father, William Godwin.

But these images of loathesomeness are fused with opposite qualities. In the film myth, the monster is all but omnipotent (it can function as a sparring partner for Godzilla), indomitable, and, for all intents and purposes, immortal (perhaps partly for the intent and purpose of sequels). It is both helpless and powerful, worthless and godlike. Its rejection spurs rampaging vengeance, combining fury and strength in infantile orgies of rage and destruction. Interestingly, in the novel this ire is directed against Victor Frankenstein's family. And even in Whale's 1931 version of the myth the monster's definition as outside (excluded from a place in) the family is maintained in a number of ways: the killing of Maria; the juxtaposition of the monster's wandering over the countryside with wedding preparations; and the opposition of Frankenstein's preoccupation with affairs centered around the monster to the interest of propagating an heir to the family barony. The emotional logic of the tale proceeds from the initial loathesomeness of the monster, which triggers its rejection, which causes the monster to explode in omnipotent rage over its alienation from the family, which, in turn, confirms the earlier intimation of "badness," thereby justifying the parental rejection.[11] This scenario, moreover, is predicated on the inherently conflicting tendencies—of being waste and being god—that are condensed in the creature from the start. It is, therefore, a necessary condition for the success of the tale that the creature be repellent.

One method for composing fantastic beings is fusion. On the visual level, this often entails the construction of creatures that transgress categorical distinctions such as inside/outside, insect/human, flesh/machine, etc.[12] The particular affective significance of these admixtures depends to a large extent on the specific narrative context in which they are embedded. But apart from fusion, another means for articulating emotional conflicts in horror films is fission. That is, conflicts concerning sexuality, identity, aggressiveness, etc. can be mapped over different entities—each standing for a different facet of the conflict—which are nevertheless linked by some magical, supernatural, or sci-fi process. The type of creatures that I have in mind here include *doppelgängers*, alter-egos, and werewolves.

Fission has two major modes in the horror film.[13] The first distributes the conflict over space through the creation of doubles, e.g., *The Portrait of Dorian Gray, The Student of Prague,* and *Warning Shadows.* Structurally, what is involved in spatial fission is a process of multiplication, i.e., a charac-

Bride of Frankenstein:
Elsa Lanchester and
Boris Karloff

ter or set of characters is multiplied into one or more new facets each standing for another aspect of the self, generally one that is either hidden, ignored, repressed, or denied by the character who has been cloned. These examples each employ some mechanism of reflection—a portrait, a mirror, shadows—as the pretext for doubling. But this sort of fission figure can appear without such devices. In *I Married a Monster from Outer Space,* a young bride begins to suspect that her new husband is not quite himself. Somehow he's different than the man she used to date. And she's quite right. Her boyfriend was kidnapped by invaders from outer space on his way back from a bachelor party and was replaced by an alien duplicate. This double, however, initially lacks feelings— the essential characteristic of being human in fifties sci-fi films—and his bride intuits this. The basic story, sci-fi elements aside, resembles a very specific paranoid delusion called Capgras syndrome. The delusion involves the patient's belief that his or her parents, lovers, etc. have become minatory *doppelgängers.* This enables the patient to deny his fear or hatred of a loved one by splitting the loved one in half, creating a bad version (the invader) and a good one (the victim). The new relation of marriage in *I Married a Monster* appears to engender a conflict, perhaps over sexuality, in the wife which is expressed through the fission figure.[14] Splitting as a psychic trope of denial is the root prototype for spatial fission in the horror film, organizing conflict through the multiplication of characters.

Fission occurs in horror films not only in terms of multiplication but also in terms of division. That is, a character can be divided in time as well as multiplied in space. *Dr. Jekyll and Mr. Hyde* and the various werewolves, cat people, gorgons, and other changelings of the genre are immediate examples. In the horror film, temporal fission—usually marked by shape changing—is often self-consciously concerned with repression. In *Curse of the Werewolf* one shot shows the prospective monster behind the bars of a wine cellar window holding a bottle; it is an icon of restrained delirium. The traditional conflict in these films is sexuality. Stevenson's *Jekyll and Hyde* is altered in screen variants so that the central theme of Hyde's brutality—which I think is connected to an allegory against alcoholism in the text—becomes a preoccupation with lechery. Often changeling films, like *The Werewolf of London* or *The Cat People*, eventuate in the monster attacking its lover, suggesting that this subgenre begins in infantile confusions over sexuality and aggression. The imagery of werewolf films also has been associated with conflicts connected with the bodily changes of puberty and adolescence: unprecedented hair spreads over the body, accompanied by uncontrollable, vaguely understood urges leading to puzzlement and even to fear of madness.[15] This imagery becomes especially compelling in *The Wolfman*, where the tension between father and son mounts through anger and tyranny until at last the father beats the son to death with a silver cane in a paroxysm of oedipal anxiety.[16]

Fusion and fission generate a large number of the symbolic biologies of horror films, but not all. Magnification of power or size—e.g., giant insects (and other exaggerated animalcules)—is another mode of symbol formation. Often magnification takes a particular phobia as its subject and, in general, much of this imagery seems comprehensible in terms of Freud's observation that "the majority of phobias . . . are traceable to such a fear on the ego's part of the demands of the libido."[17]

Giant insects are a case in point. The giant spider, for instance, appeared in silent film in John Barrymore's *Jekyll and Hyde* as an explicit symbol of desire. Perhaps insects, especially spiders, can perform this role not only because of their resemblance to hands—the hairy hands of masturbation—but also because of their cultural association with impurity.[18] At the same time, their identification as poisonous and predatory—devouring—can be mobilized to express anxious fantasies over sexuality. Like giant reptiles, giant insects are often encountered in two specific contexts in horror films. They inhabit negative paradises—jungles and lost worlds—that unaware humans happen into, not to find Edenic milk and honey but the gnashing teeth or mandibles of oral regression. Or, giant insects or reptiles are slumbering potentials of nature released or awakened by physical or chemical alterations caused by human experiments in areas of knowledge best left to the gods. Here, the predominant metaphor is that these creatures or forces have been unfettered or unleashed, suggesting their close connection with erotic impulses. Like the fusion and fission figures of horror films, these nightmares are also explicable as effigies of deep-seated, archaic conflicts.

So far I have dwelt on the symbolic composition of the monsters in horror films, extrapolating from the framework set out by Jones in *On the Nightmare* in the hope of beginning a crude approximation of a taxonomy. But before concluding, it is worthwhile to consider briefly the relevance of archaic conflicts of the sort already discussed to the themes repeated again and again in the basic plot structures of the horror film.[19]

Perhaps the most serviceable narrative armature in the horror film genre is what I call the Discovery Plot. It is used in *Dracula, The Exorcist, Jaws* I & II, *It Came From Outer Space, Curse of the Demon, Close Encounters of the Third Kind, It Came From Beneath the Sea,* and myriad other films. It has four essential movements. The first is onset: the monster's presence is established, e.g., by an attack, as in *Jaws*. Next, the monster's existence is discovered by an individual or a group, but for one reason or another its existence or continued existence, or the nature of the threat it actually poses, is not acknowledged by the powers that be. "There are no such things as vampires," the police chief might say at this point. Discovery, therefore, flows into the next plot movement, which is confirmation. The discoverers or believers must convince some other group of the existence and proportions of mortal danger at hand. Often this section of the plot is the most elaborate, and suspenseful. As the UN refuses to accept the reality of the onslaught of killer bees or invaders from Mars, precious time is lost, during which the creature or creatures often gain power and advantage. This interlude also allows for a great deal of discussion about the encroaching monster, and this talk about its invulnerability, its scarcely imaginable strength, and its nasty habits endows the off-screen beast with the qualities that prime the audience's fearful anticipation. Language is one of the most effective ingredients in a horror film and I would guess that the genre's primary success in sound film rather than silent film has less to do with the absence of sound effects in the silents than with the presence of all that dialogue about the unseen monster in the talkies.

After the hesitations of confirmation, the Discovery Plot culminates in confrontation. Mankind meets its monster, most often winning, but on occasion, like the remake of *Invasion of the Body Snatchers*, losing. What is particularly of interest in this plot structure is the tension caused by the delay between discovery and confirmation. Thematically, it involves the audience not only in the drama of proof but also in the play between knowing and not knowing,[20] between acknowledgment versus nonacknowledgment, that has the growing awareness of sexuality in the adolescent as its archetype. This conflict can become very pronounced when the gainsayers in question—generals, police

Donald Sutherland in
the toils of the delayed-
discovery plot: *Invasion
of the Body Snatchers*

chiefs, scientists, heads of institutions, etc.—are obviously parental authority figures.

Another important plot structure is that of the Overreacher. *Frankenstein, Jekyll and Hyde,* and *Man with the X-Ray Eyes* are all examples of this approach. Whereas the Discovery Plot often stresses the short-sightedness of science, the Overreacher Plot criticizes science's will to knowledge. The Overreacher Plot has four basic movements. The first comprises the preparation for the experiment, generally including a philosophical, popular-mechanics explanation or debate about the experiment's motivation. The overreacher himself (usually Dr. Soandso) can become quite megalomaniacal here, a quality commented upon, for instance, by the dizzyingly vertical laboratory sets in *Frankenstein* and *Bride of Frankenstein*. Next comes the experiment itself, whose partial success allows for some more megalomania. But the experiment goes awry, leading to the destruction of innocent victims and/or to damage or threat to the experimenter or his loved ones. At this point, some overreachers renounce their blasphemy; the ones who don't are mad scientists. Finally, there is a confrontation with the monster, generally in the penultimate scene of the film.

The Overreacher Plot can be combined with the Discovery Plot by making the overreacher and/or his experiments the object of discovery and confirmation. This yields a plot with seven movements—onset, discovery, confirmation, preparation for the experiment, experimentation, untoward consequences, and confrontation.* But the basic Overreacher Plot differs thematically from

* Confirmation as well as discovery may come after or between the next three movements in this structure.

the Discovery Plot insofar as the conflicts central to the Overreacher Plot reside in fantasies of omniscience, omnipotence, and control. The plot eventually cautions against these impulses but not until it gratifies them with partial success and a strong dose of theatrical panache.

In suggesting that the plot structures and fantastic beings of the horror film correlate with nightmares and repulsive materials, I do not mean to claim that horror films are nightmares. Structurally, horror films are far more rationally ordered than nightmares, even in extremely disjunctive and dreamlike experiments like *Phantasm*. Moreover, phenomenologically, horror film buffs do not believe that they are literally the victims of the mayhem they witness whereas a dreamer can quite often become a participant and a victim in his/her dream. We can and do seek out horror films for pleasure, while someone who looked forward to a nightmare would be a rare bird indeed. Nevertheless, there do seem to be enough thematic and symbolic correspondences between nightmare and horror to indicate the distant genesis of horror motifs in nightmare as well as significant similarities between the two phenomena. Granted, these motifs become highly stylized on the screen. Yet, for some, the horror film may release some part of the tensions that would otherwise erupt in nightmares. Perhaps we can say that horror film fans go to the movies (in the afternoon) perchance to sleep (at night).

NOTES

1. Ernest Jones, *On the Nightmare* (London: Liveright, 1971).

2. M. Katan claims that *The Turn of the Screw* also originated in a night-mare. See "A Causerie on Henry James's *The Turn of the Screw*" in *Psychoanal. Stud. Child* 17:473–493, 1962.

3. Jones, 78.

4. Frank McConnell, *Spoken Seen* (Baltimore: Johns Hopkins U. Press, 1975), 76.

5. Robin Wood, "*Sisters*," in *American Nightmare* (Toronto: Festival of Festivals Publication, 1979), 60.

6. Jones, 79.

7. John Mack, *Nightmares and Human Conflict* (Boston: Little Brown, 1970).

8. Rage is always an important component in horror films. Nevertheless, in the present horror cycle—given its fascination with telekinesis and omnipotent, Satanic children (and including the "psychoplasmic" imagery of *The Brood*)—rage has an unparalleled salience. In the America of Nixon, Ford, and Carter, the recurring cine-fantasy seems to be of pent-up, channel-less anger, welling-up, exploding, overwhelming everything.

9. Christopher Lasch, *The Culture of Narcissism* (New York: Norton, 1979). Both Lasch's and my concepts of narcissism are roughly based on Otto Kernberg, *Borderline Conditions and Pathological Narcissism* (New York: Jason Aronston, 1975).

10. Ellen Moers, *Literary Women* (Garden City, N.Y.: Anchor, 1977), 140–151.

11. The use of mythic types of fantasies to justify the parental behavior is discussed in Dorothy Block, "*So the Witch Won't Eat Me*" (Boston: Houghton Mifflin Co., 1978).

12. The slave creatures in *This Island Earth* are examples of the fusion of inside/outside and insect/human while the last apparition of the monster in

Alien—with its spring-mounted iron maw—is an example of the fusion of flesh and machine, as is the alien's stranded spaceship.

13. Robert Rogers, *A Psychoanalytic Study of the Double in Literature* (Detroit: Wayne State University Press, 1970).

14. *I Married a Monster from Outer Space* belongs to a subgenre of space-possession films including *Invasion of the Body Snatchers, It Conquered the World, They Came from Beyond Space, Creation of the Humanoids, Man from Planet X, Invaders from Mars, Phantom from Space, It Came from Outer Space, Killers from Space,* etc. Depending on the specific context of the film, the possessed earthlings in these films can be examples of either spatial or temporal fission. For an interpretation of *Invasion of the Body Snatchers,* see my "You're Next" in *The Soho Weekly News,* Dec. 21, 1978.

15. Daniel Dervin, "The Primal Scene and the Technology of Perception in Theater and Film," in *Psychoanal. Rev.,* 62, no. 2, 278, 1975.

16. In regard to shape-changing figures, like werewolves, it is important to note that metamorphosis in and of itself does not indicate a fission figure. Vampires readily shed human form to become bats and wolves; yet vampires are not fission figures. They are allotropic, varying their physical properties while remaining the same in substance. But with werewolves the change in shape betokens a change in its nature.

Another, though connected, difference between werewolves and vampires hinges on the issue of will. Werewolves—most often futilely—resist their fate while vampires, especially Dracula, prefer theirs. This is a crucial reason for having the two different myths.

17. Sigmund Freud, *The Problem of Anxiety* (New York: Norton, 1963), 39.

18. The spider, of course, has polyvalent associations. It figures importantly as a phobic object because of its ruthlessness—i.e., its use of a trap, its oral sadism—it sucks its prey, and, for men, because of its sexual practices—some female spiders feast upon their mates. In much of the psychoanalytic literature the spider is correlated with the oral, sadistic mother; its body is associated with the vagina; its legs are sometimes glossed as the fantasized penis that the mother is believed to possess. Some references concerning spider imagery include: Karl Abraham, "The Spider as a Dream Symbol," in *Selected Papers,* trans. Douglas Bryand and Alix Strachey (London: Hogarth Press, 1927); Ralph Little, "Oral Aggression in Spider Legends," *Amer. Imago* 23: 169–180, 1966; R. Little, "Umbilical Cord Symbolism of the Spider's Dropline," *Psychoanal. Quart.*; Richard Sterba, "On Spiders, Hanging and Oral Sadism," *Amer. Imago* 7: 21–28. There is also an influential reading of "Little Miss Muffet. . . ." in Ella Freeman Sharpe, "Cautionary Tales," *Int'nat. J. of Psychoanal.* 24: 41–45. In the preceding text I have also connected spiders to masturbation. I have done this not simply because spiders somewhat resemble hands but because that resemblance itself is part of our literary culture. Recall the legend of Arachne, who was punished by Minerva by being reduced to a hand which becomes a spider. Bulfinch writes that Minerva sprinkled Arachne "with the juices of

aconite, and immediately her hair came off and ears likewise. Her form shrank up, and her head grew smaller yet; her fingers cleaved to her side and served for legs. All the rest of her is body, out of which she spins her thread, often hanging suspended from it, in the same attitude as when Minerva touched her and transformed her into a spider." Thomas Bulfinch, *Mythology* (N.Y.: Dell Publishing Co., 1959), 93.

19. Some typical science fiction plots are outlined in the opening of Susan Sontag's "The Imagination of Disaster" in *Film Theory and Criticism* (N.Y.: Oxford U. Press. 1979). Sontag's first model plot is like the Discovery Plot described in this paper. However, the problem with Sontag's variant is that she does not give enough emphasis to the drama of proving the existence of the monster over skeptical objections. This, I feel, is the crux of most horror/sci-fi films of the Discovery Plot variety.

20. The theme of knowing/not knowing is important to horror films along many different dimensions. In terms of cinematic technique, it can influence the director's choice of formal strategies. For example, in recent horror films, there is a great deal of use of what I call unassigned camera movement in the context of stories about demons, ghosts, and other unseen but all-seeing monsters. In *The Changeling*, the camera begins to move around George C. Scott in his study. It is not supplying new narrative information nor is its movement explicitly correlated within the scene to any specific character. It has no assignment either in terms of narrative or characterological function. But it does call attention to itself. The audience sees it. And the audience cannot help postulating that the camera movement *might* represent the presence of some unseen, supernatural force that is observing Scott for devilish purposes. The point of the camera movement is to provoke the spectator into a state of uncertainty in which he/she shifts between knowing and not knowing.

J. P. TELOTTE

HUMAN ARTIFICE AND
THE SCIENCE FICTION FILM

The human artifice of the world separates human existence from all mere animal environment, but life itself is outside this artificial world, and through life man remains related to all other living organisms. For some time now, a great many scientific endeavors have been directed toward making life also "artificial," toward cutting the last tie through which even man belongs among the children of nature. . . . There is no reason to doubt our abilities to accomplish such an exchange, just as there is no reason to doubt our present ability to destroy all organic life on earth.

HANNAH ARENDT[1]

Vol. 36, no. 3 (Spring 1983): 44–51.

"I know I'm human," the protagonist of John Carpenter's film *The Thing* asserts, as he frantically searches for a threatening alien presence among his comrades. Taken out of context in this way, such a declaration sounds almost pointless, like an assurance of something that should be evident to the gaze of those around, as indeed it seems to the movie viewers. The very need for such an assertion, consequently, hints at an unexpected uncertainty here, even an uneasiness about one's identity and, more importantly, about what it is that makes one human. It is an uneasiness, moreover, which cannot be dispelled by a simple gaze, the means by which we typically evaluate our world, others, and ourselves. I call attention to the character McReady's predicament because it makes overt a specter which has continually haunted the science fiction film genre. Periodically throughout its history, but increasingly so in recent years, this formula has taken as its focus the problematic nature of the human being and the difficult task of being human. And as Hannah Arendt makes clear, the former concern seems to pose an ever greater barrier for the latter.

In this context, we should note the number of recent films which take as their major concern or as an important motif the potential doubling of the human body and thus the literal creation of a human artifice. Among others, films like the remakes of *Invasion of the Body Snatchers* and *The Thing, Blade Runner, Alien,* and even *Star Trek* explore some aspect of this motif, but especially a welcome or threatening capacity which inheres in this cloning or copying of the self, cell for cell, and which promises to make man both more and less than he already is. Not simply a current development, though, this motif runs throughout the history of science fiction film. Viewed from the perspective of their "mad scientist" themes, the numerous Frankenstein and Dr. Jekyll/Mr. Hyde films represent paradigms of this tendency; in fact, the enduring confusion in the popular imagination that attributes the single name of Frankenstein to both a monster and its creator underscores the effect of this doubling pattern. One of its earliest and most characteristic treatments, however, occurs in a film that many see as

the prototype for the genre, Fritz Lang's *Metropolis*. The modeling of the heroine Maria into a destructive android look-alike serves as the narrative's center-
piece and prompts its greatest display of scientific gadgetry—that which we have
come to expect to be the very core of the science fiction film. Visually indistinguishable from the real Maria, the android threatens to unleash dangerous desires in the human community and thus bring about disaster. Because she is both
alluring and potentially destructive, the artificial Maria well represents the disturbing implications of that capacity for doubling and artifice which man's science has attained.

Probably the landmark treatment of this doubling motif occurs in the original *Invasion of the Body Snatchers,* which focuses precisely upon a threatening
possibility for perfectly duplicating the human body, "cell for cell, atom for
atom," as one character explains. In this case, it is an alien life form that uses
nature wrongly, to grow seed pods which will deprive man of his own true nature, as they duplicate his body, "snatch" his intellect, but deprive him of all
emotional capacity. While films had previously presented such duplication as a
threat, the product of human aberrance or some misguided science, *Invasion*
added a disconcerting note and also laid open a desire which has frequently
moved just beneath the surface of these films, by pointing up a subtle attraction
at the heart of the doubling process. The bloodless victory of the copy, of the
pods, is actually lauded by those who have been subsumed into this emotion-
less community. This reaction suggests an elemental desire in man for the security and tranquillity which the sameness of duplication promises; as another
character notes, this transformation permits man to be "born into an un-
troubled world" and to abdicate from the many problems of modern life—problems posed, it is implied, by the very advances of science, especially in the field
of warfare, which, on the surface, usually seem a basic concern of these films.

Don Siegel, director of the original *Invasion,* admits that he sought to inject
this challenge of attractiveness in response to a widespread desire he noted to
abdicate from human responsibility in the face of an increasingly complex and
confusing modern world. To this end he

> purposely had the prime spokesman for the pods be a pod psychiatrist.
> He speaks with authority, knowledge. He really believes that being a pod
> is preferable to being a frail, frightened human who cares. He has a
> strong case for being a pod. How marvelous it would be if you were a
> cow and all you had to do is munch a little grass and not worry about
> life, death and pain. There's a strong case for being a pod.[2]

It is this "strong case" that has been repeatedly and increasingly stated in films
since the time of *Invasion. The Stepford Wives,* for instance, plays not just upon
the threat of a gradual, insidious replacement of the women in a small town by

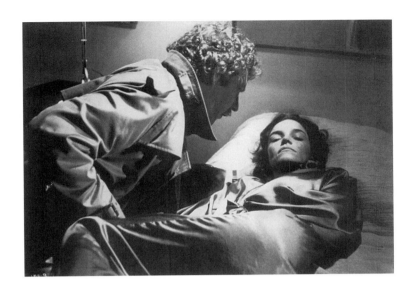

Invasion of the
Body Snatchers

mindless, dispassionate androids—apparently the perfect housewife—but also on the terror implicit in their similarity to what is held up as a cultural ideal and in the fact that this duplication is obviously desirable to those closest to the women, their own husbands. Perhaps because of our increasing concern with the potential for cloning and genetic research, such possibilities no longer seem so far-fetched, hence the recent spate of films exploring this complex proposition. They all emphasize man's fascination with knowledge and science, as has always been typical of the genre, but they link a single-minded pursuit of knowledge with that disconcerting desire to duplicate the self—or unleash the unknown power of duplication, as in *The Thing*—and its consequent rendering of the self almost irrelevant. In sum, they suggest how the human penchant for artifice—that is, for analyzing, understanding, and synthesizing all things, even man himself—seems to promise a reduction of man to no more than artifice.

This paradox also sheds some light on a subtle distinction which the science fiction film has typically sought to make in its depiction of man's attitudes towards science. As critics have frequently noted, the genre often seems to juxtapose a good and a bad science, white and black magic, as it were, with the one working to serve man and the other to threaten his position in the world. We might recall the novel *Frankenstein*'s subtitle, *The Modern Prometheus*, for it can help us to discern an even more telling distinction at work in the film genre. In its recurring manifestations, the doubling motif denotes a Faustian drive for knowledge or power, a dangerous and even self-destructive impulse behind that fascination with the power of science or some select knowledge to enable man to duplicate himself artificially. This Faustian impulse, however, typically tries to go masked as a Promethean one, that is, as a desire to bestow significant boons upon man. Of course, it is in the nature of those boons—not light but likeness, and not the potential of fire but its destructive force—that we eventually perceive the Faustian persona beneath the Promethean seeming that science and the scientist usually bear in the genre.

Why this seeming, however, and why should its ultimate expression take the very shape of seeming, namely the doubling or copying of the self? The persistence of this theme hints at a certain hubris of the mind with which the genre is concerned: a pride in a science which is seen as seeking to accommodate all things to the self, ultimately even the self, which, because of a lingering Cartesian dualism between the mind and body, thinking and feeling, has become associated with both the internal life of the mind and an external world of otherness, the not-mind.[3] The fashioning of other bodies, other forms of the self, only reinforces that split between mind and body and reasserts the hegemony of the former over the latter. What I would like to suggest, following Arendt's lead, then, is that we might see in this doubling motif the indication of a science turned inside out, a drive for knowledge and control become a desire for oblivion, although it is a blind desire, as the self unwittingly turns upon itself, even while apparently engaged in a process of valorizing the self through the ability for replication.

The full paradox and threat inherent in this artificing of life lurks just beneath the surface of a film like *Alien*. In fact, the film's central horror, a monstrous presence that thrives on man, yet is apparently invulnerable to his normal defenses, seems metaphoric of some flaw within man, perhaps the Faustian drive that increasingly seeks expression. The murderous alien is brought into the spaceship because the company sponsoring the flight has established a primary directive for the crew to gather any information on life forms that might prove valuable. Arguing for this directive, and thus directly precipitating the alien's murderous rampage among the crew, is an android, a replica of man so perfect that he fools his fellow crew members. A perfect example of the danger behind this doubling pattern, he has been programmed to ensure the mission's knowledge-gathering activities, regardless of any danger which might accrue to the human component of the expedition. In the film's most startling scene, the alien creature that has embedded itself within one of the crew members suddenly bursts through his chest, killing the human host. Born from within man, this creature metaphorically embodies the monstrous potential of the double which has made its life possible. In short, the alien represents the displaced terror and true frightening aspect of that desire for knowledge which, also arising from within man, has begun to produce life-threatening doubles. It is only through this perspective of displacement that the complex plotting of *Alien*, and especially the discomfiting relationship between android and monster, comes into proper focus. In his discussion of the nature of man's proclivity for doubles, René Girard predicts just such a link and connects the desire for doubling to man's most violent impulses; as he notes, there is "no double who does not yield a monstrous aspect upon close scrutiny."[4]

The new version of *The Thing* specifically emphasizes this "close scrutiny," that is, the visual problem posed by the double. When a scientific research team stumbles upon and accidentally unthaws an alien creature embedded in the polar ice for thousands of years, they unleash not simply a monstrous creature, one that threatens those discoverers, but a figure that seems to summarize the problems of doubling located in both *Invasion of the Body Snatchers* and *Alien*. As one character notes, this creature "wants to hide inside an imitation" and it possesses the power to "shape its own cells to imitate" any other being in its environment. That this capacity for perfect mimesis is not simply a protective mechanism, like a chameleon's color adaptation, but a very real threat to man is underscored by the gruesome scenes of possession and transformation for which the film has been scored on occasion. In fact, *The Thing* seems to draw on *Alien*'s "chest-buster" sequence as a model for these scenes—a connection which underscores the importance I have here attached to that previous scene and one which hints at an internal component in this alien doubling. What *The Thing* particularly adds to the previous formulations of this doubling motif is an emphasis on the contagiousness of this tendency, and thus its more than individual menace. As the doctor among the group calculates, at its current rate of assimilation of man, the alien polymorph could take over all of humanity in "27,000 hours from first contact." It thereby threatens rapidly to reduce man's world to a realm of imitations, to make everyone simply an extension of that alien presence.

With the awareness of this threatening possibility, an equally devastating potential also emerges, one which inheres in every act of doubling. Because man is possessed of an absolute desire for certainty or knowledge—at least, so the science fiction genre argues through its emphasis on the compulsion for knowledge—he can easily become prey to an almost debilitating anxiety in the face of whatever stubbornly resists his attempts at formulation. And when the enigma is his own double or potential double, the anxiety may take even deeper root. Almost frantically, therefore, the men at this isolated outpost reach out for some answer, some assurance, even "some kind of test," as one of them puts it, which might detect this alien presence in their midst and thus assure them that they are all just what they appear to be, truly men. Significantly, however, this task of detection and inquiry into the visible world quickly transforms into a suspicion of the human society in which they are immersed, even an uneasiness about the self; as one man asks, "How do we know who's human?" It is a question that betrays a deep-seated fear, normally kept hidden yet essentially commonplace, of all that is not the self. Calling attention to this rapid breakdown of human society which the alien visitation has precipitated, McReady notes that "Nobody trusts anybody now." What such a comment also bears witness to is an alien potential which resides in man, ever ready to be triggered by circumstance and to raise a disturbing suspicion not only about one's fellow man, but even about the self and its relationship to that human world it must inhabit.

What *The Thing* locates, therefore, is a certain *thing*-ness within man, an absence or potential abdication from the human world which can only be made present or visualized in the mirror furnished by the doubling process. The confrontation with which the film ends, as McReady and a black man, the only other survivor of the group, eye each other suspiciously, each equally sure that the other is only a double fashioned by the alien, metaphorically points up the distrust and fear which already typically mark modern society, and particularly its race relations. Of course, the doubling process which the alien initiated promised to render everyone the same, each an extension of that single intruder, and in their mutual fear of the other McReady and his comrade have already fulfilled that promise after a fashion. Moreover, that threat precipitates with both men a retreat into the private space of the mind, the one stable ground upon which they feel they can still stand. In effect, the mind is thus seen as the true repository of the self, protectively questioning all about, while asserting with ever decreasing conviction one's own humanity, as we have already seen McReady doing. If that phrase, "I know I'm human," seems to ring hollow, it is because the narrative, through its visitation of this disconcerting doubling, has managed to undercut all certainty, all dependable knowledge, certainly all reliance on appearance. Consequently, at the film's conclusion even we are unsure if one or neither of the survivors is indeed a copy, just waiting his chance to spread his mimetic reign into the outside world. Indeed, we are left to question the very future of man's life on earth, just as Arendt does.

In another sort of investigation into the nature of our modern culture, Loren Eisely has attempted to trace out the process by which "man becomes natural," that is, how he came to see himself as a part of nature and its historical processes, rather than as a strange occurrence and an intrusion into the natural world. "Before life could be viewed as in any way natural," he explains, "a rational explanation of change through the ages" was needed;[5] man had to acquire a thorough knowledge of the patterns of evolution. The recent film *Blade Runner* dramatizes the logical consequences of this mastery of evolutionary principles. The development of this understanding, the film suggests, serves as the springboard for the current concern with the possibilities of genetic engineering, which, in its turn, has generated a potential for scientifically controlled evolution: the creation and programming of perfect replicas of man, gifted with unusual beauty, strength, or intelligence, and made to serve their human creators. As a result of this original step in "becoming natural," however, apparently something has also been lost. As Eisely points out, while "man has, in scientific terms, become natural . . . the nature of his 'naturalness' escapes him. Perhaps his human freedom has left him the difficult choice of determining what it is in his nature to be."[6] The problematic nature of human nature is precisely the topic on which *Blade Runner* with its formulation of the doubling motif attempts to shed some light.

As in *The Thing*, a sense of uncertainty and the anxiety which attends it seem to color the very world of *Blade Runner* and to derive in large part from the fascination with doubling which it chronicles. The futuristic environment the film describes seems perpetually dark and rainy, as gloomy as that of film noir—the conventions of which *Blade Runner* does in fact draw on. In this bleak atmosphere we can see mirrored an interior darkness that afflicts the characters here and seems brought on by the problems arising from a culture practically predicated upon the possibilities of duplication. In this future world, man has progressed to such a point that he can genetically design and reproduce virtually anything that lives; thus we see mechanical birds, snakes, dogs, and especially people—or "replicants," as they are here termed—all of which are virtually indistinguishable from the real thing. They have been fashioned by man's science in order to satisfy his various desires, to free him from labor and the dangers of combat, or simply to amuse him. And yet in spite of these benefits, no one seems truly happy in this society; in fact, those who can do so readily abandon this world in favor of one of the "off-world colonies," doubles of the earth itself which, like so many of the copies here, are apparently perceived as being better than their original. We thus see a vision of man not only no longer at home with himself, but no longer at home with his home; and the human doubles promise to increase the level of anxiety by refusing to remain in their servile roles and demanding instead a life like that of their creators and models.

As is typically the case in the science fiction genre, then, a kind of monstrous creation has transpired, but it has gone masked as scientific advance. In the place of *Frankenstein* are two geneticists—Dr. Tyrell, master designer of replicants, and J. F. Sebastian, his chief genetic engineer. Both appear to have given that Promethean impulse free reign, pushing the desire to fashion a copy of man to its extreme in their specially designed androids for every task and every distraction. The ostensible project of providing for human needs, however, has clearly been submerged by a pride in the process of doubling itself. Tyrell, it seems, is moved solely by his fascination with creating ever more perfect copies, replicants which can defy those tests for humanity which have developed in this future world—just as *The Thing* predicts. And with the girl Rachael, whom he addresses at one point as "my child," he has nearly succeeded. Sebastian has turned his engineering skills to no less subjective end, the task of filling his lonely life with manufactured "friends," albeit small, misshapen, flawed figures—apparently various reflections of his own flawed body, which suffers from "premature decrepitude." In sum, these scientists have turned their capacities for creating copies to their own ends, and in the process have endowed their creations with a certain reflexive capacity, Tyrell's figures mirroring his own desire for perfection, beauty, and transcendence of mechanical limitation, Sebastian's reflecting not only his own defects, but also his flawed view of himself.

In these projections of the self, moreover, both have already created the conditions that must eventually render them irrelevant. Because they have programmed their replicant creations with memories of a life that never was—even providing them with photographs of supposed relations and friends—and thus tried to convince them of their humanity, these engineers have erected a potentially dangerous bridge between the human and android realms. In fact, they have succeeded too well, for they have unleashed a synthetic but powerful desire for real life, one which—as is the case in films like *Frankenstein, Invasion of the Body Snatchers,* and *The Thing*—initially places itself in opposition to the possessors of normal life, mankind. In attempting to return to Earth from the off-world colonies, the group of replicants with whom the narrative is concerned have already killed 23 humans; and after finding their way back, they predictably turn their attention to their creators, particularly Tyrell and Sebastian. What they quest for is the secret of their programmed lives, and particularly, after the fashion of men through the ages, the means to a longer life. In effect, they have embarked on a Promethean search of sorts, seeking the archetypal fire of life itself, but in that murderous trail they leave behind, we see the clearest signs of that violence which, as René Girard has noted, usually goes masked by the doubling process.[7]

An even more telling measure of the ambiguity which attaches to this doubling process is found in the absence of a sure anchor for our own sympathies in this situation. That is, in the absence of the more typical monstrous presence and as a natural outgrowth of the desire for a nearly perfect mimesis which has produced these doubles, our concern shifts uneasily about between the world-weary, alienated bounty hunter Rick Deckard and those replicants whom it is his task to hunt down and destroy. Another and equally compelling reason for these shifting sympathies, of course, is that, as we quickly recognize, both man and android here essentially share the same—a doubled—fate. Like Sebastian, the replicants suffer from their own form of premature decrepitude, a programmed mortality which ensures their inevitable death after four years of service. As a consequence, these androids face the same sort of disconcerting knowledge that man has always had to abide with, that of an inescapable and onrushing death. Fed up with his work as a bounty killer, meanwhile, Deckard meditates on the nature of his quarry and, in turn, begins to wonder about his own place in this confusing welter of being wherein everything, perhaps even himself, seems to have its double or be itself a copy. Thus

The replicant Rachael
in *Blade Runner*

he comments at one point, "Replicants weren't supposed to have feelings; neither were blade runners" like himself. It is a complex mirroring pattern which has resulted from the doubling process, as men and androids begin to see themselves in each other and, discomfitingly, prod the others into a questioning of their very nature.

In the character of Rachael, Tyrell's nearly perfect replicant, this increasingly blurred distinction between man and the copies with which he has become obsessed finds its clearest example. Accepting the testimony of his own experienced eye, Deckard is initially fooled into believing her human, and he finds himself mysteriously attracted to her. What is more unsettling is that his fascination continues even after he administers the Voight-Kampff Empathy Test, which reveals that she is a replicant. The precise meaning of those test results quickly seems to evaporate in light of Rachael's manifest "humanity," however: her love of music, desire for affection, concern for others, and apparently a love for Deckard. Her response to the test's conclusions, asking Deckard, "Did you ever take that test yourself?" only compounds his quandary; it causes him to reflect on his own humanity, on the nature, that is, of a hired killer. As a result of this reflection, the subsequent order to kill Rachael along with the other replicants prompts a marked shift in the blade runner's attitude, a questioning of that which usually goes unquestioned, namely the humanity of those who create—and destroy—these artificial lives. He thus refuses the order and instead runs off with her to spend whatever little time her short, engineered life leaves them together in a different world, as a last shot indicates, a realm of light, greenery, and life, rather than the dark, rainy cityscape which has produced them both. In effect, Deckard takes Arendt's warning to heart, abandoning "the human artifice of the world" in favor of a natural environment in which man might regain his truly human nature.

If it seems ironic that a replicant or double should provide the stimulus for such an awakening to the self and a proper sense of humanity, it may be a telling indication of how far modern man has come in his fascination with artifice and how much he has lost in exchange for that knowledge of how to double the self. No longer viewed simply as the abnormal desire of aberrant types, as in the numerous films which have focused on mad scientist types, doubling has here become the very hallmark of society, something its members take for granted—but like many things we take for granted, it is also a pernicious influence. As *Blade Runner* suggests, when this abiding fascination with doubling becomes a dominant force in man's life, he clearly runs the risk of becoming little more than a copy himself, potentially less human than the very images he has fashioned in his likeness. Man's scientific advances, in sum, threaten to render him largely irrelevant, save as an empty pattern within which knowledge might be stored and through which it might extend its grasp, further increase its capacities, and expand the realm of artifice.

At another level we should find it most fitting that a double should spur an awakening to a sense of self. In essence, another form of the doppelgänger archetype, the replicant might be expected to serve the sort of salutary function that other archetypal patterns do. In explaining the effect of archetypal images on the psyche, psychologist James Hillman notes that "reversion through likeness, resemblance," affords the mind "a bridge . . . a method which connects an event to its image, a psychic process to its myth, a suffering of the soul to the imaginal mystery expressed therein."[8] In such "resemblance," he claims, there is located a path to a psychic truth which we have forgotten or lost sight of amid the welter of modern-day experience. Because of its reflective dimension, then, the image of the double, android, replicant, or copy holds out a great promise, even as it seems rather threatening, for it carries the potential of bringing us back to ourselves, making us at home with the self and the natural world almost in spite of ourselves. We might view the combat between Deckard and the android Roy Batty in exactly this context. In the middle of their fight, Deckard slips from the top of a building and dangles precariously in the air; only the outstretched hand of Batty, grabbing Deckard at the last moment, stops his fall and brings him back from the brink of death to a possible life. It is precisely the sort of saving potential or "reversion" which always inheres in the image of the double and which may ultimately best explain the continuing fascination it holds for us.

In attempting to map out the large territory of fantasy narratives, Tzvetan Todorov identifies a singular tension at work in the form which reflects the fundamental experience of its audience. Both reader (or viewer) and protagonist, he asserts, "must decide if a certain event or phenomenon belongs to reality or to imagination, that is, must determine whether or not it is real. It is therefore the category of the real which has furnished a basis for our definition."[9] As a result of this indeterminacy, we experience "a certain hesitation" as we try to "place" the events of the narrative within a known field of personal experience or reservoir of knowledge, just as the story's characters do. In this moment of hesitation, we should be able to discern the problem of representation which lies at the genre's very core, for we hesitate because of an immediate challenge to our usual system of referents, the stock of images which lived experience normally affords. At the same time, of course, that hesitation achieves a valuable purpose in prompting this stock-taking and thus starting a most subtle reflective experience.

In its recurrent concern with a doubling motif, the science fiction film thus draws on one of the fantastic's deepest structural patterns. In those images which fall outside of our normal lexicon, the film genre admits to a mystery or enigma that is at its center; and in bracketing the image of man—through those copies or replicants—within this enigmatic category, it admits of a puzzle to which we too are a part. Even as it limns the progress or potential of science, reason, and knowledge, therefore, the genre also acknowledges an underlying mystery and ambiguity, certainly in the approximations with which our mimetic impulse has always had to content itself. The fact that these disconcerting copies are in our own shape reminds us how little science has yet learned of substance about man, how little, in essence, we know about the most alluring of models for mimesis. As Arendt noted—and as our accomplishments in genetic engineering every day point up—we already possess the potential which science fiction films have so frequently described, that for crafting artificial versions of man. What these films hope to forestall is the dark obverse of this capacity, that for making human nature artificial as well.

NOTES

1. *The Human Condition* (Chicago: Univ. of Chicago Press, 1958), p. 2.
2. Quoted by Stuart Kaminsky in *Don Siegel: Director* (New York: Curtis Books, 1974), p. 104.
3. For a more detailed discussion of this split between the rational and sensory or emotional aspects of man, see Vivian Sobchack's *The Limits of Infinity* (New York: A. S. Barnes, 1980), and Lane Roth's "The Rejection of Rationalism in Recent Science Fiction Films," *Philosophy in Context*, 11(1981), 42–55.
4. *Violence and the Sacred*, trans. Patrick Gregory (Baltimore: Johns Hopkins Univ. Press, 1977), p. 160. As Girard notes elsewhere, "mimetic desire cannot be let loose without breeding a midsummer night of jealousy and strife," "Myth and Ritual in Shakespeare," in *Textual Strategies*, ed. Josué V. Harari (Ithaca: Cornell Univ. Press, 1979), p. 192.
5. *The Firmament of Time* (New York: Atheneum, 1966), p. 72.
6. *The Firmament of Time*, p. 114.
7. In addition to *Violence and the Sacred*, see Girard's *Deceit, Desire, and the Novel*, trans. Yvonne Freccero (Baltimore: Johns Hopkins Univ. Press, 1966).
8. *The Dream and the Underworld* (New York: Harper & Row, 1979), p. 4.
9. *The Fantastic: A Structural Approach to a Literary Genre*, trans. Richard Howard (Ithaca: Cornell Univ. Press, 1975), p. 167.

SCOTT MACDONALD

CONFESSIONS OF A
FEMINIST PORN WATCHER

*Finally, here's a proper subject for the legions of feminist men: let them under-
take the analysis that can tell us why men like porn (not, piously, why this or
that exceptional man does not), why stroke books work, how oedipal formations feed the drive, and how any of it can be changed. Would that the film
[Not a Love Story] had included any information from average customers,
instead of stressing always the exceptional figure (Linda Lee herself, Suze
Randall, etc.). And the antiporn campaigners might begin to formulate what
routes could be more effective than marching outside a porn emporium.*

B. RUBY RICH, "ANTI-PORN: SOFT ISSUE, HARD WORLD,"
VILLAGE VOICE, JULY 20, 1982

*Pepe Le Pew was everything I wanted to be romantically. Not only was he
quite sure of himself but it never occurred to him that anything was wrong
with him. I always felt that there must be great areas of me that were repug-
nant to girls, and Pepe was quite the opposite of that.*

CHUCK JONES, "CHUCK JONES INTERVIEWED," BY JOE ADAMSON,
THE AMERICAN ANIMATED CARTOON, ED. DANNY AND
GERALD PEARY (NEW YORK: DUTTON, 1980), 130

Vol. 36, no. 3 (Spring 1983): 10–17.

For a long time I've been ambivalent about pornography. Off and on since early adolescence I've visited porn shops and theaters, grateful—albeit a little sheepishly—for their existence; and like many men, I would guess, I've often felt protective of pornography, at least in the more standard varieties.[1] (I know nothing at all about the child porn trade which, judging from news articles, is flourishing: I've never seen a child in an arcade film or videotape or in a film in a porn moviehouse; and though I've heard that many porn films involve women being tortured, I don't remember ever coming in contact with such material, except in Bonnie Klein's *Not a Love Story*, a film polemic/documentary on the nature and impact of porn films.) On the other hand, I've long felt and, in a small way, been supportive of the struggle for equality and self-determination for women; as a result, the consistent concern of feminist women about the exploitation and brutalization of the female in pornography has gnawed at my conscience. The frequent contempt of intelligent people for those who "need" pornographic materials has always functioned to keep me quiet about my real feelings, but a screening of *Not a Love Story* and a series of recent responses to it—most notably the B. Ruby Rich review quoted above—have emboldened me to assess my attitudes.

As I watched *Not a Love Story*, the film's fundamental assumption seemed very familiar: pornography is a reflection of a male-dominated culture in which women's bodies are exploited for the purpose of providing pleasure to males by dramatizing sexual fantasies which themselves imply a reconfirmation of male dominance. And while one part of my mind accepted this seemingly self-evident assumption, at a deeper level I felt resistant. The pornographic films and videotapes I've seen at theaters and in arcades *are* full of narratives in which women not only do what men want and allow men to do what they want, but effusively claim to love this particular sexual balance of power. Yet, given that males dominate in the culture, why would they pay to see sexual fantasies of male domination? Wouldn't one expect fantasy material to reveal the opposite of the status quo? Further, if going to porn films or arcades were emblematic of male power, one might expect that the experience would be characterized by an easy confidence reflective of macho security.

For me, however—and, I'm guessing, for many men who have visited porn arcades or film houses—these periodic visits are always minor traumas. While there is an erotic excitement involved in the decision to attend and in the experience itself, this is mixed with considerable amounts of fear and embarrassment. From the instant my car is carrying me toward pornography, I feel painfully visible, as if everyone who sees me knows from my expression, my body language, whatever, precisely where I'm going. The walk from the car to the door—and later, from the door to the car—is especially difficult: will someone drive by and see me? This fear of being seen has, in my case at least (as far as I can tell), less to do with guilt than with a fear of being misunderstood. Even though the frequency of my experiences with pornography has nothing at all to do with the success of my sex life—I'm at least as likely to visit a porn arcade when I'm sexually active as when I'm lonely and horny—I always feel the power of the social stigma against such experiences. Unless the people who see me have been in my situation, I'm sure they'll deduce that my visit to the arcade reflects my inadequacy or some inadequacy in the person I'm living with, that either I "can't get any" or I'm not satisfied with what I can get. As a result, I try to look at ease during the walk to the door: any evident discomfiture on my part, I warn myself, will only fuel whatever laughter my presence has provoked.

Once inside an arcade or a theater, this anxiety about being seen continues, though with a different slant: will I run smack into someone I know? Of course, anyone I would run into would be unlikely to misunderstand the meaning of my presence; but such a meeting would interfere with what seems to me the most fundamental dimension of going to a porn arcade or moviehouse: the desire for privacy and anonymity. Meeting someone I know would, I assume (this has never happened to me), force us to join together in the phony macho pose of pretending that our interest in the pornographic materials around us is largely a matter of detached humor, that we've come for a few laughs.

The concern for privacy determines the nature of the interaction of the men (I've seen women at porn theaters, but never in porn arcades) involved with porn. Of course, theaters are constructed so as to impede the interactions of members of the audience (I always feel a pressure not to look at people on my way out), but the structure of arcades makes some interaction between strangers almost inevitable. In retrospect, the nature and apparent meaning of this interaction always seems rather poignant. Because of our shared embarrassment about being in this place together and, perhaps, because of our awareness that our presence is a sign of an erotic impatience our casual stances belie—for whatever reason, the men I've seen in porn arcades seem to allow themselves a detached gentleness with each other. For my part—and, judging from my limited observation, I'd guess my experience is pretty standard—I move in an unthreatening way; I am careful not to make eye contact with anyone. When eye contact is unavoidable, I put my mind on erase. When I walk out of a porn arcade, I take with me no functional memory at all of the particular faces I saw there, though each visit has confirmed my feeling that in general the faces are those of quiet middle-class men pretty much like me.

I've always assumed that, essentially, those of us who co-exist with each other for a few minutes in porn theaters or arcades share the embarrassing awareness that we're there for the same thing: to look for a while at forbidden sexual imagery which excites us and, finally, to masturbate. In my experience, the masturbation itself seems less important as an experience than as a way of releasing the excitement created by the imagery. Even though most men seem to look rigorously frontward in porn theaters and even though porn arcade booths are designed so as to provide enough security for masturbation, the idea of being seen masturbating has always seemed so frightening to me (and, I assume, to others: I've never seen or heard anyone masturbate in an arcade) that I've never felt free to get deeply involved in the act the way I can when I have real privacy. Usually at a porn arcade I keep myself from masturbating for ten or twenty minutes, until I'm ready to leave; the act itself rarely takes more than fifteen or thirty seconds, and as soon as it's over, I'm on my way to my car. I move quickly because, often, despite my confidence that the other men I see have much the same experience I do, I leave terrified that someone will enter the booth I've just left, see the semen on the floor—impossible in the dimly lit booths—and yell after me. I've never masturbated in a theater (though on rare occasions I've seen others do so), but only later, outside the theater, in the privacy of a car or a men's room.

Since the reason for braving the kinesic complexity of the porn environment is exposure to the pornographic materials themselves, it's important to consider what these materials really are. Over the years I've developed what I hope is a generally accurate sense of the motifs that dominate standard porn fare directed at heterosexual men; and I've thought a good deal about why these particular motifs seem so pervasive. I'm speaking of "motifs" here rather than of "films" because the films seem centered (both in terms of the time allocated to specific imagery and in terms of the viewing gaze) on specific configurations, "acts." Even though there's always a skeletal narrative, this is so obviously a function of the need to create a context for the motifs, that one doesn't need to pay particular attention to it—except insofar as it raises the adrenaline by slightly withholding the awaited imagery.[2] The empty nature of the porn narratives is confirmed by the booths, which, in my experience, have all presented Super-8 films in loops, usually two or three films to a loop. Since each quarter, or whatever the fee is, buys only 30 seconds or so of film (then the film stops until another quarter is deposited), one doesn't automatically see a film from start to finish. The motif structure is also reconfirmed by the announcements on booth doors of the particular acts which are featured in particular booths.[3]

For me the obvious amateurishness of the production values, the acting, and the writing has generally added to the titillating mood, since what the characters do to and with each other is all the more outrageous *because* it's so patently done for the camera. In fact, some acts appear so uncomfortable and pleasureless for the actors that the camera's presence seems the only possible explanation. Our consciousness of the films as films is maintained by the camera angles, the length of shots, the lighting, all of which are usually (or at least this is how I remember them) overtly functional, providing a clear view of the sex acts between the actors and between their close-up genitals. In most films "aesthetics" are rigorously avoided in service of clarity.[4]

The motifs themselves have generally involved a relatively limited number of sexual interactions. Sexual intercourse in a variety of poses is nearly inevitable, of course, but it's rarely the clincher in a film. Judging from my limited experience, blow jobs (especially ending in ejaculation into the woman's mouth or on her face) and anal intercourse seem the present-day favorites. Sometimes they involve more than a pair of partners (two men have intercourse—one vaginally, one anally—with one woman; two women provide a blow job to one man; a woman gives a blow job to one man while another has intercourse with her) and/or a mixture of ethnic backgrounds. While the women involved seem to mirror conventional notions of attractiveness, the men are frequently quite average-looking: nearly any man will do, apparently, so long as he has a large erection.

No doubt the psychology of wanting to view sexual performances on a movie screen is complex, but over the years I've been aware of two general functions of the experience: one of these involves its "educational" value, the other its value as psychic release. When I was younger, my interest was in seeing just what the female body looked like and how it moved. Sexuality, as I experienced it as an adolescent, was something that usually occurred in the dark, in enclosed spaces, and under the pressure of time. Often I was more engrossed in the issue of "how far I was going to be able to go" than with really seeing and understanding what I was doing. In those days (the fifties) there were no porn films or arcades, but newsstands were beginning to stock *Playboy*, *Nugget*, and a variety of other girlie magazines; and my hunger to see women's bodies—and to be able to examine them without the embarrassment of being observed by the women—resulted in periodic thefts of magazines. These thefts were serious extralegal transgressions to me; I was terrified of being caught, arrested, and made an example of, until I developed the courage to try buying magazines from drugstore owners. These early magazines seemed a godsend to me, and they provided the stimulation for countless hours of masturbation. But they were also carefully censored: the focus was on breasts, though there were frequent side views of demurely posed buttocks; and all vestiges of pubic hair were, for some strange reason, erased from the photographs. (I didn't realize this until I was 17 and had the shock of my life during a heavy petting session.) One can certainly imagine a culture, like that of the Polynesians, in which the bodies of members of the opposite sex would not be visual mysteries, where we could be at ease with seeing each other. But though that has never been the case here, men continue to grow up under considerable pressure to know "how to handle" women sexually: we're supposed to know what's where and how it works. Looking at girlie magazines may seem (and be) a callous manipulation of female bodies, but its function was never callous for me. I was powerfully drawn to women, but my complete ignorance of them frightened me; the magazines were like a nightlight: they allowed me to know a little more than I otherwise would have and they allowed me the fantasy (I always knew it was an illusion) that I'd "know what to do" the next time I got to see and touch a flesh and-blood-woman.

The functioning of pornographic imagery as a means of allowing men to examine the bodies of the opposite sex seems an important aspect of porn films and videotapes, which are full of extreme close-ups of cocks thrusting into cunts. The ludicrous lack of romance in such imagery is often mentioned in condemnations of pornography, but the function seems more scientific than romantic, more like Muybridge's motion studies than a Hollywood love story. And it seems to me that the value of this visual option continues to be defensible, at least in a limited sense, given this society's pervasive marketing of rigidly defined standards of attractiveness. For one thing, direct sexual experience with a conventionally attractive woman is, or seems, out of the question for many men; and yet it's come to be one of the definers of a life worth living. Pornography provides a compromise by making visual knowledge of such an experience a possibility. Secondly, many men feel supportive enough of women to take them seriously when they complain about the invasion of privacy implicit in the unprovoked leers and comments they continue to endure on the street. I'll go to considerable lengths to avoid intruding in this way, but I have to fight the urge to stare all the time. Some of the popularity of pornography even among men who consider themselves feminists may be a function of its capacity to provide a form of unintrusive leering.

I've become conscious of a second aspect of this first function of pornographic materials, the "educational" function, during the past few years. Feminists have made us aware of the politics of staring at women, but the culture at large—particularly the culture as evident in the commercial sphere—tells us constantly that looking at women is what men are supposed to do. Looking at other men continues to be another matter entirely. Of course, spectator sports, and other forms of physical performance, allow for almost unlimited examination of how bodies function, but knowledge of the naked male body continues to be a tricky matter for heterosexual men. In conventional American life men are probably naked together more often than women: in shower rooms, most obviously. And yet, as is true in porn arcades, the kinesics of the interaction between men in such places are very precisely controlled. Men certainly don't feel free to look at other men; our lives are full of stories about how one guy catches another looking at him and punches him out. Never mind that I've never witnessed such an incident: a taboo is at stake, and potential embarrassment, if not danger, seems to hover on the edge of it. This situation is complicated further by the fact that even if men felt free to look carefully at each other in shower rooms, or wherever, a crucial element of the male body—how it functions during sexual activity—would remain a mystery. Of course, I know what my own erection looks like, but so much stress is placed on the nature of erections that it's difficult not to wonder what the erections of other men look like (and how mine looks in comparison).

One of the things that distinguishes the pornographic materials available in porn movies and arcades from what is available on local newsstands—and thus, implicitly, one of the things that accounts for the size of the hardcore porn market—is the pervasive presence of erections. In fact, to a considerable extent theater and arcade porn films are about erections. The standard anti-porn response to this is to see the porn film phallus as a combined battering ram/totem which encapsulates the male drive for power. And given the characterizations of the vain strutting men on the other ends of these frequently awesome shafts, such an interpretation seems almost inevitable. And yet, for me the pervasiveness of erect penises in porn has at least as much to do with simple curiosity. The darkness of porn houses and the privacy of arcade booths allow one to see erections close-up. The presence of women has its own power, but in this particular context one of the primary functions of the female presence is to serve as a sign—to others and to oneself—that looking at erections, even finding them sexy, does not mean that the viewer defines himself as a homosexual.

A second function of the pornographic experience involves the exact converse of a number of cultural attitudes which feminists have often seen as subtly detrimental to women. Most people now recognize that the constant attention to the "beauty" of the female body, which has been so pervasive in the arts and in commerce during recent centuries, may involve more than a respect and love for women—that it may be a tactic for keeping them more involved with how they look (and to a considerable extent, with pleasing men) than with what they do, or can learn to do. Further, the emphasis on a pristine ideal of beauty, as feminists have often pointed out, has frequently alienated women from their own bodies: real odors, secretions, processes have frequently been seen as contradictory of the Beauty of Womanhood. On the other hand, the same cultural history which has defined women as Beautiful has had, and to some extent continues to have, as its inevitable corollary, the Ugliness of men; women have been defined as beautiful precisely in contrast to men. Now, even if these definitions are seen as primarily beneficial to men, in the sense that not having to be concerned with appearances allows them more energy and time for attaining their goals and maintaining their access to power, I sense that the definition also creates significant problems for men, and especially in the areas of love and sex, where physical attractiveness seems of the essence. In recent years we've seen a growing acceptance of the idea that men, too, can be beautiful. The burgeoning homosexual subculture seems evidence of this, as does the popularity of body building. And yet, just as the pressure to see women as "the weaker sex" continues to be felt in a culture where millions of women dramatize the intrinsic bankruptcy of that notion, many men—I'd guess most men—continue to feel insecure about the attractiveness of their bodies.

Perhaps the most obvious aspect of male sexual functioning which has been conditioned by negative assumptions about male attractiveness is ejaculation. Even among people who are comfortable with the idea that men can be beautiful, semen is often (if not usually) seen as disgusting. Is it an accident that many of the substances that our culture considers particularly revolting—raw egg, snot . . . —share with semen a general texture and look? Accidental or not, I've heard and read such comparisons all my life. I remember the shock and fear that followed my first orgasm. Without knowing it, I had been masturbating in the attic of my aunt's house where I had discovered a pile of girlie magazines. The unexpected orgasm was astonishing and thrilling, but at the end of it, I discovered, to my shock, that my shirt and the magazine were covered with a substance I hadn't known existed. I cleaned myself up (even at that early point I was clear that for my relatives—especially for my mother and my aunt—the mysterious substance would be seen as a form of dirtiness), and I spent the remainder of the day walking around with my arms and hands in odd configurations in front of my shirt in the hope of avoiding detection. From that time on, I was alert to the fact that every indulgence of my desire for sex would produce evidence the discovery of which, I was sure, could be humiliating.

Now I'm well aware that to accept a mucus-like substance that comes out of one's own body is a different matter than accepting such a substance from another's body. I not only understand but can also empathize with the revulsion of many women to semen. Nevertheless, I suspect it creates the same problems for many men as the widespread squeamishness about menstruation has caused women. There are instances of course—in the midst of passion—where semen is temporarily accepted, even enjoyed by women, but these moments tend to be memorable exceptions. For the most part, even between people who love each other, the presence of semen is at best a necessary evil. Recently I mentioned this idea to a woman friend, who has had sex with many men and is proud of it, after she had indicated her contempt for men who were turned off by women's smells and secretions. "I think it depends on who you're with," she said. "If you care about the person, there's nothing disgusting about his semen." A few seconds later she added, "But who has to lie in it?" and laughed. Many women are concerned about the danger of "bleeding through" during menstruation, presumably because they feel, or fear that men feel, that menstrual secretions make them sexually undesirable; and dozens of products have been marketed to protect against such an occurrence. I feel a similar concern about semen, and must face a very special irony: the fact that it surfaces precisely at the moment of my most complete sexual abandon.

To me, the nature and function of pornography have always seemed understandable as a way for men to periodically deal with the cultural context which mitigates against their full acceptance of themselves as sexual beings. The fantasies men pay to experience in porn arcade booths and movie houses may ostensibly appear to be predicated on the brutalization of women. But from a male point of view, the desire is not to see women harmed, but to momentarily identify with men who—despite their personal unattractiveness by conventional cultural definitions, despite the unwieldy size of their erections, and despite their aggressiveness with their semen—are adored by the women they encounter sexually. Only in pornography will the fantasy woman demonstrate aggressive acceptance when a man ejaculates on her face. As embarrassingly abhorrent as it always strikes me, the hostility toward women which usually seems to hover around the edges of conventional film pornography (in the frequently arrogant, presumptive manner the male characters exhibit, for example) and which is a primary subject matter in some films, seems to be a more aggressive way of dealing with the same issues. In these instances the fantasy is in punishing resistant women for their revulsion. Of course, the punishments—usually one form or another of rape—often end with the fantasy woman's discovery of an insatiable hunger for whatever has been done to her. This frequent turnabout appears to be nothing more than a reconfirmation of the stupid, brutal myth that women ask to be raped or enjoy being raped, but—as sadly ironic as this seems—it could also be seen as evidence that, in the final analysis, men don't mean harm to women, or don't wish to mean harm to women: their fantasy is the acceptance of their own biological nature by women.[5] I've always assumed that porn and rape *are* part of the same general problem, though I've always felt it more likely that porn offers an outlet for some of the anger engendered by men's feelings of sensual/aesthetic inferiority, than that it serves as a fuel for further anger. But I'm only speaking from my own experience. I've rarely spoken frankly about such matters with men who use porn.

To try to understand the reasons for the huge business of making and marketing pornographic movies is not necessarily to justify the practice. One can only hope for increasingly definitive studies of how porn functions and what its effects are.[6] But, however one describes the complex historical factors which have brought us to our present situation, the fact remains that in our culture men and women frequently feel alienated from their own bodies and from each other. Pornography is a function of this alienation, and I can't imagine it disappearing until we have come to see ourselves and each other differently. We don't choose the bodies we are born with; natural selection, or God—or whatever—takes care of that for us. And though we can't change the fact of our difference (and regardless of whether we choose to accept and enjoy this difference by being passionate about our own or the opposite sex, or both), surely we can learn to be mutually supportive about our bodies. My guess is that porn is a symptom not so much of a sexual need, but of a need for self-acceptance and respect. If we can come to terms with that need, as it relates to both sexes, my guess is that porn will disappear.

1. During my twenties and early thirties I would guess I went to porn films and/or arcades half a dozen times a year. In the past few years (I'm 40) I've gone less frequently; it probably works out to two or three times a year at most. I assume that some men frequent such places, while others go once or twice in a lifetime. I have no information on how often or seldom an "average" man pays to see pornography. I've not been conscious of specific changes in the situations presented in the films or the attitudes which are evident in them. I assume there has been some evolution in this regard, but my experiences have been too sporadic (and too surrounded by personal anxieties) for me to be able to formulate useful conclusions about this evolution.

2. In this sense, the porn narratives seem rather similar to those of Georges Méliès's films (the acting is roughly comparable, too!).

3. Once I've decided to go to a porn theater, I go immediately, without checking to see when the movies begin or end; as often as not, I arrive in the middle of a film. (This is true only when the theater in question runs shows continuously; when a theater runs only one or two shows a day, I usually postpone a decision about going until just long enough before the beginning of the show so that the decision can be followed by immediate action.) With very rare exceptions, I've always left before a show is over; after one film has led up to and past its most stimulating motifs, I've waited only long enough to calm down and not leave the theater with a visible erection. I've never sat all the way through a double feature of porn films.

4. Recent "trash" and "punk" films—John Waters' *Multiple Maniacs, Pink Flamingos, Female Trouble, Desperate Living;* Beth and Scott B's *G-Man;* Robert Ruot's *Dr. Faustus' Foot Fetish,* for example—have exploited a similar sense of aggressive amateurishness. In fact, since *G-Man* and *Dr. Faustus' Foot Fetish* are Super-8 films, they bring with them something of the feel of Super-8 porn loops.

5.   The frequency of anal sex in porn films seems to confute this, at least if one assumes that anal sex is annoying and painful for most, or many, women. Yet, a decision not to press for fulfillment of such a desire because its fulfillment will cause pain doesn't necessarily eliminate the desire. I would guess that for many men the anal sex in porn films functions as a way of giving harmless vent to a desire they've decided not to pressure the real women in their lives about (harmless, that is, unless one assumes the women in the films feel they are being harmed, something I have no information about).

6.   One recent attempt to assess porn's effects is Dolf Zillmann and Jennings Bryant's "Pornography, Sexual Callousness, and the Trivialization of Rape," *Journal of Communication* (Autumn 1982). Unfortunately, this study's central finding—"our investigation focused on sexual callousness toward women, demonstrating that massive exposure to standard pornographic materials devoid of coercion and aggression seemed to promote . . . callousness (in particular, the trivialization of rape) . . ."—is based on testing procedures and supported by assumptions which raise nagging questions. The study's conclusions are based on a test of the impact of pornography on students exposed in groups, in a college setting, to "massive," "intermediate," and "no" amounts of conventional, nonviolent pornographic film. But in real life, porn films are seen in a very particular environment, at least in most instances I know of: in a public/private context outside the circle of one's friends and family, in places one is embarrassed about going into, and often in tiny toilet-like stalls. Wouldn't the meaning and impact of porn films be different given so different a context? Was there some reason for limiting those tested to students, and in particular to undergraduates "at a large eastern university"? Were these people users of pornography previously? What was their motivation for participating in such an experiment?

Bryant and Zillmann face some of the possible implications of their experimental procedures for their results, but they assume that, at most, students might have guessed the researchers were attempting to legitimize pornography and therefore would have distorted answers in the direction of a general social attitude which, the researchers contend, is strongly supportive of pornography, and implicitly legitimizes it by giving it legal status. My sense of the general attitude toward porn is the opposite of theirs. Certainly the legality of pornography doesn't prove that society approves of it: picking one's nose is legal, but hardly acceptable in society's eyes. My guess is that most people (including many or most of those who use porn and/or are supportive of its being available publicly to people of legal age) agree that porn is creepy and disgusting. And most people nowadays are well aware of the frequent conjecture that exposure to porn is an incentive to rape; even if we're dubious about the assumption of cause/effect in this instance, the contention creates concern. If the students tested were relatively new to porn, their massive exposure must have come as something of a shock, and if they were jolted—particularly by seeing such imagery in an institutional, unprivate context—might not some students have answered the rape questions posed later as a means of acceding to the widely held assumption that people who see porn films will be motivated by them to rape women?

LEO BRAUDY

THE SACRAMENTS OF GENRE

Coppola, DePalma, Scorsese

Vol. 39, no. 3 (Spring 1986): 17–28.

"An aesthetic of reality," André Bazin called the Italian neorealist films of the immediate postwar period, and the description has stuck. Whatever the changes in style and approach that directors like Rossellini, DeSica, Antonioni, and Fellini made later in their careers, there is still a critical tendency to root them in a film-making that stayed close to the stuff of everyday life. By respecting the integrity of the actors and objects within its gaze, it sought not to turn them into something thematic or symbolic, but to maintain their separateness and their unalloyed reality—if we take "reality" to mean that which is constantly evading our final interpretation and our subordination of it to our interpretive systems.

The now-aging younger generation of Italian-American film-makers—in which I include Francis Ford Coppola, Brian DePalma, and Martin Scorsese—at first glance could hardly be more different from the generation of neorealists in their style and preoccupations. Most striking is their commitment to genre formats in plot and style, an indication of their rootedness in an American rather than a European tradition of film-making. Genre has always been the prime seedbed of American films. The neorealists and the European school in general, with the great exceptions of the early works of the French New Wave and the more recent New German cinema, have usually treated the individual film as a work situated in the history of art, or in the eternity of nature, while even in the most ambitious as well as the most perfunctory American films it is the pressure of the history of film displayed in genre form that has been the most crucial factor. Neorealism particularly, at least in Bazin's account of it, is explicitly presented as a statement of freedom against the stylization associated with expressionist film (as part of an attack on German politics and Nazism as well). This kind of film, Bazin virtually argues, exhibits the "true" aesthetic of the medium, while the stylized sets, directorial control, broad-gesture acting, and melodramatic plots of film expressionism are a falsification of its essential nature.[1]

In such an argument, the films of Coppola, DePalma, and Scorsese, with exceptions I'll note later, almost entirely wind up on the side of the tradition that Bazin believes neorealism is attacking. They are fascinated with artifice—with genre plots, characters, and motifs that delve into the roots of popular forms—as well as with stylized sets, lighting, and an expressionist use of color that convey the emotions of the characters and the situations rather than the "reality" of the objects. In contrast to the neorealist and Soviet use of nonprofessional actors to energize the film with a "realistic" sense of character, these directors focus on both the self-stylized character and the character whose psyche film and popular culture has taken over—characters for whom all experience must be mediated by the shapes of film artifice. Instead of imitating the dynamic reticence of the ideal neorealist director, who lets reality unfold before his camera, these directors are drawn to the implications of directorial imposition and tyranny: the director as aesthetic master of his material, shaping it to his will. Rather than Renoir or Rossellini, Antonioni or DeSica, their heroes are the great independent stylists: Welles for Coppola, Hitchcock for DePalma, while Scorsese invokes the eccentric combination of Michael Powell and Sam Fuller.

Yet of course the neorealist ideal against which I am measuring the deviations of this trio of Italian-American directors who have become so prominent in the seventies and eighties is itself a myth. If there ever was a neorealist consensus, it was in the eye of the wishful-thinking observer Bazin. The operatic structures of Visconti and the directorial flamboyance of Fellini obviously also play paterfamilias to *The Godfather* and *New York, New York,* where realism is heightened rather than negated. Similarly, Bazin's too easy equation of neorealism and liberation on the one hand and totalitarianism and expressionist distortion on the other is belied by the fact that so many of the directors who came to prominence after World War II received their technical training and a certain amount of their aesthetic underpinning in Mussolini's documentary film office.[2] In fact, the neorealist commitment to "an aesthetic of reality" was never so wholeheartedly polemical as Bazin argues. Rossellini is of course considered to be the one who strayed least from the fold, descending into neither Felliniesque bravura, Viscontian theatricality, nor Antonionian modernism. But from the first Rossellini himself problematized the "reality" he was observing with calculatedly stylized effects. I mention just one example here: the torture scene in *Open City,* set in a room that, with total spatial illogic and psychic logic, is right next door to the main office of the Nazi chief as well as to the clubroom of his dissipated pleasures. Such a juxtaposition creates a rift in the documentary discourse (with its assumption that what is observed is truly happening) and makes us aware instead of the perceptual variations on "reality" through which the film is constructed. It is an incantatory moment, a mode of suprarealistic perception that I would like to call a sacramentalizing of the real, not so that it be worshipped but so that its spiritual essence, whether diabolical or holy, inflect what is otherwise a discrete collection of objects in space. Such a moment in Rossellini's early films connects them with preoccupations that appear with more elaboration later, for example, in his analysis of the signs of material status in *The Rise of Louis XIV*, or the signs of personal self-definition in such seemingly different films as *The Little Flowers of St. Francis* and *General Della Rovere*. The commerce between such moments of psychological or expressionist eruption and their surrounding documentary format can suggest as well a closer lineage between, say, Rossellini's generation of neorealists and the mingling of documentary and expressionism in Scorsese (*Raging Bull, King of Comedy*) as well as the historical melodrama of Coppola's *Godfather*.

But my purpose here is less to argue (except by suggestion) the links to an older generation of Italian film-makers than to explore the different ways Coppola, DePalma, and Scorsese adapt to the special situation of the American film what I would like metaphorically to call a Catholic way of regarding the visible world. In varying biographical degrees, they come to film, I would argue, with a specially honed sense of (1) the importance of ritual narratives, (2) the significance of ritual objects, and (3) the conferral of ritual status. Unlike the Protestant (and often Jewish) denigration of visual materiality in favor of verbal mystery, such directors mine the transcendental potential within the visual world. Objects, people, places, and stories are irradiated by the meaning from within, which as directors they seek to unlock. Sometimes the meaning, as in the work of another Catholic director, Hitchcock, is beyond the visual. But it is still linked to an effort to make visual style a mode of moral exploration, an almost priestly urge to reeducate the audience in the timelessness of ritual stories, along with the attitudes necessary for their reinterpretations.

This process takes place, as I have said, within an American film context that has always stressed the armature of genre and of film history as the presupposition of every film. It is an aesthetic approach enhanced of course by the long-lived existence of a studio system. But even with the end of the studio system (or especially with its end), we find professed anti-Hollywoodians like Coppola and DePalma seeking to set up their own version of Hollywood and in essence beating Hollywood at its own genre game. All three of them, along with most other American film-makers of their generation, received their technical training at the same time that the *auteur* theory of film was a force of radical upending of the official system of value. "No more European films of the grand style and no more Hollywood films of pretension" was the battlecry. The great American director would be defined instead as a man of personal style and vision, often working in the lowliest ranks of the studio, turning out masterpieces of tension between studio demands and personal urge. "Art" here was not the

Documentary
expressionism:
Raging Bull

grand assertion of the European artist with his tradition of craft and guild connection on the one side and masterpieces and originality on the other. *Auteur* "art" came instead from a subversive use of the paraphernalia of studio complacency to articulate a personal vision.

All three of these directors did some or a good deal of their journeyman work with that institutionalized representative of the Hollywood anti-system, Roger Corman, whose stock-in-trade was taking marginal film genres like horror or the biker films and mixing them into an almost surreal concoction of flash and action. In the midst of Hollywood, Corman represented a knowing "bad taste" that simultaneously mocked Hollywood's own upscale liberal pieties even while it studiously learned all its techniques. Corman produced Coppola's first film, *Dementia 13,* Scorsese's first substantial feature, *Boxcar Bertha*, and released DePalma's *Sisters;* he also offered a place where talented film-school graduates like George Lucas, Steven Spielberg, and Jonathan Demme could learn their craft at low pay. The previous Hollywood generations of directors had come from live television (Lumet, Frankenheimer, Penn) or filmed television (Altman, Pollack) with its symbiotic relation to

New York theater (especially in the days of the blacklist). This new generation came out of the film schools—USC, UCLA, and NYU. If the California contingent of Lucas, Spielberg, and Coppola were more oriented to Hollywood genres and studio expertise, it came in part naturally from the prejudices of their instruction, which stressed the need to fit in, if not with the Hollywood system, then with the Hollywood way of doing things—melodramatic plots and technically advanced visual style. If the New York contingent of DePalma and Scorsese was more dubious about the ultimate uses of technical expertise and often included a questioning of their own precedures, it came naturally from their nurturing in the *cinéma vérité* documentary world of New York in the fifties and sixties, with its constant arguments over the nature of cinematic truth and its New Wave city-film ambience of street-theater strutting.

But I must return from this entire generation of new directors to Coppola, DePalma, and Scorsese in particular because I believe their Catholic upbringing, literally or metaphorically, makes them the most salient film-makers of that group, heightening a self-consciousness about all aspects of film-making that is already inherent in the historical-aesthetic moment in which these young directors began to work. Each of the three emphasizes a different aspect of film self-consciousness as his own. In Coppola it is the sense of genre, which for him is attached to a feeling for family situations and family betrayals, much as the latest genre examples turn against the past in the name of bringing that past to some higher perfection. Genre for Coppola is like the rituals of religion. But in the family context those rituals are poisoned by the shadows of death and ambition, just as the christening of Michael Corleone's child in *Godfather II* is intercut with the bloodbath wave of assassinations he has ordered. The old must die so that the young can move into their places, as Brando, sinking into the garden while making faces, gives way to Pacino and DeNiro, his inheritors and his younger selves. Fred Astaire in Coppola's *Finian's Rainbow* may still spryly head off across the fields, but his day is clearly over, and like Martin Sheen contemplating Brando's Kurtz in *Apocalypse Now*, it seems easier to kill him off than to fathom his meaning. In *Godfather II* Michael the inheritor is a cold avenger, whose sword turns finally upon those he has vowed to preserve. Hymie Roth, the old Jewish gangster, may be defeated, but by the end the family has disappeared as well and Michael sits alone, while the lost voices of Sonny and Fredo and Kay echo in the empty room.

I have been recounting those elements in Coppola's films that lend themselves to an allegorical reading of his own relation to Hollywood and his past masters: a deep homage along with a simultaneous effort to replace them with his own aesthetic family—his father the composer, his sister the actress, and of course all his friends and coworkers at the (now defunct) American Zoetrope. Always there is a dream of camaraderie, and invariably that dream turns sour, often with a sentimental heaviness, for example in *The Outsiders,* where the bad boy Matt Dillon maintains his friendship with the younger boys to the point of sacrificing himself in a needless theatrical gesture. Much more than either Scorsese or DePalma, Coppola is committed to storytelling and narrative of an older sort, in accord with his commitment to genre and family ritual as structures of feeling that he wishes would still retain their ability to compel belief. But Coppola's commitment is undermined by his general unwillingness to question his own role as the director and *Wunderkind* who will pull all this together and make it work. Orson Welles is his progenitor and Wellesian control is really his ideal. But he lacks Welles's self-critical fascination with theatrical windbags and greedy fakes. In *Godfather II* Michael Corleone has clearly lost all the vitality of the past even as he has superseded it in efficiency and ruthlessness. Like Coppola's own grand projects that never quite work out—*Apocalypse Now* and *One From the Heart*—the recreation of past stories in order to squeeze them of all their possible meaning never quite gets to the core that gives them life. Too often they remain only stories, and even at his best Coppola is more a virtuoso stager of their gestures than an expounder of their meanings. *Finian's Rainbow* effectively ends one major musical tradition in film; *Godfather II* systematically dismembers and calls into question every feeling and value that animated *Godfather I; Apocalypse Now* attempts to say the final word on the whole history of European and American colonialism; *The Outsiders* will be the ultimate "bad kids are really good kids" movie, etc., etc. Instead of being energized by his self-consciousness, Coppola too often is swamped by it. His detachment from his tradition leads not to analysis so much as to compendium.

The only film that Coppola made for the short-lived Director's Company (made up of himself, Peter Bogdanovich, and William Friedkin) is *The Conversation,* a smaller film than most of his, and one that intriguingly situates Coppola in relation to the earlier generation of Italian directors, as well as to Brian DePalma. Even though, as it has often been noted, *The Conversation* owes an enormous amount to the editing and constructive skills of Walter Murch, I will treat it as connected to Coppola's own interests because, as Michael Pye and Linda Myles point out, it proceeds directly out of an intellectual context at Zoetrope where Antonioni's *Blow-up* was constantly being discussed as a key to all the most intriguing questions about the film-making process and the meaning of film that the young film-makers were setting about to explore.[3]

Blow-up was more appealing to the self-conscious young film-makers than any of Antonioni's earlier films because its theme is specifically the problematics of vision, particularly as seeing is mediated by the camera. Within a mystery plot featuring a Hitchcock-style innocent bystander who catches a glimpse

Marlon Brando
as the Godfather

of a crime, Antonioni explores similarly Hitchcockian themes of moral entrapment, in which the bystander becomes culpable through his particular way of seeing and interpreting the world. Like those of Jeff in *Rear Window*, the flaws of Antonioni's Thomas come specifically from the impulses that animate his career as a photographer. Moodily alienated from fashion photography, in which he is clearly the master over fawning, posturing women, he seeks some moral exoneration by frequenting flophouses and surreptitiously taking pictures of the bums and outcasts who are their inhabitants. By this ambiguous penance he delves into what he considers to be the "truth" of life. And he shows the photos to his agent as part of plans for a new book that will supposedly allow him to be seen as a "serious" photographer.

With his unquestioned commitment to the morality of his own perspective and style of vision, Thomas is fair game for the events that follow. By accident, he photographs what seems to be a crime and then continues to blow up his photograph in search of the elusive, consummating detail that will reveal the truth—a detail needless to say that becomes more evanescent the closer he comes to it. In *Rear Window* the newspaper photographer Jeff is drawn into the lives of the people he thinks he observes with detachment. The crucial emblem of his involvement is his discovery that he has witnessed a murder without knowing it. But there is no problem of sight for Hitchcock except for its moral valence. You have to pay for seeing; you can't be detached. In *Blow-up*, on the other hand, seeing is itself called into question, along with the minute amassing of facts that purport to lead to a solution. Unlike Hitchcock's, Antonioni's narrative does not follow even a pseudo-causal unfolding. Its story is more like a collage, a cubistic refocusing on the protagonist, who, like characters in Antonioni's earlier films, only sporadically follows his first goal. Hitchcock minimized the lost, strayed, or stolen object that was the *pretext* for so many of his plots by calling it the MacGuffin. But it nevertheless existed. In *Blow-up* the photographer tries to turn the pretext into a text and fails miserably.

Yet, although Antonioni goes beyond Hitchcock in questioning the sufficient reality of the visible world, he shares Hitchcock's final unwillingness to demystify the visual image and the director's privilege of presenting it. Thomas the photographer is not, I think, a surrogate for the director because *Blow-up* specifically characterizes the photograph as a still picture and so necessarily inferior to the cinematic way of seeing the world. By satirizing the fashion photographer's pictures of the down-and-out in a mockery of the naive neorealism that dwells only on the surfaces of reality, *Blow-up* especially implies that the photographic fetishizing of the visible is less "insightful" than that of film. Antonioni's perspective—*as director*—resembles a modernism of the Flaubertian and Joycean sort; God pares his fingernails while his characters squirm in their limited universe of immediacy. It keeps intact one of the most basic assumptions of film: that the directorial perspective is privileged, unquestioned, and almost by definition unquestionable. Hitchcock varies this assumption by making the audience, like himself and his characters, complicit in the strange goings on because of their own personal darknesses. But still it is the director who retains the edge of authority sufficient to demonstrate to us our moral lapses and epistemological blindnesses.

To return to Coppola and *The Conversation*, however, there the crime is real and the mystery can be solved—if one interprets the data properly. But Harry Caul, the sound man, who thinks that his equipment allows him to control and understand events, is in fact manipulated by his own belief in his godlike detachment. Much more than the photographer in *Blow-up*, he is a figure of the director, especially the director whose technical mastery has been his passport to success. The crucial sentence Caul has recorded he has also misheard, misread, and he had thereby totally mistaken who are the murderers and who are the victims—encouraged by his own outsider's desire to believe that the wealthy prey tyrannically on the innocent. His moral preconceptions, his belief in himself as a controlling intelligence through his expertise, and his manipulation of his technical skills themselves all turn into the agents of his failure.[4]

Yet, despite its critique of the director's technological detachment, the fact that Coppola gave up effective creation of *The Conversation* to Murch indi-

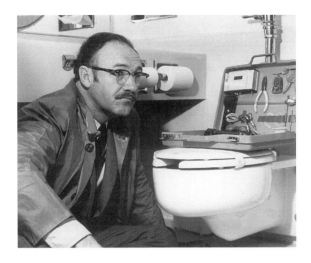

The Conversation

cates that there is some sense in which he has himself tried to escape unscathed from the film's *mea culpa*. One wonders if the maker of *One From the Heart,* with its elaborate paeans to the technology of emotion, has really watched *The Conversation* with the attention it deserves. The similarly divided aims of *Apocalypse Now,* with its simultaneous satire of American technological warfare and its exploration of dark spiritual forces in the Vietnamese jungles, follows *The Conversation* in replicating Coppola's own division between the desire to control through technique and create through imagination.[5]

I have called this interplay between the technological future and the mythic past in Coppola's films a tension, a dialectic, a Jekyll-and-Hyde split in his commitments as filmmaker and moral story-teller. But in the films of Brian DePalma, it becomes a prime theme on its own. Coppola is the genre story-teller, big daddy director, studio magnate. DePalma believes in the myth of Hollywood with a capital H and, according to all his interviews, loathes it. Yet he has become very successful making films that raise the ante in horror violence beyond even the Corman level, while mixing them with an irony about his own position as the outlaw little kid director now armed with all the technical resources and a good deal of the money of the big guys. Although brought up as a Presbyterian, DePalma acknowledges a strong Catholic cultural background. Of the three directors he is the most fascinated with significant objects, especially the knives and other instruments of cutting so favored by Hitchcock, which take their places in the rituals of the deranged. Neither Coppola nor Scorsese lavishes the attention DePalma does on a table or desk top with its array of objects that create a mood or express a personality. Objects for DePalma are close to icons, and one central icon in his films may

Holy communion in
Apocalypse Now

be the statue of St. Sebastian in Carrie's closet (not present in Stephen King's novel *Carrie*), the Saint pierced by arrows just as Carrie will by the powers of her own mind later skewer her mother with every kitchen gadget available, murdering and sanctifying her at the same time.[6]

In both *Carrie* and *The Fury,* as well as *Sisters,* DePalma celebrates the power of the mind and the imagination to move the otherwise inert objects of the world and thereby create its own reality. Telekinesis plays the same role in DePalma's films that genre references do in Coppola's and allusions to film history in Scorsese's: it invests the normal and the repetitive with the transcendent spirituality of ritual power. And DePalma particularly vests that imaginative power and strength of mind in a human being, a character, and invariably a young character at that. The young, in Coppola, can never reach the greatness of the past. They succeed primarily in turning it into a machine-like efficiency. The young in Scorsese are burdened immeasurably by their own desires for recognition and justification as dictated by movie stances and gestures from the past. But the young in DePalma have a kind of almost Wordsworthian energy that the adult world is bent on corrupting, not sexually so much as by its superior knowingness and its institutional absorption of their vitality for its own ends. The teen-age computer whiz in *Dressed to Kill* is going to use his own command of film technology to find out who killed his mother. The sound technician in *Blow-Out* is going to face down the entire police department and city government with his revelation of the criminality of a public figure. Carrie, the schlumpy teenager, falls into experience with her first menstrual period and becomes the butt of the more knowing girls around her. When she is

Non-selective destruction: *Carrie*

humiliated at the prom, she destroys everything in her path; there is no time for small distinctions about who was nice to her and who wasn't. It is personal power without an adult moral monitor, but also without the adult willingness to conciliate and beg off.

But whereas Carrie's natural magic and that of the young boy and girl in *The Fury* cause disaster to the evil (as well as a few of the good), the technical magic of the computer whiz in *Dressed to Kill*, and even more so that of the sound technician played by John Travolta in *Blow-Out*, really doesn't work. Both are more personally involved in the crime than either the photographer in *Blow-up* or the professional eavesdropper in *The Conversation*; neither has any illusions about the detachment their technology allows; both are using that technology for highly moral ends—to solve a murder or to reveal corruption. But both find their technical command to be fallible. The kid in *Dressed to Kill*, for all his minute tracking of the psychiatrist's patients, fails to understand that the killer walked out of the office rather than into it; his expertise is undermined by his youthful inability to imagine the adult depravity of the schizoid psychiatrist. The sound man in *Blow-Out*, even though he has witnessed the crime and has it on tape, is powerless to prevent the killer's erasure of his taped collection of the world's most significant sounds, just as he is powerless to prevent the murder of the prostitute who has helped him and believed in him. All he can do finally is use her scream in a horror movie—her naturalness, youth, and energy swallowed up by his own now adult and affect-less purposes. The difference here is that DePalma himself—unlike Hitchcock, unlike Antonioni, and unlike Coppola—is not left out of the indictment. The prostitute is played, in perhaps a Godardian nod, by his own wife, Nancy Allen. And there is more empathy between himself and John Travolta's sound technician than there is dissociation. Antonioni at the end of *Blow-up* makes David Hemmings disappear, blanking him out of the frame to imply his own more inclusive perspective. But Travolta at the end of *Blow-Out* resembles DePalma, sitting in the studio, opportunistically putting together a film from everything at hand.[7]

There are truths inaccessible to technique, the ending of *Blow-Out* seems to imply, and unmimeable by the seemingly lifelike creations of a spiritless technology. In DePalma, as in some Hitchcock, there is a sense that film technique, film style, the film way of seeing, can never penetrate to the real truth, which in essence is invisible. At best we have only symbols, significant objects, details, gestures, that at the crucial juncture reveal their emptiness as ways of explanation and modes of power. As Coppola hankers after the charisma of a Brando that abides technical firepower, so DePalma celebrates the psychic power from within, which technical mastery seems to corrupt or at least to stifle and to warp. He places the Hitchcockian distinction between moral control and aesthetic control further into doubt by bringing (again a bit like Godard) the film-making process itself in for some severe questioning—even of course as he glories in his manipulation of the audience as God-director.[8] In a sense DePalma's aesthetic and moral vision is closer to that of Paul Schrader, the Dutch Calvinist, than to those of Coppola and Scorsese. But his sense of sin includes neither Schrader's moral reversal of established norms nor his puritanical preoccupation with the body and its messes. Instead it is illegitimate authority, aesthetic even more than political, that is the sin for DePalma—and at his best he does not exempt his own.

Every director solves the problem of authority, on the set and in the film, in a different way. And in the unwinding of that way is his or her sense of what constitutes a coherent story. I have been characterizing the approach of Coppola as filled with an anxiety about his own authority, drawn to genre and family rituals as gardens of nostalgia amid decline; and the approach of DePalma as mocking its own authority, especially its derivation from technical mastery, even while he celebrates a psychic energy that ideally makes an otherwise inert technology actually work. In this array, Martin Scorsese is the director who most thematizes his own authority even while he explores the final and perhaps most pervasive aspect of the intersection of film with Catholicism—not ritual or significant objects, but the structure of sainthood. These distinctions are of course not hard and fast, and DePalma especially is fascinated by saint-like figures, especially the natural freak-marvels, while Coppola casts his melodrama of the generations with iconic stars like Brando. But Scorsese much more concertedly places the performer/saint/devil at the center of his films. As the first lines of *Mean Streets* insist, "You don't make up for your sins in church: you do it in the streets; you do it at home. The rest is bullshit and you know it." Like the saint in the church, the saint in the streets of Scorsese's films, so often incarnated by Robert DeNiro, makes the institutional forms into a personal order with an almost monastic fervor.

Scorsese's sense of film relies on film history and especially on the ways the film version of reality warps the consciousness of those without sufficient detachment. Saint-like in their self-sufficient isolation from the normal world, characters like Travis Bickle in *Taxi Driver* or Rupert Pupkin in *King of Comedy* dictate their own actions and responses by a world of film melodrama. They are enlarged versions of the uncle in *Mean Streets,* who is watching Fritz Lang's *The Big Heat* almost for hints on how to be a gangster, while Johnny Boy, the DeNiro character, is outside being shot. Less willing even than Rossellini to separate the natural world from his perception of it, Scorsese places his characters at the center of his films, and the look of the film radiates out from them, just as their moral conceptions of reality and their self-constructions come from the films they have already seen. Like Rossellini, Scorsese is interested in the figure of the saint as a character who moves beyond "realistic" norms, transfiguring his marginality into a kind of transcendence. The extraordinary calm of the Franciscan emissary in *The Little Flowers of St. Francis* while he is being brutalized by the bandits embodies a divine spirituality that can subsume earthly violence. In the much more pervasively violent films of Scorsese (who first wanted to be a priest because his asthma prevented him from being a gangster), the stylization of the visual form becomes a kind of skin over the eruptions within, as if to demonstrate how much chaos the rituals of seeing and story-telling can actually subdue. In a certain sense, one can thus place Scorsese in a European line that stretches from de Sade to Pasolini, in which the stories of violence and death paradoxically point to the patterns of the form that contains them and the rituals by which they are distanced and turned into meaning. Like the Neapolitan paintings of Caravaggio and others, with their incessant heads of John the Baptist and Holofernes, their pin-cushion Sebastians, and their massacred Innocents, such works disrupt in order to re-establish, breach in order to heal and re-authorize.

But Scorsese, more than Coppola or DePalma (or de Sade and Pasolini, I would say), considers the formal self-questioning of his own authority and

Taxi Driver

complicity to be part of the story he tells. Perhaps, in delivering the sacrament, the individual priest has been made eternal in his role. But Scorsese, with a modern's sense of the ersatz sainthood conferred by the media, cannot stop there. In contrast with DePalma and Coppola, and even more sharply with the blithe, control-celebrating Lucas and the director-worshipping Spielberg, Scorsese continually characterizes himself in his films as an inciting force. In *Mean Streets* he is the killer who shoots DeNiro at the end; in *Taxi Driver* he is the murderous misogynist whose appearance triggers off Travis Bickle's breakdown; in *Raging Bull* he is the barely offscreen make-up man who is preparing Jake La Motta for his stage appearance reading Shakespeare; and in *King of Comedy,* he is the a.d. who mockingly tells Rupert to ask the director if he really wants to know what's going on.

Interestingly enough, in the successive interplay between Scorsese and DeNiro, there is also a gradual emptying of the main character's moral pretensions and physical courage. With each step he turns more and more into a media figure, hungering for his place in the public eye. In the contemplation of the Italian-American director, there is some irony to be mined from the fact that in the year of *Taxi Driver,* Sylvester Stallone appeared in *Rocky.* Stallone/Travolta are an intriguing contrast with Scorsese/DeNiro: the mainstream vs. the outsider Italians, the middlebrow vs. the highbrow film-makers. The most relevant contrast to draw here is the unproblematic quality both of Stallone's thematizing of success and his celebration of winning through the self-conscious creation of a great body. True, Stallone admits that success has its pitfalls, and bodies age. But somehow those problems will be overcome. Scorsese's vision of both fame and physical fitness is much darker. In each of his films there is a progressive defacement of DeNiro—the mohawk haircut in

Taxi Driver, the bloated weight-gaining to play La Motta in *Raging Bull,* and the odd shot of hands wiping across a window-reflected face in *King of Comedy,* the implied and actual mutilations in *After Hours*—introducing a film that explores the tangle of recognition and personal identity. *Raging Bull* particularly seems to be a direct response to *Rocky,* similarly contemplating the boxer as a figure in working-class and lower-middle-class Italian-American culture. In contrast to the sweet color melodrama of *Rocky,* it is shot in a lusciously harsh black-and-white neorealist documentary style. Unlike Stallone, Scorsese does not blandly approve the benediction of visible success. In the figures of Bickle, La Motta, and Pupkin there resides instead a sense of the gaping uncertainties of public appearance and the desire for personal fame, along with a raging iconoclasm toward the performer—as if Scorsese wanted to undermine his own inclination to trust too much in the substantiality of images.

All such characters in Scorsese's films are saints of a sort, but saints as heroes *manqués.* In a way they are reminiscent of Rossellini's false General Della Rovere, the common man who becomes a hero because others think he is. But Scorsese's saints have an urge to be different and to make a difference that has been totally warped by the culture of visual media in which they try to find themselves. In Rupert Pupkin's fantasy wedding, television has become the church. As Scorsese has said of Travis Bickle's more malevolent version of this urge, he's "somewhere between Charles Manson and Saint Paul. . . . He's going to help people so much he's going to kill them." Scorsese's exploration of such upside-down spirituality is part of his own particular inclination toward the performer as the key to a social and cinematic vision. But it is the performer not in the sense of Coppola's ritually murdered Brando, but the performer as the lightning rod for all the crazy pressures on the effort to construct a self in America today. Johnny Boy and Jake La Motta are specifically Italian; Travis Bickle and Rupert Pupkin are not. But all four, like Alice in *Alice Doesn't Live Here Anymore,* as well as many minor characters in Scorsese's films, are infused with the desire to be somebody. That desire, as perhaps it must be in film, is predicated specifically on being seen and paid attention to by an audience. Johnny Boy dies among friends. But Jake La Motta leaves the film to greet a waiting audience, his career now revived, while Travis Bickle's insane shooting spree is turned by the newspapers into a heroic vendetta, and Rupert Pupkin emerges from prison for kidnapping the talkshow host to discover that he has become a celebrity, and Paul Hackett in *After Hours* is finally turned into an absurd art object himself. In *Taxi Driver* and *King of Comedy* especially, such endings are presented as part real, part fantasy, like the ending of Murnau's *The Last Laugh,* the director's salvation of characters he has otherwise presented as doomed by their own obsessive despairs. The transcendences in *Taxi Driver* and *King of Comedy,* though, are specifically examples of a media grace, as false and as true as the spotlight for

Jerry Lewis as media saint:
The King of Comedy

which the protagonists in such different ways always longed. In *Taxi Driver* the saint has become the scourge; in *King of Comedy* he is a stand-in for all those in the audience who want to be celebrated merely for being themselves.

What I have been arguing here may perhaps be extended and deepened by a consideration of the role of actual ethnicity in the works of these directors. But I'm not sure. In many of these films the ideology is not ethnicity or religion per se so much as it is the way in which those social and psychological forces are mediated by and even subordinated to visual style.[9] The crucial issue is not ethnicity but the *representation of ethnicity* by members of minority groups whose particular angle on the world has been nurtured by the world of films that they now choose to influence in their turn. In a sense, these directors and their films may therefore signal some final stage of actual ethnicity in the interplay between a specifically Italian-Catholic sensibility and the general cultural system of American film history. Instead of taking a more sociological view of evolving ethnicity, I have chosen instead to explore the possibility that the three most prominent young American directors of Italian background have a common set of aesthetic preoccupations (and therefore thematic ideology) that may be at least metaphorically considered to invoke traditionally Catholic attitudes towards the visible world. The neorealists in great part wished to step away from a cinema of stylization and control that Bazin, Rossellini, and others identified with political tyranny. They sought to create films closer to nature and thereby to natural truth. Even in their moments of stylization and artifice, they attempted to preserve the connection of their people, places, and things to a world without mediation (or at least without the mediation of the past). But the past for these young directors cannot be avoided. There is no liberation and little resistance. In this way they are similar to other directors of aspiration ever since the New Wave. The American directors especially are bound up in both the pressure of contemporary media and the need to come to terms with a film past. There is no question of being freed from history, only how to gain control of it (Coppola), mock it (DePalma), or meditate upon it and revise it (Scorsese). Thus Coppola, like Lucas, gives aid and comfort to the greats of the past (Welles, Kurosawa), Scorsese busies himself with committees to discover ways of preserving film stock and color dyes, and DePalma gives interviews denouncing Hollywood.

At the pure moment of neorealism described and idealized by Bazin, the God of nature was appealed as an escape from the devil of History. But history is now less God or devil than it is an accumulation whose compulsions can be deflected but not avoided. The only final authority is therefore not outside but within the work. Again unlike the so-called "invisible" style of the neorealists, style here is the necessary signal of personal vision. But each of these directors, in contrast with Lucas and his northern California lack of an ethnic self distinct from movie myths, has a fruitful guilty conscience about the assertion of style and the usurpation of divine or parental authority it implies. It is just that guilty conscience—that sense of the gap between secular metaphors of ritual, sainthood, authority, and their religious counterparts— that generates so much of the aesthetic and ideological richness of their films. Like so many other artists these days, Coppola, DePalma, and Scorsese are more entrepreneurs and explorers of entrapment than of freedom. But from their very best works we nevertheless emerge to puzzle out endlessly what key it was that so lavishly allowed our release.

This essay is dedicated to the memory of Dennis Turner

1.   The general assumptions about the basis of the neorealist aesthetic and particularly Bazin's version of what he believes to be Rossellini's practice has been recently challenged by Peter Brunette; see especially "Rossellini and Cinematic Realism," *Cinema Journal,* 25 (Fall 1985), 34–49. Brunette here and elsewhere in his view of Rossellini is specifically concerned with the way in which every discourse is constantly subject to erosive counter-discourses that ultimately threaten any classical sense of "unity" in the films, along with, it is implied, the conventionally moral implications of such unity. The connections I shall argue between the seemingly distinct aesthetic of the postwar neorealists and the "school" of Coppola, DePalma, and Scorsese complement some of Brunette's views, although from the angle of film history rather than that of critical theory. On the influence of Fellini's melodramatic style, see Naomi Greene, "Coppola, Cimino: The Operatics of History," *Film Quarterly,* 38 (Winter 1984–85), 28–37.

2.   Connecting a particular style with a particular politics is tricky business at best, even though theater has traditionally been the mirror of social structure, and film to a certain extent follows in its ideological wake. But I still wonder why the Nazi tendency in propaganda (with the prime exception of Riefenstahl) was toward historical melodrama, while the Fascist was toward documentary. Perhaps it has to do with the relative positions of Nazism and Fascism on the Great Man/Everyman axis, and the way each defined its audience.

3.   Michael Pye and Lynda Myles, *The Movie Brats: How the Film Generation Took Over Hollywood* (New York: Holt, Rinehart & Winston, 1979), 101.

4.   Caul's mistake has been psychologically interpreted as caused by his paranoia. But to root the explanation exclusively in his character diverts at-

tention away from the aesthetic self-criticism of *The Conversation*. In art paranoia may be just another name for aesthetic unity.

5.   The successful Ewok siege of the Death Star substation in *Return of the Jedi* contains the film's only energy because it arises from a similar tension in the imagination of George Lucas.

6.   Compare the very un-Coppolan moment in *The Conversation* when we discover that Caul has hidden the crucial tape inside a hollow crucifix.

7.   The relations between directors and stars can be arrayed on a spectrum from conflict to conspiracy. The basic question remains who is left inside the film and who is allowed to escape. With the examples mentioned above, compare Robert Altman's "erasure" of Paul Newman at the end of *Quintet*.

8.   See Pye and Myles, 168.

9.   The modernist and minimalist SoHo of *After Hours* of course geographically overlaps with the Little Italy of *Mean Streets*. Perhaps the title should appear as *After (H)ours*, to emphasize the denaturing of any ethnic characteristics in either its setting or its hero.

DAVID JAMES

HARDCORE

Cultural Resistance in the Postmodern

. . . (think of punk rock or pornography).

FREDRIC JAMESON

Vol. 42, no. 2 (Winter 1988–89): 31–39.

With the destruction or co-optation of working-class movements in the U.S. since the thirties, opposition to capitalism has increasingly been mobilized around Third World struggles of decolonization. But since the end of the invasion of Vietnam, cultural practice in the West has lost even this focus of resistance and become increasingly collusive and administered, mirroring indeed a depletion of working-class self-consciousness so devastating that it has allowed an unprecedented currency for attacks on the tenability of basic Marxist concepts, even that of class. Here, in the Baudrillardian hyperspace of the postmodern, cultural resistance seems so impossible that we are all but persuaded to rewrite the entire history of modernism around that impossibility. In the dismal glitter of our time, when the emblems of the Russian Revolution decorate our T-shirts and the Cabaret Voltaire is an only mildly fractious dance band, we wonder indeed if a real avant-garde ever existed. Despite this suspicion, we nevertheless still recognize that postmodern culture is integrated into the corporate state to an unprecedented degree. Today (and now I return my epigraph to its context), "although postmodernism is . . . offensive . . . (think of punk rock or pornography), it is no longer at all 'oppositional' . . . indeed, it constitutes the very dominant or hegemonic aesthetic of consumer society itself and significantly serves [its] commodity production" (Jameson, 1984:196).

For film and television history, a narrative form of this doxa would trace the termination of the great efflorescence of sixties avant-garde film at the end of the Vietnam war, and then a shift from film to video as the preferred high-art motion-picture medium. Though the social energies that produced the sixties avant-gardes did temporarily sustain video practices more or less modelled on structural film's exemplary negativity, they were so weakened that by the late seventies artist's video had collapsed into the backside of the beast. In short, television—video and broadcast television together—is the postmodern mutant form of film, and in it both illusionist narrative and its discontents, both the entertainment industry and opposition to it, are subsumed in the same hegemony.

Disdaining attachment to social contestation or even disaffiliation, the tropes of high modernism linger only as reflexive signs that constantly defer extra-textual engagement.

While accepting this account as generally true, I want to propose some contrary instances to what Jameson considers spurious and illusionary resistance. I argue that in the early eighties certain extremely marginal forms of punk and pornography did in fact sustain opposition to the aesthetics of the hegemony and to commodity culture. Marking a survival of sixties utopianism, these forms of erotic and music video (which I link but do not equate in the epithet "hardcore") constituted a survival of the project of the classic avant-garde— the turn of cultural practice against the status of art in bourgeois society as defined by the concept of autonomy and against the distribution apparatus bourgeois art depends on (Bürger, 1984: 22). Their demonstration of the cultural possibilities and also the limitations of the present is particularly sharp since the sixties American avant-garde film, arguably the most powerful oppositional art since World War II, was itself directly constructed upon a parallel documentation of illicit sexual and musical practices.

Simultaneously avant-garde and documentary in a way matched only by the early Soviet cinema, Underground film emancipated itself from Hollywood by reproducing in the filmic the properties of the aberrant or proscribed sexual and musical practices that preoccupied the profilmic. The quasi-vérité documentation of jazz musicians in films like *Shadows* and *Pull My Daisy* allowed improvisation, performative virtuosity, spontaneity, and the other compositional procedures of jazz to be enacted in film shooting and editing. Similarly, the transgressions of the codes of sexual representation that followed amateur documentation of domestic sexuality by, for example, Jack Smith, Stan Brakhage, and Carolee Schneemann supplied the avant-garde's formal excess and "sterility" (Lyotard, 1978), the promiscuous visual surplus to the narrative economy of industrial features.

As the New Hollywood of the late sixties appropriated sanitized forms of these innovations, so the social and aesthetic transgressions of their origins were absorbed by the culture generally. Afro-American guitarists replaced Afro-American saxophonists as the dominant influence on youth music, and the marginality of jazz gave way to the very different social dynamics of rock, which eventually became the single most important mechanism for incorporating youth dissidence. At the same time, explicit sexual representation, including a new spectacularization of the male body and more or less overt homosexual iconography (as for example in Sylvester Stallone's films), was thoroughly integrated into the entertainment and advertising industries.

While these assimilations of sixties recalcitrance do exemplify the post-modernist closure, nevertheless the industrial functions they sustain do not totally occupy the cultural field nor entirely preempt popular alternatives. During the same period, unincorporated minority video practices of musical and sexual documentary emerged—partially in reaction against them and partially negotiated in the space they have made available—which do figure resistance and perhaps even utopian alterity. In these, as in sixties avant-garde film, the formal qualities of the video-text and its social uses refract and elaborate the conditions of the music and sex they document, producing formal and operational differences from the hegemonic televisual modes. Their textual offensiveness mobilizes their challenge to both the entertainment industry and also the other institutions integrated with that industry, various journalistic and academic systems, including the one element in the postmodern hegemony that, while it has silently been speaking here, has not so far acknowledged itself: film theory.

While it may be argued that postmodern theory sustains a form of Adornian negativity lost to art proper, it is equally plausible to regard it as a symptom of the very closures it purports to diagnose. The mutually sustaining philosophical, critical, and journalistic discourses that have developed in the tow of post-structuralism and a revived Culture Criticism display a conceptual and terminological density, reminiscent of the "difficulty" of modern art, which marks their resistance to easy consumption. Yet, in the insatiable market for text, itself floated on increasingly "pure" information, these discourses themselves become commodities. Lacking any affiliation with working-class movements, they are easily institutionalized and assimilated into consumer society in general. The imbrication of allegedly radical art history in the world of corporate finance via the apparatus of museums and gallery-supported magazines is the most glittering form of this collusion; but other cultural writings have their own form of it, film criticism especially. And ever since high-modernist literature became undergraduate texts, the academy itself has been a prime agent in the construction of postmodern culture; we academics welcome a plethora of previously taboo practices with a broadmindedness that was not available to the sixties avant-gardes, certainly not to sixties film.

A crucial figuration of the incompatibility of the sixties film and the academy is preserved in a *locus classicus* of the Underground innovations I have mentioned, Jonas Mekas's *Lost, Lost, Lost*. The crisis of this film (and we inherit it as the documentation of one of the half-dozen paradigmatic shifts in the practices of cinema) occurs when Mekas and Ken Jacobs take prints of *Flaming Creatures* and *Blonde Cobra* to the Flaherty Film Seminar at Brattleboro in 1963. These two films, previously recognized by Mekas in *Village Voice* articles as "impure, naughty and 'uncinematic'" (Mekas, 1972:95), films "without inhibitions, sexual or any other kind" (ibid.:86), are refused entry to the conference, and the cinephiles are obliged to spend the night outside in their cars. But next morning, as they shoot home-movies to document their exclusion from the seminar, Mekas discovers what will henceforward be his signature improvisational style, his own form of "blowing as per jazz musician" (Kerouac, 1958:72) in film, and returns to New York and to his life's work of creating the institutions of an independent film culture.

Some 25 years later *Lost, Lost, Lost* is beginning to have a place in academic film criticism (though *Flaming Creatures* and *Blonde Cobra* do not). But given what is at stake in the film, this and similar instances of theory's openness to the avant-garde may be as discomforting to those of us who have most desired it as it is to those who have most resisted it, if for quite different reasons. If we understand the avant-garde as being of social rather than merely formal importance, we must wonder whether this new legitimacy signals the evaporation of the very alterity to which we made our commitment. On the one hand we fear that the toleration of our enthusiasms indicates their historical supercession or only an illusory offensiveness that is in fact functional within the postmodern hegemony. On the other hand, we must ask, if indeed there were a video practice today as radically innovative as the Baudelairean cinema was in its time, could—or should—we be any more receptive than the Brattleboro seminar? Would we be able to see it? And if we could see it and talk about it, what would that imply?

Questions like this forewarn me that I should not be surprised if the search for the unsayable leads to the unspeakable.

The Best of Amateur Erotic Video Volume II is a compilation of four tapes, each 15–20 minutes long, self-photographed and self-produced by middle-class, heterosexual, white couples.[1] In three of them, the couples have intercourse, while in the other first the woman and then the man masturbates separately. Each section is prefixed by a title giving the participants' first names and an identification number, usually with some form of invitation; "Debra and Earl from California," for instance, request "correspondence from anyone viewing their tape." The tape as a whole and its separate sections are briefly introduced by an unseen woman speaking for "Susan's Video," the distributing agency. The tape is available by mail without charge in direct exchange for a tape of your own sexual activity for inclusion in future collections, though it may also be obtained by purchase.

As text, the compilation differs sharply from commodity pornography. Since the tape shamelessly proclaims erotic representation as its *raison d'être*, it is not obliged to disguise itself as either narrative or documentary. The sexual encounters are not motivated by spurious narrative intrigues; without a plot, there can be no assumption of character, no role-playing which would justify the sexual activity as the representation of the behavior, deviant or not, of some other persons. Nor, apart from the minimal introductions noted, are the sexual encounters or the video photography of them framed by any normative meta-discourse that would justify their introduction as anthropological data or evidence of pathology. As a consequence of this self-sufficiency, the tape displays a diegetic steadiness, quite unlike industrial pornography's ontological tensions between fiction and the sheer *vérité* presentation of sexual activity, and its parallel formal tensions between a propulsive narrative and the interludes of its retardation.

While recent technical advances in home-video equipment allow an image quality at least as good as that of the average sixties 16mm stag film, photography and editing are rudimentary and clearly nonprofessional, with a stationary camera and deep-focus long takes being the norm (though the woman's masturbation scene is shot by her partner with a very energetic hand-held camera that suggests a direct erotic interchange). There is little use of close-ups and no intra-sequential editing, no parallel montages between genital contact and the facial response shots which register its effect. The grammatical primitiveness of this uninflected, non-suturing style culminates in a signal absence of one of the most bizarre but nevertheless ubiquitous tropes of pornography, the close-up on the man's ejaculation and the organization of patterns of formal crisis and resolution around it. Finally where (except in very specifically bracketed situations) pornography effaces its own production, here the performers recognize and address the apparatus, frequently making eye contact with the camera or watching themselves on a monitor, and comment on the fact that photography is taking place.

Distinguishing the amateur erotic video from industrial pornography, these formal differences mark the tape's deficiencies in the latter's terms, its failure to provide intensely focussed visual eroticism or to generate a compelling play of excitement and frustration. I find it less arousing and so less desirable than its industrial counterpart. But they also trace substantial differences in the social relations that the tape constructs and the activities it promotes, particularly as these realign the priorities between the pleasures of sexual contact itself and those of its optical or technical mediation and social broadcast: (1) Where in pornography the performers' pleasure is subordinated to their instrumentality in commodity film production, here those pleasures are primary and themselves determine textual organization. (2) Where in pornography the implications of observation and the consequent pleasures of exhibitionism must be repressed, here they are foregrounded. (3) Where in pornography the sexual activity depicted is always categorically unavailable to the spectator—the price of scopophilic delight is the absolute impossibility of physical contact between the performers and the spectator—here the text proposes such contact; it proposes itself as the means to it and as the means to a social network of pleasure that includes but is not limited to looking.

Pornography demands that the actors sacrifice their pleasure to the procedures of film manufacture and to the text's manipulation of its future spectators' desire. The rhythm of copulation is interrupted by the requirements of the camera set-ups, the lighting apparatus, the shooting schedules, and the other exigencies of production.[2] Indeed, the better the pornography, the more the actors' actual satisfaction is displaced into the most visually titillating display of it; the signs of sexual pleasure have a higher priority than the performance of it. Subordinating the somatic to the visual, and the experiential to the spectacular, the commodity function is thus inscribed in the photographic and editing conventions. Its demands are epitomized in the male's obligation to allow the camera to see his climax; at the point where his satisfaction would reach its fulfillment, he must withdraw; his need to make his orgasm visible obliges him to sacrifice its most pleasurable form. Some of this obligation to the filmic and the industrial tropes that accommodate it are present in the amateur tapes: the performer/photographers occasionally attempt genital close-ups and they do adjust their positions for the camera. But in general the tapes reflect the phases and drives of the performers' own activity in a less mediated way; pace and construction are dictated by their pleasure rather than by aesthetic and generic requirements or the spectators' needs, and in only one instance does the male withdraw to ejaculate; in fact Susan's guide for contributors specifically recommends that this be avoided (Meredith, 1982:83).

The performers' orientation around their own rather than the spectators' pleasure allows them both to acknowledge the apparatus and to engage the particular pleasures of exhibitionism and narcissism it allows. In pornography, which takes over the illusionist pretensions of the commercial feature film, self-consciousness is normally proscribed unless it is intradiegetically narrated in stories about film-making. Since the actors' market value depends on the conjunction of their actual unavailability to the spectator and the latter's imaginary encounter with them that the text affords, they may not admit that they are being observed by the camera, by the people on the set, or by the future spectator. But since the purpose of the amateur tapes is to introduce—perhaps even physically—the performers to the spectators, bridging the division between producer and consumer that commodity culture depends on, the vehicle of their contact may be acknowledged. The different economies correspond to different psychological states: the voyeurism of pornography depends on concealed observation, while here the performers' self-consciousness allows them the pleasures of exhibitionism, of seeing themselves reflected back by the monitor or by the more extended gaze of the tape's social distribution. Their blatant self-display releases them from guilt and invites a similarly shameless gaze for the spectator, whose participation is implicit throughout (though it is especially clear in the woman's direct address to the camera in her masturbation scene). The acknowledged visual intercourse between performer and spectator allows the tape to figure the possibility of transcending the commodity relations of pornography by adding video to one's own erotic activity and by joining the tape network as a producer.

Thus, though the sexual activity is so conventionally that of the heterosexual couple that it appears to reinforce sexual conservativism, if not the nuclear family itself, the tape implies other, more properly promiscuous, scenes, not only the "kinkier" material that the voice-over introduction mentions as being available, but the expanded circuits of promiscuous sexual adventure. The tape's final function of sexual advertising, of making sexual pleasure more available rather than repressively channelling desire into administered forms, marks then the limitations of any approach to it as representation; finally it cannot be evaluated apart from the sexual encounters it occasions,[3] even though the crucial phases in this process, the video-taping of domestic sex acts, is textually recorded.

What are the implications of introducing video into lovemaking? Initially my Luddite technophobia is checked by my inability to draw a logical line that would differentiate video from mirrors or just looking in the enhancement of erotic pleasure. But my discomfort at this mechanization of vision—my fear that sooner or later sex without Sony won't do it anymore and that this is only a last and hyperbolic instance of a culturally pandemic supplantation of the real by the simulacrum—reads it as a final step in the internalization of the ubiquitous apparatus of surveillance. As a form of autosurveillance, it completes the *industrialization* of the body, continuous with the total penetration of the spectacle and the corporation, the *incorporation* of desire itself.

These ambiguities are the ambiguities of the apparatus and so those of video in general, and they register an important difference between the epochs of film and television. Though home-movie equipment was available as early as the 1920s, the medium's development almost exclusively as an industry allowed the sixties avant-garde to be understood correctly as a *liberation* of the apparatus; conversely the alternative systems of distribution—the alternative cinemas—of the sixties were dogged by the cost of film and the unwieldiness of the machines (dependence on labs, the bulkiness and fragility of projectors). But video's popular availability, its cheapness and its ease of reproduction, means that the subcultural self-representation and the extra-industrial circulation of representations that the sixties political cinemas could only dream of are now realizable. Nothing prevents us from shedding corporate aesthetics by becoming producers rather than consumers of television except the residual prejudices of commodity art production and the internalization of industrial production values. Over the past ten or so years, this internalization has resulted in so-called artist's video, as the form of appearance of its own assimilation, fetishizing industrial-quality image manipulation. In this context,

rejection of such values with willful *video brut* can inscribe a more general ideological rejection, as indeed in its early years artist's video defined itself against
broadcast television in a negative aesthetic, partially derived from structural
film's critique of the illusionism of the commercial feature. This negativity disappeared from film and television practices of all kinds as its social precondi-
tions evaporated in the mid-seventies; but the same aesthetic model revived almost immediately in the field of music as the axiom of punk.

Since one of punk's determining strategies was its deliberately rude infrac-
tion of aesthetic and social norms, the use of the terminology of the obscene
and the illicit was entirely logical; the onomastic continuity of the term "hardcore" recalls early punk's use of bondage and fetish iconography, the use of
pornographic films in punk concerts, the use of punk iconography in industrial
pornography (e.g., *New Wave Hookers*), and more recently, certain pornographic films made within the punk subcultures (e.g., those of Richard Kern).
More precisely, "hardcore" was a purist style of the music developed initially
in Washington, DC, and Southern California in the early eighties. This, the
music's essential, its "classical," mode, mounted a deliberately anachronistic attempt to sustain early punk's negativity against its diffusion and assimilation by
the music industry as various forms of new wave. The entirely recalcitrant
music provided a besieged subculture with the basis for defensive rituals in
which the sonic (and other forms of) violence and the obstinate antiprofession-
alism that signalled rejection of overproduced corporate rock also informed
strategies of negation and antigrammaticality for everyday self-presentation
and the other cultural practices. Crucial in these intertwined social and aesthetic developments were fanzines, largely reader-written magazines which provided musical information and social exchanges of all kinds. Contributing not
just to the documentation of the subculture, but also to its formation and dissemination, fanzines provided a participatory forum, necessary as a defense
against misrepresentation in the establishment media and against regular police
rioting.

The most important fanzine in Southern California was *Flipside*, established
in 1977, which in 1984 began to distribute compilations of concert footage as
Flipside Video Fanzines. Number Nine, "When Can I Sleep In Peace,"[4] for example, has 19 cuts by 11 commercially unprofitable bands, none of whom had
corporate recording contracts. The songs all employ a brutally reductionist and
visceral musical style, whose masculinist values are summarized in the priorities,
"Faster, Louder, Shorter." When they are intelligible, the equally aggressive, blatantly agitational lyrics blast the religious right, the military-industrial complex,
the government, and the police, making explicit a categorical opposition to the
corporate state; their ideological field is announced in the songs' titles: MDC
sing "Corporate Death Burger" and "Church and State"; the Dicks sing

"Sidewalk Begging," "Hate the Police," and "No War"; the Dead Kennedys sing "Moral Majority" and "Chemical Warfare"; BGK sings "Vivisection" and "Arms Race"; and Conflict sings "From Protest to Resistance."

Like the music, the videos flaunt scorched-earth production values. Featuring live, unenhanced sound, they are shot in $1/_2$" with home cameras that lack color adjustment so that the light is not balanced and the color not always correctly keyed. They consist of rudimentary edits of footage shot at concerts simultaneously by two cameras, one placed among the audience fronting the stage, the other shooting from the side of the stage to include both performers and audience together within the frame. They contain no image manipulation, close-ups, or special effects except for the occasional superimposition of synchronous footage from the camera covering the band and that covering the audience; this trope has great symbolic weight since it figures the ritual passage of the audience over the stage and their contestation of the band's position on it and reproduces the breakdown of the distinction between audience and band that is central to punk's alterity to corporate culture. The tape does contain some other material; it opens with a crude collage of television commercials and news violence (a juxtaposition which summarizes the music's attack on consumerism and state violence) and some songs are illustrated with simple cutaways; accompanying the Dicks' "Sidewalk Begging" are shots of the homeless, while the photography of BGK's "Vivisection" is interpolated with anti-vivisectionist publicity stills. Otherwise, the tape is as raw as the music itself.

The tapes are not collectively produced and they are sold, and so in respect to the social relations their consumption mobilizes they are less radical an intervention than the erotic videos. But the commodity relations they generate are minimized; they are very cheap, costing little more than enough to return production costs and allow further compilations. Production is anonymous and since no individual authorship is announced, the art-work remains within the subculture as its autonomous self-representation and self-expression. Produced and consumed entirely within the subculture, it promotes a radically amateur aesthetic that refuses the industrial distinction between artist and market. As far as the material conditions of the medium allow, then, the fanzine reproduces in video the negative determination and positive strategies of hardcore music as well as its aesthetic and social values; denying the consensus and refusing the socialization which industrial culture merchandizes, it resists corporate assimilation and so preserves a space for social alterity.

As they document and sustain the music's resistance to the commercial functions of new wave, hardcore video fanzines define themselves generally against the panoply of corporate film and television appropriations of popular music, and specifically against the two primary forms of that appropriation:

music videos in their summary form of MTV, and feature films about punk, including ostensibly sympathetic documentaries. These industrial forms of the music correspond respectively to what Dick Hebdige noted as the two forms of recuperation of punk in general: music videos to "the conversion of subcultural signs . . . into mass-produced objects (i.e., the commodity form)" and the documentaries to "the 'labelling' and redefinition of deviant behavior by dominant groups—the police, the media, the judiciary (i.e., the ideological form)" (Hebdige, 1979:94).

Music videos' internalization of the values of industrial culture is evidenced in the correspondences between their grammar and that of television commercials, their recurrence to the most insipid and unchallenging pleasures, their exploitation of sexual stereotypes, and their flaunting of extremely expensive production values in both *mise-en-scène* and special effects. The best of the documentary films (such as Penelope Spheeris's *Decline of Western Civilization* and Lech Kowalski's *D.O.A.*, both of 1980) may be closer to the subcultures; but their mass culture function of representing punk culture to the general public obliges them to frame the others' discourse in their own. The various interview techniques establish a hierarchy of discourses in which the normativity of the film's own interpellates punk's as deviant. A summary instance of such framing, which is inevitably even more grotesque as it is narrated in mainstream Hollywood films, is the Bad Brains sequence in Scorsese's *After Hours* (1985). While this is one of the few occasions in which anything like hardcore's intensity was captured on film, the narrative denigrates the performance as aberrant, a bizarre miasma in a nightmare of irrationality.

In contradistinction to these, respectively the appropriation and the containment of punk, *Flipside Video Fanzine* places itself within the culture, sustaining and ratifying it from inside. Celebrating and enacting the aesthetic of punk music, it rejects any reconciliation with the industrial media or with the ethics of the corporate state of which those media are an integral part. This larger political contestation, implicit in the tape's form and made possible by the mode of its production, is clearly articulated in the songs' lyrics. The singer directly addresses the audience as a commonality, unified in their defiance of state militarism, and, as noted, the songs explicitly reject the domestic and foreign policies of the Reagan administration. Though all their ideas must be expressed negatively (for the aesthetic system does not allow affirmation), the songs give voice to contestation with a clarity and vehemence such as has rarely been found in American culture since the thirties. This opposition to the corporate state is most focussed where its violence is most immediately experienced, in the local police.[5]

For example, in the introduction to the Dicks' "Hate the Police" the vocalist spells out a crude syllogism; the next song, he tells the audience, "makes you a fucking Dick" because "Dicks hate the police." The outrageous puns spin language, sexuality, and the law into Möbius strips of irony: only those who lack the phallus may be the phallus or, taking the pun on "dick" in the opposite direction, only those who hate the police can be the police. As he launches into his song, warning the police to stay clear of him because he has a gun, general slamdancing mayhem among those of the audience who share his logic and recognize themselves as Dicks ensues. The next clip is from MDC, a polysemous acronym variously elaborated as "Millions of Dead Cops," "Millions of Dead Children," or "Multi-Death Corporation." It begins with the singer chanting "Dead Cops" and grasping his crotch as he mimes pissing on the cops' graves. His song, "Blue By Day," is a vitriolic attack on multinationals, and on "all the stinking rich people" who "run the police departments" and "start all the wars." The indictment of state terrorism galvanizes the audience, precipitating a frenzied but thoroughly eloquent ritual in which they climb on the stage, struggle briefly with the stagehands, perhaps share the microphone for a chorus, and then somersault back into the crowd.

Their logic is sublime: struggle violently to achieve a place in the spectacle, dance briefly in its glare, and then dive out of it, all the while celebrating resistance to authority of all kinds. But to those who are outside the subculture—those perhaps who enjoy "good" TV like "Hill Street Blues" and "Cagney and Lacey" that legitimizes state violence by representing its agents as neurotic bourgeois subjects besieged by "criminals" and the problems of "life"—to these the tape will appear as infantile and regressive as the performances it documents.

Since everywhere in postmodern culture regression is exploited for that frisson of the forbidden which creates an appearance of resistance while in fact renewing consumption, it is especially necessary that merely collusive forms of it be distinguished from others that are not reducible to corporate uses. In industrial culture, a "repressive tolerance" administers regression, channelling it to serve state interests by framing it in equally administered ideological structures (the *Rambo* films again or nubile pre-teenagers in advertising). But both the domestic erotica and the punk concert tapes do not so easily allow for vicarious or touristically secure visitation, and indeed retain a truly minatory edge to their attraction. Their threat is partly a semiological consequence of their difference from ordinary documentary, which always presents its content, its profilmic, as a curiosity different from and other than itself. But these tapes refuse that difference; the various forms of identity—ideological, environmental, functional—between the video-text and the events it records tend to collapse the signifier into the signified, the text into its context. Consequently, in both cases, one's response to the tape as art-work is overwhelmingly determined by one's assessment of the social events it depicts and incites. Since this content is unlawful, for those outside the tight subcultural circle (in which the producers and consumers are largely the same) the tapes themselves can be approved only at the cost of a double apostasy, a rejection of dominant social mores and of dominant media. Endorsing the renegades depicted or recognizing any kinship with them, which is virtually a prerequisite to liking the tapes, also commits you to a video aesthetic whose primary axiom, its *raison d'être* even, is rejection of all other regimes of television—a position which puts in crisis the discursive practices of the dominant socio-aesthetic system. And so commentary on them becomes difficult. If you don't like them, you will abruptly dismiss them as pathological. But if you do like them, especially if you *really* like them, you will be moved not to words but to action, to fucking or slamdancing. The difficulty proposed to humanist discourse, however vertiginous, is not unprecedented in cinema.

The issue has best been approached in psychoanalytic terms by Christian Metz. If cinema's pleasures are intrinsically those of the imaginary, then the theoretician's work in the symbolic, the work of distinguishing the symbolic from the imaginary, is always in danger of being "swallowed up" by the imaginary—the sliding of the *"discourse about the object"* into its opposite, the *"discourse of the object"* (Metz, 1982:5). This attraction is specifically (though surely not exclusively) a filmic one; but if its basis is in the constitutive Oedipality of the cinematic signifier (ibid.:64), how much greater must it be in texts which engage the sexual drives so directly, without sublimation.[6] Such is the case with these, with their massive affective overload, their overt pandering to the desire to see and the desire to hear. Do the erotic videos fulfill cinema by showing us the primal scene itself instead of that allegory of it which is the reference of all other films (films which it thereby violates, invalidates, and renders redundant); or do they destroy cinema by abrogating the voyeuristic precondition of such films, "a pure onlooker whose participation is inconceivable" (ibid.:64)? Similarly, is the nihilistic utopianism of hardcore—a primal scream to the other's primal scene—one that destroys music or a Dionysiac apotheosis of it? Until we have a psychoanalysis of television[7] or punk or pornography, we won't know.

But the issue is also political. The resistance these tapes propose to theory only reiterates their resistance to theory's privileged objects—bourgeois culture. As the contemporary avant-garde film has come to resemble nothing so much as broadcast television (Arthur, 1987:69), as artist's video looks more and more like broadcast television, as theory becomes a circuit in the global economy of television, whatever defines itself as *not-television* can only be talked about in reservations within (or outside) sanctioned discourse, as a rupture in its syntax. If theory can think it, it will only be (as in Jameson's remark) parenthetically.

NOTES

1. For the availability of this and other such tapes, see Meredith (1982). Similar material, which is sometimes advertised in magazines devoted to X-rated video, is referenced in Eder (1986).

2. For a humorous account of the stress of these demands on the pornographic film actor, see Gray (1985).

3. The possibility of imagining such a utopian promiscuity is, of course, severely circumscribed by external conditions; in this case, what developments in birth control in the late sixties made possible was abruptly terminated in the mid-eighties by AIDS.

4. *Flipside Video Fanzines* are available from PO Box 363, Whittier, California 90608. For a subsequent similar project, see *Suburban Relapse Fanzine*, POB 404825, Brooklyn, New York 11240. For an overview of punk fanzines in Los Angeles, see James (1984). For accounts of punk film-making, see Boddy (1981) and Buchsbaum (1981).

5. The violence of the Los Angeles Police Department is widely documented; see, for example, McCartney (1983) and Stark (1986). A collection of mid-eighties anti-police songs from Southern California was assembled as *The Sound of Hollywood: 3: Copulation* (Mystic Records, MLP 33128).

6. In their fundamental narcissism, their greater emphasis on the profilmic event and less on its subsequent observation by the spectator, these tapes document extreme instances of the first two components (*Partialtrieb*) within the sex instinct, the desire of making oneself seen and the desire of making oneself heard. Lacan (1977: 194–95) proposes that in the former the subject *"looks at himself [sic] . . . in his erotic member"* and that this delight is the "root" of the scopic drive as a whole.

7. This project has, however, been initiated in Houston (1984).

Arthur, Paul. (1987) "Last of the Machine: Avant-garde Film since 1965." *Millennium Film Journal*, 16/17/18 (Fall/Winter 1986/87): 69–93.

Boddy, William. (1981) "New York Confidential: An Interview with Eric Mitchell." *Millennium Film Journal*, 7/8/9, 27–36.

Buchsbaum, Jonathan. (1981) "A La Recherche des Punks Perdus." *Film Comment* (May), 43–46.

Bürger, Peter. (1984) *Theory of the Avant-Garde.* Minneapolis: University of Minnesota Press.

Eder, Bruce. (1986) "Mail-Order Video." *Village Voice*, 16 December, 57–58.

Gray, Spalding. (1985) "The Farmers' Daughter." *Wild History.* Ed. Richard Prince, New York: Tanam Press.

Hebdige, Dick. (1979) *Subculture: The Meaning of Style.* New York: Methuen.

Houston, Beverle. (1984) "Reviewing Television: The Metapsychology of Endless Consumption." *Quarterly Review of Film Studies*, 9, 3, 183–95.

James, David. (1984) "Poetry/Punk/Production: Some Recent Writing in L.A." *The Minnesota Review*, N.S. 23 (Fall 1984), 127–53.

Jameson, Fredric. (1984) "Periodizing the 60s." *The Sixties Without Apology.* Ed. Sohnya Sayres et al., Minneapolis: University of Minnesota Press.

Kerouac, Jack. (1958) "Essentials of Spontaneous Prose." *Evergreen Review* 2, 5 (Summer 1958), 72–73.

Lacan, Jacques. (1977) *The Four Fundamental Concepts of Psycho-Analysis.* London: Hogarth Press.

Lyotard, Jean-François. (1978) "Acinema." *Wide Angle* 2, 3, 52–59.

McCartney, Patrick. (1983) "Cops and Punks." *L.A. Weekly,* 5, 47 (21 October), 18–21.

Mekas, Jonas. (1972) *Movie Journal: The Rise of a New American Cinema.* New York: Collier.

Meredith, Raina. (1982) "The (Amateur) Shtup Tapes." *Village Voice*, 23 November 1982, 82–83.

Metz, Christian. (1982) *The Imaginary Signifier: Psychoanalysis and Cinema.* Bloomington: Indiana University Press.

Stark, Annette. (1986) "There's a Riot Going On." *Spin*, 2, 9 (December), 68–74.

PART FOUR

DOCUMENTARY

Since *Film Quarterly*'s earliest days, documentary has been one of the journal's principal interests. Besides reviews of nonfiction films in every phase of the journal's history, there have been numerous interviews and, of course, a large number of articles on the topic. Highlights have included a thirty-three-page special feature on Humphrey Jennings in the Winter 1961–62 issue; editor Helen Van Dongen's article on Robert Flaherty in Summer 1965; and Alan Rosenthal's interviews with the director, cameraman, and editor of the cinema verité film *A Married Couple* in Summer 1970.

Bill Nichols and ethnographic filmmaker David MacDougall have long been among the most thoughtful and influential writers on nonfiction film; MacDougall's "Prospects of the Ethnographic Film" appeared in the Winter 1969–70 issue. Of somewhat more recent vintage, Michael Renov's writings are also included in the list of work that must be read by those interested in nonfiction film, past and present. Linda Williams' extraordinary article on history and memory in a number of contemporary nonfiction films places her on that list as well.

A crucial feature of all four articles in this section is that despite, or through, their diverse topic areas, all are theoretical in orientation. They might easily have been included in the Theory section, as a distinctive subsection. Their placement here underscores the fact that documentary is not a genre but, like experimental film, a realm of cinema parallel to but not a subset of fictional narrative.

In "The Voice of Documentary," Bill Nichols argues that there are at least four major historical styles of documentary, each with distinctive formal and ideological qualities. These include the direct address of the Grierson era, which he calls "the first thoroughly worked-out mode of documentary"; a second mode—cinema verité—which sought to capture, through an allegedly transparent style, "untampered events in the everyday lives of particular people"; a third style that incorporates direct address (characters or narrator speaking directly to the viewer); and a more recent fourth phase, which seems to have begun

> with films moving toward more complex forms where epistemological and aesthetic assumptions become more visible. These new self-reflexive documentaries mix observational passages with interviews, the voice-over of the film-maker with intertitles, making patently clear [that] . . . documentaries always were forms of re-presentation, never clear windows onto "reality"; the film-maker was always a participant-witness and an active fabricator of meaning, a producer of cinematic discourse rather than a neutral or all-knowing reporter of the way things truly are.

Throughout much of the article, Nichols makes trenchant criticisms of the defects of the first three documentary styles. These pages are especially valuable because they treat a substantial number of specific films, including several not widely known. As for the fourth category, he makes clear that the "voice" he has in mind is "something narrower than style." It is that which conveys to us "a sense of a text's social point of view, of how it is speaking to us and organizing the materials it is presenting." It is also not restricted to any one feature such as dialogue or spoken commentary. Nichols considers the best instances of this category to be the documentaries of Emile de Antonio and some of the ethnographic films of David and Judith MacDougall.

Michael Renov's 1987 article, "Newsreel: Old and New," is a retrospective view of the first twenty years of Newsreel, "a radical film-making collective conceived during the last flush of New Left activism." Newsreel once had offices in seven major U.S. cities but at this point survives "in two versions." California Newsreel, San Francisco, makes and distributes films about the workplace and about South Africa and apartheid, with a new focus on teaching its viewers about the media. Third World Newsreel, based in New York, supports the cultural interventions of the disenfranchised.

In constructing his account, Renov consulted interviews with Newsreel members that appeared in *Film Quarterly* in Winter 1968–69 and himself conducted interviews with a number of other early Newsreel members. The New Left looked not to American radicalism of the thirties but to the utopian socialism of the very early Soviet Union and specifically to filmmaker Dziga Vertov. But unlike Vertov, with his passionate enthusiasm for the machine, the New Left media activists were mainly negative about technology. Newsreel's most successful early films, both made in 1968, were *Columbia Revolt* and *Black Panther*—also known as *Off the Pig*. Renov is excellent on the conflicts that shaped Newsreel in the early seventies. Decisions about what films would be made often depended upon who could raise money. Those who could call on family resources or were experienced fund-raisers pretty much called the shots until, between 1971 and 1973, a split developed between the haves and the have-nots. At the same time there was a split between Newsreel's growing Third World Caucus and its other operations, and a division occasioned by a radical feminist faction: most of the men left the collective over the next several months. These gender, color, and class rifts left New York Newsreel a three-person collective in 1973. But *From Spikes to Spindles*, a 1976 film about Chinese Americans in New York, established Third World Newsreel's reputation for "compact, historically situated overviews of ethnic minorities in crisis." Renov's briefer accounts of California Newsreel and of Third World Newsreel in later years are also of great interest.

"When Less Is Less: The Long Take in Documentary" is the title of David MacDougall's very thoughtful article. He pursues two sets of issues, one having to do with the pressures on documentary and ethnographic filmmakers to cut from their rushes anything that does not move the exposition forward. This is based on the terror of television producers of any "dead spots" in any program they sponsor. This fear is based on the supposed desire of viewers to move on to the next shot/point once they have grasped the preceding one and their boredom if this demand is not met. The other set of issues has to do with the values, contexts, perceptions, and uses of the long take considered in a more general cultural context. In his actual exposition, the author often mixes the two topics.

MacDougall understands the problem of rushes as one of "the ideal and the actual, the object within grasp yet somehow lost." He draws a broad analogy between the way in which individual shots are reduced in length and the way in which the entire body of footage shot for a film is reduced to produce a finished film. He also wishes to question some of the assumptions that underlie these practices. He notes that long takes are better defined by their structural qualities than by their length, and yet, he concludes, "absolute duration does finally matter." Even filmmakers "have seemed unwilling to confront perhaps the most deeply seated assumption of all: that films are necessarily superior to the rushes shot for them." A documentary filmmaker told an interviewer that "the real film was in the rushes." People would drop by his editing rooms at the BBC and become interested in all fifty hours, coming back at various times as though they were watching a serial. In a section called "Qualities Sacrificed to the Film," MacDougall lists the loss of excess meaning, the loss of interpretive space, the loss of the sense of encounter, and the loss of internal contextualization. The author concludes: "Throughout the editing process there is a constant tension between maintaining the forward impetus of the film and providing enough contextual information so that the central narrative or argument continues to make sense."

Linda Williams begins her argument with a remark by Oliver Wendell Holmes, Jr., that a photograph is "a mirror with a memory," that is, an illustration of the visual truth of objects, persons, and events. Such certainty is not possible in the era of electronic and computer-generated images, in which every photo and film is understood as a manipulated construction. Williams quotes Fredric Jameson on "the cultural logic of postmodernism" based on "a whole new culture of the . . . simulacrum." Jameson argues that it no longer seems possible to represent the "real" interests of a people or class against the ultimate ground of social and economic determinations. Citing both the Rodney King tape and the greatly increased popularity of documentary, Williams points out that the lack of faith in images goes hand in hand with a new thirst "to be moved to a new appreciation of previously unknown truth." This is a rich contradiction that she begins to explore with a number of examples that ultimately end up on one side or the other of the way out of the postmodern dilemma: *JFK, Roger and Me, Our Hitler, Hotel Terminus: The Life and Times of Klaus Barbie, Truth or Dare, Paris Is Burning, Who Killed Vincent Chin?,* and others.

Errol Morris's *The Thin Blue Line* is "a prime example of this postmodern documentary approach to the trauma of an inaccessible past." Because of its spectacular success in intervening in the truths known about this past, the film was instrumental in freeing Randall Adams from prison. The film eschews cinema verité completely, exhibiting instead an expressionist style in staging its reenactments of the versions of the murder by suspects Adams and Harris, and by several witnesses. The strategy of Morris's film is to set competing narratives alongside each other by reenacting all of them. Williams turns here to the other film she discusses in detail: Claude Lanzmann's *Shoah.* Acknowledging that the subjects of the two films are incommensurable, Williams sees a parallelism in method. What motivates both is not the opposition between absolute truth and absolute fiction, but the awareness of the final inaccessibility of a moment of crime, violence, trauma that is irretrievably located in the past. The two filmmakers do not so much represent this past as they reactivate it in images of the present. This is their distinctive postmodern feature as documentarians. In revealing the fabrications and scapegoating when fictional explanations were substituted for more difficult ones, they do not simply play off truth against lie; they show how lies function as partial truths to both the agents and witnesses of history's trauma. One of the most discussed moments of *Shoah* is the visit of Simon Srebnik to the town where he worked in the nearby death camp. The Poles on the church steps in Chelmno seem happy to see him, but in response to questions by Lanzmann, at least four of the people collaborate in providing an anti-Semitic account of the Holocaust. This fantasy, meant to assuage the Poles' guilt for their complicity in the extermination of the Jews, actually repeats their crime of the past in the present. Williams concludes that the truth of the Holocaust does not exist in any totalizing narrative, but only, as Lanzmann shows, as a collection of fragments.

BILL NICHOLS

THE VOICE OF DOCUMENTARY

Vol. 36, no. 3 (Spring 1983): 17–30.

It is worth insisting that the strategies and styles deployed in documentary, like those of narrative film, change; they have a history. And they have changed for much the same reasons: the dominant modes of expository discourse change; the arena of ideological contestation shifts. The comfortably accepted realism of one generation seems like artifice to the next. New strategies must constantly be fabricated to re-present "things as they are" and still others to contest this very representation.

In the history of documentary we can identify at least four major styles, each with distinctive formal and ideological qualities.[1] In this article I propose to examine the limitations and strengths of these strategies, with particular attention to one that is both the newest and in some ways the oldest of them all.[2]

The direct-address style of the Griersonian tradition (or, in its most excessive form, the March of Time's "voice of God") was the first thoroughly worked-out mode of documentary. As befitted a school whose purposes were overwhelmingly didactic, it employed a supposedly authoritative yet often presumptuous off-screen narration. In many cases this narration effectively dominated the visuals, though it could be, in films like *Night Mail* or *Listen to Britain,* poetic and evocative. After World War II, the Griersonian mode fell into disfavor (for reasons I will come back to later) and it has little contemporary currency—except for television news, game and talk shows, ads, and documentary specials.

Its successor, *cinéma vérité,* promised an increase in the "reality effect" with its directness, immediacy, and impression of capturing untampered events in the everyday lives of particular people. Films like *Chronicle of a Summer, Le Joli Mai, Lonely Boy, Back-Breaking Leaf, Primary,* and *The Chair* built on the new technical possibilities offered by portable cameras and sound recorders which could produce synchronous dialogue under location conditions. In pure *cinéma vérité* films, the style seeks to become "transparent" in the same mode as the classical Hollywood style—capturing people in action, and letting the viewer come to conclusions about them unaided by any implicit or explicit commentary.

Sometimes mesmerizing, frequently perplexing, such films seldom offered the sense of history, context, or perspective that viewers seek. And so in the past decade we have seen a third style which incorporates direct address (characters or narrator speaking directly to the viewer), usually in the form of the interview. In a host of political and feminist films, witness-participants step before the camera to tell their story. Sometimes profoundly revealing, sometimes fragmented and incomplete, such films have provided the central model for contemporary documentary. But as a strategy and a form, the interview-oriented film has problems of its own.

More recently, a fourth phase seems to have begun, with films moving toward more complex forms where epistemological and aesthetic assumptions become more visible. These new self-reflexive documentaries mix observational passages with interviews, the voice-over of the film-maker with intertitles, making patently clear what has been implicit all along: documentaries always were forms of re-presentation, never clear windows onto "reality"; the film-maker was always a participant-witness and an active fabricator of meaning, a producer of cinematic discourse rather than a neutral or all-knowing reporter of the way things truly are.

Ironically, film theory has been of little help in this recent evolution, despite the enormous contribution of recent theory to questions of the production of meaning in narrative forms. In documentary the most advanced, modernist work draws its inspiration less from post-structuralist models of discourse than from the working procedures of documentation and validation practiced by ethnographic film-makers. And as far as the influence of film history goes, the figure of Dziga Vertov now looms much larger than those of either Flaherty or Grierson.

I do not intend to argue that self-reflexive documentary represents a pinnacle or solution in any ultimate sense. It is, however, in the process of evolving alternatives that seem, in our present historical context, less obviously problematic than the strategies of commentary, *vérité*, or the interview. These new forms may, like their predecessors, come to seem more "natural" or even "realistic" for a time. But the success of every form breeds its own overthrow: it limits, omits, disavows, represses (as well as represents). In time, new necessities bring new formal inventions.

As suggested above, in the evolution of documentary the contestation among forms has centered on the question of "voice." By "voice" I mean something narrower than style: that which conveys to us a sense of a text's social point of view, of how it is speaking to us and how it is organizing the materials it is presenting to us. In this sense "voice" is not restricted to any one code or feature such as dialogue or spoken commentary. Voice is perhaps akin to that intangible, moiré-like pattern formed by the unique interaction of all a film's codes, and it applies to all modes of documentary.

Far too many contemporary film-makers appear to have lost their voice. Politically, they forfeit their own voice for that of others (usually characters recruited to the film and interviewed). Formally, they disavow the complexities of voice, and discourse, for the apparent simplicities of faithful observation or respectful representation, the treacherous simplicities of an unquestioned empiricism (the world and its truths exist; they need only be dusted off and reported). Many documentarists would appear to believe what fiction film-makers only feign to believe, or openly question: that film-making creates an objective representation of the way things really are. Such documentaries use the magical template of verisimilitude without the story-teller's open resort to artifice. Very few seem prepared to admit through the very tissue and texture of their work that all film-making is a form of discourse fabricating its effects, impressions, and point of view.

Yet it especially behooves the documentary film-maker to acknowledge what she/he is actually doing. Not in order to be accepted as modernist for the sake of being modernist, but to fashion documentaries that may more closely correspond to a contemporary understanding of our position within the world so that effective political/formal strategies for describing and challenging that position can emerge. Strategies and techniques for doing so already exist. In documentary they seem to derive most directly from *Man with a Movie Camera* and *Chronique d'un été* and are vividly exemplified in David and Judith MacDougall's Turkana trilogy (*Lorang's Way, Wedding Camels, A Wife Among Wives*). But before discussing this tendency further, we should first examine the strengths and limitations of *cinéma vérité* and the interview-based film. They are well represented by two recent and highly successful films: *Soldier Girls* and *Rosie the Riveter*.

Soldier Girls presents a contemporary situation: basic army training as experienced by women volunteers. Purely indirect or observational, *Soldier Girls* provides no spoken commentary, no interviews or titles, and like Fred Wiseman's films, it arouses considerable controversy about its point of view. One viewer at Filmex interjected, "How on earth did they get the Army to let them make such an incredibly anti-Army film?" What struck that viewer as powerful criticism, though, may strike another as an honest portrayal of the tough-minded discipline necessary to learn to defend oneself, to survive in harsh environments, to kill. As in Wiseman's films, organizational strategies establish a preferred reading—in this case, one that favors the personal over

Soldier Girls

the political, that seeks out and celebrates the irruptions of individual feeling and conscience in the face of institutional constraint, that re-writes historical process as the expression of an indomitable human essence whatever the circumstance. But these strategies, complex and subtle like those of realist fiction, tend to ascribe to the historical material itself meanings that in fact are an effect of the film's style or voice, just as fiction's strategies invite us to believe that "life" is like the imaginary world inhabited by its characters.

A pre-credit sequence of training exercises which follows three women volunteers ends with a freeze-frame and iris-in to isolate the face of each woman. Similar to classic Hollywood-style vignettes used to identify key actors, this sequence inaugurates a set of strategies that links *Soldier Girls* with a large part of American *cinéma vérité* (*Primary, Salesman, An American Family*, the *Middletown* series). It is characterized by a romantic individualism and a dramatic, fiction-like structure, but employing "found" stories rather than the wholly invented ones of Hollywood. Scenes in which Private Hall oversees punishment for Private Alvarez and in which the women recruits are awakened and prepare their beds for Drill Sergeant Abing's inspection prompt an impression of looking in on a world unmarked by our, or the camera's, act of gazing. And those rare moments in which the camera or person behind it is acknowledged certify more forcefully that other moments of "pure observation" capture the social presentation of self we too would have witnessed had we actually been there to see for ourselves. When *Soldier Girls*' narrative-like tale culminates in a shattering moment of character revelation, it seems to be a happy coincidence of dramatic structure and historical events unfolding. In as extraordinary an epiphany as any in all of *vérité*, tough-minded Drill Sergeant Abing breaks down and confesses to Private Hall how much of his own humanity and soul has been destroyed by his experience in Vietnam. By such means, the film transcends the social and political categories which it shows but refuses to name. Instead of the personal becoming political, the political becomes personal.

We never hear the voice of the film-maker or a narrator trying to persuade us of this romantic humanism. Instead, the film's structure relies heavily on classical narrative procedures, among them: (1) a chronology of apparent causality which reveals how each of the three women recruits resolves the conflict between a sense of her own individuality and army discipline; (2) shots organized into dramatically revelatory scenes that only acknowledge the camera as participant-observer near the film's end, when one of the recruits embraces the film-makers as she leaves the training base, discharged for her "failure" to fit in; and (3) excellent performances from characters who "play themselves" without any inhibiting self-consciousness. (The phenomenon of filming individuals who play themselves in a manner strongly reminiscent of the performances of professional actors in fiction could be the subject of an extended study in its own right.) These procedures allow purely observational documentaries to asymptotically narrow the gap between a fabricated realism and the apparent capture of reality itself which so fascinated André Bazin.

This gap may also be looked at as a gap between evidence and argument.[3] One of the peculiar fascinations of film is precisely that it so easily conflates the two. Documentary displays a tension arising from the attempt to make statements about life which are quite general, while necessarily using sounds and images that bear the inescapable trace of their particular historical origins. These sounds and images come to function as signs; they bear meaning, though the meaning is not really inherent in them but rather conferred upon them by their function within the text as a whole. We may think we hear history or reality speaking to us through a film, but what we actually hear is the voice of the text, even when that voice tries to efface itself.

This is not only a matter of semiotics but of historical process. Those who confer meaning (individuals, social classes, the media, and other institutions) exist within history itself rather than at the periphery, looking in like gods. Hence, paradoxically, self-referentiality is an inevitable communicational category. A class cannot be a member of itself, the law of logical typing tells us, and yet in human communication this law is necessarily violated. Those who confer meaning are themselves members of the class of conferred meanings (history). For a film to fail to acknowledge this and pretend to omniscience—whether by voice-of-God commentary or by claims of "objective knowledge"—is to deny its own complicity with a production of knowledge that rests on no firmer bedrock than the very act of production. (What then becomes vital are the assumptions, values, and purposes motivating this production, the underpinnings which some modernist strategies attempt to make more clear.)[4]

Observational documentary appears to leave the driving to us. No one tells us about the sights we pass or what they mean. Even those obvious marks of documentary textuality—muddy sound, blurred or racked focus, the grainy, poorly lit figures of social actors caught on the run—function paradoxically. Their presence testifies to an apparently more basic absence: such films sacrifice conventional, polished artistic expression in order to bring back, as best they can, the actual texture of history in the making. If the camera gyrates wildly or ceases functioning, this is not an expression of personal style. It is a signifier of personal danger, as in *Harlan County USA*, or even death, as in the street scene from *The Battle of Chile* when the cameraman records the moment of his own death.

This shift from artistic expressiveness to historical revelation contributes mightily to the phenomenological effect of the observational film. *Soldier Girls, They Call Us Misfits*, its sequel, *A Respectable Life*, and Fred Wiseman's most recent film, *Models*, propose revelations about the real not as a result of direct argument, but on the basis of inferences we draw from historical evidence itself. For example, Stefan Jarl's remarkable film, *They Call Us Misfits*, contains a purely observational scene of its two 17-year-old misfits—who have left home for a life of booze, drugs, and a good time in Stockholm—getting up in the morning. Kenta washes his long hair, dries it, and then meticulously combs every hair into place. Stoffe doesn't bother with his hair at all. Instead, he boils water and then makes tea by pouring it over a tea bag that is still inside its paper wrapper! We rejoin the boys in *A Respectable Life*, shot ten years later, and learn that Stoffe has nearly died on three occasions from heroin overdoses whereas Kenta has sworn off hard drugs and begun a career of sorts as a singer. At this point we may retroactively grant a denser tissue of meaning to those little morning rituals recorded a decade earlier. If so, we take them as evidence of historical determinations rather than artistic vision—even though they are only available to us as a result of textual strategies. More generally, the aural and visual evidence of what ten years of hard

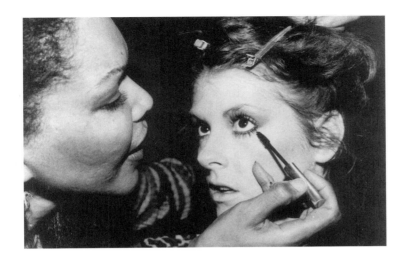

Fred Wiseman's *Models*
(Zipporah Films,
One Richdale Avenue,
Unit #4, Cambridge,
MA 02140)

living do to the alert, mischievous appearance of two boys—the ruddy skin, the dark, extinguished eyes, the slurred and garbled speech, especially of Stoffe—bear meaning precisely because the films invite retroactive comparison. The films produce the structure in which "facts" themselves take on meaning precisely because they belong to a coherent series of differences. Yet, though powerful, this construction of differences remains insufficient. A simplistic line of historical progression prevails, centered as it is in *Soldier Girls* on the trope of romantic individualism. (Instead of the Great Man theory we have the Unfortunate Victim theory of history—inadequate, but compellingly presented.)

And where observational cinema shifts from an individual to an institutional focus, and from a metonymic narrative model to a metaphoric one, as in the highly innovative work of Fred Wiseman, there may still be only a weak sense of constructed meaning, of a textual voice addressing us. A vigorous, active, and retroactive reading is necessary before we can hear the voice of the textual system as a level distinct from the sounds and images of the evidence it adduces, while questions of adequacy remain. Wiseman's sense of context and of meaning as a function of the text itself remains weak, too easily engulfed by the fascination that allows us to mistake film for reality, the impression of the real for the experience of it. The risk of reading *Soldier Girls* or Wiseman's *Models* like a Rorschach test may require stronger counter-measures than the subtleties their complex editing and *mise-en-scène* provide.

Prompted, it would seem, by these limitations to *cinéma vérité* or observational cinema, many film-makers during the past decade have reinstituted direct address. For the most part this has meant social actors addressing us in interviews rather than a return to the voice-of-authority evidenced by a narrator. *Rosie the Riveter*, for example, tells us about the blatant hypocrisy with which women were recruited to the factories and assembly lines during World War II. A series of five women witnesses tell us how they were denied the respect granted men, told to put up with hazardous conditions "like a man," paid less, and pitted against one another racially. *Rosie* makes short shrift of the noble icon of the woman worker as seen in forties newsreels. Those films celebrated her heroic contribution to the great effort to preserve the free world from fascist dictatorship. *Rosie* destroys this myth of deeply appreciated, fully rewarded contribution without in any way undercutting the genuine fortitude, courage, and political awareness of women who experienced continual frustration in their struggles for dignified working conditions and a permanent place in the American labor force.

Using interviews, but no commentator, together with a weave of compilation footage as images of illustration, director Connie Field tells a story many of us may think we've heard, only to realize we've never heard the whole of it before.

The organization of the film depends heavily on its set of extensive interviews with former "Rosies." Their selection follows the direct-cinema tradition of filming ordinary people. But *Rosie the Riveter* broadens that tradition, as *Union Maids*, *The Wobblies*, and *With Babies and Banners* have also done, to retrieve the memory of an "invisible" (suppressed more than forgotten) history of labor struggle. The five interviewees remember a past the film's inserted historical images reconstruct, but in counterpoint: their recollection of adversity and struggle contrasts with old newsreels of women "doing their part" cheerfully.

This strategy complicates the voice of the film in an interesting way. It adds a contemporary, personal resonance to the historical compilation footage without challenging the assumptions of that footage explicitly, as a voice-over commentary might do. We ourselves become engaged in determining how the women witnesses counterpoint these historical "documents" as well as how they articulate their own present and past consciousness in political, ethical, and feminist dimensions.

We are encouraged to believe that these voices carry less the authority of historical judgment than that of personal testimony—they are, after all, the words of apparently "ordinary women" remembering the past. As in many films that advance issues raised by the women's movement, there is an emphasis on individual but politically significant experience. *Rosie* demonstrates the power of the act of naming—the ability to find the words that render the personal political. This reliance on oral history to reconstruct the past places *Rosie the Riveter* within what is probably the predominant mode of documentary film-making today—films built around a string of interviews—where we also find *A Wive's Tale*, *With Babies and Banners*, *Controlling Interest*, *The Day After Trinity*, *The Trials of Alger Hiss*, *Rape*, *Word Is Out*, *Prison*

Rosie the Riveter (Clarity Films, 2600 10th St., Ste. 412, Berkeley, CA 94710)

for Women, Not a Love Story, Nuove Frontieras (Looking for Better Dreams), and *The Wobblies.*

This reinstitution of direct address through the interview has successfully avoided some of the central problems of voice-over narration, namely authoritative omniscience or didactic reductionism. There is no longer the dubious claim that things are as the film presents them, organized by the commentary of an all-knowing subject. Such attempts to stand above history and explain it create a paradox. Any attempt by a speaker to vouch for his or her own validity reminds us of the Cretan paradox: "Epimenides was a Cretan who said, 'Cretans always lie.' Was Epimenides telling the truth?" The nagging sense of a self-referential claim that can't be proven reaches greatest intensity with the most forceful assertions, which may be why viewers are often most suspicious of what an apparently omniscient Voice of Authority asserts most fervently. The emergence of so many recent documentaries built around strings of interviews strikes me as a strategic response to the recognition that neither can events speak for themselves nor can a single voice speak with ultimate authority.

Interviews diffuse authority. A gap remains between the voice of a social actor recruited to the film and the voice of the film.

Not compelled to vouch for their own validity, the voices of interviewees may well arouse less suspicion. Yet a larger, constraining voice may remain to provide, or withhold, validation. In *The Sad Song of Yellow Skin, The Wilmar 8, Harlan County, USA, Not a Love Story*, or *Who Killed the Fourth Ward*, among others, the literal voice of the film-maker enters into dialogue but without the self-validating, authoritative tone of a previous tradition. (These are also voices without the self-reflexive quality found in Vertov's, Rouch's, or the MacDougalls' work.) Diary-like and uncertain in *Yellow Skin*; often directed toward the women strikers as though by a fellow participant and observer in *The Wilmar 8* and *Harlan County*; sharing personal reactions to pornography with a companion in *Not a Love Story*; and adopting a mock ironic tone reminiscent of Peter Falk's Columbo in *Fourth Ward*—these voices of potentially imaginary assurance instead share doubts and emotional reactions with other characters and us. As a result they seem to refuse a privileged position in relation to other characters. Of course, these less assertive authorial voices remain complicit with the controlling voice of the textual system itself, but the effect upon a viewer is distinctly different.

Still, interviews pose problems. Their occurrence is remarkably widespread—from *The Hour of the Wolf* to *The MacNeil/Lehrer Report* and from *Housing Problems* (1935) to *Harlan County, USA*. The greatest problem, at least in recent documentary, has been to retain that sense of a gap between the voice of interviewees and the voice of the text as a whole. It is most obviously a problem when the interviewees display conceptual inadequacy on the issue but remain unchallenged by the film. *The Day After Trinity*, for example, traces Robert F. Oppenheimer's career but restricts itself to a Great Man theory of history. The string of interviews clearly identify Oppenheimer's role in the race to build the nuclear bomb, and his equivocations, but it never places the bomb or Oppenheimer within that larger constellation of government policies and political calculations that determined its specific use or continuing threat—even though the interviews took place in the last few years. The text not only appears to lack a voice or perspective of its own, the perspective of its character-witnesses is patently inadequate.

In documentary, when the voice of the text disappears behind characters who speak to us, we confront a specific strategy of no less ideological importance than its equivalent in fiction films. When we no longer sense that a governing voice actively provides or withholds the imprimatur of veracity according to its own purposes and assumptions, its own canons of validation, we may also sense the return of the paradox and suspicion that interviews should help us escape: the word of witnesses, un-

The Wilmar 8
(California Newsreel,
149 9th St., San
Francisco, CA 94103)

critically accepted, must provide its own validation. Meanwhile, the film becomes a rubber stamp. To varying degree this diminution of a governing voice occurs through parts of *Word Is Out, The Wobblies, With Babies and Banners,* and *Prison for Women.* The sense of a hierarchy of voices becomes lost.[5] Ideally this hierarchy would uphold correct logical typing at one level (the voice of the text remains of a higher, controlling type than the voices of interviewees) without denying the inevitable collapse of logical types at another (the voice of the text is not above history but part of the very historical process upon which it confers meaning). But at present a less complex and less adequate sidetracking of paradox prevails. The film says, in effect, "Interviewees never lie." Interviewees say, "What I am telling you is the truth." We then ask, "Is the interviewee telling the truth?" but find no acknowledgement in the film of the possibility, let alone the necessity, of entertaining this question as one inescapable in all communication and signification.

As much as anyone, Emile de Antonio, who pioneered the use of interviews and compilation footage to organize complex historical arguments without a narrator, has also provided clear signposts for avoiding the inherent dangers of interviews. Unfortunately, most of the film-makers adopting his basic approach have failed to heed them.

De Antonio demonstrates a sophisticated understanding of the category of the personal. He does not invariably accept the word of witnesses, nor does he adopt rhetorical strategies (Great Man theories, for example) that limit historical understanding to the personal. Something exceeds this category, and in *Point of Order, In the Year of the Pig, Milhouse: A White Comedy,* and *Weather Underground,* among others, this excess is carried by a distinct textual voice that clearly judges the validity of what witnesses say. Just as the voice of John Huston in *The Battle of San Pietro* contests one line of argument with another (that of General Mark Clark, who claims the costs of battle were not excessive, with that of Huston, who suggests they were), so the textual voice of de Antonio contests and places the statements made by its embedded interviews, but without speaking to us directly. (In de Antonio and in his followers, there is no narrator, only the direct address of witnesses.)

This contestation is not simply the express support of some witnesses over others, for left against right. It is a systematic effect of placement that retains the gaps between levels of different logical type. De Antonio's overall expository strategy in *In the Year of the Pig,* for example, makes it clear that no one witness tells the whole truth. De Antonio's voice (unspoken but controlling) makes witnesses contend with one another to yield a point of view more distinctive to the film than to any of its witnesses (since it includes this very strategy of contention). (Similarly, the unspoken voice of *The Atomic Cafe*—evident in the extraordinarily skillful editing of government nuclear weapons propaganda films from the fifties—governs a preferred reading of the footage it compiles.) But particularly in de Antonio's work, different points of view appear. History is not a monolith, its density and outline given from the outset. On the contrary, *In the Year of the Pig,* for example, constructs perspective and historical understanding, and does so right before our eyes.

We see and hear, for example, U.S. government spokesmen explaining their strategy and conception of the "Communist menace," whereas we do not see and hear Ho Chi Minh explain his strategy and vision. Instead, an interviewee, Paul Mus, introduces us to Ho Chi Minh descriptively while de Antonio's cutaways to Vietnamese countryside evoke an affiliation between Ho and his land and people that is absent from the words and images of American spokesmen. Ho remains an uncontained figure whose full meaning must be conferred, and inferred, from available materials as they are brought together by de Antonio. Such construction is a textual, and cinematic, act evident in the choice of supporting or ironic images to accompany interviews, in the actual juxtaposition of interviews, and even in the still images that form a pre-credit sequence inasmuch as they unmistakably refer to the American Civil War (an analogy sharply at odds with U.S. government accounts of Communist invasion). By juxtaposing silhouettes of Civil War soldiers with GIs in Vietnam, the precredit sequence obliquely but clearly offers an interpretation for the events we are about to see. De Antonio does not subordinate his own voice to the way things are, to the sounds and images that are evidence of war. He acknowledges that the meaning of these images must be conferred upon them and goes about doing so in a readily understood though indirect manner.

In the Year of the Pig

De Antonio's hierarchy of levels and reservation of ultimate validation to the highest level (the textual system or film as a whole) differs radically from other approaches. John Lowenthal's *The Trials of Alger Hiss,* for example, is a totally subservient endorsement of Hiss's legalistic strategies. Similarly, *Hollywood on Trial* shows no independence from the perhaps politically expedient but disingenuous line adopted by the Hollywood 10 over thirty years ago—that HUAC's pattern of subpoenas to friendly and unfriendly witnesses primarily threatened the civil liberties of ordinary citizens (though it certainly did so) rather than posing a more specific threat to the CPUSA and American left (where it clearly did the greatest damage). By contrast, even in *Painters Painting* and *Weather Underground,* where de Antonio seems unusually close to validating uncritically what interviewees say, the subtle voice of his *mise en scène* preserves the gap, conveying a strong sense of the distance between the sensibilities or politics of those interviewed and those of the larger public to whom they speak.

De Antonio's films produce a world of dense complexity: they embody a sense of constraint and over-determination. Not everyone can be believed. Not everything is true. Characters do not emerge as the autonomous shapers of a personal destiny. De Antonio proposes ways and means by which to reconstruct the past dialectically, as Fred Wiseman reconstructs the present dialectically.[6]

Rather than appearing to collapse itself into the consciousness of character witnesses, the film retains an independent consciousness, a voice of its own. The film's own consciousness (surrogate for ours) probes, remembers, substantiates, doubts. It questions and believes, including itself. It assumes the voice of personal consciousness at the same time as it examines the very category of the personal. Neither omniscient deity nor obedient mouthpiece, de Antonio's rhetorical voice seduces us by embodying those qualities of insight, skepticism, judgment, and independence we would like to appropriate for our own. Nonetheless, though he is closer to a modernist, self-reflexive strategy than any other documentary film-maker in America—with the possible exception of the more experimental feminist film-maker JoAnn Elam—de Antonio remains clearly apart from this tendency. He is more a Newtonian than an Einsteinian observer of events; he insists on the activity of fixing meaning, but it is meaning that does, finally, appear to reside "out there" rather than insisting on the activity of producing that "fix" from which meaning itself derives.

There are lessons here we would think de Antonio's successors would be quick to learn. But, most frequently, they have not. The interview remains a problem. Subjectivity, consciousness, argumentative form, and voice remain unquestioned in documentary theory and practice. Often, film-makers simply choose to interview characters with whom they agree. A weaker sense of skepticism, a diminished self-awareness of the film-maker as producer of meaning or history prevails, yielding a flatter, less dialectical sense of history and a simpler, more idealized sense of character. Characters threaten to emerge as stars—flashpoints of inspiring, and imaginary, coherence contradictory to their ostensible status as ordinary people.[7]

These problems emerge in three of the best history films we have (and in the pioneering gay film, *Word Is Out*), undermining their great importance on other levels. *Union Maids, With Babies and Banners,* and *The Wobblies* flounder on the axis of personal respect and historical recall. The films simply suppose that things were as the participant-witnesses recall them, and lest we doubt, the film-makers respectfully find images of illustration to substantiate the claim. (The resonance set up in *Rosie the Riveter* between interviews and compilation footage establishes a perceptible sense of a textual voice that makes this film a more sophisticated, though not self-reflexive, version of the interview-based documentary.) What characters omit to say, so do these films, most noticeably regarding the role of the CPUSA in *Union Maids* and *With Babies and Banners. Banners,* for example, contains one instance when a witness mentions the helpful knowledge she gained from Communist Party members. Immediately, though, the film cuts to unrelated footage of a violent attack on workers by a goon squad. It is as if the textual voice, rather than provide independent assessment, must go so far as to find diversionary material to offset presumably harmful comments by witnesses themselves!

Union Maids

These films naively endorse limited, selective recall. The tactic flattens witnesses into a series of imaginary puppets conforming to a line. Their recall becomes distinguishable more by differences in force of personality than by differences in perspective. Backgrounds loaded with iconographic meanings transform witnesses further into stereotypes (shipyards, farms, union halls abound, or for the gays and lesbians in *Word Is Out,* bedrooms and the bucolic out-of-doors). We sense a great relief when characters step out of these closed, iconographic frames and into more open-ended ones, but such "release" usually occurs only at the end of the films where it also signals the achievement of expository closure—another kind of frame. We return to the simple claim, "Things were as these witnesses describe them, why contest them?"—a claim which is a dissimulation and a disservice to both film theory and political praxis. On the contrary, as de Antonio and Wiseman demonstrate quite differently, Things signify, but only if we make them comprehensible.[8]

Documentaries with a more sophisticated grasp of the historical realm establish a preferred reading by a textual system that asserts its own voice in contrast to the voices it recruits or observes. Such films confront us with an alternative to our own hypotheses about what kind of things populate the world, what relations they sustain, and what meanings they bear for us. The film operates as an autonomous whole, as we do. It is greater than its parts and orchestrates them: (1) the recruited voices, the recruited sounds and images; (2) the textual "voice" spoken by the style of the film as a whole (how its multiplicity of codes, including those pertaining to recruited voices, are orchestrated into a singular, controlling pattern); and (3) the surrounding historical context, including the viewing event itself, which the textual voice cannot successfully rise above or fully control. The film is thus a simulacrum or external trace of the production of meaning we undertake ourselves every day, every moment. We see not an image of imaginary unchanging coherence, magically represented on a screen, but the evidence of an historically rooted act of making things meaningful comparable to our own historically situated acts of comprehension.

With de Antonio's films, *The Atomic Cafe, Rape,* or *Rosie the Riveter,* the active counterpointing of the text reminds us that its meaning is produced. This foregrounding of an active production of meaning by a textual system may also heighten our conscious sense of self as something also produced by codes that extend beyond ourselves. An exaggerated claim, perhaps, but still suggestive of the difference in effect of different documentary strategies and an indication of the importance of the self-reflexive strategy itself.

Self-reflexiveness can easily lead to an endless regression. It can prove highly appealing to an intelligentsia more interested in "good form" than in social change. Yet interest in self-reflexive forms is not purely an academic question. *Cinéma vérité* and its variants sought to address certain limitations in the voice-of-God tradition. The interview-oriented film sought to address limitations apparent in the bulk of *cinéma vérité,* and the self-reflexive documentary addresses the limitations of assuming that subjectivity and both the social and textual positioning of the self (as filmmaker or viewer) are ultimately not problematic.

Modernist thought in general challenges this assumption. A few documentary filmmakers, going as far back as Dziga Vertov and certainly including Jean Rouch and the hard-to-categorize Jean-Luc Godard, adopt the basic epistemological assumption in their work that knowledge and the position of the self in relation to the mediator of knowledge, a given text, are socially and formally constructed and should be shown to be so. Rather than inviting paralysis before a centerless labyrinth, however, such a perspective restores the dialectic between self and other: neither the "out there" nor the "in here" contains its own inherent meaning. The *process* of constructing meaning overshadows constructed meanings. And at a time when modernist experimentation is old-hat within the avant-garde and a fair amount of fiction film-making, it remains almost totally unheard of among documentary film-makers, especially in North America. It is not political documentarists who have been the leading innovators. Instead it is a handful of ethnographic film-makers like Timothy Asch (*The Ax Fight*), John Marshall (*Nai!*), and David and Judith MacDougall who, in their meditations on scientific method and visual communication, have done the most provocative experimentation.

Take the MacDougalls' *Wedding Camels* (part of the Turkana trilogy), for example. The film, set in Northern Kenya, explores the preparations for a Turkana wedding in day-to-day detail. It mixes direct and indirect address to form a complex whole made up of two levels of historical reference—evidence and argument—and two levels of textual structure—observation and exposition.

Though *Wedding Camels* is frequently observational and very strongly rooted in the texture of everyday life, the film-makers' presence receives far more frequent acknowledgment than it does in *Soldier Girls*, or Wiseman's films, or most other observational work. Lorang, the bride's father and central figure in the dowry negotiations, says at one point, with clear acknowledgment of the film-makers' presence, "They [Europeans] never marry our daughters. They always hold back their animals." At other moments we hear David MacDougall ask questions of Lorang or others off-camera much as we do in *The Wilmar 8* or *In the Year of the Pig*. (This contrasts with *The Wobblies, Union Maids,* and *With Babies and Banners,* where the questions to which participant-witnesses respond are not heard.) Sometimes these queries invite characters to reflect on events we observe in detail, like the dowry arrangements themselves. On these occasions they introduce a vivid level of self-reflexiveness into the characters' performance as well as into the film's structure, something that is impossible in interview-based films that give us no sense of a character's present but only use his or her words as testimony about the past.

Wedding Camels also makes frequent use of intertitles which mark off one scene from another to develop a mosaic structure that necessarily admits to its own lack of completeness even as individual facets appear to exhaust a given encounter. This sense of both incompleteness and exhaustion, as well as the radical shift of perceptual space involved in going from apparently three-dimensional images to two-dimensional graphics that comment on or frame the image, generates a strong sense of a hierarchical and self-referential ordering.

Wedding Camels

For example, in one scene Naingoro, sister to the bride's mother, says, "Our daughters are not our own. They are born to be given out." The implicit lack of completeness to individual identity apart from social exchange then receives elaboration through an interview sequence with Akai, the bride. The film poses questions by means of intertitles and sandwiches Akai's responses, briefly, between them. One intertitle, for example, phrases its question more or less as follows: "We asked Akai whether a Turkana woman chooses her husband or if her parents choose for her." Such phrasing brings the film-maker's intervention strongly into the foreground.

The structure of this passage suggests some of the virtues of a hybrid style: the titles serve as another indicator of a textual voice apart from that of the characters represented. They also differ from most documentary titles which, since the silent days of *Nanook*, have worked like a graphic "voice" of authority. In *Wedding Camels* the titles, in their mock-interactive structure, remain closely aligned with the particulars of person and place rather than appearing to issue from an omniscient consciousness. They show clear awareness of how a particular meaning is being produced by a particular act of intervention. This is not presented as a grand revelation but as a simple truth that is only remarkable for its rarity in documentary film. These particular titles also display both a wry sense of humor and a clear perception of the meaning an individual's marriage has for him or her as well as for others (a vital means of countering, among other things, the temptation of an ethnocentric reading or judgment). By "violating" the coherence of a social actor's diegetic space, intertitles also lessen the tendency for the interviewee to inflate to the proportions of a star-witness. By acting self-reflexively such strategies call the status of the interview itself into question and diminish its tacit claim to tell the whole truth. Other signifying choices, which function like Brechtian distancing devices, would include the separate "spaces" of image and intertitle for question/response; the highly structured and abbreviated question/answer format; the close-up, portrait-like framing of a social actor that pries her away from a matrix of on-going activities or a stereotypical background, and the clear acknowledgment that such fabrications exist to serve the purposes of the film rather than to capture an unaffected reality.

Though modest in tone, *Wedding Camels* demonstrates a structural sophistication well beyond that of almost any other documentary film work today. Whether its modernist strategies can be yoked to a more explicitly political perspective (without restricting itself to the small avant-garde audience that exists for the Godards and Chantal Akermans) is less a question than a challenge still haunting us, considering the limitations of most interview-based films.

Changes in documentary strategy bear a complex relation to history. Self-reflexive strategies seem to have a particularly complex historical relation to documentary form since they are far less peculiar to it than the voice-of-God, *cinéma vérité*, or interview-based strategies. Although they have been available to documentary (as to narrative) since the 'teens, they have never been as popular in North America as in Europe or in other regions (save among an avant-garde). Why they have recently made an effective appearance within the documentary domain is a matter requiring further exploration. I suspect we are dealing with more than a reaction to the limitations of the currently dominant interview-based form. Large cultural preferences concerning the voicing of dramatic as well as documentary material seem to be changing. In any event, the most recent appearances of self-reflexive strategies correspond very clearly to deficiencies in attempts to translate highly ideological, written anthropological practices into a proscriptive agenda for a visual anthropology (neutrality, descriptiveness, objectivity, "just the facts," and so on). It is very heartening to see that the realm of the possible for documentary film has now expanded to include strategies of reflexivity that may eventually serve political as well as scientific ends.

NOTES

1.   Many of the distinctive characteristics of documentary are examined broadly in *Ideology and the Image* (Bloomington: Indiana University Press, 1981), pp. 170–284. Here I shall concentrate on more recent films and some of the particular problems they pose.

2.   Films referred to in the article or instrumental in formulating the issues of self-reflexive documentary form include: *The Atomic Cafe* (USA, Kevin Rafferty, Jayne Loader, Pierce Rafferty, 1982), *Controlling Interest* (USA, SF Newsreel, 1978), *The Day After Trinity* (USA, Jon Else, 1980), *Harlan County, USA* (USA, Barbara Kopple, 1976), *Hollywood on Trial* (USA, David Halpern, Jr., 1976), *Models* (USA, Fred Wiseman, 1981), *Nuove Frontiera* (*Looking for Better Dreams*) (Switzerland, Remo Legnazzi, 1981), *On Company Business* (USA, Allan Francovich, 1981), *Prison for Women* (Canada, Janice Cole, Holly Dale, 1981), *Rape* (USA, JoAnn Elam, 1977), *A Respectable Life* (Sweden, Stefan Jarl, 1980), *Rosie the Riveter* (USA, Connie Field, 1980); *The Sad Song of Yellow Skin* (Canada, NFB, Michael Rubbo, 1970), *Soldier Girls* (USA, Nick Broomfield, Joan Churchill, 1981); *They Call Us Misfits* (Sweden, Jan Lindquist, Stefan Jarl, c. 1969), *Not a Love Story* (Canada, NFB, Bonnie Klein, 1981), *The Trials of Alger Hiss* (USA, John Lowenthal, 1980), *Union Maids* (USA, Jim Klein, Julia Reichert, Miles Mogulescu, 1976), *Who Killed the Fourth Ward?* (USA, James Blue, 1978), *The Wilmar 8* (USA, Lee Grant, 1980), *With Babies and Banners* (USA, Women's Labor History Film Project, 1978), *A Wive's Tale* (Canada, Sophie Bissonnette, Martin Duckworth, Joyce Rock, 1980), *The Wobblies* (USA, Stuart Bird, Deborah Shaffer, 1979), *Word Is Out* (USA, Mariposa Collective, 1977).

3.   Perhaps the farthest extremes of evidence and argument occur with pornography and propaganda: what would pornography be without its evidence, what would propaganda be without its arguments?

4.   Without models of documentary strategy that invite us to reflect on the construction of social reality, we have only a corrective act of negation ("this is not reality, it is neither omniscient nor objective") rather than an affirmative act of comprehension ("this is a text, these are its assumptions, this is the meaning it produces"). The lack of an invitation to assume a positive stance handicaps us in our efforts to understand the position we occupy; refusing a position proffered to us is far from affirming a position we actively construct. It is similar to the difference between refusing to "buy" the messages conveyed by advertising, at least entirely, while still lacking any alternative non-fetishistic presentation of commodities that can help us gain a different "purchase" on their relative use- and exchange-value. In many ways, this problem of moving from refusal to affirmation, from protest at the way things are to the construction of durable alternatives, is precisely the problem of the American left. Modernist strategies have something to contribute to the resolution of this problem.

5.   After completing this article, I read Jeffrey Youdelman's "Narration, Invention and History" (*Cineaste*, 12:2, pp. 8–15), which makes a similar point with a somewhat different set of examples. His discussion of imaginative, lyrical uses of commentary in the thirties and forties is particularly instructive.

6.   Details of de Antonio's approach are explored in Tom Waugh's "Emile de Antonio and the New Documentary of the Seventies," *Jump Cut*, no. 10/11 (1976), pp. 33–39, and of Wiseman's in my *Ideology and the Image*, pp. 208–236.

7.   An informative discussion of the contradiction between character witnesses with unusual abilities and the rhetorical attempt to make them signifiers of ordinary workers, particularly in *Union Maids*, occurs in Noel King's "Recent 'Political' Documentary—Notes on *Union Maids* and *Harlan County USA*," *Screen*, vol. 22, no. 2(1981), pp. 7–18.

8.   In this vein, Noel King comments, "So in the case of these documentaries (*Union Maids, With Babies and Banners, Harlan County, USA*) we might notice the way a discourse of morals or ethics suppresses one of politics and the way a discourse of a subject's individual responsibility suppresses any notion of a discourse on the social and linguistic formation of subjects" ("Recent 'Political' Documentary," p. 11). But we might also say, as the filmmakers seem to, "This is how the participants saw their struggle and it is well-worth preserving" even though we may wish they did not do so slavishly. There is a difference between criticizing films because they fail to demonstrate the theoretical sophistication of certain analytic methodologies and criticizing them because their textual organization is inadequate to the phenomena they describe.

MICHAEL RENOV

NEWSREEL

Old and New—Towards an Historical Profile

*Our films remind some people of battle footage: grainy, camera weaving
around trying to get the material and still not get beaten/trapped. Well, we and
many others, are at war. We not only document that war, but try to find ways
to bring that war to places which have managed so far to buy themselves isolation from it. . . . Our propaganda is one of confrontation. Using film—using
our voices with and after films—using our bodies with and without camera—to
provoke confrontation. . . . Therefore we keep moving. We keep hacking out
films, as quickly as we can, in whatever way we can.*

ROBERT KRAMER, NEW YORK NEWSREEL, 1968[1]

*Documentary remains the major form of political filmmaking in this country. It
has always been and probably will be in the foreseeable future. And yet, there
has been very, very little discussion of how documentary films actually function. The political efficacy of documentary is derived from the relationship of
the audience to the film—not the relationship of the filmmaker to the subject.*

LARRY DARESSA, CALIFORNIA NEWSREEL, 1983[2]

Vol. 41, no. 1 (Fall 1987): 20–33.

December 1987 will mark the twenty-year anniversary of the formation of Newsreel, a radical film-making collective conceived during the last flush of New Left activism. Once boasting offices in New York, San Francisco, Boston, Los Angeles, Detroit, Chicago, and Atlanta, Newsreel now survives in two versions: California Newsreel, San Francisco, producers and distributors of films about the workplace as well as South Africa and apartheid, with a new focus on media education (educating Americans *about* rather than *through* media); and Third World Newsreel, New York, vortex of film and video activities intended as the cultural interventions of the disenfranchised. In the following pages, I hope to suggest areas of conceptual as well as functional continuity and discontinuity between the two extant Newsreel organizations, as well as between the present enterprises and their Newsreel predecessors. In doing so, I seek to draw attention both to the achievements of a generation of American film activists and to the necessarily altered requirements for survival for politically committed documentarists in the late eighties. An historical profile of this sort can only point to a few of the most dramatic tendencies across decades of activity; this account will be supplemented by the soon-to-be-updated Third World Newsreel catalogue featuring descriptions of the Newsreel films in circulation (in addition to the hundred or so independently produced films and tapes they distribute) and by more in-depth accounts of the Newsreel infrastructure and output during its several phases.[3]

NEWSREEL PRE-HISTORY

The counterculture of the New Left tended toward negation, the issuing of shocks against presumed middle-class sensibilities, all the while reinforcing oppositional ties. Consequently, one must look elsewhere than to the culture of the American Left of the thirties for radical antecedents, perhaps to the Surrealist or

Columbia Revolt
(1968): one of
Newsreel's first films

Constructivist positions earlier in the century. If one may judge from the rhetoric of first-generation Newsreelers such as Robert Kramer, it is the utopian socialism of the immediately post-revolutionary Soviet Union that resonates most deeply with the cultural radicalism of the New Left, not the populist humanism of the American thirties.

It is the combination of youthfulness, enthusiasm, and volatility that links the work and writing of Dziga Vertov with the first wave of Newsreel practitioners. Both were dedicated to the concept of a continuing revolution and the potential of the cinema to mobilize a shared political identity necessary for broad-based social change. What separates the two and forces us to pose them in dialectical tension are their respective relations to state power and to technology. Vertov and his comrades worked at the cutting edge of a state-run revolution. Newsreel was a manifestation of the counterculture, defining itself always in opposition to the dominant, generating and encouraging resistance to the authority of the prevailing system of social, political, and economic relations.[4]

Vertov, trained as were so many other Soviet film artists for a scientific vocation, envisioned cinema as a technological vehicle for extending human powers of observation and cognition. His *kinoki* were labelled as "pilots" or "engineers" whose machine eye and radio ear could transform history. A child of his time, Vertov praised the beauty and perfection of the mechanical world and of chemical processes as the triumphant extension of natural forces.

MICHAEL RENOV

A half-century later, the relationship of New Left media activists to technology was chiefly one of negation. Early Newsreelers harbored little hope of appropriating or re-routing channels of communication to further their political goals. ("None of us are old enough to have any illusions about infiltrating the major media to reach mass consciousness and change it—we grew up on TV and fifties Hollywood."[5]) Unlike Vertov and his *kinoki,* or even the American Old Left, the founders of Newsreel in late 1967 could claim no institutional or mass-based source of support. Rather, as suggested earlier, mass base had become mass culture; party was replaced by a constituency-in-media. And yet, as with Vertov, there was within the early Newsreel movement a feverish impulse toward an elemental reconstruction for its audience—if not of perception, at least of consciousness. These radical cineastes were inspired by the enforced aesthetic privations of true guerrilla footage, documents of forces fighting wars of liberation in Vietnam, Africa, or Latin America, or by the pre-industrialized methods of the American underground film, which also offered refuge from the seamless, ideologically complicit products of the culture industry.

There is a further point of historical tangency between early Newsreel and Vertov's efforts in the pre-dawn of radical cinema. Just as the Soviet agit-trains, armed with camera equipment, film lab, and projector, traversed the land from 1919 to 1921 helping to forge a nascent cultural identity, so too did early Newsreelers mobilize their own community outreach program. Recent Academy Award recipient Deborah Shaffer (*Witness to War,* 1985) has spoken of the methods of distribution and exhibition in the Ann Arbor, Michigan chapter of Newsreel in 1969–70:

> We had two motorcycles and we put this box on the back of the motor-cycle to hold the projector. We'd go off on motorcycles with the projector and films. We would show them in dormitories, churches, people's living rooms, union halls, high school auditoriums.[6]

Vertov and his New Left cousins shared the zeal and inventiveness of the bricoleur-evangelist.

The reconstruction of consciousness for the Newsreel audience was to be achieved by a willed abdication from the standards of quality or craft; the intention was a return to an essential cinema dedicated to the requirements of building an adversarial culture. The simplicity of the appellation "Newsreel" figures a desire for a fundamental reinscription of values and practices. The unstinting revisionism which underlies this naming and its return to the blank slate of historical representation is an act of both youthful bravery and of a willing forgetfulness which breaks ties with a set of complex histories. The popular frontism of the American Left in the late 1930s and early 1940s was rooted in a hope of base-building and eventual unification while the political radicalisms of the late 1960s implied a contrary motive—the intensification of social contradiction to the point of rupture. For while the founding membership of Newsreel in New York included a core of veterans of mid-sixties community-organizing campaigns, the organization was forged in a moment of communal anger and indignation following the October 1967 March on the Pentagon. The agenda for a grass-roots, participatory democracy was buckling under the weight of a growing militancy.[7]

The altered agenda of an increasingly apocalyptic moment is expressed quite succinctly in *Garbage* (Newsreel, 1968), a film which examines a planned provocation by the members of a New York anarchist group calling itself "Up Against the Wall, Motherfuckers." During a prolonged strike of garbage collection workers, the Motherfuckers devise a plan to bring rotting garbage to the bastions of high culture and political power. They therefore dump enormous heaps of trash at the entrance-ways of Lincoln Center, home of the Metropolitan Opera and New York Philharmonic Symphony. As footage of this confrontation unspools, one demonstrator observes in voice-over that the difference between the Old Left and the New is expressed by their differing approaches to problems—the former sought to solve them, the latter to intensify them.

INSTITUTIONAL TIES—THE MYTH OF CREATION

As interviews with early New York Newsreel members indicate, the first generation of this radical film-making group represented a convergence of disparate impulses and constituencies.[8] There were the former SDS activists whose political sensibilities had been forged through a decade of community-based activism and programmatic wrangling. Of this number, Robert Kramer and Norm Fruchter, with his ties to such influential journals as *Studies on the Left* and *New Left Review*, remain the prototypes. These were the ideologues, the political "heavies" whose Movement credentials and rhetorical skills were capable of intimidating opposition in mass meetings. In addition, there were the "underground" film-makers whose concerns were loosely tied to notions of alternative art-making and self-expression, products of the boom period of the New American Cinema when the Brakhages and the Baillies commanded a sizable audience in the museums and on the campuses. The former Newsreel faction was likely to give priority to the construction of correct political organizations expressed in filmic terms while the latter tendency defined itself more directly in terms of its craft, guided by political concerns but not subsumed by them. This is, of course, a rough approximation or profile of some forty or fifty people whose idiosyncracies tended to obscure any such general tendencies.[9]

There is a larger and quite striking commonality decipherable, however; neither faction could claim for itself an organized or structurally coherent base of support—in short, an audience. Neither the Marxists nor the underground film-makers could presume to know their constituencies in any but the most abstract terms, the political activists because the Movement was undergoing a painful process of fragmentation typified by the SDS splits while the film artisans were rooted in a tradition of expressivity which valued the isolation of the artist within the hegemony of mass culture. The very values which united every Newsreel audience or potential audience were based on a fundamental negation of institutionalized frameworks (alienation from accepted social and political forms, cynicism toward the trade unionism that had been the bastion of the Old Left, a preference for vaguely articulated rather than explicit associations). A politically inflected cultural group like Newsreel, in bearing what Bill Nichols has characterized as a barometric relationship to the Left,[10] could only reproduce the soft boundaries and conceptual dissonance of late sixties political dissent typified by the rainbow of orientations and agendas that combined to protest the 1968 Chicago Democratic Convention—from the Dave Dellinger–style anti-war pacifists to the anarchic Yippie contingent.

Despite the conceptual pluralism of Newsreel's position in the early years, we can discern certain frequently unstated premises of the organization. From an interview with a range of Newsreelers published in a 1968 *Film Quarterly,* Marilyn Buck and Karen Ross gave voice to the mythic origins of the collective: "And all the TV channels and American films speak from the same mouth of control and power. We looked around . . . and Newsreel was conceived and born."[11] There is the suggestion of a kind of autochthony here, of a cleansing oracle arisen from within the belly of the mass-cultural beast. The two films which catapulted Newsreel to success in countercultural terms (*Columbia Revolt, Black Panther*—both 1968) offer further evidence of such a mythos of spontaneous generation. The films share an aura of revolutionary romanticism, offering direct contact with what appeared at the time to be the most advanced elements of the struggle—in short, news from the front. The Panther film, alternately titled *Off the Pig* (a phrase hypnotically chanted by a phalanx of Panthers during a demonstration at the Alameda County Courthouse), brought the words and images of Huey P. Newton, Eldridge Cleaver, and Bobby Seale to Movement audiences everywhere. More importantly, by its *mise-en-scène* and incantatory music track accompanying bereted and leather-jacketed Panthers-in-training, the film manages to suggest a great deal more than it can show. "No more brothers in jail/The pigs are gonna catch hell" sing the militant brothers and sisters while Cleaver speaks of the bald-headed businessmen in the

Chamber of Commerce whose exploitation will be countered by mass insurgency as soon as the rest of America catches on (which Cleaver assures us will be very soon). Here is a mixture of buoyant militancy and a political optimism which is well nigh infectious—or would have been for a sympathetic 1968 audience. In any case, hundreds of prints sold in a matter of months.

As for *Columbia Revolt,* one need only consult the published responses of student audiences to be found in the underground press of the day. According to an October 1969 account appearing in *Rat,* a New York–based organ of the radical counterculture, *Revolt* was responsible for an incendiary outburst at a college campus in Buffalo: "At the end of the second film, with no discussion, five hundred members of the audience arose and made their way to the University ROTC building [the Reserve Officer Training Corps, target of much campus protest during the Vietnam War]. They proceeded to smash windows, tear up furniture and destroy machines until the office was a total wreck; and then they burned the remaining paper and flammable parts of the structure to charcoal."[12] What the Buffalo student body had observed (and the apocryphal nature of the tale is no hindrance to a discussion of mythic contours) was the vanguard action of their Ivy League cousins, a model of energetic but sustained resistance to malign authority. The analysis contained in *Columbia Revolt* is muted in comparison to the spectacle of solidarity and community it offers. The New Age marriage rites of two students, the support marches of sympathetic faculty members, the pitch-and-catch of food stuffs holding intact the supply lines which, like the Ho Chi Minh Trail, meant sustenance for the guerrillas under siege—all these depictions of newly conceived social relations live on long after the immediate gymnasium construction issue is forgotten.

The efforts of the early Newsreel collectives aimed to inform and inspire their Movement audiences, with the balance between the two functions always in question. While a pre-Newsreel film like *Troublemakers* (1966), which follows the struggles of a community organizing group in a black neighborhood in Newark before the riots (examining the project's achievements and defeats), explores the contradictions inherent in grass-roots political activism, the post-'68 Newsreel film was likely to stress action and elicit engaged (if not educated) response. In a pronouncement that echoes the Surrealist position of the 1920s, Robert Kramer outlined the Newsreel program circa 1968: "We strive for confrontation, we prefer disgust/violent disagreement/painful recognition/jolts—all these to slow liberal head-nodding and general wonderment at the complexity of these times and their being out of joint."[13]

Given the avowedly confrontational status of the work, the emphasis upon a collective scheme of organization and production ("Newsreel is a collective rather than a cooperative; we are not together merely to help each other out

Columbia Revolt

as filmmakers but we are working together for a common purpose"),[14] what can be said about the precise division of labor of the groups in question and the material conditions of production? As every Marxist knows, consciousness does not anticipate productive relations but is conditioned and determined by them. But a major philosopher of the New Left like Herbert Marcuse was quite willing to theorize (in *An Essay on Liberation*, 1969) that, in a stage of advanced capitalism, imagination could show reason the way. Artists and free-thinkers could reshape the horizons of a society soured and desensitized by an over-rationalized ethos of thought and action. As a loosely bound group of like-minded cultural interventionists, Newsreel was the ideal manifestation of this New Age dogma.

Decision-making and the setting of policy were matters of some contestation given the lack of clear lines of authority and the diverse backgrounds of the participants. At a time that felt like a crisis period, specific goals (even ill-defined ones like "stop the war") offered sufficient binding power to keep the wheels turning and the Movement audience served. Those who, like Norm Fruchter, were accustomed to a greater precision of shared principles and a more disciplined group dynamic found the Newsreel experience a trying one. "I was . . . more of a Marxist, I think, than a lot of people in Newsreel," says Fruchter, "and so I was both interested in those congeries of different folks, and at the same time skeptical about whether we were going to hold together. The energy was awesome."[15]

So far as the mechanism for production decisions was concerned, the pattern was erratic at best. The most fundamental decisions always surrounded the initial question—what films should be made. But a second question—how to finance a given project—often proved determinant. Films could be made if there were those within the collective who could manage to make them by whatever means might present themselves. If the final result was unacceptable to the group, the film could not receive the "Newsreel" imprimatur. Several funding routes seem to have recurred in the early days. There was a core elite within the New York collective who matched the profile of the SDS leadership throughout the sixties—college-educated white males, verbal, assertive, confident, with access to funding sources both personal and institutional. Robert Kramer and Robert Machover could call upon family resources to finance projects. (Indeed, this pattern is a time-honored one in American Left circles, most recently exemplified by Haskell Wexler's anti-Contra feature, *Latino*—bankrolled in part by his mother.) The Fruchters, Kramers, and Machovers of Newsreel were the bright and persuasive young men who could function within the world of capital, either by virtue of birthright or by acquired expertise. Fruchter, for example, was well suited for fundraising given his scholarly and literary credentials (as a published novelist) and his first-hand experience with Left funding networks. Fruchter has estimated that he succeeded in raising more money for *Troublemakers*, his film about the Newark Community Union Project, than had the Project itself over its several-year lifespan. There were simmering animosities over this relative monopoly of capital-access, rooted as it was in class background. Furthermore, this same group of men (who were a key faction of the New York collective's coordinating committee) possessed far greater technical skills and experience; Fruchter, Kramer, and Machover had formed Blue Van Films several years before.

A second faction consisted of yet another group of white males who, though less likely candidates for institutional support, were well under way as independent film-makers. By 1968, Marvin Fishman and Allan Siegel had both organized film-making workshops at the Free University in New York and were able to translate their expertise into Newsreel product. At the moment of Newsreel's formation in December 1967, it was decided that a film was needed to chronicle the October 1967 March on the Pentagon; Fishman was farthest along with a personal project along those lines. Newsreel #1 (1968), entitled *No Game*, was the result, despite the fact that the film bears only a passing resemblance to the "Newsreel style" familiar from the later works—scenes of conflict; lively, non-synch music interspersed with multiple voice-over narrations from impassioned participants. There were concerted efforts made to disseminate the technical skills, but the difficulties were more deeply embedded than these well-intentioned attempts could hope to rectify. Women and minorities—after lifetimes of limited access to resources, possessing severely stunted self-images as producers of culture—were incapable of closing the gap overnight. Frustration and unspoken critiques festered beneath the surface of the organization.

And yet a necessary pragmatism reigned. In the words of Allan Siegel: "It was the kind of thing that if you came up with the money to do it [make a film], well then, you could do it. You made a film. I always used to stash myself away someplace and make things out of nothing. So I kept turning things out . . ."[16] Power and status were thus linked to the ability to produce despite the unequal distribution of the requisite tools for the task. In his discussion of Newsreel's collective process in the early days, Norm Fruchter recalls the inequities with some regret:

> Your participation depended on having another means to finance yourself. There was a group of people who worked and therefore could never stay up all night . . . and couldn't shoot certain sequences. . . . And there were a lot of arguments about the contradictions of being in, not a rich person's organization, but certainly an organization which required the leisure to be full time in it. We talked about income-sharing but never did it. We talked about finding some way to subsidize the people who had to work and never did that. All the income that was brought in and all the fundraising that was done went right into the production of more films and that perpetuated the reign of the people who had self-sufficient resources or could somehow juggle their lives or their jobs or whatever so that they could do that. And I don't think it bothered us that much at the time. I remember thinking that, yeah, it was absolutely unfair and there was nothing to be done about it.[17]

Problems arising from inequities internal to the collective—income differentials, housing, or childcare needs—were viewed as secondary to the pressing struggle for social change. The politics of sexuality and of everyday life remained issues to be addressed in a later phase of the organization.

By the early seventies, although the first-generation Newsreelers had left the organization, factionalism based on differences of privilege and access enjoyed by collective members prevailed. From 1971 to 1973, New York Newsreel members split themselves into "haves" and "have-nots," with the distinctions among ethnicity, class background, and functional class position somewhat blurred. Thus Christine Choy, a Chinese woman, at 22 the holder of a master's degree in architecture from Columbia University, was a have-not, due in part to her activities within the organization's Third World Caucus. While salary differentials posed no basis for contention—minimal stipends and rent support for collective dwellings were the extent of financial support—stratification was expressed in subtle forms: the haves edited on a Steenbeck while the have-nots made do with an old Moviola.[18]

But the rift within the collective evidenced by the have/have-not division was only one stage among a series of convulsions that left New York Newsreel a three-person collective by 1973. The success of the San Francisco–shot *The Woman's Film* (1971) had coincided with the emergence of an outspoken feminist faction within the New York organization, which began to control distribution and exhibition; most of the men left the collective in the months that followed.

As the Third World faction within the group began to focus on recruiting minorities and passing on production skills, the rift between white members and those of color intensified to the breaking point. With the dwindling of the membership, the resources capable of sustaining the collective enterprise were near exhaustion. Gone were the human resources—years of experience in shooting and assembling footage under pressure for no money, and the financial reserves—family wealth to be tapped, as well as most of the equipment.

It should be noted that while the schisms that developed within Newsreel during the early seventies around class, gender, and race effected a series of ruptures at the localized, institutional level, these organizational convulsions serve to reinforce a sense of continuity at a broader historical level. For indeed, these were the same issues (gender, race, class) that increasingly split the always tenuous coalition of New Left/countercultural forces as the focus on war resistance waned. As debates over contradictions, primary and secondary, came to occupy center stage within Movement organizations, consensus collapsed. Newsreel was never merely a reflection or conduit, that is, *about* Movement tactics and sensibilities; it has always remained *of* the Movement, a palpable index of shifting fortunes and newfound necessities.

The single factor that ensured New York Newsreel's viability in 1973 remains the material basis for twenty years of continuity despite convulsions from within—that is, the collection of films themselves. The resurgence of production in New York did not occur until 1975, when work began on *From Spikes to Spindles* (1976), a project that established Third World Newsreel's reputation for compact, historically situated overviews of ethnic minorities in crisis (in this case, Chinese Americans in New York). Until that time, the focus of collective activity remained the revival of distribution of the original Newsreel collection (achieved in part through the issuing of a new catalogue), which was recognized as the backbone of the organization. The films were the sole resources that remained to the New York organization in 1973; they have sustained the Newsreel effort since that time as financial asset and historical legacy even as the New York and San Francisco collectives move toward a reordering of goals and priorities.

The film-making collective calling itself California Newsreel was formed in 1975 from the ashes of a San Francisco Newsreel branch which had absorbed the sort of gut-wrenching political upheavals and bitter factionalism that shook the New York group during the same period. (The chief source of San Francisco's division was a move toward the Revolutionary Communist Party by certain influential Newsreel members.) By 1978, California Newsreel was comprised of three white males—Larry Daressa, Larry Adelman, and Bruce Schmiechen—none of whom had been a part of the earlier incarnation of the San Francisco Newsreel collective that produced *Black Panther* and other militant films from 1968 to 1973. Several years later, another collective member was brought on to deal exclusively with archival and distributional matters (a black man, Cornelius Moore), while only recently Schmiechen has left the collective to pursue independent projects.

No greater contrast could prevail between Cal Newsreel and its predecessors with regard to its financial underpinnings, organizational precision, and concentration on distribution over production. Unlike New York Newsreel of the early years (and to a lesser extent Third World Newsreel), California Newsreel has emphasized distribution over production. Indeed, in the twelve years of its existence, the collective has produced only two films of its own while becoming a major player within a clearly demarcated sector of the educational film market. Cal Newsreel distributes films of particular interest to an audience of economists, sociologists, and labor historians for classroom use; to labor educators and organizers within the trade union movement; and to various progressive and special interest groups at the grass-roots level (churches, action groups, campus organizations). The two films produced, *Controlling Interest* and *The Business of America . . . ,* were the results of the collective's perception of a felt need within this clearly defined audience and within the Left in general. *Controlling Interest* attempts in its 45 minutes to explain the complex nature and operating procedures of the multinational corporation and was produced at a time when no such study was available for purposes of political education. The film has sold over 800 prints since its release in 1978.

The Business of America . . . likewise aimed to fill a gap in the available public-educational resources. It was conceived in the aftermath of the Reagan victory and was intended as a more personalized treatise than the data-heavy *Controlling Interest,* capable of exposing the massive failures of the Reagan economic program and its supply-side, trickle-down ethos. Both films "found" their audience precisely because they were tailored to its particular needs—arrived at through a variety of feed-back mechanisms and close contact with the client groups.

No longer can the Newsreel audience be defined as an amorphous mass of like-minded individuals concerned to stay abreast of breaking stories of exploitation and political victories. It's now a discrete body of buyers or renters of a media product deemed vital to the educational needs of their organization or curriculum. What is interesting about this shift is that, to a certain extent, these two audiences overlap inasmuch as the 1980s generation of Left academics, organizers, and educators are largely drawn from that ill-defined body of radicalized spectators of the late sixties/early seventies. If California Newsreel seems a more briskly functional and business-like version of its progenitors, the same can be said of its audience, the Left activists who have survived into the eighties, who have withstood the onslaught of budget cuts, diminishing numbers, and the nation's mood swing to the right.

Since I have discussed the two California Newsreel productions at length elsewhere, it seems more appropriate to concentrate here on the significant features of the organization as a business enterprise.[19] The San Francisco group has remained profitable by a combination of prescience and hard work. In the months after the Soweto uprisings in South Africa (June 1976), a collective decision was made to choose a Southern African focus—to purchase the distribution rights to a variety of films about Southern Africa and related issues in order to distribute them to interested parties worldwide. At the time, no such collection of films existed; even now, California Newsreel is the world's principal source of films on apartheid, divestment, and related issues with a total of 21 documentaries acquired from independents and the BBC alike.

The escalation of apartheid aggression throughout Southern Africa over the past several years and the upswing of world interest in countering the brutality of the Botha government through sanctions and strategies of resistance have subsequently rendered these films a resource in high demand. During the recent nationwide surge of campus protests against corporate investment in South Africa, California Newsreel played a vital role in boosting the level of educated debate simply by providing a range of relevant films as well as printed material researched and developed over nearly a decade.* Once again, although perhaps in a less dramatic fashion than in 1968, Newsreel was in the right place at the right time.

California Newsreel's formula for fiscal success combines business acumen with a knack for low-budget production made possible by the shrewd recy-

---

*Over its 12-year lifespan, California Newsreel has published eight separate catalogues and five books including an 88-page text entitled *Planning Work,* a manual of resources on technology and investment for labor education funded by the Ford Foundation and the German Marshall Fund. *Using Films in South Africa: An Activation Kit on Investment* contains suggestions for post-film discussions, a series of fact sheets exposing the scope of U.S. investment in South Africa, and a packet of reprinted articles covering precise, related topics culled from newspapers, scholarly journals, and pamphlets.

cling of archival footage and, in the beginning at least, the ability to attract donated labor (crew members, editing assistants, etc.). *Controlling Interest* was
made for $30,000 with only 10% of that figure generated internally. The
Methodist Church, small foundations, and concerned individuals provided the
bulk of the funding for that project while *The Business of America . . .* was financed largely (2/3 of the $120,000 total cost) by the Corporation for Public
Broadcasting, the corporate arm of the Public Broadcasting System now firmly
controlled by Reagan acolytes. In the first year of its circulation, more than
250 prints of the film were sold to what can only be considered its secondary
market (a series of nationwide PBS airdates broadcast the film to approxi-
mately four million Americans).

The remarkable truth is that California Newsreel can boast liquid assets
sufficient to ensure its existence for years to come. In spite of its bountiful resources, each collective member draws the same salary ($25,000 annually) and
will continue to do so, no matter how bullish the Left-wing educational film
market may become. In fact, all workers—from Daressa and Adelman to the
person who sweeps the floors at the crumbling, warehouse-district office
perched in its San Francisco alleyway—receive the same base pay. This feature
of the organization is its clearest link with Newsreel's past. There is one additional point of tangency with the early days, at least with one faction of the
first New York collective. California Newsreel's activities as producer and dis-
tributor are deeply tied to the perceived requirements of the American Left and
are calculated in pragmatic, politically sophisticated terms. Like the core membership of New Left ideologues of the late sixties, Cal Newsreel (and Daressa
in particular) is equal to the task of mastering the vagaries of contemporary
Marxist theory as well as mainstream economic thought and of offering cogently argued, conceptually sound analyses and critiques of national labor
policies and long-term economic programs.

In something of a departure from its past achievements, California Newsreel
has chosen to mark its twentieth anniversary year by launching a major five-year
project aimed at deconstructing media as conventionally produced and received.
This "Media on Media" project will attempt to use the prevailing technology
(namely, broadcast television) to generate a meta-discourse on communications,
an anti-television capable of exploring new modes of expression as well as new
techniques for reading—in effect, to establish a context for exchange between
media products and their audiences. California Newsreel thus commits itself to
the creation of an environment favorable to a rejuvenated, experimental, reflexive documentary form at a moment of flagging hopes among American independent producers.

California Newsreel thus announces a dramatic shift of emphasis from
"point of production" (the workplace) to "point of reception" (the home)

consistent with its analysis of the political/cultural focus that Left organizations need to develop in present circumstances. But the concern for engaging a nationwide rather than Movement audience is in accord with the organizations's public profile for nearly a decade. As co-chair of the National Coalition of Independent Public Television Producers, Larry Daressa has lobbied strenuously in Washington for a more meaningful role for independent producers within public broadcasting's program schedule as a way of insuring the vitality of contestation within an ever more uniform cultural climate. The present "Media on Media" project, while unique to the American airwaves, is clearly consistent with the efforts of British Channel Four's Michael Jackson, producer of "Open the Box" (1986), a six-part series exploring the complexities and social effects of television, and Jean-Luc Godard, whose groundbreaking videoworks of the seventies (*Six Fois Deux* and *France/Tour/Detour/Deux Enfants*) radically challenged the French viewing public's media expectations at formal and thematic levels. Indeed, California Newsreel's ultimate aim is to intervene in the viewing habits of America, to alter not so much what we see but how we see it. This will mean working to establish a space for innovation and experimentation on American television, perhaps through the creation of an Independent Programming Service on the order of Britain's Channel Four to explore new dissemination technologies and sponsor unconventional programming. Perhaps it is the sheer scale of such aspirations that provides the clearest vector of continuity with the New Left utopianism of Newsreel's founding moment.

THIRD WORLD NEWSREEL

As we have seen, the early Newsreel operation was able to offer battlefront coverage of contemporary struggles from a recognizably Left perspective—quickly and in vast number. If that function has been lost at California Newsreel, it lives on at the Manhattan headquarters of Third World Newsreel. At a time when politically oriented documentary film-making in the United States has suffered a near-catastrophic decline, Third World has remained capable of producing films at a dizzying pace. The garment district offices of the collective are always alive with production activities at several stages; the editing rooms are in constant use for in-house projects while visiting independent film-makers frequently avail themselves of the facilities and expertise at hand. In 1985, Third World shot and completed two 50-minute films, both of them commissioned or initiated by outside sources rather than generated from within the organization. *Namibia: Independence Now* was commissioned by the United Nations Council on Namibia; distributed by Third World Newsreel, the film has been translated into seven languages. *Chronicle of Hope: Nicaragua* was a project developed in co-ordination with the Nicaraguan Peace Fleet, a Florida-based organization that regularly ships clothing and medical supplies donated by concerned Americans. The film traces a single journey from its source in upstate New York, through a series of American communities, to the point of embarkation in Florida, and at last to safe harbor in Nicaragua, thus establishing a human bridge among nations.

The primary sources of this productive momentum remain Christine Choy and Allan Siegel, who, while maintaining a long-standing personal relationship, manage to stay involved in countless projects simultaneously, all at different stages of completion. Siegel's relationship with Newsreel extends from the original December 1967 meeting through 1970 and from 1974 to the present. During that time, he has worked in a range of capacities: shooting much of *Columbia Revolt;* editing and directing such early works as *Garbage, America, Community Control, Pig Power,* and *We Demand Freedom.* Siegel's recent credits include the Nicaraguan film and one of the three segments of *The Mississippi Triangle,* a 1984 film that examines a particularly eccentric ethnic conjuncture—Chinese/black intermarriage in white Mississippi—with film-makers of each ethnic background directing the appropriate segments.

Choy has directed at a furious pace for the past decade, receiving in the process fellowships from the Guggenheim Foundation, the American Film Institute, and the National Endowment of the Arts. Having come to the U.S. as a teenager from the People's Republic of China to attend school, Choy retains something of the outsider's view of American culture and politics. She has a photographer's eye and the skills of a graphic artist refined during her years of architectural training; she designs many of the layouts for the pamphlets and booklets which Third World distributes. Choy has also maintained a high profile in the Asian-American film and art-making communities and is active in a range of related organizations, coalitions, and support groups.

Unlike its San Francisco cousin, Third World Newsreel cannot begin to support its many projects through the sales and rentals of its films. Films are financed on an ad hoc basis, each one having a life and history of its own. In answer to a question concerning the economic health of the organization, Siegel replied: "Generally, we survive. There's a certain tension to that survival which just has to do with being a marginal-type arts organization. . . . Basically, we're a small business. It's taken us a while to figure out how you survive as a small business, and in that sense, California Newsreel is much more adept. . . . We've been somewhat more anarchistic in that regard."[20]

And yet, the track record of Third World Newsreel is a tremendously solid one. When increased funding for women's and minority arts projects began to become available in the late seventies, Third World Newsreel was already a veteran organization with an impressive roster of completed films to its credit.

Choy's enduring advocacy in the field of Asian-American cultural studies and her high visibility within ongoing lobbying efforts for minority access to public funding have helped to secure for Third World Newsreel and other minority media groups some measure of financial stability. Another avenue of Newsreel's sponsorship has been the establishment of the Third World Producers Project administered by the Film News Now Foundation, conduit for a variety of Newsreel-related projects. Under the leadership of Choy and Renee Tajima (a frequent Third World Newsreel collaborator), the program provides one-on-one consultation to Third World and women media producers in all aspects of their work (fundraising, film and video production skills, distribution). Still another increasingly significant component of the Third World Newsreel portfolio is the Advanced Production Workshop. Begun in 1978, the workshop offers ten to fifteen people a year-long experience in film and video production through weekly classroom sessions culminating in several finished works. The workshops offer valuable training and experience, a community-based alternative to the competitive, industry-oriented film school model.

On another front, Third World Newsreel's exhibition programs constitute a vital sector of the collective's activities. Former Newsreel member Pearl Bowser was responsible for conceiving and programming a series of travelling film exhibitions. "Independent Black American Cinema 1920–1980" began as a retrospective of more than forty films and videotapes showcased in France in 1980 which then toured the United States over a two-year period. Other major efforts of this type have included the publication (in 1982) of a booklet entitled "In Color: Sixty Years of Images of Minority Women in the Media," which offers a series of essays intended as a contribution to the dialogue around the imaging of Third World women and the position occupied by women within the media. A related program of a dozen films ranging from Ousmane Sembene's *Ceddo* to short independent works such as Sylvia Morales's *Chicana* was organized as an exhibition event in the New York area. A more ambitious exhibition series and accompanying publication was completed in 1983— "Journey Across Three Continents," which combined a diverse selection of films by African cineastes and film-makers of the black diaspora with a lecture series and 70-page catalogue. The series toured 35 cities over a three-year period in an attempt to expose new audiences to the work as well as to convey the richness and diversity of the black experience in Africa, Europe, and the Americas. "Journey Across Three Continents," assembled and curated once again by Pearl Bowser, drew upon the research contributions of seven Black Studies scholars. Through its exhibition projects, Third World Newsreel has sought to facilitate dialogue between minority artists and concerned spectators, to develop an American audience for black and Third World media works outside the major urban centers. In this sense, Third World Newsreel shares California Newsreel's emphasis upon organizing at the "point of reception."

Spearheaded by Ada Gay Griffin, who joined Third World Newsreel through the Advanced Production Workshop, distribution has become an area of intensified focus, with the collection including more than 150 films and tapes. In addition to the early Newsreels, Cuban and Vietnamese films of the late 1960s and early 1970s, and the subsequent Newsreel projects of Siegel and Choy, the Third World Newsreel catalogue features the work of such independent producers as Arthur Dong, Charles Burnett, Steve Ning, Lourdes Portillo, and numerous lesser-known artists. By opting for nonexclusive contracts with minority producers, Third World seeks further coverage and heightened visibility for producers, while offering an average 50% return to the film-maker. Griffin has emphasized outreach to educational and community groups on a sliding scale: "I use discretion to give discounts to people I know should have access to the film."[21] The priority here is to promote the work of minority artists unable to find distributional outlets elsewhere due to the limited appeal or controversial nature of the work—or its aesthetic roughness. In Griffin's opinion, the time has not yet arrived when aesthetic standards alone can be allowed to determine the life of socially concerned programming. Training programs and consultational services rather than elitist distributional practices have been chosen as the way to raise the level of professionalism within the minority media community.

The Anthology of Asian-American Film and Video functions as an additional and ongoing distribution project for the collective. Begun in 1984, the Anthology houses some thirty films by and about Asian-Americans, making this the most significant collection of such work. Like the larger Third World distributional scheme of which it is a part, the Anthology functions as a clearinghouse and organizational vehicle for independent productions, both documentary and fiction, which would be hard-pressed to find their appropriate audiences. The Anthology is a serious contribution toward the redress of an historical imbalance, the exclusion from public view of the dreams, aspirations, and achievements of minority populations within the United States. Given its history and the tenacity of the core collective members, Third World Newsreel's position in the vanguard of cultural-political change seems assured.

CONCLUSION

In assessing the complex contributions of Newsreel in its various incarnations, we must note the relationship of the local and cultural to the macro-economic or infrastructural level which is, in the end, determinant. The unceremonious retreat of progressive forces in this decade has by now convinced us that a Marcusean analysis sacrifices explanatory or predictive power for inspirational zeal.[22] Fredric Jameson, in a recent ambitious attempt to periodize the sixties, concludes that the turbulent decade represented, after all, a moment of transition from one infrastructural or systemic stage of capitalism to another. The eighties can, according to Jameson, be characterized as global capitalism's moment of reentrenchment, the era in which the unbound social forces and liberating energies of the prior moment must be brought to heel. The sixties' unleashing of prodigious and unexpected new forces, issuing from the social movements of blacks, students, feminists, and Third Worlders, produced a kind of "surplus consciousness" disinclined to forward the multinational corporate agenda.[23] It is these emergent, relatively maverick constituencies that late capitalism must now attempt to proletarianize. But Newsreel has, from its beginnings, remained an active contributor to the development and dissemination of this "surplus consciousness," advocating resistance to the hegemonic while cultivating the values of a nascent political culture. Amidst the conservative backsliding and backlashing of the eighties, Newsreel has emerged as America's most consistent radical documentary voice. If, in the early years, its films spoke primarily to the Movement vanguard, Newsreel has moved toward a deepening of its ties with a broad spectrum of working Americans, offering a coherent Left perspective for an analysis-starved audience as well as a route to public access for minority artists. And finally, through continuing distribution of the early films of struggle and confrontation, the Newsreel enterprise has sustained the popular memory of concerted, energetic political activism. If the efforts of the sixties are to escape recuperation, to survive and, in time, to be renewed, it will be through cultural as well as political agitation. Given the history of the organization and its achievements to date, one can reasonably look to Newsreel for leadership in the struggle ahead.

The address of California Newsreel is 149 9th St., San Francisco, CA 94103; tel. (415)621-6196. Third World Newsreel is located at 545 8th Ave., 10th fl., New York, NY 10018; tel. (212) 947-9277.

1. From a series of interviews with Newsreel members in *Film Quarterly* 20, No. 2 (Winter 1968–69), 47–48.

2. Author's interview with Larry Daressa, 22 December 1983.

3. See Bill Nichols, *Newsreel: Film and Revolution,* unpublished master's thesis, UCLA, 1972. Nichols has, to date, produced the most valuable and extensive scholarship on Newsreel. In addition to the fine master's thesis cited here, see his *Newsreel: Documentary Filmmaking on the American Left* (New York: Arno Press, 1980).

4. Newsreel was but one of many Movement manifestations of the "Great Refusal." Identifying with the dispossessed, the relatively affluent first-generation Newsreelers cast their lot with those systematically excluded from privilege. By the end of the decade, the lumpen ranks were swelled by middle-class youth who rejected their birthright in order to effect meaningful social change.

5. Interview with Norm Fruchter in *Film Quarterly,* 44.

6. Author's interview with Deborah Shaffer, 19 August 1986.

7. A particularly striking index of the shift of organizing focus and radical sensibility from 1965 to 1969 is provided by contrasting two films by Norman Fruchter, one of the central figures of Newsreel's "first generation." *Troublemakers* (Fruchter and Robert Machover, 1966) chronicles an SDS organizing effort (the Newark Community Union Project led by Tom Hayden) that brought the skills and energy of middle-class college students to a black ghetto of the urban north. The film's brilliance lies in its willingness to consider the Movement's shortcomings and limitations in the period preceding the outbreaks of violence and confrontation. For further discussion of this phase of New Left

realpolitik, see Wini Breines, *The Great Refusal: Community and Organization in the New Left: 1962–69* (New York: Praeger, 1982). The second film, *Summer '68* (Fruchter and John Douglas, 1969), focuses on the several facets of cultural and political struggle within the ranks of a foundering New Left coalition (the G.I. coffee-house movement, the underground press, draft resistance organizing) which culminated in the August 1968 confrontation on the streets of Chicago at the Democratic National Convention. The shift is from community organizing to mass agitation, from fighting small battles using non-violent tactics to waging mass-mediated war with Daley's shock troops.

8. Interviews with two founding New York Newsreel members, Allan Siegel and Norm Fruchter.

9. This political/aesthetic bifurcation, though significant, obscures the relative homogeneity of the class, race, and gender composition of both factions. Neither women nor people of color tended to occupy positions of leadership in the organization prior to 1971.

10. Nichols, *Newsreel: Film and Revolution*, 73.

11. Interview with Marilyn Buck and Karen Ross in *Film Quarterly*, 44.

12. *Rat* (October 29–November 12, 1969), 8.

13. Interview with Robert Kramer in *Film Quarterly*, 46.

14. Interview with Marilyn Buck and Karen Ross in *Film Quarterly*, 44.

15. Author's interview with Norm Fruchter, 18 June 1985.

16. Author's interview with Allan Siegel, 18 June 1985.

17. Author's interview with Fruchter. In addition to the ideologues and the underground film-makers, another smaller faction of Newsreel producers existed—still primarily male—composed of those who raised funds necessary for production through illicit activities, principally drug-dealing. Pot was the ritual cornerstone of the counterculture; funds generated by its sale, when turned to the public good, were viewed as a fully legitimate source of income. The fallout from that method of fund-raising was a small but painful rate of attrition as Newsreelers were sent to prison on drug charges.

18. Author's interview with Christine Choy, 20 August 1986. Choy noted that her first Newsreel paycheck was not drawn until 1981, a full ten years after her arrival. A two-year CETA grant, welfare, and unemployment compensation furnished her means of survival for a decade.

19. See my "The Imaging of Analysis: Newsreel's Re-Search for a Radical Film Practice," *Wide Angle* 6, No. 3 (1984), 76–84.

20. Author's interview with Siegel.

21. Author's interview with Ada Gay Griffin, 8 August 1986.

22. See in particular Herbert Marcuse's *An Essay on Liberation* (1969), which contains the following succinct formulation of the "aesthetic ethos" of the sixties, a theoretical position that validated the realm of the creative imagination independent of quotidian (and frequently neglected) efforts toward mass base-building: ". . . the development of the productive forces beyond their capitalist organization suggests the possibility of freedom *within* the

realm of necessity. The quantitative reduction of necessary labor could turn into quality (freedom) . . . But the construction of such a society presupposes a type of man with a different sensitivity as well as consciousness: men who would speak a different language, have different gestures, follow different impulses . . . The imagination of such men and women would fashion their reason and tend to make the process of production a process of creation." Herbert Marcuse, *An Essay on Liberation* (Boston: Beacon Press, 1969), 21.

23. Fredric Jameson, "Periodizing the 60's," in *The 60's Without Apology,* 208–209.

DAVID MACDOUGALL

WHEN LESS IS LESS

The Long Take in Documentary

Photo Wallahs (1991)—a film by David and Judith MacDougall.
Photo © David MacDougall

Vol. 46, no. 2 (Winter 1992–93): 36–46.

There is a hidden problem in documentary film—the problem of the long camera take and what to do with it. With the exception of interview material, most of the shots in contemporary documentary films and television programs are only a few seconds long. This is in marked contrast to fiction films and television dramas, in which whole scenes are played out in a single shot. Documentary thus finds itself in the curious company of television commercials and music videos in seeking to maintain audience interest through the dynamics and variety of quick cutting. The long take has become the *terra incognita* of the modern documentary film, a blank space in a practice which devotes itself almost entirely to other properties of the shot. And this is contrary to its heritage, for documentary was born in the pleasures of watching such ordinary events as leaves shimmering on a tree or a train arriving at a station.

Not long ago I spent months filming in the streets of a small town in northern India. The finished film is intentionally one of counterpoints and disjunctions and not at all a smoothly flowing narrative.[1] Yet while I was filming, something odd occurred which I still don't fully understand. I began to shoot a kind of "shadow" film alongside the main film. This notional film—notional because it remains unmade—consists of long camera takes which quite clearly could never have been used in the main film. My main justification for shooting these long takes was that we could at least extract and use pieces of them. But in the back of my mind they actually constituted an alternative film, a counter-film to the one we were making. They formed a necessary antidote, a way of holding on to qualities which are so often lost when a film is structured for its likely audiences. I remember thinking at the time: "Is it possible to go back to zero, to film as if the cinema has just been invented? What would it be like to work like Louis Lumière when he first set up his camera on the street?"

Some of these long takes last five or six minutes (200 feet of 16mm); none are shorter than a minute or two. To watch these shots one must suspend one's usual moviegoing and television-watching expectations. But these expectations serve as a frame of reference for what I want to discuss here.

Like a spark or a stab of lightning, a shot discharges most of its meaning at once, within the first few microseconds of appearing on the screen. If we close our eyes after that first instant, the meaning survives. The mind arrests it like the shutter of a camera. What follows in our response may be very different— a sudden adherence to something happening within the shot, or a kind of coasting perusal. Or so it can be if the shot continues. But most shots are not allowed to. In film-making few shots are used in their entirety. Most are shot long and cut short.

Christopher Pinney has argued that still photographs are more indeterminate than films, offering the viewer more because they dictate meanings less. Social scientists in particular, he suggests, are afraid of still photographs and prefer film because "still images contain *too many meanings* whereas the desirability of film lies precisely in its ability to constrain meaning through narrative chains of signification. . . . They close off plural readings in the temporal flow of succession and destruction."[2] The temporal and sequential structure of film thus "provides a fortification against undesirable and 'unwarranted' readings."[3]

But applying this argument to film itself produces a curious reversal of Pinney's observations. Short camera takes resemble still photographs in their fixing of a single image, but by their very brevity they disallow the kind of perusal of the image over time permitted by photographs and by longer takes. Longer takes, which create sequential chains and the narrative cloistering of meanings, also undermine these very meanings by leaving the viewer more time to ignore or challenge them. It can thus be said that the long take comes eventually to resemble the still photograph more closely than the short take, at least in these "lexical" properties.

Just as shots may be short or long, so there are short films, long films, and occasionally very long films which are rarely seen. While no one would argue that how one reads entire films is analogous to how one reads individual shots, there is perhaps a connection between the visual context within which a shot is framed and the footage from which a finished film is extracted. Dai Vaughan writes of an ideal cinema, never to be fully achieved because tending toward an impossible conflation, "something which would attain to a narrative significance whilst remaining random."[4] The films that have come closest for him have been certain documentary films for television shot in cinéma-vérité or long-take style: "Not the rushes, yet not the fine cuts and most certainly not the transmitted versions with their cellophane wrap of commentary and captions and studio presentation, but the films as they stood when their narrative structures had just begun to emerge with the patient chipping away of the surrounding substance, yet were still perceptibly of its density and of its mass."[5]

I want to examine this problem of the ideal and the actual, the object within grasp yet somehow lost, and draw a broad analogy between the way in which shots are reduced in length in films and the way in which an entire body of footage shot for a film is reduced to produce the finished film. On the way I hope to question some of the assumptions which underlie these practices.

DISQUIET IN DOCUMENTARY

Long takes were not always the exception. In the early days of the cinema, when all films consisted of a single shot, they were the norm. Louis Lumière's first films ran for up to a full minute uncut—the length of a roll of film at the time. Some of Georges Demeny's shots (filmed in the 60mm gauge as early as 1895) ran to 40 seconds. That is very long by today's standards, even in fiction films,[6] although a few directors (Jancsó, Jarmusch) have created distinctive styles around very long takes. In television documentary the average length of a shot is closer to five seconds, excepting interviews and "talking-head" presentations. These shots tend to be cut automatically at the point where it is assumed audience attention drops, or where there is any suggestion of a pause in narrative flow.

The great enemy of documentary (and oddly, rather a taboo topic of discussion among film-makers themselves) is the "dead spot" in which nothing seems to be happening. Film producers are terrified of such moments, for they are terrified of audience impatience.[7] I suspect that the taboo status of this topic goes back to an inherent contradiction in documentary principles. In the early days of cinéma vérité and Direct Cinema, the prevailing ideology had it that dead spots weren't supposed to exist. Ordinary life was deemed to be interesting and worthy of everyone's attention. But documentary film-makers still contrived to avoid dramaturgical dead spots, cutting around them or focusing on exciting events and famous people. Documentary, whatever its ideology, still took its shape from fiction or journalism. It had to defend its interest in the ordinary by making sure that the ordinary played well. There was a tacit understanding that you didn't talk publicly about this. Who cared to admit that documentary actually concealed the lacunae characteristic of ordinary life and chose only the best bits, just like the fiction film-makers?

What constitutes a "long take" is obviously an artificial and somewhat arbitrary concept, formed in relation to an average notion of shot length and affected by content and position as well as by duration. Long takes are perhaps better defined by their structural qualities than by their length. Does the shot, for example, form an entire sequence in the film, or is it merely part of a more extended, edited sequence? In this analysis, the term "long take" refers more to a method of film construction than to actual length. Brian Henderson has pointed out that although Murnau uses a long-take style, his shots are actually quite short.[8] In his films the viewer's attention tends to be focused more upon developments within shots than upon linkages between them.

It is also evident that shots of long duration are not necessarily more revealing than if they had been shorter—for example, shots of repetitive activities or shots containing limited information which is rapidly grasped by the viewer. It is no use comparing generically different materials. Duration is perhaps the least important criterion in comparing a static, practically empty frame and a frame crowded with activity. And yet . . . and yet, as I shall argue later, absolute duration does finally matter. It is not wholly subjective and has its own measure of influence upon our reading of shots.

THE VIEWING OF IMAGES

It seems almost self-evident that how long we look at an image affects what we see in it and how we interpret it. Even if there were no other evidence of this, it has been shown that the eye successively scans an image in a series of fixations. If the time for doing this is cut short, the eye fixes on fewer points and the mind creates a less extensive version of what David Marr has called the "primal sketch."[9] In talking about viewing film images it is useful to place the process in the context of viewing practices generally. How does film-viewing differ from viewing other kinds of images, such as still photographs?

Sometimes the length of time we devote to a still photograph is determined for us, as when a train we are on flashes by a billboard with a photograph on it. The frequency with which we view photographs is also often beyond our control: it is the aim of advertisers to expose us to the same pictures as often as possible, although many photographs, such as those in newspapers, we see only once, and then usually briefly. Others, such as family snapshots, may be seen again and again—and we may choose to study them for quite long periods.

When we watch films we exchange the role of private consumer of images for that of public participant at a spectacle. Our choices become more limited. Not only are the still photographs of the film regulated to 24 or 25 per second, but the length of time we have to view each shot is precisely dictated. We thus surrender an important part of our control over the image, although not all of it. There is still the possibility of searching the shot and interpreting it to some degree independently—for example, by looking for "peripheral detail."[10] How we interpret it depends upon who we are and what assumptions we bring to it. This is a fertile process, the text of the film interacting with the texts of personality, culture, and society that define us. Despite that, there are habits of film-viewing which will hold broadly true for audiences with a shared set of cultural expectations. If the following description is in any way recognizable, it is because it applies to a quite specific set of film-making and film-viewing conventions.

RESPONDING TO THE SHOT

For Western, middle-class viewers (at least), the initial response to a shot is determined both by its content and placement in the context of the film and by various plastic and compositional elements of the shot itself. The audience, from its grasp of the context, quickly identifies the intended center of signification of the shot. In a typical character-centered film, for example, imagine that a person whom we have already seen walks down a street and encounters a stranger. Our attention attaches to this person, is then transferred to the stranger, and then perhaps shifts back again to the familiar character. We take in certain background details, but we identify the primary meaning of the shot as residing in what happens to the major character. This primary meaning—perhaps related to what Eisenstein termed the "dominant"—need not be a person, or even a specific visual object. For example, a slow pan over a city may simply signify "a sunny morning in San Francisco" (as in Hitchcock's *Vertigo*, 1958).

Dramatic films thus extend to us a challenge which is a little like a game. We are invited to participate in creating the meaning of each shot by recognizing its narrative or expository center. The length of the shot is gauged so that we must carry this out fairly quickly, leaving little time for other considerations. This contrast between a centered meaning and other coded and uncoded information in the shot may be thought of as a figure-ground relationship. What is identified as figure, and what as ground, is a result of placement and, as Nick Browne has shown for sequences of shots, may also shift and depend upon duration. Previously noted details may be brought forward retrospectively by a new context. Centered meanings may be forgotten in a process Browne calls "fading."[11]

However, there is a certain threshold of narrative or expository efficiency beyond which the motivated meaning of the shot is exhausted. If the shot unexpectedly remains on the screen without further developments, we may feel impatience or annoyance, during which we perhaps look away or withdraw our attention. If the shot continues still longer we may move to a third stage of what might be called "digressive search," when we begin to bring a very different and more idiosyncratic kind of interpretive process to bear upon the shot. In films like Andy Warhol's *Sleep* (1963) and *Blow-Job* (1964) our expectations are deliberately confounded and we are provoked into supplying the images with meaning. Audiences, however, are generally asked to stretch the rules only so far. And when they are asked to do so they are usually offered compensations.

How we respond to a shot is shaped not only by our conventional expectations but also by the rules that the film itself establishes. In Stanley Kubrick's *2001: A Space Odyssey* (1968), for instance, shots early in the film are purposely lengthened considerably beyond the norms of Hollywood editing. The result is that when the climaxes come we accept that they develop at an almost dreamlike pace.

The viewing of film shots may also be affected by largely neurophysiological processes which are still not well understood. There may be a point at which the recognition of any sign becomes subject to a certain cognitive loss or slippage. For example, after a period of time our attention may automatically shift from a particular visual figure or thematic focus to "ground" or background material. This process may be related to the directional switching that occurs when we study the diagram of a cube, or to the experience of figure-ground switching familiar from such examples in Gestalt psychology as seeing a picture alternately as a vase or two symmetrical faces. It may have to do with the different functions of the two hemispheres of the brain, or with the way in which different cells in the visual cortex respond to highly specific shapes in the environment.[12] It is possible that digressive search is triggered by such processes, so that a search for alternative configurations and meanings follows the "saturation" of an initial act of recognition.[13]

Such a schematic description of how we read film images cannot, of course, pretend to deal with the many convolutions of pattern recognition or the kinds of layered responses that may be part of reading the denotative and connotative content of complex images.

FROM RUSHES TO FILMS

Few documentary film-makers would deny that their films are highly selective and expressive of a particular culture and ideology. At the same time, when film-makers measure their films against their experience of the world they often find them lacking. What has recently been referred to as a "crisis of representation" in a broad spectrum of human studies has resulted from just such a sense of discrepancy between experience and the existing paradigms for representing it.[14] Such an intellectual climate may now encourage film-makers to pursue this sense of discrepancy a little further.

It is true that documentary film-makers have periodically questioned the inherited assumptions of their vocation. This has happened notably around the years 1935, 1960, and 1975. Ethnographic film-makers, in their brushes with other arts and rhetorics, have perhaps been particularly inclined to do so. But even they have seemed unwilling to confront perhaps the most deeply seated assumption of all: that films are necessarily superior to the raw materials shot for them.

Despite this, it is not uncommon to hear film-makers say: "The real film was in the rushes." I have an instance of this from Roger Graef, the maker of many documentary films for British television. In an interview with Alan Rosenthal he says, "In one film we shot 100,000 16mm feet. That's fifty hours. . . . These vérité films are usually best in the rushes. All fifty hours tend to be interesting. It's like a long-running serial. Strangers wandering through our viewing rooms tend to sit there and come back, and back, and back because they want to know what's going to happen next. It's got that kind of excitement to it. There *is* a problem in structuring them. The films tend to be next best at something like six or eight hours. . . . And then there's a terrible problem because all of the subplots, all the nuances, all the things that aren't going to survive, but do feed the sense of reality, all have to be cut."[15]

There is in descriptions like this, and in the experience of many film-makers, a pervasive sense of loss which is not about a quantitative difference but a qualitative one. It is as though once a film has been pruned to achieve what it actually sets out to achieve—a coherent narrative or analysis—certain qualities perceived in the rushes have been edited out of it. This contradicts the accepted notion of creative economy that "less is more," and "the work is greater than the sum of its parts." The feeling seems to be that the work has clearly become less than the sum of its parts. It is not merely a reduced semblance of the longer work but has been reduced in other important ways in achieving its final statements.

This is not to revert to the naïve view that film footage is some kind of unmediated evidence which contains the "truth" about external reality. If that were so there would be little point going beyond the rushes themselves. It would also deny that editing does in fact introduce its own higher order of truth and understanding. Rather, the sense of loss seems to identify positive values perceived in the rushes and intended by the film-maker at the time of shooting but unachieved in the completed film. It is as though the very reasons for making films are somehow contradicted by the making of them. The processes of editing a film from the rushes involve both reducing the length overall and cutting most shots to shorter lengths. I believe there is a connection between these two processes, in that they both progressively center particular meanings. Sometimes film-makers appear to recognize this when they try to preserve some of the qualities of the rushes in their films, or reintroduce those qualities through other means.

Much of what is lost from the rushes is a sense of the historical contingency of the images—the actual conditions under which films (and meaning) are produced. Film rushes are as much a chronicle of a film's production as they are of its supposed subject. The excitement Graef describes—of wondering what will happen next—is really the excitement of sensing that in the rushes *anything* can happen next. While finished films suggest a past tense, rushes seem to unfold in the present tense of a camera running. What editing removes are the stigmata of this historical moment. The shots that remain have been domesticated. They are neither tangential nor contradictory nor incontinent nor otherwise incapable of being marshalled to the film's purpose.

What does one lose, then, from the rushes? One loses, I think, qualities of spaciousness, context, and historicity, and these can be described in four different ways.

QUALITIES SACRIFICED TO THE FILM

First, one loses *excess meaning*—meaning in excess of what the film expresses and requires. This is not merely what remains unexplored in the subject that can still be found in the rushes, but all material which escapes from what might be called the "economy of signification" of the film.

Second, there is a loss of *interpretive space*—a closing-off of the legitimate areas in which the viewer is invited to supply meaning. The film dictates a certain standard of relevancy. As it moves toward its final form, the background around the centered subject is gradually whittled away. This controls the viewer's relationship to the footage in two ways: first, the background is made to appear incidental and subservient to what the film designates as a sufficient reality. Second, the background itself is physically thinned out by cutting, thus further reducing the opportunities for "irrelevant" intervention. Although different films provide different kinds of interpretive space for the viewer, this space often merely allows the audience to endorse the film-maker's meaning rather than to participate more actively in creating it. Viewers of rushes, by contrast, constantly interject their own interpretations.

Third, there is a loss of the *sense of encounter*. As the film becomes a polished, professional work, its connections with the historical act of filming, which were so evident in the rushes, gradually disappear. This is especially true of television documentaries, which typically begin with a title sequence whose purpose is to characterize the program as a fully packaged (and therefore predigested) institutional product.

Fourth, there is a loss of *internal contextualization*. In editing a film to its final length there is an inevitable loss of material which would otherwise clarify and extend the meaning of the material which is retained.

Throughout the editing process there is a constant tension between maintaining the forward impetus of the film and providing enough contextual information so that the central narrative or argument continues to make sense. As the film becomes shorter, the analysis becomes cruder. Film-makers continually sacrifice footage which they know would permit a more complex understanding of the subject but which, for reasons of length, the film cannot afford. To solve this problem, such gaps and elisions are often roughly patched over with spoken voice-over commentary.

THE WORLD WITHIN THE SHOT

Films and shots are complex structures, each evoking a larger world. Just as there are levels of contextual material within the footage shot for a film, so there are levels of contextualization within the shot itself. Loss of context can occur in discarding footage, but it can also occur when individual shots are made shorter.

Film-makers are aware of this. Sometimes they include an occasional long take simply to reinject into their film some of the qualities perceived in the rushes. But for a few film-makers the long take becomes a way of redefining the terms in which the film addresses its audience. Such an approach does not necessarily imply a realist aesthetic of the kind championed by André Bazin and many of the Italian neorealists. Brian Henderson notes this in the case of Ophuls,[16] whose long takes can be highly choreographed, and in the case of Godard. He describes a long take in Godard's *La Chinoise* (1967), which tracks past the shacks of Algerian workers in Nanterre to a modern university complex. "Eisenstein," he writes, "would have cut from a shot of the one to a shot of the other, making the juxtaposition for the viewer, obliterating time and space relations to make a clearcut social relation. Godard observes the time and space relation and lets the viewer make the social relation. . . . He does this by virtue of the long take's continuity of dramatic space and time, which this usage reveals as itself a form of argumentation or demonstration; the shot has its own internal relations, its own logic. This instance of the shot seems Bazinian but, far from fidelity to the real, Godard rips this bit of footage from its grounding in the real and puts it down in the midst of a highly abstract film essay."[17]

In this shot Godard uses a long take to create what Walter Benjamin called a "dialectical image"—an internal contextualization of a specific kind, in which one foreground element is qualified by another. But long takes permit contextualization of several kinds. They reveal relationships which link foreground with background, they reemphasize the objective presence of disparate physical objects in the shot, and they provide the "stage" for the enactment of human behavior which reveals individual identity.

Foreground/Background Relationships: A simple instance of linking between foreground and background within a shot is the way in which a moving camera defines the geography of a space. The perception of spatial relations is always a problem in the cinema because of the monocular vision of the camera, but by shifting the perspective, camera movement allows us to make sense of these relations. This movement must of necessity occur over time. A similar kind of spatial linking is produced by the quite different movement of people or objects *within* the frame. Thus the long take may be crucial to defining the geographical context within which a character exists or an action takes place. It is also obviously important in delineating actual matters of time, such as how long it takes someone to perform a particular task—something which is normally masked by the condensation of edited sequences.

Long takes can also reveal the relations between simultaneous actions and co-existing objects in one setting. These may be complex personal interactions or (as in the Godard example) connections between people and their surrounding social and economic environment. The objective conditions and historical processes which shape people's lives may often be more effectively demonstrated by appearing in the same frame than by being shown in the juxtapositions of editing, provided we are given a sufficient intellectual framework for interpreting them. This interpretation may require a conscious *reapplication of detail* from the margins of the film to its center.

The Persistence of the Physical: As I have mentioned, we sometimes subject an image to a process of digressive search. We inspect details which escape the film's inscriptions of meaning, resisting what Roger Cardinal calls the "fixation on congruity." Such details can play a role in film which goes beyond either the pleasures of discovery or a merely supportive "authenticity."

Realist documentaries have tended to rely on background detail to legitimate their choice of what is significant in the foreground, just as historical dramas provide set dressing of the proper period to make us accept their version of history. The long take, however, can serve the opposite purpose: to assert the independence and autonomy of a physical, "background" world and the constantly shifting relations, or lack of them, between material and social being. Presented in this way, physical objects reassert their stubborn and oblivious existence—what Barthes would call their "obtuse" presence. They may even appear as surreal, not because they invoke the irrational or the unconscious, but because they force upon us recognition and confrontation with the unnamed and the unremarked.

The Dimensions of Personhood: Finally, the long take can make possible a contextualizing behavior which may be essential to recognizing individual human identity. Over time, details about other human beings accumulate for us and eventually coalesce into distinct personalities. There is perhaps a parallel here with John Berger's distinction between the private photograph, produced and consumed in a context of familiarity, and the public photograph, torn out of its context and presented to strangers.[18] The challenge for the photographer, says Berger, is to restore context to the public photograph.

In daily life it is our observation of people over time which causes us to transform undifferentiated strangers (or human types) into known individuals. Film shots, unlike still photographs, can provide the necessary time frame in which sequences of behavior can unfold, allowing us to distinguish what Gombrich calls the "likeness" from the "mask." Likenesses emerge as continuities in the midst of variations. According to Gombrich, "[T]he film shot can never fail as signally as the snapshot can, for even if it catches a person blinking or sneezing the sequence explains the resulting grimace which the corresponding snapshot may leave uninterpretable."[19]

In documentary, the long take can help redress the decontextualization of the fragmentary public image, or in Berger's terms, restore the context of the private. Such recontextualization can be seen clearly in ethnographic films, which for much of their history have defined people of non-Western cultures by their roles or occupations, as anonymous actors in exotic social mechanisms. They were almost always mask, never likeness. Longer camera takes with synchronous sound and subtitled dialogue provided a means of refiguring the relationship between the person on the screen and the viewer. More effective than narrative or other humanizing strategies, it was these uninterrupted passages of behavior which, despite cultural differences, gave the necessary clues to discovering the person within the indigenous social actor.

LONG-TAKE PROSPECTS

The long take has been associated with the very earliest motion pictures and with two recent periods in the history of documentary. In the cinéma-vérité and Direct Cinema films of the 1960s it was used to record extended events and conversations. In the political and biographical films of the 1970s and 1980s it was used largely to record interviews. These latter films were strongly influenced by television journalism, which produced its own special use of the long take in building programs around eminent talking heads. The long take proved equally serviceable in discovering these heads in European cathedrals, on Andean railway journeys, or amidst the flora and fauna of African jungles.

In each of these cases, the long take has been used for quite specific and, arguably, quite narrow purposes. Even so, some of these uses have been equivocal or self-contradictory. In the period of cinéma vérité and Direct Cinema, an important model for documentary was Italian neorealist cinema—films like *La Terra Trema* (1948) and *Umberto D* (1952), which themselves borrowed ideas from earlier styles of documentary. But the attempt to reproduce in documentaries the literary qualities of fiction (as in *Salesman,* 1969) tended to confine the use of the long take to largely narrative, quasi-fictive, or authenticating functions. Paradoxically, many of the other potentialities of the long take—for articulating space and time, relating people to their environment, exploring human personality—were being more adventurously investigated in fiction, in the work of directors like Godard, Antonioni, Resnais, and Rossellini. In the second period of interview-based documentaries, the long take seems to have been devoted almost entirely to creating an oral narrative and establishing the authority of the interviewees.

There have of course been alternative tendencies and exceptions to this pattern. Leacock's *Queen of Apollo* (1970), Rouch's *Tourou et Bitti* (1971), Wiseman's *Hospital* (1970), and Kildea's *Celso and Cora* (1983) all use long takes in distinctive and sometimes idiosyncratic ways. Experimental (and "underground") films have provided other kinds of explorations. One should include here, along with the films of Andy Warhol, the work of Michael Snow, Stan Brakhage, and Trinh T. Minh-ha. In other recent documentaries, film-makers like Amos Gitai and Claude Lanzmann have used the long take to subvert the traditional construction of foreground and background. However, for most film-makers there remain serious obstacles to developing these possibilities. Film length is one of them. Films must either conform to conventional lengths, using fewer shots, or develop into much longer films. But who will watch longer films, especially if they willfully include the dreaded "dead spots" of ordinary life as legitimate content?

Segmentation suggests one possible strategy. There have been a number of experimental documentary series for television, such as Craig Gilbert's *An American Family* (1972), Roger Graef's *Police* (1982), and Melissa Llewelyn-Davies' *Diary of a Maasai Village* (1984), but so far these have tended to reproduce in documentary the interlocking story structures of drama series or have been composed of essentially self-contained episodes. In neither case has segmentation led to a noticeable expansion of conventional film time to allow for longer takes.

Ultimately the problem of film length is related to the larger problem of how to articulate longer shots to produce meanings. Without commentary, conventional documentary editing usually finds long takes intractable unless they are tracing a clear narrative line, as in Graef's films. Using longer takes gives fewer opportunities to signify by means of the cuts between them. Longer takes are also likely to be complex entities, creating problems of intellectual focus. They characteristically contain ambiguities, interruptions, and competing centers of attention. The content is mingled in ways which make it difficult for the film-maker to isolate "signal" from "noise." In scripted fiction, "noise" is generally present only when it is put there on purpose to create verisimilitude, but documentary footage is rarely so tidy. Voice-over commentary has traditionally provided one means of superimposing meanings upon such material, but always at the cost of distancing it and reducing the viewer's engagement with its physical immediacy.

These obstacles are of course only obstacles in the context of a specific set of film-making conventions and viewing practices. The real test is whether long takes can find a place in quite new communicative structures. New technologies and shifts in popular culture at least open up certain possibilities for this to happen.

First, viewers' expectations of films are likely to change as some film-making practices which are now marginal enter the mainstream. This could alter the ways in which people actually "read" long camera takes. At the moment, the tendency in commercials and music video seems toward ever shorter takes, but this could contribute to a greater tolerance for associative, non-narrative editing and eventually for more films patterned on structures other than conventional stories or arguments. Films may emerge which require greater retrospective reconstruction in the mind. Against this current must be put the way in which the formats of television journalism seem actually to have narrowed the structural repertoire of documentary.

Second, unexplored opportunities exist for combining words with images, perhaps especially with long takes. One could cite the use of multiple voices on the sound track, voices used in less regular patterns, voices addressing us in new registers. There is no equivalent in documentary, so far as I know, to the whispered commentary which accompanies live golf telecasts. Words may also be deployed more effectively in titles and intertitles, as they once were in Soviet silent films and have been occasionally since, in such films as *The Village of Furuyashiki* (1982), by Shinsuke Ogawa. The history of documentary contains other experiments worth examining and pressing further, such as the use of spoken verse in the documentaries of the 1930s. One might expect certain parallel developments to evolve from the emergence of rap videos.

Third, one can imagine more complex layerings of sound and image. As precedents one can point to Godard's "middle period" films (*British Sounds*, 1969), Clément Perron's *Day After Day* (1962), and several of Gitai's documentary films (*Ananas*, 1984; and *House*, 1980). Sounds can make us reinterpret what is nominally background and, on some occasions, reconstitute it as thematic foreground.

A fourth strategy open to documentary is to make a much more consciously analytical use of the camera. Reframing with the camera resembles a form of montage which selects, connects, and juxtaposes different images, but in "real time." In fiction films it is possible for such an approach to be scripted, as in

Hitchcock's experimental *Rope* (1948). In documentary the situation is very different, requiring on the film-maker's part an ability to impose a process of thought on the camera's movements while filming unpredictable material. So far few film-makers have adopted such a demanding interpretive stance while filming or have developed the skills to accomplish it.

But camera movement within a shot allows for certain kinds of irony which are not possible with shorter takes. In Claude Lanzmann's *Shoah* (1985), the long take makes particular reference to the fact that however long one pans over landscapes where atrocities took place, one still sees only landscapes. In effect, one looks in vain for the signified in the signifier. In a number of Godard's films (*Weekend,* 1967; *British Sounds*) long tracking shots, instead of following characters, as is usual in fiction films, track past them, fixing them not in relation to the film but in relation to their physical and social setting.

Lastly, it is worth noting that new technologies may have a profound effect upon viewing practices and, eventually, upon film form. We have yet to absorb the full implications of television. Video, an even more recent phenomenon, combines the privacy of television viewing with much greater control over the selection of viewing material. This could make possible longer works, organized in chapters or clusters of related films. Video also makes it easier to recast old films in new forms, or produce new commentaries on them. As for interactive video, it may, by giving the viewer even greater control over the investigation of material, generate much more exploratory viewing practices and eventually stimulate the new film-making practices that would allow for them.

Neither film-making nor documentary will be revolutionized by the long take alone, nor should it be claimed that the long take is in any sense the special province of documentary. But the question of what to do with the qualities which are found in long takes, and yet not found in the films derived from them, is perhaps the quintessential problem of documentary. It brings us closer to the paradox of reduction which lies at the heart of all representation, but which has none of the same implications in fiction that it does in documentary. For within every documentary is a kind of cavity, the negative imprint of the missing persons and events which are *not* there. In struggling with this material, the documentary film-maker is struggling not only with signs but quite literally with the shadows of the living and the dead. If photography does not steal the soul it steals something very like it, something deeply enough felt to generate the fraught ethical debates which uniquely surround the making of documentary films and photographs. These debates more commonly concern what is shown than what is left out. But for the film-maker the problem is truly one of disposing of the human remains.

NOTES

This is an expanded version of ideas which I first presented in a seminar as a Visiting Fellow at the Humanities Research Centre in Canberra, Australia, in 1989. I should like to thank the HRC for its support. I am indebted to E. Richard Sorenson and Allison Jablonko for the term "digressive search,"[20] which I use in a rather different sense from theirs; and to Roger Cardinal for the stimulation provided by his essay "Pausing over Peripheral Detail." I am also grateful to Leslie Devereaux, Gary Kildea, and Paul Willemen for discussions with me of some of the issues raised here.

1. *Photo Wallahs* (1991), directed by David and Judith MacDougall, Fieldwork Films, Australia.

2. Christopher Pinney, "The Lexical Spaces of Eye-Spy," in Peter I. Crawford and David Turton (eds.), *Film as Ethnography* (Manchester, England: Manchester University Press, 1992), p. 27.

3. Ibid., p. 28.

4. Dai Vaughan, "Notes on the Ascent of a Fictitious Mountain," in John Corner (ed.), *Documentary and the Mass Media* (London: Edward Arnold, 1986), p. 162.

5. Ibid., p. 163.

6. See Barry Salt, "Statistical Style Analysis of Motion Pictures," *Film Quarterly*, vol. 28, no. 1 (Fall 1974).

7. Raul Ruiz, ignoring the taboo, jokes about this in his film about documentary, *Of Great Events and Ordinary People* (1979). As the camera pans slowly along a wall after an interview, a voice remarks: "The narrator should say something in this pause."

8. Brian Henderson, "The Long Take," *Film Comment*, vol. 7, no. 2 (Summer 1971), p. 9.

9. Israel Rosenfeld, "Seeing Through the Brain," *New York Review of Books*, vol. 31, no. 15 (October 11, 1984).

10.   Roger Cardinal, "Pausing over Peripheral Detail," *Framework,* vol. 30–31 (1986), pp. 112–133.

11.   Nick Browne, "The Spectator-in-the-Text: The Rhetoric of *Stagecoach,*" *Film Quarterly,* vol. 29, no. 2 (Winter 1975–76), pp. 34–35.

12.   Howard Gardner, *The Mind's New Science* (New York: Basic Books, 1985), p. 273.

13.   One can get an idea of this by recalling a game which many of us played as children. When we repeated a familiar word over and over again—a word like "hippopotamus"—sign and referent began to separate until the sign became an unrecognizable phonetic pattern. It then became subject to the mispronunciations that occur with tongue twisters. A kind of verbal searching led to a play on alternative stress patterns (hippopo*ta*mus), picking out new signs previously hidden in the word—*hip* and *pot,* for example. Part of the pleasure of such a game for children, of course, is precisely this subversion of the linguistic codes of adults.

14.   See George E. Marcus and Michael M. J. Fischer, *Anthropology as Cultural Critique* (Chicago: University of Chicago Press, 1986).

15.   Alan Rosenthal, *The Documentary Conscience* (Berkeley: University of California Press, 1980), p. 179.

16.   Henderson, op. cit. pp. 10–11.

17.   Brian Henderson, "Towards a Non-Bourgeois Camera Style," *Film Quarterly,* vol. 24, no. 2 (Winter 1970–71), p. 5.

18.   John Berger, "Uses of Photography," in *About Looking* (London: Writers and Readers Publishing Cooperative, 1980).

19.   E. H. Gombrich, "The Mask and the Face: The Perception of Physiognomic Likeness," in E. H. Gombrich et al. (eds.), *Art, Perception and Reality* (Baltimore: Johns Hopkins University Press, 1972), p. 17.

20.   See E. Richard Sorenson and Allison Jablonko, "Research Filming of Naturally Occurring Phenomena: Basic Strategies," in Paul Hockings (ed.), *Principles of Visual Anthropology* (The Hague: Mouton, 1975).

LINDA WILLIAMS

MIRRORS WITHOUT MEMORIES

Truth, History, and the New Documentary

The Thin Blue Line © Mark Lipson

Vol. 46, no. 3 (Spring 1993): 9–21.

The August 12th, 1990, Arts and Leisure section of the *New York Times* carried a lead article with a rather arresting photograph of Franklin Roosevelt flanked by Winston Churchill and Groucho Marx. Standing behind them was a taut-faced Sylvester Stallone in his Rambo garb. The photo illustrated the major point of the accompanying article by Andy Grundberg: that the photograph—and by implication the moving picture as well—is no longer, as Oliver Wendell Holmes once put it, a "mirror with a memory" illustrating the visual truth of objects, persons, and events but a manipulated construction. In an era of electronic and computer-generated images, the camera, the article sensationally proclaims, "can lie."

In this photo, the anachronistic flattening out of historical referents, the trivialization of history itself, with the popular culture icons of Groucho and Rambo rubbing up against Roosevelt and Churchill, serves almost as a caricature of the state of representation some critics have chosen to call postmodern. In a key statement, Fredric Jameson has described the "cultural logic of postmodernism" as a "new depthlessness, which finds its prolongation both in contemporary 'theory' and in a whole new culture of the image or the simulacrum" (Jameson, 1984, 58). To Jameson, the effect of this image culture is a weakening of historicity. Lamenting the loss of the grand narratives of modernity, which he believes once made possible the political actions of individuals representing the interests of social classes, Jameson argues that it no longer seems possible to represent the "real" interests of a people or a class against the ultimate ground of social and economic determinations.

While not all theorists of postmodernity are as disturbed as Jameson by the apparent loss of the referent, by the undecidabilities of representation accompanied by an apparent paralysis of the will to change, many theorists do share a sense that the enlightenment projects of truth and reason are definitively over. And if representations, whether visual or verbal, no longer refer to a truth or referent "out there," as Trinh T. Minh-ha has put it, for us "in here"

(Trinh, 83), then we seem to be plunged into a permanent state of the self-reflexive crisis of representation. What was once a "mirror with a memory" can now only reflect another mirror.

Perhaps because so much faith was once placed in the ability of the camera to reflect objective truths of some fundamental social referent—often construed by the socially relevant documentary film as records of injustice or exploitation of powerless common people—the loss of faith in the objectivity of the image seems to point, nihilistically, like the impossible memory of the meeting of the fictional Rambo and the real Roosevelt, to the brute and cynical disregard of ultimate truths.

Yet at the very same time, as any television viewer and moviegoer knows, we also exist in an era in which there is a remarkable hunger for documentary images of the real. These images proliferate in the vérité of on-the-scene cops programs in which the camera eye merges with the eye of the law to observe the violence citizens do to one another. Violence becomes the very emblem of the real in these programs. Interestingly, violent trauma has become the emblem of the real in the new vérité genre of the independent amateur video, which, in the case of George Holliday's tape of the Rodney King beating by L.A. police, functioned to contradict the eye of the law and to intervene in the "cops'" official version of King's arrest. This home video might be taken to represent the other side of the postmodern distrust of the image: here the camera tells the truth in a remarkable moment of cinema vérité which then becomes valuable (though not conclusive) evidence in accusations against the L.A. Police Department's discriminatory violence against minority offenders.

The contradictions are rich: on the one hand the postmodern deluge of images seems to suggest that there can be no a priori truth of the referent to which the image refers; on the other hand, in this same deluge, it is still the moving image that has the power to move audiences to a new appreciation of previously unknown truth.

In a recent book on postwar West German cinema and its representations of that country's past, Anton Kaes has written that "[T]he sheer mass of historical images transmitted by today's media weakens the link between public memory and personal experience. The past is in danger of becoming a rapidly expanding collection of images, easily retrievable but isolated from time and space, available in an eternal present by pushing a button on the remote control. History thus returns forever—as film" (Kaes, 198). Recently, the example of history that has been most insistently returning "as film" to American viewers is the assassination of John F. Kennedy as simulated by film-maker Oliver Stone.

Stone's *JFK* might seem a good example of Jameson's and Kaes's worst-case scenarios of the ultimate loss of historical truth amid the postmodern hall of mirrors. While laudably obsessed with exposing the manifest contradictions of

Intervening in the process: *JFK*

the Warren Commission's official version of the Kennedy assassination, Stone's film has been severely criticized for constructing a "countermyth" to the Warren Commission's explanation of what happened. Indeed, Stone's images offer a kind of tragic counterpart to the comic mélange of the *New York Times* photo of Groucho and Roosevelt. Integrating his own reconstruction of the assassination with the famous Zapruder film, whose "objective" reflection of the event is offered as the narrative (if not the legal) clincher in Jim Garrison's argument against the lone assassin theory, Stone mixes Zapruder's real vérité with his own simulated vérité to construct a grandiose paranoid countermyth of a vast conspiracy by Lyndon Johnson, the C.I.A., and the Joint Chiefs of Staff to carry out a coup d'état. With little hard evidence to back him up, Stone would seem to be a perfect symptom of a postmodern negativity and nihilism toward truth, as if to say: "We know the Warren Commission made up a story, well, here's another even more dramatic and entertaining story. Since we can't know the truth, let's make up a grand paranoid fiction."

It is not my purpose here to attack Oliver Stone's remarkably effective deployment of paranoia and megalomania; the press has already done a thorough job of debunking his unlikely fiction of a Kennedy who was about to end the Cold War and withdraw from Vietnam.[1] What interests me, however, is the positive side of this megalomania: Stone's belief that it is possible to intervene in the process by which truth is constructed; his very real accomplishment in shaking up public perception of an official truth that closed down, rather than opened up, investigation; his acute awareness of how images enter into the production of knowledge. However much Stone may finally betray the spirit of his own investigation into the multiple, contingent, and constructed nature of the representation of history by asking us to believe in too tidy a conspiracy, his *JFK* needs to be taken seriously for its renewal of interest in one of the major traumas of our country's past.

So rather than berate Stone, I would like to contrast this multimillion-dollar historical fiction film borrowing many aspects of the form of documentary to what we might call the low-budget postmodern documentary borrowing many features of the fiction film. My goal in what follows is to get beyond the much remarked self-reflexivity and flamboyant auteurism of these documentaries, which might seem, Rashomon-like, to abandon the pursuit of truth, to what seems to me their remarkable engagement with a newer, more contingent, relative, postmodern truth—a truth which, far from being abandoned, still operates powerfully as the receding horizon of the documentary tradition.

When we survey the field of recent documentary films two things stand out: first, their unprecedented popularity among general audiences, who now line up for documentaries as eagerly as for fiction films; second, their willingness to tackle often grim, historically complex subjects. Errol Morris's *The Thin Blue Line* (1987), about the murder of a police officer and the near execution of the "wrong man," Michael Moore's *Roger and Me* (1989), about the dire effects of General Motors' plant closings, and Ken Burns' 11-hour "The Civil War" (1990) (watched on PBS by 39 million Americans) were especially popular documentaries about uncommonly serious political and social realities. Even more difficult and challenging, though not quite as popular, were *Our Hitler* (Hans-Jürgen Syberberg, 1980), *Shoah* (Claude Lanzmann, 1985), *Hotel Terminus: The Life and Times of Klaus Barbie* (Marcel Ophuls, 1987), and *Who Killed Vincent Chin?* (Chris Choy and Renee Tajima, 1988). And in 1991 the list of both critically successful and popular documentary features *not* nominated for Academy Awards—*Paris Is Burning* (Jennie Livingston), *Hearts of Darkness: A Filmmaker's Apocalypse* (Fax Bahr and George Hickenlooper), *35 Up* (Michael Apted), *Truth or Dare* (Alex Keshishian)—was viewed by many as an embarrassment to the Academy. *Village Voice* critic Amy Taubin notes that 1991 was a year in which four or five documentaries made it onto the *Variety* charts; documentaries now mattered in a new way (Taubin, 62).

Though diverse, all the above works participate in a new hunger for reality on the part of a public seemingly saturated with Hollywood fiction. Jennie Livingston, director of *Paris Is Burning,* the remarkably popular documentary about gay drag subcultures in New York, notes that the out-of-touch documentaries honored by the Academy all share an old-fashioned earnestness toward their subjects, while the new, more popular documentaries share a more ironic stance toward theirs. Coincident with the hunger for documentary truth is the clear sense that this truth is subject to manipulation and construction by docu-auteurs who, whether on camera (Lanzmann in *Shoah*, Michael Moore in *Roger and Me*) or behind, are forcefully calling the shots.[2]

It is this paradox of the intrusive manipulation of documentary truth, combined with a serious quest to reveal some ultimate truths, that I would like to isolate within a subset of the above films. What interests me particularly is the way a special few of these documentaries handle the problem of figuring traumatic historical truths inaccessible to representation by any simple or single "mirror with a memory," and how this mirror nevertheless operates in complicated and indirect refractions. For while traumatic events of the past are not available for representation by any simple or single "mirror with a memory"— in the vérité sense of capturing events as they happen—they do constitute a multifaceted receding horizon which these films powerfully evoke.

I would like to offer Errol Morris's *The Thin Blue Line* as a prime example of this postmodern documentary approach to the trauma of an inaccessible past because of its spectacular success in intervening in the truths known about this past. Morris's film was instrumental in exonerating a man wrongfully accused of murder. In 1976, Dallas police officer Robert Wood was murdered, apparently by a 28-year-old drifter named Randall Adams. Like Stone's *JFK*, *The Thin Blue Line* is a film about a November murder in Dallas. Like *JFK*, the film argues that the wrong man was set up by a state conspiracy with an interest in convicting an easy scapegoat rather than prosecuting the real murderer. The film—the "true" story of Randall Adams, the man convicted of the murder of Officer Wood, and his accuser, David Harris, who picked Adams up when he ran out of gas on the night of the murder—ends with Harris's cryptic but dramatic confession to the murder in a phone conversation with Errol Morris.

Stylistically, *The Thin Blue Line* has been most remarked for its film-noirish beauty, its apparent abandonment of cinema-vérité realism for studied, often slow-motion, and highly expressionistic reenactments of different witnesses' versions of the murder to the tune of Philip Glass's hypnotic score. Like a great many recent documentaries obsessed with traumatic events of the past, *The Thin Blue Line* is self-reflexive. Like many of these new documentaries, it is acutely aware that the individuals whose lives are caught up in events are not so much self-coherent and consistent identities as they are actors in competing narratives. As in *Roger and Me, Shoah*, and, to a certain extent, *Who Killed Vincent Chin?*, the documentarian's role in constructing and staging these competing narratives thus becomes paramount.[3] In place of the self-obscuring voyeur of vérité realism, we encounter, in these and other films, a new presence in the persona of the documentarian.

For example, in one scene, David Harris, the charming young accuser whose testimony placed Randall Adams on death row and who has been giving his side of the story in alternate sections of the film from Adams, scratches his head while recounting an unimportant incident from his past. In this small gesture, Morris dramatically reveals information withheld until this moment: Harris's hands are handcuffed. He, like Adams, is in prison. The interviews with him are now subject to reinterpretation since, as we soon learn, he, too, stands accused of murder. For he has committed a senseless murder not unlike the one he accused Adams of committing. At this climactic moment Morris finally brings in the hard evidence against Harris previously withheld: he is a violent psychopath who invaded a man's house, murdered him, and abducted his girlfriend. On top of this Morris adds the local cop's attempt to explain Harris's personal pathology; in the end we hear Harris's own near-confession—in an audio interview—to the murder for which Adams has been convicted. Thus Morris captures a truth, elicits a confession, in the best vérité tradition, but only in the context of a film that is manifestly staged and temporally manipulated by the docu-auteur.

It would seem that in Morris's abandonment of voyeuristic objectivity he achieves something more useful to the production of truth. His interviews get the interested parties talking in a special way. In a key statement in defense of his intrusive, self-reflexive style, Morris has attacked the hallowed tradition of cinema vérité: "There is no reason why documentaries can't be as personal as fiction filmmaking and bear the imprint of those who made them. Truth isn't guaranteed by style or expression. It isn't guaranteed by anything" (Morris, 17).

The "personal" in this statement has been taken to refer to the personal, self-reflexive style of the docu-auteur: Morris's hypnotic pace, Glass's music, the vivid colors and slow motion of the multiple reenactments. Yet the interviews too bear this personal imprint of the auteur. Each person who speaks to the camera in *The Thin Blue Line* does so in a confessional, "talking-cure" mode. James Shamus has pointed out that this rambling, free-associating discourse ultimately collides with, and is sacrificed to, the juridical narrative producing the truth of who, finally, is guilty. And Charles Musser also points out that what is sacrificed is the psychological complexity of the man the film finds innocent. Thus the film forgoes investigation into what Adams might have been up to that night taking a 16-year-old hitchhiker to a drive-in movie.[4]

Morris gives us some truths and withholds others. His approach to truth is altogether strategic. Truth exists for Morris because lies exist; if lies are to be exposed, truths must be strategically deployed against them. His strategy in the pursuit of this relative, hierarchized, and contingent truth is thus to find guilty those speakers whom he draws most deeply into the explorations of their past. Harris, the prosecutor Mulder, the false witness Emily Miller, all cozy up to the camera to remember incidents from their past which serve to indict them in the present. In contrast, the man found innocent by the film remains a cipher, we learn almost nothing of his past, and this lack of knowledge appears necessary to the investigation of the official lies. What Morris does, in effect, is partially close down the representation of Adams's own story, the accumulation of narratives from his past, in order to show how convenient a scapegoat he was to the overdetermining pasts of all the other false witnesses. Thus, instead of using fictionalizing techniques to show us the truth of what happened, Morris scrupulously sticks to stylized and silent docudrama reenactments that show only what each witness claims happened.

In contrast, we might consider Oliver Stone's very different use of docudrama reenactments to reveal the "truth" of the existence of several assassins and the plot that orchestrated their activity, in the murder of JFK. Stone has Garrison introduce the Zapruder film in the trial of Clay Shaw as hallowed vérité evidence that there had to be more than one assassin. Garrison's examination of the magic bullet's trajectory does a fine dramatic job of challenging the official version of the lone assassin. But in his zealous pursuit of the truth of "who dunnit," Stone matches the vérité style of the Zapruder film with a vérité simulation which, although hypothesis, has none of the stylized, hypothetical visual marking of Morris's simulations and which therefore commands a greater component of belief. Morris, on the other hand, working in a documentary form that now eschews vérité as a style, stylizes his hypothetical reenactments and never offers any of them as an image of what actually happened.

In the discussions surrounding the truth claims of many contemporary documentaries, attention has centered upon the self-reflexive challenge to once hallowed techniques of vérité. It has become an axiom of the new documentary that films cannot reveal the truth of events, but only the ideologies and consciousness that construct competing truths—the fictional master narratives by which we make sense of events. Yet too often this way of thinking has led to a forgetting of the way in which these films still are, as Stone's film isn't, documentaries—films with a special interest in the relation to the real, the "truths" which matter in people's lives but which cannot be transparently represented.

One reason for this forgetting has been the erection of a too simple dichotomy between, on the one hand, a naïve faith in the truth of what the documentary image reveals—vérité's discredited claim to capturing events while they happen—and on the other, the embrace of fictional manipulation. Of course, even in its heyday no one ever fully believed in an absolute truth of cinema vérité. There are, moreover, many gradations of fictionalized manipulation ranging from the controversial manipulation of temporal sequence in Michael Moore's *Roger and Me* to Errol Morris's scrupulous reconstructions of the subjective truths of events as viewed from many different points of view.

The Thin Blue Line
© Mark Lipson

Truth is "not guaranteed" and cannot be transparently reflected by a mirror with a memory, yet some kinds of partial and contingent truths are nevertheless the always receding goal of the documentary tradition. Instead of careening between idealistic faith in documentary truth and cynical recourse to fiction, we do better to define documentary not as an essence of truth but as a set of strategies designed to choose from among a horizon of relative and contingent truths. The advantage, and the difficulty, of the definition is that it holds on to the concept of the real—indeed of a "real" at all—even in the face of tendencies to assimilate documentary entirely into the rules and norms of fiction.

As *The Thin Blue Line* shows, the recognition that documentary access to this real is strategic and contingent does not require a retreat to a Rashomon universe of undecidabilities. This recognition can lead, rather, to a remarkable awareness of the conditions under which it is possible to intervene in the political and cultural construction of truths which, while not guaranteed, nevertheless matter as the narratives by which we live. To better explain this point I would like to further consider the confessional, talking-cure strategy of *The Thin Blue Line* as it relates to Claude Lanzmann's *Shoah*. While I am aware of the incommensurability of a film about the state of Texas's near-execution of an innocent man with the German state's achieved extermination of six million, I want to pursue the comparison because both films are, in very different ways, striking examples of postmodern documentaries whose passionate desire is to intervene in the construction of truths whose totality is ultimately unfathomable.

In both of these films, the truth of the past is traumatic, violent, and unrepresentable in images. It is obscured by official lies masking the responsibility of individual agents in a gross miscarriage of justice. We may recall that Jameson's argument about the postmodern is that it is a loss of a sense of history, of a collective or individual past, and the knowledge of how the past determines the present: "the past as 'referent' finds itself gradually bracketed, and then effaced altogether, leaving us with nothing but texts" (Jameson, 1984, 64). That so many well-known and popular documentary films have taken up the task of remembering the past—indeed that so much popular debate about the "truth" of the past has been engendered by both fiction and documentary films about the past—could therefore be attributed to another of Jameson's points about the postmodern condition: the intensified nostalgia for a past that is already lost.

However, I would argue instead that, certainly in these two films and partially in a range of others, the postmodern suspicion of over-abundant images of an unfolding, present "real" (vérité's commitment to film "it" as "it" happens) has contributed not to new fictionalizations but to paradoxically new historicizations. These historicizations are fascinated by an inaccessible, ever receding, yet newly important past which does have depth.[5] History, in Jameson's sense of traces of the past, of an absent cause which "hurts" (Jameson, 1981, 102), would seem, almost by definition, to be inaccessible to the vérité documentary form aimed at capturing action in its unfolding. The recourse to talking-heads interviews, to people remembering the past—whether the collective history of a nation or city, the personal history of individuals, or the criminal event which crucially determines the present—is, in these anti-vérité documentaries, an attempt to overturn this commitment to realistically record "life as it is" in favor of a deeper investigation of how it became as it is.

Thus, while there is very little running after the action, there is considerable provocation of action. Even though Morris and Lanzmann have certainly done their legwork to pursue actors in the events they are concerned to represent, their preferred technique is to set up a situation in which the action will come to them. In these privileged moments of vérité (for there finally are moments of relative vérité) the past repeats. We thus see the power of the past not simply by dramatizing it, or reenacting it, or talking about it obsessively (though these films do all this), but finally by finding its traces, in repetitions and resistances, in the present. It is thus the contextualization of the present with the past that is the most effective representational strategy in these two remarkable films.

Each of these documentaries digs toward an impossible archeology, picking at the scabs of lies which have covered over the inaccessible originary event. The film-makers ask questions, probe circumstances, draw maps, interview historians, witnesses, jurors, judges, police, bureaucrats, and survivors. These diverse investigatory processes augment the single method of the vérité camera.

They seek to uncover a past the knowledge of which will produce new truths of guilt and innocence in the present. Randall Adams is now free at least partly because of the evidence of Morris's film; the Holocaust comes alive not as some alien horror foreign to all humanity but as something that is, perhaps for the first time on film, understandable as an absolutely banal incremental logic and logistics of train schedules and human silence. The past events examined in these films are not offered as complete, totalizable, apprehensible. They are fragments, pieces of the past invoked by memory, not unitary representable truths but, as Freud once referred to the psychic mechanism of memory, a palimpsest, described succinctly by Mary Ann Doane as "the sum total of its rewritings through time." The "event" remembered is never whole, never fully represented, never isolated in the past alone but only accessible through a memory which resides, as Doane has put it, "in the reverberations between events" (Doane, 58).

This image of the palimpsest of memory seems a particularly apt evocation of how these two films approach the problem of representing the inaccessible trauma of the past. When Errol Morris fictionally reenacts the murder of Officer Wood as differently remembered by David Harris, Randall Adams, the officer's partner, and the various witnesses who claimed to have seen the murder, he turns his film into a temporally elaborated palimpsest, discrediting some versions more than others but refusing to ever fix one as *the* truth. It is precisely Morris's refusal to fix the final truth, to go on seeking reverberations and repetitions that, I argue, gives this film its exceptional power of truth.

This strategic and relative truth is often a byproduct of other investigations into many stories of self-justification and reverberating memories told to the camera. For example, Morris never set out to tell the story of Randall Adams's innocence. He was interested initially in the story of "Dr. Death," the psychiatrist whose testimony about the sanity of numerous accused murderers had resulted in a remarkable number of death sentences. It would seem that the more directly and singlemindedly a film pursues a single truth, the less chance it has of producing the kind of "reverberations between events" that will effect meaning in the present. This is the problem with *Roger and Me* and, to stretch matters, even with *JFK*: both go after a single target too narrowly, opposing a singular (fictionalized) truth to a singular official lie.

The much publicized argument between Harlan Jacobson and Michael Moore regarding the imposition of a false chronology in Moore's documentary about the closing of General Motors' plant in Flint, Michigan, is an example. At stake in this argument is whether Moore's documentation of the decline of the city of Flint in the wake of the plant closing entailed an obligation to represent events in the sequence in which they actually occurred. Jacobson argues that Moore betrays his journalist/documentarian's commitment to the objective portrayal of historical fact when he implies that events that occurred prior to the major layoffs at the plant were the effect of these layoffs. Others have criticized Moore's self-promoting placement of himself at the center of the film.[6]

In response, Moore argues that as a resident of Flint he has a place in the film and should not attempt to play the role of objective observer but of partisan investigator. This point is quite credible and consistent with the postmodern awareness that there is no objective observation of truth but always an interested participation in its construction. But when he argues that his documentary is "in essence" true to what happened to Flint in the 1980s, only that these events are "told with a narrative style" that omits details and condenses events of a decade into a palatable "movie" (Jacobson, 22), Moore behaves too much like Oliver Stone, abandoning the commitment to multiple contingent truths in favor of a unitary, paranoid view of history.

The argument between Moore and Jacobson seems to be about where documentarians should draw the line in manipulating the historical sequence of their material. But rather than determining appropriate strategies for the representation of the meaning of events, the argument becomes a question of a commitment to objectivity versus a commitment to fiction. Moore says, in effect, that his first commitment is to entertain and that this entertainment is faithful to the essence of the history. But Moore betrays the cause and effect reverberation between events by this reordering. The real lesson of this debate would seem to be that Moore did not trust his audience to learn about the past in any other way than through the vérité capture of it. He assumed that if he didn't have footage from the historical period prior to his filming in Flint he couldn't show it. But the choice needn't be, as Moore implies, between boring, laborious fact and entertaining fiction true to the "essence," but not the detail, of historical events. The opposition poses a false contrast between a naïve faith in the documentary truth of photographic and filmic images and the cynical awareness of fictional manipulation.

What animates Morris and Lanzmann, by contrast, is not the opposition between absolute truth and absolute fiction but the awareness of the final inaccessibility of a moment of crime, violence, trauma, irretrievably located in the past. Through the curiosity, ingenuity, irony, and obsessiveness of "obtrusive" investigators, Morris and Lanzmann do not so much represent this past as they reactivate it in images of the present. This is their distinctive postmodern feature as documentarians. For in revealing the fabrications, the myths, the frequent moments of scapegoating when easy fictional explanations of trauma, violence, crime were substituted for more difficult ones, these documentaries do not simply play off truth against lie, nor do they play off one fabrication against another; rather, they show how lies function as partial truths to both the agents and witnesses of history's trauma.

Shoah: Simon Srebnik on the church steps in Chelmno

For example, in one of the most discussed moments of *Shoah,* Lanzmann stages a scene of homecoming in Chelmno, Poland, by Simon Srebnik, a Polish Jew who had, as a child, worked in the death camp near that town, running errands for the Nazis and forced to sing while doing so. Now, many years later, in the present tense of Lanzmann's film, the elderly yet still vigorous Srebnik is surrounded on the steps of the Catholic church by an even older, friendly group of Poles who remembered him as a child in chains who sang by the river. They are happy he has survived and returned to visit. But as Lanzmann asks them how much they knew and understood about the fate of the Jews who were carried away from the church in gas vans, the group engages in a kind of free association to explain the unexplainable.

[LANZMANN]:	Why do they think all this happened to the Jews?
[A POLE]:	Because they were the richest! Many Poles were also exterminated. Even priests.
[ANOTHER POLE]:	Mr. Kantarowski will tell us what a friend told him. It happened in Myndjewyce, near Warsaw.

[LANZMANN]:	Go on.
[MR. KANTAROWSKI]:	The Jews there were gathered in a square. The rabbi asked an SS man: "Can I talk to them?" The SS man said yes. So the rabbi said that around two thousand years ago the Jews condemned the innocent Christ to death. And when they did that, they cried out: "Let his blood fall on our heads and on our sons' heads." The rabbi told them: "Perhaps the time has come for that, so let us do nothing, let us go, let us do as we're asked."
[LANZMANN]:	He thinks the Jews expiated the death of Christ?
[THE FIRST(?) POLE]:	He doesn't think so, or even that Christ sought revenge. He didn't say that. The rabbi said it. It was God's will, that's all!
[LANZMANN]:	(Referring to an untranslated comment) What'd she say?
[A POLISH WOMAN]:	So Pilate washed his hands and said: "Christ is innocent," and he sent Barabbas. But the Jews cried out: "Let his blood fall on our heads!"
[ANOTHER POLE]:	That's all; now you know! (*Shoah*, 100).[7]

As critic Shoshana Felman has pointed out, this scene on the church steps in Chelmno shows the Poles replacing one memory of their own witness of the persecution of the Jews with another (false) memory, an auto-mystification, produced by Mr. Kantarowski, of the Jews' willing acceptance of their persecution as scapegoats for the death of Christ. This fantasy, meant to assuage the Poles' guilt for their complicity in the extermination of the Jews, actually repeats the Poles' crime of the past in the present.

Felman argues that the strategy of Lanzmann's film is not to challenge this false testimony but to dramatize its effects: we see Simon Srebnik suddenly silenced among the chatty Poles, whose victim he becomes all over again. Thus the film does not so much give us a memory as an action, here and now, of the Poles' silencing and crucifixion of Srebnik, whom they obliterate and forget even as he stands in their midst (Felman, 120–128).

It is this repetition in the present of the crime of the past that is key to the documentary process of Lanzmann's film. Success, in the film's terms, is the ability not only to assign guilt in the past, to reveal and fix a truth of the day-to-day operation of the machinery of extermination, but also to deepen the understanding of the many ways in which the Holocaust continues to live in the present. The truth of the Holocaust thus does not exist in any totalizing narrative, but only, as Felman notes and Lanzmann shows, as a collection of fragments. While the process of scapegoating, of achieving premature narrative closure by assigning guilt to convenient victims, is illuminated, the events of the past—in this case the totality of the Holocaust—register not in any fixed moment of past or present but rather, as in Freud's description of the palimpsest, as the sum total of its rewritings through time, not in a single event but in the "reverberations" between.

It is important in the above example to note that while cinema vérité is deployed in this scene on the steps, as well as in the interviews throughout the film, this form of vérité no longer has a fetish function of demanding belief as the whole. In place of a truth that is "guaranteed," the vérité of catching events as they happen is here embedded in a history, placed in relation to the past, given a new power, not of absolute truth but of repetition.

Although it is a very different sort of documentary dealing with a trauma whose horror cannot be compared to the Holocaust, Errol Morris's *The Thin Blue Line* also offers its own rich palimpsest of reverberations between events. At the beginning of the film, convicted murderer Randall Adams mulls over the fateful events of the night of 1976 when he ran out of gas, was picked up by David Harris, went to a drive-in movie, refused to allow Harris to come home with him, and later found himself accused of killing a cop with a gun that Harris had stolen. He muses: "Why did I meet this kid? Why did I run out of gas? But it happened, it happened." The film probes this "Why?" And its discovery "out of the past" is not simply some fate-laden accident but, rather, a reverberation between events that reaches much further back into the past than that cold November night in Dallas.

Toward the end, after Morris has amassed a great deal of evidence attesting to the false witness born by three people who testified to seeing Randall Adams in the car with David Harris, but before playing the audio tape in which Harris all but confesses to the crime, the film takes a different turn—away from the events of November and into the childhood of David Harris. The film thus moves both forward and back in time: to events following and preceding the night of November, 1976, when the police officer was shot. Moving forward, we learn of a murder, in which David broke into the home of a man who had, he felt, stolen his girlfriend. When the man defended himself, David shot him. This repetition of wanton violence is the clincher in the film's "case" against David. But instead of stopping there, the film goes back in time as well.

A kindly, baby-faced cop from David's home town, who has told us much of David's story already, searches for the cause of his behavior and hits upon a childhood trauma: a four-year-old brother who drowned when David was only three. Morris then cuts to David speaking of this incident: "My Dad was supposed to be watching us. . . . I guess that might have been some kind of traumatic experience for me. . . . I guess I reminded him . . . it was hard for me to get any acceptance from him after that. . . . A lot of the things I did as a young kid was an attempt to get back at him."

In itself, this "getting-back-at-the-father" motive is something of a cliché for explaining violent male behavior. But coupled as it is with the final "confes-

The Thin Blue Line: Reenactment of the night in November, 1976. © Mark Lipson

sion" scene in which Harris repeats this getting-back-at-the-father motive in his relation to Adams, the explanation gains resonance, exposing another layer in the palimpsest of the past. As we watch the tape recording of this last unfilmed interview play, we hear Morris ask Harris if he thinks Adams is a "pretty unlucky fellow?" Harris answers, "Definitely," specifying the nature of this bad luck: "Like I told you a while ago about the guy who didn't have no place to stay . . . if he'd had a place to stay, he'd never had no place to go, right?" Morris decodes this question with his own rephrasing, continuing to speak of Harris in the third person: "You mean if he'd stayed at the hotel that night this never would have happened?" (That is, if Adams had invited Harris into his hotel to stay with him as Harris had indicated earlier in the film he expected, then Harris would not have committed the murder he later pinned on Adams.)

Harris: "Good possibility, good possibility. . . . You ever hear of the proverbial scapegoat? There probably been thousands of innocent people convicted. . . ."

Morris presses: "What do you think about whether he's innocent?" Harris: "I'm sure he is." Morris again: "How can you be sure?" Harris: "I'm the one who knows. . . . After all was said and done it was pretty unbelievable. I've always thought if you could say why there's a reason that Randall Adams is in jail it might be because he didn't have a place for somebody to stay that helped him that night. It might be the only reason why he's at where he's at."

What emerges forcefully in this near-confession is much more than the clinching evidence in Morris's portrait of a gross miscarriage of justice. For in not simply probing the "wrong man" story, in probing the reverberations between events of David Harris's personal history, Morris's film discovers an underlying layer in the palimpsest of the past: how the older Randall Adams played an unwitting role in the psychic history of the 16-year-old David Harris, a role which repeated an earlier trauma in Harris's life: of the father who rejected him, whose approval he could not win, and upon whom David then revenged himself.

Harris's revealing comments do more than clinch his guilt. Like the Poles who surround Srebnik on the steps of the church and proclaim pity for the innocent child who suffered so much even as they repeat the crime of scapegoating Jews, so David Harris proclaims the innocence of the man he has personally condemned, patiently explaining the process of scapegoating that the Dallas county legal system has so obligingly helped him accomplish. Cinema vérité in both these films is an important vehicle of documentary truth. We witness in the present an event of simultaneous confession and condemnation on the part of historical actors who repeat their crimes from the past. Individual guilt is both palpably manifest and viewed in a larger context of personal and social history. For even as we catch David Harris and the Poles of Chelmno in the act of scapegoating innocent victims for crimes they have not committed, these acts are revealed as part of larger processes, reverberating with the past.

I think it is important to hold on to this idea of truth as a fragmentary shard, perhaps especially at the moment we as a culture have begun to realize, along with Morris, and along with the supposed depthlessness of our postmodern condition, that it is not guaranteed. For some form of truth is the always receding goal of documentary film. But the truth figured by documentary cannot be a simple unmasking or reflection. It is a careful construction, an intervention in the politics and the semiotics of representation.

An overly simplified dichotomy between truth and fiction is at the root of our difficulty in thinking about the truth in documentary. The choice is not between two entirely separate regimes of truth and fiction. The choice, rather, is in strategies of fiction for the approach to relative truths. Documentary is not fiction and should not be conflated with it. But documentary can and should use all the strategies of fictional construction to get at truths. What we see in *The Thin Blue Line* and *Shoah,* and to some degree in the other documentaries I have mentioned, is an interest in constructing truths to dispel pernicious fictions, even though these truths are only relative and contingent. While never absolute and never fixed, this under-construction, fragmented horizon of truth is one important means of combating the pernicious scapegoating fictions that can put the wrong man on death row and enable the extermination of a whole people.

The lesson that I would like to draw from these two exemplary postmodern documentaries is thus not at all that postmodern representation inevitably succumbs to a depthlessness of the simulacrum, or that it gives up on truth to wallow in the undecidabilities of representation. The lesson, rather, is that there can be historical depth to the notion of truth—not the depth of unearthing a coherent and unitary past, but the depth of the past's reverberation with the present. If the authoritative means to the truth of the past does not exist, if photographs and moving images are not mirrors with memories, if they are more, as Baudrillard has suggested, like a hall of mirrors, then our best response to this crisis of representation might be to do what Lanzmann and Morris do: to deploy the many facets of these mirrors to reveal the seduction of lies.

NOTES

I owe thanks to Anne Friedberg, Mark Poster, Nancy Salzer, Marita Sturken, Charles Musser, James Shamus, B. Ruby Rich, and Marianne Hirsch for helping me, one way or another, to formulate the ideas in this article. I also thank my colleagues on the *Film Quarterly* editorial board, whose friendly criticisms I have not entirely answered.

1.   See, for example: Janet Maslin, "Oliver Stone Manipulates His Puppet," *New York Times* (Sunday, January 5, 1992), p. 13: "Twisted History," *Newsweek* (December 23, 1991), pp. 4–54; Alexander Cockburn, "J.F.K. and *J.F.K.*," *The Nation* (January 6–13, 1992), pp. 6–8.

2.   Livingston's own film is an excellent example of the irony she cites, not so much in her directorial attitude toward her subject—drag-queen ball competitions—but in her subjects' attitudes toward the construction of the illusion of gender.

3.   In this article I will not discuss *Who Killed Vincent Chin?* or *Roger and Me* at much length. Although both of these films resemble *The Thin Blue Line* and *Shoah* in their urge to reveal truths about crimes, I do not believe these films succeeded as spectacularly as Lanzmann's and Morris's in respecting the complexity of these truths. In *Vincent Chin,* the truth pursued is the racial motives animating Roger Ebans, a disgruntled, unemployed auto worker who killed Vincent Chin in a fight following a brawl in a strip joint. Ebans was convicted of manslaughter but only paid a small fine. He was then acquitted of a subsequent civil rights charge that failed to convince a jury of his racial motives. The film, however, convincingly pursues evidence that Ebans' animosity towards Chin was motivated by his anger at the Japanese for stealing jobs from Americans (Ebans assumed Chin was Japanese). In recounting the two trials, the story of the "Justice for Vincent" Committee, and the suffering of Vincent's mother, the film attempts to retry the case showing evidence of Ebans' racial motives.

Film-makers Choy and Tajima gamble that their camera will capture, in interviews with Ebans, what the civil rights case did not capture for the jury: the racist attitudes that motivated the crime. They seek, in a way, what all of these documentaries seek: evidence of the truth of past events through their repetition in the present. This is also, in a more satirical vein, what Michael Moore seeks when he repeatedly attempts to interview the elusive Roger Smith, head of General Motors, about the layoffs in Flint, Michigan: Smith's avoidance of Moore repeats this avoidance of responsibility toward the town of Flint. This is also what Claude Lanzmann seeks when he interviews the ex-Nazis and witnesses of the Holocaust, and it is what Errol Morris seeks when he interviews David Harris, the boy who put Randall Adams on death row. Each of these films succeeds in its goal to a certain extent. But the singlemindedness of *Vincent Chin*'s pursuit of the singular truth of Ebans' guilt, and his culture's resentment of Asians, limits the film. Since Ebans never does show himself in the present to be a blatant racist, but only an insensitive working-class guy, the film interestingly fails on its own terms, though it is eloquent testimony to the pain and suffering of the scapegoated Chin's mother.

4.   Shamus, Musser, and I delivered papers on *The Thin Blue Line* at a panel devoted to the film at a conference sponsored by New York University, "The State of Representation: Representation and the State," October 26–28, 1990. B. Ruby Rich was a respondent. Musser's paper argued the point, seconded by Rich's comments, that the prosecution and the police saw Adams as a homosexual. Their eagerness to prosecute Adams, rather than the underage Harris, seems to have much to do with this perception, entirely suppressed by the film.

5.   Consider, for example, the way Ross McElwee's *Sherman's March,* on one level a narcissistic self-portrait of an eccentric Southerner's rambling attempts to discover his identity while traveling through the South, also plays off against the historical General Sherman's devastating march. Or consider the way Ken Burns' "The Civil War" is as much about what the Civil War is to us today as it is about the objective truth of the past.

6.   Laurence Jarvik, for example, argued that Moore's self-portrayal of himself as a "naïve, quixotic 'rebel with a mike'" is not an authentic image but one Moore has promoted as a fiction (quoted in Tajima, 30).

7.   I have quoted this dialogue from the published version of the *Shoah* script but I have added the attribution of who is speaking in brackets. It is important to note, however, that the script is a condensation of a prolonged scene that appears to be constructed out of two different interviews with Lanzmann, the Poles, and Simon Srebnik before the church. In the first segment, Mr. Kantarowski is not present; in the second he is. When the old woman says, "So Pilate washed his hands . . ." Mr. Kantarowski makes the gesture of washing his hands.

Baudrillard, Jean. 1988. "Simulacra and Simulations." In Mark Poster, ed., *Jean Baudrillard: Selected Writings*. Stanford, CA: Stanford University Press.

Doane, Mary Ann. 1990. "Remembering Women: Physical and Historical Constructions in Film Theory." In E. Ann Kaplan, ed., *Psychoanalysis and Cinema*. New York: Routledge.

Felman, Shoshana. 1990. "A L'Age du temoignage: *Shoah* de Claude Lanzmann." In *Au sujet de* Shoah: *le film de Claude Lanzmann*. Paris: Editions Belin.

Grundberg, Andy. 1990. "Ask It No Questions: The Camera Can Lie." *New York Times,* Arts and Leisure. Sunday, August 12, pp. 1, 29.

Jacobson, Harlan. 1989. "Michael and Me." *Film Comment,* vol. 25, no. 6 (November–December), pp. 16–26.

Jameson, Fredric, 1984. "Postmodernism or the Cultural Logic of Late Capitalism." *New Left Review* 146 (July–August).

———1981. *The Political Unconscious: Narrative as a Socially Symbolic Act.* Ithaca, N.Y.: Cornell University Press.

Kaes, Anton. 1989. *From Hitler to Heimat: The Return of History as Film.* Cambridge: Harvard University Press.

Lanzmann, Claude. 1985. Shoah: *An Oral History of the Holocaust.* New York: Pantheon.

Lyotard, Jean-François. 1984. *The Postmodern Condition: A Report on Knowledge.* Minneapolis: University of Minnesota Press.

Morris, Errol. 1989. "Truth Not Guaranteed: An Interview with Errol Morris." *Cineaste* 17, pp. 16–17.

Musser, Charles. 1990. Unpublished paper. "Film Truth: From 'Kino Pravda' to *Who Killed Vincent Chin?* and *The Thin Blue Line*."

Shamus, James. 1990. Unpublished paper. "Optioning Time: Writing *The Thin Blue Line*."

Tajima, Renee. 1990. "The Perils of Popularity." *The Independent* (June).

Taubin, Amy. 1992. "Oscar's Docudrama." *The Village Voice*. March 31, p. 62.

Trinh, T. Minh-ha. 1990. "Documentary Is/Not a Name" *October 52* (Spring), pp. 77–98.

PART FIVE

TECHNOLOGIES

The changing technologies of film production and of film/video screening have been the subject of a number of *Film Quarterly* articles over the years. The topics treated in these pieces are necessarily of interest to the "mad keen" film lovers who read *Film Quarterly*. The art to which they devote so much of their time is almost constantly changing, both in the mode of its production and in the systems of delivery that convey it. Change occasions queries, not unmixed with anxiety, in any devotee. Will a changed cinema still love us? Will we still love it?

Charles Shiro Tashiro's article on videophilia is unusually well informed. A graduate of the UCLA film production program, he was at the time of writing a Ph.D. student in Critical Studies at the University of Southern California. Moreover, as a former producer for the Criterion Collection of videodiscs, including their edition of *Lawrence of Arabia*, Tashiro understands the technologies involved first-hand. He concedes the usefulness of home systems for the close study of films, but notes that "this apparent windfall has usually been embraced with little attention to the technical issues raised by the movement of a text from one medium to another or to the consequences of film evaluation based on video copies."

To enhance this argument, Tashiro provided *Film Quarterly* with stills of three formats of *Lawrence:* scanned, letterbox, and full film frame. The contrast between the second and the third is revealing because the depth evident in the full film frame is almost completely absent in the letterbox version. The value that Charles Barr saw in CinemaScope—a greater sense of depth than the conventional frame—is in fact negated by video or laserdisc letterboxing, which refocuses attention on the flatness of the image and hence accentuates the composition rather than, as Barr argued, effacing it.

The pieces by Charles Eidsvik and Jean-Pierre Geuens concern what Eidsvik calls "changes in film technology in the age of video." Eidsvik's exceptionally clear-eyed view is that "there is very little that is esthetically revolutionary in the new technologies, and nothing that would upset the basic film-making power structure. Changes have been conservative, a defense against inroads and threats brought by very rapidly evolving video technologies." Within this framework, Eidsvik discusses new improved film stocks, including high-speed ones, which, supplemented by six emulsions and also by advances in postproduction sound enhancements, make possible low light-level filming and, indeed, night-for-night filming. Eidsvik argues that, oddly, these changes have not affected film style. Venturing into narrative theory, however, he suggests that they may have "a discernible effect" on story and plot construction, because they allow "freer use of the kinds of settings that can be easily shown," rather than left as gaps. This is a stimulating suggestion, but later he notes more cautiously that the developments he has discussed have made "story construction a bit different in potential." Indeed, one of the conclusions of the piece is that "large theoretical claims must be put on hold," to which Eidsvik adds, very sensibly, that theory "must limit itself to a little bit of history at a time." The developments that Geuens elaborates in such elegant detail and cultural depth were anticipated by Eidsvik:

> The most obtrusive technical change outside of the area of special effects in the last decade has been in camera movement. The Steadicam, Louma-type crane, Camrail, and jibbed dolly systems that have allowed us our current period-style of perpetually moving cameras are all consequences of fitting video viewfinders to film cameras, thus making them remote-controllable.

Geuens's article on the video assist begins with a discussion of Martin Heidegger on technology and proceeds to quote the techno-perspectives of Andrew Feenberg and Herbert Marcuse as well. He traces the prehistory of movie camera viewfinders up until 1936, when the Arnold and Richter Company of Germany introduced continuous reflex viewing with its new Arriflex 35mm camera. He also discusses *Peeping Tom* (1960); Vivian Sobchack; Gilles Deleuze; independent filmmakers, including Direct Cinema practitioners, who direct and photograph their own films; Heidegger again; and Emmanuel Levinas. He then surveys the history of the use of video to support film production, which culminates in the introduction of video assist. As in Geuens's earlier article on the Steadicam, it is only after carefully building theoretical and historical contexts that he allows himself some doubt. Video assist would not have benefited Ingmar Bergman very much, but the films of James Cameron or Robert Zemeckis would have made little sense without it. In their films, "the device itself is no more than an advanced representative" of the other technologies that will be introduced in postproduction. Toward the end of the video assist piece, Geuens quotes with approval Eidsvik's account of new technologies as the industry's "defensive maneuvers" with regard to video technologies.

Stephen Prince's article contains a wealth of information about another important new technology: digital imaging or, as it is called in the industry, computer-generated imagery (CGI). Prince conducted telephone interviews with a number of practitioners in the field, research that adds significantly to the value and detail of his discussions. He distinguishes between films in which the conspicuous use of digital processes makes them evident to viewers—*True Lies*, *Jurassic Park*, and *Forrest Gump*—and others that use digital processes of which the viewer is unaware. In both categories, however, the ability of CGI to simulate movement, location, lighting, and other features creates the perceptual patterns of photographically realistic cinema.

Unlike the writers of the articles discussed above, Prince is not critical of the new technologies he discusses, either for their role in the cinema-video competitions or for their other functions in the media industry and in the national and global economies. He turns his research in a different direction—toward film theory and toward overcoming what has been called by some a realist versus formalist opposition in film theory. Given that the line between real and not real will be increasingly blurred, Prince asks, "How should we understand digital imaging in theory? How should we build theory around it?" His answer, developed at length and cogently, is what he calls a correspondence-based model of cinematic representation: film shares many of the perceptual codes that structure our everyday perception. Although CGI by definition has different origins than photographic-based imagery, the two equally correspond to our normal perception, and hence are both experienced as perceptually realistic.

Michael Dempsey's two-page manifesto against colorization is the classic statement on this galling issue. It is also classical in that one could analyze its superb rhetoric as one does a Cicero oration. He begins on a moment of rest after exhausting conflicts: "Whatever gamuts American movies have had to run during production, once made they are supposed to be secure." Studio interference, the hobbling of censorship, and other compromises impede the making of films; but there are also postrelease hazards such as pan-and-scan prints, the fading of color prints, and, most serious of all, the colorization of black-and-white films by those who own them. These include Ted Turner, who owns the MGM film library; the Hal Roach Company; and Color Systems Technology—all of whom "produce new prints of black-and-white movies with color added." (As in Cicero, the perpetrators of scandalous behavior are named.) After answering the arguments of the colorizers such as that the makers of black-and-white films could not afford color, Dempsey lists the agencies and individuals that are working to preserve black-and-white films.

Dempsey argues that the colorizers are motivated by greed and concludes, "But talking to the colorizers about things like moods of elation and reconciliation is pointless." Here the writer doubts the power of his words and arguments to have any effect on those responsible for damaging the nation's film heritage. This is known in classical rhetoric as an aporia, a point in an oration or brief in which the writer questions how to continue. This doubt itself can be used against the writer's opponents and may also reorient the argument as a whole. Thus the failure of words or arguments to have any effect upon the colorizers is at the same time his most damning indictment of them. Since money is all they understand, moreover, the writer urges his readers not to screen or broadcast colorized films: don't buy them, rent them, or watch them.

MICHAEL DEMPSEY

COLORIZATION

Vol. 40, no. 2 (Winter 1986-87): 2–3.

Whatever gamuts American movies have had to run during production, once made they are supposed to be secure. This, naturally, has not been the case. Circulating prints of Chaplin, Keaton, and Laurel and Hardy silent comedies have been corrupted with cutesy, moronic noises. TV stations concoct pan-and-scan prints of wide-screen films, destroying their compositions. Color negatives of the past three decades are subject to fading.

Now our film heritage has a new nemesis: "colorization." Using computers, such entrepreneurs as Ted Turner (who now owns the MGM film library, which he bought as fodder for his Atlanta "super station"), the Hal Roach Company, and Color Systems Technology produce new prints of black-and-white movies with color added.

Various rationales have been advanced for this disgusting cultural vandalism: black-and-white films can't draw huge TV audiences; many video store customers turn up their noses at them; "the kids" aren't interested. Shrugging "philosophically," some apologists point out that the original black-and-white negatives remain untouched. Others would protect the "classics" (these sensitive souls know all the classics intimately, of course) but let the colorizers have, say, Republic Pictures potboiler Westerns or Abbott and Costello comedies. Besides, one defense of colorization runs, most American studio pictures were shot in black-and-white only because color was too expensive. The clear implication is that black-and-white is a primitive form of cinematography which "lacks" color, and now these technocrat/hustlers will correct that deficiency. One of them, Earl Glick, the board chairman of Hal Roach Studios, has even had the gall to state that his colorizers have improved Joseph Walker and Joseph Biroc's black-and-white work on *It's a Wonderful Life*.

Color may have been too costly for most American studio movies during the 1930s and 1940s, but once black-and-white photography was chosen, the movies were designed, costumed, and lit accordingly. However, even bothering to refute arguments like these grants them undeserved dignity when in fact they are just contemptuous coverups for the one and only motive behind this rush to colorization: raw greed.

And a rush it is. Already, colorized cassettes of, for example, *Yankee Doodle Dandy, The Maltese Falcon, Topper,* and *It's a Wonderful Life* are not only flooding video stores, they are also inexorably driving the black-and-white originals into the ghettos of occasional museum or revival theater screenings in cities where such forums exist. If this situation is not reversed, no American black-and-white motion picture may ever again live in regular showings as its makers intended.

Defenders of black-and-white movies are not sitting idle. The Directors Guild has decried colorization on artistic and cultural grounds and has gone to court over the issue of copyright infringement. RKO has done the same in an effort to protect the films produced under its own name. Numerous directors, among them Billy Wilder, John Huston, Fred Zinnemann, Woody Allen, Martin Scorsese, Bertrand Tavernier, Nicholas Meyer, Peter Hyams, Martha Coolidge, and Frank Capra, have expressed outrage. James Stewart has eloquently described the grief he felt when he tried and failed to watch a colorized print of *It's a Wonderful Life* to the end. Having seen a colorized effigy of this movie's climax, I can testify that if this is how the picture is going to be presented from now on, then *It's a Wonderful Life,* in effect, no longer exists; the added color annihilates the mood of elation and reconciliation that Frank Capra and his collaborators originally sought and achieved.

But talking to the colorizers about things like moods of elation and reconciliation is pointless. Whether you are an individual viewer or a more influential person (say, a buyer or a programmer for television), the urgent message is the same: don't screen or broadcast colorized films, don't rent them, don't buy them, don't watch them. We are dealing with people who are unreachable by cultural, artistic, or social appeals because they don't care about anything except money. Therefore, let us hurt them in the way most painful to their shriveled sensibilities, by depriving them of every dollar that we can. If we do not, their bottomless avarice will deprive us and future generations of infinitely more.

[The above views are passionately endorsed by the *Film Quarterly* editorial board.]

CHARLES EIDSVIK

MACHINES OF THE INVISIBLE

Changes in Film Technology in the Age of Video

Vol. 42, no. 2 (Winter 1988–89): 18–23.

Until the early 1970s, critical discussion of film technology and practice was a preserve monopolized by film-makers and by theorists such as André Bazin and Jean Mitry who were in close contact with film-making communities and often served as intellectual spokesmen for views commonly held by film-makers. The film-making community, in trade journals such as *American Cinematographer* and *J.S.M.P.T.E.,* traded secrets, discussed craft, and celebrated its lore, myths, and mystique. Theorists and historians such as Bazin and Mitry—Mitry was himself a film-maker—built film-makers' perspectives into their views of how new technology catalyzes change in film history. This view, which permeates Mitry's *Esthétique et psychologie du cinéma* and can also be found in essays such as "The Myth of Total Cinema" by Bazin, posits an "Idealist" and "technologically determinist" view of history, with film technology allowing film-makers ever greater potential for recreating reality.[1] Though technological determinism is an understandable belief among film-makers, whose jobs depend on machines and for whom belief in technological determinism is anxiety-lessening, the position is hardly intellectually respectable.[2] Once Althusserian Marxism began to explore relationships between ideology and technology, an attack on Idealist and technologically determinist positions was inevitable. The attack, led by Jean-Louis Comolli, J.-L. Baudry, and Stephen Heath, attempted to critique technology within a "materialist" approach to cinema. Soon joined by feminist film critics such as Teresa de Lauretis, the analysis of technology and ideology has become a mainstream approach to technology at least within academe.

Though the academics (and Comolli himself) are prone to gaffes when discussing specific technological practice,[3] one cannot quarrel with their intentions or intelligence. Nevertheless, insofar as the job of historians is to account for change, their approach has little future, not because their methods—the search, for example, for codes to which technology speaks—are weak, but because they have chosen to write and work from the "position of the spectator," from what can be seen and heard on movie screens, rather than on "tainted" film-maker-generated technical histories.[4] This would be fine except for a simple problem. Not only do most movies, in George Lellis's terms, "seek to hide the methods by which they produce their illusions,"[5] new production practices often are deliberately made invisible and inaudible to film spectators. Information on new technical practices is only briefly hinted at in trade journals but primarily is passed on through actual film-making.

If the last decade is any indication of how change occurs in cinema, a lot goes on below the realm of the easily perceivable. The central fact of recent cinema is the film industry's attempt to survive in the face of overwhelming competition from video. Film can compete with video only as a producing and large-screen exhibition medium. As a producing medium it can compete only on the basis of "quality," with quality defined as something film is not trying to achieve but already *has*. Technological innovation has largely served the purpose of making that quality either "better" or easier to achieve, but not different basically from the quality that already exists. New technology thus has expanded what can be filmed but not (deliberately at any rate) how we are meant to see films. Except in the area of special effects, an area in which mainstream film-makers have been able to use the old Hollywood ploy of turning big budgets and technical prowess into a publicity stunt, conceptually conservative technological innovation has been the norm. In understanding this innovation, perhaps the only relevant theorist would be Michel Foucault, whose approach to power struggles is relevant to just about any study of technical change.[6]

But the power struggle has been basically defensive. In the last decade, the majority of technical developments in the film industry have been aimed at facilitating extant production practices rather than at changing the "look" or sound of commercial films. Just about every new product has been advertised as something that makes film-making cheaper and easier, usually by allowing smaller crews or less schlepping of equipment on location. For each problem to be solved—light levels needed for shooting, the problem of equipment weight, problems of camera mobility, or the difficulty of getting good sound on location—different companies have offered competing solutions. For low-light filming, for example, Kodak, Fuji, and Agfa have offered faster film stocks; Zeiss, Angenieux, Cooke, and Panavision have offered faster, sharper lenses; and various makers of lighting equipment have developed lights and light-control equipment that require little electricity and are highly portable. Alone, each new technology has had little effect. But in aggregate, the dozens of new technical possibilities made available have radically altered the construction and implied worlds of commercial narrative films. In terms of David Bordwell's "style-syuzhet-fabula" triad,[7] the technical developments have had surprisingly little effect on style, but a discernible effect on syuzhet (plot) construction. This has occurred because the new technologies allow more on-location film-making control, and thus freer use of the kinds of settings that can easily be shown, rather than left as syuzhet gaps, in fiction films. I will return to this issue later, after a review of the major recent changes in film technology.

How film-makers get images has been directly affected by changes in film-stock technology, lenses, and cameras meant for location use. But the primary change in visuals has been indirectly created through Automated Dialogue Replacement (ADR) in postproduction. ADR masks its own existence so well that it is not audibly detectable to a film viewer. It has been radically liberating as a catalyst for other shifts in technical practice.[8]

The most important of the visual-technology shifts has been in an expected area, film-stock technology.[9] Until the mid-1970s Eastman's 5254/7254 negative was standard for narratives; when the new 5247/7247 stock came in, films changed visually and film-making got easier: the stock had such fine grain and wide exposure latitude (7 to 10 stops of light acceptance) that it became a new standard, one still more or less prevalent. Since then Eastman, in addition to unpublicized refinements of 5247, has produced three generations of high-speed stock, a fine-grained and contrastier replacement for 7247 in 16mm (7291), a daylight-balanced version of 5247 for use with the new high-efficiency "metal-halide" arc lamps known as "HMIs," and a stock designed purely for matte work in special effects film-making. Though the newest high-speed stocks have six-layer emulsions[10] and flattened-molecule technology (which combine to allow high-speed film-making without visible grain), each stock intercuts smoothly with the basic "47." The new high-speed stocks are rated at ASA 320 (compared to 47's ASA 100) and can be rated faster, even without extended lab development ("pushing"). For example, *Full Metal Jacket* was shot with the film rated at ASA 800.[11] To the viewer, almost nothing has changed in a decade. But because of the increase in film speed without increase in grain, now very low-light scenes can be filmed easily; because of compatible tone and grain-structure architecture, interiors and even night exteriors are similar in "look." Eastman, Fuji, and Agfa stocks can coexist as stylistic variants even within a single film without a viewer noticing.[12] The effect has been on the *kinds* of shots that can be incorporated into narratives smoothly. Night-for-night filming is now relatively easy, provided the new "superspeed" lenses are used.

Low-light filming problems also were "solved" by lens and lighting manufacturers unobtrusively. Quicker and sharper zoom and prime lenses enhance the possibilities of fast stock without introducing their own "look." Where it used to take 100 footcandles of light to get sharp images a decade ago (because older lenses were only really sharp stopped down) now 25 footcandles or even 10 is common. (In Eastman's demonstration film for film-to-video transfer techniques, one romantic candle-lit scene is lit with only one ordinary candle; it looks fine.) Not only is frying no longer an occupational hazard for actors;

syuzhet construction now has very few light limitations. And because lighting problems in narrative film-making are in good part problems in schlepping lights and light-control equipment, and in getting juice to the lights, more efficient units such as HMIs have become popular. (An HMI is around five times as efficient as a tungsten lamp, twice as efficient as a carbon arc, and is daylight-temperature.) Quicker lighting set-ups with less generated heat and smaller electricity requirements expand location possibilities.

The additional location flexibility made possible by new visual tools made location work cheaper and easier; it also made story construction a bit different in potential. More low-light locations could be used, and they could be used in new ways. The city night locations of a *Desperately Seeking Susan* or *After Hours* were predicated on the new tools and stocks. Certainly night exteriors are not new; the ease with which they can be put into films is.

Complementing and accelerating the changes brought by stocks, lenses, and lights are post-production sound developments. ADR, based on "insert" electronic technology (which "ramps" the onset of the bias tone so that sounds can be inserted in a track without pops or other recording artifacts), makes it possible to clean up location sound tracks or unobtrusively to replace location sound entirely in post-production. Now so ubiquitous that almost every feature film lists ADR credits, the art of sound replacement and remixing is an unsung but central contemporary film- and video-making craft. But except for the remarkable intelligibility of dialogue made possible by ADR and new versions of sound tools such as radio microphones, the main effect of new sound technology has been to free up crews on location. No longer is a take spoiled by bad sound; no longer need a boom shadow be in the way; no longer must the sound of a moving camera be so carefully masked. But the use or non-use of ADR in a scene is undetectable.

Curiously, a by-product of ADR has been in characterization and acting styles. Actors such as Robert DeNiro now often just mumble their lines on-location, and depend on ADR sessions to get the right intonation and subtextual subtlety into the final film.[13] Before ADR, Europeans (such as Bergman) frequently "matched" dialogue either because of bad recording conditions or to re-do performance nuances;[14] with ADR this technique has become common, even everyday. Actors who do not have to project their voices can present different aspects of character than those who must be heard clearly by location microphones. Potentially this could cause large shifts in story and character construction. But the trick to the technique working is for the actor and film-maker not to get caught by viewers. Acting styles have changed since ADR. But only those within the industry know how or why.

The cameras used to shoot also have changed, and similarly, it is impossible to tell what camera has been used in any recent normal-format film. Which of the four generations of Arri 35BL or two generations of Moviecam or myriad generations of Panavision/Panaflex cameras a film was shot with is in no way visible. (Similarly it is impossible to tell what camera recent 16mm films were shot on.) Each generation in each manufacturer's line has become quieter, more reliable, more adaptable to video viewfinders, and more versatile, particularly for location filming, but no recent camera has advertised its existence to the viewer.

The most obtrusive technical change outside of the area of special effects in the last decade has been in camera movement. The Steadicam, Louma-type crane, Camrail, and jibbed dolly systems that have allowed us our current period-style of perpetually moving cameras are all consequences of fitting video viewfinders to film cameras, thus making them remote-controllable. The earliest uses of these tools were obtrusive: in *Bound for Glory* when the camera glided through a crowd smoothly and in ways not conceivable with a boom or dolly, the effect was startling; so was the camera smoothness in *An Unmarried Woman* when the camera went up flights of stairs with the actors; so were the hallway and maze and stairs moving-camera scenes in *The Shining*. But the Steadicam has become just part of current film technique, and the different devices for moving a camera by remote control are used in films almost interchangeably, usually without calling attention to themselves. The basic principle behind all the devices is that a camera can be moved more freely if its 50-lb. weight can be separated from the weight of the operator and focus-puller. Remote control and videotapes solve the problem: in the Steadicam by physically isolating the camera from the "handholding" operator; in the Louma and jib-based rigs by putting the controls at a console and locating the camera at the end of some sort of boom, with mechanical, hydraulic, or electronic servocontrol systems that allow manipulation of all camera controls.

Are developments in moving-camera technology revolutionary? They seemed so in the 1970s; now the situation is less clear. As the mobile camera became more common, the stylization apparent in a film such as *The Shining* has blended into a repertory of mobile-camera/stationary-camera paradigms. But these paradigms are not so much the consequence of technologically created opportunity as of an economics- and video-driven loss of other esthetic options. A decade ago, a film-maker could use the edges of the frame as part of compositional graphics—to lead the eye, to counterbalance other visual elements. But now cable and video distribution is the financial heart of the media storytelling business, so film-makers have to keep essential information away from the edges of the screen, and have to forget about using the graphic potentials of 2.3:1, 1.85:1 or 1.65:1 frame formats. All films must be composed for what the Europeans call "amphibious" life, for viewability both on theater and on television screens. Without control of the shape or edge of frames, visual control must be done kinetically—especially because TV screens do not carry enough visual information for long-held static shots to retain viewer attention. Glance Esthetics, our contemporary period-style, has almost completely replaced Gaze Esthetics, in which film-makers left time for the viewer to contemplate the *mise-en-scène*. Glance Esthetics (perhaps seen in purest form on music videos) requires the moving camera. But it seems far less than obvious how one might analyze stylistic changes forced by economic changes that themselves reflected new technologies and broader-scale power struggles within society. And the longer the new camera-moving technologies are with us, the less radical they seem—the more they seem mere successors to the dolly-shot esthetics championed by Max Ophuls and a whole batch of New Wave film-makers.

The sum of the technical shifts in the last decade has been to increase the possibilities of location film-making and to free film-makers from some logistical and financial production hassles. Though it would take statistical analysis to prove or disprove my impression that location exterior (and especially low-light) scenes are much more common now than they were a decade ago, and that they now more frequently form parts of the syuzhet rather than syuzhet gaps, the major drawback to such scenes (their cost) has been lessened. The film industry's ability "to turn the world into a story" (to use Mitry's famous phrase) has been increased in that more kinds of "natural" scenes can now be appropriated for fiction. But there is very little that is esthetically revolutionary in the new technologies, and nothing that would upset the basic film-making power structure. Changes have been conservative, a defense against inroads and threats brought by very rapidly evolving video technologies. Pressure from the outside rather than forces within the film industry has given us the new toys we work with on location. Each of these toys also plays to the extant power structure within the film-making community.

To grasp how new technology functions it is perhaps helpful to outline the economic and professional interests each technical shift favors. Low-budget film-makers, pushed out of the "industrial" market by video, mostly switched to video, bankrupting a lot of small 16mm equipment manufacturers and labs in the process. But at the higher budget levels, the mystique of film quality was promoted heavily by everyone from Eastman on down. Those with the most to lose by competition with video pushed the new technologies hardest. Craftspeople with a life invested in film technique were eager to try any new film tool that would make them more competitive. Rental houses could make money renting out new "top of the line" tools that changed quickly enough to keep film-makers from wanting to buy them, but still were rentable because they "worked like" older tools. Equipment manufacturers exploited film-makers' desire to survive and the willingness of rental houses to buy their stuff as a nudge to bring out "ever-better" tools. Accommodation was made to eventual video use by promoting the use of film as an originating medium and accepting the reality of Rank-Centel or Bosch video transfer. Driven by the nightmare of hearing the phrase "we could just as well have done it on tape," the film community made its internal power accommodations and promoted its mystique of quality in order to survive in the higher-budget ends of the industry. In a weird sense, the threat from video was approached with a triage mentality. What was irrevocably lost was simply accepted—films would be transferred to and shown on video. What was seen as "working" all right without change, that is, film's basic rhetoric and "tradition of quality," was deliberately *not* undermined by technical shifts but instead was reinforced. What was changed were production practices and technology. The changes made here were meant to *expand* the domain of fictionalized establishment practices into areas in which video could not compete well, such as location film-making. Video has (at least at present) real problems in dealing with on-location light contrasts. Film's light acceptance range makes it unbeatable on-location. A battery of technical changes were gradually instituted so that film's on-location advantages could be maximized. The last decade has been a power struggle between factions in the entertainment industry. Technology has simply been a tool for gaining or retaining financial power.

What can be said about the relationships between change in cinema and technical change on the basis of recent film history? Nothing very global. There have been some changes in what we see and hear and how actors act. But each change, as it came, was so subtle, so well masked, that no major change ever was "felt" by audiences. The film industry's defensive maneuvers of the 1970s and 1980s are far different from the flaunting of color, 3-D, and wide-screen in the 1950s (and judging by industry finances, far more successful). But the changes that have occurred are still not fully played out, so to argue either the parallels or differences between the last decade and preceding ones would be to deny the complexity (and complex approaches to the craft) of film as a technological medium and art form. In film, as Ingmar Bergman put it, "God is details." So large theoretical claims must be put on hold, or at least balanced with one another in recognition of the different perspectives from which cinema can be seen.

The basic problem in theorizing about technical change in cinema is that accurate histories of the production community and its perspectives, as well as of the technological options that face film-makers, must precede the attempt to theorize. And theory itself must limit itself to a little bit of history at a time. It is not that we do not need theory that can help us understand the relationships between larger social and cultural developments, ideology, technical practice, and the history of cinema. Rather it is that whatever we do in our attempts to theorize, we need to welcome all the available sources of information, from all available perspectives, tainted or not, and try to put them in balance. Anything less than that approach lessens us as students of cinema by denying the complexity of the art we study.

1. See André Bazin, "The Myth of Total Cinema," *What Is Cinema?* vol. 1. Trans. Hugh Gray. Berkeley: University of California Press, 1967, 17–21. Mitry's position, often lumped with Bazin's, puts the "advance" technology allows differently: new technology gives film-makers ever-greater means to manipulate images of reality. Mitry defended his position in virtually monthly columns in the French journal *Cinématographe* until at least 1984. Though attacks on his position often are printed in English, his defenses and counterattacks were far more interesting than the attacks. Often Mitry argued that his semiotics-trained attackers knew very little about cinema.

2. For a general put-down of technological determinism see Brian Winston, *Misunderstanding Media*. Cambridge: Harvard University Press, 1986. More specific attacks on the perspective in film history are undertaken by Barry Salt in *Film Style and Technology: History and Analysis*. London: Starword, 1983.

3. For example, Stephen Heath, in *Questions of Cinema,* attempts an attack on Liz-Anne Bawden's comment, in the *Oxford Companion to Film*, "It is technical advances which underlie stylistic innovations like handheld techniques . . ." Heath writes: "Arriflex cameras were available in Hollywood in the late 1940s but there was no particular turn to handheld sequences in response to the technical advance (nor in France at the same period in response to the Eclair Cameflex)." (230) Heath's example is silly. The old Arri and CM3 Cameflex were good handheld cameras but neither was pin-registered or self-silenced. Until recently, American professional film-makers rarely regarded a non-pin-registered camera as reliable enough for feature use. And without a blimp the Arri and Eclair could not be used for dialogue shooting; the Eclair, with its ratchet drive, was especially noisy. Blimps added between 85 and 110 lbs. to either camera's weight and made the cameras useless for hand-holding. The Arri and Cameflex caught on slowly as "wild" cameras and for European

low-budget productions where dubbing-in of dialogue was the norm. But they were technically unsuited for the mainstream industry. Bawden, in fact, is correct if one adds "self-silenced" to her "handheld" comment. The l6mm Eclair NRP and ACL and the Auricon conversions of the early 1960s did allow the *cinema vérité* movement to exist. The interplay between tools and tool-users is far more complicated than many academics such as Heath would like to admit. Even Comolli—who as a filmmaker should know better—in his essay "Machines of the Visible," attacks Mitry's defense of orthochromatic stock by defending panchromatic film (quoted from Teresa de Lauretis and Stephen Heath, eds. *The Cinematic Apparatus.* New York: St. Martin's, 1980): "A further advantage . . . the replacement of orthochromatic by panchromatic stock depends again on the greater sensitivity of the latter. Not only did the gain in sensitivity permit the realignment of the 'realism' of the cinematic image with that of the photographic image, it also compensated for the loss of light due to the change from a shutter speed of 16 or 18 frames per second to the speed of 24 frames a second necessitated by sound." (131)

The only way such compensation could occur is if the *overall* film speed (ASA) of panchromatic film were higher. As Barry Salt points out (p. 222), panchromatic and ortho stock were about the same speed (20–25 ASA), and Kodak introduced a superspeed ortho film (ASA 40–50) in 1926. Thus there was no speed advantage in panchromatic stock. Comolli apparently does not know the difference between red sensitivity and overall film speed. One hopes he has someone else do his light readings and shoot his films.

4. See Heath, *Questions of Cinema,* 226–229.

5. George Lellis, "Perception in the Cinema: A Fourfold Confusion" in *Intermedia,* ed. Gary Gumpert and Robert Cathcart. New York: Oxford, 1979, p. 388.

6. I am indebted to Gorham Kindem's unpublished paper, "Theories of Film Technology: The Case of Color Film," for the insight that Foucault's theories could be applied to specific issues within film's technical history.

7. David Bordwell, *Narration in the Fiction Film.* Madison: University of Wisconsin Press, 1985.

8. I am indebted to James Langwell, Lanco Sound, Inc., Atlanta, GA, for theoretical and practical instruction in insert re-recording techniques and for contacts with ADR specialists.

9. See Peter Wollen, "Cinema and Technology: A Historical Overview," in de Lauretis and Heath, eds., *The Cinematic Apparatus,* 14–22. Wollen correctly asserts that the most important breakthroughs throughout film history have been in film stock—in chemistry, not mechanics. Information on film stocks in my essay are from *American Cinematographer, J.S.M.P.T.E.,* and manufacturers' technical representatives.

10. See David W. Leitner, "A Look at Color Negative," *The Independent* Vol. 4, Number 10, February 1982, 5–6, for a description of six-layer negative film-stock technology.

11. Ron Magid, "*Full Metal Jacket:* Cynic's Choice," *American Cinematographer* September 1987, 74–84.

12. See George Turner, "*Out of Africa:* David Watkin," *American Cinematographer* April 1986, 84–86. Watkin used Agfa for exteriors, Kodak for interiors. Watkin claims he liked Agfa's wide latitude and soft colors; one wonders, however, if the reason might have been that with Eastman stock, shooting outside in bright light, black and Caucasian faces are difficult to expose in the same frame; with Agfa or Fuji it's no problem. Eastman's technical representatives admit it's best to use a "Half Double Fog" filter in front of the lens when filming very dark-skinned blacks and light-skinned whites under harsh sunlight. There is a case to be made for issues of skin color being built into even film-stock specifications.

13. Jean-Pierre Grasset of Les Films du Soir first informed me of DeNiro's sub-recordable sound levels; a crewmember on *Angel Heart* confirmed it. In *Once Upon a Time in America,* however, DeNiro's location dialogue was mostly usable, despite its low volume; the soundman mixed inputs from a number of hidden microphones to get usable takes.

14. See Stig Bjorkman, Torsten Manns, and Jonas Sima, *Bergman on Bergman: Interviews with Ingmar Bergman,* trans. Paul Britten Austin. New York: Simon and Schuster, 1973, 257–258. When exactly Bergman began "matching" dialogue in post-production is vague. Vilgot Sjoman reports in *L136* that Bergman was having location sound troubles on *Winter Light.* A truism in low-budget film-making is that one can hear a film's budget problems before you see them. Bergman's films, like most European films, traditionally had minuscule budgets. To cover the budget and location shooting problems they "matched" sound in post-production, even before ADR.

CHARLES SHIRO TASHIRO

VIDEOPHILIA

What Happens When You Wait for It on Video

Vol. 45, no. 1 (Fall 1991): 7–17.

Since the early 1980s, there has been a steady increase in the revenue generated by marketing of theatrical films on videocassette and disc. This mass dissemination has been a boon to those interested in close study of film texts as well as to those simply interested in owning a copy of their favorite films. However, this apparent windfall has usually been embraced with little attention to the technical issues raised by the movement of a text from one medium to another or to the consequences of film evaluation based on video copies.

This discussion is meant as a broad overview of home video, and much of it is relevant to both videocassette and videodisc. However, I have concentrated on the latter, since it has evolved into the "quality" video medium, with a greater focus on duplicating the cinematic experience and an increased sensitivity to the technical requirements of film. (As a former producer for the Criterion Collection, including their edition of *Lawrence of Arabia*, I have some insight into the factors that go into disc production.) In particular, more attention to visual matters has popularized the transfer of wide-screen films at full horizontal width, with the resulting "letterbox" shape.[1] Videodisc publishers' attempted fidelity to film originals, the theoretical problems raised by such an attitude, and its relevance to film viewing and analysis are the focus of this paper.

THE VIDEODISC MEDIUM

To some extent, videodiscs would appear to be the film enthusiast's dream come true. They are light, portable, easy to store. With the growth of the market, a larger catalogue of titles is available.[2] While not cheap, the retail price is well below fees for print rental, not to mention the astronomical sums for purchase. Moreover, discs are (at least in theory) permanent, unlike either videotape or film, which deteriorate with each use.

Film never wears out faster than when run through a flatbed editing machine, the condition best suited for close analysis. Videotape offers fast-forward and rewind, but is much slower than the nearly instantaneous access available with videodisc players. Consumer-level VCRs, in addition, cannot offer the true freeze frame that a CAV videodisc offers. Disc players can also interact with computers and offer higher picture resolution than most commercially available tape gauges.[3] And there is, finally, the greater attention paid to the video transfer true of at least some videodisc publishers.

Still, with videodiscs there are trade-offs and underlying ideological assumptions. For example, unlike compact audiodisc players (a related technology), which usually have a feature to play songs in random order, videodisc players cannot randomly "scramble" the chapter encoding included on some discs. Presumably this lack of scrambling ability is based on the assumption that the film viewer will not be interested in mixing up the linear flow of the narrative. The players also do not have a feature to play sound at anything other than regular speed, which obviously assumes that only the picture is worthy of multispeed analysis.[4]

These features are designed into (or out of) the medium. Some are more beneficial to the user than others; all are ideologically dictated. But the limitations of the machinery itself and the assumptions that go into its design must be considered (if only in the background) in any discussion of the use of discs for pedagogical, analytical, or substitute cinematic viewing purposes. We must also consider the strategies of *moving* the text from film to video.

TRANSFER/TRANSLATION

The term "film-to-video" transfer is itself an ideological mask. Its connotation of neutral movement from one location (projection in a theater) to another (viewing at home) hides the reconfiguration of the text in new terms. A more accurate expression would be "translation," with its implicit admission of a different set of governing codes. While film and video share common technical concerns (contrast, color, density, audio frequency response, etc.), their means of addressing those concerns differ. The conscientious film-to-video transfer is designed to accentuate the similarities and minimize the differences, but the differences end up shaping the video text.

We might call the ease of translating a particular film to video its "videobility." A film with high videobility translates relatively easily, perhaps even gaining in the process. (Which is to say that there are elements in the *film* that come through more clearly on video. Subtlety of performance, intricacy of design, for example, may be lost in the narrative drive of the one-time-only cinematic setting, but en-

Lawrence of Arabia (1962)

hanced at home.) A film of low videobility translates with more difficulty. There are two components to videobility: technical and experiential. Technical differences of image between film and video center around three issues: 1) brightness and contrast range, 2) resolution, and 3) color.[5] As for the sound, a sound track mixed for theatrical exhibition may, when transferred to video, have tracks that will not balance "properly" at home. (For example, dialogue tracks may be drowned out by ambience tracks, etc.)[6]

Consider the following hypothetical example. A young couple, with their baby daughter, sits next to a window covered by horizontal blinds. Next to the window is an open doorway, leading out into a garden ripe with daffodils in summer sunlight. A butterfly flits across the flowers, attracting the attention of the baby, dressed in a bright red dress. She toddles out into the sun to chase the butterfly as her parents remain in the alternating shadows and shafts of light caused by the horizontal blinds. The mother looks at the father, then says "I think it's time we called it quits" at just the moment their daughter, as she reaches for the butterfly, trips and falls giggling into the flowers.

As we work to translate this image into video, problems arise immediately. First, there is the brightness range between the garden in sunlight and the parents in shade. Film records this juxtaposition without difficulty. But as the telecine operator exposes the video for the father and mother, the baby, butterfly, and flowers disappear into a white blaze; correcting for the baby, the parents disappear into murky shadow.

A choice has to be made, but which is more important? Attention to narrative would dictate exposing for the most significant action. Reasoning that the overall film is about the couple's divorce, the operator decides that the line "I think it's time we called it quits" is more important and thus chooses to expose for the interior. The baby's giggle seems to come out of nowhere; even if the juxtaposition between the line and the baby's giggling were not there, letting the flowers go to blazes runs the risk of losing the sensual detail. This detail may not *dominate* a film, but its cumulative effect is certainly a powerful influence on our perception.

The operator decides to make an overall adjustment in contrast to bring all the brightness ranges into midrange, thus making the image more "acceptable" to video. As a result, the alternating light and shadow are readable as a pattern and the baby in the flowers reappears out of the white sun.

Just about everything is visible now, but the sacrifice has been to change all the tonal values into the middle greys. Vividness of color and detail are lost, and the image looks as if it's been washed with a dirty towel. (As an example of just such a "dirty towel" transfer, see the video release of Joseph Losey's *Don Giovanni*.) The video image is acceptable within the limitations of the medium but unsatisfactory as a reproduction of the film image. In other words, the overall contrast of the image can be "flattened" to conform to the technical limitations of video, but the visual impact has been flattened as well. Thus, films photographed in a low-key or contrasty manner might be said to have low videobility because of the difficulty in reproducing their visual styles.

But there is another problem with our scene. The horizontal blinds read perfectly well on film because of its resolving power. But on video, they produce a distracting dance as the pixels inadequately resolve the differences between the blinds and intervening spaces. In other words, film can read the interstices between the blinds and reproduce that difference; video, trying to put both the blind and the space into the same pixel, cannot. (This is why TV personalities do not wear clothing with finely detailed weave or patterns.) The only way to compensate for this "ringing" effect is to throw the image slightly out of focus.

The resolving power of the film image is almost always greater than that of video. It is this greater resolution that enables the film image to be projected great distances. It is also this resolution that allows the greater depth and sensory detail that we associate with the filmgoing experience. Therefore, a film dependent on the accumulation of fine details also has low videobility. (For example, in the MGM/UA letterboxed video release of *Ben-Hur's* chariot race, the thousands of spectators become a colorful flutter; the spectacle of *Lawrence of Arabia* is also significantly reduced by the low resolution of background detail.)

And what about color? Although photography and video color reproduction are fundamentally different (one is a subtractive process, the other additive), it is the limitations of the video image that present the greatest problems, particularly the handling of saturated reds. Too vibrant or dense, and the signal gets noisy. But since red is often used to attract attention, it cannot be muted too much in video without violating visual design. Thus, color balance on the baby's dress would have to be performed carefully to allow the red to "read" without smearing. (For examples of dissonant reds, see Juliet's ball dress in the Paramount Home Video release of Zeffirelli's *Romeo and Juliet;* also note the scenes inside HAL's brain in the MGM/UA release of *2001: A Space Odyssey.*)

On the other hand, the relative imprecision of video does have some advantages, or, at least, it can be exploited. For example, optical effects in film, such as dissolves, "announce" themselves because of a noticeable shift in visual quality as the optical begins. This shift results from the loss of a generation involved in the production of the optical effect. To some extent, because the video image lacks the same resolution, the differences between the first-generation film image and the second-generation optical image can be lessened. In effect, the difference takes advantage of video's inferior resolving power to make the first-generation image look more like the second-generation image.

There are other problems, though, that result indirectly from the relatively low fidelity of the video image when compared with the high-fidelity sound reproduction possible with only a modest home stereo. Classical narrative is structured on the notion of synchronization between image and sound. This synchronization has a temporal component: we expect words to emerge from lips at the moment they form the letters of those words; when a bomb goes off, we expect to hear an explosion, etc. But there is also a *qualitative* component to synchronization. A big image of an explosion should be loud; a disjuncture occurs if the audio "image" remains large when that big image is reduced to a small screen. Imagine attending the opera and sitting in the last row of the upper balcony but *hearing* the music as if sitting in orchestra seats.

Home stereo is not equal to a theater. But subjectively, it is much closer in effect to the theatrical experience than a television image is to a projected film image. Moreover, when the sound tracks maintain some aspects of theatrical

A spinner in
Blade Runner

viewing/hearing that are easy to maintain in audio but impossible to duplicate in picture, we're once again conscious of the differences, not only between picture and sound, but between video and film. For example, in the opening scene of *Blade Runner*, a spinner (flying car) appears in the background, flies toward the foreground, then disappears camera left. As it retreats into the distance behind us, the sound continues (at least in those theaters equipped with surround stereo), fading into the distance, even though the image is no longer on the screen.

When this effect is duplicated in the Criterion Collection's letterboxed edition of the film, the audio decay of the spinner goes on too long or not long enough, depending on where you've placed your speakers. While the speakers can be moved, doing so runs the risk of throwing *other* sounds out of "synch." Even if it doesn't affect other sounds, however, the labor of moving speakers around for each viewing session takes the home video experience a long way from the passive enjoyment of sitting in a darkened theater, allowing yourself to be worked over by sight and sound.

"Improving" the film original by correcting optical effects, "fudging" the video when it can't handle the superior resolving power of film images, "flattening" the contrast ratio in order to produce an image that registers some version of the information contained in the original, together with audio that by its technical superiority reinforces our awareness of the video image—at what point do these differences produce a product no longer a suitable signifier of the film signified? Colorizing, for example, while damned as an obvious distortion of the film, can also be defended as improving the original. Is the conscientious transfer any less of a distortion? Preserving the "original" film text may prove as elusive a goal as the "unobtrusive" documentary camera.

THE DISINTEGRATING TEXT: VIDEODISCS AS CLASSICAL RUINS

Reconstructions of ancient architecture can be attempted from the fragments scattered across a landscape. But a rebuilt Parthenon is still a product of the archaeology that researched it. Videocassettes and discs are like large shards— hints of the original. But discs are not just the ruins of their forebears, they are the guns that destroy the temple by taking the archaeological process further, breaking the flow of a film into sides, segmenting the programming into "chapters," halting it altogether with freeze frames, encouraging objective analysis.

Film viewing, of course, is not genuinely continuous, since a feature film is divided into several reels. The theatrical experience, however, represses the disruption of reel breaks by quick changeovers of projectors, producing an illusion of continuous action. Videotape maintains that flow, at least for average length films. Discs cannot,[7] and publishers are thus faced with the problem of where to break the narrative. The decisions are governed by two concerns: 1) length limitations of the side—one hour for a CLV (Constant Linear Velocity) disc, 30 minutes for a CAV (Constant Angular Velocity) disc, and 2) suitability of the break.

Choice of breaks is not as simple as it might seem. For example, with a 119-minute film, it is not just a matter of putting 60 minutes on one side, and 59 minutes on another. If the 60-minute mark occurs in the middle of dialogue or a camera movement, then the break has to be pushed back to the previous cut. If there's an audio carryover over that cut (particularly a music cue), then other problems arise. If aesthetic considerations suggest going back before the 59-minute mark, it will no longer be possible to fit the film on a single disc, which means a rise in production costs. Faced with such an alternative, aesthetic considerations become secondary. (For example, consider the break between sides one and two on the Criterion CAV *Lawrence of Arabia*, which occurs in the middle of a dissolve between Lawrence and Tafas in the desert and their retrieval of water from a well. This break subverts the linkage function of a classical dissolve, here intended to bridge two disparate times and locations. On the disc, the desert and the well remain distant, separated by the time necessary to change sides.)

The disruption to narrative is inevitable, though, wherever the break is placed. It can be *ignored*, but it cannot be *overcome*. The jolt created by the side breaks becomes an integral part of the text. Moreover, the passive watching of the theatrical experience is replaced by one involving labor, however minimal (getting up and switching sides), encouraging a literal, physical interaction with the medium. (Imagine what it would be like if in the middle of every theatrical viewing you had to wait a few seconds before the film continued; imagine further what it would be like if *you* were responsible for continuing the experience.) This physical interaction involves the *proletarianization* of the video viewer by forcing him/her to become, in effect, a projectionist. And any suppression of the knowledge of technology thus requires a conscious activity: we cannot pretend that the discourse will proceed without us, because it won't until we get off the couch and flip sides.

This fragmentation of the viewing experience gets reinforced by the chapter encoding (although most discs are still produced without chapters). By their very name, chapters call attention to the hybrid nature of the medium. The obvious comparison is with a book. But book chapters are chosen by their authors; however much they segment the narrative, that choice arises at the moment of composition. As such, they are an integral part of the book's form.

Videodisc chapters are not cinematic composition, they are videodisc imposition. They aren't chosen at the point of film production, but after the fact, a voice from outside the text.[8] While common sense might lead one to expect chapters to be equivalent to the cinematic "sequence," in fact they often do not conform to any breakdown of the cinematic action, and there is no single pattern or rationale for their placement. They do, however, encourage the user to think of the text as something other than an unrolling, uninterruptible narrative. (For this reason, at least one well-known producer/director refuses to allow chapter encoding on disc releases of his films.)

Furthermore, while the chapter metaphor evokes books, their function is more similar to the track or cut of an LP or CD. The visual appearance of the videodisc, obviously intended to evoke the LP,[9] reinforces this hybrid association. Scenes or segments of the film end up getting treated like individual pop songs on a record or CD: no longer related to their immediate surroundings, they become isolated as discrete units. Chapter stops run like a mine field under the linear development of classical narrative. Fans of a film no longer have to sit through the parts they don't like; they can jump to their favorite scenes, in whatever order they choose. Imagine how different an experience it would be to enter a movie theater and be able to skip the tedious parts or scramble the order of the reels. "I came for the waters . . ." zip "We'll always have Paris." And I suspect even the viewer interested only in watching the movie will use the chapter encoding for quicker access. Isn't one of the consequences of the repeated viewings encouraged by home video *boredom?* The significance of chapters is that viewers are beginning to think in these terms, to feel *in control* of a film's tedium.

If chapters evoke books and records, freeze frames turn a film into a sequence of stills or paintings. In so doing, they further destroy linear development. A single CAV side contains 54,000 frames. That's 54,000 possible points of fixation, alternative entries into an imagistic imaginary. The film's characters and story can be discarded in favor of new narratives inspired by the images. Just as photographs and paintings arrest our gaze and inspire us to invent, so too the frozen film image, isolated in time, loses its context and creates a new one.

With motion removed, the film image becomes subject to a different critical discourse. No longer is it enough to talk about an image getting us from point A to B (the narrative prejudice). Criticism of the image's frozen form, composition, lighting, color are invited. Individual images can be subjected to the standards of photography and painting. Of course, few film images can withstand such scrutiny, since most are *composed* in movement.

> Of course cinema cannot be reduced to its still frames and the semiotic system of cinema cannot be reduced to the systems of painting or of photography. Indeed, the cinematic succession of images threatens to interrupt or even to expose and to deconstruct the representation system which commands static paintings or photos. For its succession of shots is, by that very system, a succession of views.[10]

To the extent that they encourage a criticism based on alternative codes, freeze frames threaten the very basis of classical narrative, in effect reversing the semiotic power relationship noted by Dayan.

"YOU HAVE TO SEE IT IN A THEATER"

An undergraduate film-appreciation class at the University of Southern California is taught on the basis that films, in order to be understood fully, must be seen under theatrical conditions. Great expense is taken to obtain good prints; screenings occur in a large facility analogous to first-run theaters in the Los Angeles area. Stress is placed on the larger-than-life aspect of film-going. And yet, when a scheduled film is unavailable in 35mm, dirty, murky, 16mm prints are used. Is this part of the theatrical experience?

Yes, although in ways not likely to be on the minds of anyone prejudiced toward theatrical exhibition. This attitude implies that theatrical viewing conditions, even at their worst, are preferable to viewing a decent video version at home. But film exhibition is subject to a range of factors—print quality, film gauge, optical vs. magnetic sound, stereo vs. mono, screen size, aspect ratio,

High "videobility":
The Wizard of Oz

the quality of the reproductive machinery—beyond the control of the consumer. So—which violates the film more, a good video or a bad print?

Most video transfers are made from technically superior film sources. At their best, the resulting tapes or discs have a uniform gloss that is generally not true of theatrical prints outside of initial runs. The benefit of this uniformity is a standardization of presentation, dependent only on the hardware used for reproduction. Of course, all forms of standardization involve loss as well as gain. The variability of theatrical projection can have unintended benefits, when elements not noticed in one circumstance show up under others. But it seems unlikely that anyone would *prefer* a scratchy, inaudible reduction print made from a third generation negative to a video copy made carefully from an early generation source.

Earlier, I introduced the concept of videobility to describe the ease of translating a film into video. But videobility involves more than just questions of whether or not a decent video image can be produced. Some films have high videobility (*The Wizard of Oz* probably seems *more* familiar on video than in a theatrical screening, since most of us know the film through television broadcast). Others strike us as impossible to imagine on video without significant loss (Bondarchuk's *War and Peace,* for example). Is there, then, something in the viewing experience that *depends* on theatrical conditions for full effect of a given film? Or, more properly, what does video lack that film possesses that makes the theatrical experience "essential"?

In "The Work of Art in the Age of Mechanical Reproduction," Walter Benjamin wrote that

> The cult of the movie star, fostered by the money of the film industry, preserves not the unique aura of the person but the "spell of the personality," the phony spell of a commodity.[11]

Is the quasi-religious aspect of film viewing, induced by capital or not, "phony"? If a film succeeds in moving us to ecstasy, does it matter in *experiential* terms whether or not it is a "true" sensation? The ecstatic component of (some) filmgoing cannot be dismissed, particularly when discussing it in relationship to home video. For this religious aspect of filmgoing is clearly lacking in home video viewing.

One obvious reason for this lack is the difference in scale. As the cliché has it, film is larger than life, television smaller. And yet the difference between video and film experiences is not scale *as such,* but the depth that greater size gives to film's sensory extravagance. It is that richness, sensual saturation, and euphoria that video cannot duplicate. But if video is excluded from the Dionysian, it gives access to the excess that *creates* ecstasy through the capacity to repeat, slow, freeze, and contemplate. Savoring replaces rapture.

LETTERBOXING, MON AMOUR

The problem of scale has, from the first, been linked to the related issue of aspect ratio. CinemaScope and other wide-screen processes were developed (along with high-fidelity stereo sound) with the purpose of overwhelming viewers with an experience not available on their televisions at home. On the other hand, sale of broadcast and video rights of theatrical features represents a lucrative source of revenue, necessitating a means of squeezing wide-screen images into the TV frame. But you cannot fill the TV frame without either cutting off edges of the film picture, or through anamorphic compression, turning the films into animated El Grecos.

In recent years, there has been a growing interest in maintaining the theatrical aspect ratio for video viewing. Unfortunately, this interest has bred the fallacious notion that there is a single "correct" aspect ratio. In fact, it is the *rule,* not the exception, that there is no single "correct" aspect ratio for any wide-screen film. For example, during photography, it is common for directors and cinematographers to "hard matte" some, but not all, of their shots if they expect to exhibit in 1.85 or 1.66. If you examine the negative, some shots would be matted for 1.66, say, and others at full frame 1.33. Which is "correct"?

Full reproduction of *Lawrence* frame, without matte

Frequently, too, the ratio of photography will be altered when a film changes gauges. A film might be shot in nonanamorphic 70mm at 2:1, reduced to anamorphic 35mm at 2.35:1, then reduced to 16mm at 1.85:1. (The *Lawrence of Arabia* disc, for example, was produced from a 35mm source, meaning a slight loss of vertical information.) Then there are those processes, like VistaVision, that were *designed* to be shown at different ratios. As if that weren't complex enough, most projectionists show *everything* at 2:1. Is "correct" based on intention, gauge, exhibition, breadth of distribution, amount of visual information, . . . ?

While it might be more prudent to think of an "optimal" aspect ratio, rather than a "correct" one, who should choose the optimum? Asking the director or cinematographer perpetuates the auteurist mystique while assuming that the filmmaker knows best how a film at home should be watched. This approach further assumes that these people are best equipped to translate film images into video images. To privilege film technicians, then, subordinates video to film.

Prior to the involvement of the film's technicians, optimality was visually determined by concentrating on significant dramatic action and sacrificing composition and background detail (by cropping the edges of the frame). When composition made such reframing impossible (when, for example, two conversing characters occupied opposite edges of the frame), then a "pan-and-scan" optical movement was made; or the frame was edited optically into two shots.

"Full frame" TV image with pan-and-scan

"Full frame" TV image with letterboxed full film frame

Pan-and-scan transfers are performed largely to preserve narrative and to approximate the theatrical experience by keeping the entire television frame filled. There is an implicit assumption that the *vertical* dimensions of the film frame must be maintained. Letterboxing maintains the full *horizontal* dimension of the wide-screen image. In effect, pan-and-scan transfers privilege the television (thus subordinating film to video). It is more important to fill the TV frame than it is to maintain cinematic composition. Letterboxing reverses that priority by preserving the cinematic framing.

But a transformation occurs in maintaining composition. (If it didn't, letterboxing wouldn't be controversial.) In his essay "CinemaScope: Before and After," Charles Barr writes:

> But it is not only the horizontal line which is emphasized in CinemaScope. . . . The more open the frame, the greater the impression of depth: the image is more vivid, and involves us more directly.[12]

If Barr is correct, letterboxing, by merely maintaining the horizontal measurement of the 'Scope frame, cannot duplicate the wide-screen experience. Letterboxing equates the *shape* of the CinemaScope screen with its *effect*.

In fact, while letterboxing subordinates the TV screen to cinematic composition, it simultaneously *reverses* that hierarchy. If film is usually considered larger and grander than TV, wide-screen film letterboxed in a 1.33 TV frame subjects film to television aesthetics by forcing the film image to become *smaller* than the TV image. Thus, in the act of privileging film over video, video ends up dominant. (The movement from 70mm theatrical exhibition to 19-inch home viewing is one long diminuendo of cinematic effect.)

Moreover, letterboxing is an ambiguous process, with all the resistance ambiguity encounters. A letterboxed image is neither film nor TV. Its diminished size makes it an impossible replacement for the theatrical experience; at the same time, the portentous black bands at the top and bottom of the screen remind the video viewer not only of the "inferiority" of the video image to the film original (it can only accommodate the latter by shrinking it) but also of a lack. What is behind those black bars? Edward Branigan makes the point that the frame is "the boundary which actualizes what is framed" and that "representation is premised upon, and is condemned to struggle against, a fundamental absence."[13]

The absent in film is everything outside the visual field. In a letterboxed transfer of 'Scope films, the matte hides the bottoms and tops of the outgoing and incoming frames. Viewing the film without the matte would make it impossible for us not to be aware of the "cinematicness" of the image, since we would be viewing frame lines in addition to the picture. The mattes for "flat" wide-screen films (1.85:1 and 1.66:1) frequently blot out production equipment such as microphones, camera tracks, and so on, that the director or cinematographer assumed would be matted out in projection.

Both frame lines and extraneous equipment are part of the repressed production process. To see them ruptures the classical diegesis. And the fact that such a violence to our normal cinematic experience is necessary in video would call attention once again to the differences between the media. A double exposure of ideology would occur: of the repressed aspects of cinematic projection (frame lines, equipment)[14] and of the presumed neutrality of the transfer procedure.

Yet there is no useful alternative to letterboxing.[15] Form and composition *are* important; useful analysis of films on video cannot be performed when 43 percent of the image has been cropped, and certainly no one can claim to have seen(!) the film on video under such circumstances. If maintaining the horizontal length of the image creates the fiction that the cinematic experience has been approximated, it is nonetheless a fiction worthy of support. Besides, letterboxing introduces aesthetic effects of its own.

The frame created by the matte contributes one more effect toward treating the cinematic image as an object of analysis. Just as the frame of a painting directs our gaze toward the painting enclosed, so too the letterbox calls attention to the aesthetic qualities of the image framed. But that may be the problem; if people object to letterboxing, it's because it turns their classical narratives into formalist galleries. (Consider how the ponderously pseudo-epic qualities of *Lawrence of Arabia* get lost in a background blur on video, refocusing attention on the flatness of the image and compositional precision.) In fact, letterboxing does precisely the *opposite* of what Barr likes about wide-screen:[16] it ends up *accentuating* composition, rather than effacing it.

"I'LL WAIT FOR IT ON VIDEO"

Who, after becoming used to the flexibility of home video, has not wanted to fast-forward past bits of a boring or offensive theatrical film? Doesn't this desire suggest a transformation of the cinematic experience by home video? What we once might have endured, we now resent. Hollywood continues to offer plodding, linear narratives wilted with halfhearted humanism as the staple of its production. But doesn't our itchy, reflexive reaching for the remote control suggest a complete *saturation* by classical narrative?

Whether we like it or not, home video turns us all into critics. Instead of being engulfed by an overwhelming image that moves without our participation, we're able to subject film texts to our whims. And by allowing the viewer greater insight into an object of cultural production, home video starts to break the hold of individual texts and, possibly, of cinema in general. This conscious participation in film viewing can only be helped by the widespread dissemination of film texts, even in hybrid form.

We're back to Benjamin again. Having a good reproduction of the *Mona Lisa* does not substitute for the actual painting but it "enables the original to meet the beholder halfway," and in so doing, the copy "reactivates the object reproduced."[17] Well-produced home video performs the same function for film texts, which, the "phoniness" of the theatrical experience notwithstanding, *are* invested with an aura by classical practices of obfuscation, suppression, and capitalist investment in the commodity of the image. As home video allows us to meet the film text halfway, it does to film what film-makers have done to the world for years: turns it into an object for control.

At the same time, a conscious video consumer must confront the reality that home video is a luxury, that the possession of the equipment results from a position of privilege, thus perpetuating the very economic relations the active viewership (might) help undermine. Does this reality turn any video viewing into a guilty pleasure? One answer to this dilemma may reside in the writings of Epicurus, whose philosophy of pleasure derived from moral calculation may be the best guide for the aware consumer:

> The flesh perceives the limits of pleasure as unlimited and unlimited time is required to supply it. But the mind, having attained a reasoned understanding of the ultimate good of the flesh and its limits . . . supplies us with the complete life, and we have no further need of infinite time: but neither does the mind shun pleasure.[18]

Videodiscs make us into proletarians and encourage criticism through physical interaction and segmentation. But, produced with care to maintain some aspect of the scopic pleasure of the cinematic image, they make possible a connoisseurship of form that theatrical viewing discourages. Videodisc viewing sits at an awkward juncture between criticism and experience, analysis and ecstasy, progress and privilege. As we participate in this ambiguous vacillation between oppositions, we become a post-modern contradiction: the Proletarian Epicure.

Moreover, home video gives us a means of almost literally "deconstructing" films, helping us remake them to our own ends. Even those who deny their proletarian position by viewing these film/videos in a linear fashion end up, as they change sides or put the VCR in pause, participating in the creation of an alternative text. Videodiscs, as a hybrid medium dedicated to reproducing an experience alien to it, standardizes, fragments, commodifies, objectifies, and segments that experience. You can "wait for it on video," but "it," like Godot, will never arrive, because the discs' high-tech insouciance offers, despite their truckling to the capitalist realities, a revolutionary hope: the destruction of classical cinema.

1. Consider this note on the back of 20th Century–Fox videodisc packages: "Special Wide Screen Edition. The film contained on this laserdisc is being presented for your enjoyment in the wide screen format, or 'letterbox,' allowing you to experience the film at home as closely to the original version as possible." All the major video publishers have some variation on this note, stressing the disc's fidelity to the theatrical original and the normality of the shape of the letterboxed image.

2. Though still far fewer than are available on tape. Neither medium has really made a dent in the library of available film titles. Who, what, and why decides which titles are available on video is a subject unto itself.

3. Super VHS, Hi-Band Video 8, and ED-Beta offer the same number of lines of horizontal resolution as videodiscs. However, all of these magnetic media suffer from an immediate wear and tear not true of discs.

4. This particular limitation is not only frustrating for anyone interested in sound/image relationships, it's downright odd. CD players, which are designed for audio *only*, allow us to hear samples of the music as we scan. Why is there no equivalent for film listening?

5. Brightness range is the difference between the brightest and darkest parts of the shot. Contrast is the brightness range between any two given spots in the shot. For a concise description of the technical inequities of the two media, see Dominic J. Case, "Telecine-Compatible Prints," *SMPTE Journal*, June 1989, pp. 415–54. For a discussion of color sensitometry, see H. J. Bello, "An Introduction to the Technology of Color Films (Film Colorimetry)—A Tutorial Paper," *SMPTE Journal*, November 1979.

6. See Graham Carter, "Mastering of Dolby Stereo Film Material for Videocassette Release," *Audio Plus*, March 1991.

7. Some videodisc players are capable of playing two sides, but the disruption remains since the viewer has to wait as the laser repositions at the beginning of the second side.

8. The Criterion Collection frequently provides literal "voices from outside the text" by recording audio commentary running with the film. Obviously, these commentaries encourage an alternative perception as well.

9. For a short discussion of the early reaction to videodiscs, see Barry Fox, "Video discs—too late for the gravy train?" *New Scientist,* vol. 91, no. 1260, pp. 277–80. Videodiscs, in fact, were the parent technology of CDs; the latter's success has given videodiscs their second market life.

10. Daniel Dayan, "The Tutor-Code of Classical Cinema," *Film Quarterly,* vol. 28, no. 1, p. 28.

11. Walter Benjamin, "The Work of Art in the Age of Mechanical Reproduction," in *Film Theory and Criticism: Introductory Readings,* ed. Gerald Mast and Marshall Cohen, 3rd ed. (New York: Oxford University Press, 1985), p. 686.

12. Charles Barr, "CinemaScope: Before and After," *Film Quarterly,* vol. 16, no. 4, p. 9.

13. Edward Branigan, *Point of View in the Cinema: A Theory of Narration and Subjectivity in Classical Film* (Berlin and New York: Mouton Publishers, 1984), p. 65.

14. Consider the following comment: "Note that in 1971 an ANSI specification was published to limit the projector aperture to a height of 0.700" (instead of the 0.715" previously specified) to limit the screen appearance of splices." Fred H. Detmers, "Photograph Systems," *American Cinematographer Manual,* ed. and comp. Charles G. Clarke, 5th ed. (Hollywood: American Society of Cinematographers, 1980), p. 44.

15. Even if an HDTV standard is introduced that produces a ratio wide enough to accommodate Panavision and CinemaScope, there will still be a need for *vertical* masking of films (and videos?) shot in the 1.33 ratio. May I propose we call this vertical matting "keyholing"?

16. Barr, op. cit.

17. Benjamin, op. cit., p. 678.

18. *Epicurus: The Extant Remains,* trans. Cyril Bailey (Oxford: Clarendon Press, 1926), p. 99.

[Other sources used for this piece were David Bordwell, Janet Staiger, and Kristin Thompson, *The Classical Hollywood Cinema: Film Style and Mode of Production to 1960* (New York: Columbia University Press, 1985); and Matt McGillicuddy, *Color Television Fundamentals, NTSC, PAL and SECAM,* s.l., Ampex Corporation, s.d.]

JEAN-PIERRE GEUENS

THROUGH THE LOOKING GLASSES

From the Camera Obscura to Video Assist

The original video assist apparatus put together by Bruce Hill in 1970

Vol. 49, no. 3 (Spring 1996): 16–26.

The studio is finally quiet. The actors are restless. The crew is ready. "Sound." "Camera." The slate is taken. A voice calls "Action." A voice? Is this really the director, "with his back to the actors,"[1] looking at the scene on a little video monitor? Isn't the director, at least the solid Hollywood professional of old, supposed to sit just next to the camera, facing the action? What's happening here?

Following the trajectory that led from the old-fashioned parallax viewfinders to the contemporary use of video-assist technology, I will argue that "looking through the camera" is never a transparent activity, that each configuration has distinctive features whose design and implementation resonate beyond the actual use of the device. In his still seminal essay "The Question Concerning Technology,"[2] Martin Heidegger warned us that "technology is no mere means,"[3] that the adoption of a new method of production often expresses more than the simple substitution of one tool by another. In Andrew Feenberg's words, "modern technology is no more neutral than medieval cathedrals or the Great Wall of China; it embodies the values of a particular civilization. . . . "[4] Herbert Marcuse is even more radical. For him, "specific purposes and interests of domination are not foisted upon technology 'subsequently' and from the outside; they enter the very construction of the technical apparatus. Technology is always a historical social project: in it is projected what a society and its ruling interests intend to do with men and things."[5] Thus, as far as the camera is concerned, the very appearance of a novel gizmo could itself be significant of cultural or economic changes that have taken place in the film industry prior to the use of the new technology and, in turn, the actual practice of the supplemental device may help shape a different kind of cinema.

In the first years of cinema, getting access to the image that was to be recorded on film was no easy matter. The early cameras could never provide such necessary information. Indeed, not only the pioneer cameras of the 1890s and the

1900s but also the first truly professional cameras used by Holly-wood—the Bell and Howell 2709 and the Mitchell Standard Model—had to resort to peeping holes, miscellaneous finders, magnifying tubes, swinging lens systems, and rack-over camera bodies to give any information at all about the image produced by the lens.[6] At best, the operators were allowed to survey the scene before or after actually shooting it. Crucially missing from their arsenal was the capability to check on exact framing, focusing, lighting, depth of field, and perspective while filming. Although a lens could be precisely focused on an actor's position ahead of time, what happened during the shot, especially if there was any movement, remained a mystery. The operators, in effect, were shooting blind. As they watched through the parallax viewfinder on the side of the camera, a device that produced but a pallid, lifeless, uninviting substitute for the real thing peeked at seconds earlier, they remained outsiders to what was truly going on inside the apparatus. In a way, the mystery of what happened inside the camera during the shooting acted as a synecdoche for the further magic that would be worked on the film in the lab, where it was to be chemically treated and its content at last exposed to view. Only at the screening of the dailies could one know for sure whether the scene was good or needed to be reshot. Such a daunting situation therefore required steady professional types and, indeed, this is how the "operative cameramen" were described by their peers in the American Society of Cinematographers: "They must be ever on the watch that no unexpected or unplanned action by the players or background changes from the originally planned movement and lighting on the set, occur during shooting. They sit behind the camera, like the engineer at his throttle, ever watching for danger signals."[7] These brave men behind the camera, despite their vigilance, thus stood in a hermeneutic relation to their instrument. The otherness of the machine remained unassailed, its viewing apparatus a numinous, hermetic object standing as a third party between the operator and the world. The best one could do was stand next to the thing, maybe controlling its mishaps or its surges, but, throughout, acknowledging the actual film process as a thorough enigma.

The situation changed in 1936, when the Arnold and Richter Company of Germany introduced continuous reflex viewing with its new Arriflex 35mm camera. The solution was truly elegant: by mirroring the side of the shutter that was facing the lens and tilting it at a 45-degree angle, the light that was not used by the film when the latter was intermittently moving inside the camera was now made available to the operator for viewing purposes. Suddenly, the deficiencies that had marred the early camera systems were eliminated as operators, looking through the lens during the filming, gained maximum control over the images they were shooting. In fact, the smoothness of the Arriflex solution hid a paradox. Even though the operator may believe he or she sees what the film gets, technically speaking one never actually witnesses the same instant of time that is recorded on film because of the fluctuating movement of the shutter—when the operator gets the light, the film does not, and vice versa. More importantly, this means that the access to the lens is punctuated by the blinking presence/absence of the mirrored shutter. In my view, this flickering implies more than a simple technical chink; it radically transforms the linkage between the operator, the camera, and the world by literally embodying the eye within the technology of the apparatus itself.

Indeed, if we go back to the early years of still photography for a moment, there was always a sense of awe when the operator's head finally disappeared under a large black cloth in order to take the picture. "What do you have there: a girlfriend?" a model asked of Michael Powell's protagonist in *Peeping Tom* (1960), a comment that clearly exposes the prurience of the act. In a similar fashion, on the motion picture set, the view through the reflex viewfinder quickly became fetishized, the actual practice exceeding the useful aspect of checking on the parameters of the scene. Crew hierarchy determined who got to take a peek. Yet the static image one could witness when the camera was at rest had finally little to do with what happened during the real shooting, when the operator alone received the full force of the system. Then the impact was truly stirring; due to the saccadic nature of the shutter's rotation, the effect on the eye was nothing less than phantasmagoric. Because the other eye of the operator remained closed during the filming, the flickering light on the ground glass became thoroughly hypnotic, even addictive.[8] For the time of the shot, with only one eye opened onto the phantastic spectacle on the little screen, the operator was very much lost in another world, a demimonde, a netherworld not unlike a dream screen for the wakened.

It is not so much that the frame provides for the operator a "synoptic center of the film's experience of the world it sees," as Vivian Sobchack has suggested,[9] but that what is being seen and the way it is seen combine in bringing forth a unique experience for the person at the camera. Let us consider for a moment the ramifications of what is actually taking place. A scene is rehearsed, then shot a number of times until the director declares him/herself satisfied. Through it all, the same general actions are performed with little change by the actors (basic gestures are duplicated, more or less the same lines enunciated) and the crew moves in sync with the action—a swinging of the boom that keeps abreast of an actor; a short dolly movement that accompanies an action; a dimming of the light level at the proper moment by an electrician; a change of focus by the camera assistant; and, for the operator, maybe a pan or other small readjustment that keeps the scene within the frame. What we have here, then, is no less than a ritual, a ceremony of sorts that also involves repetition, reenactment, and specific gestures carried out by "practitioners specially trained."[10] On a macro scale, the effect of a ritual is to bond a group, to create a sense of *communitas* when all participants find themselves sharing an experience. And, characteristically, this is a well-known effect experienced by all in a film crew as the constant repetition of specific actions, performed with only minimal variations, gives each member the sense both of cultic participation in a grand project and of sharing in a larger, collective identity. For the operator who most intimately experiences it all as an eye mesmerized by the spectacle on the little screen, the effect is even more hallucinatory. The sense of time is altered; there is no past or future any more, only a flux, a duration, an endless synchronic moment with actions many times repeated, an epiphany punctuated only by "eternal poses," to use Gilles Deleuze's descriptive words.[11] Because it stands outside mechanical time and physical space, the experience recalls the "oceanic" early moments of life. During that moment, the operator, neither here nor there, stands liminally between two worlds. As he or she merges, to some extent, with the phantom action on the little screen, a communion takes place that integrates the self within an ideal reality. Not surprisingly a certain *Ekstase* can be reached. The effect then is not unlike that of a trance in a ritual, an experience that also momentarily transforms the individual. No wonder that, after the shot, different members of the crew turn toward the operator and ask: "How was it?"

Others have been sensitive to the reflex feature of the camera for distinct reasons as well. For instance, independent film-makers functioning simultaneously as directors and operators have worked both in fiction and in documentary. Among others, Nina Menkes, Ulrike Ottinger, and Werner Schroeter have always insisted on controlling the camera. In their kind of moviemaking, it makes a lot of sense not just to be present but also to participate in the moment of creation and help deliver the scene through the camera. For Direct Cinema practitioners, however (Richard Leacock, D. A. Pennebaker, and Albert Maysles in the heyday of the movement), the situation is somewhat different. As the subject here belongs not to fiction but to the real world, and the situation, by choice, cannot be rehearsed, there is no question of experiencing a ritual. Instead, the film-maker and the camera seem to merge into one persona that absorbs the scene and responds to it. For the Drew team, for instance, not only is the scene "unscripted, it's unrehearsed . . . for the first time the camera is a man. It sees, it hears, it moves like a man."[12] In other words, through its heartbeat, the pulse of its shutter, the camera now breathes as a human being. And the film-maker, operating like the expert craftsperson of old, carves up the world for the benefit of the viewer, dereifying the structures of daily life, eventually revealing what was either unseen or just obscure moments before. In this case, therefore, the look through the camera functions very much as an example of what Heidegger refers to as *techne*, the Greek practice of the craftsperson which brings forth *poesis* through the work. For Heidegger, the decisive factor is not the tool itself but the "unconcealment" of the world that results from its use.[13]

However, because the rigid division of labor in the Hollywood cinema forbids it, the typical director is almost never the person behind the camera (often sitting, instead, just underneath it). For him or her, therefore, nothing really changed in the substitution of the original apparatus by the reflex camera. The director remains exterior to the camera's process. After orchestrating everybody else's actions, the director gauges the results of the take instantly, *in vivo*, by gut instinct. Precisely because such directors do not look through a viewing screen during the filming, they literally function as metteurs-en-scène: their scene indeed is the stage, the space where fellow beings move about. What they must be sensitive to is the human intercourse at hand, the social space between people, the presence of objects as well as the flesh of the individuals. All the senses of a director are imbricated in this evaluation. Although the scene is shot in pieces and staged to be captured in a certain way on film, the dramatic action has a reality of its own. It is thus experienced by the director as (to borrow another notion from Heidegger) *Zuhandenheit*, the ready-at-hand, an involvement with the world through technique that actually supersedes the use of the equipment.[14] Expressly because the director is not looking through the camera, the technology associated with directing remains somewhat in the background, only a subordinate accessory. For Heidegger, what is experienced in this fashion is ontologically quite different from what could be observed through *Vorhandenheit*, the present-at-hand, the contemplation of a decontextualized subject matter. Directors functioning in the traditional mode thus depend mostly on human rather than exclusively cinematic skills: this does not feel right, that timing is a little off, this character would not really do that.

Furthermore, if we listen to Emmanuel Levinas for a moment, when a face-to-face encounter among human beings takes place, the contact involves more than a mere recording of an action by the eyes.[15] It embodies the most fundamental mode of being-in-the-world. A face, for Levinas, expresses the vulnerability of the being; it is an appeal, a call. The face solicits a human contact beyond cold rationality or calculative thinking. Its sheer presence impinges on the other person's autocratic tendencies. In this light, the director's "vision" of the scene becomes compounded by his/her own presence among the actors. Sharing a unique moment of time, the director becomes thoroughly wedded to the players as fellow human beings who carry their load of pain or distress. Can the director in these conditions (to recall well-known cases in our cinema) remain unaware of the wooden leg of one actor even if it remains off-camera? Can the director not respond to the cancer that is eating up this other actor? Even if we abandon these dramatic examples, is it really possible for the director to leave entirely behind the lunch shared with some actor, the conversations that went on, the hopes that were disclosed or the fears that were expressed? To go back to Heidegger, the director here does more than take a look (*Sicht*) at the scene professionally; emotion is involved as well (*Ruchsicht*), a look that involves sympathy, concern, and responsibility. Furthermore, the sharing of a human space and the mutual recognition that takes place between people automatically involve moral claims. One individual temporarily gives something of him/herself to another. Trust matters deeply. Ethics are involved. As a result, the director functions both as a participant in a shared exchange and as a shaman who guides others through a difficult process of shedding off. For such a director, the scene clearly takes place in front of his or her eyes, not behind where the camera is. After the take, the information that originates from the crew is certainly important, but it is purely technical in nature: did the action remain in focus, was the pan smooth, did the mike get in the shot, was the jolt to the dolly noticeable?

A radical departure to this long-standing mode of directing came about as a result of Jerry Lewis's introduction of video as a guide for the director to evaluate the quality of a take. There were of course good reasons for Lewis to do so: this was a logical solution to the problem of the actor/director, who was otherwise unable to check his performance. Buster Keaton would surely have been an ardent practitioner of the new technology. What Lewis did was elegant in its simplicity: he positioned a video camera as close as possible to the film camera, allowing him to view what he had just shot on playback. Although the technology was primitive and the equipment, at the time, heavy and cumbersome, Lewis persevered, and others eventually picked up on the idea. As early as 1968, some motion picture cameras that incorporated plumbicon tubes in the viewfinder (thus splitting the light that normally would go to the operator alone), were used to film a tennis championship in Australia.[16] The next year, videotape playback was used in the film *Oliver!* (Carol Reed, 1968) to check on the lip sync or the movement of performers. If the tape showed the actor or dancer to be in sync after all, it saved the retake of a difficult and expensive dance number.[17] By most accounts, though, credit for the integration of the video "camera" within the motion picture camera by means of a pellicle (a thin, partial mirror that split the light coming to the operator) goes to Bruce Hill, an engineer/tinkerer who had worked at Fairchild and Mitchell.[18] By 1970, working independently, Hill had modified a Mitchell BNCR and used a one-inch-videotape recording and playback system by Ampex. The subsequent image could be observed on a 17-inch monitor. A variation of this package was used for the helicopter sequences of *The Towering Inferno* (John Guillermin and Irwin Allen, 1974), the first time such a device was used by the Hollywood establishment.

Not surprisingly, directors shooting commercials were the first to embrace the new technique, for in their work in particular it is very important to check on the exact placement of a product in relation to many other coordinates. With the help of video, minute details could be discussed between representatives of the advertising agency and the technicians. Today, practically all commercial productions use video assist and playback on the set. In contrast, feature directors were distinctly slower in adopting the new apparatus: only 20 percent or so of the productions in the early 1980s used video assist. And although today most do, no more than 40 percent of the shoots bother with a playback system.[19]

On the surface, the use of video assist on the set provided only positive benefits for the director and the crew. For directors, being able to see the picture of the scene being rehearsed meant gaining back some of the control that historically had been lost to operators. For a crew, the advantages could be measured in terms of efficiency. During a shoot, questions keep flying to the operator: is the boom in the shot, where is the frame line, do I need to prop that area, are these people in the shot, how high do I need to light that wall, etc.? A lot of production time is lost as the operator attempts to make clear the parameters of the shot to the gaffer, the assistant director, the boom person, or the prop master. Once video assist becomes available and a large monitor is provided for the various crew members, all they have to do is look at it to answer their own question. In a similar fashion, the light split itself can be subdivided so as to provide a mini-image to the operator's assistant or the dolly grip. It might be more practical indeed for these technicians to look at an image on a monitor than to the scene itself to decide exactly when to initiate a rack focus or a dolly movement. All of these advantages end up saving time, and thus money, for the production.

There were, however, some technical mishaps that initially limited the appeal of the novel apparatus. The early grievances were mostly concerned with the disappearance of the director, who might be locked in a trailer loaded with equipment and who would communicate with the crew and actors only through a loudspeaker. Helen Hayes, for instance, was heard complaining about such a "disembodied voice" when working on *Raid on Entebbe* (Marvin Chomsky, 1977). And Garrett Brown grumbled that, when he was shooting the maze scene in *The Shining* (Stanley Kubrick, 1980), "Stanley mostly remained seated at the video screen, and we sent a wireless image from my camera out to an antenna on a ladder and thence to the recorder,"[20] in effect forcing Brown to go back and forth between the maze and the trailer, quite a distance away, just to find out if the take was good. That problem was eventually worked out when directors were able to use the monitor on the set itself. Another difficulty involved the operator: as the video system taps the light that would normally go to the eye of the camera person, a loss of clarity can be experienced by the operator, in effect making the job more difficult. One reason black-and-white taps have been traditionally preferred over color models is that the former could function with much less light intake compared to the latter. A new color tap though, the CEI Color IV, is said to be almost as economical as the black-and-white models and is thus gaining in popularity. Flickering was another "annoyance" that marred some of the viewing. But there are now new models, such as those factory-installed by Arriflex on its new 535 camera, which incorporate a totally flicker-free tap. Although more traditional directors of photography, such as Haskell Wexler, have indicated their preference for a video image that reproduces the flicker of the motion picture camera, most directors of photography shooting commercials go for the enhanced version, perhaps to soothe the apprehension of clients or agency people who might wonder about the misfiring on the monitor.[21] A fourth difficulty concerned the matching of the image received on the monitor to specific aspect ratios when shooting wide-screen or when using an anamorphic lens. Here the solutions could be makeshift in nature (paper tape can be applied directly on the monitor so as to delimit the 1.85:1 aspect ratio), or electronic (monitors can now switch easily from a squeezed to an unsqueezed image). Finally, using videotape playback after each take may slow down the impetus of the crew because it interrupts everyone's activity—a situation that has limited the use of that particular technique. It might indeed be cheaper to redo a shot immediately than to break the momentum of the cast and crew. For this reason, videotape playback, when used at all, is looked at only after several takes have been shot so as to minimize the disruption.

Moving now from a technical to a cultural evaluation of video assist, we focus on its similarities to the camera obscura, a tool used by many painters in the seventeenth century to replace or supplement their own human viewpoint. Significantly, in both machines, the observer (the painter or the director) no longer confronts the world directly but looks instead at an image formed through an optical contraption. In other words, a mediation is taking place. If the technology remains transparent to its user, he or she, in the words of Svetlana Alpers, "is seen attending not to the world and its replication in [an] image, but to . . . the quirks of [a] device."[22] In his analysis of Vermeer's work, Daniel A. Fink has pointed to a number of optical phenomena directly related to the use of a camera obscura.[23] They are all consequential for the image being produced. For example, whereas in daily life the eye continually refocuses as it engages objects located at different distances, the camera obscura equipped with a lens forces the operator to view the scene through a single plane of focus, in effect making some objects sharper than others. Likewise,

Margo, with
Burgess Meredith,
looking through
the camera
(*Winterset*, 1936)

whereas Vermeer's contemporaries represented relatively large and sharp mirror images of objects, very much like the eyes would see them, Vermeer's own mirror reflections are comparatively small and slightly out of focus, as they would appear through a lens focused on a different plane. All in all, Fink points out ten such "distortions" introduced by the instrument used by Vermeer.

In the same manner, today, the limitations of video keep interfering with the work of directors of photography because of the differences between what is seen on the monitor and what will be in fact recorded on film. The main culprit here is the lack of resolution of the video image and the fact that its contrast ratio does not match that of the film stock. Shadow detail, for instance, does not show up on the monitor, a situation that inevitably creates doubt about the handling of the lighting scheme. For the same reason, directors have been known to complain when low light levels may simply make it too dark for them to see the expressions of the players on the monitor. And, when using color, everyone frets about the differences between the colors on the set, those on the monitor, and those that will show up on film. In addition, directors of photography have noted that the usual size of the monitor (typically a 9-inch set) used by the director may also make it less likely that action will take place in the background in a long shot or even on the sides of the frame, as the miniaturized or peripheral action would not play well on such small screens.

The action therefore often ends up enlarged and more centered. Beyond this, if the movie is going to be cut digitally, it makes little sense for the production to pay for regular film dailies. As a result, the director will not be aware of the large-screen effect of the film until it is prepared for release in the theaters: a definite drawback. Lastly, the fact that the scene is observed through video technology as opposed to film may have consequences of its own. Film images' fascinatingly rich appearance originates in the random distribution of the silver molecules on the film surface. Each individual frame in effect configures the subject slightly differently. When played back, the scene is reconstructed twenty-four times per second, bringing forth more "livingness" to the eye of the spectator than any single frame could provide on its own. In contrast to this, as Vivian Sobchack describes it, "electronic technology atomizes and abstractly schematizes the analogic quality of the photographic and cinematic into discrete pixels and bits of information that are then transmitted serially . . . ,"[24] a design responsible for the "sameness" of the electronic image. In other words, a picture so constituted may not prompt the kind of investment associated with the older technology. And this in turn may produce a viewing situation for the director that demands quick renewal and change, shorter scenes, a point of view that Charles Eidsvik has described as "glance esthetics" in lieu of the older, more traditional "gaze esthetics."[25]

Looked at another way, employee relations on the set have also gone through a subtle restructuring. The operator is no longer the sole source of vision. Someone is now watching over the very guardian of the sight. The situation is not unlike a contemporary version of Taylorism, where work is carefully meted out into distinct components that can be precisely measured through scientific management techniques. Early in the century, for example, Frank Gilbreth, a disciple of Frederick Taylor, determined through the use of photographs a bricklayer's ideal working position. He then attempted to enforce this position on other bricklayers, thus hoping to eliminate minor but wasteful divergences from the more effective stand.[26] However, as work is rationalized and systematized, a subtle de-skilling of the worker's craft occurs. In fact, it is no longer trusted at face value, it is verified through technology until it matches very precisely the demands of management. Andrew Feenberg put it this way: whereas earlier "the craftsman possessed the knowledge required for his work as subjective capacity . . . mechanization transforms this knowledge into an objective power owned by another."[27] On the set then, the camera operator ceases to function as an independent agent who is counted on to execute a difficult move. He/she becomes merely the mechanical arm of the director. The operator, having lost some of the creativity associated with his/her own work, is thus transformed into a semiautomaton. The change eliminates the trust in someone's craft. It reinforces the industrial aspect of film-making, the manufacturing of a marketable commodity where the picture represents the surplus value of the labor performed by the operator.

Another characteristic shared by the camera obscura and video assist is the apparent objectivity and finality of the image they provide. Because the scene was captured by an optical device, the camera obscura's picture was thought to be necessarily truer to the model than that obtained through traditional human effort. In a similar fashion, the contemporary film director imagines gaining access to the truth of the scene when he or she abandons the actors and watches the take, no longer face-to-face from underneath the camera but indirectly on the monitor. After all, isn't this image the very picture that is being simultaneously recorded on film, the one that will be seen later by the viewers? As Jonathan Crary puts it, in each situation "the observer . . . is there as a disembodied witness to a mechanical and transcendental re-presentation of the objectivity of the world."[28] As a result, the camera obscura and video assist can be said to incorporate within their machinery the Cartesian ideal of the partition between pure body sensations and the mind, with the latter, the true self, inspecting the observations gleaned by the senses. Paul Ricoeur best described this mode of thinking when he called it "a vision of the world in which the whole of objectivity is spread out like a spectacle on which the cogito casts its sovereign gaze."[29] What is at stake here is the authority of an ideal observer, removed from the scene, someone who is no longer operating as a body-in-the-world sharing a space/time continuum with the actors. The latter, instead, are objectified, appropriated for the director's use. As it plucks the scene out of that common, human context, video assist fragments the total experience specific to the traditional directing mode. What takes place in fact duplicates the calculative thinking of the traditional scientific experiment that first sets measurable goals for itself, then authenticates their presence in an ensuing test, thus "guaranteeing the certainty and the exactness"[30] of the project as a whole. Similarly, the contemporary director ends up verifying on the monitor what he/she expects to find there in the first place. The attention, in other words, is on what Heidegger called *Vorhandenheit,* the foregrounding of technology, of the actual, of what has been worked out during the rehearsals, at the expense of the film still as a project (his notion of *Zuhandenheit*), a potential, something not quite yet there, something that remains a becoming, that is still in flux. The present-at-hand, what is already there, takes precedence over what is still outstanding, what could still be created. A metaphysics of presence-through-the-image in effect dominates the day.

What I am suggesting here is that getting access to the image is not an automatic panacea for the director. To illustrate this point, let us look at two films produced and directed by Francis Ford Coppola. On the one hand,

Conrad Hall behind the camera (*Tell Them Willie Boy Is Here*, 1969)

Apocalypse Now (1971) emerged from complete chaos and three years of shooting—perhaps the ultimate example of "how not to make a film"—a masterpiece. On the other hand, *One from the Heart* (1981) was conceived most rationally with the help of the latest electronic wizardry available at the time. From the very beginning of the production, an audiotape of the actors' read-through of the script was combined with storyboard images and temporary music to help the pre-visualization of the film as a whole. Polaroids of the actors' early rehearsals then replaced the drawings, followed by videotapes of the scenes shot on location in Las Vegas. As a result, long before a single foot of film was actually shot, "the whole movie could be seen at any time,"[31] by anyone involved in the film. Furthermore, when the film was ultimately shot in a Hollywood studio, Coppola could watch each take with music and sound effects. And he "was able, at the beginning of each production day, to view an edited version of the previous day's shooting, complete with music and sound effects."[32] The idea was to be able to handle immediately any kink in a scene, any difficulty with the pacing within or between scenes. As each segment of the project could be looked at, analyzed, dissected, film-making in effect became a totally rational enterprise, with the director-engineer at the helm calculating, quantifying, mastering the impact of each and every effect. This total involvement with the ever-present image, the absolute elimination of the mystery of shooting, should have produced the most successful film ever. What Coppola forgot though, in his all-out effort at demagicizing the film process,

James
Cameron
looking at the
video assist
(*True Lies*,
1994)

is that, paraphrasing Maurice Merleau-Ponty, the director's "vision is not a view upon the 'outside,' a merely physical-optical relation with the world."[33] No more than a poem can be said to exist in the words per se, a film does not reside solely in an image that can be observed on a little screen. During the shooting, it remains instead a becoming, an opening, a possibility that may or may not be realized later on. A film, in other words (still paraphrasing Merleau-Ponty), is as much in the "intervals" between images as it is in the pictures themselves.[34] Fleeing the mystery of creation, the challenges and the claims involved in a face-to-face transaction, the contemporary director thus functions as a distant subject who masters and objectifies others through the supremacy of technique. The lingering of the body in time and space has been replaced by what Nietzsche called an Apollonian frenzy with the eye.[35] The mise-en-scène has turned into mere mise-en-image, a soulless play of isolated, context-free commodities.

Technology must never be accepted at face value. It is not because the science is there that the invention or the use of a machine will automatically follow suit. And not all novel techniques are successfully adopted by the practitioners in the field. One cannot, David F. Noble reminds us, ever simply state that the best existing technology is automatically being used at all times. Instead, we must always replace that assumption with more probing questions: "The best technology? Best for whom? Best for what? Best according to what criteria, what visions, according to whose criteria, whose visions?"[36] Hence, insofar as video assist is concerned, what are the historical conditions that made its use so widespread? When Jerry Lewis used it there was little interest on the part of other directors to emulate him. Yet, not so many years afterward, in remarkable unison, most American directors ended up adopting his method. What happened in between that brought about this radical change? The answer lies in what Charles Eidsvik has called "the film's industry's defensive maneuvers of the 1970s and the 1980s,"[37] when, to repel the thrust of both television as a competing source of entertainment and videotape as a contending recording medium, changes were made in the kind of cinema that was produced. The writing in effect pushed the plots "into areas in which video could not compete well. . . ."[38] Practically speaking, this meant that the small movies, the psychological films, the non-action pictures, were abandoned to television. Conversely, the theatrical experience was redefined as the larger-than-life action spectacle. Although Eidsvik identifies location film-making as the main beneficiary of these changes, location per se did not prove itself enough of a draw to sell the real movie in the theater over the TV movie of the week. More was needed, and camera pyrotechnics were quickly enlisted to divert and bedazzle the spectator's eyes. These technological advances, however, also eroded the traditional control of the director on the set. First, the very mobility of the Steadicam created a dilemma for the director.[39] What was he or she supposed to do: run after the Steadicam operator or remain ineffectually behind? Second, the Louma crane isolated the camera at the extreme end of its reach, all the time maneuvered from afar by an operator working at a console. Third, cable contraptions of one type or another followed, flying the camera far above the scene. Fourth, helicopters equipped with gyrostabilized systems further extended the reach of the apparatus. Finally, the ease of digital technology pushed film-making toward ever more complex and demanding composite images. All in all, as the "scene" became less and less accessible, directors had no choice but to look at a remote image on a video monitor.

"In choosing our technology," Feenberg suggests, "we become what we are, which in turn shapes our future choices."[40] And so it is that a scene that required an improbable camera position would also benefit from graphic action and various kinds of pyrotechnics, traditional or otherwise—all situations that incidentally also showed up best on the monitors. In other words, whereas it is unlikely that the cinema of Ingmar Bergman would have significantly benefited from the use of video assist, that of Jim Cameron or Robert Zemeckis makes little sense without it. In this type of film-making, in fact, the device itself is no more than an advanced representative of other, more intensive technologies that will later on enhance the surface appeal of the film in postproduction: digital-image processing, digital editing, digital sound enhancing, etc. And in turn this superior technology, this dazzling maneuverability, this extraordinary display of breathtaking technique is widely advertised, thus staking new claims for the global hegemony of Hollywood. The fire power of the contemporary American film may be less physically destructive than that of the old gunboat, but it nevertheless forces its superiority on the technologically backward national cinemas of Europe, Asia, and elsewhere, threatening their very survival.

For the new American director, however, success speaks for itself and money speaks best of all. Hence, no rejection of the power of technology should be expected. Needed or not, video assist is here to stay, not because it is necessarily the best tool for the job, but because, more than ever, we implicitly trust a machine more than ourselves to tell us about the world. As the objectification of the world through the domination of technique is pushed one notch further, the *cogito* of old can be said to have been given a more contemporary twist: *video, ergo est.*

NOTES

1. This attack was made twice by directors of photography during the "New Perspectives" seminar sponsored by the American Society of Cinematographers and Eastman Kodak Worldwide Student Program at the University of Southern California on February 18, 1995. Although the charge might have been exaggerated for the sake of effect, no one on the panel bothered to soften it.

2. Martin Heidegger, "The Question Concerning Technology," trans. William Lovitt, in *Basic Writings,* ed. David Farrell Krell (New York: HarperCollins, 1977), pp. 283–317.

3. Heidegger, p. 294.

4. Andrew Feenberg, *The Critical Theory of Technology* (New York: Oxford University Press), p. v.

5. Herbert Marcuse, *Negations,* trans. Jeremy J. Shapiro (Boston: Beacon Press, 1968), p. 224.

6. I am very grateful to Wesley Lambert, who showed me his marvelous collection of antique cameras and spent much time pointing out the different viewing devices in use.

7. Gib., "Close-Ups: Guy Bennett: Operative Cameraman," *International Photographer,* vol. 11, no. 3 (April 1939), p. 5.

8. The effect I am describing in this essay is unique to cameras equipped with a mirrored shutter. The look through the lens is certainly less fascinating when shooting with a camera designed with a partial mirror that splits the light before it reaches the shutter, thus providing an uninterrupted flow to the operator.

As for operators shooting with their other eye closed, an informal survey with camera instructors at USC (Woody Omens and John Morrill, among others) revealed an operating difference between fiction and documentary work. Most operators prefer to shoot narratives with the other eye shut so as to concentrate on the scene in the viewfinder with, from time to time, a quick check toward an actor about to enter the frame, a car that may be getting too close, or the bustling of the focus puller. In documentaries, however, the consensus is that an operator should keep the other eye open so as to be aware of what is happening in the field at all times.

9. Vivian Sobchack, *The Address of the Eye: A Phenomenology of Film Experience* (Princeton, NJ: Princeton University Press, 1992), p. 134.

10. Ron G. Williams and James W. Boyd, *Ritual Art and Knowledge: Aesthetic Theory and Zoroastrian Ritual* (Columbia, SC: University of South Carolina Press, 1993), p. 70.

11. Gilles Deleuze, *Cinema 1: The Movement-Image,* trans. Hugh Tomlinson and Barbara Habberjam (Minneapolis, MN: University of Minnesota Press, 1986), p. 7.

12. In A. William Bluem, *Documentary in American Television* (New York: Hastings House, 1965), p. 194.

13. For Heidegger's full argument, see "The Question Concerning Technology," in *Basic Writings,* pp. 287–317.

14. In Martin Heidegger, *Being and Time,* trans. John Macquarrie and Edward Robinson (San Francisco, CA: HarperCollins, 1962), chap. 4.

15. For Emmanuel Levinas's ideas, check his *Totality and Infinity: An Essay on Exteriority,* trans. Alphonso Lingis (Pittsburgh, PA: Duquesne University Press, 1969).

16. See Stan Meredith, "The Electronic-Cam System," *American Cinematographer,* vol. 49, no. 4 (April 1968).

17. In David Samuelson, "Electronic Aids to Film Making," *American Cinematographer,* vol. 50, no. 8 (August 1969).

18. I am indebted to Lindsay Hill of Hill Production Services for information about his father and his research.

19. I am truly grateful to Terry Clairmont of Clairmont Camera for sharing with me his knowledge of the industry's reaction to the introduction of video assist technology.

20. Garrett Brown, "The Steadicam and *The Shining,*" *American Cinematographer,* vol. 61, no. 8 (August 1980), p. 853.

21. In James B. Brandt, "Video Assist: Past, Present and Future," *American Cinematographer,* vol. 72, no. 6 (June 1991).

22. Svetlana Alpers, *The Art of Describing: Dutch Art in the 17th Century* (Chicago: University of Chicago Press, 1983), p. 31.

23. In Daniel A. Fink, "Vermeer's Use of the Camera Obscura—A Comparative Study," *The Art Bulletin,* vol. 53, no. 4 (December 1971), pp. 493–505.

24. Vivian Sobchack, "The Scene of the Screen: Envisioning Cinematic and Electronic 'Presence,'" in *Materialities of Communication,* ed. Hans Ulrich Gumbrecht and K. Ludwig Pfeiffer (Stanford, CA: Stanford University Press, 1994), p. 100.

25. Charles Eidsvik, "Machines of the Invisible: Changes in Film Technology in the Age of Video," *Film Quarterly,* vol. 42, no. 2 (Winter 1988–89), p. 21.

26. See Milton J. Nadworny, *Scientific Management and the Unions* (Cambridge, MA: Harvard University Press, 1955), pp. 54 ff.

27. Feenberg, p. 27.

28. Jonathan Crary, *Techniques of the Observer: On Vision and Modernity in the Nineteenth Century* (Cambridge, MA: MIT Press, 1991), p. 41.

29. Paul Ricoeur, *The Conflict of Interpretations,* trans. Don Ihde (Evanston, IL: Northwestern University Press, 1974), p. 236.

30. William Barrett, *The Illusion of Technology: A Search for Meaning in a Technological Civilization* (Garden City, NY: Anchor Press/Doubleday, 1978), p. 191.

31. Thomas Brown, "The Electronic Camera Experiment," in *American Cinematographer,* vol. 63, no. 1 (January 1982), p. 76.

32. Brown, p. 79.

33. Maurice Merleau-Ponty, *The Primacy of Perception,* trans. Carleton Dallery (Evanston, IL: Northwestern University Press, 1964), p. 181.

34. Maurice Merleau-Ponty, *Sense and Non-Sense,* trans. Hubert L. Dreyfus and Patricia Allen Dreyfus (Evanston, IL: Northwestern University Press, 1964), p. 48.

35. *The Portable Nietzsche,* ed. and trans. Walter Kaufmann (Harmondsworth, England: Penguin Books, 1982), p. 519.

36. David F. Noble, *Forces of Production: A Social History of Industrial Automation* (New York: Oxford University Press, 1986), p. 145.

37. Eidsvik, p. 22.

38. Eidsvik, p. 22.

39. On the subject of the Steadicam, see my article "Visuality and Power: The Work of the Steadicam," *Film Quarterly,* vol. 47, no. 2, pp. 8–17.

40. Feenberg, p. 14.

STEPHEN PRINCE

TRUE LIES

Perceptual Realism, Digital Images, and Film Theory

Digital compositing in *Forrest Gump*

Vol. 49, no. 3 (Spring 1996): 27–37.

Digital imaging technologies are rapidly transforming nearly all phases of contemporary film production. Film-makers today storyboard, shoot, and edit their films in conjunction with the computer manipulation of images. For the general public, the most visible application of these technologies lies in the new wave of computer-generated and -enhanced special effects that are producing images—the watery creature in *The Abyss* (1989) or the shimmering, shapeshifting *Terminator 2* (1991)—unlike any seen previously.

The rapid nature of these changes is creating problems for film theory. Because the digital manipulation of images is so novel and the creative possibilities it offers are so unprecedented, its effects on cinematic representation and the viewer's response are poorly understood. Film theory has not yet come to terms with these issues. What are the implications of computer-generated imagery for representation in cinema, particularly for concepts of photographically based realism? How might theory adapt to an era of digital imaging?

Initial applications of special-effects digital imaging in feature films began more than a decade ago in productions like *Tron* (1982), *Star Trek II: The Wrath of Khan* (1982), and *The Last Starfighter* (1984). The higher-profile successes of *Terminator 2, Jurassic Park* (1993), and *Forrest Gump* (1994), however, dramatically demonstrated the creative and remunerative possibilities of computer-generated imagery (CGI).

Currently, two broad categories of digital imaging exist. Digital-image processing covers applications like removing unwanted elements from the frame—hiding the wires supporting the stunt performers in *Cliffhanger* (1994), or erasing the Harrier jet from shots in *True Lies* (1994) where it accidentally appears. CGI proper refers to building models and animating them in the computer. Don Shay, editor of *Cinefex*, a journal that tracks and discusses special-effects work in cinema, emphasizes these distinctions between the categories.[1]

As a consequence of digital imaging, *Forrest Gump* viewers saw photographic images of actor Gary Sinise, playing Gump's amputee friend and fellow Vietnam veteran, being lifted by a nurse from a hospital bed and carried, legless, through three-dimensional space. The film viewer is startled to realize that the representation does not depend on such old-fashioned methods as tucking or tieing the actor's limbs behind his body and concealing this with a loose-fitting costume. Instead, Sinise's legs had been digitally erased from the shot by computer.

Elsewhere in the same film, viewers saw photographic images of President Kennedy speaking to actor Tom Hanks, with dialogue scripted by the film's writers. In the most widely publicized applications of CGI, viewers of Steven Spielberg's *Jurassic Park* watched photographic images of moving, breathing, and chomping dinosaurs, images which have no basis in any photographable reality but which nevertheless seemed realistic. In what follows, I will be assuming that viewers routinely make assessments about the perceived realism of a film's images or characters, even when these are obviously fictionalized or otherwise impossible. Spielberg's dinosaurs made such a huge impact on viewers in part because they seemed far more life-like than the miniature models and stop-motion animation of previous generations of film.

The obvious paradox here—creating credible photographic images of things which cannot be photographed—and the computer-imaging capabilities which lie behind it challenge some of the traditional assumptions about realism and the cinema which are embodied in film theory. This essay first explores the challenge posed by CGI to photographically based notions of cinematic realism. Next, it examines some of the problems and challenges of creating computer imagery in motion pictures by drawing on interviews with computer-imaging artists. Finally, it develops an alternate model, based on perceptual and social correspondences, of how the cinema communicates and is intelligible to viewers. This model may produce a better integration of the tensions between realism and formalism in film theory. As we will see, theory has construed realism solely as a matter of reference rather than as a matter of perception as well. It has neglected what I will term in this essay "perceptual realism." This neglect has prevented theory from understanding some of the fundamental ways in which cinema works and is judged credible by viewers.

Assumptions about realism in the cinema are frequently tied to concepts of indexicality prevailing between the photographic image and its referent. These, in turn, constitute part of the bifurcation between realism and formalism in film theory. In order to understand how theories about the nature of cinematic images may change in the era of digital-imaging practices, this bifurcation and these notions of an indexically based film realism need to be examined.

This approach to film realism—and it is, perhaps, the most basic theoretical understanding of film realism—is rooted in the view that photographic images, unlike paintings or line drawings, are indexical signs: they are causally or existentially connected to their referents. Charles S. Peirce, who devised the triadic model of indexical, iconic, and symbolic signs, noted that "Photographs, especially instantaneous photographs, are very instructive, because we know that in certain respects they are exactly like the objects they represent . . . they . . . correspond point by point to nature. In that respect then, they belong to the second class of signs, those by physical connection."[2]

In his analysis of photography, Roland Barthes noted that photographs, unlike every other type of image, can never be divorced from their referents. Photograph and referent "are glued together."[3] For Barthes, photographs are causally connected to their referents. The former testifies to the presence of the latter. "I call 'photographic referent' not the *optionally* real thing to which an image or sign refers but the *necessarily* real thing which has been placed before the lens without which there would be no photograph."[4] For Barthes, "Every photograph is a certificate of presence."[5]

Because cinema is a photographic medium, theorists of cinema developed concepts of realism in connection with the indexical status of the photographic sign. Most famously, André Bazin based his realist aesthetic on what he regarded as the "objective" nature of photography, which bears the mechanical trace of its referents. In a well-known passage, he wrote, "The photographic image is the object itself, the object freed from the conditions of time and space which govern it. No matter how fuzzy, distorted, or discolored, no matter how lacking in documentary value the image may be, it shares, by virtue of the very process of its becoming, the being of the model of which it is the reproduction; it *is* the model."[6]

Other important theorists of film realism emphasized the essential attribute cinema shares with photography of being a recording medium. Siegfried Kracauer noted that his theory of cinema, which he subtitled "the redemption of physical reality," "rests upon the assumption that film is essentially an extension of photography and therefore shares with that medium a marked affinity for the visible world around us. Films come into their own when they record and reveal physical reality."[7] Like Bazin, Stanley Cavell emphasized that cinema is the screening or projection of reality because of the way that photography, whether still or in motion, mechanically (that is, automatically) reproduces the world before the lens.[8]

For reasons that are alternately obvious and subtle, digital imaging in its dual modes of image processing and CGI challenges indexically based notions of photographic realism. As Bill Nichols has noted, a digitally designed or created image can be subject to infinite manipulation.[9] Its reality is a function of complex algorithms stored in computer memory rather than a necessary mechanical resemblance to a referent. In cases like the slithery underwater creature in James Cameron's *The Abyss*, which began as a wireframe model in the

Jurassic Park: Not the real T. Rex

computer, no profilmic referent existed to ground the indexicality of its image. Nevertheless, digital imaging can anchor pictured objects, like this watery creature, in apparent photographic reality by employing realistic lighting (shadows, highlights, reflections) and surface texture detail (the creature's rippling responses to the touch of one of the film's live actors). At the same time, digital imaging can bend, twist, stretch, and contort physical objects in cartoonlike ways that mock indexicalized referentiality. In an Exxon ad, an automobile morphs into a tiger, and in a spot for Listerine, the CGI bottle of mouthwash jiggles, expands, and contracts in an excited display of enthusiasm for its new formula.[10]

In these obvious ways, digital imaging operates according to a different ontology than do indexical photographs. But in less obvious ways, as well, digital imaging can depart from photographically coded realism. Objects can be co-present in computer space but not in the physical 3-D space which photography records. When computer-animated objects move around in a simulated space, they can intersect one another. This is one reason why computer animators start with wireframe models which they can rotate and see through in order to determine whether the model is intersecting other points in the simulated space. Computer-simulated environments, therefore, have to be programmed to deal with the issues of collision detection and collision response.[11]

The animators who created the herd of gallimimus that chases actor Sam Neill and two children in *Jurassic Park* were careful to animate the twenty-four gallis so they would look like they might collide and were reacting to that possibility.[12] First, they had to ensure that no gallis actually did pass into and through one another, and then they had to simulate the collision responses in the creatures' behaviors as if they were corporeal beings subject to Newtonian space.

In other subtle ways, digital imaging can fail to perform Kracauer's redemption of physical reality. Lights simulated in the computer don't need sources, and shadows can be painted in irrespective of the position of existing lights. Lighting, which in photography is responsible for creating the exposure and the resulting image, is, for computer images, strictly a matter of painting, of changing the brightness and coloration of individual pixels. As a result, lighting in computer imagery need not obey the rather fixed and rigid physical conditions which must prevail in order for photographs to be created.

One of the more spectacular digital images in *True Lies* is a long shot of a chateau nestled beside a lake and surrounded by the Swiss Alps. The image is a digital composite, blending a mansion from Newport, Rhode Island, water shot in Nevada, and a digital matte painting of the Alps.[13] The compositing was done by Digital Domain, a state-of-the-art effects house created by the film's director, James Cameron. The shot is visually stunning—crisply resolved, richly saturated with color, and brightly illuminated across Alps, lake, and chateau.

Kevin Mack, a digital effects supervisor at Digital Domain who worked on *True Lies* as well as *Interview with the Vampire*, points out that the image is unnaturally luminant.[14] Too much light is distributed across the shot. If a photographer exposed for the lights in the chateau, the Alps would film too dark, and, conversely, if one exposed for the Alps in, say, bright moonlight, the lights in the chateau would burn out. The chateau and the Alps could not be lit so they'd both expose as brightly as they do in the image. Mack points out that the painted light effects in the shot are a digital manipulation so subtle that most viewers probably do not notice the trickery.

Like lighting, the rendering of motion can be accomplished by computer painting. President Kennedy speaking to Tom Hanks in *Forrest Gump* resulted from two-dimensional painting, made to look like 3-D, according to Pat Byrne, Technical Director at Post Effects, a Chicago effects house that specializes in digital imaging.[15] The archival footage of Kennedy, once digitized, was repainted with the proper phonetic mouth movements to match the scripted dialogue and with highlights on his face to simulate the corresponding jaw and muscle changes. Morphs were used to smooth out the different painted configurations of mouth and face.[16]

When animating motion via computer, special adjustments must be made precisely because of the differences between photographically captured reality and the synthetic realities engineered with CGI. Credible computer animation requires the addition of motion blur to simulate the look of a photographic image. The ping-pong ball swatted around by Forrest Gump and his Chinese opponents was animated on the computer from a digitally scanned photographic model of a ping-pong ball and was subsequently composited into the live-action footage of the game (the game itself was shot without any ball). The CGI ball seemed credible because, among other reasons, the animators were careful to add motion blur, which a real, rapidly moving object passing in front of a camera will possess (as seen by the camera which freezes the action as a series of still frames), but which a key-framed computer animated object does not.

In these ways, both macro and micro, digital imaging possesses a flexibility that frees it from the indexicality of photography's relationship with its referent.[17] Does this mean, then, that digital-imaging capabilities ought not to be grouped under the rubric of a realist film theory? If not, what are the alternatives? What kind of realism, if any, do these images possess?

In traditional film theory, only one alternative is available: the perspective formulated in opposition to the positions staked out by realists like Kracauer, Bazin, and Cavell. This position, which might be termed the formalist outlook, stresses cinema's capacity for reorganizing, and even countering and falsifying, physical reality. Early exponents of such a position include Rudolf Arnheim, Dziga Vertov, and Sergei Eisenstein. In his discussion of classical film theory, Noël Carroll has pointed out this bifurcation between the camps of realism and formalism and linked it to an essentializing tendency within theory, a predilection of theorists to focus on either the cinema's capability to photographically copy physical reality or to stylistically transcend that reality.[18]

This tension in classical theory between stressing the ways film either records or reorganizes profilmic reality continues in contemporary theory, with the classical formalist emphasis upon the artificiality of cinema structure being absorbed into theories of the apparatus, of psychoanalysis, or of ideology as applied to the cinema. In these cases, cinematic realism is seen as an *effect* produced by the apparatus or by spectators positioned within the Lacanian Imaginary. Cinematic realism is viewed as a discourse *coded* for transparency such that the indexicality of photographic realism is replaced by a view of the "reality-effect" produced by codes and discourse. Jean-Louis Baudry suggests that "Between 'objective reality' and the camera, site of inscription, and between the inscription and the projection are situated certain operations, a *work* which has as its result a finished product."[19] Writing about the principles of realism, Colin McCabe stresses that film is "constituted by a set of discourses which . . . produce a certain reality."[20]

Summarizing these views, Dudley Andrew explains, "The discovery that resemblance is coded and therefore learned was a tremendous and hard-won victory for semiotics over those upholding a notion of naive perception in cinema."[21] Where classical film theory was organized by a dichotomy between realism and formalism, contemporary theory has preserved the dichotomy even while recasting one set of its terms. Today, indexically based notions of cinema realism exist in tension with a semiotic view of the cinema as discourse and of realism as one discourse among others.

In some of the ways just discussed, digital imaging is inconsistent with indexically based notions of film realism. Given the tensions in contemporary film theory, should we then conclude that digital-imaging technologies are necessarily illusionistic, that they construct a reality-effect which is merely discursive? They do, in fact, permit film artists to create synthetic realities that can look just like photographic realities. As Pat Byrne noted, "The line between real and not-real will become more and more blurred."[22] How should we understand digital imaging in theory? How should we build theory around it? When faced with digitized images, will we need to discard entirely notions of realism in the cinema?

The tensions within film theory can be surmounted by avoiding an essentializing conception of the cinema stressing unique, fundamental properties[23] and by employing, in place of indexically based notions of film realism, a correspondence-based model of cinematic representation. Such a model will enable us to talk and think about both photographic images and computer-generated images and about the ways that cinema can create images that seem alternately real and unreal. To develop this approach, it will be necessary to indicate, first, what is meant by a correspondence-based model and, then, how digital imaging fits within it.

An extensive body of evidence indicates the many ways in which film spectatorship builds on correspondences between selected features of the cinematic display and a viewer's real-world visual and social experience.[24] These include iconic and noniconic visual and social cues which are structured into cinematic images in ways that facilitate comprehension and invite interpretation and evaluation by viewers based on the salience of represented cues or patterned deviations from them. At a visual level, these cues include the ways that photographic images and edited sequences are isomorphic with their corresponding real-world displays (e.g., through replication of edge and contour information and of monocular distance codes; in the case of moving pictures, replication of motion parallax; and in the case of continuity editing, the creation of a screen geometry with coherent coordinates through the projective geometry of successive camera positions). Under such conditions, empirical evidence indicates that naive viewers readily recognize experientially familiar pictured objects and can comprehend filmed sequences, and that continuity editing enhances such comprehension.[25]

At the level of social experience, the evidence indicates that viewers draw from a common stock of moral constructs and interpersonal cues and percepts when evaluating both people in real life and represented characters in the media. Socially derived assumptions about motive, intent, and proper role-based behavior are employed when responding to real and media-based personalities and behavior.[26] As communication scholars Elizabeth Perse and Rebecca Rubin have pointed out, "'people' constitutes a construct domain that may be sufficiently permeable to include both interpersonal and [media] contexts."[27]

Recognizing that cinematic representation operates significantly, though not exclusively, in terms of structured correspondences between the audiovisual display and a viewer's extra-filmic visual and social experience enables us to ask about the range of cues or correspondences within the image or film, how they are structured, and the ways a given film patterns its represented fictionalized reality around these cues. What kind of transformations does a given film carry out upon the correspondences it employs with viewers' visual and social experience? Attributions of realism, or the lack thereof, by viewers will inhere in the ways these correspondences are structured into and/or transformed by the image and film. Instead of asking whether a film is realistic or formalistic, we can ask about the kinds of linkages that connect the represented fictionalized reality of a given film to the visual and social coordinates of our own three-dimensional world, and this can be done for both "realist" and "fantasy" films alike. Such a focus need not reinstate indexicality as the ground of realism, since it can emphasize falsified correspondences and transformation of cues. Nor need such a focus turn everything about the cinema back into discourse, into an arbitrarily coded reorganization of experience. As we will see, even unreal images can be perceptually realistic. Unreal images are those which are referentially fictional. The Terminator is a represented fictional character that lacks reference to any category of being existing outside the fiction. Spielberg's dinosaurs obviously refer to creatures that once existed, but as *moving photographic images* they are referentially fictional. No dinosaurs now live which could be filmed doing things the fictionalized creatures do in *Jurassic Park*. By contrast, referentially realistic images bear indexical and iconic homologies with their referents. They resemble the referent, which, in turn, stands in a causal, existential relationship to the image.[28]

A perceptually realistic image is one which structurally corresponds to the viewer's audiovisual experience of three-dimensional space. Perceptually realistic images correspond to this experience because film-makers build them to do so. Such images display a nested hierarchy of cues which organize the display of light, color, texture, movement, and sound in ways that correspond with the viewer's own understanding of these phenomena in daily life.

Forrest Gump: Computer-generated crowd

Perceptual realism, therefore, designates a relationship between the image or film and the spectator, and it can encompass both unreal images and those which are referentially realistic. Because of this, unreal images may be referentially fictional but perceptually realistic.

We should now return to, and connect this discussion back to, the issue of digital imaging. When lighting a scene becomes a matter of painting pixels, and capturing movement is a function of employing the correct algorithms for mass, inertia, torque, and speed (with the appropriate motion blur added as part of the mix), indexical referencing is no longer required for the appearance of photographic realism in the digital image. Instead, Gump's ping-pong ball and Spielberg's dinosaurs look like convincing photographic realities because of the complex sets of perceptual correspondences that have been built into these images. These correspondences, which anchor the computer-generated image in apparent three-dimensional space, routinely include such variables as surface texture, color, light, shadow, reflectance, motion speed and direction.

Embedding or compositing computer imagery into live action, as occurs when Tom Hanks as Gump "hits" the CG ping-pong ball or when Sam Neill is "chased" by the CG gallimimus herd, requires matching both environments. The physical properties and coordinates of the computer-generated scene components must be made to correspond with those of the live-action scene. Doing this requires precise and time-consuming creation and manipulation of multiple 3-D perceptual cues. Kevin Mack, at Digital Domain, and Chris Voellmann, a digital modeller and animator at Century III Universal Studios, point out that light, texture, and movement are among the most important cues to be manipulated in order to create a synthetic reality that looks as real as possible.[29]

To simulate light properties that match both environments, a digital animator may employ scan-line algorithms that calculate pixel coloration one scan line at a time, ray tracing methods that calculate the passage of light rays through a modelled environment, or radiosity formulations that can account for diffuse, indirect illumination by analyzing the energy transfer between surfaces.[30] Such techniques enable a successful rendering[31] of perceptual information that can work to match live-action and computer environments and lend credence and a sense of reality to the composited image such that its computerized components *seem* to fulfill the indexicalized conditions of photographic realism. When the velociraptors hunt the children inside the park's kitchen in the climax of *Jurassic Park,* the film's viewer sees their movements reflected on the gleaming metal surfaces of tables and cookware. These reflections anchor the creatures inside Cartesian space and perceptual reality and provide a bridge between live-action and computer-generated environments. In the opening sequence of *Forrest Gump,* as a CG feather drifts and tumbles through space, its physical reality is enhanced by the addition of a digitally painted reflection on an automobile windshield.

To complete this anchoring process, the provision of information about surface texture and movement is extremely important and quite difficult, because the information provided must seem credible. Currently, many of the algorithms needed for convincing movement either do not exist or are prohibitively expensive to run on today's computers. The animators and renderers at Industrial Light and Magic used innovative software to texture-map[32] skin and wrinkles onto their dinosaurs and calibrated variations in skin jostling and wrinkling with particular movements of the creatures. However, while bone and joint rotation are successfully visualized, complex information about the movement of muscles and tendons below the skin surface is lacking.

Kevin Mack describes this limit in present rendering abilities as the "human hurdle"[33]—that is, the present inability of computers to fully capture the complexities of movement by living organisms. Hair, for example, is extremely difficult to render because of the complexities of mathematically simulating properties of mass and inertia for finely detailed strands.[34] Chris Voellmann points out that today's software can create flexors and rotators but cannot yet control veins or muscles.

Multiple levels of information capture must be successfully executed to convincingly animate and render living movement because the viewer's eye is adept at perceiving inaccurate information.[35] These levels include locomotor mechanics—the specification of forces, torques, and joint rotations. In addition, "gait-specific rules"[36] must be specified. The *Jurassic Park* animators, for example, derived gait-specific rules for their dinosaurs by studying the movements of elephants, rhinos, komodo dragons, and ostriches and then making some intelligent extrapolations. Beyond these two levels of information control is the most difficult one—capturing the expressive properties of movement. Human and animal movement cannot look mechanical and be convincing; it must be expressive of mood and affect.

As the foregoing discussion indicates, available software and the speed and economics of present computational abilities are placing limits on the complexities of digitally rendered 3-D cues used to integrate synthetic and live-action objects and environments. But the more important point is that present abilities to digitally simulate perceptual cues about surface texture, reflectance, coloration, motion, and distance provide an extremely powerful means of "gluing" together synthetic and live-action environments and of furnishing the viewer with an internally unified and coherent set of cues that establish correspondences with the properties of physical space and living systems in daily life. These correspondences in turn establish some of the most important criteria by which viewers can judge the apparent realism or credibility possessed by the digital image.

Obvious paradoxes arise from these judgments. No one has seen a living dinosaur. Even paleontologists can only hazard guesses about how such creatures might have moved and how swiftly. Yet the dinosaurs created at ILM have a palpable reality about them, and this is due to the extremely detailed texture-mapping, motion animation, and integration with live action carried out via digital imaging. Indexicality cannot furnish us with the basis for understanding this apparent photographic realism, but a correspondence-based approach can. Because the computer-generated images have been rendered with such attention to 3-D spatial information, they acquire a very powerful perceptual realism, despite the obvious ontological problems in calling them "realistic." These are falsified correspondences, yet because the perceptual information they contain is valid, the dinosaurs acquire a remarkable degree of photographic realism.

In a similar way, President Kennedy speaking in *Forrest Gump* is a falsified correspondence which is nevertheless built from internally valid perceptual information. Computer modelling of synthetic visual speech and facial animation relies on existing micro-analyses of human facial expression and phonetic mouth articulations. The digital-effects artist used these facial cues to animate Kennedy's image and sync his mouth movements with the scripted dialogue. At the perceptual level of phonemic articulation and facial register, the correspondences established are true and enable the viewer to accept the photographic and dramatic reality of the scene. But these correspondences also establish a falsified relationship with the historical and archival filmic records of reality. The resulting image is perceptually realistic but referentially unreal, a paradox that present film theory has a hard time accounting for.

The profound impact of digital imaging, in this respect, lies in the unprecedented ways that it permits film-makers to extend principles of perceptual realism to unreal images. The creative manipulation of photographic images is, of course, as old as the medium of photography. For example, flashing film prior to development or dodging and burning portions of the image during printing will produce lighting effects that did not exist in the scene that was photographed. The tension between perceptual realism and referential artifice clearly predates digital imaging. It has informed all fantasy and special-effects work where film-makers strive to create unreal images that nevertheless seem credible. What is new and revolutionary about digital imaging is that it increases to an extraordinary degree a film-maker's control over the informational cues that establish perceptual realism. Unreal images have never before seemed so real.

Digital imaging alters our sense of the necessary relationship involving *both* the camera and the profilmic event. The presence of either is no longer an absolute requirement for generating photographic images that correspond to spatio-temporally valid properties of the physical world. If neither a camera nor an existent referent is necessary for the digital rendition of photographic reality, the application of internally valid perceptual correspondences with the 3-D world *is* necessary for establishing the credibility of the synthetic reality. These correspondences establish bridges between what can be seen and photographed and that which can be "photographed" but not seen.

Because these correspondences between synthetic environments and real environments employ multiple cues, the induced realism of the final CG image can be extraordinarily convincing. The digital-effects artists interviewed for this essay resisted the idea that any one cue was more important than others and instead emphasized that their task was to build as much 3-D information as possible into the CG image, given budgetary constraints, present computational limitations, and the stylistic demands of a given film. With respect to the latter, Kevin Mack pointed out that style coexists with the capability for making the CG images look as real as possible. The Swiss chateau composite in *True Lies* discussed earlier exemplifies this tension.

The apparent realism of digitally processed or created images, then, is a function of the way that multiple levels of perceptual correspondence are built into the image. These establish reference points with the viewer's own experientially based understanding of light, space, motion, and the behavior of objects in a three-dimensional world. The resulting images may not contain photographable events, but neither do they represent purely illusory constructions. The reliability or nonreliability of the perceptual information they contain furnishes the viewer with an important framework for evaluating the logic of the screen worlds these images help establish.

The emphasis in contemporary film theory has undeniably shifted away from naive notions of indexical realism in favor of an attention to the constructedness of cinematic discourse. Yet indexicality remains an important point of origin even for perspectives that reincorporate it as a variant of illusionism, of the cinema's ability to produce a reality-effect. Bill Nichols notes that "Something of reality itself seems to pass through the lens and remain embedded in the photographic emulsion," while also recognizing that "Digital sampling techniques destroy this claim."[37] He concludes that the implications of this "are only beginning to be grasped,"[38] and therefore limits his recent study of the filmic representation of reality to non-digitized images.

Digital imaging exposes the enduring dichotomy in film theory as a false boundary. It is not as if cinema either indexically records the world or stylistically transfigures it. Cinema does both. Similarly, digital-imaging practices suggest that contemporary film theory's insistence upon the constructedness and artifice of cinema's discursive properties may be less productive than is commonly thought. The problem here is the implication of discursive equivalence, the idea that all cinematic representations are, in the end, equally artificial, since all are the constructions of form or ideology. But, as this essay has suggested, some of these representations, while being referentially unreal, are perceptually realistic. Viewers use and rely upon these perceptual correspondences when responding to, and evaluating, screen experience.

These areas of correspondence coexist in any given film with narrative, formal, and generic conventions, as well as intertextual determinants of meaning. Christopher Williams has recently observed that viewers make strong demands for reference from motion pictures, but in ways that simultaneously accommodate style and creativity: "We need films to be about life in one way or another, but we allow them latitude in how they meet this need."[39] Thus, Williams maintains that any given film will feature "the active interplay between the elements which can be defined as realist, and the others which function simultaneously and have either a nonrealist character (primarily formal, linguistic or conventional) or one which can be called anti-realist because the character of its formal, linguistic or conventional procedures specifically or explicitly tries to counteract the cognitive dimensions we have linked with realism."[40] Building 3-D cues inside computer-generated images enables viewers to correlate those images with their own spatio-temporal experience, even when the digitally processed image fails in other ways to obey that experience (as when the Terminator morphs out of a tiled floor to seize his victim). Satisfying the viewer's demand for reference permits, in turn, patterned or stylish deviations from reference.

Computer imaging in *The Mask*

Stressing correspondence-based transformational abilities enables us to maintain a link, a relationship, between the materials that are to be digitally transformed (elements of the 3-D world) and their changed state, as well as providing a means for preserving a basis for concepts of realism in a digitized cinema. Before we can subject digitally animated and processed images, like the velociraptors stalking the children through the kitchens of *Jurassic Park,* to extended meta-critiques of their discursive or ideological inflections (and these critiques are necessary), we first need to develop a precise understanding of how these images work in securing for the viewer a perceptually valid experience which may even invoke, as a kind of memory trace, now historically superseded assumptions about indexical referencing as the basis of the credibility that photographic images seem to possess.

In the correspondence-based approach to cinematic representation developed here, perceptual realism, the accurate replication of valid 3-D cues, becomes not only the glue cementing digitally created and live-action environments, but also the foundation upon which the uniquely transformational functions of cinema exist. Perceptual realism furnishes the basis on which digital imaging may be carried out by effects artists and understood, evaluated, and interpreted by viewers. The digital replication of perceptual correspondence for the film viewer is an enormously complex undertaking and its ramifications clearly extend well beyond film theory and aesthetics to encompass ethical, legal, and social issues. Film theory will need to catch up to this rapidly evolving new category of imaging capabilities and grasp it in all of its complexity. To date, theory has tended to minimize the importance of perceptual correspondences, but the advent of digital imaging demonstrates how important they are and have been all along. Film theory needs now to pay closer attention to what viewers see on the screen, how they see it, and the relation of these processes to the larger issue of how viewers see. Doing this may mean that film theory itself will change, and this essay has suggested some ways in which that might occur. Digital imaging represents not only the new domain of cinema experiences, but a new threshold for theory as well.

NOTES

Thanks to Carl Plantinga and Mark J. P. Wolf for their helpful suggestions on an early version of this paper.

1. Telephone interview with the author, October 19, 1994.

2. Quoted in Peter Wollen, *Signs and Meanings in the Cinema* (Bloomington, IN: Indiana University Press, 1976), pp. 123–24.

3. Roland Barthes, *Camera Lucida: Reflections on Photography,* trans. Richard Howard (New York: Hill and Wang, 1981), p. 5.

4. Ibid., p. 76.

5. Ibid., p. 87.

6. André Bazin, *What Is Cinema?* vol. 1, ed. and trans. Hugh Gray (Berkeley, CA: University of California Press, 1967), p. 14.

7. Siegfried Kracauer, *Theory of Film: The Redemption of Physical Reality* (New York: Oxford University Press, 1960), p. ix.

8. Stanley Cavell, *The World Viewed* (Cambridge, MA: Harvard University Press, 1979), pp. 16–23.

9. Bill Nichols, *Representing Reality: Issues and Concepts in Documentary* (Bloomington, IN: Indiana University Press, 1991), note 2, p. 268.

10. The design and creation of these ads are profiled in detail in Christopher W. Baker, *How Did They Do It? Computer Illusion in Film and TV* (Indianapolis, IN: Alpha Books, 1994).

11. See Ming C. Lin and Dinesh Manocha, "Interference Detection Between Curved Objects for Computer Animation," in *Models and Techniques in Computer Animation*, ed. Nadia Magnenat Thalmann and Daniel Thalmann (New York: Springer-Verlag, 1993), pp. 43–57.

12. Ron Magid, "ILM's Digital Dinosaurs Tear Up Effects Jungle," *American Cinematographer*, vol. 74, no. 12 (December 1993), p. 56.

13. Stephen Pizello, "*True Lies* Tests Cinema's Limits," *American Cinematographer*, vol. 75, no. 9 (September 1994), p. 44.

14. Telephone interview with the author, October 25, 1994.

15. Telephone interview with the author, October 25, 1994.

16. Ron Magid, "ILM Breaks New Digital Ground for *Gump*," *American Cinematographer*, vol. 75, no. 10 (October 1994), p. 52.

17. I do not wish to imply that photography was ever a mere mechanical recording of the visual world. During shooting, printing, and developing, photographers found ways of creating their own special effects. Despite this, theorists have insisted upon the medium's fundamental indexicality.

18. Noël Carroll, *Philosophical Problems of Classical Film Theory* (Princeton, NJ: Princeton University Press, 1988).

19. Jean-Louis Baudry, "Ideological Effects of the Basic Cinematographic Apparatus," in *Narrative, Apparatus, Ideology,* ed. Philip Rosen (New York: Columbia University Press, 1986), p. 287.

20. Colin McCabe, "Theory and Film: Principles of Realism and Pleasure," in *Narrative, Apparatus, Ideology*, p. 182.

21. Dudley Andrew, *Concepts in Film Theory* (New York: Oxford University Press, 1984), p. 25.

22. Telephone interview with the author, October 25, 1994.

23. Noël Carroll has urged film theory in this direction by recommending smaller-scale, piece-meal theorizing about selected aspects of cinema rather than cinema in toto and on a grand scale. See *Philosophical Problems of Classical Film Theory*, p. 255, and Carroll, *Mystifying Movies: Fads and Fallacies in Contemporary Film Theory* (New York: Columbia University Press, 1988), pp. 23–34.

24. For a fuller discussion of this literature, see my essays "The Discourse of Pictures: Iconicity and Film Studies," *Film Quarterly*, vol. 47, no. 1 (Fall 1993), pp. 16–28 and "Psychoanalytic Film Theory and the Problem of the Missing Spectator," in *Post-Theory: Reconstructing Film Studies*, ed. David Bordwell and Noël Carroll (Madison, WI: University of Wisconsin Press, 1996).

25. See Uta Frith and Jocelyn E. Robson, "Perceiving the Language of Films," *Perception,* vol. 4 (1975), pp. 97–103; Renee Hobbs, Richard Frost, Arthur Davis, and John Stauffer, "How First-Time Viewers Comprehend Editing Conventions," *Journal of Communication*, no. 38 (1988), pp. 50–60; Julian Hochberg and Virginia Brooks, "Picture Perception as an Unlearned Ability: A Study of One Child's Performance," *American Journal of Psychology*, vol. 74, no. 4 (December 1962), pp. 624–28; Robert N. Kraft, "Rules and Strategies of Visual Narratives," *Perceptual and Motor Skills* no. 64 (1987), pp. 3–14; Robert N. Kraft, Phillip Cantor, and Charles Gottdiener, "The Coherence of Visual Narratives," *Communication Research*, vol. 18, no. 5 (October 1991), pp. 601–16; Robin Smith, Daniel R. Anderson, and Catherine Fischer, "Young

Children's Comprehension of Montage," *Child Development* no. 56 (1985), pp. 962–71.

26.   See Austin S. Babrow, Barbara J. O'Keefe, David L. Swanson, Renee A. Myers, and Mary A. Murphy, "Person Perception and Children's Impression of Television and Real Peers," *Communication Research*, vol. 15, no. 6 (December 1988), pp. 680–98; Thomas J. Berndt and Emily G. Berndt, "Children's Use of Motives and Intentionality in Person Perception and Moral Judgement,"*Child Development* no. 46 (1975), pp. 904–12; Aimee Dorr, "How Children Make Sense of Television," in *Reader in Public Opinion and Mass Communication*, ed. Morris Janowitz and Paul M. Hirsch (New York: Free Press, 1981), pp. 363–85; Cynthia Hoffner and Joanne Cantor, "Developmental Differences in Response to a Television Character's Appearance and Behavior," *Developmental Psychology*, vol. 21, no. 6 (1985), pp. 1065–74; Paul Messaris and Larry Gross, "Interpretations of a Photographic Narrative by Viewers in Four Age Groups," *Studies in the Anthropology of Visual Communication* no. 4 (1977), pp. 99–111.

27.   Elizabeth M. Perse and Rebecca B. Rubin, "Attribution in Social and Parasocial Relationships," *Communication Research*, vol. 16, no. 1 (February 1989), pp. 59–77.

28.   I am indebted to Carl Plantinga for clarification of some of these distinctions.

29.   Telephone interviews with the author, October 25, 1994.

30.   Stuart Feldman, "Rendering Techniques for Computer-Aided Design," *SMPTE Journal*, vol. 103, no. 1 (January 1994), pp. 7–12.

31.   With respect to digital-imaging practices, rendering is distinct from the phases of model-building and animation and refers to the provision of texture, light, and color cues within a simulated environment.

32.   Texture-mapping is a process whereby a flat surface is detailed with texture, such as skin wrinkles, and can then be wrapped around a three-dimensional model visualized in computer space. Some surfaces texture-map more easily than others. Pat Byrne, at Post Effects, points out that spherical objects are problematic because the top and bottom tend to look pinched. Telephone interview with the author, October 25, 1994.

33.   Telephone interview with the author.

34.   Author's interview with Kevin Mack. See also Tsuneya Kurihara, Ken-ichi Anjyo, and Daniel Thalmann, "Hair Animation with Collision Detection," in *Models and Techniques in Computer Animation*, pp. 128–38.

35.   See Stephania Loizidou and Gordon J. Clapworthy, "Legged Locomotion Using HIDDS," in *Models and Techniques in Computer Animation*, pp. 257–69.

36.   Ibid., p. 258.

37.   Nichols, *Representing Reality*, p. 5.

38. Ibid., p. 268.

39. Christopher Williams, "After the Classic, the Classical and Ideology: the Differences of Realism," *Screen*, vol. 35, no. 3 (Autumn 1994), p. 282.

40. Ibid., p. 289.

PART SIX

HISTORICAL REVISIONS

The five articles and one interview in this section have to do with historical revisions in quite different senses. The Hans Barkhausen and Gösta Werner pieces employ archival research to cast doubt on claims made by two filmmakers concerning their roles in history. Barkhausen's short article on Leni Riefenstahl was based on extensive research that he did in the then newly available "voluminous documentary material of the former Ministry of Propaganda and Public Enlightenment [headed by Joseph Goebbels] and . . . the former Reich Ministry of Finances." The evidence that he found overwhelmingly refuted, and exposed as a lie, Riefenstahl's longtime claim that, although her earlier film *Triumph of the Will* (1936) had been commissioned by the Nazi Party, *Olympia* (1938) was financed by her own company with no support by the Third Reich. When the same Goebbels earlier offered Fritz Lang the directorship of the film industry for the Third Reich, Lang left Berlin for Paris that night—he didn't even have time to withdraw his money from the bank. This Lang anecdote—it's the one to tell if you're telling only one—has been passed on by several generations of film teachers and film textbooks. Doing some archive work of his own, as well as consulting secondary sources, Swedish scholar Werner has come up with a more complex story.

Lincoln Perry, who took his stage name, Stepin Fetchit, from a racehorse, may well have been the most important black performer in the first forty years of American film history and was, up to that time, by far the most successful, critically and financially. Among the high points of his career were two films he made with Will Rogers: *Judge Priest* (1934), also featuring Hattie McDaniel, and *Steamboat Round the Bend* (1935), both directed by John Ford. As early as 1946, black groups objected specifically to the Stepin Fetchit screen persona, which they regarded as degrading to blacks. Hence he made only one other film—Ford's *The Sun Shines Bright* (1953). In an interview with Joseph McBride in 1971, Perry argued persuasively that in the course of his event-crowded life, he had broken barrier after barrier not only for black film actors, but also for black people generally. This view was confirmed when Perry was among the first group of inductees into the Black Filmmakers Hall of Fame in 1974.

The Beverle Houston, Leonard J. Leff, and David Ehrenstein articles pursue historical revisions in the realm of the criticism of films and filmmakers. Houston develops an alternative approach to and interpretation of the films of Orson Welles. Leff examines less the narrative events and visual perspectives of *Citizen Kane* than a number of interpretations of that film. Ehrenstein's essay on *Desert Fury* most certainly rereads a forgotten film and thereby restores it to public discourse, but this is only the beginning.

In her influential study of Welles, Houston notes that Charles Foster Kane is forced to leave his family too early, but that George Minafer in *The Magnificent Ambersons* (1942) leaves his family too late. At the center of these two films and a third—*The Stranger* (1946)—are family-centered narratives that focus on what Houston calls the Power Baby,

> the eating, sucking, foetus-like creature who, as the lawyer at the center of *The Trial* [1963], can be found baby-faced, lying swaddled in his bed and tended by his nurse; who in *Touch of Evil* [1958] sucks candy and cigars in a face smoothed into featurelessness by fat as he redefines murder and justice according to desire; . . . and who, to my great delight, is figured forth explicitly in *Macbeth* [1948] where, in a Wellesian addition to Shakespeare, the weird sisters at the beginning of the film reach into the cauldron, scoop out a handful of their primordial woman's muck, shape it into a baby, and crown it with the pointy golden crown of fairy tales.

Returning to the moment of Mrs. Kane's decision to send her son away— and her blaming it on her husband—Houston notes the son's running to his father until his mother stops his progress with a sharp "Charles!" She speaks of the camera's dwelling on the mother's enigmatic look at this moment as "one of the film's most powerful and puzzling images." Of the scene generally, she concludes that we "must accept the overdetermination [i.e., undecidability] of this genuinely ambiguous moment." When Isabel Amberson marries dull Wilbur Minafer rather than dashing, amusing Eugene Morgan, she lavishes her love on young George, creating for him a "state of uncontested love with the mother, secure inside a warm, dark house. . . . No reason to get a job or a profession. No reason ever to leave this nest of complete dependence and desire." When George finally ventures forth, a car hits him and both his legs are broken. This reminds us of Kane's final years in a wheelchair and prefigures maimed legs in other Welles films: Arthur Bannister's limp and double canes in *Lady from Shanghai* (1948), Mr. Clay's immobility in *The Immortal Story* (1968), and the bullet in the leg that Hank Quinlan took for Pete in *Touch of Evil*—Hank later leaves his cane at the hotel where he murders Joe Grande.

Houston's discussion of women in Welles's films develops striking new perspectives. After she leaves Kane, "Susan's real return has been to her position within another social class." Lucy Morgan in *Ambersons* is forced into a more regressive return: life with her father, and celibacy. Especially interesting is Houston's account of *The Stranger*: Mary Longstreet has married a man who turns out to be a Nazi; how could a nice girl have make this bizarre choice? Nazi hunter Wilson wants Mary to be shown the kind of man she married, and he is willing to put her in danger, by using her as bait, to accomplish this. Her father and her brother agree and keep her under surveillance. This makes the control of the woman complete: "The dangers of active female sexuality and choice-making take on the resonance of a national and cultural disaster." The husband dies and deserves to do so "at the rational plot level," but the point is that "the aroused woman, the sign of difference as danger," is subject to "a struggle to force her into passivity and return, and often a lethal one."

Despite what the title "Reading *Kane*" might suggest, Leonard J. Leff does not provide yet another interpretation of *Citizen Kane*. On the contrary, his purpose is to question the assumptions and practices that scholars and critics have pursued for decades. In this bracing enterprise, he draws upon reader-response criticism, particularly the work of Stanley Fish, including his call to "*slow down* the reading experience so that 'events' one does not notice in normal time, but which do occur, are brought before our analytical attentions." Leff looks especially at *Kane*'s narrators—Thatcher, Bernstein, Leland, Susan, and Raymond—in order to see if other commentators, such as Bruce Kawin in *Mindscreen*, are correct in treating the sections of the film associated with each as a unified presentation of that character's perception. Leff argues that the Thatcher section does not remain within the banker's mindscreen, but deviates frequently and rapidly—sometimes within a time span of sixty seconds—to the mindscreens of others—now Mrs. Kane, now Charles, now a "supra-narrator." Reviewing various critical theories as to why Mrs. Kane sends her son away, Leff concludes, "These and other interpretations, though not unreasonable, miss the point. At this moment, the text has slipped out of our control: we may not say with any certainty why Mrs. Kane sends away her son."

"*Desert Fury*, Mon Amour": David Ehrenstein is the author of the article that bears this title, but the remarkable voice that we hear in it is a creation of the text itself. "*A Film of No Importance*: In the end it all comes down to *Desert*

Fury. Desert Fury? You haven't heard of it? Of course you haven't. Why should you? . . . [T]his turgid melodrama . . . figures in no known pantheon or cult. Its director, Lewis Allen, is devoid of *auteur* status. [*Desert Fury:*] Not good. Not bad. Mediocre. In fact, one might even go so far as to call it *quintessentially* mediocre."

The voice of the text is often furious, or *Fury*ous. Furious at theoretical critics whose bad faith deflects the auteur status of the films they choose to analyze. Furious that it is devoting so much time and attention to this resplendently blah film; but furious also at pretentious art films that critics still claim to admire, such as *Hiroshima, Mon Amour,* a film that, for all its merits, is devoid of humor. And while we're on the subject, humor is something in which this reading abounds: dry wit, belly laughs, and more than the seven types of irony that William Empson distinguished. All that said, the text's voice is genuinely interested in *Desert Fury,* at least fitfully—the strange plot, Lizabeth Scott's displacements of affect from straight Tom (Lancaster) to the dangerous and implicitly bisexual Hodiak, and the most charged relationship of all: the daughter-mother (Mary Astor) conflict that runs straight and crooked through all but the film's final pairing. Along the way, the voice also analyzes the film's running "fashion-show" of everyday sportswear; the pre-film build-up of the Scott-Lancaster romance; why a film of this kind is in color; and the character of Johnny (Wendell Corey), explicitly a homosexual, who warns Scott away from Hodiak for reasons that the text does not even try to hide.

It is possible to argue, or to recognize, that the kind of close textual reading of an individual film that began with *Cahiers du Cinéma*'s *Young Mr. Lincoln,* and includes quite a few stops along the way, comes to an end, or at least to a serious cessation, with Ehrenstein's article.

JOSEPH McBRIDE

STEPIN FETCHIT TALKS BACK

Stepin Fetchit (sometime in the 1930s). Courtesy of the
Academy of Motion Picture Arts and Sciences.

Vol. 24, no. 4 (Summer 1971): 20–26.

To militant first sight, Stepin Fetchit's routines—all cringe and excessive devotion—seem racially self-destructive in the rankest way, and his very name can be a term of abuse. And yet, in looking at his performances (for instance as the white judge's sidekick and looking-glass in Ford's The Sun Shines Bright) *cooler second sight must admit that Stepin Fetchit was an artist, and that his art consisted precisely in mocking and caricaturing the white man's vision of the black: his sly contortions, his surly and exaggerated subservience, can now be seen as a secret weapon in the long racial struggle. But whatever one makes of Stepin Fetchit's work, he was one of the few nonwhites to achieve status in American films, and he deserves to be remembered.*

Like all American institutions, Stepin Fetchit is having a hard time these days. The legendary black comedian, now 79 years old but looking decades younger, has found himself a target of ridicule from the very people he once represented, almost alone, on the movie screen. A revolution has erupted around him, and he has been cast not in the role of liberator (as he sees himself), but as a guard in the palace of racism. The man behind the vacant-eyed, foot-shuffling image is Lincoln Perry, a proud man embittered by scorn and condescension.

Once a millionaire five times over, he now lives modestly in Chicago and takes an occasional night club gig. He hasn't acted in a movie since John Ford's *The Sun Shines Bright* in 1953, though he appeared in William Klein's documentary about heavyweight champion Muhammad Ali, *Cassius le Grand*, while acting as Ali's "secret strategist" during the Liston fights. Perry once served in a similar capacity for Jack Johnson, and Ali's gesture of kinship has given a massive boost to the comedian's self-esteem.

I encountered him in a garish bottomless joint in Madison, Wisconsin, on the night of Ali's fight with Oscar Bonavena. Before we talked, I sat down to watch his 20-minute routine, which was sandwiched on the program between Miss Heaven Lee and Miss Akiko O'Toole. Audiences at these Midwestern nudie revues behave like hyenas in heat, but there is one very beautiful thing about a place like this, and I mean it: nowhere else in America today will you find such a truly democratic atmosphere. Class distinctions vanish as hippie and businessman, hard-hat and professor, white and black and Indian and Oriental unite in a common impulse of animal lust. Women's liberationists would object, of course, but not if they could observe the audience at close range—Heaven Lee had us enslaved.

When Step appeared, in skimmer and coonskin coat, there was a wave of uneasy tittering, and his first number, an incomprehensible boogie-woogie, stunned the audience into silence. What's this museum piece doing out there? Better he should be stored away where we can't think about him. But as he launched into his routine, a strange thing happened. Slowly, gradually, people began to dig him. Stepin Fetchit is, first and last, a funny, funky man. It isn't that his jokes are so great (a lot of them were tired-out gags about LBJ, of all people), it's the hip way he plays them. What made Step and Hattie McDaniel outclass all the other black character actors of bygone Hollywood was their subtle communication of superiority to the whole rotten game of racism. They played the game—it was the only game in town—but they were, somehow, above it: Step with his otherworldly eccentricities and Hattie McDaniel with her air of bossy *hauteur*. A tableful of young blacks began to parry back and forth with Step as he talked about the South. "You know how we travel in the South?" "No, how we travel in the South?" "Keep quiet an' I tell you." "That's cool. That's cool." And Step drawled: "Fast. At night. Through the *woods*. On top of the *trees*." The irony may have been a shade too complex for the rest of the audience, but everybody understood when he laconically gave his Vietnam position—"Flat on the ground"—and explained the situation of the black voter: "Negroes vote 20 or 25 times in Chicago. They don't try to cheat or nothin' like that. They just tryin' to make up for the time they couldn't vote down in Mississippi. When you in Mississippi you have to pass a test. Nuclear physics. In Russian. And if you pass it, they say, 'Boy, you speak Russian. You must be a Communist. You can't vote.'"

Out flounced Akiko, and we went downstairs to a dusty storage area which had been hurriedly transformed into a dressing room. Stepin Fetchit may be funny, but Lincoln Perry isn't. "Strip shows are taking over everything," he lamented. "You're either at the top or you're nothing." The stage he was using, a rectangular runway, forced him to turn his back on half of the audience, and he was trying to improvise a new means of attack. (It was sad and strangely appropriate that the lighting was so bad he had to carry his own spotlight around with him.) His heart, moreover, was with Ali. "That's where I should be, with that boy," he said. Jabbing his finger and circling me like a bantamweight boxer, Perry quickly turned the interview into a monologue.

Under a single swaying light bulb, the sequins on his purple tuxedo flashing, he moved in and out of the shadows like a restless ghost. I began to get the eerie feeling that I was serving as judge and jury, hearing the self-defense of a man accused of a cultural crime. This is what the man said:

I was the first Negro militant. But I was a militant for God and country, and not controlled by foreign interests. I was the first black man to have a universal audience. When people saw me and Will Rogers together like brothers, that said something to them. I elevated the Negro. I was the first Negro to gain full American citizenship. Abraham Lincoln said that all men are created equal, but Jack Johnson and myself *proved* it. You understand me? I defied white supremacy and proved in defying it that I could be *associated* with. There was no white man's ideas of making a Negro Hollywood motion picture star, a millionaire Negro entertainer. Savvy? I was a 100% black accomplishment. Now get this—when all the Negroes was goin' around straightening their hair and bleaching theirself trying to be white, and thought improvement was white, in them days I was provin' to the world that black was beautiful. *Me.* I opened so many things for Negroes—I'm so *proud* today of the things that the Negroes is enjoying because I personally did 'em myself.

People don't understand any more what I was doing then, least of all the young generation of Negroes. They've made the character part of Stepin Fetchit stand for being lazy and stupid and being a white man's fool. I never did that, but they're all so prejudiced now that they just can't understand. Maybe because they don't really know what it was like then. Hollywood was more segregated than Georgia under the skin. A Negro couldn't do anything straight, only comedy. I did more acting as a comedian than Sidney Poitier does as an actor. I made the Negro as innocent and acceptable as the most innocent white child, but this acting had to come from the *soul*. They brought Willie Best out there to make him an understudy for me. And he wasn't an actor, he wasn't an entertainer or nothin' like that. I didn't need no understudy, because I had a thing going that I had built my own. And the worst thing you'll hear about Stepin Fetchit is when somebody tries to imitate what I do, the first thing they're gonna say is "Yassuh, yassuh, boss." I was way away from that.

Do I sound like an ignorant man to you? You made an image in your mind that I was lazy, good-for-nothing, from a character that you seen me doin' when I was doin' a high-class job of entertainment. Man, what I was doin' was hard *work!* Do you think I made a fool of myself? Maybe you might *want* me to. Like I can't be confined to use the word black. For a comedian, that takes the rhythm out of a lot of jokes and things. So when I use the words colored and Negro I'm not trying to be obstinate. That's what I'm going around for—to show the kids there are a lot of people that's doin' things to confuse them.

I'm just trying to get the kids today to have the diplomacy that I had to when I was doing it, and I think they'll come out first in everything. I didn't fight my way in—I *eased* in.

Humor is only my alibi for bein' here. Show business is a mission for me. All my breaks came from God. You see, I made God my agent. Like it's a coincidence that I'm here talking to you now. They bring a lot of people here, they pay 'em to talk to these students. They teachin' these students to go against law and order, they teachin' 'em to go against God, against their country, and they're *payin'* 'em. They wouldn't pay me to come to town to talk to the students. Are you one of these college boys? No? That's good. All these college boys, the first word they think of when they write about me is Uncle Tom. I was lookin' for the word to come up but it didn't. Uncle Tom! Now there's a word that the Negro should try to wipe out and not use. Uncle Tom was a fictional character in a story that was wrote by Harriet Beecher Stowe. And Abraham Lincoln said that this thing was one of the propaganda that put one American brother against his other.

Kids is eccentric. They think they want to hear all these eccentric things. Like I see beautiful kids—I went to a place near where I'm working called the Shuffle and the reason they're using all this long hair and these whiskers, looking like apostles, that's because they're leanin' towards God, instinctively. Good kids, and a lot of old men is foolin' 'em. I want to let 'em know how I as a kid, a small Negro kid that was a Catholic too—so I had eleven strikes against me in them days—became a millionaire entertainer. Now these kids, they think that I'm unskilled and I'm uneducated, you know, and I don't have no diplomas or anything like that. But they must remember that they're listening to 79 years of experience.

I was an artist. A technician. I went in and competed among the greatest artists in the country. When I was about to make a movie with Will Rogers, Lionel Barrymore went to him and said, "This Stepin Fetchit will steal every scene from you. He'll steal a scene from anything—animal, bird, or human being." That was Lionel *Barrymore*, of the *Barrymore* family!

John Ford, the director, is one of the greatest men who ever lived. We was at the U.S. Naval Academy in 1929 making a picture called *Salute*, using the University of Southern California football team to do us a football sequence between the Army and the Navy. John Wayne was one of their football players. And in order to be seen by the director at all times, because Ford wanted to make him an actor, John Wayne taken the part of a prop man. That director made him a star. And on that picture, John Wayne was my dresser! John Ford, he was staying in the commandant's house during that picture, and he had me stay in the guest house. At *Annapolis!*

I was in *Judge Priest*, that Ford did with Will Rogers in 1934. Did you see that? Well, remember that line Will Rogers says to me, "I saved you from one

Stepin Fetchit (on right, with coonskin coat) as Jeff Poindexter in John Ford's *Judge Priest* (1934). Courtesy of the Academy of Motion Picture Arts and Sciences.

lynching already"? We had a lynching scene in there, where I, as an innocent Negro, got saved by Will Rogers. They cut it out because we were ahead of the time. In 1953 we did a remake of that picture, called *The Sun Shines Bright*. And John Ford, he did the lynching scene again. This time the Negro that gets saved was played by a young boy—I was older then. But they kept it in. That was my last picture.

I filed a $3 million lawsuit against something that Bill Cosby said about me in a show called *Of Black Americans*. But I didn't make Cosby a defendant. Know the reason why? Because that's not the source of where the wrong come. It's CBS, Twentieth Century–Fox, and the Xerox Corporation, the men that sponsored it, that's responsible for distortin' my image. Cosby was just a soldier. He was not a general. I know all the black comedians. Bill was the onliest one I hadn't met. I met him for the first time in Atlanta at the Cassius Clay–Jerry Quarry fight. Cassius called me and say, "Hey, Step, I want you to meet Bill." I just said hello, because I was busy, and then he said, "Bill *Cosby!*" I went back and I say, "Well, Cosby, I hope that you help to put a happy ending to my damages that has been done." He says to me, "Yeah, I told my wife, I hope that you win this suit, because it was taken out of context." Cosby's a great comedian, but for the educated classes. Savvy? A few years ago he wouldn't have been able to be where he is—I was the one who made it possible for him. The worst thing in America today is not racism. It's the way the skilled classes is against the unskilled classes. You understand me?

Now, if we don't get this country straight, your next president is going to be George Wallace. They figure everybody is being turned idiot and they gonna all agree it's gonna be a man like George Wallace to help our problems if we don't straighten them out ourselves.

Ain't but two things in the world today. That's good and bad, right and wrong. Now if we follow everything down to them two things, and we are either on one of them sides, it ain't no white, no colored, no Black Panthers, no Ku Klux . . . we either for good or for bad! We ought to have a National Association for the Advancement of *Created* People and not think about each nationality that represents 50 percent of America. When God made Adam, he didn't make all these different nationalities. Man did it. There is no mules in heaven. Now let me explain this to you. Mules are man-made, made from crossing a jackass with a horse. So when man got mixed up, it wasn't the work of God, it was the work of man. Racism? Remember when there wasn't but four people on earth, Cain killed his brother Abel and started unbrotherly love. God didn't have nothin' to do with unbrotherly love.

To show you how fate works—Cassius Clay, none of these great liberals would touch him and give him a chance to fight again. And who do you think give him a chance to fight again? Senator Leroy Johnson of Georgia, a man that is associated with Lester *Maddox*. Without Lester Maddox, Cassius Clay wouldn't have fought today, although the image they gave to you was that Lester Maddox was against it. You get the idea? You understand me? The greatest example of *Americanism* was shown to Cassius Clay by a proxy, through Lester Maddox! That's the way the world is running. So let's face these things right, not like we pitchin' things, or like we want it to go. God's gonna work in a mysterious way! We have had men supposed to be great all down the line—Alexander, Moses—and we still found the world all messed up. Ain't nobody in good shape. Ain't nobody got no sense or nothin'.

It was Satchel Paige that opened the major leagues to the Negro ball players. Not Jackie Robinson. *No* suh! Satchel Paige did the dirty work. He used to go and play in counties where they didn't allow a Negro in the county. He did the good work—what I did—made good will and good relations. Jackie Robinson was the politician, you understand me, the skilled one that walked in and got the benefits. Satchel Paige broke down the whole deal and hasn't got credit for it yet, just because he was unskilled labor. He was 100 years ahead of his time, like I am, like Johnson was.

The reason why Cassius sent for me was because he found out that I was the last close intimate of Jack Johnson. Jack told me a lot of things. Cassius always said they wasn't but one fighter that was greater than him, and that was Jack Johnson. And so he wanted to know *everything* about him. He got me in and he would ask me all the different things that Jack would tell me about. I taught him the Anchor Punch that he beat Liston with—that was a punch that Jack improvised. Cassius dug up some pictures of Johnson and I told him about this out-of-sight punch that Jack Johnson said he had. He said he could use it any time he wanted on Willard. See, Willard did not knock Johnson out. Johnson sold the heavyweight champion of the world for $50,000. Johnson accepted $15,000 in Europe and told them to give his wife $35,000 at ringside. He wanted the heavyweight champion title to belong to America. They had ran Jack into a lot of things, you get the idea . . . be too long to talk about.

They promised him with the $15,000 they would wipe off this year that he's supposed to serve. But they didn't do that, so he came back and served the year himself. You get the idea? I saw that play, *The Great White Hope*. I think it's terrible as far as telling the truth about Jack Johnson. It's not about Jack. Jack Johnson had noble ideas. They had him beating this girl—Jack never did a thing like that. And they showed where he was defeated and knocked out, but they didn't show that he sold out the heavyweight champion and that he wanted the championship to belong to America.

We were going to do this picture of his life story, called *The Fighting Stevedore*. You know—from Galveston, Texas, where he used to be a stevedore. While we was waiting to write the story—we was making it just for colored theaters, in them days things weren't integrated and the big companies wouldn't want to buy it because everything had thumbs down on Jack Johnson like things tried to be with Cassius, although I'm sure Cassius is coming out of it—while we was waiting to write this thing, we sent Jack down to lead the grand parade of Negro rodeos in Texas. That was the trip he got killed on. I booked him on it.

I always call Cassius "Champ" because I used to call Jack Johnson "Champ." The way Jack and me met, we was both celebrities, and I used to sit in his corner when we was fighting. We became friends especially when he found out that the same priest had taught both of us. His name was Father J. A. St. Laurent. He taught also the Negro student that became the first Negro Catholic priest in America. Here's a picture of me preachin' to Martin Luther King. I was telling him that I was in Montgomery, Alabama, *before he was born* playing with white women. This priest was the head of the school I went to, St. Joseph's College. It was a Catholic boys' school. And this priest used to have the nurses come from St. Margaret's Hospital to play with us—that's where Mrs. George Wallace was a patient before she died. They had picnics, spent a whole day on our campus with these colored boys, playing ball with us, eating in our dining room, and things like that. This priest he taught us a technical education—Tuskegee used to teach manual labor—and so he left those boys with something. We had no inferiority complex. Jack always wanted to show that all men were created equal, so he goes into Newport News society and married a white woman out of the social register, a *blue-blood!*

My father named me Lincoln Theodore Monroe Andrew Perry. Told me he named me after four presidents—he think I'm gonna be a great man. But I can't see how in the world he named me after Theodore *Roose*velt. He wasn't even president yet! I was born in 1892—here's my birth certificate—in Key West, Florida, the last city in the United States. I'm a descendant of the West Indies. My mother was born in Nassau, my father was born in Jamaica. I had talent all my life—my father used to sing. He was a cigar maker. I got in show business in 1913 or '14. The people who had adopted me and sent me off to this school, something happened to them, and so this priest told me I could work my way through school. In summertime he let me go to St. Margaret's Hospital to work. When time to go back to school, there was a carnival that used to winter in Montgomery. Turned out to be the Royal American Shows. So I joined it, joined the "plantation show." The plantation shows started to call themselves minstels, but minstrels was white men made up. Plantation shows was black men made up.

I got my name Stepin Fetchit from a race horse. The plantation show minstrels, we went down in Texas and there was a certain horse we used to go and see at the fair. We knew these races because they went to the same fairs as we did. There was a horse that we knew would never lose, so we would go out and give the field and the odds. Well, people thought we was crazy—he would always win. But one day they entered a big bay horse on us, and *he* won. We went and grabbed the program, looked, and it was Stepin Fetchit, horse from Baltimore. And so I goes back to show business in Memphis, and hear "Stepin Fetchit! Stepin Fetchit!" from everyone. I wrote a dance song of it called "The Stepin Fetchit, Stepin Fetchit, Turn Around, Stop and Catch It, Chicken Scratch It to the Ground, Etc."

Me and my partner was introducing this new dance. We were Skeeter and Rastus, The Two Dancing Crows from Dixie. Jennifer Jones's father booked us in a white theater in Tulsa, Oklahoma, which was unusual. And in place of putting our names Skeeter and Rastus, he put Step and Fetchit and he made that our names. When my partner, he wouldn't show up, I would tell the manager, "No, it's not two of us, it's just one of us, the Step and Fetchit." And then I'd go out and do just as good as the two of us. I fired him, since I had wrote the song, see, and in place of The Two Dancing Crows from Dixie, I was the Stepin Fetchit. I got the lazy idea from my partner. He was so lazy, he used to call a cab to get across the street.

I was in Ripley's "Believe It or Not" as the onliest man who ever made a million dollars doing nothing. Anything money could buy, I had. I had 14 Chinese servants and all different kinds of cars. This one, a pink Rolls Royce, it had my name on the sides in neon lights. My suits cost $1,000 each. I got some of them from Rudolph Valentino's valet after he died. I showed people that just because I had a million dollars, the world wouldn't come to an end. But then I had to file a $5 million bankruptcy and didn't have but $146 assets. No, I wasn't held up by no robbers, and I wasn't in any swindling gambling games. It was all "honest" business people I trusted who took the money, all good, upstanding people. I was too busy makin' it to think about savin' it. I started with nothin' and I got nothin' left, so I've come full circle. But I'm rich. I'm a millionaire. Know the reason why? Because I go to Mass every morning. I have been a daily communicant for the last 50 years. Everything I've accomplished I've accomplished in believin' that seek ye first the kingdom of heaven and all things will be given to thee. Consider the lilies of the field . . .

HANS BARKHAUSEN

FOOTNOTE TO THE HISTORY OF RIEFENSTAHL'S *OLYMPIA*

Vol. 28, no. 1 (Fall 1974): 8–12.

Leni Riefenstahl has maintained that her two 1936 Olympics films, *Fest der Völker* and *Fest der Schönheit,* were produced by her own company, commissioned by the organizing committee of the International Olympic Committee, and made over the protest of Nazi Minister of Propaganda Joseph Goebbels. In "Olympia, the Film of the Eleventh Olympic Games in Berlin, 1936," a paper written to defend herself in 1958, she says: "The truth is that neither the Ministry of Propaganda nor other National Socialist party or government bodies had any influence on the Olympic Games or on the production or design of the Olympia films."

The voluminous documentary material of the former Ministry of Propaganda and Public Enlightenment and the materials of the former Reich Ministry of Finances, today deposited in the Federal Archives in Koblenz (the central depository of the Federal Republic of Germany), tell a different story.

These records show that the two Olympia films were financed by the Nazi government, that the Olympia Film Company was founded by that government, that the government made money by distributing the films through the Tobis-Filmkunst Company, and that the government, finally, ordered the liquidation of the Olympia Film Company, in which Leni Riefenstahl and her brother were partners.

The true story of the origin of the two Olympics films of 1936 begins with a short memo written in the Reich Finance Ministry on October 16, 1935, saying: "On the order of Herr Minister Goebbels, Ministerial Counselor Ott, on October 15, proposed the following special appropriations to me: (1) for promotion of the Olympic Games: RM 300–350,000; (2) for the Olympic film: RM 1,500,000."

Ministerial Counselor Ott was the budget expert in the Propaganda Ministry, much respected, and rather liberal by the standards of the times. A carbon of the memo was sent to him by the Finance Ministry, and he initialed it on October

17, 1935. The words "to me" evidently refer to the section chief in charge in the Finance Ministry; his name in the note is recorded only by his initial "M."

The memo continues, with reference to point (2), that is, the Olympic film:

The Ministry of Propaganda submits the draft of a contract for the production of a film of the Olympics, according to which Miss Leni Riefenstahl is commissioned to produce a film of the summer Olympics. The cost is budgeted at RM 1,500,000.

I have pointed out that this film is certain to bring revenue, so that there would be no difficulty in financing the costs by private enterprise, for example by the Film-Kredit-Bank. This method would avoid government financing. But Ministerial Counselor Ott replied that Herr Minister Goebbels requests the prefinancing with *government* funds.

According to information from Ministerial Counselor Ott, Herr Minister Goebbels will request the proposed funds in the cabinet meeting of October 18, 1935. [Emphasis in the original.]

This is what actually happened.

In the contract mentioned in the memo Leni Riefenstahl is commissioned to produce and direct the film of the Olympics. The contract repeats the costs of RM 1,500,000. This amount was to be disbursed in four installments:

RM 300,000 on November 15, 1935

RM 700,000 on April 1, 1936

RM 200,000 on November 1, 1936

RM 300,000 on January 1, 1937

We shall soon see that these amounts were not enough to produce the film.

Section 3 of the contract with Riefenstahl says:

"From the amount of RM 1,500,000 Miss Riefenstahl is to receive RM 250,000 for her work, which is to cover expenses for travel, automobile, and social affairs." The contract stipulated—and this turned out to be an important provision—that Leni Riefenstahl was "to account to the Reich Ministry for Propaganda and Enlightenment for the disbursement of the RM 1,500,000 by presenting receipts." The contract specifically reconfirms that "she is solely responsible for the general artistic direction and overall organization of the Olympic film."

In her 1958 defense paper she writes: "On higher orders (Dr. Goebbels), the German news cameramen, who were the most important elements in the making of documentary pictures, were removed from Leni Riefenstahl's control."

Section 6 of the contract says:

"The Reich Ministry for Propaganda and Public Enlightenment undertakes (as previously in the production of the Reich Party Day film *Triumph des Willens*) to place the German weekly news shows [*Wochenschauen*] of the Ufa, Fox, and Tobis at the disposal of Miss Riefenstahl and to obligate them to make accessible the material filmed by them for the Olympia film."

The amounts that Riefenstahl was to pay for this material were spelled out by the Propaganda Ministry.

I presume the *Wochenschau* companies were not enthusiastic about having their cameramen take orders from Riefenstahl. But *Wochenschau* material was in fact delivered to her, as shown by the "Itemized List for Herr Minister, April 1937." It states all costs incurred until then for the Olympia film, with a total of RM 1,509,178.09, which includes as item 11: "Raw film and *Wochenschau* material: RM 220,003.41." Whether Riefenstahl actually used this material in her film is a different question. But in her distribution contract with Tobis this possibility is specifically spelled out for legal reasons.

In her postwar interviews Riefenstahl consistently referred to "her own company" that produced the Olympia film. In her 1958 defense paper she also says: "Goebbels did not want Leni Riefenstahl to show the victorious black athletes in the Olympia film. When L. R. refused to comply with these requests and did not honor them later either, Goebbels ordered the Film-Kredit-Bank, which was answerable to his Ministry, to refuse all further credits to the Olympia-Film Company (a private firm)." The parenthesis is in the original. These statements, however, are products of Leni Riefenstahl's imagination. What are the facts?

When a film company was funded, it was general practice to deposit in a court of law an initial capital of RM 50,000, after entering the firm in the official Trade Register. The funds for the founding of the Olympia Film Company were provided by the Reich government. But the Reich, in this case, was parsimonious. Hence Ministerial Counselor Ott, on January 30, 1936, wrote to the Berlin-Charlottenburg Court: "The Olympia Film Company is being set up at the request of the government and financed by funds supplied by the government. The means needed by the company to produce the film are likewise supplied exclusively by the government. The company has had to be established because the government does not wish to appear publicly as the producer of this film. It is planned to liquidate the company when the production of the film is concluded."

Evidently this was still not spelled out with sufficient clarity for the Court. Therefore the Reich Film Chamber, the body responsible for the founding of film companies, wrote to the Court on February 12, 1936: "We are not talking, then, about a private enterprise, or about an enterprise with ordinary commercial aims, but about a company founded exclusively for the purpose of external organization and production of the said film. It appears unwise [*untunlich*] for the government itself to appear as the producer." Hence Leni Riefenstahl's fictitious company was required to pay no more than RM 20,000 as original capital, from the funds provided by the government. Still, the Examination Board of the Propaganda Ministry complained on October 16, 1936, that "the original capital has not been paid in up to now."

The report of the General Accounting Office which contains these words was an embarrassment for Riefenstahl which she never got over. It was probably one reason why she hated the Propaganda Ministry. Hence I will have to discuss that report further.

The auditors of the GAO, like those of any official agency, even in the Third Reich, were petty bureaucrats. The GAO had tackled audits for other agencies of the government, but presumably it had never dealt with a film production, and certainly never had to deal with such a temperamental and self-assured film artist as Riefenstahl. The auditors, however, chose to treat her strictly as the manager of the Olympia Film Company.

The auditors complain that as early as September 16, 1936, of the government-agreed RM 1,500,000 "RM 1,200,000 were requested by the Company and paid out, although by that time only RM 1,000,000 were due." They complain further that "the use of these funds contradicts the order concerning government economies to administer official funds economically and carefully." They add that there were no economies "in general expenses such as per diem payments, tips, meals, drinks, charges, and special charges." "Rarely," they say, "was there a meeting in which the company did not pay for breakfast, lunch, or dinner." The auditors take issue with the fact that the Geyer Works, where Riefenstahl edited the Olympia film and had it printed, on the occasion of its business anniversary was presented with two flower baskets and a gift, valued together at RM 117; that the firm paid RM 202.40 for a business course attended by Leni Riefenstahl's secretary; that RM 10.17 was paid without specification for the "Reich Race Research Office"; that "Miss Riefenstahl and her business manager Grosskopf were reimbursed RM 18 and 15.75 for lost fountain pens." It goes on in this way for pages—thousands of bills or receipts were examined, and where the auditors saw fit were commented on. A few passages read like comedy: those administering money are chided by the sentence: "The company has no strongbox." Business manager Grosskopf, being responsible for the safety of the cash, "was obliged to take the money home with him" and during the examination on October 3, 1936, "had produced RM 14,000 to 15,000 in various amounts from different pockets of his clothing." The outraged auditors state: "Such practices are verboten."

Incidentally, I happen to know Grosskopf and met him on occasion during the months when the Olympia film was in production. He was a solid, conscientious older businessman, visibly bothered by a situation that was beyond his control.

Goebbels treated this report, presented to him by Ministerial Counselor Hanke, chief of the Ministerial Secretariat (later Gauleiter in Breslau), far more generously than Riefenstahl will allow today. With a green pencil he wrote across the report "Let's not be petty" and ordered Hanke to talk with Riefenstahl. However, when Ministerial Counselor Ott presented Goebbels with an additional request for RM 500,000 because the RM 1,500,000 "presumably will not be sufficient," he wrote: "RM 500,000 are out of the question." But one can sense that this phrasing left the door open. At any rate, he approved an additional RM 300,000.

He refused Ott's suggestion "to include the Film-Kredit-Bank in the future, because it can factually check on the expenditures of the Olympia Film Company," but shrewd Ott has added to his suggestion: "One will have to assume, of course, that Miss Riefenstahl will fight such an order with all means at her disposal." Besides, observes Ott, "it could be undesirable for a private firm, such as the Film-Kredit-Bank, to have intimate information about a company entirely set up by the government." He suggests that perhaps the Reich Film Chamber should do the auditing.

It was undoubtedly disconcerting for Riefenstahl to have to answer the various criticisms of the auditors. Her annoyance was understandable; but there was a second reason to be annoyed. Goebbels ordered the Reich Film Chamber to make available "Judge Pfennig of the Reich Film Chamber as advisor to the Olympia Film Company." He was to ensure the "purposeful and economic use of the means of this company." The Reich Chamber, on its part, was to report to him, Goebbels, "about Judge Pfennig's activities and observations." Goebbels signed this order with his own hand.

Pfennig was the Legal Counsel of the Reich Film Chamber. Earlier he had worked for the major German film producing company, the Ufa. After Hugenberg in 1927 had taken over the Ufa and had appointed the Director General of the Sherl Publishing Company, Ludwig Klitzsch, as Director General of Ufa, economy was demonstrably practiced. As early as April 1927 Klitzsch appointed Pfennig, then a law clerk, as director of his secretariat and informed the Board of Directors accordingly (Ufa, Board of Directors protocol No. 18, April 28, 1927). Klitzsch, however, could economize only as long as Goebbels would let him. But after about 1937 Goebbels increasingly prevented economy. It must have been Leni Riefenstahl's second great grief to have Judge Pfennig appointed to supervise her, even though disguised as observer.

In her paper of 1958 Riefenstahl says that she concluded a distribution contract with Tobis, but this tells little about the ownership of the Olympia Film Company. A government-owned company needed a distribution contract just as much as a privately owned one. The contract, concluded December 4, 1936, between Olympia Film Company, represented by Leni Riefenstahl, and Tobis-

Olympia

Cinema Company, represented by production chief Fritz Mainz, specifically points out that the production costs will be about RM 1,500,000. Tobis agreed to a guarantee for RM 800,000 for the first part and at least RM 200,000 for the second part of the film. What this contract did not mention, however, was the obligation by Tobis to account not only to Olympia Film Company but also to the Ministry of Propaganda. This was duly done, however; one copy of the accounting went to Olympia Film Company and two copies to the Ministry of Propaganda, one of which was routed to Ministerial Counselor Ott.

It took Leni Riefenstahl eighteen months to complete the two films, a period of time envisioned by the contract with Tobis. The première took place on April 20, 1938, Hitler's 49th birthday, at Ufa Palace at the Zoo in Berlin in festive surroundings. There was no indication of a rift between Goebbels and Leni Riefenstahl, such as she has talked and written about.

As early as September 26, 1938, Ministerial Counselor Ott was able to report to the Ministry of finance that "a million Reichsmark of unplanned revenue have flowed into the coffers of the Reich treasury."

At that time the *Rechnungshof* (General Accounting Office) remembered that the understanding had been to liquidate the Olympia Film Company on the completion of its task. On November 5, 1938, the agency inquired of the Reich Minister for Propaganda and Public Enlightenment "when the liquidation of the Olympia Film Company is to be expected." On November 21 the reply came, saying that "according to present developments the end of business is to be expected in fiscal year 1939."

Barely six months later, on May 17, 1940, that is, after the start of the war, the Propaganda Ministry was able to report to the Reich Finance Ministry that the RM 1,800,000, "needed for the production of the Olympia films and advanced by the government, had been repaid in *full* to the Reich." The liquidation of the Olympia Film Company, the report added, had been decided in a company meeting on December 6, 1939, to be effective December 31; the liquidation was to be carried out by business manager Grosskopf. Future revenues from the film would "as up to now be paid into a holding account of the Reich Treasury."

The liquidation process, in fact, took two more years. In the middle of Hitler and Goebbels' "total war," the tireless Ministerial Counselor Ott, still in the same position at the Propaganda Ministry (remarkable in view of the frequent changes in other departments of the agency), on February 1, 1943, reported to the Reich Finance Ministry that "the liquidation of the Olympia Film Company has been completed." According to the accounting submitted "the total net gain transferred to the Reich amounted to RM 114,066.45."

When a king dies another must be immediately proclaimed; hence the final paragraph states: "The further utilization and administration of the two films of the Olympics have been transferred to the *Riefenstahl Film Company* [my emphasis], which will report quarterly about the financial status." No inkling, indeed, of hostility between Propaganda Ministry and Riefenstahl.

Thanks to Adolf Hitler the German Reich has ceased to exist, but Leni Riefenstahl is still permitted to exploit her two Olympia films of 1936/1938. She does so now on the basis of a thirty-year contract concluded ten years ago between her and the Transit Film Company, which administers the film rights of the German Federal Republic. Of course, from time to time, she has to settle accounts.

BEVERLE HOUSTON

POWER AND DIS-INTEGRATION
IN THE FILMS OF ORSON WELLES

No movie is made by a complete adult. First of all,
I don't know any complete adults.

ORSON WELLES

I, señor, am not one *of anything, but, like you, señor, I am unique.*

THE SECOND (DYING) ART FORGER, TO PICASSO, IN *F FOR FAKE*

Vol. 35, no. 4 (Summer 1982): 2–12.

In a scene of snowfall before a small house, Charles Foster Kane is cast out of his family by his newly rich mother. As generations of moviewatchers are well aware, it is to this snow scene that he returns upon his death as the text itself returns to the "No Trespassing" sign. In *Magnificent Ambersons,* on the other hand, family and friends spend years trying unsuccessfully to dislodge Georgie Minafer from the family mansion and the bosom of his mother. When the infant is finally forced out, he breaks both his legs. In the same film, Lucy Morgan is forced by Georgie's refusal to enter the world of men and money to return to her father and a lifetime of celibacy. Mary Longstreet in *The Stranger* is forced into a similar return.

Both *Citizen Kane* and *Magnificent Ambersons* reveal a central male figure who is extremely powerful in certain ways, who can charm, force, or frighten others into doing what he wants. But the desire for control is haunted by everything that evades it. The opening of *Citizen Kane,* with its decayed golf course and terraces, its moss-covered gothic magnificence, reveals to us two aspects of this pattern: both the overreaching ambition and its failure—a grand life, now in ruins. Even at the height of their powers, these men are revealed to be helpless in certain realms of life, unable finally to live out their desires. Focusing on *Citizen Kane, Magnificent Ambersons,* and *The Stranger* as family-centered narratives set in the United States, with substantial reference to *Touch of Evil, Immortal Story,* and *Chimes at Midnight* for close parallels of theme and/or narrative strategies, and with passing glances at a number of other Welles films, this essay will examine the ways in which the boundless fear, anger, and desire of these figures power both narrative and image in these films.

In my own years of obsession with the Welles films,[1] I have come to call this central figure of desire and contradiction the Power Baby, the eating, sucking, foetus-like creature who, as the lawyer at the center of *The Trial,* can be found baby-faced, lying swaddled in his bed and tended by his nurse; who in *Touch of Evil* sucks candy and cigars in a face smoothed into featurelessness by fat as he redefines murder and justice according to desire; who in his bland and arrogant innocence brings everybody down in *Lady from Shanghai;* who, in the framed face of Picasso, slyly signals his power as visual magician and seducer and who is himself tricked in *F for Fake;* but who must die for the sake of the social order in *Chimes at Midnight* and who dies again for his last effort of power and control in *Immortal Story;* and who, to my great delight, is figured forth explicitly in *Macbeth* where, in a Wellesian addition to Shakespeare, the weird sisters at the beginning of the film reach into the cauldron, scoop out a handful of their primordial woman's muck, shape it into a baby, and crown it with the pointy golden crown of fairy tales.

Who are these infant kings who return to early scenes, whose narratives are deflected, and whose situations are finally reversed? What do they have, and what lack? How are they both more and less than they wish to be, sometimes never reaching, but more often losing their once-great powers in the world of men and money? And what is the pattern of possibilities for their women, who are so often denied or forced into returns, whose fates are so extreme, yet so limited?

The mother of Charles Foster Kane becomes rich and powerful in a moment of transformation. She uses this power to reject Charles utterly. He is ripped untimely from a scene where he could reach whatever combination of love, fear, acceptance, and rejection that might come from the child's living out the drama of sex and power with his parents. The untimeliness of this change is suggested perfectly by the exaggeration of size relations in the Christmas shot where Charles, with his unwanted new sled, gazes up defiantly at a huge Thatcher, the money monster, on that most familial of holidays, the one based on the birth of a perfect son into a perfect family.

In the name of what does Charles's mother commit this horribly wrenching act, for which she is so eager that she has had her son's trunk packed for a week? It is true that the father moves as if to strike Charles when he pushes Thatcher. And it is true that he says: "What that kid needs is a good thrashing," moving Mrs. Kane to reply: "That's what you think, is it; Jim? . . . that's why he's going to be brought up where you can't get at him." Apparently Mrs. Kane thinks he is "the wrong father" for little Charles. Yet we have little evidence that the father has ever harmed or frightened the child. As the four talk outside the cabin, Charles moves eagerly toward his father's arms; the mother must stop him by calling his name sharply. Thus it is one of the film's most powerful and puzzling images when, at the moment of her insistence, Mrs. Kane slowly turns her head to the side as the camera dwells on her enigmatic look. Is it one of confidence for having freed her son from a struggle he couldn't win? Or one of cruel pleasure in having triumphed over father and son for their very maleness? Is she the terrible mother of myth and nightmare? Joseph McBride suggests: "It is simply that the accident which made the Kanes suddenly rich has its own fateful logic—Charles must 'get ahead.' What gives the brief leave-taking scene its mystery and poignancy is precisely this feeling of pre-determination."[2] It must be emphasized, however, that the logic is not that of fate but of money and social class. Insisting that "this isn't the place for you to grow up in," the newly empowered mother pursues her son's "advantages" by removing him from an impoverished rural environment. She turns her son over to an agency—the bank—that she believes will protect and promote him better than the family. Yet we cannot fully escape the hint of a revenge and must accept the overdetermination of this genuinely ambiguous moment.

The role of the father needs to be understood in a different way as well. It is not his cruelty that is most significant. The fact that Fred Graves, the defaulting boarder who knew both Mr. and Mrs. Kane, left the fortune exclusively to Mrs. Kane, somehow brings Charlie's paternity into question. Did Graves leave it all to Mrs. Kane because he found the father wanting in some way—weak and whining, dependent on his wife, perhaps? Or is it Graves himself, in his unpredictable act of generosity, who is the right ("real") father? Even though we are made sympathetic with Mr. Kane—"I don't hold with signing my boy away. . . . Anyone'd think I hadn't been a good husband. . . ." (Why doesn't he say, "Good *father*"?)—still other negative qualities are revealed. He first tries to get little Charles to believe that his forced migration from country/family to city/bank is going to be a wonderful adventure: "That's the train with all the lights. . . . You're going to see Chicago and New York. . . ." But when Charles refuses to be fooled, the father threatens to thrash him. Thus even this "wrong father" has two faces: he who promises deceitfully, who promises pleasure where there is abandonment, and he who later threatens violence. For the boy, the father becomes the promise of worldly experience and the threat of danger, both exaggerated. Longing to cling to the beloved but mysteriously rejecting mother, unable to trust the weak and deceitful father, the boy Charles reacts with rage as his life is captured in this frozen moment.

And what of Georgie Minafer, who got out, not too early, but too late? Within the basic reversal, there are a number of similarities, particularly concerning the father. In this film, money also brings about the constitution of the "wrong" family. The agency of business is this time substituted, not for the family as a whole, but for the emotional participation of the father through Isabel Amberson's choice of husband. She marries Wilbur Minafer, a "steady young businessman," instead of Eugene Morgan, "a man who any woman would like a thousand times better." Though the local women opine that Isabel's "pretty sensible for such a showy girl," they prophesy correctly the return of the passions denied by Isabel's choice: "They'll have the worst spoiled lot of children this town will ever see. It'll all go to her children and she'll ruin them." An only child receiving the full adoration of a mother who married for

"This nest of complete dependence and desire": *The Magnificent Ambersons*

dollars and sense, so puny he nearly dies as an infant, young Georgie also has a father who is virtually absent. Later, when the father dies, the voice-over narrator tells us: "Wilbur Minafer. A quiet man. The town will hardly know he's gone." And Georgie hardly knew he was there. But this time the young man with the wrong father, with *no* father to love and hate on a regular basis, has not been sent away by the mother. Instead, we find that Georgie lives fully in a mutual state of uncontested love with the mother, secure inside a warm, dark house and a rich and fabled family. No reason to get a job or a profession. No reason ever to leave this nest of complete dependence and desire.

The theme of the wrong or displaced father is explicit in *Immortal Story* as well, where the primacy of money (over friendship rather than passion this time) once caused old Mr. Clay to drive away his partner, the father of Virginie. When he brings her back to her father's house (which Clay now occupies) to play out her role in his fable of seduction, he functions as a cruel "wrong father" over whom she is able to triumph. Throughout the Welles canon, fathers and mothers are doubled and tripled, offering, through displacement, the multiplications and contradictions of identity and representation. *Falstaff (Chimes at Midnight)* offers one of the richest and most fluid exercises in doubling and multiplicity of father/identity. Very early in the film we are presented with Falstaff as an old man who is at the same time an innocent, the one who has been shaped by the "son" he is supposed to have corrupted. As he tells us: "Before I knew thee, Hal, I knew nothing." Later on, Falstaff puts a pot on his head and plays the role of Hal's other father, the king, chastising the boy for his bad friends and wastrel's life. Then they change roles and Hal plays his own father, the king. All the way through the film, Hal's knowledge of his impending power as future king has run concurrent with his boyish playfulness and has made all his jokes and insults to Falstaff painfully cruel, as they now are in this exchange of roles. This cruelty is, of course, prophetic of his final assumption of a fixed identity as king, which entails the rejection of Falstaff after Hal has become his own father in earnest.

The main trajectory of the plot of *Citizen Kane, Magnificent Ambersons,* and *The Stranger* turns in on itself in the pattern of a return. The child/man, unable to continue his movement toward social participation and "maturity," falls back into a childhood situation, and the woman in *The Stranger* is forced into a similar return. In *Citizen Kane*, Charlie instantly defies his substitute father and the more or less innocent energy of this rebellion carries him well into young manhood. He travels, starts to run a newspaper, behaves like an aggressive young man in the world. This phase reaches a kind of peak in his "Declaration of Principles," where he lays down the law of the sons against the corrupt fathers of the money agencies (as Thatcher had earlier laid down the law of the "Trust" to his mother), his rebellious liberalism creating a link between the youthful and the poor. But he is not content to let the words and actions of the newspaper speak for themselves. He insists on foregrounding the enunciation, as it were, revealing himself as "author" of the newspaper, unmediated by an editorial persona. This authorial gesture is merely one of the ways that young Charles reveals his huge ambition. This boy, thrown out of many elegant schools, sees himself as becoming "champion of the people." His actions reveal the exaggerated picture he has of himself and his powers, which will later be revealed in the huge poster of himself at the rally, as he sets out to win everybody's love.

Love on a personal level reveals both his overarching aspirations *and* his limitations. The announcement of his engagement is read in a room full of statuary he has been sending to the office—"the loot of the world"—gifts given to no one, and never enough to fill the huge empty spaces that he and the others in his life will occupy as they grow older. In his bride to be, he has acquired another high element of culture—the president's niece. But like Isabel Amberson's, Charlie's attention is only briefly engaged by his new mate. McBride suggests that Charles has a need for affection that Emily "could not gratify," but I suggest that it is Kane who will not "gratify," turning from relations within his family to activities in which he need function only as a source of verbal or financial power, where he is never called upon to act as husband/lover/personal father. (In *Immortal Story*, Mr. Clay tells us that he has always avoided all personal relations and human emotions, which can "dissolve your bones.")

One night, his uncharged marriage a boring failure, his vaunting political ambitions uncertain, Charles decides to make a return to the place where his mother's goods, and his own truncated development, lie in storage. But instead, he is splashed by mud and because of this accident, the return is delayed. He comments to Susan on this deflection: "I was on my way to the Western Manhattan Warehouse—in search of my childhood."

Georgie Minafer's dream-like intimacy with his mother (as signalled by the long, slow take and dark depth of field) is suddenly threatened by a second father (the "right father?"), Eugene Morgan, who has made a return of his own. Morgan has come back to the town of his romantic defeat to try again with the soon-to-be-widowed Isabel, bringing with him a daughter (the mother is never mentioned) and a number of transformations that will be devastating for Georgie, who clings to his fixed identity as an Amberson. Trying to resist Eugene in the world of men, Georgie is ineffectual because of such misconceptions. He overestimates the power of his family identity to guarantee his superiority (or, indeed, his survival). He is wrong when he tries to ridicule Gene's invention of the automobile, and wrong again when he tries to enlist his father against the usurper by absurdly accusing him of wanting to borrow money. But he is not wrong with his mother. Oh, no. With Isabel, practically all he has to say is: "You're my mother," and she agrees to call it off with Eugene, despite his plea not to allow their romance to be ruined by "the history of your own perfect motherhood."

As in *Citizen Kane*, it is a sudden and unexpected change of fortune—this time a loss—that finally breaks up the family. Georgie is faced with an entirely new situation. He is alone and must support himself. His mother has died of a nameless wasting disease, having been devoured by Georgie's ravening orality. (All these Power Babies eat and eat.)[3] Furthermore, his Aunt Fanny, who has been a kind of shadowy mother double, loving instead of being loved, seeking instead of evading, who has lived only to yearn after Eugene and to feed Georgie, is now completely dependent upon him. As he goes out in the world, one prospective employer notes that he has become "the most practical young man," but only very, very briefly. Praying at his mother's empty bed, the new Georgie begs forgiveness from the Father of Fathers, but no fathers hear, for in the next cut, Georgie has an accident. An automobile knocks him down and breaks both his legs.

Let us recall here that Kane's son was killed in an automobile accident (which also claimed his wife) and that maiming of the legs is common in the Welles canon. Recall the extreme limp and double canes of Arthur Bannister in *Lady from Shanghai,* the greatly reduced mobility of Mr. Clay in *Immortal Story,* and perhaps most complex, the bullet in the leg that Quinlan took for his friend Pete Menzies in *Touch of Evil.* And if the leg wound can be taken as suggesting deflected or impeded sexuality, then we must note the role of Quinlan's cane in bringing about his downfall.

Georgie has always known where the danger lies. The first night he meets Eugene and Lucy, he denigrates the automobile and wishes her father would "forget about it." Later he scorns it as useless and, prophetically in more ways than one, says it should never have been invented. Georgie's insistent and perverse dismissal of this most powerful agent of transformation is, of course, thoughtless and superficial at the rational level; he appears foolish and self-defeating, moving his Uncle Jack to remark on how strange it is to woo a woman by insulting her father. But Georgie is reacting to the car as symbol of Gene's phallic power to take away the mother love on which Georgie sustains himself so voraciously and on which, as an untried emotional infant, he believes his life depends. While others enter into mature speculation about how the automobile will change the world—Eugene himself is most confident that it will: "There are no times but new times," he says—Georgie is terrified for his life. In his identity as a new man of the future, Eugene has benefitted from an exchange of power with the Ambersons; their great fortune is gone, their living space (the home, the woman's place) is taken away, while Eugene's fortunes rise, his factories and power transformers consuming the Amberson space and returning it as a city. To move from rural safety to urban danger, Georgie Minafer need only leave the house. In his own life and in the society at large, Georgie's world of women has given way to a world of men. This shift in economy threatens him at the deepest level. Georgie has begun to fear that he will soon take his "last walk," as the narrator puts it. In the reversal implied by his *seeking* a "dangerous job," Georgie signals us that his fear is becoming unbearably acute.

As the automobile accident fulfills Georgie's prophetic panic, he is returned to the state of complete dependency that marked his place in the family of origin. But this time, it is a strangely smiling Eugene Morgan upon whom he must depend. Worse than Georgie's worst fears, this outcome brings, not the death that might even be wished for, but a bitter substitute for the ecstatic plenitude of mother love. For Eugene, his rival/double, it constitutes a triumph.

As the new money and usurping father brought terror and helplessness to Georgie Minafer, they bring rage and isolation to Charles Foster Kane. Once a dirty accident has deflected him from his return and brought him together with Susan, their relationship takes a strange turn. Kane almost seems to act out the role of her mother. Susan's youth is established—"Pretty old. I'll be twenty-two in August"—and we learn that her mother had operatic aspirations for her small, untrue voice. Immediately after this revelation, we see several of the film's few conventional, romantic close-ups as Susan declares sweetly: "You know what mothers are like," and Kane answers dreamily: "Yes, I know." The mention of the mother is linked with the sign values of shallow depth, key and back lighting, and slightly soft focus, signalling Romance even more strongly than the early scene with Emily, and suggesting that Susan has tapped into Kane's deepest desires—perhaps a fantasy of a mother staying with a child, watching over it and nurturing it, causing it to grow and flourish. Susan's reaction to this impossible program is another matter, to be spoken of later.

The meeting with Boss Jim Gettys, the other key encounter of Kane's life, turns upon the role of yet another father in the family and in culture. As his mother and Mr. Thatcher seemed to be in cahoots long ago against the little boy whose weak and unreliable father did nothing to help him, now another Mrs. Kane and another usurping father move to dislodge him once again from a place where he is perhaps living out *all* the roles of his frozen moment, but according to a new script of his archaic desires.

With inadequate experience of father and family to mediate between his infant rage and the world of signification, Kane has imagined his rival Gettys as a monster and put that monstrous image into the public realm—newspaper pictures of Gettys "in a convict suit with stripes—so his children could see. . . . Or his mother."[4] Now Gettys must wipe out the representational power of these images. To do so, he must discredit Kane completely. Thus Gettys as powerful and successful father and son punishes Kane, not for his transgression with Susan, which stands in for the move against the father and which might have stayed a childish secret forever, but for his unbridled excess in attacking Gettys so viciously in the newspaper. Even so, Gettys is formidable but not cruel, urging Kane to do his duty and avoid family disaster by withdrawing from the race. Finally, when Kane can do nothing but scream his child-like defiance, Gettys's words are those of the elder instructing the younger: "You need more than one lesson, and you're gonna get more than one lesson." Like Georgie's, Kane's comeuppance has swept over him suddenly in a wild moment.

The image of Kane screaming down his impotent rage from the top of the steps suggests an attempt to reverse the size relations of the Christmas shot with Thatcher, and evokes similar images in a number of Welles's other films, most notably where his Macbeth, having destroyed a number of families, including that of the Kingdom itself, finally stands alone on the high wall, seeming to find a perverse ecstasy in his impotent defiance of Macduff, the outraged father (himself "untimely ripped") who has come to bring him down. In *The Stranger*, Charles Rankin, exposed as the Nazi Franz Kindler, screams down his defiance of Mr. Wilson, the Nazi-hunter/father figure, from the top of a clock tower.

Charlie Kane's impotent
defiance of Boss Jim Gettys

Kane's destruction of the bedroom after Susan leaves is perhaps the most famous scene of rage in American film. Kane had tried to insert himself into the
culture as a "celebrity" through public office—a space somewhere between that
of a commodity and a well-known friend or family member. To the child of
banks, being elected is perhaps like being loved. But his excess of anger cost him
that public affirmation. Now the saving fantasy with Susan has failed, bringing
on the wild rage. As he picks up the glass ball, Kane completes the return begun
on that night when he started for the warehouse. We have already seen Kane in
the newsreel with useless legs, swaddled in white like an old baby. The narrative will now offer no more events involving Kane before death causes him to
release his frozen scene of trauma. After he passes through the hall of mirrors,
the camera holds on the empty reflector; his identity is erased by its repetition.
As Baudry says: "An infinite mirror would no longer be a mirror."[5] With his
smooth head, pouting lips, and single tear, Kane is almost foetus-like, back in
a primordial isolation before language, before family, before self.

As Susan walks away from Kane (and from her doll, seen in the extreme foreground as they quarrel, and seen again next to Kane's sled among the final images—he longed for his; she didn't long for hers) she also walks away from the
return forced upon her by Kane. As indicated by her attempt at suicide, she

doesn't wish to continue as the child, living out her mother's fantasy or Charles's desire. Perhaps punished by her "alcoholism" for her aggressiveness in leaving Kane, certainly childishly imprudent in having spent all the money, Susan's real return has been to her position within another social class. But she is surviving, capable of working, playing, and feeling deep sympathy. Lucy Morgan in *Magnificent Ambersons* is also forced into a return, but a far more regressive one, and certainly of a different style. Georgie wouldn't enter the world of men and money, and Lucy certainly couldn't join him in the closed world of mother love. Therefore, as she tells him, "Because we couldn't play together like good children, we shouldn't play at all." In an idyllic out-of-doors scene, paralleling the one in which Morgan tried to convince Isabel to marry him, Lucy describes her situation to her father in the story of Ven Do Nah. This Indian was hated by all his tribe, so they drove him away. But they couldn't find a replacement they liked better. "They couldn't help it." So Lucy declares her intention to stay in the garden with her father for the rest of her life: "I don't want anything but you."

In several of Welles's films, a daughter, having made the wrong sexual choice, must return to the father. Perhaps the success of the fathers represents a displacement of the Power Baby's desired return, a metonymy in which the intensely longed-for power is muted as it moves into the quiet certainty and control of imagined patriarchal authority (yet another move in the representation of the diffuse subject). The most extreme version of the daughter's situation is developed in *The Stranger*. Mary Longstreet has chosen as her sexual partner not a dependent infant, not a half-baked crook like the daughter (of a white slaver) in *Mr. Arkadin*, but the worst possible enemy of everyone in the whole world—a NAZI! And how could this perfectly nice girl make this bizarre choice, which even her brother can't believe: "Gee, Mr. Wilson, you must be wrong. Mary wouldn't fall in love with that kind of a man." But Nazi-hunting father doubles like Mr. Wilson are not wrong. "That's the way it is," he later says, because "people can't help who they fall in love with." For "people," of course, read "women." (Remember Lucy and Ven Do Nah?)

This odd choice (and the presence of a Nazi in this New England town in the first place) can perhaps be understood by recognizing Kindler as representing difference, not only because he is a German, but in another way, because he is so closely associated with Mary. She is isolated in her connection with him. Only she has chosen him; only she supports him. In a strange way, he represents her insofar as she is one who makes a sexual choice. He is Mary's difference. For fathers, and for small-town America, this difference must be contained. In this deeply conservative film, Kindler's/Mary's difference must bring about his own downfall and her return. But his difference will also be recuperated. His exotic European hobby of fixing clocks will reinvigorate rural American tradition and law, as represented by the old town clock with its scenes of justice and revenge.

Control of the woman:
The Stranger

Wilson neatly describes the trajectory of the film: "Mary must be shown what kind of man she married, even though she'll resist hearing anything bad about Charles." And despite this resistance, they are sure that her "subconscious" is their "ally," that deep inside her she has a strong "will to truth." This resource of unconscious health will, of course, lead her to relinquish her own willful difference and allow herself to be returned to her father. Thus family (again with no mother) and town will return to their original situation. A triumph of personal and social stasis.

Touch of Evil offers a more ambiguous answer to the question: can the continued presence of woman-as-difference be tolerated? One of the strangest features of this film is the often comical forced separation of Suzie and Vargas which results from the pervasive contradiction between power and impotence, the search for and denial of sexual difference in Quinlan's character. Quinlan's regression to murder and other acts of vengeance was apparently triggered by the transgression of his young wife (with a sailor, as in *Immortal Story* and *Lady from Shanghai*). He now seeks to rewrite his own history by preventing Vargas (the double of his younger, potent self) from taking the risks of coupling. Having become a candy eater whose memory of sexuality draws him into Tanya's place, Quinlan now tries to hold on to his conservative power, which effaces sexual difference in his second partnership—with Pete Menzies—in his racism, and in his excessive acts of fixing the fate of all transgressors (they are all "guilty as hell"). We must remember that the entire action of the film was triggered by the murder of a father by his daughter's Mexican lover—from the point of view of the father, so to speak, surely a wrong choice and indication of the dangers of difference. Thus Suzie, the often absurd woman-as-sexual-difference, is drugged, and possibly raped (though even this sexuality is denied; she is lifted off the bed at the peak of the orgy scene, thus substantially altering the logistics of rape) and almost killed for expressing desire in the way she looks and acts. Throughout the film, she is pressured by both her husband and Quinlan's people to give up the promise of sexuality and return across the border to the U.S., to "safety," to the known, the predictable, the place of before-her-sexuality—the place, ostensibly, of her father. Mexico itself, like Vargas the Mexican, represents the exercise of difference, which is constantly exploding and making trouble. In the end, it is only partially controlled. When Suzie is finally reunited with Vargas in the car, his first moves toward her are not sexual, but like those of a child who needs to lean on his mother's breast. Yet the fact of the reconciliation itself implies that the conservative force of return has been resisted to some extent. Difference has been allowed some play.

In *The Stranger,* the control of the woman is far more complete. The dangers of active female sexuality and choice-making take on the resonance of a national and cultural disaster. Mary's father is a New England Supreme Court Justice named Adam, and her brother is named Noah. To defy them is to endanger all that's best in American culture and in the Bible as well. To prevent this, to bring the daughter back into the fold, the two fathers, Justice Longstreet and Detective Wilson, are willing to take extreme risks—with Mary's life, that is. They decide that Kindler's attempt to kill her will be the best "evidence" to convince her of whom she has really married, so they decide to use her as bait. Wilson: "Naturally, we'll try to prevent murder being done. . . . He may kill her. You're shocked at my cold-bloodedness. That's quite natural. You're the father. . . ." Thus the fathers are split so that one can be conventionally horrified at the lengths to which the other is willing to go to bring her back into line. Then, since no other proof against Kindler exists, the gathering of evidence becomes a matter of watching Mary. Wilson: "From now on, we must know every move that Mrs. Rankin makes." Fathers, brother, and servant combine to watch and control her, but even so, she eludes them, rushing off through the graveyard to kill or be killed on the clock tower. In the end, at the top of the tower, the Nazi gets his comeuppance, brought about by the fathers, but executed by a female avenging angel just as deadly as the daughter in *Touch of Evil.* Kindler is impaled on the sword of the clockwork angel, screaming in pain during this dreadful parody of an embrace. Kindler deserves it, of course, at the rational plot level. But the point is that in these films, the aroused woman, the sign of difference as danger, evoking the threat of lack (inadequacy?), is not often so genteel as Lucy in *Magnificent Ambersons.* It is usually a struggle to force her into passivity and return, and often a lethal one.

The conservativism revealed in some of these narratives is often contradicted in the films' means of expression, which is also marked by a kind of excess. It is, of course, well known that in the Welles films, the conventions of classical cinema are either abandoned or exaggerated to fascinating extremes. The discreetly moving or subjective camera, the illusion of three-dimensionality through depth of field, become the bizarre angles, sweeping crane shots, and dwarfing depth and scale that mark several of these texts. Even expressionistic features are taken further as light and shadow become patches of saturated darkness and blinding brightness. *Citizen Kane* particularly is marked by the excitement of what Julia Kristeva calls "an excess of visual traces useless for the sheer identification of objects."[6] In the projection room sequence, where light is used not to illuminate, but as having sign value in itself, and in other sequences like the travelling shot up the facade and through the sign of Susan's night club, and the shot up to the stagehand "critics" at the Opera House, these visual excesses and special effects convey a pleasure taken at the point of enunciation, an exuberance in the aggressive wielding of the language of film. Like Charles with his "Declaration of Principles," this enunciation declares itself boldly.

Later on, as Kane receives his "more than one lesson," the power of youth to transform aggressiveness into exuberance seems diminished and the tone changes. In relation to the negative narrative changes that they mark in scenes like the party with the dancing girls or Susan's suicide attempt, the wide-angle lens and extreme camera positions now seem to invite reading as signals of distress, an enunciative energy somehow grown perverse. Sometimes, as in the eerie, empty space of Jed Leland's hospital, visual work and characterization would suggest that seeing has now become the mutual recognition of grotesquery. The long, slow-moving, sinuous takes in *Magnificent Ambersons*, particularly in the party sequence, suggest not freedom of choice in processing a simulacrum of reality,[7] but enunciative awareness of the hopelessly desirable dream of seamless flow and oneness in the world of the mother. This movement is prefigured in the flowing overhead shots of Kane's fragmented plenitude at the end of *Kane,* and would have been even more pronounced in its seemingly endless withholding of expected cuts in the party sequence had the film been released as Welles intended, with reel-length shots during this portion of the film.

The excess of these images also raises the question of "evidence," which is central to a number of Welles films and which becomes dominant in all the foregrounded systems of *F for Fake*. In the projection room sequence of *Kane,* for instance, light is the elusive stuff of which delusive biography is made, no more reliable than the various embedded tales of unfulfilled desire (Leland's, Susan's, Bernstein's—remember the girl in white on the ferry boat?) that make up the film's narrative. Excessive light and shadow actually deny access to images as representations, and raise the question of how they can be used as evidence, and evidence of what, setting the act of seeing over against the structuring absence of knowledge or explanation. In *The Stranger,* though Wilson offers Mary filmed images of the concentration camps as evidence of her husband's evil, he does not let them stand on their own. Instead, he places himself in the image or projects the images onto himself, making his body and the field of his features into the evidence, as if asserting: "Even if the images are functional representations, trust and believe *me*. I who speak am the greater authority." *The Stranger* is one of Welles's more visually and narratively conventional films. As its "realism" is less distressed, so the power of the law is not undermined. Wilson's authority as enunciator of diegetic truth is allowed to remain, at the partial cost of Welles's authority and presence as the film's enunciator. We observe a similar substitution of bodies (Hastler's and K's) for the "pin-screen" images of the "Law" fable where Hastler is trying to convince K of its immutability in *The Trial*. As Mary's body was to be watched for the invocation of evidence in *The Stranger,* so Virginie's sexual act will become the "final evidence" of Clay's guilt in *The Immortal Story*. And Pete Menzies's wiretapped body becomes the site of aural evidence in *Touch of Evil*, the reliability of so-called "concrete" evidence having been disposed of in the planting of the dynamite and in the history of Quinlan's entire career of manipulating "evidence." The authority of the enunciation, the aggressiveness of the intention, is substituted for the trustworthiness of the evidence itself (perhaps suggestive of the particular way in which Welles has loved to use make-up as clearly enunciated, nonrealistic masking throughout his career, combining the contradictory qualities of an identity always recognized and a disguise insisted upon with equal clarity).

The figure of the Power Baby condenses certain irreconcilable contradictions and diffusions that we have been examining in plot, character, and visual development. These can be represented through various discourses about the subversion of the unified subject. The Power Baby's constitution in doubleness is exaggerated by the failure of the family experience to mitigate the father-related excess and rage on the one hand, and the mother-related helpless dependency on the other. The family's failure, in turn, is often seen as produced not only by the woman's ability to confound the issue of paternity in a number of different ways, but also by the changing patterns of money and urbanization at different points in American history, by the ideologies that say banks are better than families for promoting children, that move Isabel to choose Wilbur Minafer, that conflate law and vengeance in border towns.

As we learn from the voice-over narrator at the beginning of *Magnificent Ambersons*, this ideology uses fashion, money, and media to create the only possible categories of identity into which the sexed subject must be forced. It also conflates female sexuality and lethal threats by posing difference as danger or disruption that is sometimes fully contained, sometimes a little too powerful for conservative strategies, and sometimes ironically (*Immortal Story*) or fully (*F for Fake*) triumphant.

In each Power Baby, we have found an imagined social self with aspirations to greatness and total love that can only be dreams, founded in misrecognitions of both self and the social world. These mistakes are perfectly expressed in *Immortal Story,* where the clerk, Levinsky, tells us that Mr. Clay wants "to demonstrate his omnipotence—to do the thing which cannot be done." And within the "I" together with this overreaching social self, one and the same and

The Immortal Story

yet another, is a wildly flailing infant (we see him destroy Susan's room) fixed in incomprehension, terror, and rage, who returns to undo all social work and to reduce the organism to blank helplessness: the Wellesian "I" as the extremes of power and powerlessness.

The various stories of the Power Baby can also be seen as the refusal of the subject to be constituted in continuous narrative. Both Charles and Georgie are presented through versions of the *Bildung* structure that typically would move the subject from childhood through young manhood to "maturity." This form carries the conventional assumption of the infant born in powerlessness, a tabula rasa who gains experience and knowledge that become integrated into the increasing wisdom and power of the mature self. Thus in the insistence on the return to earlier scenes and conditions, these narratives deny this trajectory, using the *Bildung* narrative no less ironically than that of the retrospective biography.

For himself, his family, and his women, the Power Baby refuses the myth of personal harmony. Sometimes struggling for conservation and stasis, sometimes, as in *F for Fake,* flaunting multiplicity and difference, Welles the enunciator asserts the primacy of the individual without the comfort of the unified self.

NOTES

1. At least ten years ago, Stanley Crouch, then of Pomona College, now of the *Village Voice*, called me up in the middle of the night to discuss some Welles films we had recently seen. Then, as now, the urgency of a 3 a.m. phone call on this subject seemed perfectly reasonable, and our conversation began to move my thoughts in their present direction.

2. *Orson Welles* (New York: Viking Press, 1972), p. 43.

3. Freud sees this characteristic as signalling an infantile fixation in the "'cannibalistic' or 'oral' phase, during which the original attachment of sexuality to the nutritional instincts still dominates the scene." "From the History of an Infantile Neurosis (The Wolf Man)," *Three Case Histories* (New York: Macmillan, Collier Books, 1963), p. 299.

4. In his analysis of "The Wolf Man," Freud notes that "a father is the prototype . . . of the caricatures that are drawn to bring derision upon someone." *Three Case Histories*, p. 256.

5. Jean-Louis Baudry, "Ideological Effects of the Basic Cinematographic Apparatus," *Film Quarterly* (Winter 1974–75), p. 45.

6. "Ellipsis on Dread and the Specular Seduction," *Wide Angle*, Vol. 3, no. 3 (1979), pp. 42–47.

7. For a discussion of Welles's films in terms of realism, however, see André Bazin, *Orson Welles* (New York: Harper & Row, 1978). For further discussion of all aspects of Welles's work and biography, see: Joseph McBride (see note 2); Ronald Gottesman, ed., *Focus on Orson Welles* (New Jersey: Prentice-Hall, Inc., 1976); James Naremore, *The Magic World of Orson Welles* (New York: Oxford Univ. Press, 1978); Charles Higham, *The Films of Orson Welles* (Berkeley: Univ. of Calif. Press, 1970); Pauline Kael, *The CITIZEN KANE Book* (Boston: Little, Brown, 1971); Peter Cowie, *A Ribbon of Dreams: The Cinema of Orson Welles* (New York: A. S. Barnes, 1973); Peter Bogdanovich, *The Cinema of Orson Welles* (New York: Museum of Modern Art, 1961); Robert Carringer, "Rosebud Dead or Alive: Narrative and Symbolic Structure in *Citizen Kane*," *PMLA* (March 1976).

I should like to thank the UCLA film archive for its generous cooperation in providing me access to these films.

LEONARD J. LEFF

READING *KANE*

All this happened in much less time than it takes to tell, since I am trying to in-terpret for you into slow speech the instantaneous effect of visual impressions.

JOSEPH CONRAD, *HEART OF DARKNESS*

Vol. 39, no. 1 (Fall 1985): 10–21.

Charles Foster Kane's second wife has left him. In mute frustration, he throws down her suitcases and begins wrecking her overdecorated bedroom. When he comes to a glass paperweight, he stops. He shakes it and says, offscreen, "Rosebud." With his butler and other servants watching silently, he walks into one corridor, then another, out of his employees' range of vision, until he passes between two full-length mirrors. This last image of Charles Foster Kane is multiplied again and again into infinity, a powerful envoi to *Citizen Kane*'s visualization of its main character.

After Kane walks offscreen, emptying the frame of people, the camera slowly advances toward the mirror. The mirror cannot reflect Kane's servants, for they have been left behind in an adjacent corridor; but since it is a mirror and has reflected Kane's image, it must reflect something. As the camera continues its forward progress, it promises to expose—what? Raymond, the flashback's putative author? The narrator? The camera? The spectator? Here we directly confront two questions: Who is the arranger of the images? And who is watching the film? In the following essay, I wish to explore the reasons that previous answers to these questions have seemed somehow unsatisfying; I would also like to suggest a method of reading *Citizen Kane* that will allow us to understand our reactions to the film even if it does not permit us to speak conclusively of the "meaning" of the film and its surprisingly inconstant point of view.

Although critics Bruce Kawin, Nick Browne, Seymour Chatman, Brian Henderson, and others have at length discussed point of view as well as the relationship between point of view and the spectator, Kawin has focused specifically on *Citizen Kane*. (See the "Works Cited" at the conclusion of this essay.) *Kane* portrays its narrators in the third person, Kawin says in *Mindscreen: Bergman, Godard, and First-Person Film*, but accords their narratives a first-person bias. In Thatcher's story, for example, the banker's "narrating mind is offscreen. The film presents not Kane's life with Thatcher in third-person flashback but Thatcher's tale (which is presumed to be both biased and accurate) in mind-screen" (34); consequently, we understand Thatcher's intent through his deployment of camera position, montage, etc., and recognize through "the logic of their changes" his narrative bias (14).

But are *Kane*'s narrators capable of generating the film's often sophisticated *mise-en-scène*? In his interview with the *News on the March* reporter, the butler reveals an inarticulateness (Kane "did crazy things sometimes"), a limited vocabulary, a tendency to repeat himself, and a condescension toward his employer that make him, at best, a doubtful author of the "infinity of Kanes" image and its provocative coda. Thatcher's flashback presents similar problems. Through studied compositions that use deep focus, forceful images outside the banker's ken, and shots or sounds obviously from another character-narrator's sensibility, Thatcher's flashback posits the voices of other characters as well as that of a "supra-narrator," an awkward but necessary term in discussing *Citizen Kane*'s layered text. At some point in each of the flashbacks, not only does each narrator relate events at which he or she was not present, each also employs a visual and narrative style wholly at odds with his or her personality or state of mind. What these shifts in point of view *mean*, however, may ultimately matter less than what they *do*. To demonstrate, I turn to a stimulating if controversial methodology articulated by literary critic Stanley Fish.

For Fish, author of *Is There a Text in This Class? The Authority of Interpretive Communities* (1980), a text does not contain meaning, a reader produces it. Books are thus *objects* that readers translate into *events*. Consider the final line in Milton's "On His Blindness": "They also serve who only stand and wait." How far, we wish to know, has the speaker moved from an earlier impatience with God? To some Milton scholars, this line constitutes a profound trust in God; to others, a qualified, perhaps even forced note of affirmation. According to Fish, however, no conclusions are possible. Reading "On His Blindness" line by line, we execute a series of assumptions about the speaker and his relationship with God, each of which is undercut and no one of which is determinant. In short, the reader's experience of the uncertainty of the sonnet's last line constitutes the poem's very meaning. The parallels between literature and film are at once implicit and attractive.

Answering their detractors, reader-response critics like Fish have carefully defined "the reader." In the examination of *Citizen Kane* that follows, I have stipulated a composite "we" modelled after Michael Riffaterre's reader of "Les Chats," an informed "we" alert to what one of the cinema's most stimulating works *does*. Just as the *News on the March* reporter negotiates the post-Kane world, we negotiate *Kane;* we engage in a series of anticipations, reversals, revisions, and recoveries that forces us to examine the cognitive tasks that we as readers perform and that finally urges us to assume our role in the work's creation. The reporter opens his investigation into the mystery of Rosebud by reading a manuscript whose "objectness" is exaggerated during its presentation. He expects the diary to "make sense," but it does not: readers make sense, not texts. Accordingly, as we make our way through a "slowed down" version of a *Kane* flashback, we may evaluate each shift in point of view as it occurs and thereby not extract a meaning from the sequence but, instead, locate the moments that frustrate assumptions or expectations about point of view, describe our experience of those moments, and discover in them how if not what *Citizen Kane* means.

"She won't talk," Thompson tells his boss after his first visit to Susan Alexander Kane. Thompson's search (really Rawlston's search, for Thompson resists going) takes the reporter from the El Rancho nightclub and its torpid singer to the Thatcher Memorial Library and the marble statue of its benefactor, Walter Parks Thatcher; thus the image of a woman who will not communicate fades to the image of a man who cannot communicate. Neither augurs well for solving the mystery of Rosebud. A litany of restrictions on hours, page numbers, and quoted matter precedes Thompson's entrance through a door that closes in our face. We read this last action as prohibiting *our* entrance. Almost at once, though, the image of the door dissolves to that of the library's inner sanctum. Outside Hollywood, to dissolve means to disintegrate, disunite, break up; the film's dissolve here does indeed separate us from our *expectation* of denied admittance, but it does not alter the *experience* of denied admittance. *Citizen Kane* continually draws us on. Will we come to know Kane or will we not? Will the film "let us in" or will it not? This and countless other moments in *Citizen Kane*, including the revelation of the flaming sled, suspend the answer, at last indefinitely. But even if we decide that we know something of Kane (or Rosebud or the little glass snow scene), the impediments to that knowledge remain part of our reading experience. In the conclusion of the essay, the implications of this point will be examined.

Aside from a portrait of Thatcher, the reading room qua vault houses the library's meager collection—one book, a "private diary." The setting's rigidity, formality, and containment suggest that even if Thatcher knew the secret of Rosebud, he might not divulge it. Nevertheless, the guard extracts the manuscript from the wall safe and, accompanied by a deathly cadence, bears it to Thompson. The library's pretensions are borne out in the halation of the diary, which along with the dramatic ritual of the receptionist and the guard may amuse us. Yet the presentation of the diary mirrors in reverse the door shut in our face; where the door frustrated our expectation of intimate knowledge of Kane, the diary promises it. "Thompson bends over to read the manuscript," states the shooting script. "Camera moves down over his shoulder onto page of manuscript" (168). Thompson, his face never seen, remains in shadow throughout the film; at once there and not there, he approaches the embodiment of what the Germans call the "fiktiver Leser"—the "fictive reader." In going "over his shoulder" to reach the narrative agency, a script direction that the film heeds and replicates with each succeeding internal narrator, camera movement denotes a text reached *through* Thompson and explicitly *read* by him. We are to identify not with Thompson but with his task, reading.

We begin our reading, literally, with the section of the Thatcher manuscript entitled "Charles Foster Kane." Thompson quickly scans a prefatory note that we hardly see, much less read. (From its text, which can be read when the film is run frame by frame, one understands at once that Thatcher's diary is really a memoir, a recollection of events written well after the date of their occurrence.) Then, at a slower speed, the camera sweeps across a page, directing us to read, "I first encountered Mr. Kane in 1871." Despite the third-person title, "Charles Foster Kane," the narrative has opened in the first person. "I," stirring a nascent assumption about tellers telling their own tales, suggests that the story will center on Thatcher, rather than "Charles Foster Kane," not a hopeful sign for a reporter or a viewer in search of an intimate view of Kane. From the news short, we know that young Charles Kane assaulted Thatcher upon their first meeting; the banker's use of "encountered" connotes also the immediate adversial relationship between the two. "Mr. Kane," referring to Charles when he was a boy, reinforces "encountered" as a lexical gesture of contempt. In short, by the time the shot of the sentence begins to dissolve, we have reached an assumption about the forthcoming image, conventionally the opening of a flashback. "I," "encountered," and "Mr. Kane" have established the emotional distance and dissonance between the writer and his fractious subject. Along with the author's personality as indicated by the surroundings and the news short, the diction promises us a ponderous, self-serving narrative, wholly without sympathy for young Kane and dominated by Thatcher's jaundiced perspective.

The opening of the Thatcher section, focusing on the young Charles Kane playing in the snow, has a distinct point of view. But whose is it? Bruce Kawin argues that each of the film's narrators maintains his equivalent of "first-person discourse"; without distortion, "Thatcher's mind dominates those portions of the film that relate his part of Kane's story" (34–35). Our moment-to-moment experience of the sequence, though, suggests a disquiet overlooked in Kawin's interpretation. In *The Magic World of Orson Welles*, James Naremore sees what happens: "At first the black dot, against pure white [Charles against the snow] echoes the manuscript we have been looking at, but it swoops across the screen counter to the direction the camera has been moving, in conflict with the stiff, prissy, banker's handwriting, suggesting the conflict between Kane and Thatcher that runs through the early parts of the movie" (41). During the dissolve from the library to Colorado, we experience a shift in expression, if not also perspective. The lighting, the music, and the very content of the opening shot argue against Thatcher's authorship. Music keyed to the gloom of the banker and his memorial, for example, lightens at Charles's appearance. A crisp three-note refrain, delicately percussive, becomes a satiny theme played legato on the strings; along with a glissando on the harp, it introduces not "Mr. Kane" but a carefree child, at one (Ira Jaffe says in "Film as the Narration of Space") with the natural universe (103). Charles's initial depiction and especially the romantic music accompanying it void our assumption that "Thatcher's mind" exercises sovereignty over his narrative.

As the spirited young boy continues playing his Civil War game, the camera draws back to reveal, sequentially, Charles's mother, future guardian, and father standing at the Kanes' window, through which we and—we now discover—they have been looking. The framing of the youth, walling him at once in and out, has been variously interpreted; Jaffe, for example, suggests that the camera's movement fixes Charles and renders "his physical existence suddenly . . . exceedingly fragile" (104). But what do the appearance of additional characters in the scene and the camera movement that effects it *do*? At first, especially as we reflect on the contrasts in music and lighting on either side of the dissolve, we perceive the scene as narrated not by Thatcher but by a supranarrator. The moving camera's introduction of Mrs. Kane, however, causes us to revise: all along, apparently, the image of the happy child has been from his mother's perceptual point of view, one that seemingly unites the perspective and the expression. Or has it? The continued reverse tracking of the camera soon adds Thatcher to the frame. Like the weak-willed Jim Kane, he looks at Mrs. Kane, not Charles. Though she may dominate Charles ("Be careful, Charles. . . . Pull your muffler around your neck, Charles"), Thatcher dominates her. His mindscreen manifests itself not only in the room's gloomy atmosphere (which we gradually see) but in his direction of the scene's focus away from matters of the heart and toward the affairs of business: "Mrs. Kane," he says, "I think we'll have to tell him now." Mary Kane accedes. In the course of sixty seconds, the film has offered us three different points of view—a narrator's, Mary Kane's, and Thatcher's. Although we are back where we began, those moments when our assumptions about the narrative proved premature, if not false, remain part of our experience of *Citizen Kane*.

As Mrs. Kane turns from the window, she faces Thatcher, their profiles opposite one another in the frame. "I'll sign those papers now, Mr. Thatcher," she says, and begins to walk forward. Her fixed expression, a triumph of determination over emotion, seems to drive the camera down a path that she has willed it to travel. But when the camera comes to rest, we recognize that its

Welles shooting the
first Thatcher scene

movement from the window has been constant and that it has led unfailingly
toward the papers, Thatcher's papers, awaiting their signature. Thatcher con-
centrates on financial decisions, Kawin says, "not just because he is Kane's
banker but because he is *a* banker" (33); the inevitability of the camera's direction, we assume, relocates the perspective and the expression in a single
mindscreen, Thatcher's. A stable camera, providing us with the first of the celebrated deep-focus shots in *Citizen Kane,* now clearly frames four characters:
Mary Kane renouncing her son, Thatcher busily pushing the papers to her, Jim
Kane pacing in the middle ground, and Charles—to whom all except us seem
oblivious—playing happily in the snow. Once again, though, the point of view
and the voice have splintered. A banker of narrow vision, Thatcher is incapable of generating the contrasts and emotions so richly elaborated through
the use of deep focus. Meticulously organized, this long-enduring shot has an
"authoritarian effect," James Naremore says, "the actors and the audience
under fairly rigid control" (42–43). *Whose* control matters less than the implications of the shift: our assumption again proves erroneous, our expectation
unfulfilled. Less than a minute into the flashback, the perceptual and the "interest" points of view as well as the perspective and the expression have fused

and diverged more than three times. From whose point of view is Thatcher's story told? Our experience of the text makes any response problematic.

Having signed the papers, Mrs. Kane returns to the window. The camera, via a cut, points into the house from its position at the porch. Mrs. Kane's previous insistence on orchestrating the event ("It's going to be done exactly the way I've told Mr. Thatcher"), her resolve ("I've had [his trunk] packed for a week now"), and her expression make her the scene's dramatic center. Although deep focus is again employed, the composition offers us little of interest beyond the foreground and Mrs. Kane. Jim Kane and Thatcher stand in the middle distance where, uncharacteristically for this narrator, Thatcher hesitantly remains. Mrs. Kane's seemingly blank expression draws significance from the music, somber chords in the low register of the strings. She responds to Thatcher's comments on the practical aspects of Charles's departure, but her thoughts are obviously elsewhere. This time, the camera moves only after she does. When Mrs. Kane turns screen left to walk outside, the camera tracks left to follow her. The prevailing mindscreen seems hers. The pan across the log face of the house cuts off Thatcher in the middle of a speech: "I've arranged for a tutor to meet us in Chicago. I'd have brought him along with me. . . ." The banker chooses his words too carefully and regards himself as too important to leave any thought incomplete; the interruption of a line of his dialogue does nothing to reestablish his mindscreen. But neither does it support our assumption that Mrs. Kane narrates. We could read the incident as a representation of Mrs. Kane's selective hearing, her preoccupation with Charles obliterating the world around her. The music does suggest this continuity in point of view. The disappearance of the dialogue track, however, directly parallels only those moments when Thatcher and Mrs. Kane are out of view and thus suggests a narrating presence outside of both characters. The suspension of sound might thus signal the return of the supra-narrator or—as the camera's placement outdoors may already have anticipated—the emergence of Charles.

When Mrs. Kane exits from the door, she calls, "Charles." Her son replies from off-screen, "Lookee, Ma." Charles beckons his mother and readies us to see what he sees, perhaps *as* he sees. The camera, already outside, pulls back to position itself just behind Charles. Mrs. Kane, the only character inadequately dressed for the cold (a noteworthy point), says, "You better come inside, son." The camera's deference toward Mrs. Kane (though outside, it has centered on her) and the association of Charles with the natural world (he has even a snowy complexion) as well as his insistence that we see what he sees lend each character some claim to point of view. Just as we are tempted to anticipate the dominance of one or the other, Thatcher steps forward: "Well, well, well, that's quite a snowman." In this shot, which lacks multiplaned clarity and momentarily the

Citizen Kane

scene's expressive music, an ingratiating man tries to cajole a peevish child into the adult world ("Now can we shake hands . . . what do you say? Let's shake"). The camera foregrounds the action and moves only to contain it. The image of Charles's assault on the unsuspecting banker, photographed efficiently, with no musical accompaniment, seems derived from Thatcher's mindscreen. For only the second time in the scene, we have the sense that the putative narrator and the actual narrator are one.

At Jim Kane's awkward attempt to strike Charles ("what that kid needs is a good thrashing"), Mrs. Kane enfolds her son in her arms. All of the scene's conflict between mother and father and, later, guardian and child has not obscured a question that we have been formulating and that now will be answered: why is Mrs. Kane sending away her son? The film cuts to a tight close-up of her, accompanied by a musical crescendo, as she says: Charles is "going to be brought up where [his father] can't get at him." Many consider her reason inadequate, yet it supports a common assumption about the flashback. Along with Kawin, virtually every critic regards Thatcher as the scene's constant narrator. ("The point is not that Thatcher is photographed from outside his physical viewpoint," Kawin says, "but that every scene corresponds with his personal conception of Kane, and illustrates this conception rather than subjectively records 'what happened'" [34].) If we truly regarded Thatcher as the narrator of the moment being discussed, we would celebrate Mrs. Kane's chilly response because its very tenuousness validates Thatcher as narrator. She translates her feelings into a pragmatic business decision that Thatcher would understand, accept, and unemphatically report. But the cut to the close-up does something that no critic has acknowledged: it compromises Thatcher's mindscreen. The transfer of guardianship represents the banker's opportunity to manage a fortune, period. He has no interest in probing for the situation's psychological dimension, the possible but unarticulated reasons underlying Mrs. Kane's decision. His sensibility calls for retention of the long shot, an appropriate distance for incorporating but not highlighting what Mrs. Kane says.

More than a division between the perspective and the expression, the close-up of Mrs. Kane and the evocative music originate with a narrator eager or prepared for her response; they focus our attention exquisitely and ready us for emotions laid bare, for intimate truth. When the dialogue frustrates that expectation, we are left with a problem that the text has raised but declined to solve. Here the critics have stepped in. "The accident which made the Kanes suddenly rich," Joseph McBride explains in *Orson Welles,* "has its own fateful logic—Charles must 'get ahead'" (43). In "Power and Dis-Integration in the Films of Orson Welles," Beverle Houston argues that Mrs. Kane exacts a "cruel pleasure" by defeating the prerogative of husband and son; in her action lies "the hint of a revenge" (3). These and other interpretations, though not unreasonable, miss the point. At this moment, the text has slipped out of our control: we may not say with any certainty why Mrs. Kane sends away her son. To insist upon one reason over another is to attempt to return the responsibility for meaning to the text when it belongs with the reader. Our experience of the apparent inadequacy of Mrs. Kane's response coupled with the shift in point of view is finally the meaning of this moment in *Citizen Kane.*

Mrs. Kane explains her reason for sending away Charles and turns toward him. Moving—not tilting—down, the camera exchanges a close-up of the mother for one of the child. Charles's scowl as he looks up initially suggests again Thatcher's mindscreen. A downward angle of the camera rather than an eye-level shot would underscore this point, but Charles's defiant expression surely squares with Thatcher's perception of him. May we be sure, however, that Charles glowers at Thatcher? The boy's glance up and right could be directed at Jim Kane, who just now verbally and (almost) physically abused him and who now stands at Thatcher's immediate left. Whether Thatcher or Kane, the object of Charles's scorn becomes an ambiguity that we expect to be resolved. Jean-Pierre Oudart and Daniel Dayan's theory of the "absent one," set forth in "The Tutor-Code of Classical Cinema," suggests that the next cut (or, alternatively, further movement of the camera) will provide the necessary reaction shot. If Jim Kane is its subject, it will support Mrs. Kane's explanation for apparently spurning Charles, a justification that Thatcher would be likely to accept at face value and duly report. If Thatcher is its subject, it will reveal yet a different object of the hostile young Kane's wrath. Thatcher's mind-screen, of course, could project either shot.

From Charles's sullen face, the film cuts to neither Thatcher nor the father. Instead, it dissolves to the boy's sled. The sound of a train whistle far in the distance, connoting Kane and his guardian's movement east, temporally links Thatcher to the on-screen image; the insistent, hurrying whistle punctuates his earlier haste to catch the train. But even though the sound track might reflect Thatcher's aural perspective, the imagery makes his origination of the shot problematic. To Thatcher, the sled is a weapon in his "encounter" with "Mr. Kane"; he refuses even to discuss the sled when directly questioned about it during a congressional investigation (depicted in the *News on the March* short). The tremulous music and the long duration of the shot (actually two shots subtly joined by a dissolve) give the image an almost melancholy placidity, one whose tone conflicts with the banker's attitude toward Charles and his desire to put Colorado behind them. So the dissolve from Charles's face to the sled not only frustrates our expectation that we will discover the object of the boy's scorn but also calls into question Thatcher's mindscreen.

The image of the sled could well be Mrs. Kane's projection. Throughout the preceding scene, she has frequently appeared distant. When she watches Charles playing in the snow ("I've got his trunk all packed"), her look is fixed, contemplative. The sled tells us nothing more about why she sends away her son, but in its lingering stillness, perhaps evoking the absent boy, it seems a perfect object of her gaze. And though Thatcher has gone, the Colorado setting remains, making her a viable choice as narrator. Because it follows the shot of Charles's face, however, the image of the sled could also be his projection. Earlier we felt the imminence of his mind's eye; perhaps here we discover not *who* he looks at but *what,* in mindscreen. In the parlor car with Thatcher, listening to the plaintive whistle of the train carrying him far from home, he might be thinking of the sled. Read from his mental perspective, the image might seem to embody his loneliness. Finally, of course, a supra-narrator might generate the image of the sled. In tone, it resembles many similar shots in the film's opening scene, presumably authored by the supra-narrator; like them, it is bracketed by dissolves and accompanied by an unmelodic musical theme. In brief, the shot of the sled proceeds from an author whom we may not identify with any certainty. The shot thus doubly frustrates expectation.

In the next scene, we see paper being torn from a package. A still youthful Charles is opening his Christmas present, a new sled. "Well, Charles," Thatcher says offscreen. A pause follows this line, which concludes, "Merry Christmas." "Well, Charles," the line may mean, "here's exactly what you asked for." This scene privileges Charles: a head-on shot of him looking up at Thatcher concludes with a tilt up to a low-angle shot of Thatcher looming over him. Thatcher's mindscreen predominates. Charles's "Merry Christmas," which connotes surly ingratitude and is photographed from Thatcher's point of view, squares with Thatcher's view of the boy as presented at the congressional investigation. The next two scenes, showing Thatcher's increasing exasperation with Charles's profligacy and his foolish belief that "it would be fun to run a newspaper," also suggest his mindscreen; the camera moves in tandem with him as he dictates a letter to urge responsibility on his charge, and when the scene concludes, Thatcher's eye directly meets the camera's lens, as if to bond the narrator and the narratee. In the succeeding montage, however, Thatcher's dyspepsia while reading issues of the *Inquirer* becomes the butt of a cinematic joke. The dynamic visuals, the pulsating editing rhythm, and the high-spirited music convey none of the dryness of Thatcher's prose; they lead us, in short, to conclude that in this most unstable of texts, the narrator has again changed.

The montage functions as a lively curtain-raiser to Thatcher's first direct confrontation with the adult Kane. The film's second-time viewer draws an inescapable conclusion from the scene. An "emperor of newsprint," Kane galvanizes the *Inquirer*, a sleepy daily paper with a genteel staff. On one occasion, as Bernstein's flashback shows, he has his reporters impersonate the police, bully the husband of a presumably missing Brooklyn woman, and trump up a front-page story where no story exists. Kane calls this "the truth" and delivers it "quickly and simply and entertainingly." The montage that drives Thatcher into Kane's office mirrors Kane's philosophy of yellow journalism— it is entertaining, zestful, and inflammatory. The montage represents the pounding of Thatcher as the young Kane might imagine it, perhaps through "the field of the mind's eye."

Linked seamlessly to the montage, the scene in the *Inquirer* office moves Kane center screen. If, as Bruce Kawin argues, Thatcher narrates it through mindscreen, the banker chooses uncharacteristically to minimize his presence. "Bernstein appears in all the scenes he relates," Kawin tells us, "and the camera continually pays attention to him" (35); Kawin can make no such statement about Thatcher. The banker, dressed in black, appears at the periphery of the frame, almost blending in with the screen's dark border. Kane, on the other hand, appears in the center in white. Although the parallel placement of Thatcher and the camera might seem to bond these two as narrators, Kane dominates the scene and sets the tone. The "I" of the Thatcher manuscript is simply in eclipse.

Again, James Naremore describes what we see:

[Kane] is at his most charming and sympathetic during the early scene in the newspaper office, where his potential danger is underlined, but where he is shown as a darkly handsome, confident young man, loyal to his friends and passionate about his work. This is, in fact, the point of Welles's full-scale entry into the film, and it is predictably stunning. . . . Here at last, greeted by a triumphal note of Herrmann's music, is the young Welles of Mars panic fame (79–80).

But which Welles? The celebrity? Though he may be drawing on his confrontations with naysayers in radio or the theater, Welles seems to be doing more than "playing himself." In this scene Kane assumes the role in which he has cast himself, the crusading journalist whose pleasure it is both to "look after the interests of the underprivileged" and in the process, apparently, to thwart his ex-guardian. As he will win over the *Inquirer's* subscribers, he wins us over by letting us experience his exuberance, his power to captivate the readers of newspapers and films. Naremore calls Kane's (Welles's) entrance "predictably stunning." What stuns us, even in a text whose inconstancy of point of view has been established, is the exchange of Thatcher's harsh perspective for a point of view so strongly indicative of Kane's mindscreen.

Countering his guardian's protest that the *Inquirer* will drain his capital, Kane admits that he will lose at least $3 million on the paper. "You know, Mr. Thatcher, at the rate of a million dollars a year . . ." (at this point, the film cuts from the medium shot of the two men to a close-up of Kane, his eyebrows lifted in mockery of Thatcher) ". . . I'll have to close this place in sixty years." When audiences laugh at this punch line, as they invariably do at screenings I have attended, they are responding positively to this "charming and sympathetic" man. Kawin might have argued (though he does not) that the close-up proceeds from Thatcher's mindscreen in order to demonstrate what a smart aleck Kane really is. Yet the music that punctuates Kane's line—a muted horn playing a presto version of the "newspaper theme"—snickers (as Kane does) at Thatcher's narrow conservatism. This witty, idealistic newspaper publisher conjures up an appealing persona in this scene of the film, and after taunting Thatcher throughout it, he even gives himself the last spoken word. From the driving energy of the montage to the conspiratorial intimacy of the close-up, we seem to experience through Kane's own perspective the Kane that Bernstein, Leland, Susan, and so many others fell for. The close-up, excluding Thatcher, the newspaper office, and the rest of the film's world, brings us into such close proximity to Kane that we neither desire nor expect a return to a narrative frame whose existence has all but been forgotten. A very rapid dissolve, however, exchanges Kane's smiling face for our second glimpse at Thatcher's manuscript: "In the winter of 1929 he . . ." This entry hardly gives Thatcher "the last word": it describes an event that occurred over thirty years after his confrontation at the *Inquirer,* when general economic conditions, not

Citizen Kane

the management of the newspaper, disabled Kane. Thatcher's cheerless control of the narrative has nonetheless returned and with it the need for our renegotiation of the text.

Some may reject the notion that *Citizen Kane* asserts Kane's mindscreen; after all, Kane dies in the opening scene. Yet the film's framing structure has only a superficial integrity, whose violation we experience less than sixty seconds into the first flashback. (Note, too, that although we *assume* that the dying man is Kane, we *see* only his silhouette and a fragment of his face.) Throughout *Citizen Kane*, we experience a divergence between perspective and expression and, moreover, between the putative narrator and the actual narrator that seems to make tenable, however unexpected or improbable, the presumably dead Kane's somehow being brought to life. Exhilarating and perplexing in the short run, what do these glimpses into Kane's world through Kane's mind's eye do? They return us to the film, again and again, to discover what we already know to be true but cannot quite accept. Each interpreter of *Citizen Kane* has a different slant on it: James Naremore tells us that Rosebud is important, Robert Carringer (in "Rosebud, Dead or Alive") that the glass paperweight is important, Ira Jaffe that window imagery is important. The fact that essayists continue to argue for a thematic center in *Citizen Kane* suggests the weaknesses of the formalists' approach: no one answer can satisfy us. Despite what these and other critics tell us, the text does not stand still; it continually challenges us *not* to settle on sleds, paperweights, or windows. The sporadic, ephemeral, yet insistent suggestions of the Kane mindscreen constitute a major index to the text's instability, which response-centered criticism allows us to apprehend. As Stanley Fish says, it permits us to "*slow down* the reading experience so that 'events' one does not notice in normal time, but which do occur, are brought before our analytical attentions" (28). What we know of *Citizen Kane*, whether its symbolism or its point of view, we know only through the activity of reading, our making of assumptions, revisions, and new expectations. In a temporal interpretation of the film, based on our moment-by-moment experience of it, we finally discover all that we know of the text.

From its opening credits and first sequence, with its persistent advancing camera, *Citizen Kane* raises and frustrates the reader's expectation of coming to know Kane. Our consistently revised assumptions, however, permit us to experience and learn the work's very object lesson, the danger of closing on the text. This strategy of reader education continues to the end of *Citizen Kane*. In Xanadu's Great Hall, a frustrating search behind us, we believe with Thompson that no word can explain a man's life; as the camera retreats from Thompson and his colleagues and we see the clutter that Kane has left behind, we recognize that Rosebud is indeed "a"—not "the"—missing piece to a jigsaw puzzle. But a dissolve to the cellar changes the camera's direction, from withdrawal to advancement. Above the boxes and crates, we move forward, apparently *toward* something. The camera probes, the music builds, and suddenly the sled and its emblazoned name appear before us. Robert Carringer warns us against accepting the sled as "the principal insight into Kane" (185), while Joseph McBride argues that the shot of the sled "does in fact solve nothing" (43). If not "the principal insight," however, "Rosebud" is *an* insight. And although it may not unlock the psychology of Kane's character, it provides a referent for the film's first spoken word and grants us at least nominally what for almost two hours we have longed to know.

Irrespective of "meaning," the shot of the sled gives many viewers a rush; it *does* something to them. With the roll on the timpani and the swelling ritardando, we experience a long-delayed pleasure that we perhaps had assumed, especially given the film's lack of convention, would be denied us. The shot of the sled is particularly felicitous because it seems just compensation for the disappointments and frustrations that we have endured. It may not "solve" anything of major significance in Kane's life, but it gives the film—and us—a sense of closure. Indeed, the shot of the sled concludes with a fade-out, leading us to expect a title card that reads "The End." But a fade-in returns us to the exterior of the mansion, where black smoke rises from the furnace chimney. With a dissolve we are immediately before the chain link fence, and as the music becomes eerier, more somber, we follow the camera down to the "No Trespassing" sign. Draining the excitement of the shot of the sled, this anticlimactic sequence seems to introduce a more restrained voice into the narrative. Let us consider, moment by moment, the film's proffered solutions to the Kane enigma: Thompson argues inexplicability. To formalist critics, the audience's euphoria on discovering at least the identity of Rosebud means nothing in light of the recognition that the audience is back where it began. Yet the experience of having the ostensibly conclusive answer to Kane's character superseded by the unsettling image of the sign draws attention to our wish for compact solutions to complex problems. The act of knowing, we come to realize, is a temporal process, based on assumptions ever subject to question, challenge, and revision.

Superimposed over a shot of the mansion and its massive initialled iron gate, the words "The End" appear. A trumpeting resolving chord concludes the music as the image fades out. Five seconds pass, the screen silent and dark. We do not assume, we know: the film has at last ended. Then, however, a title card fades in; The Mercury Theater, it notes, proudly introduces the cast. Outtakes have recently been used as codas to some Burt Reynolds films and, more trenchantly, to *Being There* (1979). The tail credits for *Citizen Kane,* though, contain no gaffes. On screen, the principals reprise a line of dialogue. Though each shot seems to have been lifted from the film proper, all of the footage comes from alternate takes, most of them containing less incisive readings than those in the body of the film. These visual tail credits constitute pieces of a rough draft designed by the implied author to reveal for the last time his strategy of betrayed expectations. We may infer from them the existence of not only other Kanes but other *Kane*s. Who is Kane? As even the music suggests, we can never know. The rhythmic theme that accompanies the tail credits resembles the spirited "chasers" used to empty theaters between screenings in the nickelodeon era; it is heard earlier, of course, as the song that attempts to build the myth of "good old Charlie Kane." Its words carry an insistent refrain: "Who is this one . . . who is this one . . . what is his name . . . what is his name?" The very opening of *Citizen Kane,* which teasingly heralds the name and apparently the identity of the film's central character, also introduces through its truncated credits the first frustrated expectation. Although the tail credits now fulfill one aspect of that expectation, they do not include Orson Welles/Charles Kane among the images of the "principal actors." The absence of Kane and the reprise of that rousing campaign song with its interrogative lyrics signal for one last time Kane's elusiveness. Where is Kane? Who is that man? These two implied and unanswered questions, part of our experience of the film's last moments, suspend, indefinitely, our closing on *Citizen Kane.*

All of us who study *Citizen Kane* share an intellectual pleasure in it, but do we return to the film because we seek fresh support for our theses (Rosebud is/is not significant) or because we find our theses inadequate to explain the film's hold over us? Each of the work's putative narrators claims special knowledge of Kane. Thatcher entitles his journal entry "Charles Foster Kane," suggesting its comprehensiveness. Leland remembers "absolutely everything" about Kane, and even after a night of drinking, Susan tells Thompson that "a lot comes into my mind about Charlie Kane." The supra-narrator descends upon the burning sled with complete confidence in its unifying symbolic value; the shot provides the visual equivalent of Raymond's assured boast, "I tell you about Rosebud." Critics of *Citizen Kane* close on the film with no less certainty. But how valid is their analysis? In interpreting *Citizen Kane*, they neglect our experience of *Citizen Kane*, of the cinematic techniques—the long take, moving camera, deep focus—that lead to assumptions unfulfilled, of the shifting points of view that promise and ultimately frustrate our ability to draw definite conclusions about Kane, of our impossible goal of extracting a meaning from this or any work.

Tennyson's Ulysses calls "experience . . . an arch wherethrough / Gleams that untravelled world whose margin fades / Forever and forever when I move." Ulysses' experience of life resembles our experience of this remarkable film. As we read *Citizen Kane*, the "meaning" seems never present but always ahead. In any reader-centered text, inexhaustible and forever potential, closure is impossible. Thompson's conclusion says as much for *Citizen Kane:* no "word [read 'text'] can explain a man's life." Since readers, not words, produce meaning, the reading of Kane (and *Kane*) will never be finished. Nor should it be. "Coming to the point," Stanley Fish writes, "is the goal of a criticism that believes in content, in extractable meaning, in the utterance as a repository. Coming to the point fulfills a need that most literature deliberately frustrates (if we open ourselves to it), the need to simplify and close. Coming to the point should be resisted . . ." (52). Each time we watch *Citizen Kane*, we have at hand the answer to its ambiguities. The very activity of reading brings *Kane* into existence: in the making and revising of assumptions about the text, its point of view and other myriad complexities, we actualize it, and when we have concluded our reading of *Kane*, only our experience of *Kane* remains.

WORKS CITED

Browne, Nick. "The Spectator-in-the-Text: The Rhetoric of *Stagecoach.*" *Film Quarterly* 29, no. 2 (1976): 26–38.

———. "Narrative Point of View: The Rhetoric of *Au Hasard, Balthazar.*" *Film Quarterly* 31, no. 1 (1977): 19–31.

Carringer, Robert. "Rosebud, Dead or Alive: Narrative and Symbolic Structure in *Citizen Kane.*" *PMLA* 91 (1976): 185–193.

Chatman, Seymour. *Story and Discourse: Narrative Structure in Fiction and Film.* Ithaca: Cornell University Press, 1978.

Citizen Kane. Dir. Orson Welles. RKO, 1941.

Dayan, Daniel. "The Tutor-Code of Classical Cinema." *Film Quarterly* 28, no. 1 (1974): 22–31.

Fish, Stanley. *Is There a Text in This Class? The Authority of Interpretive Communities.* Cambridge: Harvard University Press, 1980.

Henderson, Brian. "Tense, Mood, and Voice in Film (Notes After Genette)." *Film Quarterly* 36, no. 4 (1983): 4–17.

Houston, Beverle. "Power and Dis-Integration in the Films of Orson Welles." *Film Quarterly* 35, no. 4 (1982): 2–12.

Jaffe, Ira S. "Film as the Narration of Space: *Citizen Kane.*" *Literature/Film Quarterly* 7 (1979): 99–111.

Kawin, Bruce. *Mindscreen: Bergman, Godard, and First-Person Film.* Princeton: Princeton University Press, 1978.

McBride, Joseph. *Orson Welles.* New York: Viking Press, 1972.

Naremore, James. *The Magic World of Orson Welles.* New York: Oxford University Press, 1978.

Riffaterre, Michael. "Describing Poetic Structures: Two Approaches to Baudelaire's 'Les Chats.'" *Reader-Response Criticism from Formalism to Post-Structuralism.* Ed. Jane P. Tompkins. Baltimore: Johns Hopkins University Press, 1980. 26–40.

Welles, Orson, and Herman J. Mankiewicz. *Citizen Kane.* In Kael, Pauline. *The Citizen Kane Book.* Boston: Little, Brown, 1971.

DAVID EHRENSTEIN

DESERT FURY, MON AMOUR

For Vito Russo and Richard Dyer

Vol. 41, no. 4 (Summer 1988): 2–12.

It would seem that we *know something* about the cinema. The past decade has witnessed no end of theoretical incursions—linguistic, psychoanalytic, technohistorical, feminist—into an audiovisual technique heretofore seen solely as the province of wild-eyed devotees less concerned with whys and wherefores than sensations and sensibilities. Reams of copy have shot from an ever-growing academic superstructure armed to the teeth with methodological weaponry designed to blast apart not merely the nature of the cinematic beast but human consciousness itself. Yet for all of the work that's been done, critical theory has failed to evolve into critical *practice*. The cinema today remains as essentially unexamined as it was at the inception of this analytical jamboree—a quandary, a mystery, a mess.

"Like critics, like historians, but in slightly different ways, theoreticians often help to maintain the cinema in the imaginary enclosure of a pure love," claims Christian Metz.[1] But in truth the ways of critics, historians, and theoreticians aren't different. Theory has consistently claimed for itself a place apart—a cultural higher ground above the fray of common strife that Metz has so justly identified as the "institution" of cinema. "To be a theoretician of the cinema," Metz writes, "one should ideally no longer love the cinema and yet still love it: loved it a lot and only have detached oneself from it by taking it up again from the other end, taking it as the target for the very same scopic drive which had made one love it. Have broken with it, as certain relationships are broken, not in order to move on to something else, but in order to return to it at the next bend in the spiral. Carry the institution inside one still so that it is in a place accessible to self-analysis, but carry it there as a distinct instance which does not over-infiltrate the rest of the ego with the thousand paralyzing bonds of a tender unconditionality. Not have forgotten what the cinephile one used to be was like, in all the details of his affective inflections, in the three dimensions of his living being, and yet no longer be invaded by him: not have lost sight of him, but be keeping an eye on him. Finally, be him and not be him, since all in these are the two conditions on which one can speak of him."[2]

The language suggests a lover attempting to renegotiate a relationship with a mistress "needed" yet not quite "desired" as before. Metz—elegant, passionate, decorous, precise—can't help but give the impression of a writer caught up in a vast preamble to a subject whose discussion he fears elucidating fully. To speak more frankly would risk engagement with that "tender unconditionality" of the cinema's affectivity. And to do so would burst the bubble of quasi-scientific objectivity theorists hold so dear. Metz's Hamlet-like "Be and not be" is a frank admission of his awareness of this epistemological cul-de-sac—an awareness not at all apparent among others theoretically disposed. They're too busy whipping up methodological smokescreens to disguise or deny the critical proscriptiveness inherent in their projects. Yet like some low-grade cultural infection, clear critical biases continue to inhabit these discourses, wending their way through the most blandly bloodless prose—dust-dry treatises invariably opening with that most dreaded of academic invocations: "This paper . . ."

What is to be done, after all, with articles claiming to address notions of cinematic Space, Time, and History, that insist on promulgating the works of Oshima and Straub-Huillet as untouchable ideals?[3] What gain is to be made with theories trafficking amidst the deified likes of Ford, Sternberg, or Cukor—ostensibly examining "form" yet keeping the content of *auteur*-based idealism intact?[4] How is the study of narrative served by taking the terminology of the Russian formalists, then skewering it on some three decades of traditionally received wisdom regarding the evolution of Hollywood, the "New Wave," Soviet cinema in the twenties, etc.?[5] How can feminist battles with the "male gaze"[6] be waged by exposing Michael Snow's enthrallment to it on the one hand, then falling back to embrace the likes of Nicolas Roeg on the other?[7] In short the Question Cinema: Is theory at base nothing more than a somewhat ostentatiously rarefied exercise in nostalgia?

No need to ask about the *actual* progress of the cinema amidst this academic wool-gathering round retro Hollywood "classicism." It's gone its own way, serenely indifferent, instinctively decadent. Expanding itself on the one end—thanks to increasingly expensive production procedures—it's contracted on the other, the better to squeeze itself into its new home-video format. As this grotesque cyborg bellows and wheezes its way across the culture its means and ends become increasingly difficult to gauge. It's not merely the bipartite beast of FilmVideo that must be addressed, but the hydra-headed monster of "Media" as well: network television, newspapers, magazines, tabloids, opinion polls, and computerized informational data banks. All these areas, intimately interconnected, subdivide as well into such multicellular organisms as fashion layouts, rock videos, talk shows, pop recordings, live televised news reports, and made-for-TV "Movies of the Week."

Desert Fury

The hesitancy and doubt swirling about Metz's "attempt" at bringing together "Freudian psychoanalysis" and the "cinematic signifier" to produce what he, with touchingly tremulous modesty, refers to as a mere "contribution" to film theory speaks volumes. *Everything* remains to be said about the cinema. The problem, never really faced, is that there is no simple way to say it.

A FILM OF NO IMPORTANCE

In the end it all comes down to *Desert Fury*. *Desert Fury*? You haven't heard of it? Of course you haven't. Why should you? A 1947 Paramount release starring Lizabeth Scott and Burt Lancaster, this turgid melodrama about a gambling casino owner's daughter infatuated with an underworld gambler suspected of murder figures in no known pantheon or cult. Its director, Lewis Allen, is devoid of *auteur* status. Its performances are, by and large, not of award-winning stature. Its composer, Miklos Rozsa, has surely written more interesting musical scores.

Shot in color largely on studio sets representing outdoor locales (there was some actual location shooting as well), *Desert Fury*'s not-quite-*noir* plot makes it the odd-film-out among the equally florid programmers produced during the same period (*I Walk Alone, The Strange Love of Martha Ivers, The File on Thelma Jordan*). You aren't likely to find *Desert Fury* listed on a revival or repertory house schedule. It isn't available on home video. At best you might be able to catch it in some 3 a.m. slot on local television, or unspooled some afternoon when rain cancels a baseball game. And why not? It's "just a movie"—produced, consumed, forgotten. Not good. Not bad. Mediocre. In fact, one might even go so far as to call it *quintessentially* mediocre.

Of course to invoke notions of mediocrity is to evoke the specter of critical qualitativeness so dreaded by theoretical cadres, committed as they are to the promulgation of the notion of "value-free" analyses. Still, it wouldn't be going out on much of a limb to state that the diegesis of *Desert Fury* lacks the textual complexity found in such pantheon favorites as *Young Mr. Lincoln, The Pirate, Touch of Evil, North by Northwest,* or that most persistently picked of theoretical plums, *Letter From an Unknown Woman.*

The production of *Desert Fury* plainly involved choices of camera placement, focal length, lighting, sound mixing, musical scoring, and the like, perfectly commensurate with studio practices of the late forties at their most routine. The script by Robert Rossen, adapted from a *Saturday Evening Post* serial by Ramona Stewart, is workmanlike but formally quite undistinguished, holding as it does to a simple linear dramatic progression, unities of Time, Place, and Action, and such time-honored melodramatic conventions as "Fate" and "Ironic Coincidence" in the pulling together of otherwise unlinked aspects of plot and characterization. You've seen its like before, and all things being equal you'll doubtless see it again.

And yet something lingers over *Desert Fury*—hangs on, suspended in the studio indoor/outdoor air. For this writer (critic? journalist? theorist? historian? film buff?—the terms begin to slip, as well they might as the text begins to pull astride specified object of desire) cannot quite be *done* with *Desert Fury*. The heavy-lidded, smokey-voiced ambiance of Lizabeth Scott certainly plays a part in this—particularly in those scenes where she's set against the gleamingly dentalized muscularity of the young Burt Lancaster.[8] A certain Pop Art palimpsest common to late forties product observed in retrospect is part of this picture as well—especially as *Desert Fury*'s color gives actors, backgrounds, and objects the polished sheen so prized by Richard Hamilton.[9] Mary Astor's performance as Scott's mother is also there to be enjoyed, albeit in a much more straightforward way—the one element of *Desert Fury* whose quality is not in question. And last but not least there's the novelty of the character played by Wendell Corey—a homosexual psychopath given to dryly cynical asides and sudden violent rages. But then, we're getting ahead of ourselves.

Make no mistake, there's no avoiding the fact that critical congress with *Desert Fury* risks trafficking with nostalgic indulgence at its most absolute. Yet this is precisely why a *Desert Fury* is of such intense interest. Standing clear of the swamp of mass-media affection that forever grounds the likes of *Casablanca*, *Gone With the Wind*, and *Citizen Kane*, *Desert Fury* can be dissected with cool remove. It speaks to cinematic desires barely formed and only half-uttered—that vague itch for "a movie" answered by a compendium of images and sounds that never reach a level that could be called "memorable" yet somehow manage to "divert."

For any theorist worth his or her salt, the next step would be, of course, to scramble for a proper analytical position. All you have to do is scout a specified ground for study, then nail *Desert Fury* down with an appropriate abstract. Surely there's a *grande syntagmatique* to scrutinize here. Or perhaps a simple two-shot or two containing some quirk of psychoanalytic import. Feminist interest goes without saying. How does the figure of Lizabeth Scott "speak castration"? Let me count the ways . . .

But the simple, brutal fact of the matter is that all these techniques are very much beside the point.

TROUBLE IN CHUCKAWALLA

It's 1947. Let's go to the movies. What's playing? It's *Desert Fury*. Who's in it? Burt Lancaster and Lizabeth Scott. What's it about? Well . . .

After having been thrown out of her fifth finishing school, Paula Haller (Lizabeth Scott) has come home to the small desert town of Chuckawalla where her mother Fritzie (Mary Astor) runs the local gambling casino. Paula wants to go to work for her mother. Fritzie would prefer that Paula marry Tom Hanson (Burt Lancaster), the local deputy sherrif. Paula's attracted to Tom but isn't sure she's ready to settle down, especially as Eddie Bendix (John Hodiak) has just come to town. A gambler/gangster from the big city, Bendix and his henchman Johnny Ryan (Wendell Corey) are staying at a ranch outside of town. Years before, Bendix's wife had been killed in a mysterious auto accident on the Chuckawalla bridge, with suspicions of foul play. Paula is attracted to Eddie, and he to her, as she resembles his late wife. Fritzie is opposed to Paula's seeing Eddie, and so is a very possessive Johnny Ryan. Both (separately) plot to keep the pair apart. Eddie and Paula get together nevertheless and defiantly confront Fritzie. In a last-ditch attempt to stop them, Fritzie tells of her own past romance with Eddie. Paula leaves with Eddie nonetheless. On the way out of town the couple run into Johnny. At a roadside restaurant Johnny tells Paula the truth about Eddie—that he arranged his wife's death. Eddie shoots Johnny. Paula drives off with Eddie in pursuit. Tom joins the chase, which ends with

Eddie crashing his car into the Chuckawalla bridge—exactly where his wife died years before. Tom pronounces Eddie dead at the scene. Fritzie arrives and she and Paula make amends. She leaves, and Tom and Paula—also reconciled—walk off together into the setting sun. The end.

It goes without saying that the above summary provides only the most general overview of *Desert Fury*. It establishes a basis for further discussion, a point of possible entry. But it is only *one* point. Plot alone can't deal with the morass of images and sounds that calls itself *Desert Fury*. Consider, for example, the quasi-hypnotic effect created by the blindingly bright shade of blue sky behind Hodiak and Corey's heads as they stand by the bridge in the film's first scene where they enter town, or the dazed look on the face of an extra standing behind Scott in a scene in the casino. Then there's a visual *frisson* created by cutting between an actual outdoor locale and a studio set of the same place. Think of the picture window in Scott's bedroom—creating a picture-within-a-picture on a screen already chockablock with iconographical bric-a-brac. Then there's that framed black-and-white photo of Scott in Astor's office and the disturbing effect created when Scott stands astride it—which image is more "real"? All of these factors, naturally, come under the heading of "distractions" or "accidents"—they're not "meant" to be seen as narrative integers. But they're nonetheless *there*.

There too is *Desert Fury*'s advertising pitch. Itself a narrative, it runs parallel to whatever fragments of the film's actual story it chooses to disclose, playing on a series of alternate associations—roles played by the performers in the past, films *Desert Fury* hopes to recall as a possible point of appeal. And it is here that we find yet another *Desert Fury*: "A story that sweeps with sinister and growing menace thru sun-baked desert towns, luxurious ranches, colorful gambling houses to the greatest chase climax ever recorded by cameras."

TERMS OF ENDEARMENT

"Everyone went to the movies in the late forties," claims critic Andrew Sarris: "A disaster like the Gable-Garson *Adventure* grossed five million domestic, and musical atrocities like *Holiday in Mexico* and *The Dolly Sisters* drew lines instead of the flies they would attract today."[10] Consequently most viewers out for an evening's entertainment weren't likely to be deterred by the almost unanimously unfavorable notices *Desert Fury* received when it made its debut.

"The picture as a whole makes you think of a magnificently decorated package inside which someone has forgotten to place the gift," wrote Archer Winsten in the *New York Post*. "If you can accept all these automobiles and clothes as a substitute for a story that makes good sense, here's your picture," noted Alton Cook in the *World Telegraph*. Forty years haven't altered critical evaluations in any significant way. "Mild drama of love and mystery among gamblers, stolen by Astor in a bristling character portrayal," says the 1987 edition of Leonard Maltin's *TV Movies*.[11] Audiences exiting *Desert Fury* in 1947 would very likely have agreed with him. But these same audiences didn't in all likelihood go *in* to *Desert Fury* for Mary Astor. Their attention was directed elsewhere—to Lancaster and Scott.

Under contract to the film's producer, Hal Wallis, Lizabeth Scott (born Emma Matzo), with her dusky voice (doubtless modeled after Lauren Bacall) and wave-encrusted hair (echoing the likes of Veronica Lake), was clearly being promoted as the latest in a long line of sultry siren types. In 1941 she made her debut in an undistinguished programmer called *Frightened Lady*. After a brief hiatus she returned in *You Came Along* (1945), followed by *The Strange Love of Martha Ivers* (1946). She next made her biggest splash opposite Humphrey Bogart in *Dead Reckoning* (1947). The career of Burt Lancaster was progressing even faster at the time of *Desert Fury* though he had only two previous films to his credit—*The Killers* (1946) and *Brute Force* (1947). Inevitably *Desert Fury*'s ads boasted "That *Killers* guy and that *Dead Reckoning* dame come together as a team of dynamite-and-fire."

What the ads fail to mention is that as far as the film's scenario is concerned the "dynamite-and-fire" is supposedly between Scott and John Hodiak. Hodiak, curiously, gets top billing on the film's credits—*over* both Scott and Lancaster. One of a number of male not-quite-leads-not-quite-stars of that era, Hodiak's most notable appearances were in *Lifeboat* (1943), *Marriage Is a Private Affair* (1944), and *The Harvey Girls* (1946). His *Desert Fury* billing bespeaks a canny agent. Yet no agent, however influential, could forestall the onslaught of Scott-Lancaster associations that accrued round *Desert Fury*'s ads. Couples being the coin of the cinematic realm, *Desert Fury*'s promotional copy could not help but create one.[12]

But why Scott-Lancaster rather than Scott-Hodiak as the script clearly indicates? And what about those specially posed Scott-Lancaster photos that go even further in underscoring the relationship between characters who don't truly function as a couple until the film's last few shots? These ballyhoo glossies show Scott and Lancaster in a series of dramatic clinches that have no parallel within the diegesis that calls itself *Desert Fury* (Scott resting her head on Lancaster's chest, looking up at him rapturously—the "French seam" of her blouse slightly ripped. Lancaster struggling to wrest a gun from Scott's hand, her eyes closed shut as if in an erotic reverie). Clearly Scott-Lancaster are viewed as *appealing* in a way that Scott-Hodiak are not. Consider Scott's and Lancaster's comparably wavy hair. Consider Lancaster's strapping physique in comparison to Hodiak's, particularly as the latter's far less impressive chest is put on open display in a scene where Scott finds him taking the sun. What's going on here?

John Hodiak in *Desert Fury* offers us the spectacle of cinema at its most paradoxical. Lancaster is Hodiak's obvious superior on every level. How can Lizabeth Scott even so much as *think* of preferring John to Burt? One tries to imagine what the film might have been like had the contest been—for want of a better term—more evenly balanced. Imagine, for example, a *Desert Fury* with Kirk Douglas in the Hodiak role.[13] It certainly would have been a logical choice. Douglas was in fact posed between Scott and Lancaster in their next film, *I Walk Alone*. However, the center of *I Walk Alone* is Lancaster's character, not Scott's, and the Douglas character in that film is a wily on-his-game ganglord, not the testy indecisive neurotic played by Hodiak in *Desert Fury*. Moreover *Desert Fury*, need we be reminded, is entirely about Lizabeth Scott.

Scott's Paula has to choose between two men—one "good," one "bad." Consequently the concise logic of Hollywood dictates the terms for this choice by making it *for* her. Plainly the casting of as uncharismatic an actor as John Hodiak serves *Desert Fury*'s ends. Though the script and dialogue indicates a veritable torrent of passion flowing between Scott and Hodiak, what emerges is an almost palpable lack of lust—particularly in the scenes in which they're required to kiss. The pair set to work with the dogged determination of would-be outdoorsmen who've suddenly had a change of heart while white-water-rafting in the Rockies.

Still, Scott's comminglings with Lancaster aren't much of an improvement. They seem to salute one another like ships passing in a fog—icons of "Male" and "Female" more aware of their individual image power than any conjoined forces that might be negotiated to some other erotic end. Only when placed next to Astor does Scott really convey some sense of the passion the film's title suggests. But as far as *Desert Fury*'s plot is concerned, the Scott-Astor relationship is simply an engine driving Scott's character toward the resolution Lancaster provides. Dust-dry though it may be, this Scott-Lancaster pairing is the plateau on which *Desert Fury* is destined to settle.[14]

Desert Fury's advertising is a lie. But this lie only serves to underscore a deeper truth. For like Poe's (and Lacan's and Derrida's) "Purloined Letter," the "message" of *Desert Fury* is always in plain sight. Even before the story begins, the discrimination of "desirable" Lancaster over "undesirable" Hodiak has been set in place. The performers' particular qualities (or in this case lack of same) are slipped into the folds of the scenario like a hand in a kidskin glove. The ads aid this effort, suggesting an atmosphere redolent with danger and intrigue—as it is in the film for Scott-Hodiak but not for Scott-Lancaster. Thus the "good" couple is iconographically intermingled with the "bad" one—safety conflating with danger the better to promote the product.

This "ideal" movie couple isn't the only cozily familiar element *Desert Fury* has to offer. Reassurance also figures in the narrative's echoes of other films. Here's a mother-daughter conflict right out of *Mildred Pierce* or *Possessed*.

Desert Fury

The recurring automobile accident recalls *The Postman Always Rings Twice*. The criminal-out-of-his-element subplot harks back to *High Sierra*. The color cinematography, particularly in the scene where Scott and Lancaster go riding, recalls *Leave Her to Heaven*. And that's not all vis-à-vis the color.

"Luscious new colors will be introduced by Lizabeth Scott in her new film *Desert Town* which Hal Wallis is producing," gushes *Paramount News*.[15] "Armed with a set of artists' paints, Edith Head, Paramount's chief designer, spent several week-ends in the desert near Sedona, Arizona, where the cast of *Desert Town* was on location, in order to study some of nature's own colors." The results of her labors were the creation of no less than "16 gowns to be worn by Miss Scott in the film, which is in Technicolor." Thus the oddity of filming a minor potboiler like this one in color is explained—it's more than a melodrama, it's a fashion show.

Not surprisingly, in keeping with this new-found sense of splendor a title like *Desert Town* simply won't do anymore, and as *Paramount News* notes,[16] it's changed to *Desert Fury*. "Producer Wallis and his associate, Joseph H. Hazen, with Paramount sales and advertising executives, decided upon the new title to underscore the strong dramatic action and emotional conflict in the story of a group of modern characters which is enacted in the colorful setting of today's desert country."

CONSPICUOUS CONSUMPTION

Early on in *Desert Fury* Paula pulls into downtown Chuckawalla and spies two of its more well-heeled female citizens. "Window shopping?" she asks them breezily. "Yes," they reply, looking pointedly at her, "but we don't like what we see. It's too cheap." Cut to Paula looking hurt. She starts up her car and drives off in a huff, nearly knocking the two women down.

The scene establishes a major plot conflict—Paula's estrangement from the town's "upper crust" substrata, an "outsider" status that she alternately resents and enjoys (when Tom in the very next shot says he should have arrested her for her conduct she replies, "It would have been worth it"). Yet at the same time the scene's meaning proceeds from another more obvious level. Like almost everything in *Desert Fury*, the subject of the scene is *shopping*.

"Come with me to Los Angeles and we'll buy some new clothes," Fritzie says to Paula, hoping to bring her out of a funk. "But I don't need any new clothes," Paula replies. "A girl always needs new clothes," says Fritzie, offering up a mother's wisdom, consumerist-Hollywood-style. And it's true, for in the world of *Desert Fury* women always require the new—clothes, adventures, backgrounds, romance. We don't need to go to Los Angeles to go shopping in *Desert Fury*, the film is *already* shopping. As *Newsweek* magazine noted, "Lizabeth Scott, impersonating a petulant daughter, changes costume so frequently that one forgets she is an actress, not a model."[17] Obviously the film makes no distinction between these dual functions. And why should it? The scene in which Paula is sent to her room to be kept away from Eddie alone involves five complete costume changes. One wonders whether this blatant "fashion pitch" was written into the script beforehand or presented itself at some later point in the production—perhaps when it was decided that Edith Head was to play a more important role than usual in *Desert Fury*'s making.

With *Desert Fury* we're deep in the heart of that Hollywood where studio "showmanship" declares that audience interest in "the clothes" carries equal—if not greater—weight with "the stars" or "the story." The clothes put so pointedly on display in *Desert Fury* are just the sort of casual "sport" ensembles an average middle-class woman in the late forties would be likely to wear. They stand in sharp contrast to the glamour duds featured in such films as *The Women* (1939), *Woman's World* (1954), *Written on the Wind* (1956), or *Funny Face* (1957). In *Desert Fury* "practical" purchases predominate. And so it goes with the "purchase" of men.

If all the "classical" cinema has to offer is a "male gaze" forever epoxied to an image of the female seen by definition as "inauthentic," then the audiences for which *Desert Fury* was expressly designed would have few means at their disposal for getting beyond the film's first scene. There's John Hodiak gazing—like so many movie males—rapturously at Lizabeth Scott as she drives up to the Chuckawalla bridge. But if his gaze is so central, why does the film continue to be in relentless pursuit of Scott irrespective of Hodiak's visual purview? Obviously someone *else* is looking at Lizabeth Scott—a female spectator whose ability to see with her own two eyes hasn't as yet been accounted for by a theory that would have us all crashing headlong into the Chuckawalla bridge along with Hodiak's wife.

The image of Lizabeth Scott in *Desert Fury* is quite plainly up on the screen for *other women* to gaze at. She is a model whose presence bespeaks make-up "secrets," hair-care "tips," a fashion "forecast." The actual relevance of this figure in relation to the lives of women in the postwar era is, naturally, open to question. But it is quite without question that the character of Paula means to address those women and their lives as directly as possible. *Desert Fury* is a "woman's picture" offering its audience the image of an *homme fatal* to parallel the *femmes fatales* of the forties *film noirs*.

As critic Barbara Deming has noted,[18] the *film noir* is in many ways something on the order of an allegorical morality play—its heroes' trafficking in criminal activity standing in for killings on the battlefields, its *femmes fatales* a paranoid evocation of soldiers' fears of returning to "unfaithful" wives and sweethearts. *Desert Fury*, dealing as it does with the postwar *Zeitgeist* from "a woman's point of view," highlights these problems with fewer disguises. The war's end brought with it a pool of men for women to choose from. Picking the "good" from the "bad" is *Desert Fury*'s principal subject. But there is another force at play here as well—equally ideological in nature. For with the return of men came the demand for the return of women to "traditional" roles—removing them from the work force in which they had been placed of necessity during the war.

"You look kinda nice emptying out those ashtrays," Eddie tells Paula, as she adds her "woman's touch" to clear the squalor of Eddie's living arrangements with Johnny. Shortly afterward she's seen sitting at Eddie's feet in front of a roaring fireplace, reading a romance novel. That Paula *herself* is in a romance novel gives the scene an exceedingly cryptic literary *trompe l'oeil* quality—as if Alain Robbe-Grillet had momentarily hijacked the scenario. Paula's a party to an object lesson being staged for the viewer's benefit—how to recognize, organize, and direct the process of her desires along accepted social lines.[19]

Of course, it shouldn't be forgotten, Paula has also expressed a wish for a career. But with incredible deftness *Desert Fury* forecloses this wish by tying it inextricably to Fritzie's insistence on Paula's social betterment. The job at the casino would be a step down—forever barring Paula from the social approval she guiltily craves. Only marriage to Tom would set things aright. "They've accepted you," Fritzie tells him, "and in time they would accept Paula—she'd get her friends." And as with everything else in *Desert Fury* this process is all a matter of purchasing power—and consumer integrity.

Fritzie wants to "buy" Tom for Paula. His market "value" is clear. Moreover, she'll sweeten the deal. She promises Tom a ranch for his pains. But Tom doesn't want to be an object of exchange, particularly in a woman's eyes. Still he knows where the social cutting edge lies—who are the dealers in this world and who are the dealt. This is why he lets Eddie go in the scene where he picks him up on the highway. Paula ends up "buying" Tom, but on her own terms—after first inspecting the "brand X" of Eddie Bendix.

Still in the midst of this buyer's market there's one bit of damaged goods that stands out in sharp relief against the background of all the others bought and sold across the film's trajectory: Johnny Ryan.

NO LOVE FOR JOHNNY

  —"Why would there be some of me apart from Eddie?"
  —"Two people can't fit into one life."
  —"That's what you think."
  —"Someday he'll leave you."
  —"He'll never leave me."

A standard bit of dialogue for a late-forties melodrama, perfectly suited for a scene in which the heroine fights for "her man," forestalling the troublesome intrusion of "another woman." The only difference is that the "other" in *Desert Fury* is male.

There's nothing *particularly* novel about the presence of a homosexual character in a postwar Hollywood film—especially a crime melodrama. Think of *The Maltese Falcon* (1941) with its Joel Cairo (Peter Lorre), Mr. Gutman (Sydney Greenstreet), and his "gunsel" Wilbur (Elisha Cook, Jr.). Think too of the pair of inseparable hit men played by Lee Van Cleef and Earl Holliman in *The Big Combo* (1955). And that's not to mention George Macready in *Gilda* (1946), John Dall and Farley Granger in *Rope* (1948), Robert Walker in *Strangers on a Train* (1951), and many other Hollywood films in which the presence of a homosexual character adds a touch of spice to an otherwise routine scenario. The difference with *Desert Fury* is the remarkable degree of specificity with which sexual status is detailed.

"I was about your age or older," Eddie tells Paula, recalling how he first met Johnny. "It was in the Automat off Times Square about two o'clock in the morning on a Saturday. I was broke, he had a couple of dollars, we got to talking. He ended up paying for my ham and eggs." "And then?" Paula inquires with expectant fascination. "I went home with him that night," Eddie continues. "I was locked out. I didn't have a place to stay. His old lady ran a boarding house. There were a couple of vacant rooms. We were together from then on."

How touching this subtle integration of the notion of "a *couple* of vacant rooms"—like the twin beds for married couples required by the Hays Code (in force at the time of *Desert Fury*'s making). As the immortal Inspector Truscott in Joe Orton's *Loot* remarks, "Two young men who knew each other very well, spend their nights in *separate* beds? Asleep? It sounds highly unlikely to me." And so it is, what with Johnny snarling a terse "Getoutahere!" every time Paula so much as glances toward Eddie. Then there's his pathetic pleading to "stay" with Eddie, even after the latter has taken Johnny off his payroll. The relationship couldn't be spelled out more clearly. And it's also clear that this same relationship provides a prime source of attraction to Eddie for Paula.

Curious that such a configuration should find its way into an otherwise mundane scenario. *Desert Fury* cleanly establishes Eddie's unsuitability for Paula through his organized crime associations, the murder of his wife, and his past affair with Fritzie. Bisexuality, it would seem, would only serve to gild this lily. But as the subject of *Desert Fury* is proper sexual object-choices and social roles for American women in the postwar era, Eddie's sexual predilictions have an additional plot function. The attraction held by certain heterosexual females for bisexual males was plainly of some significance to that period's social life, otherwise a film like *Desert Fury* would have been inconceivable. Hollywood, particularly in the studio heyday of the late forties, was never in favor of the advancement of narrative strategies unfamiliar to the masses. *Desert Fury* may seem novel today, but apparently no one in the front office blinked back in 1947.

In a way *Desert Fury* was the *Making Love* of its time. Like *Desert Fury*, *Making Love* was designed largely in terms of female spectatorship. The clear speculation in 1982 was that the sight of two men physically intertwined might have the same voyeurist currency as that of the sight of two women. This in turn brings up the fact that lesbianism has always been regarded as well within the purview of the "gaze"—the eyes of men "legitimizing" what would otherwise be an "aberration." The same does not hold for men. The first words a homosexual hears indicative of his newly won pariah status are "What are *you* looking at?" The "you" emphasized in this rhetorical accusation serves to arrest through the sheer force of its own specification the notion that male voyeurism would even so much as *conceive* of a male object.

This voyeuristic threat plays no part in *Desert Fury*. Our views of both Hodiak and Lancaster are quite conventional in that whatever physical attractions they may possess, their power and legitimacy *as men* are their true source of sexual fascination. Likewise for Wendell Corey as Johnny. He's simply the lynch-pin of the plot—the key to its mystery. As for his expression of desire, it's ever so carefully interwoven into the film's network of dramatic conflicts. In keeping with the "classical" cinema's tendency to ground desire within a force-field of point-of-view shots for purposes of spectator identification, *Desert Fury* is especially scrupulous about restricting Johnny's expressions of ardor toward Eddie to two-shots in which the men appear together. The only exception to this rule is the breakfast scene mentioned previously, where Johnny pleads to stay on with Eddie at no salary. The depth of Johnny's feelings are plain for all to see, but in the exchange of looks between Johnny, Eddie, and a silent, pensively smoking Paula, they are prevented from falling within the viewer's sightline. Paula, without speaking, dominates here. It is the regulation of *her* vision that dictates the *mise-en-scène* of emotions. Johnny nonetheless leaves his mark on the narrative on another level.

It is Johnny who controls Eddie. He "created" him (as Eddie's climactic confession makes clear) and introduced him to a life of crime. It was Johnny who drove Eddie to kill his wife. "*I'm* Eddie Bendix!" he declares moments before his death. And even after death Johnny looms across the action—his final speech is repeated on the sound track as Eddie races after Paula in his car, crashing it into the Chuckawalla bridge.

"They never fixed it," Paula says to Tom, referring to the bridge's railings, shattered in the wake of the first accident and gaping open at the moment of the second. She could, of course, be referring just as well to a sociosexual schema that allows the likes of an Eddie or a Johnny. "They will [fix it] one day," says Tom, reassuring her. But forty years later, nothing about *Desert Fury*, or the culture that spawned it, has been "fixed."

PRISONER OF THE DESERT

Just how far have we come since the fall of 1947? The bulk of *Desert Fury*'s plot (mother-daughter conflict, woman in thrall to "unsuitable" male) has long served as the stuff of television "soap opera"—both daytime and "prime-time" variety. Fashion "pitches" have their place in this narrative schematic— recently having revived the shoulder pads common to the late forties. Women in these mainstream scenarios are presented as having the "option" of "career" or "family"—though the bias towards domestic "choices" are plain, with attendant "guilt" over "lack of fulfillment *as a woman*." "Having it all" is the catch-phrase surrounding this cultural cul-de-sac.

Homosexuality has likewise found its "place" as well. Once confined to the margins of experimental cinema, it's been upgraded to the tributaries of the

Desert Fury

mainstream—"art" and "independent" cinema, and over-the-counter hard-core pornography. Figures like Johnny Ryan no longer "work" here. And why should they? What role is there for a Johnny in an era of Bruce Weber blatancy, or the lip-smacking, towel-snapping sensuality of a *Top Gun*?

Johnny Ryan belongs precisely where he is—a late forties programmer called *Desert Fury*. A compendium of medium-two-shots (with a handful of long shots and close-ups for spice) ceaselessly pursuing one another round a fixed locale. Here are five figures locked inside a scenario so claustrophobic that they need not move more than a few feet before slamming into one another. Here are a series of problems to be dealt with, demands to be answered: Overbearing parents, social stigma and snobbery, dangerous acquaintances, unsuitable swains, a woman not sure about what she wants to do with her life, homosexual desire. Nothing new here. Nothing "old" either. It's the world in which we live, "brought to life" by the Cinema we love. And in our working through it all, it's still possible to isolate the bases of our fascination, our frustration, our boredom, our obsession, our*selves*. But ahistorical "close analysis" can't reach it alone, nor can any other theoretical framework that deals with film solely at the level of narrative logic, or as a vast preamble to a psychoanalytic technique that can function at best only as a metaphor for cinematic interaction.

Metz seems aware of this when he writes that "the problem of the cinema is always reduplicated as a problem of the theory of the cinema and we can only extract knowledge from what we are (what we are as persons, what we are as culture and society)."[20] But who are these persons, this culture, this society?

"Cinematic images," comments Jean-Louis Schefer, "exercise a powerful preemption over the living being, not simply because he is made to feel present at the spectacle, but because he can't see the spectacle unless he's part of it in some way, or unless he himself is the absolute reason for the spectacle, its profoundest passion. That's the real question for cinema. It's never a partial phenomenon based on a split; it's a participatory phenomenon, generalized and indeterminate, working across *all* the objects of the spectacle. A cinematic projection has to be diffused—across the hero, and the villain, and the animals, and the objects, and the places on the screen—over the whole world. It's with the entirety of that world on screen that the spectator participates or identifies himself, and it's there that he's most sensitive to the effects of spatial dislocation, temporal distortion, and especially emotions."[21]

There is no set theoretical formulation, no royal road to chart this course of cinema. There are only a series of byways and backalleys—some connecting directly to the narrative at hand, others intersecting with advertising, commerce, and current events. Some of these routes connect. Others are cul-de-sacs. But it's only by following them that we can possibly see our way through this detritus, this Technicolor swamp, this two-penny fashion show, this absurd confluence of fixity and drift, this *Desert Fury*.

NOTES

1. Christian Metz, *The Imaginary Signifier*. Indiana University Press, 1982, p. 13.

2. Ibid., p. 15.

3. Stephen Heath, *Questions of Cinema*, Indiana University Press, 1981. Particularly the essay "The Question Oshima."

4. "We wanted to re-read Ford, not Huston, to dissect Bresson and not René Clair, to psychoanalyze Bazin and not Pauline Kael," T. L. French, "*Les Cahiers du Cinéma 1968–1977*, Interview with Serge Daney," *The Thousand Eyes #2.*

5. David Bordwell, *Narration in the Fiction Film*, University of Wisconsin Press, 1985.

6. Laura Mulvey, "Visual Pleasure and Narrative Cinema," *Screen* Volume 15, Number 3, Autumn 1975.

7. Teresa de Lauretis, *Alice Doesn't: Feminism, Semiotics, Cinema*, Indiana University Press, 1984.

8. "What interests me . . . in Lizabeth Scott films," Alloway writes, "are those properties specific to popular movies which can be validated by comparison with other films and other mass media." Lawrence Alloway, *Violent America: The Movies 1946–1964*, The Museum of Modern Art, 1971.

9. "A still from a 40's movie called *Shockproof* had a fascination that I spent some time analyzing. Everything in the photograph converged on a girl in a 'new look' coat who stared out slightly to the right of the camera. A very wide-angle lens must have been used because the perspective seemed distorted, but the disquiet of the scene was due to other factors. It was a film set, not a real room, so wall surfaces were not explicitly conjoined; and the lighting came from several different sources. Since the scale of the room had not been unreasonably enlarged, as one might expect from the use of a wide-angle lens, it could be assumed that false perspective had been introduced to counteract its effect . . . , yet the foreground remained emphatically close and the reces-

sion extreme. All this contributed more to the foreboding atmosphere than the casually observed body lying on the floor, partially concealed by a desk. The three collages . . . are about this image of an interior space—ominous, provocative, ambiguous; with the lingering residues of decorative style that any inhabited space collects. A confrontation with which the spectator is familiar yet not at ease." (*Richard Hamilton,* The Solomon R. Guggenheim Museum, 1973, page 46.) "I've been looking at the catalogue. There is a wonderful clarity in Hamilton's work. And looking at these pictures some things have come back to me—Pat Knight's rather angular handsomeness, the pale lipstick face, with eyes trying to hide something, and an attitude of sameness about her against the changing backgrounds and melodramatic action." (*Sirk On Sirk* by Jon Halliday, The Viking Press, New York, 1972, page 79.)

10. "Pop! Go the Movies," *Moviegoer* #2, Spring, 1964.

11. *Leonard Maltin's TV Movies and Video Guide,* 1987 Edition, Signet Books.

12. In his video presentation *L'Image du Cinéma,* Raymond Bellour provocatively describes the cinema as a "machine that produces couples."

13. See John O. Thompson, "Screen Acting and the Commutation Test," *Screen,* Volume 19, Number 2, Summer, 1978.

14. And even this plateau is in a sense provisional, for Scott and Lancaster—dressed in their costumes from *Desert Fury*—make an appearance in *Variety Girl,* another 1947 Paramount release. Directed by George Marshall, *Variety Girl* is a revue-style musical—ostensibly about the charitable organization "The Variety Clubs of America,"—thrown together much along the lines of such wartime musical reviews as *Thank Your Lucky Stars, Stage Door Canteen,* or *Star Spangled Rhythm.* A slim plot (coscripted by Frank Tashlin) follows the adventures of Olga San Juan and Mary Hatcher in Hollywood as an excuse to showcase Paramount stars and personalities (among those making cameos: Ray Milland, Paulette Goddard, Bob Hope and Bing Crosby, Alan Ladd, Dorothy Lamour). The film's finale is a nightclub show with a carnival motif. Ringmaster William Demerest takes us to one exhibit featuring "Buffalo Burt Lancaster and Lizabeth 'Texas' Scott." Lancaster is to shoot a pair of cigarettes out of Scott's mouth from over his shoulder, using a mirror. "Stop breathing," he tells her. "Who's breathing?" she asks. The camera is on Lancaster when he shoots. He turns about looking disappointed. He walks over to where Scott was standing. The space is empty. He looks down indicating he has felled her. He takes a card and places it on a post nearby. It reads "Girl Wanted."

15. *Paramount News,* September 23, 1946.

16. *Paramount News,* November 11, 1946.

17. "No, My Desert Daughter," *Newsweek,* September 15, 1947.

18. *Running Away from Myself: A Dream Portrait of America Drawn from the Films of the 40's,* Grossman Publishers, 1969.

19. "We've been begging them on our knees—I mentioned previously women analysts—to try to tell us, well, not a word! Never been able to get

anything out of them," Jacques Lacan, *Le Seminaire* Volume XX, *Encore,* Editions du Seuil, 1975, page 69.

20. Christian Metz, *The Imaginary Signifier,* Indiana University Press, 1982, page 5.

21. Paul Smith, "Our Written Experience of the Cinema: An Interview with Jean-Louis Schefer," *Enclitic* Volume VI, Number 2, Fall, 1982.

GÖSTA WERNER

FRITZ LANG AND GOEBBELS

Myth and Facts

Fritz Lang—unknown date, but probably when he
was still in Berlin

Vol. 43, no. 3 (Spring 1990): 24–27.

Myths are born and grow and flourish. Those who unthinkingly pass them on end up believing that they are facts. Repetition creates a cloak of seeming veracity which confuses gullible minds so that they cannot detect the truth underneath.

Thus every knowledgeable member of the film trade believes in the story of film director Fritz Lang's precipitate flight from Germany following on the banning of his film *The Testament of Dr. Mabuse.* The story goes that Dr. Goebbels, who was responsible for the banning, offered Lang the post of managing director of the entire German film industry. He stuck to his offer, maintains Lang himself, even after being told by Lang that he was a Jew—in actual fact Lang was half Jewish, his mother being Jewish. The story then goes on to say that Lang was given 24 hours to reconsider Goebbels' generous offer. Before nightfall Lang fled Berlin for Paris. He did this so precipitously that he did not even have time to draw money from the bank—banks closed in those days in Germany at half-past two.

But is this the true story? Thanks to material recently made available by the Deutsche-Kinemathek in Berlin—which placed it at the disposal of the German Film Museum (*Deutsches Filmmuseum*) in Frankfurt and its young and very able program director Ronny Loewe—we are now able to discover the facts. These are as follows.

The Nazi seizure of power occurred on 30 January 1933. For some time traditional German censorship continued without a break as if nothing had happened. It was not until six weeks later, on 14 March, that the *Ministerium für Volkserklärung und Propaganda* was set up, with Dr. Joseph Goebbels as its head. At that time the *Testament des Dr. Mabuse* was not quite completed, so the film had not been submitted to the censors.

No one expected the film to be banned, however, and on 21 March the official film journal *Der Kinematograph* was able to report that the premiere was to be on Friday 24 March at the large picture palace called Ufa-Palast am Zoo.

Fritz Lang, near the end
of his life, at the Pacific
Film Archive in Berkeley

Two days later, i.e., 23 March, *Der Kinematograph* informed its readers that
the premiere had had to be put off as the film only that same day would reach
the censors. The day after, 24 March, the same journal wrote that the post-
ponement of the premiere had been due to "technical reasons."

Nothing further was revealed about the film until not quite one week later.
On 30 March *Der Kinematograph* announced that the German Board of Film
Censors had banned the film on the preceding day. The decision had been
reached at a meeting of the Board, "under the chairmanship of Counsellor
Zimmerman." The reason given was that it constituted a threat to law and
order and public safety—in accordance with a regulation to be found in the
Law of Censorship.

The film was passed, however, for distribution abroad—there was both a
German and a French version. The German version was first shown in Vienna
on 12 May 1933, but the French version had its premiere a month earlier in
Paris. The cutter of the film, Lothar Wolff, had even earlier taken the French-
speaking material to Paris during the final stages of the making of the film and

had completed the editing of the French version there. This gives the lie to the story that appears from time to time about the negative of the film having been smuggled to France in suitcases filled with dirty linen.

The film had also been sold to a number of European countries (besides Austria and France). Among them was Sweden, where, however, on 26 April 1933, the German version of the film was banned by the Swedish Board of Film Censors in accordance with paragraph six of the Royal Ordinance for Cinema Productions, the paragraph against the depicting of violence on the screen.

In Germany the last week of March 1933 turned out to be an eventful and momentous one for the German film industry. Goebbels had lost no time in preparing a large-scale drive to "renew" German film production as a whole. On 28 March, the day before the banning of the *Testament des Dr. Mabuse,* Goebbels had invited in the entire top personnel of the German film industry to a *Bierabend* in the Hotel Kaiserhof. Among those present were producers, directors, and technical staff. Certain reports have it that Fritz Lang was among those present.

It was in the course of this private party that Goebbels expressed his admiration for four films: he said they had made an indelible impression on him. The four were Eisenstein's *The Battleship Potemkin,* the American *Anna Karenina* (with Greta Garbo in the lead), Fritz Lang's *Die Nibelungen,* and Luis Trenker's *Der Rebell.* The last-mentioned film, whose motif is the struggle for freedom of the Tyrolese, had been released in Berlin two months earlier and was still being shown. Goebbels professed his admiration for Eisenstein's film for the power with which a political idea permeated the film. This, he thought, should set an example for the new, ideologically conscious and politically engaged film that he expected from all German producers, directors, and manuscript writers—though of course the political overtones would have to be different!

It is very likely that Lang was present at this party. He was known to be a fierce nationalist and had at this time no intention of leaving Germany. The day before, 27 March, he had taken part in the founding of the "direction group" of the NSBO (= *Die Nationalsozialistische Betriebsorganisation*). Three other major film figures were also involved: Carl Boese, an experienced and highly successful director of comedies; Viktor Jansen, a young director of comedies for whom Billy Wilder had written a number of scripts; and Trenker, an actor and director renowned for his dramatic "mountain pictures" with strongly nationalistic undertones.

Thus Lang can hardly have been surprised when, one day in April, shortly after the Kaiserhof party, he was summoned by Goebbels and offered the leadership of the entire German film production—instead of being only one of the four placed at the helm of the NSBO. It was not just a highly attractive offer. It was logical as well.

A Goebbels favorite: *Anna Karenina*

It was at this point, according to the story, that Fritz Lang, penniless and with Goebbels' offer ringing in his ears, fled headlong to Paris, only to return to Berlin and the Fatherland after the end of World War II.

Which parts of this story are facts and which are the "story"?

(A) *The contact between Goebbels and Fritz Lang:* Even though it is highly probable that Goebbels *did* offer Lang the post as head of the entire German film production, there is not a word about it in Goebbels's usually meticulous diary for the year 1933. Lang is not mentioned there at all.

(B) *Lang's headlong flight to Paris:* The answer is to be found in Lang's passport. The passport, numbered 66 11 53.31, was issued in Berlin on 11 September 1931, and valid until 11 September 1936. It contains a large number of stamps and Fritz Lang's name is to be found alongside nearly every one of them. There are no visas or exit stamps for the months of February, March, and the beginning of April 1933. There is only one exit visa for Fritz Lang. It is made out by *Der Polizeipräsident in Berlin* and dated 23 June 1933. It is valid for exits for a period of six months. Up to that date Lang had therefore never left Germany.

The passport also contains several visas for entry into Belgium, every one issued in Berlin and at the end of June and July 1933. Further, during the same period Lang purchased foreign currency repeatedly at the *Weltreisebureau Union* in Unter den Linden in Berlin, totalling 1,366 *Reichsmark*. All these transactions are duly registered in the passport in dated stamps: 26 June, 27 June, 20 July. These days Lang must have been in Berlin.

According to the testimony of entry and exit stamps, in June and in July 1933 Lang visited England and Belgium, inter alia by air. He had a two-year visa for repeated entries into France. It was issued in London 20 June 1932 and was valid until 20 June 1934. The entry stamps for 1933 are all from June and July 1933, the first being dated 28 June, the last 31 July.

The foreign currency stamps from Berlin testify, as do the various entry and exit stamps, that between the journeys abroad in the summer of 1933 Lang returned to Berlin, which city he left finally only on 31 July 1933—four months after his legendary meeting with Goebbels and supposed dramatic escape.

Dr. Goebbels did not forget Lang and his films. When in October 1933 he celebrated his thirty-sixth birthday in his new and elegant official residence in Berlin he entertained himself and his guests in the evening by showing them the banned *Testament des Dr. Mabuse*. Lang, meanwhile, was in France, where he was shortly to begin filming *Liliom*.

SOURCES

Fritz Lang's passport: Deutsche Kinemathek, Berlin. Berlin in March 1933: Gerd Albrecht, *Nationalsozialistische Filmpolitik* (1969), pp. 12–13.

Goebbels' speech in Kaiserhof, 28 March 1933: given *in extenso* in Albrecht, pp. 439 ff.

Lang's part in NSBO: *Cinegraph, Lexikon zum deutschsprachigen Film* (1984), p. D3, also *Cahiers du Cinéma*, no. 99, September 1959, p.29.

Interview with Lang giving his version of the story: *Movie* no. 4, November 1962, pp. 4–5.

For statements made by Lang: Francis Cortade, *Fritz Lang* (1963), p. 21. See also P. M. Jensen, *The Cinema of Fritz Lang* (1969), p. 104; Lotte Eisner, *Fritz Lang* (1976), p. 131; Ludwig Maibohm, *Fritz Lang* (1981), pp. 164–169; N. Simsolo, *Fritz Lang* (1982), p. 46; M. Töteberg, ed., *Fritz Lang in Selbstzeugnisse* (1985), p. 78, p. 136.

For embellishments: Lotte Eisner, in *Ich hatte einst ein schönes Vaterland* (1984), relates how Lang was wont to tell with great delight about his conversation with Goebbels and how "each time he embellished it a little more." (pp. 127–28)

PART SEVEN

GROUP TEXTS

The films made by Maya Deren, Kenneth Anger, Bruce Baillie, Stan Brakhage, and many others—what do we call them? Underground cinema? That term refers both to midnight showings at feature film theaters and to literally fugitive showings in the days of censorship, when a hostile society sent police to enforce its disapproval. Experimental cinema? This suggests a process of trial and error that never does resolve itself aesthetically. Independent cinema? Independent these filmmakers certainly were, but the term must be shared with many postwar documentaries and with feature films of the low-budget variety. Indeed, four of the five feature films nominated for an Academy Award in 1997 were "independently produced." Avant-garde is probably the best term, if only because it is the one most used by filmmakers and critics in this area. Whatever the name of this cinema, it is doing well: new avant-garde filmmakers emerge every year, and several of the pioneers have been honored. Among the first 100 films selected for permanent preservation in the National Film Registry of the Library of Congress are *Meshes of the Afternoon* (1943), by Maya Deren; *Dog Star Man* (1964), by Stan Brakhage; and *Castro Street* (1966), by Bruce Baillie.

Unfortunately, there is not always an easy way to see even these well-known avant-garde films and such films, even when available for study, are notoriously difficult to write about. Even though all four of the films discussed in the Spring 1976 Special Feature were highly regarded, the essays by the three writers included here were an act of faith in the future. It is worth noting that *Film Quarterly* has been interested in avant-garde film for most of its forty years, a commitment that has remained constant at least since the early 1970s. In Spring 1971 Bruce Baillie appeared on the cover in a still from his film *Quick Billy;* and an image from Tom DeWitt's *Fall* appeared on the Spring 1972 cover, with an accompanying essay by John Fell. Later highlights include a dossier on Yoko Ono's film work in the Fall 1989 issue and numerous other essays and/or interviews by Scott MacDonald concerning Ernie Gehr, Andrew

Noren, Anne Severson, Yvonne Rainer, Martin Arnold, and others. There have also been interviews of Holly Fisher and Barbara Hammer, as well as attention to a number of figures poised in diverse ways between the avant-garde and the independent feature, including Peter Greenaway, Jan Lenica, Todd Haynes, Sally Potter, Maggie Greenwald, Gregg Araki, and Monika Treut.

Lucy Fischer's essay on *Castro Street* correctly calls the film "fundamentally an abstract composition." The anecdotal comments she quotes from the film-maker tell us only where he gathered the images for his work, including some of the stunning shapes and colors of the final film:

> Castro Street running by the Standard Oil Refinery in Richmond, California . . . switch engines on one side and refinery tanks, stacks, and buildings on the other—the street and the film ending at a red lumber company.

A series of oppositions define the film—a phase of movement of camera and/or objects moving right is countered with another moving in the opposite direction. Color and black-and-white images are continually opposed and/or superimposed in whole or part. "Clearly it is this sense of oppositions confronted and synthesized which one perceives as dynamic resolution" in viewing the film. An additional subtlety in the film is Baillie's blurring the distinction between the movement of the camera and the movement of its object. Is the train in a shot moving or is the camera moving across it?

To Parsifal (1963) is an early Baillie film—his fourth overall and his most serious work to that time. (Virtually all of Baillie's best work was completed between 1961 and 1971: twelve films in eleven years.) As Alan Williams points out, the sixteen-minute film is divided equally into two parts of eight minutes each:

> Part one depicts a sunrise, a journey out to sea in a boat, then gulls flying around the boat while fish are cleaned, and finally the journey back and the reappearance of land. [The bright red blood of the fish stains the predominantly blue and white images of the film to that point.] In part two the setting changes from sea and coastline to a mountain forest traversed by railroad tracks. Workmen are seen repairing the tracks, after which a train passes through the forest while a nude woman stands nearby. The woman washes herself in a stream as insects move on ground and water. Then the workmen are seen repairing the tracks; a train appears and a man's hand pulls the woman away from the camera as the train continues through the forest, illuminated by a setting sun.

What we see of the woman is mainly limbs, hands, and feet; what is shocking, as nearly always in Baillie's work, is the contrast between colors: the tones of her skin and those of the forest. Thematically, the woman and forest, on the one hand, are opposed to the tracks, workers, and train, on the other. The conjunction of woman and nature is at once classical, ideological, and banal. The conjunction of man with thrusting technology is presented explicitly here as the rape of nature. The extensive use that Williams makes of Wagner's *Parsifal*— excerpts of which are played in both parts of the film—is most illuminating.

William R. Barr's four-page note concerns two Brakhage birth films, *Window Water Baby Moving* (1959) and *Thigh Line Lyre Triangular* (1961). The earlier film, included in many college campus collections, is seventeen minutes long; the second is five minutes. P. Adams Sitney classifies both as "lyrical films," but Barr plausibly insists that the first is half-lyric and half-documentary. Barr sees the second film, which uses extensive painting on the images, as "a layered, integrated affirmation of all creativity." He sees it also as an important step toward Brakhage's later work.

A refreshing aspect of Barr's piece is his willingness to criticize Brakhage for "the egocentricity of his commentary" on *Window*. It is clear from Jane Brakhage's testimony and from Stan's own accounts that she contributed importantly to the planning and execution of the film, which he is at pains to claim as his own alone. Barr's firmly expressed reservations go hand in hand with his affirmation of Brakhage's power and importance as an artist.

Had it been written twenty years ago, *Thelma & Louise* might well have ended up as a Roger Corman picture; it would have fit right in with Corman's own *Bloody Mama* (1969) and the Corman-produced *Boxcar Bertha* (1972) and *Crazy Mama* (1975), directed by Martin Scorsese and Jonathan Demme, respectively. In those tough, low-budget films there was no Ansel Adams lighting and no policeman who seems to be bucking for the Nobel Peace Prize. Also, needless to say, the women in those films committed and ran from actual crimes, not self-defense against a brutal attempted rape.

That was then, and it is precisely its relation to the now that makes *Thelma & Louise* so fascinating. It seems that most films these days are either hits or flops—the middle range has narrowed considerably. It took a big production, big stars, and a big director and cinematographer to make even such a well-crafted, nicely judged script into a successful film. Or, more precisely, to attract enough initial attention to reach Friday–Saturday moviegoers.

A number of our eight contributors devote attention to the question of genre in *Thelma & Louise*. Harvey R. Greenberg recalls Ridley Scott's earlier work as using "popular genre toward revisionist ends": *The Duellists* (1977), *Alien*

(1979), and *Blade Runner* (1982). But *Thelma & Louise* "arguably wins the prize for sheer number of genres interrogated against the grain in a single Scott picture." Greenberg identifies classic and contemporary Westerns, various subgenres of road movies, and seventies buddy movies. Leo Braudy suggests Westerns and film noir. Peter N. Chumo II sees the film as what he calls a "road screwball comedy," of which *It Happened One Night* is the prototype. Other outlaw films, even those with deadpan humor, nevertheless lack "the self-awareness or growth typical of the smart, witty screwball heroine." Screwball's "liberation and growth through role-playing" are seen, for instance, in Thelma's robbery of the market. The scene with the policeman and other scenes reveal the "smart, sassy lines of a screwball heroine who has a sense of humor about her situation." However, whereas the screwball couple "normally achieve a clarity of vision that enables them to be reintegrated into society," in *Thelma & Louise* this does not happen.

Brian Henderson's contribution deals with the narrative organization of *Thelma & Louise.* Although, like most films, it tells its story chronologically, it organizes narrative time, and the distinct temporalities that result, in a way that powerfully enhances its theme. The heroines are always shown together, with the exception of two scenes that create contrasts by crosscutting between them. The main body of the film is structured by crosscutting between the escaping protagonists and their reluctant pursuer, the FBI agent who is monitoring their case. Both the police scenes and the scenes with Thelma and Louise are temporarily indeterminate. This is a worry-free scheme that allows the filmmakers to elide what they wish in each story, but it also serves to immerse us in the divided temporality of the heroines: a continual motion forward and a continual reflection backward.

Linda Williams compares *Thelma & Louise* not only to *Butch Cassidy and the Sundance Kid,* with which it shares a final, all-but-fatal freeze-frame, but also to "that most resonant of revenge Westerns, John Ford's *The Searchers.*" Like Ethan, Louise has a clouded past that is referred to vaguely and never explained. We suspect, from her angry, vengeful reaction to her friend's imminent rape, that rape was likely her trauma in Texas. She notes also:

> The sheer surprise of *Thelma & Louise* is to have shown, in a way that serious films about the issue of rape (cf., *The Accused*) could never show, how victims of sexual crime are unaccountably placed in the position of the guilty ones, positioned as fair game for further attack.

Carol J. Clover emphasizes not those men who disliked *Thelma & Louise,* as early debate about the film did, but the far more significant fact that large numbers of men saw it and liked it. Indeed, she believes that "a real corner in gender representation has been turned in mainstream film history." But the same corner was turned fifteen years ago in so-called exploitation cinema. Horror fans recognize the "tough-girl heroes" in various mainstream films as "upscale immigrants from slasher and rape-revenge movies of the eighties—forms that reveal in no uncertain terms the willingness, not to say desire, of the male viewer to feel not just *at* but *through* female figures on screen."

Albert Johnson's piece—"Bacchantes at Large"—and Leo Braudy's—"Satire into Myth"—are oddly parallel and complementary, not least in taking a large view of *Thelma & Louise.* Johnson calls the film "an entertaining and picaresque tragicomedy" and a vivid portrait of an America in which women are still struggling to define their individualities: "it is a symbolic perusal of feminine inconsistencies." He notes Louise's "totally realistic" version of the world, and her exasperation with Thelma's naivete becomes a bitter commentary on the failure of her own hope. He also notes an aspect of the film that has escaped notice. "Much attention is given to landscape; the imitation Hollywood motels off the highways; a conglomerate of oil wells in dusty twilights; and faces of aged, displaced people, seen briefly in doorways and windows, remnants of lost dreams (particularly for Louise, who notices them)."

In the country-western bar the characters visit, Leo Braudy observes, "men and women alike wear the paraphernalia of fantasy western individualism. In this atmosphere of the ersatz and the fallen," the attempted rape of Thelma and Louise's killing of the rapist "cuts through like an icy blast, announcing the violence and brutality under the celluloid-thin mists of self-sufficiency and heroism." On the road, the camera stresses the "choking inevitability of the world they are trying to escape," not just the massive machinery, the oil drills and trucks, but even Monument Valley: the benevolent spaces of John Ford Westerns are shot as walls constraining the heroines. As opposed to Scott films centering on "romantically posturing men," *Thelma & Louise* opts "more for wisecracks and the techniques of comic exaggeration than for self-important despair." The film's "violence erupts within a hard-edged satire of wannabe heroism and consumer identity" and builds to a conclusion that moves the duo "out of this heightened satiric reality into myth."

Marsha Kinder's piece is a fascinating comparative study of *Thelma & Louise* and *Messidor* (1979), a film by Swiss filmmaker Alain Tanner, whose works "address feminist concerns within a broad political context that also includes issues of class conflict, racism, and transnationalism." Both films are road movies about a pair of women who "abandon their traditional place in patriarchal culture, a transgression that at first seems trivial but soon turns them into gun-toting outlaws and that ultimately leads to death." In both films also, the women's journey takes them from the city to the country, where they have a communion with nature that makes them realize there is no going back.

The true glory of *Thelma & Louise* is that, in a phrase of the Roland Barthes era, it has made the culture speak. Not since the classics of the sixties and seventies, and perhaps *Blade Runner* (1982), have on-screen events so buzzed the volubility centers of so many viewers.

SPECIAL FEATURE

Independent Cinema

Vol. 29, no. 3 (Spring 1976): 14–34.

THE SHORT AND THE DIFFICULT

Because of its analogies with drama and novel, the analyst of fictional narrative film can draw upon literally thousands of years of critical analysis—stretching back through Aristotle's *Poetics,* which laid out the fundamental critical categories (plot, character, spectacle, and so on) which go echoing on, even now, through the columns of your daily paper's film review section. Generations of Hollywood practitioners have put down on paper their accumulated how-to-do-it structural wit and wisdom. More recently theoreticians have attempted to deploy the machinery of linguistic and folk-tale analysis in order to understand how narrative films are put together. Though individual films continue to offer puzzles that tax even brilliant critics, there do not seem to be any greatly challenging theoretical lacunae in this area.

But astonishingly little work has been done on non-narrative forms. It is as if, in the history of literary study, virtually no attention had been paid to lyric poetry or the short story—only to novels and plays.

It seems likely that the structures of short, lyric forms are distinctly different from those of longer forms. The familiar, reliable devices of tension and suspense do not seem to apply, at least not in any easily recognizable way. Effects are often more akin to those of song than of drama. Visual considerations carry relatively more weight than in the story film where "action" tends to predominate, yet they are hard to describe and assess. In short, if we are to understand how the lyric film "works," we evidently need an entirely different sort of critical and theoretical approach than we use for the narrative film. Yet even the devotees of independent or experimental or "underground" cinema have failed to develop the new ideas that might enable us to understand such works on a more than impressionistic basis.

It is time to begin to try to remedy this situation. Here are several articles which attempt to deploy a critical methodology appropriate to non-narrative works. Perhaps significantly, two of these deal with films by Bruce Baillie—whose works are among those in our independent cinema that most resist paraphrase into verbal structures.

[*Ed. note*]

LUCY FISCHER

CASTRO STREET: THE SENSIBILITY OF STYLE

I do not place the artist on a pedestal as a little god. He is only the interpreter of
the inexplicable, for the layman the link between the known and the unknown, the
beyond. This is mysticism, of course! How else can one explain why a combination
of lines by Kandinsky or a form by Brancusi, not obviously related to the cognized
world, does bring such intense response . . . granted the eye becomes excited, why?

Edward Weston, *The Flame of Recognition*

In making this entry of April 7, 1930, in his classic *Daybooks*, Edward Weston
touched upon one of the central mysteries of our response to art: the manner in
which pure forms can speak to us and impress us with a sense of their meaning.
He characterizes the process as essentially mystical; but his consciousness of the
materiality of form and structure seems to render him somewhat uneasy with
that conclusion and he ends the passage much as he began, still questioning why.

It is thoughts of this nature which inflect our response to *Castro Street,* by
Bruce Baillie. Like the works of a Brancusi or Kandinsky, it is fundamentally
an abstract composition. For the rhetoric of pure line and form it substitutes
the orchestration of photographic images treated as graphic elements within a
complex montage design. And like the response to abstract art expressed by
Weston in his remarks, our reaction to *Castro Street* involves a level of questioning. For the potency of its address inspires us to fathom the means by
which its plastic abstractions communicate a sense of their significance.

On the surface, *Castro Street* presents an audiovisual tapestry in which footage
of a railroad yard and oil refinery are subtly interwoven. Strands of imagery (of
trains, smokestacks, industrial landscapes) appear on the screen to the accompaniment of a score of muted mechanical sounds. Discrete shots, however, seem devoid of autonomous, representational status. Rather each becomes a pictorial
thread intertwined with others in the fabric of an overall pattern.

In this manner *Castro Street* creates for the spectator an experience which
transcends the nature of its literal subject. As we watch graceful figures of train
cars float by, and listen to the dampened sounds of engine-whistle screams,
what we apprehend is not a picture of the industrial décor. Rather what we experience is something more vague and ethereal; it is a sense of profound and
dynamic resolution.

What we perceive in our viewing of *Castro Street* finds reverberations in
certain experiences Baillie seems to have had at the time of the film's creation.

We know that it was made during a severe period in the artist's life, one in which he felt as if he "were being born";[1] hence his cryptic epithet for the film—"the coming of consciousness."

Although the exact nature of that experience is known to Baillie alone, two enigmatic notes he made at the time offer us entree to his private sensibility as well as an approach to the aesthetics of the film. One appears in the form of a hand-written entry on a printed program for a screening of *Castro Street* and reads:

> the confrontation of opposites (Carl Jung)
> "the strength or conflict of becoming"[2]

Clearly the quote implies a relationship in Baillie's mind between the process of becoming ("the coming of consciousness") and the psychic confrontation of opposites. Its use on a program note suggests a further link between this conception and the formal structure of the film. This is substantiated by a reading of Baillie's catalogue description of *Castro Street*. For its language makes clear the sense of dialectical interactions imposed upon the configuration of the work:

> Castro Street running by the Standard Oil Refinery in Richmond, California . . . switch engines on one side and refinery tanks, stacks, and buildings on the other—the street and the film ending at a red lumber company. All visual and sound elements from the street, progressing from the beginning to the end of the street, one side is black-and-white (secondary) and one side is color—like male and female elements.[3]

But Baillie's perceptions of the period were of a more complex and resonant character. For in addition to a sense of the confrontation of opposites, Baillie postulated their ultimate dissolution. Thus while the world presents apparent polarities, true consciousness affords the perspective from which to apprehend their resolution. This notion seems best articulated in a second note by the artist, one which constitutes an entry in his *Castro Street* journals:

> now in my work, beyond sequence
> beyond distinctions. . . .
> way of conceiving reality
> sequence/knowledge
> beyond to
> real consciousness (ego loss)
> = agitation-less (loss)[4]

Clearly it is this sense of oppositions confronted and synthesized which one perceives as dynamic resolution in one's viewing experience of *Castro Street*. To inscribe this "way of conceiving reality" within the design of the film, Baillie has abstracted his photographic imagery to such a degree that it no longer presents an external depiction of reality. Rather it seems to have penetrated the surface of worldly appearance in order to render a vision of its deeper structures.

In grappling with the issue of our response to abstract art Weston had relegated its power to the realm of mysticism, thus avoiding a fruitful answer to the question. He had, however, concluded with a critical challenge, by asking "how *else*" we might explain art's cogent effect. In many ways an examination of *Castro Street* provides an occasion to engage that challenge. For rather than some "inexplicable link . . . between the known and the unknown," we find, upon analysis of the cinematic text, concrete relationships between Baillie's "metaphysical" postulations and his methods of plastic organization. Thus the dynamic of oppositions confronted and resolved which Baillie enunciated in his writings is manifested in the film on the level of formal interactions between color, movement, and sound.

While for Baillie the "coming of consciousness" arose in the domain of spiritual revelation, for the viewer of *Castro Street* it transpires in the realm of critical insight. For not only does the film afford us access to Baillie's particular sensibility; it occasions a consciousness of the means by which a sensibility can be articulated in a rigorous artistic form.

On all its complex tectonic levels the central mechanism of *Castro Street* involves the construction of formal oppositions in order ultimately to deconstruct them and dissolve the very notion of opposition itself. In this regard Baillie departs from the Eisensteinian conception of montage as collision. For while the Eisensteinian aesthetic calls for the intensification of oppositions, Baillie's editing style works toward the nullification of oppositions. If for Eisenstein "art is always conflict according to its methodology,"[5] for Baillie *Castro Street* encompasses a gesture in the direction "beyond sequence, beyond distinctions. . . ."

But, of course, to "go beyond" implies at first being "there"; and it is by examining the modes of articulating formal polarities within *Castro Street* that we arrive at a vision of how they are ultimately transcended into unity.

Castro Street is, above all else, a film of hyperbolic superimposition; from beginning to end it creates a uniform texture of densely enmeshed imagery. It would seem that implicit in the very mechanics of superimposition would be the kind of dialectical conflict that formed the basis of Eisenstein's theory of montage. After all, in superimposition it is as though the myriad oppositions that Eisenstein had posited as arising between the shots are encompassed literally within the frame itself.

If one examines the course of Baillie's career, however, one seems to witness a growing dissatisfaction with the dialectical quality of superimposition, and an evolution in the contrary direction. He speaks, for example, in disparaging terms of his use of "gross" superimpositions in *Quixote* and refers to his technical endeavor as "crudely trying to combine images on the screen at the same moment."[6]

Despite its perceived failures, however, *Quixote* did mark for Baillie the initiation of an attempt to neutralize the oppositions inherent in superimposition. It signaled a move in Baillie's work toward allowing diverse imagery to "share the frame."[7] This stylistic trend would ultimately culminate in the creation of *Quick Billy* in 1970, but *Castro Street* stands as a major aesthetic plateau along the way. The making of *Castro Street* in fact seems to have embodied Baillie's shift in formal direction:

> I used two projectors when I edited. . . . When I first projected it, the two things together, it was a beautiful film just as it was. I projected on the same spot on the screen not side by side as it would be when I finally had done it.[8]

In *Castro Street*, therefore, Baillie veers from a heavily layered style of superimposition to a style of superimposed contiguity. Through this technique images are planted in neighboring segments of the frame—either by direct superimposition or by the more elusive strategy of matting.

Castro Street begins in darkness with Baillie's name handwritten across the screen. The center of the frame then opens up in muted color to reveal what appears to be a camera lens. The frame contracts once more and closes. A slit of light becomes visible in the lower portion of the frame. Gradually, the light pattern shifts and we realize that what we have seen has been light reflected off a glass surface, through which we now vaguely perceive the outline of smoke. The glass is then pulled away and bares the image of industrial smokestacks. Two matted areas (in upper and lower right-hand corners of the frame) fade in. Each one records a slightly different view of a commercial landscape as seen from the window of a moving vehicle. Next a faint diagonal wipe takes away the large-scale image of the smokestacks; the twin mattes remain. Another portion of the frame then unfolds to display a more defined image of industrial chimneys. This matted area travels upward in the frame while simultaneously the two earlier corner mattes fade out. Eventually a diagonally composed negative image of a high-tension wire (as seen from a moving car) fades in and inhabits the frame with a circular matte containing the image of a smokestack.

What becomes apparent from this description is the seamlessness of Baillie's design (a seamlessness which makes the attempt at verbal translation an act of critical hubris). Rather than creating a sense of superimposed images in dialectical conflict, Baillie works against this to create a sense of coherent union. He embeds one image within another and fuses them so that they "come out as though they were married."[9]

Perhaps the most mystifying example of this technique occurs towards the end of the film. The sequence begins with a low-angle shot of a man standing on an industrial machine against the background of a blue sky. At a certain point the center of the frame gapes open (like a wound) and shows us a yellow-tinted image of a metal pipe. Magically the image of the man (which has become the matting environment of the second shot) transforms to a monotone blue, then to a solid black, and finally returns to the image of the man. The central yellow area then closes up and disappears.

It is this organic sense of the connection of shots that is so crucial to the power of *Castro Street*—the sense of a shot opening up and closing to reveal a second shot, much as the iris of the eye expands and contracts to delineate the boundaries of the pupil.

Thus we find that the heightening of shot distinctions that traditionally occurs in layered superimposition becomes an annihilation of distinctions in the kinetics of matting. Matting is, after all, the quintessential Hollywood illusionist technique; it allows the fluid combination of images without the telltale traces of superimposition. It accomplishes the merging of images while blurring our consciousness of the act of fusion.

The intention to combine shots was at points inscribed within the very process of shooting the film itself. For in recording images Baillie used his black-gloved hand to reserve spaces which would later be occupied by other shots.

Concomitant with the elimination of shot differentiation in *Castro Street* is the weakening of temporal distinctions. Often the images so joinlessly share the frame that it is difficult to establish whether they were photographed simultaneously as one shot or represent two separate temporal moments joined only in the editing process. As Baillie has phrased it in relation to *Quick Billy*, his matting strategy is one of overlaying imagery so that it "looks like it was all invented or occurring at the same moment."[10]

But it is not purely the technique of matting that creates the sense of image resolution; it is also Baillie's means of rhythmically choreographing the images in succession. What one notices in analyzing *Castro Street* are the "transactions" that take place between shots. As one matte fades out, another, perhaps, fades in. Thus one set of imagery is continually exchanged for another in intricate patterns of balanced and symmetrical progression. At one point in the film, for example, we have a shot involving two layers of superimposition. The first presents a negative image of the ground, and the second a negative representation of trains in motion. As the latter image remains on the screen the former fades out; but as it does so it is replaced by a shot of flowers in close-up. Through this technique of

Raw footage showing matting process used in *Castro Street* (Canyon Cinema)

the interchange of imagery, shots are joined not only by their compression within the boundaries of the frame but by the kinetics of the editing process itself. Baillie seems to be alluding to this sense of montage when he formulates his notion of the cut as the moment "when one thing *becomes another* in succession."[11]

This sense of one thing becoming another is further accentuated by the fact that the pace of movement from shot to shot in *Castro Street* is one of lulling uniformity. Thus the rhythm of a tracking shot on one image level of the frame will be synchronous with a panning action on another. The similarity of tempo works to nullify the disjunction in form and subject.

Not only does the matting process minimize the boundaries between discrete shots, it works as well to soften the rigid quadrilateral borders of the frame. Thus Baillie utilizes the biomorphically shaped matte provided by his hand to "get away from geometry" and create a "moving amorphous form."[12]

Another formal opposition that Baillie simultaneously activates and neutralizes is that of black-and-white versus color. His engagement of the tonal conflict is even apparent in his description of the film: " . . . picture and sound taken on one street—the color side female, the black-and-white side male, in opposition (creation)."[13]

But it is characteristically ambiguous that Baillie has chosen a sexual analogy to illustrate this formal polarity. For implicit in the invocation of discrete sexual elements is the possibility of their fusion in sexual union.

Most often in *Castro Street* tonalities are opposed through the technique of superimposition; thereby, one of the layers of imagery will be recorded in color while the other will be shot in black-and-white. Frequently this disparity is heightened by the fact that the black-and-white layer has been realized in high-contrast negative. One example of this pattern occurs midway through the film in a multi-tiered composite image of objects in movement. On one layer a yellow train car moves left to right across the screen while on another a black-and-white train wheel floats by in the same direction.

Given this virtually textbook case of montage "collision," what accounts for the fact that our experience of the tonal dialectics of *Castro Street* is one of essential tranquillity? It would seem that several formal strategies are at work to dampen the potential sense of chromatic tension.

First of all, Baillie begins the film in highly muted color, the kind that barely reaches consciousness as such. It is a ghostly color that forms a vaporous immaterial hue, like that of a rainbow. On this level Baillie's subdued chromatics tend to accentuate the ethereality of his images, as well as to blur the perceptual distinction between color and black-and-white.

Having established this diluted tonality, Baillie then begins quite carefully to introduce "true" colors, almost as "characters" into the abstract narrative. Red is the "star" of the film; it comes as the first rich color on the caboose of a train and it reappears in the middle of the film, at first anamorphically, and then as a red steering wheel. Characteristically it closes the film with the climactic image of the dome-roofed lumber barn at the end of the street.

Significantly, blue and yellow play supporting roles as the other major colors in which *Castro Street* is painted. Blue appears as the hazy background in which so many images are planted and also as the sky. Yellow hues occur on industrial pipes, in an anamorphic vision of rocks, and, most strikingly, in a field which neighbors Castro Street.

Blue, yellow, and red are, of course, the primary colors. Thus *Castro Street* is tinted in archetypal tones: black (the absence of color), white (the presence of all colors), and the primary colors (those which are parents to all the rest).

Certain theoretical speculations arise from this formal choice. First of all, it seems telling that in utilizing black-and-white Baillie saw fit to invert their values through negative printing. In so doing, the comfortable opposition of the absence or presence of color is turned on its head and disarmed. Moreover, at times during the film Baillie chooses to dissect white light through prismatic lenses, thereby revealing the presence of variegated spectral hues in its apparently monochrome band. Finally, the selection of primary colors adds further complexities to the tonal structure. For although primary colors in "montage collision" create all other chromatic hues, theirs is essentially a seamless union. As R. L. Gregory explains it in *Eye and Brain*: " . . . two colours give a third colour in which the constituents cannot be defined. Constituent sounds are heard as a chord and can be separately identified . . . but no training allows us to do the same for light."[14] Thus primary colors work in montage in a manner similar to that of Baillie's imagery: distinctions are apparently there and not there at the same time.

Another formal conflict which is engaged and then released within the dynamics of *Castro Street* is the directional opposition of movement. Once more its primary means of formulation is the technique of superimposition. Throughout the film when images share the frame we often find that they embody movement in opposing screen directions. Typical of this pattern is a shot involving directly superimposed images of trains in motion: one image layer moves horizontally left to right, while the other moves diagonally into the depth of the frame. Perhaps the most hyperbolic instance of editing for antagonistic movement comes rather early in the film. A variety of moving-train images in high contrast negative are edited in split-screen format so that they seem to crash together in the central axis of the frame.

This moment, however, in its climacticism, is essentially uncharacteristic of the mode in which Baillie handles movement in the rest of the film. For in general in *Castro Street* Baillie works to resolve rather than heighten the sense of polarity of movement; and he does so by employing a variety of techniques. To begin with, when editing images of opposing motion Baillie most often juxtaposes movements executed in quasi-identical rhythms. Thereby the synchronicity of the pace of movements seems to blur our recognition of their antipathetic directions. Rather than collide, the images tend to cancel each other out and leave us with a sense of quiescent stasis. One is reminded of an exchange between Baillie and an interviewer that appeared in *Film Comment*:

BB: I have to say finally what I *am* interested in, like Socrates: peace . . . rest
      . . . nothing.

FC: No movement at all?

BB: Nothing. Okay, that's enough.[15]

Exceptions do occur when Baillie utilizes a sense of syncopation in the rhythm of objects in motion. Ironically, however, the example that comes to mind is one in which the objects depicted are moving in the *same* direction. Toward the end of the film we have an image of a right-to-left tracking shot over signs plastered on a wall. Next the image of a train moving in the same direction fades in, superimposed. The pace of the train, however, is slower than that of the track and at points its movement seems to be reversed.

Thus when directionally contrary movements are involved Baillie works to buffer their sense of opposition; where similarity exists, distinctions are maintained. "Different" is the "same" and the "same" is "different" until the very poles of the semantic equation become meaningless.

But movement in *Castro Street* involves a greater subtlety as well; for central to our experience of its ambiguity is Baillie's blurring of the distinctions between the camera and its object as a source of movement. This is possible because of the phenomenon of relativity of movement in film. As Rudolf Arnheim explains it in *Film As Art:*

> Since there are no bodily sensations to indicate whether the camera was at rest or in motion, and if in motion at what speed or in what direction, the camera's position is, for want of other evidence, presumed to be fixed. Hence if something moves in the picture this motion is at first seen as a movement of the thing itself and not as the result of a movement of the camera gliding past a stationary object. In the extreme case this leads to the direction of motion being reversed.[16]

Thus throughout *Castro Street* even the secure notion of directionality is confounded. We may see objects move by from screen right to left but more often than not, examination reveals them to be stationary objects photographed by a camera moving from left to right.

Inherent in this paradox are certain theoretical overtones. For by employing this perceptual ambiguity Baillie generates confusions between the traditional antipathies of stasis and motion, and left and right. And the reason that these polarities can be questioned is that he has dissolved a third and more profound distinction: that between the perceiver and the perceived. Thus because of the ambiguity concerning whether it is the perceiver (i.e., the camera eye) or the object perceived (or both) that is in motion, it is possible that what is moving within the frame may, in fact, be static; and what "moves" left may have been photographed by a camera moving right.

A unifying sensibility is also apparent in two final parameters of the film's construction. *Castro Street* embraces a variety of modes of vision yet works to resolve any tension engendered by their disparity. Where "clear" images prevail, Baillie works against their sense of realism and definition by using matting, damped coloration, negative printing, or the slurring effect of an improperly threaded camera.[17] Where anamorphic photography occurs, Baillie often subverts its sense of abstraction by removing the distorting, mediating gel and revealing the subject in sharp focus. Obviously, the mutually exclusive perceptual modes implied by the polarities of color versus black-and-white, negative versus positive registration, are contained as well within the incorporative vision of the film.

In many ways the confounding of styles of vision mirrors the conflation of perceptual modes that we find in Baillie's diaries and notebooks. Just as clear and anamorphic sections intermix within the film, so fragments from waking and dreaming states flow together in the journals.

Baillie also works in *Castro Street* to nullify any sense of disjunction between the sound and image tracks. He does so, however, without resorting to the facile technique of illusionistic sync sound. Rather *Castro Street* creates a highly abstract sound track that, while never illustratively coinciding with the images, provides an almost synaesthetic aural equivalent for them. The texture of the sound track parallels that of the image and follows a similar "narrative" line. In sections where the editing of the shots creates a regular lulling rhythm (e.g., the opening of the film), the sound track heightens this mode of temporality by intoning monotonous chugging train sounds. At moments of visual climax (e.g., when a mass of superimposed images "crashes" in the center of the screen) the sounds take the form of louder, harsher, shrill whistle screams.

This formal unity of sound and image is characteristic of other films by Baillie. The highly montagist section of *Mass* which presents an assertive visual collage translates this strategy to the aural parameter as well. Thus Baillie accompanies images from old movies and television with fragments of dialogue from commercials, newscasts, and television dramas. The total fusion of sound and image in *All My Life* (which consists of a single tracking shot of a fence accompanied by Ella Fitzgerald's rendition of the title song) is apparent in Baillie's characterization of the film as "a singing fence."[18]

Just as sound-to-image dichotomies are blurred in *Castro Street*, so sound-to-sound distinctions are elided. Disparate mechanical sounds blend together and those ostensibly from the train yard merge indistinguishably with those from the oil refinery, forming a unified aural composition.

Ultimately even the subject matter of *Castro Street* reveals its own impulse toward bracketing contradictions. Like the industrial landscape of *Red Desert* the mise-en-scène of *Castro Street* stands as a hybrid cross of barren technological sordidness and stark arresting beauty. As P. Adams Sitney noted: "When we look at the whole of [Baillie's] work we see in alternation two incompatible themes; the sheer beauty of the phenomenal world and the utter despair of forgotten men."[19]

Yet central to the magic of *Castro Street* would seem to be its power to make the incompatible compatible—to contain contradictions both on a formal and thematic level. It is, perhaps, even more profoundly the point of *Castro Street* to refuse us the comfort of such categorical polarities at all. One is curiously reminded of Eisenstein's discussion of Japanese culture and of his analysis of their traditional synthesis of the oppositions of auditory and visual material:

> audio visual relationships . . . derive from the principles of Yang and Yin, upon which is based the entire system of Chinese world outlook and philosophy . . . Yang and Yin . . . depicted as a circle, locked together within it *Yang* and *Yin*—*Yang*, light; *Yin*, dark—each carrying within itself the essence of the other, each shaped to the other—*Yang* and *Yin*, *forever opposed, forever united*.[20]

Bruce Baillie's *Castro Street*

It is precisely this sense of unity revealed in disunity, of resolution in opposition that reigns supreme on all levels of *Castro Street*—on the level of shot-to-shot superimposition, directionality of movement, tonal composition, sound-image relation, and spiritual sensibility.

As Baillie has told us, *Castro Street* is a film "in the form of a street." Implicit in this notion seems the concept of the film as path, or even journey. We know from Baillie's autobiographical notes that the film was for him a "coming of consciousness—a recognition of the confrontation of opposites as part of the 'conflict of becoming.'" But throughout the film itself, embedded within the opaque imagery, have been signs which seem to bear hidden messages relevant to Baillie's concerns. Thus the graphic "X" of the railroad crossing sign seems a symbolic diagram of the structure of the film (which is, after all, an intersection point of formal and thematic oppositions). And the appearance of the railroad name of "Union Pacific" emblazoned on a passing car seems tinged by a vague, metaphysical resonance.

But it is the final emblem of the film that warrants our most attentive reading, and it appears in the form of a sign for *Castro Street* that floats by on the screen. For contained within the graphics and articulation of that closing image is inscrolled the very dynamics that have informed the style and meaning of the film. It is an image that speaks a language of resolved oppositions: It is one of the final images of the work yet presents to us for the first time the title of the film. It is recorded in black-and-white negative yet is superimposed over a positively registered red-colored barn dome image. It *moves* across the screen, yet was, of course, in reality, *static*. It drifts past us right to left but depicts an arrow which points left to right.

Thus the sign which bears the name of *Castro Street* is clearly more than a street sign. Its pregnant mode of presentation proposes it as truly exemplary of the formal and thematic energies of the film.

NOTES

1. Richard Whitehall, "Interview with Bruce Baillie," *Film Culture*, No. 47, pp. 17–18.
2. Bruce Baillie, Program for *Castro Street*. File: Museum of Modern Art.
3. Bruce Baillie in P. Adams Sitney, *Visionary Film* (New York: Oxford University Press, 1974), p. 208.
4. Bruce Baillie, Notebook entry, May 22, 1966.
5. Sergei Eisenstein, *Film Form* (New York: Harcourt, Brace and World, 1949), p. 48.
6. Bruce Baillie, MOMA Cineprobe Tape, April 7, 1970.
7. Richard Corliss, "Bruce Baillie: An Interview," *Film Comment*, Vol. 7, No. 1 (Spring 1971), p. 25.
8. Whitehall, *op. cit.*, p. 7.
9. Bruce Baillie, MOMA Cineprobe Tape, April 7, 1970.
10. *Ibid.*
11. Corliss, *op. cit.*, p. 26.
12. Bruce Baillie, MOMA Cineprobe Tape, April 7, 1970.
13. Bruce Baillie, in *Harbinger*, Vol. 1, No. 1 (July 1967), p. 32.
14. R. L. Gregory, *Eye and Brain* (New York: McGraw-Hill, 1973), p. 119.
15. Corliss, *op. cit.*, p. 31.
16. Rudolf Arnheim, *Film As Art* (Berkeley: University of California Press, 1957), pp. 131–32.
17. Sitney, *op. cit.*, p. 208.
18. Bruce Baillie in *Harbinger*, Vol. 1, No. 1 (July 1967), p. 34.
19. Sitney, Museum of Modern Art Circular #66.
20. Eisenstein, *Film Sense* (New York: Harcourt, Brace and World, 1947), p. 93.

ALAN WILLIAMS

THE STRUCTURE OF LYRIC: BAILLIE'S *TO PARSIFAL*

It's difficult to say exactly where or how *To Parsifal* is a lyric film and where or how a narrative work. For this reason, ordinary critical vocabularies (based on certain "types" of films) do not apply with much usefulness to Bruce Baillie's abstractly assembled color images, nor to the nature and functions of his sound track. To get a sense of how this film *works* it will be necessary first to break it down, *outline* it, in order to see how the (implied) viewer puts it together.*

The 16-minute film falls neatly into two nearly equal parts, separated by fades to and from black.

Part one depicts a sunrise, a journey out to sea in a boat, then gulls flying around the boat while fish are cleaned, and finally the journey back and the reappearance of land. This is, narratively, a reasonably clear presentation of a fishing voyage; the only strange thing, informationally, is the absence of human beings (except for the hands seen cleaning fish). In part two the setting changes from sea and coastline to a mountain forest traversed by railroad tracks. Workmen are seen repairing the tracks, after which a train passes through the forest while a nude woman stands nearby. The woman washes herself in a stream as insects move on ground and water. Then the workmen are again seen repairing the tracks; a train appears and a man's hand pulls the woman away from the camera as the train continues through the forest, illuminated by a setting sun.

The two parts function as one larger unit by similar patterns of development and by a strong sense of temporal progression. Part one begins at sunrise and seems to end during the afternoon. The second part begins at some time in the morning and ends with a sunset. Whether we are to take the film as occurring during a single day or during two days seems beside the point; the work has an almost mythic sense of time. As the beginning of part one and the end of part two are connected by the presence of the sun, the end of the first part and the beginning of the second are connected by the presence of mist (subtly underlined by the foghorn on the sound track during the darkness which separates the two units).

Both parts exhibit a circular (symmetrical) construction which also contributes to the mythic—ritualistic—aspects of the work. This is most striking

---

* The "viewer" here, strictly speaking, means the principle of possible meanings built into the work, the ways in which structures outside the film *must* be brought to bear in order for its reading to be coherent, to make "sense" of some sort. In this way, the text *needs* the implicit "viewer."

From the opening of Baillie's *To Parsifal* (Canyon Cinema)

in the ABA movements of the fishing voyage: land to water to land again—voyage out, fish and gulls, voyage back. There is another large ABA structure at work in part one, not specifically connected with the story as such (though it contributes to the overall formal structure). This is the alternation on the sound track between music and "natural" sounds. The film begins with a coast-guard weather report, recorded (seemingly) on the boat. This continues to the fourth shot of the film, where it slowly fades out as music fades in—an excerpt from Wagner's *Prelude* to *Parsifal*. This music continues almost until the end of part one, when foghorns and boat noises are heard, continuing through to the dark screen which divides the work.

Part two is more complex, as may be seen merely from its density of shots (65 as opposed to part one's 43) and from the more frequent alternations on the sound track. Nevertheless, the same formal principles are at work. The workmen and the train appear twice, at the beginning and end. The middle portion (woman bathing and the insects) is not repeated and does not incorporate any elements which precede or follow it—except for the woman, who is seen in a different place, in a different light (this being the brightest tonality in part two), and from a different camera angle and position. The principal elements new to the repeated "A" section in part two are the man's hand and the sunset, but both have their equivalents in part one: the hands which clean the fish, and the rising sun. What is lacking in the forest scenes is a means of "explaining" the images, as part one can be called a fishing expedition. (We will see later that much clarification of this part's "story" can be obtained by relating it to Wagner's opera.)

The sound track for part two is more complex than that of part one, but it still proceeds by an alternation of music and "natural" noises. There are four sections of music, drawn from the body of the opera, which alternate with three types of sounds associated with the train: the voices of the workmen, wheels on the tracks, and the train whistle. This grouping is similar to that in part one where all "real" sound was connected with the boat. Thus we can represent the structure of part two as an expansion of the circular pattern already noted in connection with part one. If A signifies music and B natural sound, the pattern is AB ABA BA. Part one begins and ends with natural sound-effects, whereas part two begins and ends with music.

So far I have been indulging in what would most frequently be called a "formal" analysis of *To Parsifal*. The question most frequently raised by such a procedure (and rightly so) is: where does it lead? What does this analysis say about the text and its production of meaning? The ABA structure (and its expansion) which we have isolated, first of all, *does* contribute to the "mythic" feeling of Baillie's film. But more importantly, the heavy formal equivalences between the two sections of the work permit us to draw some tentative conclusions about the visual and thematic equivalences between these sections.

The boat with its wake and the train with its track have similar places in the formal configurations of parts one and two. The fish and the woman, as well as the animals that surround them—gulls and insects—appear only in the "B" sections of the two parts. Constant in both sections are the functional equivalences between ocean and land, masts and trees. Thus, the formal parallels we have noted have repercussions on what might be termed a thematic level. Significantly, the visual treatment of these same elements (particularly masts = trees, wake = tracks, and ocean = land) matches up through composition within the image.

These tentative conclusions will have to suffice until we have investigated the formal structure of the film a bit further. The patterns we have observed have analogues at levels beyond the global movement of each section of the film. Our brief summary of the fishing expedition as presented in *To Parsifal* may be summarized as follows:

1. Prelude (sunrise): land, water, boat
2. Journey out to sea
3. Gulls and fish cleaning
4. The journey back

But are there any other criteria than narrative structure which make this grouping more valid than any other? For example, how do we separate segments 1 and 2, by what principle and at what moment?

There are some important formal principles differentiating the various segments which we have identified. Aside from shot content (which is still quite important), these segments are distinguished by emphasis on movement within the frame (segments 1 and 3) and movement—generally tracking—of the camera (segments 2 and 4). This is a distinction which will remain important for the second part of the film. Segments 2 and 4 are composed almost exclusively of tracking shots taken from the side of the boat. To this moving depiction of immobile objects is contrasted the fixed-camera shots of the moving sun, grass, and hands cleaning the fish in segments 1 and 3. This general tendency is contradicted by occasional shots, but as an overall structure device it remains remarkably constant.

The passage from one type of shot (and segment) to another is accomplished so smoothly as to be almost imperceptible. Shots 8 and 9 of the film, which demarcate what we have termed segments 1 and 2, are a good example. The camera, fixed, shows a close-up of water in motion, all white, taken from the shore. The new shot begins as apparently the same thing, until an upward pan to smoothly moving blue water reveals that we are now tracking with the boat, the first of a series of such shots which will continue until the beginning of the third segment, where lateral tracking is either absent or considerably de-emphasized, depending on the shot.

Another way in which these segments are differentiated is by their internal coherence. When we examine groupings of shots in *To Parsifal* we find a precise, almost abstract way of juxtaposing images and forming larger units with them. Two principles of coherence seem to be at work (these are common, it should be said, in many types of film). The first we might call a principle of alternation: given two types of shots—from different angles, distances, of different subjects, and so on—the two elements may alternate, ABAB and so on. The second principle we might term variation by distance: given a single subject or type of shot, the camera distance may change from long shot to medium to close-up or vice versa. In *To Parsifal* these two procedures occur sometimes independently, sometimes in combination. Breaks in the narrative structure and significant individual shots are emphasized by the absence of these two types of coherence.

Described in this fashion, these two principles of organization may well seem artless and mechanical. Their action within the film, however, is subtle and balanced. Perhaps the easiest way to demonstrate the work's artful manipulation of such formal principles is to study the "fish and gulls" segment in part one. The core of this segment is formed by the perfectly symmetrical development of images of the fish being cleaned:

> Medium shot, camera up: many gulls flying by the boat; the rope swings briefly into the foreground, with water seen at the end of the shot (20 seconds)

> Extreme close-up, camera down towards table: bloody fish's mouth, very red (1.7 seconds)

> Medium shot, up: sky and a gull flying alongside the boat, mast and cable (11 seconds)

> Close-up, down: fish's body, knife cutting both the frame and the fish's belly (3.3 seconds)

> Medium close-up, down: three fish on a table, hands cleaning one of them (6 seconds)

> Close-up, down: one fish, split open; the knife passes through its body and the frame of the shot (4.0 seconds)

> Medium shot, up: sky and gull, mast and cable (same set-up as the third shot of this series; 2.7 seconds)

> Medium close-up, up: gulls flying, sky, no boat parts (1.7 seconds)

> Extreme close-up, down: a fish's head, its yellow eye in the right center of the frame (1.3 seconds)

> Medium shot, horizontal: empty sky framed by a doorway; the gulls fly in and out of the frame (8.3 seconds)

We may see that these shots are centered on the most distant (medium close-up) and longest (6 seconds) image of the fish. This shot is surrounded by briefer, closer images of fish, and this group of three is in turn surrounded by other shots of fish and of gulls, arranged symmetrically.

Thus, the appearance of the fish is regulated both by alternation with shots of gulls and by variation by distance. This new material—the fish—is introduced in a manner typical of the film as a whole: alternation is the rule, with subjects and formal procedures held over from the part of the film which immediately precedes. This is true, for example, in the distinction which we already made between movement in the shot (fish and gulls) and movement of the camera (tracking with the boat): the latter does not totally disappear in this segment but is phased in and out through the principle of alternation.

The use of color and shot duration in this segment is also characteristic of the development of the film as a whole. The first introduction of the fish motif is accomplished in a brief shot, particularly short in comparison to the 20-second shot which precedes it. The tonality of the film to this point has been largely blues and greens, with some yellow in the introductory segment, and the first shot of the bloody fish introduces an extreme hue of red which, in contrast, is nothing short of shocking. The last (equally brief) extreme close-up of the fish introduces a brilliant yellow not seen previously.

This "fish and gulls" segment is more rigidly developed than others in the film, in keeping with its central thematic importance. The opening (what we have labeled segment 1 of part one) of *To Parsifal*, on the other hand, shows much freer construction, even though it is still based on the same sorts of development and linking of images. This segment consists of:

Long shot, horizontal (vertical motion with boat): silhouette of boat on left in foreground; water, shore, sky lit by sun behind hills; title fades in and out over boat (27 seconds)

Medium long shot, horizontal: grass, hills, sky lit from behind hills (5 seconds)

Very long shot, horizontal: grass rustling, fence, hills, grey sky (8.6 seconds)

Long shot, horizontal (vertical motion with boat): boat parts in right foreground; water, hills, the sky lit by more light than previously (20 seconds). Dissolve to:

Long shot, horizontal: grass in foreground, hill, sea, sky (looking towards the sea; 10.8 seconds)

Long shot, horizontal: grass in foreground, moving furiously, hills, sky, no water (9.8 seconds)

Medium long shot, horizontal: rocks (one in foreground at right), sea, sky (10 seconds)

Close-up, downward camera: rocks, water in rapid movement, no sky (6.4 seconds)

We can see the principles of alternation and variation by distance at work in these shots. The second image, for example, appears to be (though from its lack of movement evidently is not) a closer shot of the hill with the sun behind it seen from the boat at the film's very beginning. Shot 3 introduces a new type of image—hills and grass, not at dawn—and is followed in shot 4 by a return to the elements of shot 1. Shots 5, 7, and 8 are successively closer views from a new vantage point (looking towards the sea) of rocks, shoreline, and water. Shot 6, on the other hand, is a closer view of the same elements seen in shot 3. In terms of content we could schematize this series as AABACBCC. This complex yet symmetrical pattern recalls the careful construction of baroque music or certain types of rhyme schemes in French poetry. Lest we give the impression of too much formal rigor we should note that duration of shots varies considerably in this segment. In general, it follows the film's tendency to accord more running time to more distant or complex shots at the expense of close-ups or simple visual groupings.

One more comment should be made about this opening to Baillie's film. The shots which we identified as types "A" and "C" are essentially the same type of shot taken from two directions, which will be the two directions of the film as a whole. Shots 1, 4, and presumably 2 are taken from the sea looking toward shore and rising sun. Shots 5, 7, and 8 are taken from the shore looking toward the sea. Thus the division we may note between shots 4 and 5, which is the point at which the segment folds back on itself formally (this emphasized by a dissolve), is explicable as the meeting of water and land—and the two different directions (and angles—up and down) from which they can be viewed. (Shots 4 and 6 are distinct in this series by including no reference to the sea or to direction at all; they seem to have been taken at an entirely different location and time of day. Indeed, they seem to refer to the second half of the film, particularly since they are strikingly similar to several of its shots.)

The second half of *To Parsifal* is, as we noted, more complex than the first. It is possible to carry out the same operation of segmentation as we did with part one, though the result is a bit less elegant. What is more important here is to explore further the structuring principles of the work and its possible meanings.

In examining the overall structure of parts one and two we posited an equivalence between the nude woman and the fish being cleaned. As the position of the woman will lead us into the central problems of an interpretation of Baillie's film, we will note the stages of her presentation. She first appears in a very brief close-up of the back of her head. This shot is surrounded by two almost identical shots of the train in motion. This procedure is comparable to the position of the first close-up of the fish (also, significantly, of its head), which is surrounded by shots (looking up, as with the train) of gulls. Use of color is analogous in the two cases: the red of the fish is the first use of this color in the midst of dominantly blue and white images, while the woman's blond hair is an almost equally great contrast to the muted greens and browns of the shots which surround it. Both woman and fish are introduced in shots of such short duration that it is only with their second, longer appearances that the initial shots can be identified, in retrospect.

But the development, on a shot-to-shot basis, of the motif of the woman does not continue to parallel that of the fish. Later, where we might expect a more distant shot of the woman's hair and body, we see instead a tracking/panning shot of the woman as seen from the train. There is only one similar shot, in terms of movement, in the film. This is in part one, where we see a gull on the water from the moving boat. Paradoxically, these links establish a sort of formal equivalence between woman and gull, as well as between train and boat, ground and water.

In the center of what we termed the large, "B" section of part two the woman reappears. Shots of her are cut into a series depicting mainly water-strider insects on the mountain stream. She is in the water in these shots, and no train or tracks are visible. Again, she appears only twice, briefly, and then is not seen for ten shots, when she is shown in medium shot, from the back as before. This is a more distant shot from the same position as the previous ones, and is followed later by a return to the original distance, giving a progression by symmetrical variation of camera distance similar in method to the development of the images of the fish in part one.

Finally, in the return to the "A" segments of part two, the woman is again alternated with shots of the train. These images work by an opposition of camera angles similar to that in the fish/gulls segment of part one: shots of the train (and from the train) are angled up, whereas shots of the woman emphasize a downward angle.

Near the end of the film, we see the first shot of the man's hand, which will be present in all subsequent images of the woman. The last three shots of woman and hand (always alternating with shots of the train) are particularly intriguing because they introduce a change of direction. These are the first images of the woman from the other side of the "action"—of her belly and neck rather than back. In the first shot of this type, leaves and foliage frame the grasping hand, a composition which recalls the first appearance of the train in part two, where small leaves on the edge of the frame surround the more distant train. This comparison implicitly gives support to the idea of the train as "masculine" principle—as phallus. We should note in connection with this shot that the hand is not pulling the woman out of the path of the train, as has been suggested in some commentaries on the film. Rather, it pulls her out of the stream (and, if we are to believe the matches established previously in the film, *towards* the train). But here we encounter problems beyond the level of segmental structures and formal oppositions.

The question arises: to what extent can we use this brief study of structural features of *To Parsifal* as part of an attempt at a general interpretation of the

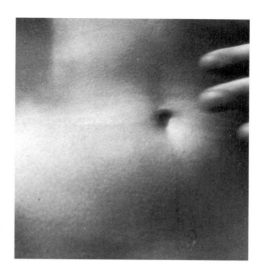

From part two of
Baillie's *To Parsifal*

film? To approach this problem we must begin by placing the film in a larger context, that of the Parsifal legend. For Baillie has, by the title of his film and by the use of music from Wagner's opera, grafted his relatively abstract images onto a traditional Western narrative. In its essentials the Parsifal story begins with a kingdom mysteriously laid barren by the illness of its ruler, the Fisher King. The king suffers from a wound of unknown origin, and the land of his kingdom is infertile by response. The king and land can only be restored to health by the quest of a pure knight for the Holy Grail, the vessel in which Christ's blood was gathered during the crucifixion. The knight must resist the seductions of a temptress (Kundry, in the Wagner opera) and perform various acts of bravery.

Even from this brief summary we can see points of congruence with Baillie's *To Parsifal*. There is a "wounding," as we have seen, quite prominent in part one—that of the fish. What better representation of the "Fisher King"? And a naked woman appears in part two—accompanied on the sound track by an excerpt from Act II of the opera, in which Kundry sings seductively to Parsifal to stay with her and abandon his quest. We could postulate, therefore, that part one of the film depicts the wounding of king and land and that part two concerns the quest for redemption and fertility. But this interpretation raises many questions. Should we therefore see *To Parsifal* as an anti-technology film, depicting the "rape" of nature by man's interference? Who or what in the work is Parsifal? Why the presence of the train in part two? Is the quest successful? These questions can only be approached in conjunction with a consideration of internal relations in the film and its place in the larger body of Baillie's cinema.

We can begin by considering the parallels established between parts one and two. These parallels have profound effects on meaning (indeed, such structures *create* meaning). The insistence on modes of transportation, on water, the similar introductions of woman and fish, the resemblances between many shot-types and visual elements common to both parts, the repeated oppositions established by parallel editing between up and down, moving and non-moving shots, and so on—all suggest that the two parts of the film depict similar states, or perhaps different aspects of the same problem.

If part one depicts the wound (rape) of nature and part two the quest for renewed fertility (and it would seem that this is a reasonable assumption, considering the mythic context Baillie has given the film), then the parallels between parts one and two suggest that in *To Parsifal* the rape of nature and the return of fertility are different aspects of the same act. We should note in this regard that some versions of the Parsifal legend indicate that the knight who must search for the Grail is also originally responsible for the wounding of the Fisher King. This interpretation—the continuity and interdependence of the wound in nature and the quest for health (the "freeing of the waters" in the legend)—would help explain the establishment of a mythic time in the film, marked by sunrise and sunset. The work depicts not a closed series of events but a cycle, a process continually in play, and not a redemption found once and for all.

This set of meanings is put in explicitly sexual terms. Many aspects of the film's structure suggest a basic division of its elements into cultural stereotypes of masculine and feminine forces—yin and yang. The woman and the fish are both strikingly associated with water and are presented as comparatively static ("passive"). They both are only seen from horizontal or downward camera angles. The boat and the train, on the other hand, both ride over land and water, on tracks and wake, and are presented as causing motion ("active") and are only seen in horizontal or upward angles of the camera. A number of shots suggest that boat and train leave not only marks but *wounds* on the surface of land and water. We might generalize from these associations to see nature as a "feminine" element (given the prevailing mythology of our culture) and technology as a "masculine" one. But this notion in no way makes *To Parsifal* an anti-technology film. Rather, the work seems to be a song, a hymn (in ideologically suspect terms . . .) to the cycle of infertility and fertility, wounding and healing, intercourse and childbirth.

We can find some justification for this point of view in the singularly sexual connotations of many images in the film. Examples in part one include the boat's masts, the knife which passes through the red lateral opening in the fish, and the boat passing under the bridge. In part two we might cite the train seen moving through the framing leaves, the trees set off at a marked upward angle, the workman's wrench by the tracks, and, of course, the man's hand clutching the woman's body and the long tracking shot from the train forward through the trees—after the woman has been pulled from the water (like a fish).

To examine these hypotheses, it would seem reasonable to broaden the corpus under examination to include all of Baillie's films. Is what we have suggested about *To Parsifal* contradicted or supported by the structures and themes of his other work? *To Parsifal* (1963) is the first of three films concerned, as Baillie has said, with problems of "the hero." The other two works in this series are *Mass for the Dakota Sioux* (1963–64) and *Quixote* (1964–65). One of the major problems of *To Parsifal* is finding in it any "hero" at all. Likewise, in the two other films there is no single Hollywood-style protagonist. Rather, the heroes of these films are collectivities, mythically linked in each case with a legendary hero—Don Quixote and Christ—just as the Parsifal story supports the images of *To Parsifal*. Thus Baillie's conception of the hero in these works seems not that of any individual *actor*, but rather of a *force* at work in many guises. The only existence allowed the "hero" as distinct individual in Baillie's cinema is in the myths which structure the films. But the forces at work in *To Parsifal* seem hardly human at all. The two centers of the film are the boat and the train. If a hero is to be found it would seem that they are its active representatives. The boat journeys to sea and causes (in terms of what we see) the wounding of the fish; the train passes through the forest without stopping as a nude woman stands seductively by the tracks. These are precisely the actions of the legendary Parsifal. The hero is the "masculine" principle here embodied by technology.

Despite the frequent beauty of its images of nature, Baillie's cinema is not one of protest and contestation of "progress." *Castro Street* (1966) seems particularly relevant here, because its central image is the train. Shots of switch-engine, street signs, factory buildings, and other elements of the locale are superimposed in a contrapuntal fashion; nothing in the film suggests any commentary other than a reveling in the abstract beauty of these forms. Baillie has said that one image of a train engine near the end of this film represents "for the film-maker the essential of consciousness." Tracks and a cablecar also figure prominently in his first film, *On Sundays* (1960), though their thematic position in that film is not clearly defined.

We should note, finally, in considering *To Parsifal* in the light of Baillie's work in general, a pervasive differentiation between male and female. Whether these films should be considered as overtly sexist is not a concern here. We should note, however, that all of Baillie's films indicate an adherence to cultural stereotypes of masculinity and femininity which we found helpful in decoding *To Parsifal*. In particular, the women in *On Sundays*, *Valentin de Las Sierras*, and *Quick Billy* (1971) are presented as passive objects of men's more active interest.

Thus, we can find in Baillie's other work three of our centers of interest in reading *To Parsifal*—the hero, technology, and male/female differentiations.

All these topics seem to reinforce our analysis of the film: through a traditional grid of "masculine" and "feminine" elements, the work celebrates the eternal cycle of death and rebirth, sterility and rejuvenation.

It remains to be seen how we can justify the project of such a reading. None of these ideas are literally "in" the film. At the beginning of this study I attempted to read the implicit viewer *into* the film text. The viewer, it will be recalled, is that system or set of systems which may "make sense" of the work. This operation is far from being innocent or "natural," for the text by itself is a set of fragments. Without some notion of the viewer, criticism risks reducing any text to its discontinuities.

There is a certain sort of structuralist criticism which pretends to totally evacuate the viewer from the study of film. Such an operation is, to my way of thinking, illusory. To pretend that in film the spectator is wholly passive is sheer nonsense, a form of elitism worse than the bourgeois individualism of the "every person sees his/her own film" point of view. Thus, in this study of *To Parsifal*, I have frequently referred to the "viewer," but not to my own or anyone else's *direct* experience of the film. Rather, what is here called the "viewer" is in fact the set of ways of *giving meaning* to the work. The film text *needs* the spectator, and the spectator's function is to create coherence from it.

To Parsifal, like any film, cannot be studied without first giving an approximation of how it is read. In this study I have suggested, hopefully, part of this operation. The objective of structuralist criticism is not the negation of experience; rather, we must account for experience *outside of its own terms*. Binary oppositions, ideological schemas, and the like are useless without some explanation of what happens to us when we go to the movies.

The independent American cinema is a worthy object of study for such a criticism precisely because so much is left to the implicit (textually defined) viewer. A critique of the cinema of Bruce Baillie is impossible without a notion of how his films "work." Movies, to use Godard's formulation, are machines. You pay your money and take the effects. You like them or not. But we as viewers are part of the machine, and nowhere more so than in films such as *To Parsifal*. The machine exists *through* us, as well as through other factors—ideology first of all—beyond any immediate perception. But to understand it all, even to begin to understand what happens, we first must know what happens at the most basic levels—at our end of the machine.

WILLIAM R. BARR

BRAKHAGE: ARTISTIC DEVELOPMENT
IN TWO CHILDBIRTH FILMS

"Never trust the artist. Trust the tale," wrote D. H. Lawrence about uncovering significance in narrative fiction. Lawrence was protecting his work from his own remarks that, applied insensitively or maliciously, would distort meaning or even replace the texts themselves. His advice holds true as well for avant-garde film, especially when it seeks to reveal the workings of an artistic consciousness; with its relatively closely knit practitioners and small (but growing) number of followers, experimental film is dependent upon an oral tradition of communication and discussion. Stan Brakhage shares Lawrence's view of the autonomy of the individual work of art and the novelist's distrust of the artist as critic, declining any exceptional position he might otherwise claim by virtue of his acts of creation: " 'Even when I lecture at showing of past Brakhage films I emphasize the fact that I am not artist except when involved in the creative process AND that I speak as viewer of my own. . . —I speak . . . as viewer of The Work (NOT of . . . but By-Way-of-Art), and I speak specifically to the point of What has been revealed to me AND, by way of describing the work-process, what I, as artist-viewer, understand of Revelation.' "[1] Granting the authority of the autonomous work of art, one can yet bring forth extra-artistic information which clarifies both the intention and the "work-process" behind and within the work; although one may not finally believe the teller one must listen carefully to him.

Understanding the context in which Brakhage operates is particularly important because of the extensive use he makes of his family in his films. For example, "Open Field," one of the *Sexual Meditations*, might appear to be simply a parody of the stereotyped experimental film which shows a young, nude girl running through a field in slow motion. But the information that the girl is Brakhage's daughter entering adolescence and that the film is in part the father's attempt to come to terms with her emerging sexuality and his own feelings towards her leads to a less sterile interpretation. "Open Field" becomes, through its depiction of the psychological processes that make the film-maker human, a universalized and even mythic dramatization of the powers of time.

Context plays a more complex role, however, in the comprehension of Brakhage's first two childbirth films, *Window Water Baby Moving* (1959) and *Thigh Line Lyre Triangular* (1961), which David Curtis considers to be among Brakhage's "most widely appreciated works."[2] The juxtaposition of remarks made by Brakhage and his wife about the genesis of *Window Water*, depicting the birth of their first child, validates Brakhage's awareness of the limitations which his intensely personal, self-directed artistic vision confer upon him. Jane Brakhage saw the decision to film the birth at home rather than in a hospital as extrinsic to the couple, dictated rather by nervous hospital administrators.[3] Stan, on the other hand, believed the choice to have been made within the family. More significantly, Jane emphasized her share in the conception and creation of *Window Water*. Her husband, though admitting her to be a consistent "inspiration," asserted with equal emphasis that Jane was completely absorbed in the dynamics of childbirth and that the finished film, which includes shots made by Jane of the relieved father, was solely his work.[4] Jane Brakhage's statements are invariably the more convincing because they reflect the totality of the environment; Brakhage's, by contrast, limit the context of the film to himself and formal or technical concerns. Given such illustrations of the fallibility of the critical perceptions of even a great artist, one is entitled to wonder whether Brakhage's widely quoted remarks about "closed-eye vision," which he saw as so important to the second birth film and which critics have since assumed to define the significance of the work, are not also in some measure reductive in terms of the finished artifact.[5] One purpose of this paper is, therefore, corrective; but in its more important aspect it tries to reach beyond the merely negative to arrive at a fuller understanding of Brakhage's artistic achievement as it is revealed through the relationship between the two birth films.

"Crisis" is an integral part of Brakhage's work and his perceptions as theoretician and human being. At times what qualifies as critical seems trivial, but in general biological milestones fascinate him. Death in particular haunts him; in *Anticipation of the Night* (1958), which includes an abstract birth sequence, a suicide jarringly concludes what is otherwise an unmistakably joyous hymn to life. The inconsistent closure demonstrates the dominance of the idea in one way, but Brakhage's retrospective explanation of the technique to be employed is even more startling: the death by hanging was to be his own, the film-maker shooting footage until he strangled.[6] The question of death is carried over in *Window Water*, too, but there it emerges as background rather than as substantive filmic material. Brakhage wondered, in a fantasy that inverts the usual parental vicariousness, whether the newborn child—especially if it were a boy, would "take my place in life and leave me free to die."[7] Such an anxiety may account for the result that both techniques and selection of material to be filmed make the audience and the film-maker more distant from the event of parturition, which is depicted in awe-inspiring, purely physiological and "realistic" images.[8] P. Adams Sitney states, for example, that "throughout the film Brakhage uses black and white leader to affirm the screen and the cinematic illusion . . . for relieving the dramatic tension built up as the moment of birth approaches."[9] Other techniques, though, are explicitly and almost sentimentally theatrical, more characteristic of Hollywood films than of experimental cinema. The film's early sequences, showing a laughing, pregnant Jane in a bathtub, prepare in a conventional way the antithesis between idyllic bliss and the physiological pressures and visceral knowledge of parturition. Likewise, the intercutting of these images with the more anguished later shots accentuates the mythic journey from innocence to experience in the naively romantic terms of the commercial flashback. If, as Sitney argues, *Window Water* conforms to the definition of lyrical films—"the lyrical film postulates the film-maker behind the camera as the first-person protagonist of the film" (*VF*, p. 180)—then one corollary is that the finished film primarily reflects the artist's consciousness, drawing attention to his craftsmanship. Such, clearly, is the case with the use of black and white leader and especially with the intercutting of early and late images, where memory's recall destroys chronometric and historical time. But the camera's emergence as a quasi-character which can unblinkingly record the visual details of labor and birth (unlike the humans who need relief from the naked event) implies a central ambiguity about the film-maker's position in this film. Jane Brakhage's remarks about filming *Window Water* are useful here, not least because her husband supports them: " 'He calls the hospital and gets the nurse who says she'll be right there. . . . Stan starts worrying. I continue roaring and panting. Stan stops filming he's so upset. He gets nervous. He tells me to relax and pant. He needs to relax; I'm doing fine. I tell him how much I love him and ask him if he's got my face when I'm roaring and this sets him off again and reassures him, and he clickety-clackety-buzzes while I roar and pant.' "[10] Not only has the agent in the film reminded the film-maker to do his job, but the film-maker, nearly paralyzed by his confrontation with raw life, finds refuge from the phenomenal world and its attendant, primal anxieties by retreating behind the camera. It would appear, then, that *Window Water* is at least as much a traditional dramatic or documentary enterprise as a lyrical film for two reasons. First, the filmmaker is not the protagonist, since the camera ultimately replaces and obliterates rather than affirms his consciousness. Second, the film is made powerful less by the film-maker's craft than by the sheer presence of Jane Brakhage and the unavoidable fact of the experience which she undergoes. *Window Water* is, as a result, a generic hybrid; it includes two major foci without developing any relationship between them.

Like *Window Water*, the second birth film (of the couple's third child) is silent and in color. Otherwise, *Thigh Line* is very different from its predecessor. Its setting is a hospital rather than a home. In contrast to *Window Water*'s 17 minutes, *Thigh Line* is only five minutes long; and the later film lacks the urgency and intensity of the earlier one. *Thigh Line Lyre Triangular* underscores the cinematic illusion through anamorphic shots of Jane Brakhage in labor and of the doctor and nurse in attendance, through prominent use of leader, through intercutting of birds and animals with hospital sequences, and especially through painting directly on the film. "Realistic" sequences are, consequently, rarely in evidence. Sitney, in somewhat disapproving tones, argues that "although we do not see him in this film there is no doubt that we are looking at the birth through the eyes of the artist, whose eccentric vision is ecstatic to the point of being possessed" (*VF*, p. 191). Although it is true that *Thigh Line*, more than *Window Water*, attempts to reproduce in visual terms the consciousness of its maker, the later film does not support a charge of either eccentricity or possession, both of which imply a greater or lesser loss of control. More important, it does not encourage a sense of discontinuity between the film-maker and the material with which he works. Instead, *Thigh Line* achieves a profound fusion of the two.

One method of attaining this fusion is through the introduction of birds and animals as natural symbols. Brakhage explained that these "were easily represented by taking material only out of *Anticipation of the Night*."[11] While their connection with vitality is apparent, equally significant is their having had a previous existence in another film. The imagistic reiteration implicitly acknowledges creative and historical continuity as analogous and interrelated; the symbolic potential further refines the former component to include organic development. But the painting on film is of greater centrality in linking the artist with his material. In *Metaphors on Vision*, Brakhage stated that "only at a crisis do I see both the scene as I've been trained to see it (that is, with Renaissance perspective, three-dimensional logic—colors as we've been trained to call a color a color, and so forth) and patterns that move straight out from the inside of the mind through the optic nerves. In other words, in intensive crisis I can see from the inside out and the outside in. . . . I wanted a childbirth film that expressed all my seeing at such a time."[12] In general terms, Brakhage's famous statement articulates any artist's ability to see in both conventional and idiosyncratic ways, and by extension to construct a work which is generically categorizable (and therefore accessible to the audience) but also made unique by an individual's signature. In this sense, the theoretical explanation applies as well to *Window Water* as to *Thigh Line*. But the signature in the latter film lies in its expression of the "patterns that move straight out from the inside of the mind through the optic nerves"—Brakhage's "closed-eye vision" that results from the interplay of light and eye when the eye is closed, from external pressure on the eyeball, and even from the electrical impulses along the optic nerves themselves. In this lies the peculiar problem of the passage quoted. No one can underestimate the importance of the contribution of "closed-eye vision," but by the same token the device should not be taken out of context, isolated, and proferred as absolute truth. While "closed-eye vision" enormously expands the optical possibilities of film, unintegrated emphasis upon it reduces vision to mechanical operations. Devoid of any organic connection with the film, the technique is merely a tour de force; and Brakhage's reference to "all my seeing," when it is taken to be limited to the radical form of presentation in its formalistic aspects, leads only to an unfair charge of solipsism.

It is possible to suggest that the film has a different, less exclusive significance, based on the implications of "all my seeing." Brakhage has spoken of how his work changed after he married Jane Collum:

> I would say I grew very quickly as a film artist once I got rid of drama as prime source of inspiration. I began to feel all history, all life, all that I would have as material with which to work, would have to come from the inside of me out rather than as some form imposed from the outside in. I had the concept of everything radiating out of me, and that the more personal and egocentric I would become, the deeper I would reach and the more I would touch those universal concerns which would involve all man. What seems to have happened since marriage is that I no longer sense ego as the greatest source for what can touch on the universal. I now feel that there is some other concrete center where love from one person to another meets; and that the more total view arises from there. . . . It's in the action of moving out that the great concerns can be struck off continually. . . . Where I take action strongest and most immediately is in reaching through the power of all that love towards my wife, (and she towards me) and somewhere where those actions meet and cross, and bring forth children and films and inspire concerns with plants and rocks and all sights seen, a new center, composed of action, is made. (quoted in *VF*, p. 185).

Brakhage seems to have underestimated the tenacity of his premarriage views, since they are evident in *Window Water*'s concern for conventional drama and the egocentricity of his commentary. But between *Window Water* and *Thigh Line*, the major shift in perspective began, for the later film is clearly representative of his more developed vision. Its use of painting on film is a pure cinematic symbol for the movement from drama to other modes of organization and from a Whitmanesque egocentricity ("I am vast, I contain multitudes") to a more balanced sensibility. Optically, the painting mediates between the objects filmed and the film-maker himself. This mediation suggests, along with the emphatically anamorphic shots of the objects, a change of focus from far to middle distance—or from representation of objects either as themselves or as the artist's perceptions to a concern for the interaction between the other and the self, an interaction only vaguely implied by the dual focus of *Window Water*. Metaphorically, the painting becomes the triangulated representation of "some other concrete center where love from one person to another meets; . . . somewhere where those actions meet and cross, and bring forth children and films." Where *Window Water* tries to emphasize the artist and to imply that the distance and patterning of the aesthetic product are superior to the turmoil of biological creativity even while it reveals the latter's irresistible force, that lopsided discontinuity disappears in *Thigh Line*. The second childbirth film is a layered, integrated affirmation of all creativity, and its visual symbolism evokes the metaphysical forces that have involved two people in two different but related collaborative efforts.

NOTES

1. "Respond Dance," in P. Adams Sitney, ed., *Film Culture Reader* (New York: Praeger, 1970), pp. 239–40.
2. *Experimental Cinema* (New York: Universe Books, 1971), p. 132. "Song V," a third childbirth film, cannot be divorced from the aesthetic context of the complete *Songs* and is therefore omitted from this discussion.
3. "The Birth Film," in *FCR*, p. 231.
4. "Interview with Stan Brakhage," *FCR*, pp. 208–10.
5. See, for example, Sheldon Renan, *An Introduction to the American Underground Film* (New York: Dutton Paperbacks, 1967), p. 122; and Sitney, *Visionary Film* (New York: Oxford U.P.,1974), p. 191.
6. "Interview with Stan Brakhage," pp. 202-03.
7. *Ibid.*, pp. 208–09.
8. Just so, Carol Emshwiller pointed out to me that the beauty of "The Act of Seeing with One's Own Eyes" ("Autopsy"), the third segment of *The Pittsburgh Trilogy*, derives from the pattened rituals of dissection opposed to the nearly intolerable vision of humans reduced to meat.
9. Sitney, *Visionary Film*, p. 189. Subsequent references to this edition will be included in the text (as *VF*).
10. "The Birth Film," pp. 232–33.
11. "Interview with Stan Brakhage," p. 225.
12. *Ibid.*, p. 225. See also *Film-Makers' Cooperative Catalogue No. 6* (New York: Harry Gantt, 1975), p. 27.

FQ ROUND TABLE

The Many Faces of Thelma & Louise

Vol. 45, no. 2 (Winter 1991–92): 20–31.

Some of the spirit of Ridley Scott's 1991 breakaway hit has entered the realm of public discourse: the *New York Times* spoke of "... the press ... beginning to hear from fellow Republicans that Bush's top aides are squandering precious political capital as if on a 'Thelma-and-Louise'-style spree." (Nov. 22, 1991, p. A11.) In light of the sometimes vehemently differing reactions to this film, *FQ* invited a number of its contributors to offer their impressions—not as reviews but as brief illuminations of a facet each found particularly interesting. These are their responses.

[*Ed. note*]

HARVEY R. GREENBERG

THELMA & LOUISE'S EXUBERANT POLYSEMY

Like Robert Altman and Blake Edwards, Ridley Scott often works with popular genre toward revisionist ends. His first commercial effort (*The Duellists*, 1977) deployed the swashbuckler's derring-do to advance an ironic pacifism. He went on to critique the greed of contemporary corporate practice, first with a canny blending of horror and science-fiction strategies (*Alien*, 1979), then by marrying science-fiction conventions to the tropes of noir (*Blade Runner*, 1982).

The director's latest project, *Thelma & Louise*, arguably wins the prize for sheer number of genres interrogated against the grain in a single Scott picture. I mark the signature of classic and contemporary Westerns, sundry types of road film (doomed/outlaw/lovers subgenre in particular), and the seventies "buddy" movie.

Thelma & Louise's ideological agenda has caused exceptionally polarized debate. The film has been variously interpreted as feminist manifesto (the heroines are ordinary women, driven to extraordinary ends by male oppression) and as profoundly antifeminist (the heroines are dangerous phallic caricatures of the very macho violence they're supposedly protesting). Some critics have discerned a lesbian subtext (that final soul kiss at the abyss); others interpret this reading

Taking pictures:
Susan Sarandon (left)
as Louise and
Geena Davis as Thelma

as a demeaning negation of feminine friendship that flies in the face of patriar-chal authority.

These vehemently opposed critiques own, as it were, a piece of the ideological action. One is reminded of the blind men in the folk tale, each of whom affirmed that his description of the elephant—based on the part he grasped—was the only true account of the beast. By the very historical grounds of their creation, big, popular entertainments like *Thelma & Louise* often contain both reactionary and progressive elements, more or less ajar.[1]

A director of liberal inclinations like Scott still functions within an industry and culture profoundly saturated with the premises of corporate capitalism. The latter may intrude upon a project directly, or through subtler invasions of the creator's psyche. The result is a highly *polysemic* text: such a film typically offers a wide range of possibility for contestation across the political spectrum over issues "whose time has come" out of one contemporary circumstance or another (e.g., *Easy Rider*, 1969; *The Deer Hunter*, 1978).

Thelma & Louise's ideological polysemy is abetted by the director's charac-teristic dense cinematic and artistic intertextuality (central quotations on the lat-ter score include Ansel Adams and the nineteen-eighties Hyperrealists). Callie Khouri's script also enhances the film's ambiguous openness for interpretation by sharply scanting information about the protagonists' prior lives, except for a few bold strokes. What one gets of the women is essentially what one sees.

Scott is a formidable entertainer, but he lacks Edwards' or Altman's sub-versive boldness (at their best). His critiques are increasingly vitiated by tidy "with the grain" resolutions (in this sense, *Thelma & Louise*'s unhappy end-ing is as problematic as *Blade Runner*'s infamous happy ending). It may nevertheless be argued that we should feel lucky for *Thelma & Louise*'s raucous probe of the Second Sex's still dismal status in Bush-y America, given Hollywood's current gentler, kinder predilection for the bimbos (and bitches) of *Working Girl* and *Pretty Woman*.

But one must wonder if—Gramsci, thou art with us yet—we're supposed to feel lucky, and let it go at that. . . .

1. See my earlier critique of *Star Trek* in "In Search of Spock: A Psychoanalytic Inquiry," *Journal of Popular Film and Television*, vol.12 (1984), pp. 52–65; and Douglas Kellner's work along these lines in "*Blade Runner*: A Diagnostic Critique," *Jump Cut*, no. 29 (1984), pp. 6–8, and Michael Ryan and Douglas Kellner, *Camera Politica: The Politics and Ideology of Contemporary Hollywood Film* (Bloomington: Indiana University Press, 1988).

CAROL J. CLOVER

CROSSING OVER

To focus, as the debate about *Thelma & Louise* did, on those men who disliked it is to miss what I think is the far more significant fact that large numbers of men both saw and did like it. Precious few American films have had women at the center and men on the periphery, and what ones there are have not, for the most part, drawn large male audiences—a pattern that has sustained the claim that whereas women are willing to "identify" with screen males, the converse is not the case. What the success of *Thelma & Louise* with male audiences suggests is that if you write the parts right and execute them with conviction, the sex of the players is no object: if the buddy-escape plot is conventionally male, it is not intrinsically so, and lots of men were evidently happy to enter into that very American fantasy even when it is enacted by women, even when the particulars are female-specific (rape, macho husband, leering co-worker), and even when the inflection is re-markably feminist. And although the film showed signs of defensiveness on this point (the *niceness* of the Harvey Keitel figure struck me as something of a sop to the men in the audience) it was on the whole surefooted in its assumption that its viewers, regardless of sex, would engage with the women's story. When someone can say, as Geena Davis did in an interview, that "If you're threatened by this movie, you're identifying with the wrong person," a real corner in gender representation has been turned in mainstream film history. I emphasize "mainstream" here, for the same corner was turned in so-called exploitation cinema some 15 years ago. Fans of horror recognize the "tough-girl heroes" of films like *Thelma & Louise*, *Silence of the Lambs*, *Sleeping with the Enemy*, and *Mortal Thoughts* as upscale immigrants from slasher and rape-revenge movies of the eighties— forms that reveal in no uncertain terms the willingness, not to say desire, of the male viewer to feel not just *at* but *through* female figures on screen. Perhaps the mainstreaming of that operation, in films like *Thelma & Louise*, will call it to the attention of theory, which has not done full justice to "wrong-direction" cross-gender imaginings.

ALBERT JOHNSON

BACCHANTES AT LARGE

Not only is *Thelma & Louise* an entertaining and picaresque tragicomedy, but it is also a vivid portrait of contemporary Americana, where women are still struggling to redefine their individualities: it is a symbolic perusal of feminine inconsistencies. Louise Sawyer (Susan Sarandon) and Thelma Dickinson (Geena Davis) are aspects of female escapism, an urgent undercurrent in American society that seems to cultivate a mostly unfulfilled yearning for women to run away from the boredom and sexual entrapment to which they are condemned.

Here is a film that reveals a sad decline in American culture, with its facile acceptances of empty pleasures and demoralized sexual chauvinism toward women. Dennis Hopper's *Easy Rider* and Monte Hellman's *Two-Lane Blacktop* displayed the male attraction for a wayward, motorized sort of outlaw wandering across America, with freedom of highways correlated to a promise of adventure and, most of all, hedonistic fun. The heroines of *Thelma &*

Thelma and her
rebel without a cause
(Brad Pitt as J.D.)

Louise offer the same thing, but with the pathetic fallacy of American open
spaces mainly representing precursors of doom beyond desire.

Callie Khouri' s screenplay manages to offer detailed, believable characters in
Thelma and Louise themselves and in the various men who surround them during their escapades. Sarandon had already captured the essence of hard-edged
self-assurance as the tart-tongued waitress in *White Palace*, and her portrayal of
Louise rounds out and explores feminine defiances. Davis's vulnerable Thelma
(reminding one of a younger version of Shirley Booth's Lola in Inge's *Come Back
Little Sheba*) is a perfect complement to Louise's personality. The director (Ridley
Scott at his most visual) deftly contrasts Louise's neat kitchen with Thelma's
fridgefull of half-eaten Snickers bars, as well as their variant styles of packing suitcases. It is Thelma's jubilant rush toward freedom from her husband, Darryl
(Christopher McDonald), a perfect example of the Playboy Philosopher, that sets
the tone of recklessness as the women set forth. Thelma's near-rape by redneck
Harlan (Timothy Carhart) at the Silver Bullet, a roadside country-western bar
that is more-Texan-than-Texas, is the catalyst for sudden violence and death; this
changes their original exuberance to anxieties which gradually strengthen bonds
of love and loyalty between them as they continue their flight from the law.

Louise's version of the world around them is totally realistic, and her continued exasperations with Thelma's naiveté become bitter commentaries on
the failure of her own hope and a particular world-weariness regarding any future happiness for either of them.

When Louise's boyfriend, Jimmy (Michael Madsen), finds them and offers her marriage she is too resigned by disillusioned romances to accept him, and Thelma finds the James Dean–Bruce Weber image of J.D. (Brad Pitt), a handsome drifter, too irresistible a sex symbol to dismiss, causing further disruption of Louise's plan for an escape to Mexico. The director and his cinematographer (Adrian Biddle) wrap beautiful visions around the errant women racing along in their dusty convertible, singing out their calls-of-the-wild.

Much attention is given to landscape; the imitation Hollywood motels off the highways; a conglomerate of oil wells in dusty twilights; and faces of aged, displaced people, seen briefly in doorways and windows, remnants of lost dreams (particularly for Louise, who notices them). The eternal desert monoliths add to the isolated status of the women's flight toward the border.

Thelma and Louise's ultimate gestures of feminine liberation are exemplified by their total humiliation of a lewd truck driver and the subsequent subjugation of an arrogant young state trooper (Jason Beghe), who is reduced to tears by their domination. These are episodes of high humor, leaving one unprepared for the denouement. The essential humanity of *Thelma and Louise*, for all their luckless travails, wins one's sympathies, and although a happy ending is desired, their leap into the void is a final stamp upon one's conscience: they are only two beautiful, easygoing women who recognize that they can no longer tolerate a deepshit status in a man-made American universe.

PETER N. CHUMO II

THELMA & LOUISE AS SCREWBALL COMEDY

The elements are familiar: the killing, the robbery, the flight from the police, the high-speed car chase. It is little wonder that many critics see Ridley Scott's *Thelma & Louise* as an outlaw film. However, it also displays key elements of a screwball comedy, of which the "road screwball" is an important subgenre (best exemplified by *It Happened One Night*, 1934) whose themes include

Role reversal:
Jason Beghe
as the state trooper

escaping the constraints of authority for the freedom of the open road, playing out different roles, and ultimately shedding one's old identity for a new one.

While outlaw films like *Bonnie and Clyde* and *Butch Cassidy and the Sundance Kid* have scenes of deadpan humor, these moments generally do not suggest the self-awareness or growth typical of the smart, witty screwball heroine. In *Thelma & Louise*, however, when J.D. suggests that Thelma's husband is an "asshole," and Thelma agrees, "He *is* an asshole. Most of the time I just let it slide," we see a classic screwball heroine assuming a certain control over her life while also maintaining a sense of irony toward her childish husband.

Liberation and growth through role-playing—distinctive features of the screwball tradition—figure prominently in *Thelma & Louise*, especially in Thelma's robbery of the market, her personal turning point when she casts aside all inhibitions, takes on the persona of an outlaw, and gains a new sense of freedom. She uses the theatrical "robbery speech" that J.D. has taught her, but does not become a copy of a male outlaw. Rather, she makes the role her own and adjusts the robbery to suit her own tastes when she asks for a couple of bottles of Wild Turkey, which has become her favorite drink on the road. Thelma, then, sheds her identity as a timid, even childlike housewife by relying on her own instincts and creativity within the outlaw role. Although Thelma's crime initially shocks Louise, she soon gets caught up in the fun, and their laughter and sense of exhilaration as they drive away from "the scene of our last goddamn crime!" (as Louise enthusiastically puts it) solidifies them as a screwball couple having fun with their outlaw personae, goofing off on the road, and taking control of their lives in the process.

In the encounter with the state trooper, a wisecrack defuses a potentially violent moment as Thelma, holding a gun on the officer as he explains that he has a wife and kids, advises him, "You be sweet to 'em, especially your wife. My husband wasn't sweet to me. Look how I turned out"—the smart, sassy lines of a screwball heroine who has a sense of humor about her situation. Instead of a disturbing confrontation, we have a prank (they lock the officer in his trunk) and sharp, funny dialogue, more akin to the fun of a screwball couple defying authority (perhaps Cary Grant and Katharine Hepburn in *Bringing Up Baby*) than outlaws at odds with society in general.

While Susan Sarandon and Geena Davis have entered the pantheon of great screwball couples, their sense of freedom poses a generic problem, since the screwball couple normally achieve a clarity of vision that enables them to be reintegrated into society. As a female screwball couple who have no desire to return to their old lives and are actually being hunted by male society, Thelma and Louise cannot follow this pattern, but the film itself finds a way of going beyond the usual screwball marriage. Finally surrounded by police and choosing to drive over the edge of the Grand Canyon rather than be captured, Thelma and Louise first kiss and then clasp hands in a mystical marriage that distinguishes the film as the most unique screwball ever made—not simply because it presents a marriage of females but because it is a transcendent, not a social, marriage and ultimately an apotheosis, a mythic flight into forever.

BRIAN HENDERSON

NARRATIVE ORGANIZATION

Thelma & Louise has no voice-over narration, makes no use of the frequentive, and has no flashbacks or flash-forwards. Like many, perhaps most, films, it tells its story in chronological order, in what might be described as an unfolding present. What is unlike other films, however, are the ways in which *Thelma & Louise* organizes narrative time and the distinc-

Louise with Jimmy (Michael Madsen)

tive temporalities, fundamental to all the effects and meanings of the film, that result.

The killing of Harlan turns the lives of Thelma and Louise upside down: suddenly their relation to the past is uncertain; their future unknown. They flee to the open road, "not so much bound to any haven ahead as rushing from all havens astern" (Melville). The film itself fissures at this point, launching a parallel montage between investigating police and escaping women that is sustained until the film's-end face-off at the Grand Canyon.

The time dimensions of the title characters' flight are surprisingly indeterminate—not only the hour and the day of any given scene but also how much time is supposed to have elapsed between any two successive scenes and how long it has been since their journey began. The few clues provided are retrospective. Thelma says well after the fact that it was 4:00am when she first tried to reach Darryl by telephone—where was he? Later she tells the state trooper they hold at gunpoint that she and Louise would never have pulled a stunt like this three days ago—they seem to have been gone much longer than that. The alternation of filmic night and day usually time-orients viewers but this too is undermined, and time stretched out, by the women's driving around the clock;

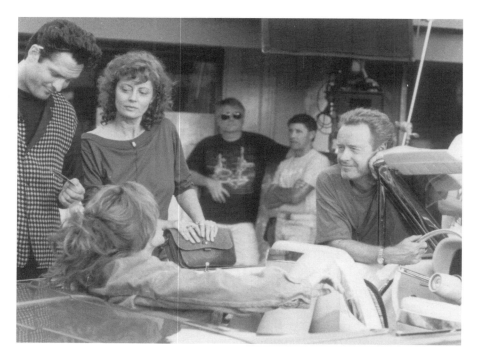

Ridley Scott (right) on the set of *Thelma & Louise*

the Oklahoma City episode—Louise in one room with Jimmy; Thelma in another with J.D.—is their single off-road night.[1]

Fiction-film police work is often shown in a pseudo-documentary manner, sometimes even with the date and hour stamped on the beginning of scenes. However, the police scenes in *Thelma & Louise* are as temporally indeterminate as the women's scenes—we do not know when they take place or how much time elapses between them. How can the film sustain a floating time scheme in each of its two narrative strands? Because the two strands prop each other up: the considerable ellipses within each strand intersperse with those of the other, filling in its gaps and thereby covering for it. Thus the film-makers can break away from Thelma and Louise to the police at any time they wish and come back to them at any later point in their journey they choose. This is a worry-free formal scheme that allows the film-makers to skip what they want to skip and to show what they want to show. A single-stranded *Thelma & Louise* would have had to account for its ellipses, perhaps by dialogue, by time-passing montages, by dissolves, and/or by other devices: a different film.

What is the point of this scheme? It serves to immerse us radically in Thelma and Louise's divided temporality. The characters exist simultaneously in two temporal modes—a continual motion forward and a continual reflection backwards. "Go!" "Go, Go!" and "Go, Go, Go!" are words we hear frequently in the film, even, when Thelma jumps in the car after robbing a convenience store, "Go! Go! Go, Go, Go!" Each of the women has a paralyzing crisis in the course of the film: Thelma after the killing lies inert on a motel bed, then sits in a daze by the pool; Louise after the theft of the money sits on the floor of another motel room in a stupor. The solution in both cases, effected by the other character, is to get the stalled one back in the car and on the road. It is the road itself, regardless of destination, which is curative.[2]

In the other temporal mode, awareness lags behind events but comes more forcefully for that reason. (Knowledge that follows action is common in Western literature, especially in tragedy.) Louise shoots Harlan, then, addressing his sitting-up corpse, cautions him to change his behavior: "You watch your mouth." By this point, of course, he cannot speak or hear her words—Louise is temporarily denying the knowledge that will change her life. Thelma seems quicker on the uptake; when Darryl offers neither support nor trust, she understands her fate instantly. "When do we get to Mexico?" she says to Louise, in effect signing on for the long drive. Thelma's most profound realizations come later, however, reflecting her character's astonishing growth. Near the end she understands that Louise was raped in Texas some time ago and that this event still shapes her life. Thinking of the rape that she herself barely escaped, thanks to Louise, Thelma ratifies ex post facto the killing of Harlan, wishing only that she had done it herself. She then says, in the film's crowning realization, "My life would have been ruined much worse than it is now."

1.   The film cuts back and forth between the women's rooms here, as it did between their preparations to leave at the beginning of the film; otherwise they are shown together. A partial exception is Thelma's robbery of the convenience store. The camera holds on the waiting Louise while it is occurring, but later we see the event on the videotape from the store's camera that the police and Darryl are watching. In the police narrative strand, the viewing of Thelma in action is a present scene. In relation to the Thelma-Louise narrative strand, however, it is the filling-in of what Gérard Genette calls a lateral ellipsis (or paralipsis), in which a narrative does not skip over a moment in time but sidesteps an element of it. Thus the robbery scene has a dual status—a present scene in the police narrative and a filling-in of a lateral ellipsis in the narrative of Thelma and Louise.

2.   Thelma and Louise's destination changes several times in the course of the film: to get away from the scene of the crime; to get out of the state; to reach

Oklahoma City where Louise's money is; to escape to Mexico without crossing Texas; then, with the police on their trail and their Mexican plan known, heading further west, and north, to what turns out to be the Grand Canyon.

LINDA WILLIAMS

WHAT MAKES A WOMAN WANDER

Thelma and Louise have been much criticized for behaving, in the time-honored tradition of most American heroes, violently and without reflection. Male critics have been especially critical of this violence, claiming that to put women in the male outlaw mold of Butch and Sundance is nihilistic, "toxic feminism" with a fascist theme. Obviously there is something unsettling to male viewers about women with guns. Obviously there is something exhilarating about this same vision to women viewers. But the gender gap that has widened in discussions of this film has, I think, missed the crucial cultural reference. If *Thelma & Louise* offers a gender-bending revision of a basic American myth it is not simply that of the going-out-in-a-blaze-of-glory of Butch and Sundance but something closer to a complex revision of that most resonant of revenge Westerns, John Ford's *The Searchers*.

The Searchers is a revenge saga in which Ethan Edwards, hooked up with a younger male sidekick, obsessively hunts and kills the Indians who raped and killed his brother's wife, Martha, and abducted his niece. *Thelma & Louise* re-imagines the revenge narrative from the point of view of the women who were once its victims. (The exhilaration for women viewers is in the difference.)[1] In both films melancholy, mature heroes (Louise and Ethan) have mysterious, guilty pasts about which they do not speak. Ethan, haunted by an unlawful desire for his brother's wife, shares a measure of guilt with the savages who have raped and abducted her. Though victim of the Indians' violence, Ethan shares in it as well.

Louise too has a clouded past. Something happened to her in Texas and it seems to have been rape. When she sees this crime repeated upon her young friend she, like Ethan, turns mad and vengeful, becoming angry at men the way

Ethan is angry at Indians. But the revenge of the women victims is different. It is as if Martha and Debbie in *The Searchers* set out to revenge themselves.

Revenge stories grip us because of their mythic excess. Watching *The Searchers*, we become aware, as Ethan and Martin wander over the Southwestern landscape, of the depth of the revenge-seeking hero's alienation from the "sivilization" once equated with things feminine. And watching *Thelma & Louise*, we thrill to another form of alienation—from things masculine. Lighting out for the Territory, or leaping into the void, are no more nihilistic, or toxic, when women do it than men. But they are different. For women to close themselves off to the comforts of home, the alienation and anger must run deep. And the exhilaration of the release from this "sivilization" amounts to something like pure joy. The sheer surprise of *Thelma & Louise* is to have shown, in a way that serious films about the issue of rape (cf., *The Accused*) could never show, how victims of sexual crimes are unaccountably placed in the position of the guilty ones, positioned as fair game for further attack. The thrill of watching this film is the thrill of seeing our deepest and most contradictory myths reworked with female victim-heroes at their center.

1.   See Carol J. Clover, *Men, Women, and Chain Saws: Gender in the Modern Horror Film* (Princeton, NJ: Princeton University Press, 1992).

LEO BRAUDY

SATIRE INTO MYTH

Part of *Thelma & Louise*'s heritage as a belated Western is to begin with a lament for lost space that the main characters only gradually realize *has* been lost. So much of the early part of the film is set in familiar post-Hopper (Edward or Dennis) interiors: roadside cafés, motels, and crowded apartments; Western space, with all its potential for self-enhancement and beginning again, fallen into the sordidness of small-town limitation. The bar where the adventure starts

Thelma . . .

loos like an emblem of fallen romanticism hardly up to the already postheroic *Urban Cowboy*. In the cowboy bootheel slamming of the communal dancing, like some chorus-line crossover of Michael Kidd and Albert Speer, men and women alike wear all the paraphernalia of fantasy western individualism.

In this atmosphere of the ersatz and the fallen, the attempted rape of Thelma in the parking lot and Louise's killing of the rapist cuts through like an icy blast, announcing the violence and brutality under the celluloid-thin myths of self-sufficiency and heroism.

As they escape, when the film truly hits the road, the promise of space and freedom lures them on. But the camera still continues to stress the choking inevitability of the world they are trying to escape, not just the massive machinery, oil drilling equipment, and trucks that constantly threaten to squeeze them out of our vision, but even the seemingly more benevolent spaces and spires of John Ford's Monument Valley.

It's easy enough in many Ford films to point out how narratives that are supposed to cover hundreds of miles all seem to take place within the confines

. . . and Louise

of Monument Valley. But when similar things happen in *Thelma & Louise*, the effect is not the creation of a special world, but a sense of being walled in by expectations and walled in by fate, like the grainy television screen catching Thelma's robbery of the convenience store, making her "famous."

Like so many film noir couples, Thelma and Louise finally head for Mexico, the old place of nature and freedom, where you go when the West closes down. Louise's refusal to go to Texas may supply a psychological validity to her killing—the possibility that she herself was raped in Texas. But on the level of the Western and the road film, the refusal of Texas is a refusal of those wide open genre spaces as a solution.

Ridley Scott seems drawn in many of his films to the self-enclosed male character, like Harrison Ford in *Blade Runner* or Harvey Keitel in *The Duellists*, whose fragile identity rests on a suffocating pride. The gloomy setting of the films enwraps and restricts him even as he struggles to be free. But in *Thelma & Louise*, with its female duo of friends, there is a more intense dialectic of enclosure and openness. The sense of fate is qualified by an almost exact existential luxuriance in knowing that fate and facing it.

But unlike Scott's tales of romantically posturing men, *Thelma & Louise* goes in more for wisecracks and the techniques of comic exaggeration than for self-important despair. Many of the more ridiculous attacks against the film took its assertions as somehow realistic arguments about women, men, guns, and violence. But however real *Thelma & Louise* may be, it's not realistic. Its violence erupts within a hard-edged satire of wannabe heroism and consumer identity, and it builds to its conclusion through a series of scenes that emphasize the way in which Scott and Callie Khouri's main characters move out of this heightened satiric reality into myth.

First appears the Rastafarian bicyclist in Monument Valley, who blows ganga into the trunk that holds the motorcycle cop. Then comes the broadly painted incident of the truck driver (with its echoes of Steven Spielberg and Richard Matheson's wonderful *Duel*). And finally the concluding scene itself, as Harvey Keitel, here the sympathetic cop, watches helplessly as Thelma and Louise launch themselves into space and turn, not into magic heroines who manage to land on the other side, or angelic martyrs who crash into the canyon, but into a brightly colored magazine illustration. This last image echoes, as many have noted, Redford and Newman at the end of *Butch Cassidy*. But I think more of the freeze-framed Jean-Pierre Léaud at the end of *400 Blows*, faced with the threatening freedom of the sea. Not gun-toting heroes turning into legends, but hand-holding heroines of thwarted energy turning into a myth of blood, escaping the frame that confines them.

MARSHA KINDER

THELMA & LOUISE AND *MESSIDOR* AS FEMINIST ROAD MOVIES

Thelma & Louise bears a striking resemblance to *Messidor* (1979), a film by Swiss filmmaker Alain Tanner, most of whose works address feminist concerns within a broad political context that also includes issues of class conflict, racism, and transnationalism. I don't know whether Callie Khouri or Ridley Scott have seen or were influenced by *Messidor*, or whether it is merely included within the film's rich reservoir of intertextual relations, but a comparison of the two films highlights how deeply rooted *Thelma & Louise* is within its own cultural movement.

Like *Thelma & Louise*, *Messidor* is a road movie about a pair of women who abandon their traditional place in patriarchal culture, a transgression that at first seems trivial but soon turns them into gun-toting outlaws and that ultimately leads to death.[1] While in *Thelma & Louise* the women are two close friends distinguished by age and marital status, in *Messidor* they are two single strangers of the same age (18 and 19) who meet on the road. In both films the "turning point" comes with an attempted rape, which the women avert and avenge with violence.

In *Messidor*, the primary target of the women's rebellion is respectable bourgeois institutions like the patriarchal family, *not* media culture as in *Thelma & Louise*. Scott's spunky heroines encounter a veritable postmodernist parade of treacherous male characters from well-known movies and popular male action genres—including the James Dean look-alike who, despite his useful lessons on sex and robbery, proves to be a rebel without a cause; the foulmouthed trucker without his convoy; and the well-meaning, sensitive cop whose bad timing contributes to their death.

In both films, the women's journey takes them away from the city and into the countryside, where they have a moment of communion with nature that makes them realize there is no going back, and where they move through a mythic landscape that both masks and delineates the nature of their final entrapment. In *Messidor*, the idyllic Swiss landscapes promise an illusory freedom—exaggerated in sweeping aerial shots. These overviews both contradict and disguise the rigid social repression imposed on all inhabitants below; they inspire flight yet provide no way out.

Thelma and Louise's chase is played out against the familiar landscapes from the Western genre—especially Monument Valley and the Badlands. But unlike Jeanne and Marie, who never have a clear destination and whose options and energy wind down, they don't wander aimlessly but rather choose the appropriate generic destination that is known to all those familiar with the Western genre: the Mexican border. One begins to suspect that they are purposely avoiding Texas not only because that was the site of Louise's secret trauma but also to motivate their ending up in the Grand Canyon. For, ultimately, their goal is to perform a sex change on Western mythology—to outdo those macho buddies, Butch Cassidy and the Sundance Kid, by making their grand suicidal leap into that great vaginal wonder of the world.

Thelma & Louise begins where *Messidor* ends—in the same kind of small-town restaurant where Jeanne and Marie have their final, fatal showdown with the law. Instead of making a romantic leap into a new feminist mythology, these Swiss outlaws senselessly shoot a customer who they mistakenly think has called the police. They make no attempt to get away. They are never empowered like Thelma and Louise, for they lack their exuberant energy and good humor; as hitchhikers, they have no glamorous shiny convertible and no final gesture of romantic defiance.

Messidor belongs with other European feminist road movies that explore the repression of women in the context of larger issues of history and class conflict and because of this political analysis their tone and conclusions are uncompromising and grim. Avoiding such analysis, *Thelma & Louise* reinscribes a male action genre with gutsy, hyperfeminine heroines who succeed in outshooting their macho antagonists, and thus the film is more like Cassavetes' *Gloria* (1980) and Ridley Scott's own *Alien* (1979).

In the nineteen-nineties, there is no longer the widespread belief that incisive political analysis can help one control the process of rapid restructuring that the world is undergoing. Instead there is a growing confidence in making endless revisions in the basic paradigm. And in the case of cinema and mass media the prevailing paradigms are Hollywood genres, for American pop culture is now our only remaining successful world export. Once these films, television programs, and genres were reconceptualized as software, they became more malleable and vulnerable to appropriation and ideological reinscription, not only by American independents but also by multinational corporations, spectators, and emigrés—including a British import like Ridley Scott. Perhaps that's why *Thelma & Louise*—with its glamorous images of gun-toting female buddies who stand up to rape and sexual harrassment—might ultimately prove to be more politically effective in the nineties than *Messidor* was in the seventies.

1.   The following description of *Messidor* is influenced by Beverle Houston's essay "*Messidor*: A Post-Structuralist Reading," *Women and Literature* (Fall 1984).

NOTES ON CONTRIBUTORS

Hans Barkhausen, at the time of writing, was a film scholar and writer in Germany.

William R. Barr, at the time of writing, was Professor of English at St. Lawrence University, Canton, New York.

Leo Braudy is the author of *Jean Renoir, The World in a Frame,* and *Native Informant,* as well as the editor of *Focus on* Shoot the Piano Player and co-editor of *Great Film Directors* and *Film Theory and Criticism.* He is a member of the *FQ* editorial board.

Ernest Callenbach founded *Film Quarterly* in 1958 and edited it until his retirement in 1991; during those years he was also the editor responsible for the distinguished film books published by the University of California Press. Author of the environmental classic *Ecotopia,* he continues to write and lecture in the ecology field. He is a member of the *FQ* editorial board.

Noël Carroll is the Monroe C. Beardsley Professor of Philosophy at the University of Wisconsin–Madison and President of the American Society for Aesthetics. His books include *Philosophical Problems of Classical Film Theory, Mystifying Movies, The Philosophy of Horror, Theorizing the Moving Image, Interpreting the Moving Image,* and *The Philosophy of Mass Art.*

Peter N. Chumo II's article in *Film Quarterly* on *Thelma & Louise* launched his writing career. His work has appeared in *Bright Lights Film Journal, Journal of Popular Film and Television, Post Script, Films in Review, Literature/Film Quarterly, Cinema Journal,* and *Creative Screenwriting.* He is currently on the writing staff of *Magill's Cinema Annual.*

Carol J. Clover is Professor of Rhetoric (Film) and Scandinavian (Medieval Studies) at the University of California, Berkeley. She is the author of *Men, Women, and Chain Saws* as well as books and articles on medieval subjects. She is currently working on two books: one on Anglo-American trials and entertainment, and one on *Pulp Fiction*.

Michael Dempsey has written for *Film Comment, Sight and Sound*, the *Los Angeles Times*, and *Film Heritage*. His name appears in the end credits of such films as *March or Die* and *Death Valley* (both directed by Dick Richards) and a West German film, *Comeback* (directed by Cristel Buschmann). He was for many years the Los Angeles editor of *FQ*.

Manthia Diawara is Professor of Comparative Literature and Film at New York University. He is the editor of *Black Renaissance/Renaissance Noire*.

David Ehrenstein is the author of *Open Secret: Gay Hollywood 1928–1998, The Scorsese Picture: The Art and Life of Martin Scorsese*, and *Film: The Front Line—1984*. His writings have appeared in such publications as *Film Culture, Film Comment, Sight and Sound, Cahiers du Cinéma, Los Angeles*, the *Los Angeles Times, Out*, and *The Advocate*. He is the Los Angeles editor of *Film Quarterly*.

Charles Eidsvik teaches film production and history at the University of Georgia, in Athens. He is an independent filmmaker and computer-based animator.

Lucy Fischer is Professor of Film Studies and English at the University of Pittsburgh, where she is Director of the Film Studies Program. Her books include *Cinematernity: Film, Motherhood, Genre; Shot/Countershot: Women's Cinema and Film Tradition; Imitation of Life*, and *Jacques Tati*. Forthcoming is a book on *Sunrise* for the British Film Institute.

Jean-Pierre Geuens teaches film at the University of Southern California.

Harvey R. Greenberg is Clinical Professor of Psychiatry at Albert Einstein Medical College, Bronx, New York, and the author of *Screen Memories: Hollywood Cinema on the Psychoanalytic Couch*.

Brian Henderson is Professor of Film in the Department of Media Studies at the State University of New York at Buffalo. His books include *A Critique of*

Film Theory and two editions of screenplays by Preston Sturges; his articles have been reprinted in many books and translated into many languages. He is a member of the *FQ* editorial board.

Beverle Houston chaired the University of Southern California's Critical Studies Department and co-edited *Quarterly Review of Film Studies* from 1982 until her death in 1988. Best known for her essays on television spectatorship and her 1978 issue of *QRFS* on feminist theory, she was one of the first American film scholars invited to China.

David James's essay in this collection, "Hardcore," also appears in his most recent book, *Power Misses: Essays Across (Un)Popular Culture,* a collection of essays on practices constructed in opposition to capitalist culture.

Albert Johnson was Professor of African-American Studies and Film Studies at the University of California, Berkeley. He was a former director of the San Francisco International Film Festival, a consultant to the Munich International Film Festival, and film critic for, among other magazines and journals, *Sight and Sound*. He was a member of the *FQ* editorial board.

Marsha Kinder is Professor of Critical Studies at the University of Southern California and Director of the Labyrinth Project at the Annenberg Center for Communication. Her books include *Blood Cinema* and *Refiguring Spain,* and the forthcoming *Kids' Media Culture* and *Luis Buñuel's* Discreet Charm of the Bourgeoisie. She is the general editor of the USC Electronic Press and of a series of bilingual CD-ROMs on national media cultures, and is a member of the *FQ* editorial board.

Leonard J. Leff teaches film and literature at Oklahoma State University. His most recent book is *Hemingway and His Conspirators: Hollywood, Scribners, and the Making of American Celebrity Culture.*

Scott MacDonald is working on *A Critical Cinema 4,* the fourth in a series of books of interviews with independent filmmakers, published by the University of California Press. He teaches film at Hamilton College.

David MacDougall, the author of *Transcultural Cinema,* has made some twenty documentary and ethnographic films, including *To Live with Hands* (1972) and *Tempus de Baristas* (1993). He is Queen Elizabeth II Research Fellow and Convenor of the Program in Visual Research at the Australian

National University in Canberra. His most recent filming concerns a school in northern India.

Joseph McBride is the author of such books as *The Book of Movie Lists*, *Steven Spielberg: A Biography*, *Frank Capra: The Catastrophe of Success*, *Orson Welles*, and *John Ford* (with Michael Wilmington). A founding member of the Los Angeles Film Critics Association, he contributes film reviews regularly to *Cinemania Online* and *Boxoffice* magazine.

Bill Nichols is editor of the two-volume anthology *Movies and Methods*. *Blurred Boundaries: Questions of Meaning in Contemporary Cinema* is his most recent book; it extends concepts from his earlier book, *Representing Reality*, which has set the standard for investigations of nonfiction and social representation.

Stephen Prince, Associate Professor of Communication Studies at Virginia Tech, in Blacksburg, is the book review editor of *Film Quarterly*. His latest books are *Savage Cinema: Sam Peckinpah and the Rise of Ultraviolent Movies* and *Sam Peckinpah's* The Wild Bunch.

Michael Renov is Professor of Critical Studies in the University of Southern California School of Cinema-Television. He has written extensively on documentary film and video, and is the editor of *Theorizing Documentary* and co-editor of *Resolutions: Contemporary Video Practices* and *Collecting Visible Evidence*.

Charles Shiro Tashiro is a research associate at the University of Southern California's Annenberg Center for Communication. A former producer for the Voyager Company's Criterion Collection, he currently produces CD-ROMs, directs short videos, and is the author of *Pretty Pictures: Production Design and the History Film*.

J. P. Telotte is Professor of Literature, Communication, and Culture at the Georgia Institute of Technology, in Atlanta, where he teaches courses in film and cultural studies. His publications include books on Val Lewton, film noir, cult films, the science fiction film, and the Machine Age.

Gösta Werner is a Swedish scholar, screenwriter, and director of shorts and features who has published books on film history and theory, Eisenstein, James Joyce, Marcel Proust, and others.

Virginia Wright Wexman is Professor of English at the University of Illinois at Chicago and the author of *Creating the Couple: Love, Marriage, and Hollywood Performance*. She is currently writing a book with the working title *Compromised Positions: Hollywood Directors and the Cultural Construction of the Artist*.

Alan Williams is Professor of French and Cinema Studies at Rutgers University. He is the author of *Republic of Images: A History of French Filmmaking* and has written numerous articles and a monograph on Max Ophüls. He is currently working on a history of American studio system films.

Linda Williams is Professor of Film Studies at the University of California, Berkeley. She is the author of *Hard Core: Power, Pleasure and the "Frenzy of the Visible"* and of the forthcoming *Melodramas of Black and White*. She is a member of the *FQ* editorial board.

Esther C. M. Yau is Associate Professor of Film in the Department of Art History and the Visual Arts at Occidental College. Her work has appeared in several anthologies, as well as in *Discourse*, *Quarterly Review of Film and Video*, and *Wide Angle*. She is co-editor of *New Chinese Cinema: Forms, Identities, Politics*, and is completing an anthology on contemporary Hong Kong cinema.

INDEX

In creating this index, every effort was made to include all film titles, individual and organization names, and subjects for which there is a substantial or significant mention. Film stills and quotes are also indexed. Omitted are titles, names, and subjects that are mentioned in passing or as part of a list. Film titles appear in the index as they do in the text, with cross-references to all alternative titles.

Wizard of Oz, The, 362
Woman's Film, The, 278
Women, representation of, 49–50, 78–84, 86, 101–103, 116–118, 144–145, 191–202, 284, 285–286, 534, 545–550, 554–560
Wood, Robin, 78, 161
World, The Flesh and the Devil, The, 24–25

Xala, 115–116

Yellow Earth, 50–51, 92–111
Youngblood, Gene, 40–45

Zapruder film, 311, 315
Zillmann, Dolf, 201–202n6

Compositor: Publication Services
Text: 10/13 Sabon
Display: Sabon
Printer: Data Reproductions
Binder: Data Reproductions